eBay® PowerSeller Business Practices For Dummies®

Cheat Sheet SM

To Become an eBay Power...

- ✔ Be an active seller on eBay for at least 90 days.
- ✔ Sell a minimum of 2 items on the site per month for the past 3 months.
- ✔ Have a minimum 100 Feedback rating.
- ✔ Maintain a Feedback percentage of at least 98 percent.
- ✔ Keep a DSR (Detailed Seller Rating) of 4.5 or higher for the past 12 months in all 4 classification ratings.
- ✔ Keep your eBay seller's account current and paid on time.
- ✔ Comply with all eBay listing policies.
- ✔ Run your business by upholding eBay's community values.
- ✔ Sell a minimum average of $1,000 in gross merchandise sales (GMS) or 100 items per month on eBay.com, Half.com, eBay Express, or eBay Motors.

Ten+ Essential PowerSeller Skill Areas

For More About . . .	See These Practices . . .
Maintaining an impeccable reputation in the eBay community	2, 4, 32, and 35
Planning your selling on eBay	7 and 9
Controlling your shipping costs	10, 27, and 28
Pulling in customers with attractive listings and images	18 and 21
Marketing online	11, 13, and 26
Getting control of your presentation with HTML	17
Taking advantage of powerful eBay and PayPal features	12, 13, 19, 39, and 40
Riding herd on insurance and taxes	30, 43, and 44
Running your business with a professional attitude	7, 36, 44, and 45
Using technology to its best advantage	20, 28, 38, and 47
Exploring your options for doing business on — and beyond — eBay	14, 15, 44, and 46

For Dummies: Bestselling Book Series for Beginners

eBay® PowerSeller Business Practices For Dummies®

Cheat Sheet

eBay Time in International Time Zones

eBAY	HAWAII	BUENOS AIRES	ENGLAND	GERMANY	JAPAN	SYDNEY
00:00	10:00 p.m.	5:00 a.m.	8:00 a.m.	9:00 a.m.	5:00 p.m.	6:00 p.m.
01:00	11:00 p.m.	6:00 a.m.	9:00 a.m.	10:00 a.m.	6:00 p.m.	7:00 p.m.
02:00	Midnight	7:00 a.m.	10:00 a.m.	11:00 a.m.	7:00 p.m.	8:00 p.m.
03:00	1:00 a.m.	8:00 a.m.	11:00 a.m.	Noon	8:00 p.m.	9:00 p.m.
04:00	2:00 a.m.	9:00 a.m.	Noon	1:00 p.m.	9:00 p.m.	10:00 p.m.
05:00	3:00 a.m.	10:00 a.m.	1:00 p.m.	2:00 p.m.	10:00 p.m.	11:00 p.m.
06:00	4:00 a.m.	11:00 a.m.	2:00 p.m.	3:00 p.m.	11:00 p.m.	Midnight
07:00	5:00 a.m.	Noon	3:00 p.m.	4:00 p.m.	Midnight	1:00 a.m.
08:00	6:00 a.m.	1:00 p.m.	4:00 p.m.	5:00 p.m.	1:00 a.m.	2:00 a.m.
09:00	7:00 a.m.	2:00 p.m.	5:00 p.m.	6:00 p.m.	2:00 a.m.	3:00 a.m.
10:00	8:00 a.m.	3:00 p.m.	6:00 p.m.	7:00 p.m.	3:00 a.m.	4:00 a.m.
11:00	9:00 a.m.	4:00 p.m.	7:00 p.m.	8:00 p.m.	4:00 a.m.	5:00 a.m.
12:00	10:00 a.m.	5:00 p.m.	8:00 p.m.	9:00 p.m.	5:00 a.m.	6:00 a.m.
13:00	11:00 a.m.	6:00 p.m.	9:00 p.m.	10:00 p.m.	6:00 a.m.	7:00 a.m.
14:00	Noon	7:00 p.m.	10:00 p.m.	11:00 p.m.	7:00 a.m.	8:00 a.m.
15:00	1:00 p.m.	8:00 p.m.	11:00 p.m.	Midnight	8:00 a.m.	9:00 a.m.
16:00	2:00 p.m.	9:00 p.m.	Midnight	1:00 a.m.	9:00 a.m.	10:00 a.m.
17:00	3:00 p.m.	10:00 p.m.	1:00 a.m.	2:00 a.m.	10:00 a.m.	11:00 a.m.
18:00	4:00 p.m.	11:00 p.m.	2:00 a.m.	3:00 a.m.	11:00 a.m.	Noon
19:00	5:00 p.m.	Midnight	3:00 a.m.	4:00 a.m.	Noon	1:00 p.m.
20:00	6:00 p.m.	1:00 a.m.	4:00 a.m.	5:00 a.m.	1:00 p.m.	2:00 p.m.
21:00	7:00 p.m.	2:00 a.m.	5:00 a.m.	6:00 a.m.	2:00 p.m.	3:00 p.m.
22:00	8:00 p.m.	3:00 a.m.	6:00 a.m.	7:00 a.m.	3:00 p.m.	4:00 p.m.
23:00	9:00 p.m.	4:00 a.m.	7:00 a.m.	8:00 a.m.	4:00 p.m.	5:00 p.m.

For Dummies: Bestselling Book Series for Beginners

eBay® PowerSeller Business Practices
FOR DUMMIES®

eBay® PowerSeller Business Practices

FOR DUMMIES®

by Marsha Collier

Wiley Publishing, Inc.

eBay® PowerSeller Business Practices For Dummies®

Published by
Wiley Publishing, Inc.
111 River Street
Hoboken, NJ 07030-5774
www.wiley.com

WILEY

About the Author

Marsha Collier, one of the foremost eBay experts and educators in the world, is also a top-selling eBay author with over 1 million copies of her books in print. She is especially proud of two books: *eBay For Dummies,* the bestselling book for eBay beginners, and *eBay Business All-in-One Desk Reference For Dummies,* the bestselling title on operating an eBay business. Marsha co-hosts the *Computer and Technology Show* on wsRadio.com along with Marc Cohen of KABC. She also shares her eBay business expertise through video training segments at Entrepreneur.com's *Entrepreneur's Coaches Corner.* Her column that appears on Entrepreneur.com is also syndicated on many other major news sites.

Marsha intermixes her writing about eBay with her role as experienced spokesperson on the subject. She was one of the original eBay University instructors, as well as a regular presenter at eBay's annual convention, eBay Live. Marsha also hosted the highly acclaimed "Making Your Fortune Online," a PBS special highlighting online business. While traveling across the United States and around the world, she makes regular appearances on television, radio, and in print to discuss online commerce.

Marsha earned her eBay stripes as a longtime seller on the site. She began her eBay selling career in 1996 to earn extra money for her daughter's education (and eventually paid for university with her eBay earnings). She grew her business to a full-time venture and was one of the first eBay PowerSellers. Nowadays, you can find everything from autographed copies of her books to photo supplies, pet toys, and DVDs in her eBay Store ("Marsha Collier's Fabulous Finds") and on her Web site.

Marsha currently resides in Los Angeles, CA. You can contact Marsha via her Web site, coolebaytools.com.

Dedication

This book is dedicated to all you prospective eBay PowerSellers out there who have the dream and the drive to succeed. I wrote this book for you, and I share my expertise so you can skip the trial-and-error and go straight to work gaining the most profits. Those who succeed join me in knowing that hard work and loving what you do get the job done — and lead you to financial achievement and contentment.

Good luck in your endeavors. I know this book will help you get to the next level.

Author's Acknowledgments

Writing a book is a monumental task. Lots of people have helped, but the lion's share of assistance comes from the encouragement that I receive from the eBay community and those I've met when "doing it eBay."

If it weren't for Patti "Louise" Ruby's friendship and support as the tech editor for this book, I think I might have lost my mind. She helped me keep on top of the many changes on the eBay site and never said no to my seemingly endless requests.

Leah Cameron and Barry Childs-Helton (with whom I've been lucky enough to work before) were my editors on this book. Working with Leah is a dream. She's there to lend her unique style of savvy to my words. She truly "gets it" like no one else. And Barry cleans up after us both. You'd almost think there's no one on earth with such vast experience with the English language — especially Victorian nouns. *(If anyone is really reading this and you find the Victorian noun in the book, e-mail me and I'll send you a prize.)* I'm honored to have them as my editors; they help create the very best in the *For Dummies* series. Thank you, Leah and Barry.

Then, of course, I thank the management at Wiley. My publisher, Andy Cummings, and my acquisitions editor, Steven Hayes, both work hard to fill the world with instructional and entertaining books.

Publisher's Acknowledgments

We're proud of this book; please send us your comments through our online registration form located at www.dummies.com/register/.

Some of the people who helped bring this book to market include the following:

Acquisitions, Editorial, and Media Development

Project Editors: Leah Cameron, Barry Childs-Helton

Executive Editor: Steven Hayes

Technical Editor: Patti Louise Ruby

Media Associate Project Manager: Laura Atkinson

Media Assistant Producer: Shawn Patrick

Media Quality Assurance: Kit Malone

Editorial Assistant: Amanda Foxworth

Sr. Editorial Assistant: Cherie Case

Cartoons: Rich Tennant (www.the5thwave.com)

Composition Services

Project Coordinators: Erin Smith, Katherine Key

Layout and Graphics: Claudia Bell, Carrie A. Cesavice, Stephanie D. Jumper, Erin Zeltner

Proofreaders: John Greenough, Caitie Kelly, Christine Sabooni

Indexer: Cheryl Duksta

Publishing and Editorial for Technology Dummies

Richard Swadley, Vice President and Executive Group Publisher

Andy Cummings, Vice President and Publisher

Mary Bednarek, Executive Acquisitions Director

Mary C. Corder, Editorial Director

Publishing for Consumer Dummies

Diane Graves Steele, Vice President and Publisher

Joyce Pepple, Acquisitions Director

Composition Services

Gerry Fahey, Vice President of Production Services

Debbie Stailey, Director of Composition Services

Contents at a Glance

Table of Contents

Introduction

What can I say? eBay is habit-forming, and I've got the habit big time. I've been writing about eBay since its early days in 1998. I've been selling on the site since 1996, was one of the first PowerSellers, and I'm still a PowerSeller; watching the online market change over the years has been an enriching experience in more ways than one. I've noticed that the buyers and the sellers (no less than eBay itself) are constantly changing — especially in the ways they buy, sell, and trade on the site. eBay was once a homespun site where collectors would sell and buy things mostly to fill their collections — but now it's a full-on e-commerce behemoth, selling everything from cars to ladies' vintage silk fans.

If you're selling on eBay, this book will bring you up to date with the best practices necessary to succeed in the current marketplace. In its press releases, eBay likes to say it's vibrant. If *vibrant* means "ever-changing," then it certainly is! Hundreds of vendors are pushing products that offer to help eBay sellers improve their sales. In this book, I show you the important tools, many of the business tasks you can perform yourself, and some strategies that integrate the tools and tasks into sound business practices. The point is to fill you, my reader, with just enough information to thrive on the site. Making the leap from part-timer (yes, a PowerSeller *can* be a part-timer) to high-revenue producer just got easier.

Keep in mind that an eBay business is full blown e-commerce. People who start selling on eBay with the idea of creating a successful home-based business generally have no concept of what it takes to run their own businesses — and virtually no background in retailing. Understanding how a business works takes study and practice (some people even spend six years at college to learn about running a business). So don't be disappointed if (at first) all your eBay sales don't immediately skyrocket. There's a definite learning curve, and that's why I write my books. I pull from my years of marketing and advertising work and my current full-time occupation — writing and teaching about eBay — to offer insights and help you through the rough spots.

By buying this book, you'll be investing two things I truly respect: your money and your time. In return for your money and the time you spend reading the book, I'll give you lots of solid information (without a sales pitch that you don't really want). I'm confident that putting this information into practice will be invaluable, and I point you in that direction every chance I get.

Putting Business Skills into Practice

That's what this book is all about — showing you the important skills that are unique to eBay businesses. Over 241 million confirmed registered users are on the site — and most of them are buyers. And these buyers are waiting to buy your products; all you need to do is "set the bait" with a few of the practices you encounter in this book. Sellers are growing too — it seems everyone wants a piece of the eBay pie. So I show you how to combat the competition and get a leg up on their sales.

I started my own business from home, way back when, when I left the newspaper business to stay at home and take care of my daughter. Those were the days when you kept it a secret that you worked from home, because no one would take you seriously unless you had an office — and extra rent to pay. I took the skills I'd learned from managing a marketing department at a major metropolitan newspaper to my small business at home — and thrived. Over the years I've studied the e-commerce market and kept up with the newest tools.

The practices in this book guide you through growing and profiting as an eBay PowerSeller. All you need to do, when you have a question, is look it up in the index or the Table of Contents and then read the related practices. If you like, read the book cover to cover. Try not to skip over too much; you never know when there's been a change in something you think hasn't changed since the last Ice Age.

eBay changes its *modus operandi* constantly. So do the eBay service providers. To be on the safe side, stick with me through some of the stuff you may consider basic. Remember, back when you were in school, how reviewing the work you did solidified the facts in your mind? Same deal here. Many of the ideas may be new to you, but they *all* will help your business take care of its bottom line.

In *eBay PowerSeller Business Practices For Dummies*, you find out how to

- **Master what it takes to make a profitable income.** I try to demystify the inner workings of running an e-business. There's lots of conflicting information out there about what it takes to make the grade; this book separates the wheat from the chaff. I'll discuss different business models, and you'll see the tools you need to make it big.

- **Take your eBay business up a notch.** Discover how top online retailers know what goods to buy for resale, and when to buy them. I've included in these pages the straight goods — the information that all those get-rich-quick e-mails *claim* to give you — except here you get the real facts.

- **Organize and fine-tune your tedious tasks.** Many online sellers waste precious time (and money) on doing things "the right way." My goal is not only to show you how to do things the "right way," but also to save your precious resources for a little personal time as well.

- **Set up listings that do the selling for you.** I get hundreds of e-mails from people wanting referrals to people who can design templates for their auctions or eBay stores. In this book, you'll get the short version on how to do this yourself — and save buckets of money.

- **Customize your eBay business to suit you.** Here's where you get a handle on the eBay Certified Provider tools that can work as an adjunct to the best of businesses (I let you know which ones). I also outline some of my favorites — the excellent tools that eBay supplies.

Foolish Assumptions

The target of all these revelations: those of you who've sold on eBay, perhaps even made PowerSeller status, but want to ratchet up your sales and make a bit more hard-earned cash. If that's where you find yourself, this book was written just for you. Here are some other silly assumptions I've made:

- You have a decent amount of feedback on eBay (hopefully very positive — if not, I show you how to fix that).

- You have a PayPal account (and I'll bet you're not using it to its fullest potential benefit).

- You're thinking seriously of starting (or expanding) your e-commerce Web site.

- You have an existing small business or you'd like to start one.

- You like the idea of not having to work set hours.

- You feel that working from a home office in jeans and a T-shirt is a great idea.

I assume you've been selling on eBay for a while, maybe for years. You may be selling on eBay part time and feel that you've become successful enough to take your business up a notch. Maybe you're running a full-fledged business on eBay, and know how to use the site; but occasionally there will be a certain new feature that escapes you. I've demystified some of eBay's newest tools for you in this book.

There's a lot of get-rich propaganda on the Internet, coming from people who *claim* to have the inside track on how to make big money online. There seems to be a new site popping up weekly willing to sell you something — your ticket to riches online. Guess what? These folks are getting rich on what they make from those who buy their products, or who pay a monthly fee for their services. I'm not saying they're all bogus — not by any means — but this book gives you a clearer look at some of the valuable heavy-hitters.

I also assume you want to know some solid retailing and e-commerce plans for your business. I've made a point to put those in this book, too.

From what I've heard from the eBay community, you're probably comfortable with the site, but want to make more of it. That's the basis of this book: Making more money online without wasting time *or* money.

What's in This Book

There's a term that's swept the business world: Best Practices. A buzzword, no denial, but you need to know what it means. *Best practices* are defined as programs, initiatives, or activities that are considered leading-edge, or exceptional models for others to follow.

I haven't merely interviewed a bunch of PowerSellers and reported their ideas on these pages. I actually test various tactics in my own eBay store and on my Web site. Sometimes I get e-mails from readers asking why I haven't sold much lately — even though I still remain a PowerSeller. Well, my business has sprouted some new activities these days:

1. I've been too busy writing to really list, list, list the way I should.

2. I'm testing out the new hot "tactic" and it isn't working. (Yet.)

3. I'm on the road, teaching at eBay University, or talking to PowerSeller groups.

This book gives you the benefit of my human mistakes and victories in groups of "practices." Each practice tackles just one subject and lays it out succinctly. It's a way to get your answer quickly, without a lot of extraneous verbiage. Some of the practices go into running Web sites and sourcing inventory. But if those topics aren't relevant for your current business, just skip past them and come back when you need to know those particular facts.

When I come to an idea that cross-references another, I give you a practice number to go to and check out if you want more in-depth information. Also, if an idea comes to you while you're reading, check out the index in the back of the book. It helps you pinpoint your question's answer.

Part I: Power Up to PowerSeller Status

Here's where you and I get together. We talk about PowerSeller status and what it really means. We figure out just how much of a commitment you want to make to your online business. Aside from refreshing your view of the updated nuances of trading on eBay, I examine what type of merchandise can work the best for you — and give you guidance on right-pricing your goods. Countless e-mails come to me all the time to ask me what to sell. My stock answer is "sell what you *know*," but in this part of the book, we examine how to get a line on what really is "right" for you.

Part II: Hit Your Sales Targets

Here's where the finesse comes in. I tip you off to some of the best research tools. There are plenty of tools that work, but I'll single out a few to show you ones that work best for particular merchandisers. I'll help you find out what's hot and how to find the merchandise you need. Interested in importing? Drop-shipping? Liquidation sales? I've lived through selling in all those ways — and I'll give you the benefits — and the drawbacks — to each. I name names and give you the straight scoop.

Buying wholesale all by yourself? You can buy almost anything — without a middle man if you just read this practice. Put this information into play for your business, and you'll be hip to those hokey "wholesale list" e-books and other gimmicks — and you'll be harder for them to tempt!

Here we talk about some not-so-sexy (but essential) things like merchandise, business plans, getting the best prices for your items, and more. Your eBay store will come in here, too, and we'll talk about finding new ways to bring in customers and how to market your business on the Web.

Part III: Build Better Listings

It's no secret that better-looking listings sell — but that doesn't necessarily mean going into a graphics frenzy. Here we talk about what really works — and why even some top PowerSellers have confusing listings that actually hinder their sales.

There's an in-depth discussion of photographing the goods for eBay *and* handling your own image-hosting. I take you, step by step, through professional (but doable) photography methods for getting quality images. You also get an HTML tutorial that answers your questions about setting up your listings to foster good, clean, high-bidding auctions.

I also show you how to use some very handy (and free) eBay tools — such as Turbo Lister — that offer effective, inexpensive help with listing your items.

Part IV: Become a Model Seller

No, no, no, you don't have to lose 40 pounds — just trim your *business* and become more efficient. In this part, you find out the secrets of getting your item from one place to the next — safely! Know when and where to use insurance, and how to handle returns.

I also address the problems of dealing with fraudulent buyers. Yes, folks, eBay's full of human beings, some of them bad apples — and though sellers usually get the bad rap, I've found there are possibly more bad buyers out there than bad sellers! Again, I've made the mistakes myself, so I'll show you how to avoid some nasty situations and what to do if (despite your best efforts) you find yourself in a mess.

Your security comes into play here — selling online exposes a lot about you to the world. Okay, I'm basically a paranoid sort, but here it comes in handy: I give you some tips about staying safe while you do a big business online.

Part V: Manage Your Business

This is the pitfall for a lot of folks. Here's where — even if you're selling lots of items — you can fall down into the big hole of failure. So don't pass by this part. It's about staying organized, staying legal, and following proper accounting practices — even where to get initial financing to start your business. These essentials are all in this part.

We often neglect thinking about the little things (they generally turn into big things unless they're addressed) like insurance, taxes, and legal forms. I deal with all that here.

eBay has a couple of companies that can really get your business going. *Skype* is one of them — an over-the-Internet phone service that helps sellers save time and communicate economically with their buyers. You may have no idea of what Skype can do for your bottom line, but stay tuned (and no, you don't *have* to talk into a hokey microphone). You'll also get the lowdown on *PayPal* and just how much this payment handler can do to improve your bottom line. I answer the complaints of those who have issues with PayPal, and tell you how you can profit from using this incredible service.

Conventions Used in This Book

Conventions? I love conventions! Late-night cocktail parties, free gizmos, lots of learning and fun. Sadly, this isn't what the publisher has in mind (and you thought the *For Dummies* team had a sense of humor, eh?). Here *conventions* means the varied ways we've used typefaces to make things stand out for you while you read this book.

- ✔ The online experience has lots of abbreviations: GMS, NWT, URLs. If I come across an abbreviation you need to know, I give you the definition and the abbreviation together. That way, if you see the abbreviation again, you know what it means. (Also, check out the glossary in the back of the book — remember, the answers are *always* in the back of the book.)

- ✔ To show you things you have to type, I put them in **boldface** text. That way you can type the commands exactly as needed.

- ✔ If I show you Web sites or e-mail addresses, they're set in `monospace` text. For example, my Web site can be found at `www.cool ebaytools.com`.

Icons Used in This Book

One thing I love about *Dummies* books is that authors can use icons to draw your attention to things they want to point out. I've noticed that other recently published books on eBay have incorporated the icon philosophy — but I want you to know who started the standard — the *Dummies* crew, laying it out for the smartest readers anywhere (but you knew that, right?).

You'll see the ones I use:

 This is when my mind wanders to something I really want you to know, but it doesn't fit into the text at that point. It's an important thing that's important to know, so I'll put in the little "tip" icon. Think of it as a personal note from me.

 When you see this icon, I've interjected an idea that's something you need to keep in mind while proceeding with the task at hand or applying the idea down the road.

 Yikes! When you see a Warning icon, know that you're treading in some delicate territory. Many of these represent situations that can come back to bite you in the rear if you're not careful. Please note the warnings and stay safe!

 InsiderSecrets are nuggets of wisdom that aren't commonly known in the eBay community or are kept secret by those in the know. When you see this icon, please take note. It's a piece of knowledge that you will find extremely useful.

Where to Go from Here

As you read the book, I'd love for you to immediately put an idea you glean into practice and see how it works for you. Of course, you may already know about similar good business practices — but those may be worth revisiting to get some more ideas. Check out the links when you find them in the book; you may find some up-to-date information.

I'd love to give you a super-fast way to contact eBay, but the site is so big — and changes so fast — that such a boon isn't practical yet. For now, this book gives you all the links I know. If you have any better contacts, please let me know.

You can reach me at my e-mail address, mcollier@ coolebaytools.com. Please realize that I'm a one-woman show; often the number of e-mails I receive can be overwhelming. I really do read every one and will answer e-mail when I can. Often, lots of readers have the same question — in that case, I address it in my newsletter, which you can sign up for on my Web site, www.coolebaytools.com. (I promise you'll never get spam, and I will not sell or give away your e-mail address to anyone.) My newsletter comes out *about* every six weeks — and I use the word *about* on purpose. But hey, it's free.

My publisher also has a very helpful Web site, www.dummies.com. You can visit the site and get tips on all sorts of *Dummies* subjects, including tips from me on eBay.

At this point, why not give the Table of Contents a look and see what interests you? If you have a particular question, check the index and visit the practice that tickles your fancy. From there, just hop around. Enjoy this book. I wrote it to help you, and I really hope you find some new insights — and solid practices — for running and profiting from your eBay business.

Part I

Power Up to PowerSeller Status

The 5th Wave   By Rich Tennant

"The divorce was amicable. She got the Jetta, the sailboat and the recumbent bike. I got to keep the feedback rating on eBay."

Understand What It Takes to Be a PowerSeller

As buyers browse through the items on eBay, they're bound to notice that PowerSeller icon next to a seller's user ID. When buyers shop on eBay, this is the icon they want to see next to the seller's name. The icon gives sellers an air of trustworthiness and credibility; it makes the buyer comfortable to do business with this person. It's like the symbol on the front of a Mercedes or the crest on the hood of a Cadillac: There's a perception of quality. It's true, the eBay PowerSeller status is given only to those sellers who uphold the highest levels of professionalism on the site — and this enhanced reputation translates into more sales.

eBay refers to PowerSellers as "pillars of the community," and they rank among the most successful sellers in terms of gross sales and customer satisfaction. Bottom line? They're smart businesspeople. PowerSellers have to maintain certain monthly levels of Gross Merchandise Sales (total dollar amount of eBay sales — GMS in eBayspeak), and they get there by providing good items for sale and excellent customer service.

It's not only that eBay respects PowerSellers — it also actually acknowledges them in a positive fashion. Customer-oriented sellers get benefits that other eBay sellers don't. You'll be able to save cold, hard cash for treating your customers right; read on.

In this practice, I outline the requirements for mounting the PowerSeller pedestal, warn you about mistakes that could knock you off the pedestal, and disclose the benefits of staying atop it.

Meeting PowerSeller Qualifications

Actually, becoming a PowerSeller isn't as difficult as most new sellers believe. The requirements are basic, and almost anyone who sells on the site on a regular basis can become a PowerSeller. eBay reviews eligibility for the program's applicants on a monthly basis, although gross sales are averaged on a *quarterly* basis (every three months). You'll receive an e-mail from eBay acknowledging your status once the master computer at eBay reviews your account and says you've made it.

To be sure you get the PowerSeller-eligibility e-mail, you must opt to receive advanced selling communications for PowerSellers by mail, e-mail, and telephone. You can find this opt-in setting in the Notification Preferences area of your My eBay page. See Practice 2 for more information on My eBay.

To become a PowerSeller on eBay, you must fulfill the following requirements:

✔ Be an active seller for at least 90 days

✔ Sell a minimum of two items on the site per month for the past three months

✔ Have a minimum of a 100 feedback rating

✔ Maintain a feedback percentage of at least 98 percent

✔ Keep a DSR (Detailed Seller Rating) of 4.5 or higher for the past 12 months in all four classification ratings (see the upcoming section, "DSRs and What They Mean to You")

✔ Keep your eBay seller's account current (read: pay your bill to eBay on time)

✔ Comply with all eBay listing policies

✔ Run your business by upholding eBay's community values (see the sidebar "eBay community values," later in this practice)

✔ Sell a minimum average of $1,000 in gross merchandise sales (GMS) or 100 items a month on eBay.com, Half.com, eBay Express, or eBay Motors

 PowerSeller Feedback scores and DSRs are calculated based on *total* feedback. This, in reality, provides a better picture of the seller; it reflects the fact that they've satisfied many repeat buyers. eBay works out PowerSeller Feedback by taking the total number of positive Feedback entries and dividing them by the total number of Feedback entries (both positive and negative).

DSRs and What They Mean to You

I've been bandying the term DSR around a lot already, and it may not seem familiar to you. These *Detailed Seller Ratings* (DSRs) are strong indicators of customer satisfaction.

Buyers can (aside from leaving a positive, neutral, or negative feedback) now leave an anonymous rating of your performance in four areas: item as described, communication, shipping time, and shipping and handling charges. You won't see who left specific ratings.

Buyers can post these ratings when leaving regular feedback by clicking one to five stars (as in Figure 1-1). These stars do not impact your feedback score but are very important to your reputation on eBay.

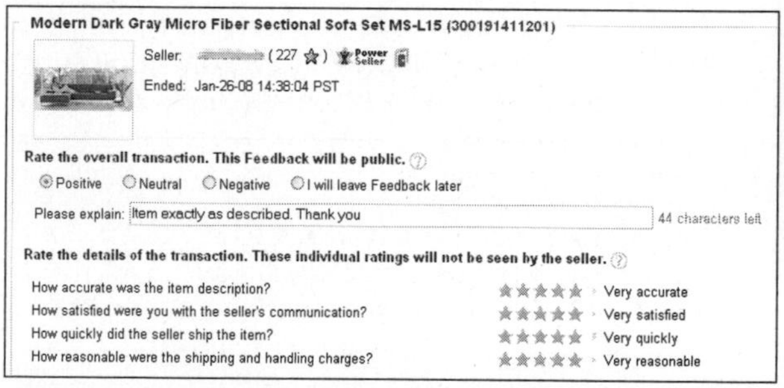

Figure 1-1: Leaving Feedback now includes rating the seller in four areas.

As buyers leave DSRs with their Feedback, the ratings will show up on your Feedback profile in a chart. Figure 1-2 shows my current chart.

 If a buyer (due to multiple transactions) leaves more than one set of detailed seller ratings, the average of that buyer's ratings will be used when calculating the seller's DSRs.

Detailed Seller Ratings (since May 2007)		⊙
Criteria	Average rating	Number of ratings
Item as described	★★★★★	214
Communication	★★★★★	214
Shipping time	★★★★★	214
Shipping and handling charges	★★★★★	212

Figure 1-2: As you can see, some buyers don't realize that shipping is more expensive from LA to NY. Bah!

Avoiding DSR pitfalls

Buyers now need to take feedback in a serious manner and must allow for the realities of buying online. As a PowerSeller, perhaps you can help educate buyers through your e-mails or listing descriptions. And definitely pay special attention to your business practices related to the following DSR rating areas:

- **Item Description:** Sellers need to be more careful in describing an item exactly without using misleading text or phrases. Don't describe reconditioned or refurbished items as *new*. When customers see the word *new*, they expect *new*, not *like new*.

- **Communication:** Many sellers don't check e-mail over the weekend. If this is your practice, instruct your buyers to consider only regular business days when evaluating communication.

- **Shipping Time:** Buyers should rate sellers on the time it takes them to actually ship out the item, not the time it takes to receive it. Postmarks come in handy as proof to buyers that shipping was timely. Sellers shouldn't be held responsible for delays in shipping services, customs delays, or for the time required for a payment to clear.

- **Shipping and handling charges:** Buyers need to be aware that sellers have shipping expenses over and above the actual postage cost. Costs for packing materials and reasonable handling fees (to cover a seller's time and direct costs associated with shipping) need to be considered normal.

Getting discounts on Final Value fees

DSRs are important to more than your reputation. Aside from your PowerSeller status hinging on your continually maintaining a 4.5 average DSR rating, your pocketbook is impacted as well.

When you sell regularly on eBay, a big part of your expense is your Final Value fees. As a top-notch PowerSeller, you get a discount on that unavoidable expense, as follows:

- Sellers with an average DSR rating of 4.8 or more (based on the previous 30 days) receive a *15 percent Final Value Fee discount* on their monthly bill.

- If you have DSRs of 4.6 or more (based on the last 30 days) you get a *5 percent Final Value Fee discount.*

These discounts can amount to significant savings and should boost your desire to provide the very best of customer service possible.

 Ramp up your communication with your buyers, as recommended in the previous section, "Avoiding DSR pitfalls." I firmly believe that this is the best way to keep your DSR ratings high.

Improving search visibility

A seller's visibility in eBay's search or browse feature is tied to customer satisfaction. eBay measures your customer satisfaction by combining your DSRs, Feedback score, and number of complaints (hopefully few) filed in these categories: SNAD (where an item is "significantly not as described") or INR (for "item not received").

eBay calls its tinkering with the search results (based on customer satisfaction indicators) *Best Match*, which is the default sort in a search. For PowerSellers, this means the following:

- Item exposure in search increases for sellers having DSRs 4.6 and above, and at least 95 percent customer satisfaction in the last 30 days.

- Item exposure decreases for sellers with low customer satisfaction or shipping and handling DSRs.

Safeguarding Your Feedback Rating

You may notice that many sellers on the site with feedback ratings in the tens of thousands don't have the PowerSeller embellishment on their auctions. That's not because they're not good people, it's just that some of their transactions may have gone awry. (Just so you know, eBay does acknowledge these sellers internally, and refers to them as "Top Sellers.") In this case, buyers can check the seller's feedback and thoughtfully evaluate it before placing their bids or doing a Buy It Now (BIN) purchase.

I have to note it here: Oftentimes new buyers just don't take the time to read the seller's policies before they buy — and then, at the slightest dissatisfaction, give the seller a negative feedback entry. Not fair, but not uncommon. A typical example: When buyers don't read the seller's warnings about the risks of buying liquidation merchandise.

 It's good to know, at this point, that if you run into a situation that results in your getting undeserved negative feedback, you can avail yourself of eBay's Mutual Feedback policy.

Minding eBay Policies

Complying with eBay's policies may seem a rather esoteric regulation, but there it is. You can't expect *not* to make a mistake now and then (okay, I've had a couple of oops-moment policy violations over the years — we're all human). I often get e-mails from sellers desperate because they've been called on a violation from eBay — they worry about how it will hurt them on the site. Will they be thrown off?

 The PowerSeller arena gives us some hard and fast rules. The preeminent rule you must never break relates to *shill bidding* — bidding on your own listings. That's an unforgivable sin in the eBay world — and shill bidding has one other little problem: It's a violation of federal law.

At the level of PowerSeller (which is based on the volume of transactions per month), eBay allows a little room for error, as follows:

- ✔ **Bronze level:** 4 violations in a 60-day period.
- ✔ **Silver and Gold levels:** 5 violations in a 60-day period.
- ✔ **Platinum:** 6 violations in a 60-day period.
- ✔ **Titanium:** 7 violations in a 60-day period.

I say that allowing a little human leeway for some degree of violation is more than lenient. It's really quite fair. Aside from the absolutely-no-shill-bidding rule, potential violations generally come from certain substandard selling activities:

- ✔ **Charging buyers too much,** for example, by levying excessive shipping and handling charges or adding payment surcharges.
- ✔ **Misrepresenting yourself or your goods,** including misrepresenting your identity, using misleading titles or inaccurate listing categories, and getting false hits by keyword spamming.
- ✔ **Hindering the buying experience,** for example, with site or transaction interference, or by spamming customers, maintaining no item listings, putting the wrong links in your listings, and so on.
- ✔ **Accepted Payments.** Stick with the eBay standard, PayPal. If you don't accept payments through PayPal, you'll loose a large percentage of customers, and you won't be protected against the majority of buyer scams.
- ✔ **Choice Listings,** specifically, one item per listing. If an item comes in three different sizes, it requires three different listings. That's one of the reasons to have an eBay store — so you have a place to accommodate buyers who require different sizes.

In addition to violations of eBay's listing policies, other User Agreement violations crop up that don't relate to listing practices. (I explain all these violations and discuss the basics of eBay's policies — so you can stay on the straight and narrow path — in Practice 32.)

PowerSeller Tiers

Being a PowerSeller provides membership in an exclusive club, and there are five different levels of membership. Members of the different tiers must average a certain level of sales every month; reviews happen every three months.

Each PowerSeller tier gives the Seller more privileges from eBay. One of the most valuable benefits is that when an issue needs to be addressed with eBay, the PowerSellers can access priority customer-service support (see Table 1-1).

 Another great benefit for PowerSellers is eBay's "Unpaid Item Protecton Program." This gives PowerSellers additional protection against losses from nonpaying bidders. The standard rule is that after you file for an unpaid item, you receive a refund of your listing fees. As a PowerSeller, you can get your money back for any listing-feature fees (boldface type, a gallery plus, and such) when the buyer doesn't pay for the item and you file an Unpaid Item claim.

What's the difference between these two PowerSellers?

Here are screenshots from two completed listings from two different eBay PowerSellers. Both sellers are successful on the site; both have good reputations. Which one do you think has to work harder to maintain PowerSeller status?

Seller #1

Seller #2

To maintain that small icon on the listing, Seller #1 would have to sell only one item per month! Seller #2 would have to put in a lot more sales effort to sell a minimum $1,000 a month. Notice also that Seller #1 doesn't even have an eBay Store — no little-red-door icon next to the user ID). Oddly enough, it's often easier for a seller like #2 than it is for a seller like Seller #1. Sourcing and efficiency are the keys here; I cover merchandise sourcing in Practice 6.

TABLE 1-1: POWERSELLER LEVELS AND SUPPORT BENEFITS

Tier	Monthly Average GMS	E-mail Support	Toll-free Phone	Manager Support
Bronze	$1,000 or 100 items sold per month	*	(not toll-free)	
Silver	$3,000 or 300 items sold per month	*	*	
Gold	$10,000 or 1,000 items sold per month	*	*	*
Platinum	$25,000 or 2,500 items sold per month	*	*	*
Titanium	$150,000 or 15,000 items sold per month	*	*	*

Other Program Benefits

In addition to receiving premium support, eBay PowerSellers have other benefits:

- ✔ **Access to the Reseller Marketplace:** A special eBay area, just for PowerSellers, the Reseller Marketplace opens up a large supply of merchandise that can be bought for resale on eBay.

- ✔ **Health care:** PowerSellers and their immediate families have the opportunity to purchase exclusive health insurance.

- ✔ **Approved use of PowerSeller logo:** eBay supplies PowerSellers with templates for business cards and stationery so they can print custom stationery and business cards that include the official PowerSeller logo.

- ✔ **Discounts:** eBay partners offer special service discounts to eBay PowerSellers.

Becoming an eBay PowerSeller is an important step to eBay professionalism. It's something worth aspiring to!

eBay community values

There's a clear set of eBay community values that are taken seriously by the eBay community and by eBay employees. These values were set out early on by the company's founder, Pierre Omidyar:

- ✔ We believe people are basically good.

- ✔ We believe everyone has something to contribute.

- ✔ We believe that an honest, open environment can bring out the best in people.

- ✔ We recognize and respect everyone as a unique individual.

- ✔ We encourage you to treat others the way that you want to be treated.

All eBay sellers are expected to uphold these tenets in all their dealings on the site.

Okay, no snickering from the peanut gallery. We all know that there are quite a few sellers who don't follow these precepts. But then, they're not PowerSellers, are they?

Knowing eBay Inside and Out

Practice 2

In This Practice

✔ Checking out the entire system

✔ Looking beyond the "core" (that is, auctions)

✔ Selling in different areas

As eBay sellers, we generally have an attitude of "yeah, yeah, I know all about eBay, I sell on it every day." But do you, do you *really*? Okay, I'll roll with it, you know eBay. But indulge me here. Let me run through the very basics of where PowerSellers can sell on eBay. As part of your PowerSeller practices, I'm guessing that you routinely engage in more than one kind of eBay transaction. Perhaps a quick refresher on what's available to you on the site might just spark another new idea for your business.

www.eBay.com

The Web page shown in Figure 2-1 displays the eBay home page — at least the way it looked when I took the screen shot. Sellers rarely take the time to view the home page, but it's important for you to check it once in a while. That way you'll know what the *buyers* see when they come to the site.

Figure 2-1: The eBay home page — as of right now.

Buyers — get it? This is the way they first look at eBay and get an impression of what's happening on the site. There are several versions of the home page; if you refresh your browser two or three times, you'll see them all and get the gist of what's going on.

The home-page layout changes a couple of times a year, but one thing stays the same: The special promotions change by season on the home page, providing links that go to related item searches on the site.

Get Where You Want to Go with the Nav Bar

On the top of every eBay page is a navigation bar, as shown in Figure 2-2. From this bar, you can access all the most important points on the eBay site. If, for some reason, you can't find what you're looking for, a link to the Site Map is just waiting to help out (near the top of the home page). You will probably find what you want by clicking there.

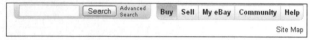

Figure 2-2: You can get wherever you want to go from here.

The navigation bar (no matter how often eBay tries to change it) will always point to the most important places on eBay. On the current navigation bar, buyers find the tools to help them locate items for sale. As a PowerSeller, you can use these same tools to research your competitors' offerings:

- ✔ **Search box:** Just type in a word or series of keywords and click Search to look for a particular item.

- ✔ **Advanced search link:** This thinly disguised link takes you to a place where you can truly define your searches on eBay. You can also perform additional searches on the site:

  - ▶ *Items by Seller*

  - ▶ *Items by Bidder*

- ▶ *By Item number*

- ▶ *Items in stores*

- ▶ *Find Stores*

- ▶ *Find a member:* If you know someone's e-mail address but don't know the User ID — and if you haven't participated in a transaction with that person — eBay will only let you know whether he or she is registered on eBay.

- ▶ *Find Contact information:* Here's where you can get the phone number of someone who's bid on or won one of your items.

- ▶ *Find a Trading Assistant:* Someone to sell your excess stuff for you — or maybe to hire some extra holiday sales help!

In addition to the search tools, you see a group of links in a single graphic. If you hover your mouse pointer over one of them, a drop-down menu appears, as in Figure 2-3.

Figure 2-3: Just click the link you'd like to visit.

The five links divide out like this:

- ✔ **Buy** (where all those potential customers look for direction):

  - ▶ **Browse categories:** Takes you to a page of the main categories, and links to the subcategories

  - ▶ **Help with buying and bidding:** For the real newbies with lots of time on their hands. This links to a page of videos so you can sit in front of your computer and learn about eBay.

  - ▶ **Buyer Tools:** Believe it or not, there's a whole bunch of gizmos and gimcracks for buyers to use — and further confuse them about eBay.

▶ **Reviews and Guides:** Here you'll find eBay user reviews on products and various media. There's also a section of "Guides" written by eBay users. As far as the guides, go, be careful about putting into practice what you learn here, unless you're absolutely sure that the person that wrote the guide *is* an expert. Example? I'd trust the ones on "choosing fabrics for quilting" versus "How I Succeed on eBay" (written by someone who clearly has plenty of time to rewrite what they've learned elsewhere).

✔ **Sell** (where even PowerSellers go for tools and tips):

▶ **Sell an item:** Takes you to the beginning of the Sell Your Item form.

▶ **Getting Started:** A nice primer of how to start selling on eBay (you'll find that and much more in my book, *eBay For Dummies*, published by Wiley — sorry, I couldn't help the shameless plug).

▶ **What to Sell:** Takes you to an area where eBay will give you some advice.

▶ **Seller Tools and eBay Stores:** A quick connection to the subscription services offered by eBay; I discuss these in depth later in this book.

▶ **Shipping Center:** A hub to the shipping-information area of eBay. The most useful link here takes you to an easy-to-use eBay shipping calculator so you can estimate your shipping costs before listing an item. Keep in mind that much of what you see here is "partner" or paid advertising.

✔ **My eBay** (a place for buyers and sellers to manage eBay interactions):

▶ **Summary:** Takes you to your My eBay Summary page.

▶ **Watching:** Here you can jump to the items you are watching in My eBay.

▶ **Bidding:** Takes you to the items you're bidding on.

▶ **Selling:** Here's where you can jump directly to the items you have up for sale.

▶ **Favorites:** Your favorite pages on the eBay site.

✔ **Community** (where PowerSellers can keep themselves in the know about eBay developments):

▶ **News:** This is a spot I visit regularly. Here's where the eBay employees post information on upcoming changes to the site and special promotions.

▶ **Answer Center:** A link to eBay's member-to-member Q-and-A area.

▶ **Workshops/Discussion Forums:** If you enjoy hanging out in chat rooms, eBay has its share. You'll find all sorts of folks hanging around to chat and answer questions. Unfortunately, you may find a bunch of people giving very bad advice.

▶ **My World:** eBay's version of MySpace. Whoever clicks your User ID from anywhere on the eBay site will be taken to your My World page. (Hmmm, don't have a My World page? Go to Practice 11 for information about what it really does and how to use it.)

▶ **eBay Blogs:** As if there aren't enough spaces for blogs on the Web — eBay offers its members even more space to air their feelings. I checked it out: A blog entry asking for eBay advice got six incorrect answers posted in reply — on something that's just plain eBay policy. What a waste of time!

▶ **Groups:** If you've special interest in a subject, you can join a group and sit around and chat — or just stop by to take a look at what's up. Why don't you just sell something?

▶ **eBay Giving Works:** A valuable link! Click this link to see the current fabulous charity items currently up for sale. Buy something fun and help someone in need.

✔ **Help** (where buyers and PowerSellers alike find answers and advanced instruction):

▶ **Help Topics:** Never mind the suggested topics. Write in your question and you'll find the eBay policy answer.

▶ **Learning Center:** Watch more videos on your computer.

▶ **Security and Resolution Center.** A valuable link where you can report violations.

▶ **eBay University:** If you'd like to attend an eBay University class, you can check here to see when they'll be in your city. I am a lead instructor with Griff, so click the link to see instructors, and maybe we can have a chance to meet!

▶ **Contact Us:** To save you headaches, you can chat online with eBay support.

If you're a PowerSeller (and have logged in), you can get a toll-free number to call for one-on-one support.

eBay Transactions — the Short Version

eBay has grown into this massive mega-marketplace that even the best of eBay experts can find daunting from time to time. For PowerSellers, knowing what transactions are available and most suitable for their business is just good practice. This section looks at the available types of eBay transactions and gives you the goods on how they work.

The core of eBay — traditional auctions

Single-item auctions are the mainstay of eBay; they're also the easiest to recognize. Unlike "traditional" live auctions that end with the familiar phrase "Going once, going twice, sold!" eBay auctions are controlled by the clock. The seller pays a fee and lists the item on the site for a predetermined period of time; the highest bidder when the clock runs out takes home the prize.

Auctions are the bread and butter of eBay. You can run a traditional auction for one, three, five, seven, or ten days, and when the auction closes, the highest bidder wins. I'm sure you've bid on several, and I hope you've won a few.

But more importantly, if you run auctions as a PowerSeller, I'm sure you've successfully concluded *more* than a few. You begin the auction with an opening bid, and bidders bid up your opening price, competing with one another and building a healthy profit for you on your item.

Reserve-price auctions

A *reserve price* protects sellers from having to sell an item for less than the minimum amount they want for it. You may be surprised to see a sports car up for auction at eBay with a minimum bid of only a dollar. It's a fair bet that the seller has put a reserve price on this car to protect himself from losing money.

As a PowerSeller tool, setting a reserve price allows you to start with a lower minimum bid, and lower minimum bids attract bidders. Unfortunately, if you make the reserve price too high and it isn't met by the end of the auction, no one wins.

eBay charges a fee for sellers to run these auctions. Nobody knows (except the seller and the eBay computer system) what the reserve price is until the auction is over, but buyers can tell from the auction page whether they're dealing with a reserve-price auction. Reserve-price auctions are in the listings alongside the other items, so you have to click and open an auction to find out whether it has a reserve. A message also appears on the page, saying whether the reserve price has been met. Once bids have been made on an item, that message is especially relevant to the bidders.

Multiple Item (Dutch) auctions

Multiple Item (or Dutch) auctions offer more than one of the same item in an auction-style format. Although Dutch auctions seem to be a dying breed on eBay (some PowerSellers just don't bother with them), you occasionally still come across them while browsing — and they can be a bit confusing. Normally you see a quantity of available items (more than one).

In a Dutch auction, bidding progresses just as in normal eBay auctions. The bidder may bid on one or more of the items available, and the highest bidders win (based on the quantity bid for and won). The only trick to this type of auction is that more than one bidder can win — and all bidders win their items at the *lowest* successful bid — *not* the highest!

Auctions with the Buy It Now option

Buyers don't have to participate in an auction on eBay to buy something. By clicking the Buy It Now button, any interested party can close the sale at the listed Buy It Now price and end the auction immediately. Buy It Now is the fastest choice for buyers who are certain they can't live without the auctioned item and they're okay with the Buy It Now price. If buyers seek this kind of instant gratification on eBay, they can visit the eBay Stores. Or they can isolate these items by clicking the Buy It Now tab when browsing categories or performing searches.

As a PowerSeller, using the Buy It Now option is helpful for offering a fixed-price option to those who only browse through the auctions (and newbies rarely visit the stores).

Selling with Fixed Price sales

Selling with fixed prices on eBay offers yet another way to move your items. Buyers can make purchases quickly and easily on the eBay site as Fixed Price sales or directly in eBay Stores. Buyers can easily recognize these sales because they have no

Place Bid option. As a PowerSeller, offering Fixed Price sales lets you sell off items you wish to quickly unload or stock in depth.

Restricted-access auctions

If you're interested in selling items of an adult nature, eBay has an adults-only *(Mature Audiences)* category, which has restricted access. Although buyers can peruse the other eBay categories without having to submit credit-card information, they must have a credit-card number on file at eBay to view and bid on items in this category. Restricted-access auctions are run like the typical timed auctions. To bid on adult items, the bidder must first agree to conditions listed on a terms-of-use page after entering his or her User ID and password. This page pops up automatically on the next attempt to access this category.

Private auctions

Some sellers choose to hold private auctions because they know that some bidders may be embarrassed to be seen bidding on a dozen lace panties in front of the rest of the eBay community. Others sellers may go the private route because they are selling big-ticket items and don't want to disclose their bidders' financial status.

Private auctions are run like the typical timed auctions, except each bidder's identity is kept secret. At the end of the auction, eBay provides contact info to the seller and to the high bidder — and that's it.

Previously, sellers used the private auction to cloak the identities of bidders in high-dollar auctions. These days, eBay hides the identities of bidders automatically when the reserve or Buy It Now price is set at or above $200. Bidders are assigned anonymous names, such as a***b.

Also, if highest bid, reserve, or Buy It Now price on an item reaches a certain level, bidders' names become anonymous. Only the seller and the bidder can view real User IDs in their respective My eBay pages. That information isn't available in a bidder or seller search.

 Private auctions are a good choice, especially if you're selling item of an intimate nature.

Selling in eBay Stores

Thousands of eBay sellers have set up stores with merchandise meant for Buy It Now, fixed-price transactions. In these stores, buyers can find anything from socks to jewelry to appliances. For a PowerSeller, having an eBay Store offers an additional opportunity to build a reputation and a return-customer base. (I give you the full story on how to sell in eBay Stores in Practice 12.)

 The new feedback system allows feedback to count toward your total when posted by returning customers. Previously, the system enabled a member to have only one impact on another member's score. The important thing to remember is that *only one Feedback per week from a trading partner* will count toward your total.

eBay Live Auctions

If one yearns for that traditional, going-going-gone (highest bidder wins) sort of auction, buyers can participate in auctions that are running live at a gallery in real time. In *eBay Live Auctions,* prospective buyers can bid via eBay's Internet hook-up just as if they were sitting in chairs at the auction house. These auctions are usually for unique and interesting items that may not be likely to turn up in your locality. You can find Live auctions at www. ebayliveauctions.com (that's the home page in the Figure 2-4).

Figure 2-4: eBay Live Auctions — bidding action in real time!

To sell on eBay Live Auctions, you must be a licensed auction house or a seller using a licensed auctioneer to control the bidding. eBay Live Auctions supply buyers with exciting, nonstop, live auction action right on their desktops. Joining a live auction is a lot of fun. These auctions happen in real time; you can see (and participate in) the bidding action on your screen as it's happening. PowerSeller, licensed auctioneers, sometimes use Live Auctions to liquidate large stocks of merchandise in a very short period of time.

Automotive? Sell in eBay Motors

Anything and everything automotive can be sold on eBay Motors (see Figure 2-5). PowerSellers, get ready to roll! I give you more information on selling your wheels through eBay Motors in Practice 3.

Figure 2-5: eBay's online car lot, eBay Motors.

Selling on eBay Express

eBay Express is eBay's new answer to eBay shopping simplified. A shopper can go to the site (www.express.ebay.com) and shop from many sellers all at once. The eBay Express home page is also different from the eBay site, as Figure 2-6 demonstrates.

Sellers must meet special criteria to be eligible to sell on the eBay Express site. As you can tell from the upcoming list of requirements, it's pretty much a shoe-in for PowerSellers to have their items listed on the site.

Figure 2-6: The face of eBay Express.

If you want to take advantage of selling on eBay Express, you must

- Maintain a Feedback score of 100 or more, *and* a Positive Feedback rating of 98 percent or better.
- Not have your feedback profile set to "private."
- Have a PayPal Premier or PayPal Business account.
- Be registered as a U.S. registered seller, or Canadian registered seller.
- Allow shoppers to pay for multiple items with a single payment. (You can specify this on your My eBay Preferences page within Shipping and Discounts section).

Your listings also have to fulfill a set of criteria. To qualify for eBay Express, they must

- Be in one of the following formats (no auctions): Fixed Price, Store Inventory, or Auction-style with Buy It Now.

✔ Indicate, in the Item Condition field, whether the item is New or Used. (Some categories are exempt, but eBay doesn't tell you which ones.)

✔ Use the Pre-Filled Item Information if you're selling any sort of media.

✔ Include shipping costs (flat, calculated, or free) in the shipping fields.

✔ Include a picture with your description (once again, some categories are exempt from this requirement — and eBay doesn't say which ones).

✔ Represent items located in the United States with an individual item cost that does not exceed $10,000.00.

Sell on Half.com

Selling at Half.com is different from selling on eBay because you're selling in a solely fixed-price marketplace. Your item is listed head-to-head against more of the same item from other sellers.

Half.com currently lists millions of items, but only books, CDs, DVDs, video games, and game systems. Because Half.com is part of eBay, your feedback follows you to the site. The Half.com home page is shown in Figure 2-7.

Figure 2-7: Half.com is powered by eBay.

From a seller's point of view, the best features of Half.com are these:

✔ The item listing is free.

✔ The item stays on the site until it's sold or until you take it down.

Half.com charges a commission after your item sells (frugal PowerSellers don't use it much). Commissions for items sold in the Books, Music, Movies, and Games categories are a percentage of the selling price of the item. The shipping cost is not added to the selling price for calculating this commission.

As you can see, there are varied ways to make a buck on eBay. In the next practice, I refresh you on the costs of doing business on eBay.

Practice 3

Discerning the Many Faces of eBay

In This Practice

✔ Seeing how buyers browse for items

✔ Selecting one (or more!) listing categories

✔ Checking out the subsites

eBay used to be a homey little site, with (as I can remember) about 20 categories. That was it — just 20. When I started writing about eBay, each year, with each new book, I'd manually count the categories so I could show the growth of the site. Today there are 34 top categories, but the subcategories and the sub-subcategories must be well into the six-figure numbers. eBay has grown to such an incredible marketplace that counting the categories would take much more time than it's worth. Take a look for yourself.

Click the Categories link on the topmost eBay pages (just below the search bar), and you'll come to a page that looks something like Figure 3-1.

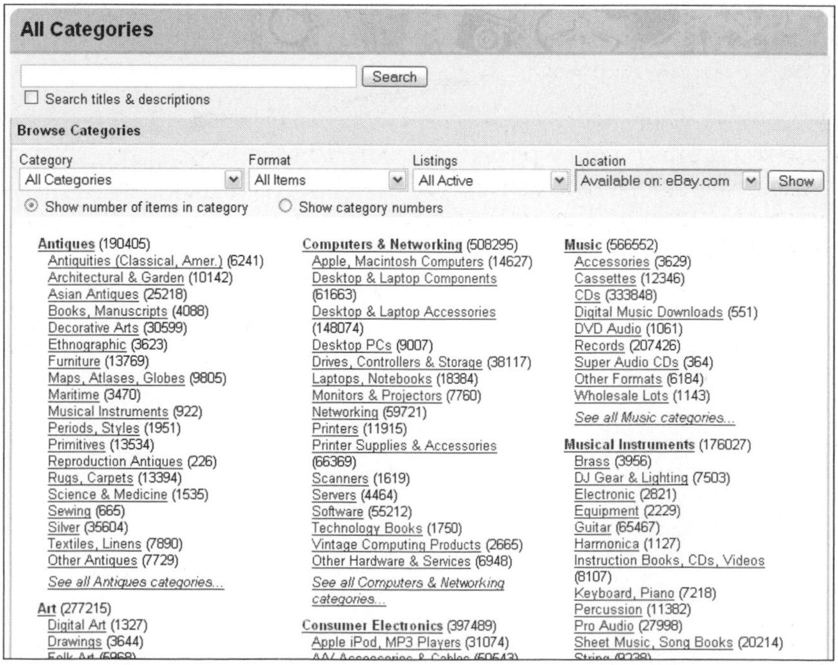

All Categories

[Search] ☐ Search titles & descriptions

Browse Categories

Category	Format	Listings	Location	
All Categories	All Items	All Active	Available on: eBay.com	[Show]

◉ Show number of items in category   ○ Show category numbers

Antiques (190405)
Antiquities (Classical, Amer.) (6241)
Architectural & Garden (10142)
Asian Antiques (25218)
Books, Manuscripts (4088)
Decorative Arts (30599)
Ethnographic (3623)
Furniture (13769)
Maps, Atlases, Globes (9805)
Maritime (3470)
Musical Instruments (922)
Periods, Styles (1951)
Primitives (13534)
Reproduction Antiques (226)
Rugs, Carpets (13394)
Science & Medicine (1535)
Sewing (665)
Silver (35604)
Textiles, Linens (7890)
Other Antiques (7729)
See all Antiques categories...

Art (277215)
Digital Art (1327)
Drawings (3644)
Folk Art (6968)

Computers & Networking (508295)
Apple, Macintosh Computers (14627)
Desktop & Laptop Components
(61663)
Desktop & Laptop Accessories
(148074)
Desktop PCs (9007)
Drives, Controllers & Storage (38117)
Laptops, Notebooks (18384)
Monitors & Projectors (7760)
Networking (59721)
Printers (11915)
Printer Supplies & Accessories
(66369)
Scanners (1619)
Servers (4464)
Software (55212)
Technology Books (1750)
Vintage Computing Products (2665)
Other Hardware & Services (6948)
See all Computers & Networking categories...

Consumer Electronics (397489)
Apple iPod, MP3 Players (31074)
A/V Accessories & Cables (59543)

Music (566552)
Accessories (3629)
Cassettes (12346)
CDs (333848)
Digital Music Downloads (551)
DVD Audio (1061)
Records (207426)
Super Audio CDs (364)
Other Formats (6184)
Wholesale Lots (1143)
See all Music categories...

Musical Instruments (176027)
Brass (3956)
DJ Gear & Lighting (7503)
Electronic (2821)
Equipment (2229)
Guitar (65467)
Harmonica (1127)
Instruction Books, CDs, Videos
(8107)
Keyboard, Piano (7218)
Percussion (11382)
Pro Audio (27998)
Sheet Music, Song Books (20214)
String (9238)

Figure 3-1: The first third of the first screen of eBay's sales categories.

See those huge numbers next to the categories? They represent the number of active listings in each category. Also note the link at the bottom of the main category listing; you can click it to see *all* sub-categories in that category.

Speaking of active listings, Figure 3-2 is from Medved.net, showing a graph of the number of auctions hosted on eBay during the month of December 2007. It's a huge amount, at one point exceeding 18 million auctions in one day! You can check this chart on a daily, monthly, or yearly basis from `www.medved.net/cgi-bin/cal.exe?EIND`.

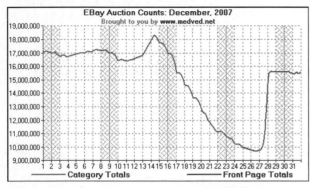

Figure 3-2: eBay Auction counts from Medved.net.

All of the above just illustrates the giant swath that eBay has cut across the Internet environment. Not only is eBay doing a huge job in their categories, but they've also named some *super*categories as well.

Then there's growth. Aside from owning PayPal (the worlds largest online payment service), eBay purchased and invested in other retail-oriented sites. You can find links to them on the eBay Home page, as in Figure 3-3.

All this growth and expansion makes eBay a bustling marketplace with varied outlets for PowerSellers' wares. Whether you stick with the regular auction categories or branch out into the special supercategories, you're sure to find a location that fits the items you sell. In this practice, I show you the way around the many faces of selling on eBay — and help you evaluate just where you can make more cash.

Figure 3-3: eBay's family of companies.

Maneuvering through Categories

So how does eBay keep track of the millions of items that are up for auction at any given moment? The brilliant minds at eBay decided to group items into a nice, neat little storage system called *categories*. The home page lists most of the main categories, but currently eBay offers sellers tens of thousands of subcategories, ranging from Antiques to Weird Stuff. And don't even ask how many sub-subcategories (categories within categories) eBay's got — I can't count that high.

Locating the perfect sub-subcategory

Well, okay, I *could* list all the categories and subcategories currently available at eBay — if you wouldn't mind squinting at a dozen pages of really small, eye-burning text. But a category browse is an adventure that's unique for each seller, and I wouldn't think of depriving you of it. Suffice it to say that if you want to find that perfect spot to list your items, you're in browsing heaven now.

Here's how to navigate around the categories — just the way a buyer would:

1. **Click the category that fits your merchandise, such as Books or DVDs & Movies.**

   You're transported to the category's page. You see categories and subcategories listed next to each heading. Happy hunting.

2. **After the category page appears, you find subcategories listed underneath the main category title. Click the subcategory, and keep digging through the sub-subcategories until you find items similar to those you sell.**

   For example, if you offer your customers items honoring their favorite television shows, click the Entertainment Memorabilia category or the DVDs & Movies category. The Entertainment Memorabilia category has many links, including the Television Memorabilia subcategory. Below the TV Memorabilia link, you find the subcategories Ads, Flyers, Apparel, Clippings, Photos, Pins, Buttons, Posters, Press Kits, Props, Scripts, Wardrobe, and Other.

3. **Make note of the specific sub-subcategory that represents your items so you can list them accordingly.**

   Congratulations — you've just navigated through several million items to find that one TV-related collectible item that matches what you plan to sell.

Many eBay sellers will tell you that selecting the exact category isn't crucial to achieving the highest price for your item — and they're right. The bulk of buyers (who know what they're looking for) just input search keywords into eBay's search box and find their items that way. Potential buyers, though, will select a category, peruse the items, and see whether one strikes their fancy — it's just like going to the mall.

Specifying listing category(ies)

On the first page of the Sell Your Item form, you need to select the main category for your item.

 To find where other sellers have successfully sold items that are similar to yours — and see the prices the items sold for — you can perform a completed item search from the More Search Options page. Just type your item keywords into the Search box, click the box to search Completed Listings Only, and indicate to have your results sorted by highest prices first. After you have your results, click the completed listings with the highest prices. At the top of the auction page, you'll see the listed category. You may find that your item is listed successfully in more than one category.

Also check the active listings; are lots of people selling your item? If you see that you're one of forty or fifty selling the item, you need to get creative as to where to list your item. Evaluate the item and its potential buyers — in what categories would someone who's shopping for your item search?

eBay provides some features to help you think outside the category box, as follows:

- **Find Suggested Categories:** Who says that a box of Blue Dog note cards (with the famous doggie icon painted by Cajun artist George Rodrigue) belongs only in *Everything Else: Gifts & Occasions: Greeting Cards: Other Cards?* If you use the Find Suggested Categories tool in the upper-right corner of the Select Category area on the Sell Your Item page, you may find some other creative places to list your item.

- **Search Categories:** As part of the Sell Your Item form, eBay gives you a tool to find where the bulk of sellers are selling your item. Put your keywords in the Search Categories text box and click Search. Figure 3-4 shows how many categories I can list my Blue Dog cards in.

SELL YOUR ITEM   **1. SELECT A CATEGORY**   2. CREATE YOUR LISTING   3. REVIEW YOUR LISTING

Select a category

Help buyers find your listing by selecting a category that best describes your item.

| Browse categories | Search categories | Recently used categories |

george rodrigue   [Search]

Categories

☐ Art > Prints > 1950-Now > Limited Editions > Original
☐ Books > Nonfiction Books
☐ Books > Antiquarian & Collectible
☐ Art > Other Art
☐ Books > Magazine Back Issues
☐ Art > Posters
☐ Art > Prints > 1950-Now > Limited Editions > Other
☐ Books > Fiction Books
☐ Collectibles > Advertising > Retail Establishments > Department Store
☐ Art > Paintings > 1950-Now > American
☐ Collectibles > Animation Art, Characters > Animation Art > Production Art
☐ Art > Prints > 1950-Now > Open Editions
☐ Books > Children's Books
☐ Collectibles > Advertising > Distillery > Absolut
☐ Everything Else > Gifts & Occasions > Greeting Cards > Christmas, Holiday

Tip: Reach more buyers by selecting two categories. (Fees apply)

[Continue ▶]

Figure 3-4: Let eBay do some of the categorizing work.

Listing your items in two categories

Suppose you've found two perfect categories in which to list your item. eBay allows you to list an item in two categories, but does that mean it's the best marketing decision for your auction? That depends, so consider the following:

✔ When you list an item in two categories, you must pay two listing fees. Depending on the time, the season, the availability of your item, and how much you paid for it, you may or may not have the budget for listing an item twice.

✔ Many eBay buyers are savvy in their use of the search engine. If they search for your item by using the search engine rather than by browsing the categories, listing the item in two categories might be a needless expense.

 You can change your category mid-auction if your item hasn't garnered a bid, starting with your item in one category and ending with it in another. And at the end of an auction in which your item doesn't sell, you can use the relisting feature to run the auction again in another category.

Finding where to sell your stuff

The Internet is crowded with auctions. Every major portal seems to now include auctions as part of its site. The bottom line is that most bidders and sellers go to eBay. Why? Because more computers and electronics are sold on eBay than at Buy.com; more used cars are sold on eBay than at Autotrader; and more toys are probably sold at eBay than at KBToys.com. Even the United States Post Office has found a niche on eBay, selling the contents of undeliverable packages in odd lots.

Whether you're selling auto parts, toys, fine art, or land, you too must find your niche on eBay. Sounds easy enough. After all, deciding where to put your stuff for sale is straightforward, right? Not necessarily. After taking a look at the eBay Category Overview page, you can see that the inclusion of thousands of subcategories complicates this task.

Consider the *Star Trek* toys that enjoyed a surge of popularity as the continuing saga unfolded in TV series and movies. The easy choice is to list the item under Toys, Bean Bag Plush: Action Figures: Star Trek. But what about the category Collectibles: Pop Culture: Science Fiction: Star Trek? This is the point where you must decide whether you want to list in two categories (and pay more) or count on the fact that your beautifully written auction title will drive those using the search engine directly to your item.

So you aren't into selling Star Trek toys? Suppose you're selling a VHS of the movie *The Red Violin*. Would listing it in Movies: Movies: Videos: General, be the right choice? Or would you hit the proper audience of category browsers in Music: Musical Instruments: String: Violin, Viola? A book on 1960s fashion? Better in Books: Antiquarian, Rare: General or in Books: Nonfiction: Collectibles? Actually I have my best luck going direct to the fans of '60s fashion in the category Collectibles: Vintage Clothing, Accessories: Clothing: Women: Other Women's Clothing.

Believe it or not, the popularity of categories themselves varies from time to time. Potential buyers may search one category more than others, and their preferences depend on which way the wind blows. News stories, the time of year, hot trends, or whether Katie Couric makes a comment about something can change a particular category's popularity. Keeping up on these trends is sometimes tough, so you must do some research.

So how can you possibly know the best category for your item? Research your items on a regular basis by using my favorite tool: the awesome eBay search engine. After you've found the right category for the item you're listing, give it a try. But be sure (occasionally) to try alternatives as well; the popularity of different areas of the site can come and go with time.

 Even when you've been selling a particular item for a while — and doing well with it — you might be surprised to hear that changing to another related category can boost your sales. A little research now and then can go a long way to increasing your eBay sales.

eBay's Supercategories

On the eBay home page, take a look at the long list of links on the left. You'll even find some supercategories on the list of links at the very bottom of the eBay home page.

The eBay gurus put together specialized categories to encompass areas of interest that cover more than one category. On the eBay home page, you'll currently find these (eBay will no doubt add more in the future):

- ✔ Real Estate
- ✔ eBay Motors
- ✔ eBay Express
- ✔ Giving Works (Charity)
- ✔ Live Auctions

These supercategories come in very handy when you're selling cross-category merchandise.

Handling Real Estate Sales

American farmland sprawls across the country, and there's plenty of open space. But because of urbanization and many other factors, large areas of land have had to be subdivided and sold. People buy land for investment, vacations, or retirement. It's no longer common for a family to spend an entire lifetime in one home. We move, and often live in many different places. Real estate, although a major purchase, is becoming more and more an everyday transaction.

The smart people at eBay are sly trend-spotters, so they opened an official category for real estate transactions in fall 2000. You can access eBay's Real Estate category through the category link on the left side of the home page or by going directly to

`http://pages.ebay.com/realestate/`

Not really an auction

eBay Real Estate auctions aren't really auctions. Because of the wide variety of laws governing the sale of real estate, eBay auctions of real property aren't legally binding offers to buy and sell. Showing your real estate on eBay is an excellent way to advertise and attract potential buyers. When the auction ends, however, neither party is obligated (as they are in other eBay auctions) to complete the real estate transaction. The buyer and seller must get together to consummate the deal.

Nonetheless, eBay real estate sales are popular and the gross sales are growing by leaps and bounds. You don't have to be a professional real estate agent to use this category, although it may help when it comes to closing the deal. If you know land and your local real estate laws, eBay gives you the perfect venue to sell your subdivided acreage in Wyoming that Uncle Regis left you in his will.

Getting a break on realtor fees

For less than the cost of a newspaper ad, you can sell your home, condo, land, or even timeshare on eBay Real Estate in the auction format. You can also choose to list your property in an ad format, accepting not bids but inquiries from prospective buyers from around the world. On the Sell Your Item form, you must specify special information about your piece of real estate.

In Tables 3-1 and 3-2, I provide a listing of fees that you can expect to encounter on eBay Real Estate. Note that the reserve fee charges are the same as on regular eBay auction listings. (See Practice 8 for a list of those fees.)

TABLE 3-1: eBay Real Estate Fees

Type of Fee	Fee Amount
Insertion (listing) for 1-, 3-, 5-, 7-, or 10-day auction (or fixed price)	$35
30-day auction	$50
Ad format 30 days	$150
Ad format 90 days	$300
Reserve under $200 (refundable if reserve is met)	$2
Reserve over $200	1% of reserve (maximum $100)

TABLE 3-2: eBay Real Estate Residential & Commercial

Type of Fee	Fee Amount
Insertion (listing) for 1-, 3-, 5-, 7-, or 10-day auction	$100
30-day auction	$150
Ad format 30 days	$150
Ad format 90 days	$300
Final value fee	none

When buyers participate in a listing that is listed in ad format, they don't place bids. At the bottom of the item's description page is a form to fill out that sends the buyer's information to you (the seller). After you receive this information, you can contact the buyer, and the two of you may negotiate privately. When browsing the Residential Homes for Sale category, buyers see a small ad icon in the bids column to indicate items that are listed as advertisements. Most residential home sales are handled in this manner. Land and timeshares are typically sold in the auction format.

Note that neither eBay Inc. nor eBay Real Estate Inc. (real estate advertising services on eBay are offered by eBay Real Estate Inc., a wholly owned subsidiary of eBay Inc.) provides real estate broker services. Even so, eBay Real Estate Inc. maintains real estate licenses in at least 45 states in the U.S.

To own a piece of land outright is a great feeling. (To *sell* a piece of land at a profit feels even better!) Plenty of virgin land is showing up on eBay, in lots and acreage, on a daily basis. Add your real estate offering to the mix and help more eBay buyers get the "happy landowner" feeling.

Selling on eBay Motors

If there's one purchase that I don't enjoy making it's buying a car. Please don't misunderstand. I love cars, and I have a personal attachment to every car I've ever owned. It's just that each time I'm approached by a car salesman, I get intimidated. The minute the salesman says "I've got to check with my sales manager to see if I can do that," I just know I'm a goner.

And when I've finally decided on the car model I want, I still have to face *the deal,* when Mr. Sales Guy calls in the finance manager to try to sell me warranties, alarms, ups, and extras, which I never wanted or needed. I guess I'm not a good car buyer — I feel the need to run out of the dealership — and I usually do.

I've known many people who have successfully purchased cars on eBay Motors (as pictured in Figure 3-5). They couldn't have found deals like these at their home dealerships, and are very, very happy with their purchases.

Figure 3-5: The eBay Motors (home for almost anything with a motor) home page.

Many of the cars on eBay Motors are private party sales. But when you sell a car on eBay, you may compete against bank cars (repossessions) and cars that have been cherry-picked by wholesalers and dealer overstocks. There are also the professional car dealers selling their rare, hard-to-find cars to a marketplace that draws millions of visitors per month. You can't get that many people through the door at a local dealership! Dealers put up the rare colors and limited edition vehicles because this *is* an auction site, and the rarer an item the more likely bidders are to get excited. The more excited bidders are, the more they lose their heads — and the higher the price goes.

Yes, this *is* an auction — and the bidding goes hot and heavy, an average of seven to eight bids per sale. It's a very competitive environment for the most desirable cars. Dealers can sell cars for less on eBay, because it costs them less to sell. (They don't have to pay the finance manager to twist your arm to buy the ups and extras.) Cars sell quickly on eBay, and they're making money on volume, not by picking your pockets.

Offering car parts

Got used car parts? eBay has an enormous market in used car parts. One seller I know goes to police impound sales and buys wrecks — just to salvage some valuable parts that he can resell on eBay.

New car parts are in demand, too. If you catch a sale at your local auto-parts store when it's blasting out door handles for a 1984 Corvette (a vehicle for which it's hard to find parts), it wouldn't hurt to pick up a few. Sooner or later, someone's bound to search eBay looking for them. If you're lucky enough to catch the trend, you'll make a healthy profit.

Supplying the market with used cars

Yes, *you* can sell cars on eBay. In fact, used-car sales have skyrocketed online thanks to all the people who find eBay to be a trusted place to buy and sell used vehicles. Selling vehicles on eBay is a natural business for you if you have access to good used cars, work as a mechanic, or have a contact at a dealership who lets you sell cars on eBay for a commission or on a consignment basis.

Here are just a few things to keep in mind if you plan to sell cars on eBay:

- Selling a car on eBay Motors is a bit different from selling on regular eBay, mainly in the fees area. Take a look at Tables 3-3 and 3-4 for significant differences.

- To sell a vehicle on eBay Motors, you must enter the Vehicle Identification Number (VIN) on the Sell Your Item page. This way, prospective buyers can always access a Carfax report to get an idea of the history of the car. Figure 3-6 shows that eBay even has a simple vehicle checklist to help you with your listing; you can get it here:

  http://pages.motors.ebay.com/sell/
  sell_your_vehicle_checklist.pdf

✔ Although many people who have found the vehicle of their dreams on eBay are more than happy to take a one-way flight to the vehicle location and drive it home, shipping a vehicle is a reasonably priced alternative. You can make arrangements to ship a car quickly and simply.

Figure 3-6: eBay Motors checklist.

eBay Motors   **Sell Your Vehicle Checklist** ☑

Part ① : Vehicle Information
VIN: ☐☐☐☐☐☐☐☐☐☐☐☐☐☐☐☐☐ *(17-digit if 1981 or later)* **Mileage:** _____
Year: _____ Make: _____ Model: _____ Sub-Model: *(if applicable)* _____
Engine Cylinders: *(circle one)* 3 | 4 | 5 | 6 | 8 | 10 | 12 **Title Type:** *(circle one)* Clear | Salvage | Other
Transmission: *(circle one)* Manual | Automatic **Warranty:** *(circle one)* Existing | None

Major Vehicle Equipment
☐ Anti Lock Brakes (ABS)   ☐ Air Conditioning   ☐ Cruise Control   ☐ Dual Front Air Bags   ☐ Dual Power Seats
☐ Leather Seats   ☐ Moon Roof   ☐ Multi Compact Disc   ☐ Navigation System   ☐ Power Door Locks
☐ Power Windows   ☐ Premium Sound   ☐ Tilt Wheel   ☐ Traction Control

Photo Checklist
Exterior
☐ Left side   ☐ Right side   ☐ Front   ☐ Rear
Interior
☐ Front seats   ☐ Back seats   ☐ Trunk   ☐ Dashboard
Special
☐ Engine bay   ☐ Odometer close-up   ☐ Customization   ☐ Wear/damage

Part ② : Vehicle Description
Vehicle description and history: Helps answer common questions about the vehicle.
☐ Are you the original owner or know the ownership history?
☐ Have you made any modifications to the car: accessories, wheels, etc.?
☐ Do you have maintenance records on the vehicle?
☐ Do you have a warranty? (If so, provide details about remaining coverage and transferability.)

Vehicle condition: Helps buyers know what to expect when purchasing and bidding.
☐ Is there any condition not shown in your vehicle photos: mechanical, interior, exterior, cigarette odor?
☐ Does your vehicle feature any unique customization or added accessories that you'd like to showcase?
☐ Have you performed any recent maintenance on the vehicle, such as tire replacement or major service?
☐ Are there any current mechanical or cosmetic issues or near-future needed maintenance (like tires)?

Terms of sale: Helps make the sale easier and quicker if the buyer is prepared.
☐ Do you have the title available? If not, specify timing and availability.
☐ Any specific time frame for sale or payment conditions?
☐ Will you accept escrow payments?
☐ Any other paperwork required for a legal sale of a vehicle in your area (such as smog inspection)?

Part ③ : Vehicle Pricing
Starting Price
Setting it low will encourage the most bidding activity.

Reserve Price
The Reserve Price should be set at the minimum price you will accept. Don't have a Reserve Price in mind? Consider researching similar vehicle values at eBay Motors, or try other vehicle pricing resources such as Kelley Blue Book.

Buy It Now
You can stimulate immediate sales with Buy It Now. If a buyer wants your vehicle at your Buy It Now price, they can click to buy it directly instead of bidding on the vehicle. It can be a fast way to sell your vehicle since anyone can accept your Buy It Now price at any time. Avoid setting the Buy It Now too high such that no bidders would ever consider Buy It Now.

If your reserve isn't met in an eBay Motors auction, you may still offer the vehicle to the high bidder through the Second Chance option. (Find more information on that option in Practice 26.) You may also reduce your reserve during the auction if you feel you've set your target price too high.

TABLE 3-3: EBAY MOTORS VEHICLE-SPECIFIC FEES

Type of Vehicle	Listing Fee	Transaction Services Fee*
Passenger Vehicle	$40	$50
Motorcycle	$30	$40
Powersports	$30	$40
Powersports under 50cc	$3	$3
Other vehicles	$40	$50
Parts & Accessories (regular eBay fees apply)		

There is no Final Value Fee for selling on eBay Motors. The Transaction Service Fee is what you pay when your item gets a bid (or if you've used a reserve, when bidding meets your reserve price).

TABLE 3-4: EBAY MOTORS RESERVE FEES

Reserve Price	Fee
$0.01 – $5,000.00	$5.00
$5,000.01 – $10,000.00	0.1% of reserve price
$10,000.01 and up	$10.00

An item you've listed on any eBay supersite will appear in any search, whether a potential buyer conducts a regular eBay search or executes a search in eBay Motors.

Participating in eBay Live Auctions

The Live Auctions area of the eBay site is one of the most exciting places for buyers to visit, especially during an auction. If you look in this area (as in Figure 3-7), you'll see that buyers have the opportunity to bid or watch an auction — in live action — on some of the finest and most unusual items in the world. I have personally spent many a fun afternoon with the smallest dream that I might be able to bid with the big boys on some of these special auctions.

To sell your items on eBay's real-time Live Auctions, you must be a licensed auction house — or, as an individual seller, you must use a licensed auctioneer to control the bidding. To apply to sell on Live Auctions, go to

```
http://cgi3.liveauctions.ebay.com/ws/
    eBayISAPI.dll?LAApplicationFormV4
```

and fill out the form. eBay will notify you if you are approved.

Figure 3-7: eBay Live Auctions home page.

Donating through GivingWorks Sales

In Practice 16, I thoroughly cover the GivingWorks selling process. Sellers wishing to raise money are able to pick a benefiting nonprofit from a certified list, and designate a percentage of the proceeds

(from 20–100 percent) to donate, when they list an item on eBay. These items will appear in the search results with a "charity auction" icon. When you go to the item page, you'll see the name of the non-profit and some information about them, and the percentage of the final bid that the seller is donating. You can search eBay for your favorite nonprofits by name.

Selling in Other eBay Zones

There's more to eBay than just the auction site; don't lose a selling opportunity by not checking into the other viable selling area owned by eBay.

Peddling goods on eBay Express

eBay set up the Express site to attract the casual or new-to-eBay shopper. Most are afraid of big-bad-eBay and feel more comfortable shopping at a standard e-commerce Web sites. So here they won't seem as overwhelmed as they do on eBay proper; that's because it doesn't *appear* to have thousands of sellers. The key for them is they have one shopping cart — and Express turns their eBay shopping experience into a one-stop shop.

Buyers make selections at eBay Express and can put as many items as they want into their individual shopping carts — even though the items come from different sellers. The buyer makes one payment, and eBay and PayPal divvy up the payments between the individual sellers in the transaction behind the scenes. The transition from click to buy is seamless, and the buyer experience is just the same as shopping at one of the other huge e-commerce stores. There's only one catch: If a buyer buys from a large number of sellers, the shipping costs will go sky-high, so it's still a benefit to buyers to buy more items from one seller in order to take advantage of combined shipping.

eBay has been desperately trying to make Express a place for new shoppers to feel comfortable and safe, so if you want to sell on Express, here's what you need to know:

✔ eBay feedback rating must be a minimum of 100.

✔ You must have at least a 98 percent positive rating (and your feedback can't be private).

✔ Your items (which will appear automatically in Express) must be in Buy It Now, Fixed Price, or Store Inventory format.

✔ Your listing must include a photo, the item's condition (in the Item Specifics area — not just the description), and you must quote any shipping costs.

✔ You must accept PayPal for payments from a Business or Premier account.

For more information and the latest requirements, go to

```
pages.ebay.com/express/service/
   about/checklist.html
```

If you want to find your listings on Express, use this URL:

```
http://search.express.ebay.com/
merchant/marsha_c
```

Be sure to use your User ID instead of mine (marsha_c) when you run your search.

If you qualify to sell on Express, your listings will automatically port to the Express site with no effort on your part.

eBay's half brother: Half.com

Selling at Half.com is different from selling in your eBay (or other online) personal store because you're selling in a fixed-price marketplace. Your item is listed head-to-head against more of the exact same item that other sellers are selling. Half.com isn't a home for your store; you might say that each item has its own store, complete with competing sellers.

You can sell many things at Half.com, which presently ranks as one of the Internet's most-visited sites. Half.com currently lists millions of items, including new or used books, music, DVDs and VHS, video games, and game systems. Half.com, shown in Figure 3-8, is part of eBay, and your feedback follows you to the site.

Figure 3-8: The Half.com home page.

From a seller's point of view, the best features of Half.com are

✔ The item listing is free.

✔ The item stays on the site until the item is sold or until you take it down.

Half.com charges a commission after your item sells, as shown in Table 3-5. Commissions for items sold in the Books, Music, Movies, and Games categories are a percentage of the selling price of the item only. The shipping cost is not added to the selling price.

TABLE 3-5: HALF.COM SALES COMMISSIONS

Selling Price Plus Shipping	Half.com Commission
Less than $50	15%
$50.01 – $100.00	12.5%
$100.01 – $250.00	10%
$250.01 – $500.00	7.5%
More than $500	5%

To list an item for sale at Half.com, first you need to locate the item's Universal Product Code (UPC) or a book's International Standard Book Number (ISBN). In case you're wondering what an ISBN is, turn this book over and find the bar code on the back. The number written below it is this book's ISBN number.

If you don't want to bring all your books, CDs, movies, or games to your computer, you can use an inexpensive hand-held scanner (that holds memory) and bring it over to your stacks of items. Scan away all the ISBN numbers until the scanner memory fills up. Go back to your computer and download the data to input for sale.

When someone searches for an item, a book for example, at Half.com, a listing of all sellers who are selling that book appears. The listings are classified by the condition of the book — categorized as "Like New" or "Very Good" — depending on what the seller entered. The list price of the book is included, as well as a comparison of selling prices throughout the Internet at various book dealers.

You'll find that once you add the UPC or ISBN in your listing, Half.com comes up with an image of your item, so you don't have to take a picture for your sale. When an item is out of print, Half.com may not have an image to upload with the listing. In this case, the text "Image not available" appears in the area where the picture would appear.

Half.com Sell It Now

On Half.com, buyers can pre-order an item that's not listed on the site. This lets you make a sale without finishing your listing! The *Sell It Now* option will appear during the listing process of your item; just before you specify the amount you desire to list your item for. If your seller rating and item condition match the criteria that the buyer specified in a Pre-Order, the *Sell It Now* option will appear.

If you receive a notice that a buyer would like to Pre-Order the item — and you agree to the amount they wish to purchase the item for — check the box next to "Sell It Now for $<amount specified by the buyer>". After your Pre-Order sale has processed, within the next few hours you will receive a "You've Made a Sale" e-mail notification.

When a prospective buyer searches and finds an item for books or other items, a list of the sellers with the lowest prices appears on the page (see Figure 3-9).

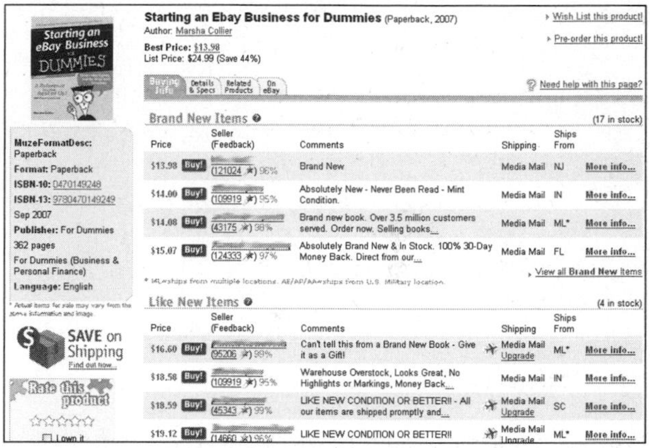

Figure 3-9: A book listing at Half.com.

When you list an item at Half.com, you have the opportunity to list a 500-character note describing the item's condition. Your selling price can be whatever you like, but keep it low enough to stay competitive with other sellers' items.

For example, if you're selling a hardcover book for $37, here's what happens:

1. Buyer buys the book that's priced at $37.

2. Half.com charges the buyer $3.99 for Media Mail shipping and handling costs.

3. You pay Half.com a 15 percent commission, which is $5.55 on a $37 item.

4. You get a shipping reimbursement of $3.07.

    See Table 3-6 for Half.com shipping reimbursements.

5. Half.com sends you a net payment of $34.52.

TABLE 3-6: HALF.COM SHIPPING REIMBURSEMENTS

Item	Media Mail	Expedited (Usually Priority Mail)
Hardcover book	$3.07 for first item; $1.40 for each additional item	$5.24 for the first item; $3.49 for each additional item
Paperback book	$2.64 for the first item; $1.15 for each additional item	$5.20 for the first item; $2.24 for each additional item
Music & DVDs	$2.39 for the first item; $1.19 for each additional item	$5.20 for the first item; $1.99 for each additional item
VHS Movies	$2.14 for the first item; $1.19 for each additional item	$5.20 for the first item; $1.99 for each additional item
Audio Books	$2.64 for the first item; $1.15 for each additional item	$5.20 for the first item; $1.94 for each additional item
Games	$2.89 for the first item; $1.15 for each additional item	$5.20 for the first item; $1.99 for each additional item

Practice 4

Benefiting from the Community and Certified Providers

In This Practice

✔ Checking out Certified Providers

✔ Learning from others on the boards

It seems that once something gets "big" there are a zillion experts out there to help you through the maze. One of my favorite Web sites, www.wikipedia.com, is full of information on almost every topic. I can "mostly" rely on their information, because they generally require citations (references to other sources which document both influence and authority). When a *wiki* (an online resource that allows users to add and edit content) is properly moderated, it can be highly useful. As a matter of fact, there's an entry in the Wikipedia that was posted about me (see Figure 4-1), interestingly; people are constantly updating and changing it — it looks good to me!

Figure 4-1: I looked up, and there I was. . . .

The book you are reading is also "moderated" in a similar way. All my books, although I am an eBay seller, eBay University Lead Instructor, e-commerce consultant, and active in many sellers' groups, are double-checked by one of the smartest eBay experts I know, Patti Louise Ruby.

I never want my readers to get the wrong message from my recommendations, but that's not necessarily the case in 99 percent of what you see and hear on the Web today. Many people's advice has an underlying tone of trying to sell you something.

The eBay world is no exception. At last count, there were over 120 books in print giving you *the word* on eBay. Some of the biggest-selling books are from people who have only casual experience with eBay (or are no longer on eBay — they just write about it). Too many rely on interviews and second-hand knowledge, which may be tainted if someone has something to sell or an axe to grind (and lots of folks do).

As an eBay PowerSeller, make it one of your standard practices to double-verify the credentials of any person or company you decide to deal with on eBay. In this practice, I tell you about the eBay certifications that give you a good place to begin checking out services and solutions — and about how to distinguish good advice from the eBay community at large.

Picking up Info on eBay

Speaking of axes to grind, you really need to be careful of the advice you receive on the eBay boards. Many posters use alternate User IDs to disguise their identities so you can't be sure where your information is coming from. The posters who use their real sellers' IDs may have a bit more credibility. But do keep in mind that some shady sellers figure the best way to thwart the competition is to give out bad information.

On the other hand, I don't want to scare you completely. There are many great people who post on eBay's boards, who are willing to help the newbie with a question and answer. My personal favorite is *Bobal*, who's been a long-time eBay member and booster of new sellers on the boards. Figure 4-2 shows one of his helpful posts.

Even PowerSellers — who should know the rules — break eBay policies in their listings. Figure 4-3 shows a seller listing the breeds of dogs that will fit into

the dog collar they're selling. Oh, come on — that's keyword spamming, and it's against eBay policies — though I'm sure that if these sellers were on an eBay discussion board, they'd recommend the use of this description type. Bad idea.

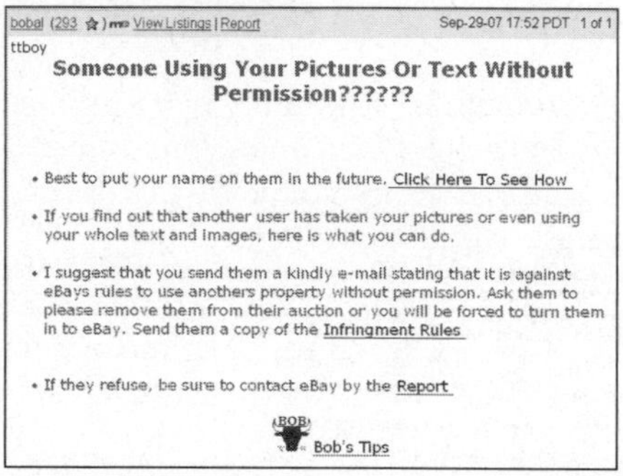

Figure 4-2: Members of the eBay community often lend a helping hand.

You see, anyone looking for the particular dog breeds listed in the description could find that breed of dog just by running a title and description search. This keyword spamming wastes the buyer's time by attempting to fool the search engine. The description in the listing for the collar should give the manufacturer's sizing and the actual measurements, perhaps tell the buyer where to measure on the dog to get the collar size — and that's it.

COLLAR 3/8" FITS NECKS 8" TO 14"

(SMALL BREEDS)

AUSTRALIAN TERRIER

BICHON FRISE

CAIRN TERRIER

FOX TERRIER

ITALIAN GREYHOUND

LHASA APSO

MALTESE

MANCHESTER TERRIER

MINIATURE DACHSHUND

MINIATURE PINSCHER

MINIATURE SCHNAUZER

Figure 4-3: Keyword spamming is just irritating.

The bottom line here is that the quality of the information you get is based on where and whom it comes from.

Certifying a Certified Provider

eBay endorsement is something I've wanted to talk about for a long time. I get e-mails upon e-mails from people asking me about one company or another, telling me a particular company is

- ✔ Recommended by eBay
- ✔ Endorsed by eBay
- ✔ Owned by eBay (because the eBay logo appears in the Web site)

None of the above is ever true. There is a Certified Provider program from eBay where eBay qualifies businesses who want to do business with the eBay community. Note that I used the word *qualify*. That does not mean *endorse*.

 By having the Certified Provider program, eBay manages to keep the very worst of the worst from aligning themselves with eBay.

I discuss the complete requirements for qualifying as a Certified Provider later in this practice, but for now, recognize up front what eBay says:

> *Participants [in the program] must have extensive experience with eBay, pass a strict certification exam and provide a number of proven customer references that are checked by eBay.*

That description (again) does not say *endorsed*, *approved*, or any other title implying formal authorization by eBay. It only says that participants have passed an eBay exam, proved references, and paid their fee. The best way to check out one of eBay's providers is to find other sellers who've done

business with them and get their feedback (not necessarily the ones the provider supplies to you). Whenever I do business with someone who gives eBay advice, I run a Google search on the company's name and the word *fraud* to see whether they've been involved in any fraudulent activities that haven't been made widely public.

🎯 Be careful when checking out any company. Many businesses deliberately use the word *fraud* on many of their Web site pages to trip up a Google search. If businesses have the correct combo of words on their site, they can literally fill up the first two pages of a Google search — and most people won't check further. Be a smart seller. Before you think of doing business with someone, investigate! Investigate as if it's your last dollar going to that person or company.

eBay has a handy new directory that makes finding a provider easy. Go to `certifiedprovider.ebay.com` and you'll be able to find a company that meets your needs. Again, before hiring someone, be sure to check independent references.

There are two types of certified eBay providers:

- ✔ **Certified Services Providers** perform business functions for eBay sellers. For example, these providers might offer customer-service support by responding to buyer inquiries, or they may supply graphics and design store and listing templates to improve seller brands. They may also provide recommendations to help you find the best ways to sell on eBay. Certified Services Providers can display the logo pictured in Figure 4-4 in their advertising.

Figure 4-4: The Certified Services logo.

Requirements for Certified Providers include having at least one company member (or 50 percent of the employees) pass the eBay Certified Consultant exam (exam costs $150 per person) for certification and supplying verifiable customer references. The information covered in the exam can be accessed online in the eBay Help system. eBay also offers a class to buff up eBay skills.

✔ **Certified Solutions Providers** are the people who produce the code and the software used as third-party applications on eBay. They not only provide technology, they also create solutions and programs from data they license from eBay. The requirements for this certification are clearly more stringent. They have to be well-versed in all that techie programming stuff and know how to integrate the eBay API into the applications they invent. Still a minimum of one (that is, 50 percent of employees) must pass an eBay Certified Engineer test (cost: $150). They also must supply verifiable references and be committed to programming for the eBay platform. Figure 4-5 shows you what the Certified Solution Provider logo looks like.

Figure 4-5: A Certified Solution is eBay-compatible.

 A *compatible* application means that eBay has checked the Provider's software or tool, and it works with eBay's programming requirements. But compatibility is not a measure of a company or of their business.

Becoming a Certified Provider

If, after reading the regs, you have an interest in serving (and making money from) the eBay community, you might consider hanging up your shingle as a Certified Provider. This designation carries lots of benefits other than displaying an official-looking logo in your ads and Web site. One of the best perks is that Certified Providers are invited to speak at eBay events and online. Many of the speakers at eBay Live are providers — and have the benefit of teaching their approaches to eBay sellers in an organized educational format. Table 4-1 shows you the basic plan.

If all these benefits sound good to you, just know that the cost to be a provider (after the $150 certification per person) is $3,000 a year. If you fail your initial test, there is a $75 retesting fee. To balance out all that sticker-shock, know also that there are lots more benefits when you join this program. For more of the straight story — and all the details — on becoming a Certified Provider (and building your bottom line), go to

```
http://developer.ebay.com/programs/
certifiedprovider
```

 This does not mean that you speak for eBay. Here's the relevant quote from the terms of the Certified Provider program: "You will not represent yourself as an eBay employee or agent of eBay. Further, you will not imply an affiliation with eBay or in any way suggest that eBay is involved with or endorses your products or services. "

TABLE 4-1: eBay-Certified Provider Benefits

Benefit	What It Gives You
Free placement in Solutions Directory	You will be listed in the eBay Solutions Directory.
Upgraded search display	Your certification logo will appear on both the search-results and details pages where your entries appear in the Solutions Directory. You will also get credits toward advertising in the Directory.
Solutions Finder inclusion	Sellers looking for products like yours will be able to find you in the Solutions Finder, generating many possible sales leads to build your revenue.
Internal account advocate	You get an internal account advocate to tout your company and the services you provide to key eBay staff, thereby providing high internal visibility.
eBay staff training and awareness	You can meet — and present your services to — key eBay employees, including Customer Service, Seller Development, and other eBay staff. You have the opportunity to familiarize them with your offerings, and you can provide training materials and giveaways to the eBay Customer Service Resource Center.
Education Specialist training and awareness	You can get the attention of eBay's Education Specialist Program instructors through placement in the Education Specialist resource center. You can give 'em the chance to fall in love with what you're doing and speak to thousands of their students about the benefits of your services.
Certified Provider-led workshops	You can get new business leads and promote your company through eBay's online workshops. This allows you to interact with the eBay community directly, by showcasing your company's area of expertise.
eBay Live! special opportunities	Generate leads with special treatment at eBay Live! You can use your Certified Provider logo on your booth property. You can gain new customers by being included in eBay's "Using Certified Providers" class, and also apply to teach a class yourself through Certified Provider–led panels.
eBay Radio	Qualify for discounts on eBay Radio. Also, select Certified Providers may be invited to appear on the eBay Radio Developer Showcase.
News flash	Receive news about new benefits in the program, new advanced certification offerings, and upcoming co-marketing opportunities available only to Certified Providers.

Part II

Hit Your Sales Targets

The 5th Wave — By Rich Tennant

KNOB BROS.
- Paint Drying Equip.
- TV Test Pattern Design
- Sap Buckets

"Maybe it would help our eBay sales if we perk up the listings with images of our products in action."

Practice 5

Deciding What to Sell and the Tools That Help You

In This Practice

- Looking for trends outside eBay
- Taking eBay's temperature
- Checking in with portals
- Getting serious with data-gathering tools

In Practice 6, I talk about where the professional sellers find the items they sell online; in this practice, I talk about getting yourself centered on which product lines you'd like to sell. Once you've figured out what kind of merchandise you're comfortable with, you can use the tools I discuss in this practice to home in on the latest bestsellers.

Just as successful stockbrokers need to know about individual companies, they also need to know about the marketplace as a whole. Sure, I know about the over 1,500 Webkinz up for sale on eBay — and so does nearly everyone else who's interested in that category. To get a leg up on your competition, you need to know the bigger picture as well — for example, how Webkinz stack up in the world of collectible and virtual pets.

Here are some questions you should ask yourself as you contemplate turning merchandise into cash by selling items on eBay:

- **What items are currently hot?** If you see everyone around you rushing to the store to buy a particular item, chances are good that the item will become more valuable as stocks of it diminish. The simple rule of supply and demand says that whoever has something everyone else wants stands to gain major profits.

- **Do I see a growing interest in a specific item that might make it a big seller?** If you're starting to hear talk about a particular item, or even an era ('80s nostalgia? Baseball cards making a comeback? Who knew?), listen carefully and think of what you own or can get your hands on that can help you catch a piece of the trend's action.

- **Should I hold on to this item and wait for its value to increase, or should I sell now?** Knowing when to sell an item that you think people may want is a tricky business. Sometimes you catch the trend too early and find you could have commanded a better price if you'd waited. Other times, you may catch a fad that's already passé. It's best to test the market with a small quantity of your hoard, dribbling items one-by-one into the market until you've made back the money you spent to acquire them. When you have your cash back, the rest will be gravy — *and* you'll have a good feel for the market.

✔ **Is a company discontinuing an item I should stockpile now and sell later?** Pay attention to discontinued items, especially toys and novelty items. If you find an item that a manufacturer has in limited supply, you could make a tidy profit. If the manufacturer ends up reissuing the item, don't forget that the original run is still the most coveted and valuable.

✔ **Was there a recall, an error, or a legal proceeding associated with my item?** If so, how will it affect the value of the item? For example, a toy discontinued for reasons *other than safety* may no longer be appropriate, but it could be rare and collectible if sealed and intact.

 Some people like to go with a gut feeling about when and what to buy for resale. By all means, if instinct has worked for you in the past, factor instinct in here too. If your research looks optimistic but your gut says, "I'm not sure," listen to it; don't assume you're just hearing that lunchtime taco talking. Test the waters by purchasing one of the prospective items for resale and listing it on eBay. If that sale doesn't work out satisfactorily — drawing the proper profit margins at your ultimate purchase price — you won't have a lot of money invested, and you can credit your gut feelings with saving you effort and cash out of pocket.

Exploiting your talent

If you're talented in any way, you can sell your services on eBay. Home artisans, chefs, experts with advice to share, and even stay-at-home psychics are transacting business daily on the site. What a great way to make money on eBay — make your own product or advise someone on your expertise! Even Life Coaches are selling their time on the site.

Many custom items do well on eBay. People go to trendy places (when they have the time) such as Soho, the Grove, or the Village to find unique custom jewelry. They also go to eBay. There's a demand for personalized invitations, cards, and announcements — and even return address labels. Calligraphic work or computer-designed items are in big demand today, but no one seems to have the time to make them. Savvy sellers with talent can fill this market niche.

Studying the Media

Catching trends is all about listening and looking. You can find all kinds of inside information from newspapers, magazines, television, and of course, the Internet. Believe it or not, you can even find out what people are interested in these days by bribing a kid. Keep your eyes and ears open. When people say, "Britney Spears is *everywhere* these days," instead of nodding your head vacantly, start getting ideas.

In newspapers

Newspaper reporters (Internet bloggers, too) are bombarded by press releases and inside information from companies the world over. Look for stories about celebrities and upcoming movies and see whether any old fads are making a resurgence (you can sell such items as *old school*).

Read the accounts from trade conventions, such as the New York Toy Fair or the International Consumer Electronics Show. New products are introduced at such events, and immediately journalists give them thumbs-up or -down. Use the information to help determine the direction of your favored merchandise.

On television

No matter what you think of television, it has an enormous effect on which trends just come and go and which ones stick. Why else would advertisers sink billions of dollars into TV commercials? For example, one Oprah appearance for an author can turn a book into an overnight bestseller. (If you're reading this, Oprah, I'm still waiting for the call back.)

Consider the swath cut by all those popular reality shows on the tube. Memorabilia and related items-of-the-moment can bring in some serious cash.

Tune in to morning news shows and afternoon talk shows. The producers of these shows are on top of pop culture and move fast to be the first to bring you the Next Big Thing. Take what they feature and think of a marketing angle. If you don't, you can be sure somebody else will.

Catch up with youth culture . . .

. . . or at least keep good tabs on it. If you remember cranking up The Beatles, Styx, or The Backstreet Boys (say what?) until your parents screamed, "Shut that awful noise off," you may be at that awkward time of life when you hardly see the appeal of what young people are doing or listening to. But if you want tips for hot auction items, tolerate the awful noise and listen to the kids around you.

 Children, especially preteens and teens, may be the best trend-spotters on the planet. Remember, before they turn 21 or so, young people know everything. If you doubt it, just ask them.

Check out magazines

Magazines geared to the 18-to-34 age group can help you stay on top of what's hot. See what the big companies are pitching to this target audience (and whether they're succeeding). If a celebrity is suddenly visible in every other headline or magazine, be on the lookout for merchandise relating to that person. (Are we talking hysteria-plus-cash flow here, or just hysteria?)

Finding Soon-to-Be Hot Sellers on eBay

Everyone wants to know what the hot ticket is on the eBay site. They want to know what's selling best so that they can run out, buy it, and *make big money* on eBay. Whoa, there, big fella.

As you may know, I'm not a believer in the notion that eBay is anybody's get-rich-quick program. Nobody can give you secret information that magically transforms you from a garage seller to a warehouse tycoon overnight. You get there by studying the market and finding out what works and what doesn't. There are no shortcuts. That said, here's where you can use eBay to find information on what's currently hot or going to *be* hot.

 Keep in mind that I ask you to rely on current data. Tutorials or suggestions from eBay are fine, and are written by well-meaning employees with a solid business background — who are (more than likely) not sellers on the site. A PowerSeller with experience can look at the data and derive the proper message of exactly what's going on. That's *you*. Make your own decision and save time and money. Trust your gut.

Taking the pulse of eBay

A little-known (and über-valuable to sellers) part of the eBay site is the eBay Pulse. On this page, located at `pulse.ebay.com`, you can find the most popular ten searches in any major category. Figure 5-1 takes you to the page and shows the top ten searches for the entire site.

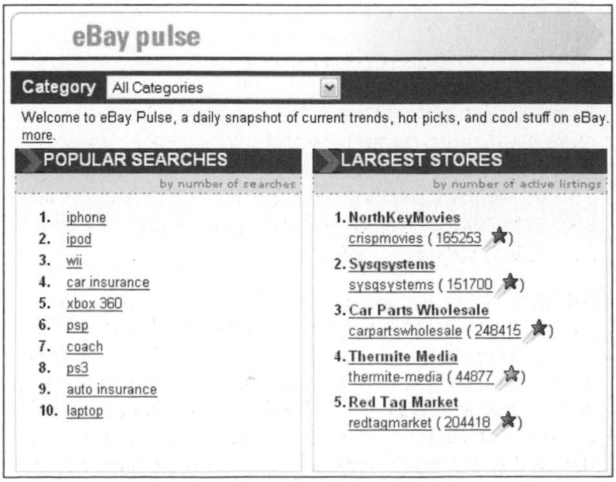

eBay pulse

Category: All Categories

Welcome to eBay Pulse, a daily snapshot of current trends, hot picks, and cool stuff on eBay. more.

POPULAR SEARCHES
by number of searches

1. iphone
2. ipod
3. wii
4. car insurance
5. xbox 360
6. psp
7. coach
8. ps3
9. auto insurance
10. laptop

LARGEST STORES
by number of active listings

1. **NorthKeyMovies**
   crispmovies (165253)
2. **Sysqsystems**
   sysqsystems (151700)
3. **Car Parts Wholesale**
   carpartswholesale (248415)
4. **Thermite Media**
   thermite-media (44877)
5. **Red Tag Market**
   redtagmarket (204418)

Figure 5-1: The daily updated "pulse" of eBay.

For amusement value (not solid selling data) at the bottom of the main Pulse page (all categories) you can find the Most Watched items in all categories. Here's where you can find the auctions that amuse those who visit eBay: get-rich-quick plans, toast with Jesus' image, and all the fun items.

On the other hand, when you select your category to examine, as in Figure 5-2, you'll not only see the top ten searches, but you get to see which hot items are most watched by eBay buyers (Figure 5-3). Here's where you can catch a break and see what's hot — right now.

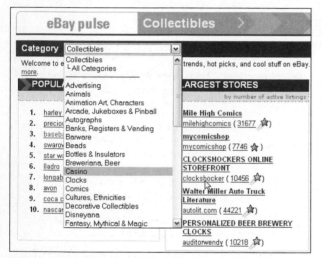

Figure 5-2: Taking the pulse of your selected category.

Figure 5-3: Seeing exactly what the peeps are watching.

Home-page promotions

Now, wouldn't you be the smart one if you were to list items that coincided with the promotions that show up on the eBay Home Page? Oh yeah — and I'll tell you where you can find out just what eBay plans to display ahead of time.

You can go to eBay's Seller Central for that data. Since eBay is constantly changing the location of links, make it easy on yourself by going directly to `pages.ebay.com/sellercentral/calendar.html`. Type the URL directly in your browser, and you'll come to the Seller Central calendar.

You'll find a current list of items that will be featured in the next couple of months, as shown in Figure 5-4.

 To find the home page for all the features I mention here, just type `pages.ebay.com/sellercentral` into your browser and you can click the appropriate links.

Merchandising Calendar

The following promotions will be highlighted on eBay's home page in the coming months.* Check back often for updates and be sure to stock up by visiting the eBay Wholesale Lots portal.

Events	Dates	Featured Categories
Halloween	10/1-10/31	Clothing, Shoes & Accessories, Everything Else
Thanksgiving	11/1-11/22	Home & Garden
Holiday	11/1-12/25	All
Get What You Really Wanted	12/26-12/31	All

Figure 5-4: eBay's Merchandising Calendar in Seller Central.

eBay's monthly hot sellers

eBay maintains an area that evaluates category sales on a monthly basis. Before you start thinking this data is all you need "to make big bucks on eBay," keep in mind that trends change by the moment and hot items on eBay can change by the day (for example, between the initial launch of a new product — when it's rare — and when it goes into full distribution across the country).

This data is broken down by category, so you can see which subcategories are hot. The Hot Categories Report is presented in a PDF file in Seller Central. You can go to the page directly at

```
pages.ebay.com/sellercentral/
    hotitems.pdf
```

Figure 5-5 shows you a sample page of this report and how eBay breaks things up by category level. There is a page for each major listing category; on that page, eBay breaks down the hot-selling items by level-2 through level-4 subcategories. This level of detail shows exactly what merchandise is moving off the site.

Cameras & Photos		
Super Hot		
Level 2	Level 3	Level 4
Camcorders	MiniDV	Sharp
Film Cameras	35mm Point & Shoot	Leica
Wholesale Lots	Cameras	Digital Cameras
Very Hot		
Level 2	Level 3	Level 4
Binoculars & Telescopes	Eyepieces & Telescope Accs.	Mirrors, Prisms & Holders
Binoculars & Telescopes	Telescopes	Schmidt-Cassegrain
Digital Cameras	Point & Shoot	8.0 Megapixels & More
Film Cameras	35mm Point & Shoot	Canon
Film Cameras	35mm Point & Shoot	Olympus
Flashes & Accessories	Film Camera Flash Units	Vivitar
Lighting & Studio Equipment	Portable Flash/Strobe	Flash Units
Printers, Scanners & Supplies	Photo Printers	Hewlett-Packard
Printers, Scanners & Supplies	Photo Printers	Kodak
Hot		
Level 2	Level 3	Level 4
Camcorder Accessories	Blank Tapes & Memory	8mm, Hi8
Digital Camera Accessories	Accessories	Camera & Printer Docks
Digital Camera Accessories	Memory Cards	xD Picture Card
Digital Cameras	Parts & Repair	Parts & Repair
Digital Cameras	Point & Shoot	2.0 to 2.9 Megapixels
Film Cameras	Large Format	5x7 & Smaller
Projection Equipment	Accessories	Slide Viewer

Figure 5-5: Seems there's still money to be made by buying old film cameras at garage sales and selling them on eBay.

EBay's methodology for this report is precise and displays results updated monthly (down to a level-4 subcategory) items that

- ✔ Have a Month-over-Month bid growth of at least 1 percent.

- ✔ Show a bid-per-item figure greater than the average for the relevant level-3 category.

- ✔ Show a Conversion rate (rate of listings to sales) of at least 50 percent for the level-4 category in the most recent month.

- ✔ Receive at least 100 bids per week for items in the level-4 category.

eBay's degrees of "Hotness"

- ✔ **Super Hot:** These items show at least a 35 percentage spread between bid growth and listing growth. eBay describes the spread decision this way:

  For instance, month-over-month bid growth for the L4 Category may be 50 percent, while month-over-month listing growth for the L4 Category may be 10 percent. Because the percentage-point spread (40 percentage points) is greater than 35 percent, this category is deemed "Super Hot."

  Read that four or five times and you'll understand why eBay needs a For Dummies book.

- ✔ **Very Hot:** These items show a percentage-point spread between 15 percent and 35 percent.

- ✔ **Hot:** These are the remaining hot level-4 subcategories with spreads up to 15 percent.

Is It the "Buzz" or the "Zeitgeist?"

That's a tough call. Yahoo has its Buzz page and Google labs has its Zeitgeist page. These two daily pages will give you an up-to-the-second look at what the world is looking to buy at any particular moment — in real time. Deciding who's right or wrong isn't an issue. I think the difference in the results of each report show the difference between Google and Yahoo! users. (Hey, what do I know, I just study this stuff.)

The eBay site is the world's host for popular culture. If it's hot, people come to eBay to look for it. You should also look on the Internet to find the buzz or the Zeitgeist. There is a difference:

- By *buzz* I mean the latest gossip, rumor, or thing that's talked about at the water cooler at work. Something that's the buzz can become a trend — and trends are what you look for to find profits in the world of eBay.
- Google defines *Zeitgeist* (pronounce "ei" like a long *i* sound) this way: "Etymology: German, from Zeit (time) + Geist (spirit) . . . the general intellectual, moral, and cultural climate of an era."

Checking out the buzz on Yahoo!

You can find the beginnings of buzz in any news report or on your Internet provider's home page. Yahoo! has Yahoo!'s Buzz Index, at `buzz.yahoo.com/overall/`. It's a daily compilation of items that have received the largest number of searches on their system. You can see what's new on the list, what's going up, and what's going down. Figure 5-6 shows the Overall Searches from January 17, 2008.

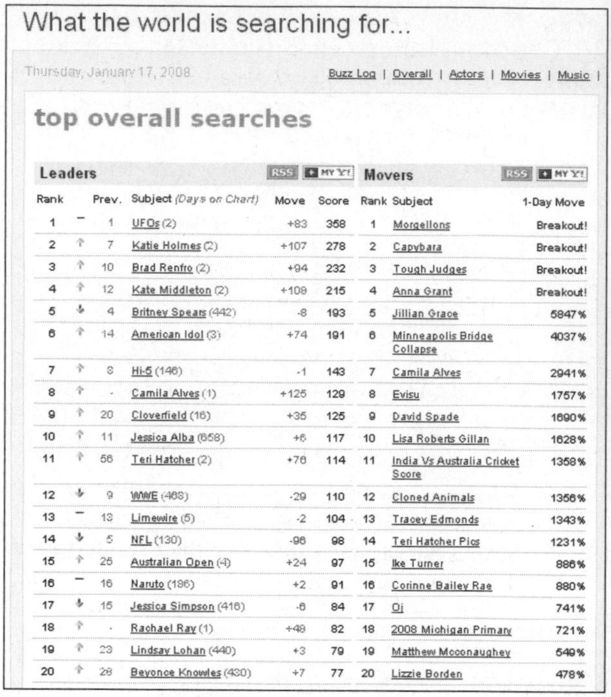
What the world is searching for...

Thursday, January 17, 2008 — Buzz Log | Overall | Actors | Movies | Music |

top overall searches

Leaders: Rank		Prev.	Subject (Days on Chart)	Move	Score	Movers: Rank	Subject	1-Day Move
1	—	1	UFOs (2)	+83	358	1	Morgellons	Breakout!
2	↑	7	Katie Holmes (2)	+107	278	2	Capybara	Breakout!
3	↑	10	Brad Renfro (2)	+94	232	3	Tough Judges	Breakout!
4	↑	12	Kate Middleton (2)	+108	215	4	Anna Grant	Breakout!
5	↓	4	Britney Spears (442)	-8	193	5	Jillian Grace	5847%
6	↑	14	American Idol (3)	+74	191	6	Minneapolis Bridge Collapse	4037%
7	↑	8	Hi-5 (146)	-1	143	7	Camila Alves	2941%
8	↑	-	Camila Alves (1)	+125	129	8	Evisu	1757%
9	↑	20	Cloverfield (16)	+35	125	9	David Spade	1690%
10	↑	11	Jessica Alba (658)	+6	117	10	Lisa Roberts Gillan	1628%
11	↑	56	Teri Hatcher (2)	+76	114	11	India Vs Australia Cricket Score	1358%
12	↓	9	WWE (463)	-29	110	12	Cloned Animals	1356%
13	—	13	Limewire (5)	-2	104	13	Tracey Edmonds	1343%
14	↓	5	NFL (130)	-96	98	14	Teri Hatcher Pics	1231%
15	↑	25	Australian Open (4)	+24	97	15	Ike Turner	886%
16	—	16	Naruto (186)	+2	91	16	Corinne Bailey Rae	880%
17	↓	15	Jessica Simpson (416)	-6	84	17	Oj	741%
18	↑	-	Rachael Ray (1)	+48	82	18	2008 Michigan Primary	721%
19	↑	23	Lindsay Lohan (440)	+3	79	19	Matthew Mcconaughey	549%
20	↑	28	Beyonce Knowles (430)	+7	77	20	Lizzie Borden	478%

Figure 5-6: What's hot on Yahoo!, a snapshot of the day's pop culture.

Who's hot on the Zeitgeist page?

My personal favorite is the Zeitgeist; perhaps because my pop-culture thoughts are deftly reflected in the Google users' searches. Google's search index does not reflect your personal searches (who makes the searches is unidentified), but the daily searches, like the Hot Trends shown in Figure 5-7, are pulled daily from Google's massive hard drives.

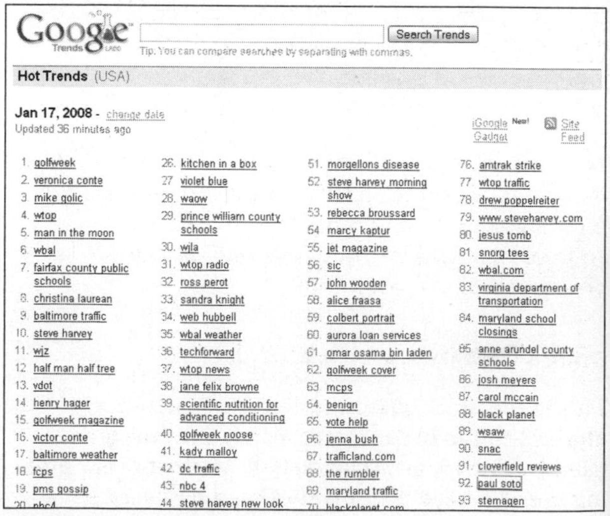

Figure 5-7: Hot Trends on Google.

If you're in a fun mood to see some of Google's crazy, self-deprecating humor, check out their undeniable sense of fun at their spoof "PigeonRank" page (originally posted for April Fools' Day 2002):

```
www.google.com/technology/pigeon
rank.html
```

"When a search query is submitted to Google, it is routed to a data coop where monitors flash result pages at blazing speeds. When a relevant result is observed by one of the pigeons in the cluster, it strikes a rubber-coated steel bar with its beak, which assigns the page a PigeonRank value of one. For each peck, the PigeonRank increases. Those pages receiving the most pecks are returned at the top of the user's results page with the other results displayed in pecking order." You gotta love those guys at Google.

Tools to Gather Exclusive Data

Okay, we've taken a look at data that's offered on a silver platter — and although I've shown you trusted sources, there's nothing that beats getting data that you alone have access to. When you do your own research, you're more likely to find the golden nugget you've been really looking for.

The tools below can be used when you're planning on making a purchase (the best time), or once you have a giant lot of merchandise to sell. These sources can help you decide when, where, and for how much to sell your stuff.

eBay's Completed Item search

This is the most basic and the most accurate barometer of what is selling on eBay. It's the tool most used by PowerSellers when they're timing and pricing their listings. Since you're on the advanced track, I won't give you a step-by-step on how to do an eBay search. But, as a reminder, once you've searched for the item you want to sell, look to the left side of the page; click the *Completed Listings* link and repeat the search.

Marketplace Research from eBay

This under-respected eBay tool lets you gather current data on selling trends, as well as view and analyze top searches, average start prices, average sold prices, and more. It's a subscription product (you have to pay for it), but if you get organized you can get in at nominal cost.

With Marketplace Research, you can view how many items are listed and how many of those sold successfully within a prescribed time period. This will alert you to trends that will help you decide what, where, and when to sell. When you perform a Marketplace search on an item, you'll see charts and graphs that illustrate sale price and bidding trends. Some of the things Marketplace shows include the following:

- Average number of bids/item
- Average sold price
- Number of items sold
- Number of completed items
- Average starting price
- Number of items sold

The service is available at three tier levels, and the most economical is the two-day pass (access data back 60 days on eBay's servers) for only $2.99. For $9.99 a month you can get daily access along with extra features. For $24.99 you can go back 90 days and get oodles of extra data. The question is, since eBay is constantly changing, why would you go *back* 90 days? And would oodles of data waste a whole lot of time? Your call. To make your own decision, go to the level comparison page at

```
pages.ebay.com/marketplace_research/
    detailed-comparison.html
```

Mining your data with Terapeak

I really like Terapeak (as you can tell by my references to them elsewhere in the book). Using Terapeak, eBay sellers can instantly research up-to-the-minute prices and demand for items sold on eBay. Terapeak gets this secret information as a member of eBay's data licensing program with access to all of eBay's completed auction metrics. Terapeak data helps deliver the information you need to get a better grip on predicting the performance of your items for sale.

Using Terapeak, sellers can compare the previous sales success of different listings for exactly the same items. Yes, this is a pay-for-play service, but Terapeak also features a free eBay research package that offers members complete, detailed reports: You get the scoop on products sold, including information on the best times to sell, pricing, listing formats, features that maximize sales, and keyword and title recommendations. (If you can get all that for free — can you imagine how much you get when you pay for the service?)

Figure 5-8 shows a snapshot from Terapeak's free service on recent sales of my new and used books in the past seven days.

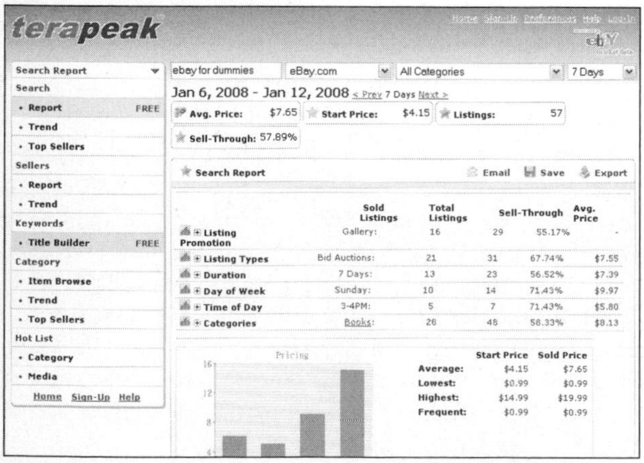

Figure 5-8: Seven days' worth of sale of new and used books.

The full-blown Terapeak service costs $197.95 a year (a 34 percent savings over their $24.95 per month subscription fee). Check the entire home page because often you'll find a considerable discount deal.

To see what you get for your money, go to `www.terapeak.com/signup`.

Personal listing information from Sellathon ViewTracker

ViewTracker from Sellathon answers the most popular questions I'm asked by eBay sellers. It works differently from the other services I've mentioned: When you enter a small amount of supplied HTML code into your descriptions, ViewTracker analyzes your listings to teach you what's working — and not working.

Before ViewTracker, trying to figure out the exact time and day to end a particular auction was a chore: You had to do a considerable amount of research by running test auctions on the eBay site. Now you can follow the "body clocks" of your buyers and find out when *they* search for your type of item.

Here's a partial list of the type of data you can get by using the ViewTracker system:

- ✔ Sequential number of the visitor. Is this the 19th visitor or the 104th — and will this person come back again?

- ✔ Date and time the visitor arrived at your auction.

- ✔ Visitor's IP address. By clicking the IP address in the Sellathon screen, you can see only those visits originating from this IP address.

- ✔ What City, State, and Country your visitor is from.

- ✔ Whether the Reserve Price was met when the visitor arrived.

- ✔ When the item receives a bid (and how many have been placed to that moment).

- ✔ Whether the current visitor is the high bidder, a bidder who has been outbid, or no bidder at all.

✔ Whether the visitor has chosen to watch this listing in his or her My eBay page.

✔ Whether the visitor browsed a category, searched a category, searched all of eBay, used eBay's Product Finder Utility, came from "See Seller's Other Items," or some other page.

▶ If the visitors were browsing, which category were they browsing when they clicked into your listing?

▶ If they were searching, what search terms did they use to find your item?

▶ If they were searching when they came upon your item, did they search Titles Only or Titles and Descriptions?

✔ Did they elect to view Auctions Only, Buy It Now, or both?

✔ Did they refine searches using specific parameters? These include Show/Hide pictures, Sellers that accept PayPal, Price Range, International Availability, Regional Searching, Gallery View, and Show Gift Items.

✔ Was there a preference in the way they sorted the search results? Did they search items from High Price to Low Price?

Amazing stuff, eh? By applying the information from ViewTracker, you can change tactics to help your little business grow into a big one. You'll be able to customize your items to match your very own eBay market.

There's a whole lot more to ViewTracker. The cost for the program starts at $49.95 a year. For a free trial, go to www.sellathon.com/coolebaytools.

6 Finding Merchandise to Sell

Practice

In This Practice

- ✓ Finding merchandise like a pro
- ✓ Visiting marts and trade shows
- ✓ Learning the players without a scorecard
- ✓ Buying off-price goods
- ✓ Looking overseas
- ✓ Drop-shipping or not

If anything vexes the up-and-coming eBay seller, it's the question, "*What* do I sell?" And the second question that then jumps to mind is "Where am I going to *find* merchandise?" These queries, of course, morph into the standard "What can I sell to make the most money on eBay?" These are all good questions. Actually the answers are obvious — or will be, after I outline them in this practice. But think about the situation and consider this question: "What successful seller has answers that they want to share with the competition?"

When profitable eBay PowerSellers have a good, solid source of merchandise, they're not likely to share the name of that source with anyone — nor would any brick-and-mortar retailer. (Think about it a minute.) When I was teaching a class for advanced sellers at eBay Live (the annual eBay convention), I was asked *the* question in an auditorium-size room filled with PowerSellers. I answered a question with a question: Were there any PowerSellers in the audience who would like to share their sources with the rest of the group? You could have heard a pin drop. So I upped the ante — "I'll pay anyone $10 for one solid source" — still silence. Business is business.

And as an eBay seller, you find yourself inundated with e-mail — as well as seeing auctions on eBay — offering wholesale source lists. These messages guarantee that you'll find items you *can* sell on eBay, purportedly very lucratively. Yes, but *will* they sell? More importantly, will they sell at a profit? Not everything on eBay sells like hotcakes.

The bottom line here is that all successful sellers tweak out their own sources. What works for one may not work for another; different types of financial transactions and personal relationships work for different vendors. I gleaned the methods for finding goods that I include in this practice from my own research, as well as from interviews with successful online retailers.

Don't make the liquidation mistake

I once got an e-mail from a young couple planning to borrow money to purchase a pallet of liquidation goods to start an eBay business. I immediately wrote back to try to dissuade these young people. They had no idea of what *liquidation merchandise* meant — and the challenges involved in making a profit with it. They just thought they were buying a load of new and like-new merchandise for pennies on the dollar. Don't make that mistake. If a deal seems too good, the goods usually aren't worth what you're paying for them. (Be sure to read on for information on how to make informed decisions about liquidation merchandise.)

Always exercise some caution (and a little healthy skepticism) when someone sells (along with his or her "wholesale" merchandise) tips or newsletters on how to "get rich quick" or "make big money" on eBay. Legitimate wholesalers are there to move goods quickly from their warehouses to retailers. Their business is not to teach you how to "make it big" on eBay. And before you stock up on *anything*, consider this bit of wisdom from Danny Goodman (the Dodger baseball marketing wizard from the O'Malley days): When a vendor told him that an item would "sell like hotcakes," Danny replied, "Hotcakes don't sell at all in stadiums."

Finding out Where Stores Buy Their Merchandise

Okay, you've set up shop on eBay, and you want to ramp up to PowerSeller status. You kind-of-know what type of merchandise you want to ramp up with, but you don't know where to turn to get the volume and the quality you need. Anyone in

the brick-and-mortar world who plans to open or expand a store faces the same quandary: finding merchandise that will sell quickly at a profit.

Merchandise that sits around doesn't give you cash flow — which is the name of the game in any business. (*Cash flow* = profit = money to buy better, or more, merchandise.) I spoke to several successful retailers, and they all gave me the same answers about where they began their quest. The upcoming sections give you a look at the answers these retailers shared.

To gain access to legitimate wholesale sources, you must be a licensed business in your city or county. You also have to have a resale permit and tax ID number from your state.

When you do become a PowerSeller, you'll be able to shop for merchandise on eBay's Reseller Marketplace. It's a place where you can buy excess inventory directly from many manufacturers, liquidators, and wholesalers. Admittance to this site is only for **PowerSellers** at `http://reseller.ebay.com`.

Finding merchandise locally

Always remember that the cost of shipping the merchandise to you adds a great deal of expense. The higher your total expense per item, the lower your profit will be. The more you buy locally to resell, the more profit you can make.

The first place most potential retailers go is to their local wholesale district. You can find yours in your yellow pages (remember that giant brick of a book they drop in your driveway once a year?) under the name of your item. For example, suppose you want to sell women's apparel. You'd look up *Women's Apparel* in the yellow pages and find the subcategory of *Wholesale*. Bingo! Immediate merchandise sources, within driving distance of your home! Also be sure to check the directories in neighboring communities as well. The value of this printed (and usually overlooked) resource is immeasurable when you're starting up a business.

Newspaper auction listings

Another excellent source of merchandise for resale is your daily newspaper — in particular, the listings of major liquidation and estate auctions (usually on Saturday). Check out your daily newspaper each day and look for this page or section.

You may want to sell women's apparel, but if you can get a great deal on office or pet supplies, paying cents on the dollar, you just may bend your way of thinking!

Don't miss the daily classified section — look for ads that announce local business liquidations. Do not confuse any of this with garage sales or flea-market sales (run by individuals and often a great source for one-of-a kind items). Liquidation or estate sales are professionally run, usually by licensed liquidators or auctioneers and involve merchandise that may be new but is always sold in *lots* (in a quantity).

 If your local newspaper has a Web site, use its online search to view the classifieds for major liquidations, estate auctions, or other similar deals. Right there online, you can often find just what you are looking for locally.

Regional merchandise marts

Your next stop, should you be lucky enough to live in close proximity, is a regional merchandise or fashion mart near you. These marts are giant complexes that hold up to several thousand lines of merchandise in one area.

Merchandise marts are hubs for wholesale buyers, distributors, manufacturers, and independent sales representatives. They have showrooms within the property for manufacturers or their representatives to display their current merchandise. Under one roof, you may find both fashion and gift merchandise for your eBay business.

See Table 6-1 for a representative sprinkling of the many marts across the country. Realize that this is not a comprehensive list, just one to get your mind moving. You can contact the individual marts for tenant lists and more information. If you are a legitimate business, they will be more than happy to teach you the ropes and get you started.

My very favorite, the California Market Center has tons of useful information to help newbies get going. Also, some of the showrooms at the CMC honor a historical habit of selling samples to the general public on the last Friday of the month. This sample sale occurs only when the timing does not conflict with a major market event, which is when retailers are here to shop the market for future deliveries to their stores.

TABLE 6-1: WHOLESALE MERCHANDISE SOURCE MARTS

Name	Location	Web Site Address	Trade Shows
Americas Mart	Atlanta, Georgia	`www.americasmart.com`	Apparel, jewelry, shoes, fashion accessories, gifts, home furnishings
California Market Center	Los Angeles, CA	`www.californiamarketcenter.com`	Apparel, accessories, textiles, toys, gifts, furniture and décor, garden accessories, stationery, personal-care products
The Merchandise Mart	Chicago, Ill	`www.mmart.com`	Apparel, office, home, decorative accessories, textiles, gifts
The Chicago Market	Chicago, IL	`www.giftandhome.com`	Apparel, home furnishings, antiques, gifts, bridal
Columbus Marketplace	Columbus, OH	`www.thecolumbusmarketplace.com`	Gifts, garden, home furnishings, décor
Dallas Market Center	Dallas, TX	`www.dallasmarketcenter.com`	Apparel, gift products, decorative accessories, home furnishings, lighting, garden accessories, floral, and gourmet
Denver Merchandise Mart	Denver, CO	`www.denvermart.com`	Apparel, gifts, souvenirs, gourmet, collectibles, home décor
International Home Furnishings	High Point, NC	`www.ihfc.com`	Home furnishings and décor of all types
Kansas City Gift Mart	Kansas City, MO	`www.kcgiftmart.com`	Gifts, gourmet, design, home décor
The L.A. Mart	Los Angeles, CA	`www.lamart.com`	Gifts, home décor, furnishings
Miami Merchandise Mart	Miami, FL	`www.miamimart.net`	Apparel, gifts, accessories, home décor
Minneapolis Gift Mart	Minneapolis, MN	`www.mplsgiftmart.com`	Gifts, home décor, accessories
New York Merchandise Mart	New York, NY	`www.41madison.com`	Gifts, home décor, accessories
7W	New York, NY	`www.225-fifth.com`	Gifts, home décor, accessories, stationery
San Francisco Gift Center	San Francisco, CA	`www.gcjm.com`	Apparel, jewelry, home furnishings, gifts, jewelry, stationery
The New Mart	Los Angeles, CA	`www.newmart.net`	Contemporary clothing and accessories

In the month of December, sample selling happens each Friday except when Friday falls on a holiday or the eve of a holiday. To get a peek at the California Market Center's partial 2008 calendar, check out Table 6-2.

TABLE 6-2: 2008 CALIFORNIA MARKET CENTER SHOW DATES*

Month	Date	Event name
January	11-15	LA Fashion Market Summer '08
	12-14	TRANSIT | LA Footwear & Accessories Show
	15-21	CMC Gift & Home Market
March	14-18	LA Fashion, Gift & Home Market Fall '08
	15-17	TRANSIT | LA Footwear & Accessories Show
April	7-09	LA Majors Market Fall '08
	14-16	LA Int'l Textile Show Spring/Summer '09
June	6-10	LA Fashion Market Fall II/Holiday '08
	7-09	LA Footwear & Accessories Show
July	15-21	CMC Gift & Home Market
August	8-12	LA Fashion Market Holiday/Resort '08
	9-11	TRANSIT | LA Footwear & Accessories Show
October	5-07	LA Majors Market Spring '09
	17-21	LA Fashion, Gift & Home Market Spring '09
	18-20	TRANSIT | LA Footwear & Accessories Show
	27-29	LA Int'l Textile Show Autumn '09/Winter '10

*All dates are subject to change.

When you go to each mart's Web site, you find hundreds of links to wholesale sources. Many marts also send you a directory of the manufacturers represented in the mart.

One of my favorite Web sites, `www.greatrep.com`, has hundreds of sources for the newest, hottest merchandise. To see these sources, you will have to register with your reseller's permit as identification. This service is for The Trade only *(and yes, you are The Trade!)*.

A cool feature on the greatrep.com site can be accessed without registering. The site offers a fairly complete calendar of all the merchandise trade shows across the U.S. This is excellent information, because many cities don't have marts, but do host merchandise shows. (The Salt Lake Gift Show is a perfect example.) Find the link on the home page, or go directly to `www.greatrep.com/trade_shows.asp`.

Wholesale trade shows

By checking out the links to the marts listed in Table 6-1, you also end up with links to the thousands of wholesale trade shows that go on across the country each year.

Trade shows are commonly held in convention centers, hotels, and at the local merchandise marts.

When visiting a show or a mart, view all merchandise before you place an order. Bring a notebook with you to make copious notes of items you find interesting and where you find them.

These trade shows are gargantuan bourses — hundreds of wholesale vendors all lined up and ready to take your orders. The vendors have samples of the merchandise in the lines they carry, and are delighted to answer all your questions about their products, credit applications, and minimum orders. These shows are designed to move product to retailers like you!

Very few trade shows are more exciting than the Consumer Electronics Show (CES), sponsored by the Consumer Electronics Association. If you buy breakthrough technologies to sell online, this show is a must! You'll find the latest in everything high-tech — including digital imaging, electronic gaming, home electronics, car audio, home theater, satellite systems, and much, much more. It takes days to see this show. You'll see what's new, but more importantly, you'll see what will be passé in a hurry — great merchandise to sell fast on eBay!

CES draws over 100,000 buyers each year, and the vendors are there to sell their goods to you. Visit the CES Web site at www.cesweb.org to get an idea of the excitement that the show generates.

 Find out whether the merchandise you're interested in is selling on eBay *before* you make your purchase. Bring a laptop with a wireless connection (to take advantage of the hot spot at the show) or make notes for purchases on another day. Getting a good deal on merchandise is one thing — selling it on eBay is another.

Figuring out Who's Who in the Industry

It would be very simple if you just bought merchandise from a manufacturer. But that's rarely the case. A full team of players participates in the wholesale game, and each player performs a different task. So you'll understand how to follow the plays without a program, here's a brief rundown:

- ✔ **Manufacturers:** Buying directly from a manufacturer may get you great prices, but may not be a place for a beginner to start. Manufacturers usually require large minimum orders from retailers. Unless you have a group of other sellers (perhaps a friend who owns a retail store?) to split your order with, you may have to make your purchase from middlemen who've marked up the item for their own profit.

 An exception to the large-quantity requirement may be in the apparel industry. Because apparel has distinct, rapidly changing fashion seasons, a quick turnover in merchandise is a must. Apparel manufacturers may allow you to make small purchases toward the end of the current season to outfit your eBay store. It never hurts to ask.

✔ **Wholesalers (also Distributors):** Here's your first step to finding your "middleman." Wholesalers purchase direct from the manufacturer in large quantities. They sell the merchandise to smaller retailers who cannot take advantage of the discounts from manufacturers for large orders.

The important thing is to find a wholesaler who is familiar with (or better yet, specializes in) the type of merchandise you want to sell. Obviously, someone who specializes in prerecorded DVDs and videos will not have much of a clue about the fashion market, and vice versa.

Don't forget to check local wholesalers (as described in "Finding merchandise locally," earlier in this practice) to find some good sources.

✔ **Manufacturer's reps:** These are generally the type of people you'll meet at trade shows or marts — the traditional Willy Loman kind of salesman. They represent one or many noncompeting manufacturers and sell their merchandise to retailers for a commission.

✔ **Jobbers or brokers:** Jobbers and brokers are independent businesspeople who buy merchandise from anywhere they can at distressed prices. They mostly deal in liquidation or salvage merchandise.

Don't forget to negotiate. Almost *everything* in the wholesale merchandise world is negotiable. Although merchandise may have a set price, you may be able to get a discount if you offer to pay on delivery, or within ten days. Ask whether your sources can help you out with shipping costs (and perhaps promotions). You just may get a discount if you promote their products through banner ads. Ask, ask, ask. The worst that can happen is that they say no.

Selecting Your Merchandise

You're likely to find various levels of quality when you look for merchandise to resell on eBay. If you take time to evaluate the condition of the merchandise you're getting, you save time (and money) in the long run. Receiving a box of ripped or stained goods when you expected first-quality merchandise can be pretty disheartening. Know what the industry language tells you about the quality of the merchandise you're looking to buy. And ask, ask, *ask* — about the condition of the merchandise, that is. Before you put down your money for goods, qualify 'em.

In addition to qualifying the goods you buy, take the time to qualify the processes and partners you use. For example, *drop-shipping* (shipping goods straight from a stockpile to the consumer) is ever more popular as a method to move the merchandise sold on eBay — but it comes with many caveats. For example, eBay has a policy about pre-selling items, so be sure to check it out — and make sure your drop-shipper has the merchandise ready to go when you place your order. Read on to get the goods on what to check out *before* you get the goods from a drop-shipper.

Know the Lingo of Merchandisers

Yes, you know that *apparel* is clothing, but did you know that the wholesale industry has its own vocabulary? Here are some terms you're likely to run across:

✔ **Job lots:** The word *job* appears randomly throughout the wholesale industry. A manufacturer may want to "job out" some merchandise that's off-season. In this use, a *job lot* simply refers to a bunch of merchandise sold at once. The goods may consist of unusual sizes, odd colors, or even some hideous stuff that wouldn't blow out of your eBay store if a hurricane came in. Some of the merchandise (usually no more than 15 percent) may be damaged.

 A good way to find a *jobber* (someone who wants to sell you job lots) on the Internet is to run a Google search on *wholesale jobber*. Another great place to find them is the phone book or industry newsletter classifieds.

There are super discounts to be had on job lots — and if the lot contains brand names from major stores, you may be able to make an excellent profit.

✔ **Off-price lots:** If you can get hold of top-quality, brand-name items in off-price lots, you can do very well on eBay. These items are end-of-season *overruns* (they made more items then they could sell through their normal retailers). You can generally find this merchandise toward the end of the buying season.

Many eBay sellers, without having the thousands of dollars to buy merchandise, make friends with the salespeople at manufacturers' outlet stores (that's where the merchandise may land first). Others haunt places like TJ Maxx, Marshall's, and Burlington Coat Factory for first-rate deals.

 Search genuine trade publications' classified ads for items to buy in bulk. Publications like *California Apparel News* have classifieds that are accessible online. Visit their Web site, www.apparelnews.net and click *classifieds*.

✔ **Liquidations:** All the eBay sellers think of liquidations as the mother lode of deals. And, yes, they may be the mother lode of deals if you can afford to buy and store an entire truckload (that's an 18-wheeler's container) of merchandise. That takes a great deal of money and a great deal of square footage. Not to mention the staff to go through each and every piece.

You could end up with close to 50 *pallets* (the wooden platforms that measure 4'×4', stacked as high) of merchandise from a liquidation purchase.

You may be able to buy a single pallet or two, rather than a full load, from a liquidator, but a single pallet is even more of a gamble — you won't have the breadth of merchandise to amortize the damaged goods that could be in the load. Check for any of the following when dealing with these wares:

▶ This merchandise can be an assortment of liquidations, store returns, salvage, closeouts, shelf pulls, overstocks, broken items and surplus goods.

▶ As much as 40 percent (if not more) of a truckload may be totally useless to your business.

▶ Some items may be damaged but repairable; others *may* be perfectly saleable.

Buying liquidation merchandise is a gamble but can have advantages. By buying a full truckload, you have a wide breadth of merchandise, you'll pay the lowest amount for it, and some of it may be good for spare parts.

 Save yourself some money. Don't go on eBay and buy some "list" of wholesalers for $5. You can get the same names by running a Google search on the term *wholesale*.

Staying Safe when Buying Liquidations

 Nobody offers a quality or fitness guarantee when you buy liquidation merchandise. You could end up with pallets of unsalable merchandise, and you must steer quickly away from anyone who "guarantees" you'll make money.

Because all liquidation merchandise is sold "as is," here are a few suggestions for dealing with the uncertainties:

- **Get an anonymous free e-mail address** from Yahoo! before signing up for any "mailing lists" or "newsletters." Some Web sites that offer these publications make most of their money by selling your e-mail address to spammers. If you give them an anonymous e-mail address, the all-too-frequent buckets of spam that result will never end up in your real mailbox. (I learned about that the hard way.)

- **Raise your shields.** If the "wholesalers" also link their Web sites to miscellaneous make-big-profits-at-eBay Web sites, beware. They may be making most of their money from commissions when the e-book of "road-to-riches" secret tips is sold to you.

- **Be sure there is a phone number on the site.** Give them a call and see how you're treated. It's no guarantee of how they'll treat you if you're unhappy with a purchase, but you may get a human being on the phone (rare and precious these days).

- **Look for a physical address.** Do they have a place of business or is the company running out of some guy's pocket cell phone? (Often it's not a good sign if there's no place to *hang* a sign.)

- **Ask for references.** Seeing the Better Business Bureau Online, TrustE, or SquareTrade logo on the Web site can bolster trust in the company. (They actually have to qualify for those seals.)

- **Before you purchase anything, go to eBay and see whether that item will sell — and for how much.** Use eBay's search engine and check the completed listings (as I describe in Practice 5). Often you find hundreds of listings for an item with no bids. Check completed auctions and be sure that the item is selling for a solid profit over what you expect to pay for it (including shipping).

- **Never buy anything just because it's cheap.** That was true in Thomas Jefferson's day and it's still true today. Be sure you can actually *sell* the merchandise. (I also learned this the hard way.)

- **Look for the word FOB.** That means *freight on board*. You will be charged freight from the location of the merchandise to your door. The shorter the distance, the cheaper your freight costs.

 Before doing business on any Web site, be sure its owners have a Privacy Policy that protects your personal information. Also check for an About Us page. Be sure the About Us page really talks about the business and the people behind it. I hate to be repetitive, but be sure you can reach a human being on a phone or in person (with a street address) if need be.

Internet Shopping for Resale Merchandise

I've come across many legitimate sources of goods on the Internet. There are some really good ones. But as I mentioned in the preceding section, the Internet is loaded with scam artists; it's up to you to check vendors out for yourself before spending your hard-earned money. Even if I mention sellers here, I want you to check them out as if you knew nothing about them. I cannot guarantee a thing; all I know is that at the time of writing, they were reliable sources for eBay merchandise.

 You must have a Federal Tax ID number (that's your identification to do business) — and possibly a State Reseller's Permit number — to even register on the most legitimate wholesale sites. Finding wholesale Web sites with this restriction is a *good* thing. It's another way to verify that you're the dealing with a legitimate supplier.

Liquidation.com

If you like auctions (and I *know* you do), check out `Liquidation.com`. This is a massive all-auction Web site that has incredible deals on all types of merchandise.

One of the things I love about this site is that when you're inspecting the individual auctions, often you find that many auctioneers provide a link to the *manifest* — a list of every piece of merchandise in the lot. Then, if you click the word *Manifest* at the top of the auction page, you see an exact, piece-by-piece list of the items included in the lot you're bidding on.

Liquidation.com also has a shipping calculator to help you know ahead of time how much your shipping costs may be.

Wholesale Central

One of the largest sites of wholesalers on the Internet is `Wholesalecentral.com`. You'll find everything from women's apparel to flea-market items — all with their own clickable links and phone numbers. The site is the brainchild of Sumner Publications. They have a linked online directory of thousands of wholesale sources selling all types of merchandise. They also publish a monthly magazine called *Web Wholesaler*.

Big Lots Wholesale

If you're familiar with the Big Lots stores scattered around the country, then you have an idea of what you can buy at `biglotswholesale.com`. A quick click took me to their Web site — and showed me they were loaded with great deals on everything from health and beauty items to toys to lawn and garden tools! Before placing an order, be sure to check and see whether the item is selling on eBay. If many eBay sellers are trying to sell the item now, why not place an order and sell when the other sellers have exhausted their stock? When fewer sellers are selling, the price usually goes up. "Supply and demand" is the name of the game.

 Sites like Big Lots Wholesale change merchandise quickly, so when you find something that piques your interest, research it quickly and buy it. It may not be there when you check back.

Great Rep

Established in 1999, GreatRep.com is an Internet directory of wholesale giftware, home furnishing, and furniture industry. You can easily view new sources on the site, and even order catalogs and place orders at `www.greatrep.com`.

Bargain Wholesale

Bargain Wholesale is an incredibly fun site that has loads and loads of high-quality, low-priced merchandise. It's the wholesale unit of the famous 99¢ Only stores that started in their City of Commerce California offices. They sell directly to retailers, distributors, and exporters.

If you live in Los Angeles, Houston, or Chicago, you can visit one of their showrooms. If not, you can purchase merchandise online on their Web site at `www.bargainw.com` and shop for your business. To be able to buy at the site, however, you must have a business license or a resale number from your state. They also have a minimum order; if it's too high for you, why not split an order with another seller?

 On a visit to CES, you can connect with distributors who sell wholesale consumer electronics to small legitimate resellers. A good company that I've discovered is **D&H Distributing** (`www.DandH.com`). With six national warehouses to drawn on, it's a one-stop source for IT, consumer electronics, and gaming products. Another good source is **Evertek** (a discount distributor found online at `www.evertek.com`). Evertek offers wholesale distribution of excess and close-out consumer electronics, computer hardware, and peripherals.

Importing Your Merchandise

I know this is possibly one of the scariest things eBay sellers do — and if the thought of importing doesn't scare you, then you'd better get your scare-o-meter checked. Dealings with a company that's oceans away are based on a whole new level of trust. There's no PayPal to protect you, no credit-card warranties to watch your back. It's just you and the cash that you wire overseas. I have imported items to sell on eBay, and after my first nail-biting transactions . . . I'm ready to do it again.

You can find some Web sites that are directories that connect you with manufacturers overseas, but they don't guarantee the performance of the vendors that sell on the site. Just like eBay, they can't. Some nightmares that go along with importing merchandise range from receiving an incomplete order to getting word that the vessel carrying the goods sank on the way to its destination. (I swear, I really saw that on a bulletin board.)

When you purchase goods from overseas, it is customary to pay in advance, through a bank, using wire transfer. Say goodbye to your cash and pray delivery occurs in a timely manner. Sending that transfer is a simple task — and with most major banks, you can do this all online.

The best way to import items is to do business with a manufacturer that comes to you with recommendations from other businesses you know personally and can call to confirm. (*Personally* is the key word here — anyone can come up with a bogus list of references.)

Another way is to find a vendor at a trade show. Often a company is required to become a member of the organization behind the show to purchase a booth. At least *someone* checks them out. This is how I found my vendor in Taiwan.

After you've got the vendor and have selected the merchandise you want to buy, you pay for it and it's sent to you in one of several ways. Pretty

straightforward. My personal experience is with air freight and items sent by ship:

- ✔ **Air freight:** Expensive! But a viable alternative if you are buying your items at a very reasonable price (you've confirmed this by researching the market) and there's plenty of room to add a buck or so to your cost.

- ✔ **Slow boat from China (or fill in your products' country of origin here):** This method is really, really reasonable. Don't let anyone tell you that you have to order a full container of merchandise to ship by sea. I've received orders as small as 2 pallets. Note, however, a couple of things to keep in mind when shipping by sea:

  - ▶ **There's a lot more paperwork.** Your manufacturer is used to doing all this so expect that you be e-mailed PDF files of your invoice, packing lists, and Bill of Lading.

  - ▶ **You need another partner in this transaction.** That's a freight-forwarding company. These people also receive copies of your documents and have representatives at the receiving dock. They handle any customs or other regulatory bureaucratic chores. They also handle the transportation of your merchandise to your office (or, if your business is like mine, your garage).

All in all, if you have the right suppliers, importing merchandise can be a pleasant and profitable way to add to your product offerings.

Dealing with Drop-Shippers

The second-most-asked question I get wants the lowdown on drop-shippers. A *drop-shipper* is a business that stocks merchandise and sells it to you (the reseller) — but ships the merchandise directly to your customer.

By using a drop-shipper, you transfer the risks of buying merchandise, shipping it, and storing it to another party. You become a *stockless* retailer with no inventory hanging around — which can be an economical, cost-effective way to do business.

 The eBay User Agreement has firm rules about selling items that are not in the control or possession of the seller at the time of the listing. This situation is covered under eBay's Pre-Sale policy. Generally, pre-sale listings consist of items that are sold in advance of a delivery date to the public, but, in the case of drop-shipping, you are not in possession of the item and you must follow these same rules.

If you decide that selling merchandise before you actually have it is something you want to try, here are the rules you must follow:

✔ You must guarantee that the item will be available for shipping within 30 days from the date of purchase.

✔ You must clearly indicate in your description the fact that the item is a pre-sale item (not in your possession) and quote a delivery date. The text that displays this information must be no less than the default font size of the eBay Sell-Your-Item form (HTML font size 3).

Some vendors specialize in selling to online auctioneers via a drop-shipping service or through warehouses. There are even a few crafty eBay sellers who make money by selling lists of drop-shipping sources to other sellers — I hope not to you. Rather than actually seeing the merchandise you sell, you're given a photo. After you sell the item, you give the vendor the address of the buyer. The vendor then charges your credit card for the item plus shipping and ships the item to your customer for you.

This way of doing business can cost *you* more and lowers your profits. If you're in business, your goal is to make as much money as you can. Because drop-shippers are in business, too, they mark up the merchandise they sell to you (and the shipping cost) so that they can make their profit.

 Drop-shipping can work to *supplement* your basic eBay business by helping you offer additional items. It can also work well if you regularly purchase merchandise directly from a manufacturer that offers to drop-ship additional items from its product lines for you. In that case, you know who you're dealing with – and what the merchandise is like.

Always be careful when using a drop-shipper. Following are some good practices to use if you decide to do so:

✔ **Ask for references** and then check them.

✔ **Don't give the drop-shipper your credit card number** or allow a month-by-month charge to your account if you're not benefiting from the services.

✔ **Check for direct competition.** Find out whether a zillion sellers are selling the same merchandise on eBay — and not getting any bites.

✔ **Verify an acceptable cost.** Check that the price you will pay for the item leaves you room for profit.

I've researched some drop-shipped items on eBay and noted that many inexperienced sellers mark up these goods by only a fraction. They seem to be happy making $5 per sale and don't take into consideration how much the listing fees for other unsold items cost them. That's just not the smartest business practice, and these sellers can ruin the market for similar items for everyone else.

✔ **Have contingency plans for sold-out merchandise.** Be sure to consider what happens if the drop-shipper runs out of an item that you've just sold. You can't just say "oops" to your buyer without getting some nasty feedback.

Your reputation as a seller is at stake. If you find a solid source and believe in the product, order a quantity and have it shipped to your door. Don't pay for someone else's mark-up for the privilege of shipping to your customers.

Practice 7

Building a Business Buying Plan

In This Practice

✔ Getting your sales data together

✔ Evaluating your six-month merchandise plan

We all like to think of online enterprises as something special, but eBay businesses have a lot in common with their brick-and-mortar cousins.

There are so many types of business models that sellers use on eBay. Some sellers are constantly on the prowl for new products, and stock their merchandise as soon as they find a deal. Others follow the trends and try immediately to get stock of the latest and greatest gizmo that's hopefully going to sweep the country (and eBay). Plenty of sellers run their businesses by selling for others, and constantly beat the pavement for new customers to serve. Then there's the new eBay e-tailer.

The eBay *e-tailer* (electronic retailer) buys merchandise to sell on eBay. Though they're always looking for new wholesalers, e-tailers usually specialize in a particular type of stock item, such as dolls, sports cards, lighting fixtures, or apparel. Their eBay business is organized; they sell their merchandise and then buy more to replenish their stock. But is this the best way to handle things? It definitely works for most sellers, but those who actually went to school and studied retailing know there's a better way.

One of the first things you learn when studying retail buying is the use of a six-month merchandise plan. It's the ultimate tool in the arsenal of a successful retail buyer. Although this plan was originally designed for brick-and-mortar retailers, I've adapted it here for eBay e-tailers.

Filling out the plan may not seem like a lot of fun, but after you do it, you'll be able to combine the result with the reports generated by your bookkeeping program. This report package gives you a clear, concise picture of your eBay business. This is a business, not a guessing game — and handling your business in a professional manner will save you a great deal of time and money.

Understanding the Six-Month Merchandise Plan

Business means not running by the seat of your pants — although that may be fun and exciting, it's really not a solid business practice. One of the reasons I started my own business is that an unorganized business format appealed to me. But that was then. To my dismay, I soon learned that organization and planning really *did* make a difference in my bottom line.

Anyone who has participated in management in a corporation knows about the annual "plan." Every year, at every business, management gets together (with Ouija boards and dartboards) to project sales, expenses, and profits for the coming year. From this annual exercise, the "budget" for the coming year arises. These are the magic numbers that form everyone's annual raises — along with the company's plans for growth.

So, assuming that eBay sellers are online retailers, it follows that retail evaluation could help eBay sellers make sound business decisions. Making a merchandise plan is a good step in that direction. A *merchandise plan* covers six months at a time and sets sales goals. It also helps estimate how much money must be spent on merchandise (and when) so that a particular season's success can be replicated and magnified.

Questions to Ask Yourself

Planning out a timeline for your sales and promotions, product offering, and buying is really tough. The Ouija board may seem like a good idea to you, but ask yourself the following questions before you get started (if you have the answers set in your head first, the rest will be a bit easier):

✔ **Evaluating your current sales trends**. Are your sales up a certain percentage from last year? Are you expecting that figure to go higher? Although there is no guarantee to this, factoring in an increase or ☹ decrease in sales may help you predict which times of year you can expect a rise in sales.

✔ **Planning upcoming sales and promotions.** You should (really, you should) decide when you will run sales in your eBay Store. Will you have a pre-holiday sale? A Mother's Day Sale? Even though you may cut some prices, the extra volume may cause a boost in sales.

✔ **Examining your customer profile and product appeal.** Is your customer base changing? Is your product line becoming passé? If so, include a plan for offing dead or soon-to-be-dead merchandise in a sweeping liquidation.

✔ **Identifying major changes in the economy.** Are customers getting stingy with their disposable cash? If you're selling luxury items and the dollar is plunging, consider adding some lower-priced items to your store's offerings.

Getting the Data

You need to gather a few numbers before putting your plan on paper. You should be able to get these numbers from your bookkeeping software program's Inventory Valuation report:

✔ **BOM:** The value, in dollars, of your **beginning-of-month** inventory.

✔ **EOM:** The dollar amount of your **end-of-month** inventory.

✔ **Gross sales:** Total revenue from sales (not including shipping and handling).

✔ **Markdowns:** Total revenue of merchandise you have sold at eBay below your target price.

The EOM figure for a specific month is the same as the BOM figure for the following month. Example: The end-of-month figure for April is the same as the beginning-of-month figure for May.

To put together your six-month plan, you need to have sales history for a six-month period. To get a good historical picture of your sales, it's beneficial to have an entire year's worth of figures.

 Your six-month plan can be based on your total eBay sales, or only one segment of your business. For example, if you sell musical instruments, along with many other sundry items, but you want to evaluate only your musical-instrument sales, you can use just those figures for a six-month plan for your "music" department.

What you're going to establish is your inventory turnover. You'll measure how much inventory sells out in a specified period of time. The faster you "turn over" your merchandise, the sooner you can bring in new merchandise and increase your bottom line. You can also evaluate whether you need to lower your starting price to move out stale inventory so you can get cash to buy *new* inventory.

When you prepare your six-month plan (Table 7-1 shows an example), set out the months not by the regular calendar but by a *retail calendar*, which divides the year into the seasons of Fall/Winter (August 1 through January 31) and Spring/Summer (February 1 through July 31). That way, if you want to refer to top national performance figures in trade publications (or on the Internet), you're basing your figures on the same standardized retail seasons as the rest of the business world.

Formulas That Calculate Your Data

Okay, I can admit that bigger minds than mine came up with these standard formulas. Magically, they

work and are used by retailers around the world. If you're not pulling the figures from a bookkeeping program, here's how you make the calculations.

You can make your calculations in dollar amounts or number of units of the item. In order to figure out how much of this item to buy, you must know how much you have left in stock.

- ✔ EOM Stock = BOM Stock + Purchases — Sales

- ✔ BOM Stock = EOM Stock from the previous month

- ✔ Sales + EOM — BOM = Monthly Planned Purchases

Prepare a chart for your own business, similar to the one shown in Table 7-1. Study your results and find out which months are your strongest. Let the table tell you when you might have to boost your merchandise selection in lagging months to (in turn) boost sales. Compiling and analyzing your sales data will help bring your planning from Ouija board to reality.

Let your figures talk to you. Study them (if possible) over a couple of years of your business's operation. They'll give you a solid history on how your style of retailing works. Look for

- ✔ **Bursts of income**. Use this figure to salt away some cash for the times when you'll need income to carry you over the humps.

- ✔ **Sales slowdowns**. Use this figure to plan sales and promotions. There's no guarantee that they'll work (perhaps the market is just dead at that time of year), but at least you'll have a fighting chance to bring in extra cash.

- ✔ **Benefit of discounts**. I can't stress enough that sticking to your "regular price" on some items may be your downfall. You may have to (and be able to) charge different amounts at different times of year. Things may even up after a year — you'll never know till you try.

TABLE 7-1: SAMPLE SIX-MONTH EBAY MERCHANDISE PLAN

Fall/Winter	Aug	Sept	Oct	Nov	Dec	Jan	Total
TOTAL SALES	$2,875.00	$3,320.00	$3,775.00	$4,150.00	$3,950.00	$4,350.00	$22,420.00
+ Retail EOM	$1,750.00	$3,870.00	$4,250.00	$3,985.00	$4,795.00	$4,240.00	$22,890.00
+ Reductions	$575.00	$275.00	$250.00	$175.00	$425.00	$275.00	$1,975.00
– Retail BOM	$3,150.00	$1,750.00	$3,870.00	$4,250.00	$3,985.00	$4,795.00	$21,800.00
= Retail Purchases	$2,050.00	$5,715.00	$4,405.00	$4,060.00	$5,185.00	$4,070.00	$25,485.00
Cost Purchases	$3,310.00	$3,540.00	$4,725.00	$5,150.00	$2,775.00	$3,450.00	$22,950.00
% of Season's Sales	12.82%	14.81%	16.84%	18.51%	17.62%	19.40%	
% of Season's Reductions	29.11%	13.92%	12.66%	8.86%	21.52%	13.92%	
Average Stock	$3,815.00						
Average Sales	$3,735.00						
Basic Stock	$1,000.00						

Recoup the Costs of Selling on eBay — and Then Some

8

Keeping track of the bottom line is a practice where many business-people fall into trouble. Sellers can get carried away with tasks — listing items, relisting items, shipping items, depositing the money — and they may lose track of their bottom line. These sellers don't know whether the money they take in from sales does the two things it must do: (1) cover the cost of making the sale and (2) give them a little extra (a profit!). Making a profit is essential for running a business; *not* making one is traditionally the cause of the bulk of nationwide Chapter 11s, no matter what the size of the business.

In this chapter, I'm looking to refresh your memory about exactly what you're paying every time you list on eBay — and to remind you of the links to check back from time to time. (Keep this information at the top of your memory bank.) I have even put together a sample spreadsheet that reflects my common price points — with the costs involved. So I immediately know that when I sell a store item at $24.99, it's going to cost me $2.53 in total fees — plus PayPal fees.

In this practice, I give you tips on pricing strategies that help you cover expenses and make a profit, too. The first item on the agenda is to understand all the fees involved with running an e-business on eBay.

Keeping an Eye on the Bottom Line

It doesn't seem so much, $.55 or so to list an item, and a small Final Value fee. Of course, a few cents go to PayPal. One by one, these minute amounts tend to blast past your eyes. You don't really see your eBay fees, because they're not directly deducted from your sales. eBay bills you at the end of the month, and unless you are keeping *very* good books, it's easy to lose track of your costs.

All those nickels, dimes, and quarters build up. The hundreds (thousands?) of sellers who are selling items on the site for $1 can't be making much of a profit — not even enough for a pack of gum! Perhaps they mark up their shipping by a couple of bucks — but that's still only . . . a couple of bucks. To avoid this low-profit trap, you must be keenly aware of every penny you spend on eBay listing fees, eBay Final Value fees, listing options, and PayPal fees.

Keeping an Eye on Listing Fees

eBay *listing fees* (and *reserve* fees) are based on your starting bid price, or your amount for a Fixed Price sale. Although eBay listing fees have remained somewhat stable over the years, eBay raised the rates and changed their pricing levels traditionally in February. For a very long time, the most you would pay to list a regular item on the eBay site was $3.30. Now, that figure has gone up to $4.00.

Table 8-1 shows you the current listing fees. The base auction-listing fee of $.10 (for any item priced from $.01 to $9.99) looks pretty cheap. Fees for Media (books, music, DVDs and movies, and video games) are lower, see Table 8-2 for those numbers.

Notice that the higher your starting price is, the higher your actual fee. And as the second column in Table 8-1 shows, the *little guy* (the seller with lower-priced items to sell) has a lower listing fee.

But as the rightmost column shows, this same little guy takes a higher hit (percentage-wise) than the seller selling higher-priced items. That is, the percentage of starting price paid in fees is higher for lower-priced items.

 If you're planning to start your auctions at $1.00, consider starting them at $.99 instead. You save 57 percent in listing fees! One seller I know made that change to his auctions and saved $2,400 a month!

The midpoint figures indicated in the charts shown here are there because we thought you might like seeing (at a glance) approximately what percent the fees are, based on the price at which you've chosen to start your listing.

TABLE 8-1: eBay Listing Fee Comparison

Starting Price	Listing Fee	Price-Range Midpoint (rounded)	Fee as Percentage at Midpoint (rounded)
$0.01 — $0.99	0.15	.50	30%
$1.00 — $9.99	0.35	5.50	6.36%
$10.00 — $24.99	0.55	17.50	3.14%
$25.00 — $49.99	1.00	37.50	2.67%
$50.00 — $199.99	2.00	125.00	1.6%
$200.00 — $499.99	3.00	350.00	.86%
$500 and up	4.00	$750.00 (not midpoint)	.53%

TABLE 8-2: eBay LISTING FEE COMPARISON (MEDIA CATEGORIES)

Starting Price	Listing Fee	Price-Range Midpoint (rounded)	Fee as Percentage at Midpoint (rounded)
$0.01 — $0.99	0.10	.50	20%
$1.00 — $9.99	0.25	5.50	4.55%
$10.00 — $24.99	0.35	17.50	2%
$25.00 — $49.99	1.00	37.50	2.67%
$50.00 — $199.99	2.00	125.00	1.6%
$200.00 — $499.99	3.00	350.00	.86%
$500 and up	4.00	$750.00 (not midpoint)	.53%

Hmmm, perhaps I'm seeing a pattern here. Just a thought — maybe we should only sell items that sell below $24.99 or above $49.99? Yep, that's the ticket!

Take a look at Figure 8-1; I don't think the seller made much money in this sale — especially when the spot price of silver (as of this writing) is $17.82 an ounce!

• **Figure 8-1: Not a very profitable sale.**

Using reserve fees

Perhaps now you're thinking, *I can use a low listing fee to attract the bargain hunters, but tack on a reserve price.* You can always work the reserve to your advantage, but remember: Bidders get edgy when they see a reserve-price auction — they start

to wonder whether they should spend their time bidding on the auction or maybe find a better deal elsewhere.

Placing a reserve price on one of your auctions, as pictured in Figure 8-2, means that the item will not sell until the bidding reaches the reserve price. A reserve price may also add a hefty fee to your listing, should the bidding not meet the reserve. For example, if you list a poster at a $.99 starting price with a reserve price of $21.99, your combined listing and reserve fees total $2.15. When your reserve-price item sells for above the reserve price, two good things happen: You've sold your item at a good profit and you get more storage space.

1/3 Carat Diamond Solitaire w/platinum band
Purchased from Blue Nile

You are signed in

Current bid:	US $0.99 Place Bid >
	Reserve not met
End time:	Sep-30-07 09:28:41 PDT
	(6 days 17 hours)
Shipping costs:	US $4.60
	US Postal Service Priority Mail® Service
Ships to:	United States
Item location:	Coos Bay, OR, United States
History:	1 bid
High bidder:	____ (481 ☆)

1 of 4
View larger picture

You can also: Watch This Item

Get mobile or IM alerts | Email to a friend

• **Figure 8-2: I'll bet this auction has a serious reserve!**

Keep in mind that you may lower the reserve price on an item as many times as you like, as long as the reserve price has not been met and there are at least 12 hours left on the listing.

The reserve fee is based on the reserve price you set, as outlined in Table 8-3.

 Put the amount of your reserve price at the top of your listing description. That way there's a good chance the buyers will see it and know what they're in for. You could also offer free shipping in a reserve auction to take the edge off.

TABLE 8-3: EBAY RESERVE AUCTION FEES

Reserve Amount	Fee
$0.01 — $199.99	$2.00
$200 and up	1 percent of reserve price (maximum of $50.00)

The key here is to calculate, *before* you list your item, whether it costs you more in fees to use a reserve or to list with a higher starting price.

Table 8-4 compares the same item sold with different listing strategies. Notice that the Final Value fee (explained in the upcoming section "Adding In the Final Value Fees") stays the same regardless of the listing strategy used.

TABLE 8-4: COMPARISONS OF TWO COMPLETED AUCTIONS — WITH AND WITHOUT RESERVE

	Starting at $24.99	Starting at $9.99 with $24.99 Reserve
Listing fee	$.55	$.35
Reserve fee	0	$2.00
Final Value fee	$2.19	$2.19
Total	$2.74	$4.54

If the reserve item in Table 8-4 does not sell, listing and reserve fees would total $2.35!

Wow! Aren't you surprised? (I was too!)

 If your item doesn't sell the first time at the higher starting price, you can always relist it at a lower starting price and *then* use a reserve. If it sells, you'll still get the listing fees waived and you won't have to pay a reserve fee at all.

Using Second Chance Offer

If you have an item up for sale on the site, and the auction goes above your target sales price and you have more of the item in stock, you can offer another of the item to an underbidder.

At the end of a multiple-bidder auction, you can click a box on the page to offer the item to any of the underbidders — for his or her high bid. After you click the box, the resulting page looks something like the figure below.

My Messages: Second Chance Offer

To send a Second Chance Offer for this item, select a duration and bidder(s) below.

Item: NEW Palm Treo 680 AT&T GSM GPRS EDGE QBAND Sealed CING (Original Item ID: 120153884090)

Subject: **eBay Second Chance Offer for Item #120153884090: NEW Palm Treo 680 AT&T GSM GPRS EDGE QBAND Sealed CING**

Duration
1 day

Select bidders who will receive your offer
The number of bidders you select can't be more than the number of duplicate items you have to sell. The Second Chance Offer price is a Buy It Now price determined by each bidder's maximum bid. Learn more.

Select	User ID	Second Chance Offer Price
☐	(2)	US $250.00
☐	(69 ★)	US $240.00
☐	(62 ★)	US $221.00
☐	(57 ★)	US $215.85
☐	(766 ★)	US $203.30
☐	(133 ★)	US $200.00
☐	(13 ★)	US $150.00

It's the underbidder's lucky day.

You will be charged only Final Value fees — not additional listing fees — if the bidders purchase the item.

Adding listing upgrades

eBay listings, just like anything that comes with extras (your new car, for example), have many options and upgrades. But also like your new car's options, they cost you money. eBay's optional upgrades are almost as fun as heated car seats in the winter — but only if they make you money!

Figure 8-3 shows how even a random search on eBay listings can yield examples of some very popular listing options:

- ✔ **Gallery.** This option definitely draws attention to your item. Gallery listings show a small picture next to the item title. The tempting glimpse grabs the gaze of potential buyers right away; a listing with the camera icon simply indicates that a picture of the item is available in the listing description. The gallery option costs you nothing — if you don't take advantage of it you're missing the boat.

- ✔ **Buy It Now.** In our immediate-gratification society, the But It Now option is very attractive to savvy eBay shoppers. Of course, those very same savvy eBay shoppers know just how much they want to spend, and if your Buy It Now price is too high, they may blast right by your listing. Use Buy It Now for items you have in stock, with a clear target price. For twenty-five cents or less, Buy It Now can move your merchandise quickly. Table 8-5 shows you the fees eBay charges to run a Buy It Now listing.

93.34 CT RARE JEWELRY RING GEM GREEN AMETHYST 0.99 $ NR *Resizing Available*	𝓟	$26.00	10	3h 43m	$8.00	110171144096
160K A MONTH! MAKE IT ONLINE GUARANTEED! NO JOKE!	𝓟	$0.01	Classified Ad	3h 45m	Pickup only	190145240309
10K gold three stone diamond pendant chain earring set 0.99 NR! Anniversary pendant w/ chain & dangle earrings	𝓟	$62.00	10	3h 46m	$9.00	200151432866
ADVERTISE ON HUGE TRUCK WHERE 30,000 CARS PASS EVERYDAY PRIME BILLBOARD SPACE IN NEW YORK FOR ADVERTISING!!!!!	𝓟	$2,199.00	*Buy It Now or Best Offer*	3h 51m	Pickup only	260161113912
Essick Multiquip Cement and Mortar Mixer 12 CF TOWABLE TOWABLE MIXER 12 CF Gasoline Driven/ FREE SHIPPING	𝓟	$3,950.00 $4,450.00	*Buy It Now*	3h 52m	Free	300152984583
ANTIQUE Rare 1700s Royal Czar Russian Enamel Trunk Box	𝓟	$331.89	18	3h 54m	Not specified	300151357921

• **Figure 8-3:** A piece of a search page, including various eBay upgrades.

TABLE 8-5: COSTS FOR A BUY IT NOW LISTING

Buy It Now Price	Fee
$0.01 — $9.99	$ .05
$10.00 — $24.99	$ .10
$25.00 — $49.99	$ .20
$50.00 or more	$ .25

- ✔ **Bold:** Applying boldface type to your item title really spices it up and pulls it off the page right into the reader's eye. Unfortunately, bold adds an additional $1 to your listing cost, so you better be in a position to make some good profit from the item. Make sure your research shows that it can sell for your target price.

- ✔ **Best Offer:** There's no charge to add Best Offer to your item, but expect that you may get some ridiculously low offers. But if you really want to get rid of the item — it's eBay's best answer to Craigslist.com (only on eBay you can at least make a couple of dollars on the shipping).

- ✔ **Item Subtitle:** Notice the subtitle under one of the auctions. This is your opportunity to add additional text to your title, readable by prospective buyers as they scan a search or browse a category. The fee for adding a subtitle is 50 cents.

 A couple of caveats on subtitles: This additional text will be picked up only if the searcher is searching both titles and descriptions. The additional text does not get pulled up in a title-only search — and all the text in the world won't help if your starting price is far above what your competition's asking.

Tables 8-6 and 8-7 show you the additional fees involved in the eBay listing upgrades and in Featured Plus!

TABLE 8-6: eBay Upgrades and Their Fees

Listing Upgrade	Its Fee
Home Page Featured (single quantity)	$39.95
Home Page Featured (quantity of 2 or more)	$79.95
Highlight	$5.00
Item Subtitle	$0.50
Bold	$1.00
Listing Designer	$0.10
Gallery	Free
Gallery Featured	$19.95
10-Day Listing Duration	$0.40
Scheduled Listings	$0.10
Gift Services	$0.25

TABLE 8-7: Featured Plus! Fees for Auction and Fixed-Price Listings

Item Starting Price	Fee
$.01 to $24.99	$9.95
$25.00 to $199.99	$14.95
$200 to $499.88	$19.95
$500 and above	$24.95

eBay offers discounts on some features when they're purchased in a package. The Value Pack at $.65 combines a Gallery Plus ($.35), an Item Subtitle ($.50), and Listing Designer ($.10), thereby saving you $.30. There's also the Pro Pack, which combines Bold ($1.00), Border ($3.00), Highlight ($5.00), Gallery Featured ($19.95), and Featured Plus! (can vary from $9.95 to $24.95) for a discounted rate. That many features may be a bit of overkill — but still a considerable savings. (The Pro Pack is available only to sellers with a Feedback score of 10 or greater.) See Table 8-8 for the costs involved.

TABLE 8-8: Pro Pack Fees for Auction and Fixed-Price Listings

Item Starting Price	Fee
$.01 to $24.99	$19.95
$25.00 to $199.99	$24.95
$200 to $499.88	$29.95
$500 and above	$34.95

eBay Picture Services

If you are shopping the site or even researching your competitor's auctions, you'll notice that some sellers have preview pictures of their items at the top of their listing pages, as shown in Figure 8-4.

What a great selling point this is. The prospective buyer can see your item the second they click the page! Best of all there's no additional cost to the seller.

eBay offers the first picture free of cost to all sellers. It's definitely something you should take advantage of. Any additional pictures (easily uploaded to your item page) cost $.15 each. Discount packages are available for 1 to 6 photos at $.75 and 7 to 12 photos at $1.00. If you want the picture to be displayed larger (Gallery Plus) when the buyer mouses over it in Search or Browse, add an additional $.35 to your fees.

• **Figure 8-4:** A free top-of-the-page preview photo is available from eBay's Picture Services.

Always use the free picture — after all, it's free! But why not save extra fees by uploading your own additional pictures for your sales? (See Practice 25 for full instructions on how to do this on your own.)

Adding In the Final Value Fees

Final Value fees (FVFs) are charges on the amount that your item sells for — *not* including whatever you charge for shipping. Table 8-9 shows the basics of the Final Value fee and how it's calculated.

The table shows FVFs for auctions and fixed-price listings, but not for store inventory (that's another whole can of worms), eBay Motors, real estate, or classified ads.

PowerSellers can get up to a 15 percent discount on Final Value Fees (FVFs) when they maintain high detailed seller ratings (DSRs). (See Practice 12 for more info about FVFs.)

TABLE 8-9: FINAL VALUE FEES FOR AUCTIONS AND FIXED-PRICE LISTINGS

Final Item Price	Final Value Fee
$.01 to $25.00	8.75% of the selling price
$25.01 to $1,000.00	8.75% on the first $25, plus 3.5% on the difference between $25.00 and a final item price up to $1,000
$1,000 and up	8.75% on the first $25, plus 3.5% on the difference between $25.00 and $1,000, plus another 1.5% on a final item price over $1,000

So how do all these percentages translate to real dollars? Take a look at Table 8-10, where I calculated fees for some random closing prices.

TABLE 8-10: SAMPLE PRICES AND COMMISSIONS

Closing Bid Price	Percentage	What You Owe eBay
$10	8.75% of $10	$.88
$256	8.75% of $25 plus 3.5% of $231	$10.27
$1,284.53	8.75% of $25 plus 3.5% of $975 plus 1.5% of $284.53	$40.58
$1,000,000	8.75% of $25 plus 3.5% of $975 plus 1.5% of $999,000	$15,021.31 (whew!)

PayPal Gets Its Cut of the Action

When you've sold your item, you think that's the end of the fees? Nope! If your customer pays via PayPal, you're faced with fees for using the PayPal service.

Having a PayPal Premier or Business account is important to building your commerce, for these reasons:

- ✔ eBay buyers look for the PayPal option because it offers them another level of protection against fraud.

- ✔ Most customers prefer to pay with a credit card, either to delay the expense or to have complete records of their purchases.

- ✔ From a seller's point of view, using PayPal can be cheaper than having a direct-merchant credit card account.

- ✔ PayPal helps with your paperwork by offering downloadable logs of your sales that include all PayPal fees. eBay fees are not included; you're on your own for those.

The difference between a Premier and a Business account is that a Premier account allows you to do business under your own name. A Business account requires the account to be registered in a business name.

PayPal fees are fairly straightforward: Every transaction is charged a $.30 transaction fee, plus a percentage of the total collected — *including* your shipping charges. The percentage collected at the standard rate is 2.9 percent; for a merchant rate, it's 2.2 percent.

The standard rate is charged to all new users of PayPal. After you've been accepting PayPal for a while and have received at least $1,000 a month through PayPal for three months, you qualify for a Merchant rate.

 Even after you're qualified, you won't get the Merchant rate automatically. As you attain the needed level of sales, you must e-mail PayPal (after you've logged in to your account) to point out that you've attained it, ask the service to put the lower rate into effect, and request that your account be converted to a Merchant account.

Set Your Pricing to Cover All Costs

When you know all the fees involved in selling your item, you can play around with the pricing and figure out how much your Buy It Now (or target selling) price should be.

Remember to include all these costs when pricing your items:

- How much you paid for the item you want to resell.

- All your Listing and Final Value fees.

- The Freight In amount (the cost of shipping the item to you).

- The cost of shipping the item to your buyer. (Visit Practices 27 and 28 for information on how to calculate the cost involved in your shipping the item out to your buyers.) This cost should be covered by your shipping charges to the buyer.

Deciding on your price is a very personal thing. It all depends on the type of business you have and how much of your income depends on your eBay business.

Some sellers insist on a 50-percent profit — but I honestly think that's unrealistic. A 35 to 40 percent profit is more realistic. Keep in mind, though, that as you grow, you need to pay salaries and administrative costs out of your "net" sales.

Selling Costs in eBay Stores vary; Stores have their own (very different) listing fees. The lowered listing fees are backed up by the fact that you have to pay a monthly fee for your store (see Table 8-11).

TABLE 8-11: eBay Store Subscription Costs

Store Level	Fee
Basic	$15.95 / month
Premium	$49.95 / month
Anchor	$299.95 / month

Listings for an eBay Store are lower, as shown in Table 8-12. Some listing-upgrade features are lower (and some aren't), as noted in Table 8-10, and Final Value fees are actually higher (about double!) for items sold in stores than for regular item listings (see Table 8-13).

TABLE 8-12: STORE LISTING FEES

Listing or Reserve Price	Listing
$1.00 – $24.99	$0.03 / 30 days
$25.00 – $199.00	$0.05 / 30 days
$200.00 and above	$0.10 / 30 days

TABLE 8-13: STORE-LISTING UPGRADES

Upgrade Option	Cost per 30 Days of Listing Duration
Gallery	Free
Item subtitle	$.02
Gallery Plus	$.35
Listing Designer	$.10 (same as auctions)
Bold	$1.00 (same as auctions)
Border	$3.00 (same as auctions)
Highlight	$5.00 (same as auctions)
Featured Plus!	Same as auctions (refer to Table 8-7)

And don't forget the Final Value fees that apply to goods in your eBay Store. Table 8-14 lists those.

TABLE 8-14: STORE FINAL VALUE FEES

Final Item Price	Final Value Fee
$.01 to $25.00	12% of the selling price
$25.01 to $100.00	12% of the first $25.00, plus 8% of the remaining balance ($.01 to $75.00)
$100.01 to $1000.00	12% of the first $25.00, plus 8% of $75.00 and 4% of the remaining balance ($.01 to $900)
$1000.00 and up	12% of the first $25.00, plus 8% of $75.00, plus 4% of $900 and 2% of the remaining balance ($.01 and up)

Having an eBay Store to house your goods has some compelling aspects. For example, you can sell multiples of an item without incurring multiple listing fees. Here are some advantages I find with having my eBay Store:

- ✔ Buyers browse and buy related items in one purchase
- ✔ Listings for individual sizes and/or colors are far more economical that auction listings
- ✔ You can list slower-selling items at a lower cost.

The (thankfully) last table for this practice (Table 8-15) gives you a handy comparison of your costs for items with the same selling price, but sold through an eBay store rather than through regular item listings. Because shipping costs should be basically the same, I've not included those costs in the comparison.

TABLE 8-15: STORE SALES VERSUS REGULAR LISTING SALES

Final Item Price	Starting Price	Regular Listing and Final Value Fees	Store Listing and Final Value Fees
$10.00	$.99	$1.03	$1.23
$256.00	$49,99	$11.27	$15.34
$1,284.53	$199.99	$42.58	$50.79
$1,000,000	$200,000	$15,025.31	$20,025.10

Practice 9

Building a Selling Strategy

In This Practice

- ✔ Setting starting prices and length of auctions
- ✔ Picking the day to start and end your auctions
- ✔ Finding out how people find your auctions
- ✔ Seeing what days your items are visited

You can buy the "inside secrets" of eBay from lots of places. Generally the "most-watched" items on eBay site are the *Get Rich Now — Buy this and you'll be a millionaire* e-books. Some e-book sellers try to convince you that only *they* have the surreptitious bits of knowledge — gleaned from years (months?) of experience on the site — that reveal what's really going on. Truth be told, the online retail market changes so quickly that eBay can barely keep up with it — the profile of the online shopper changes constantly. However, there are some basic laws of retail that do not change — and they may be new to those who haven't studied the cycles. How likely is it that anybody has the ultimate answer? Sure, mysterious rumors crop up — do you hear some eerie music playing? — magical means to sure-fire auctions. Start an auction at a certain day and time, and you'll automatically make more money? Please! The only one who rakes in profits with that information is the guy selling it to you!

To illustrate the variety of the strategies that actually *do* work, I include screen shots from my current ViewTracker eBay data. These graphs reflect real-time hits and traffic for my sales. At the end of this practice, I show you some more features of this service and how they can improve the bottom line on your listings. I also use a service — Terapeak.com — that provides site-wide data (Sellathon's ViewTracker is based on a seller's personal sales).

Strategies for Running Your Sales

I've interviewed many eBay high-volume sellers and almost all agree that some popular eBay theories are . . . well . . . . bunk. However, these sellers do have some practical preferences for when and how they conduct their eBay transactions, and those are well worth knowing. This section gets to the gist of these preferences and the corresponding practices.

The basic plan for running an auction is the same for everyone, except for decisions regarding the timing of the auction and the starting price. If you speak to 20 eBay sellers, you'll probably get 20 different answers about effective starting bids and when to end your auction. Until you develop your own philosophy, I'd like to give you a look at my research — and some tools to help you make a sound decision.

The ideas in this practice come from my own experience and discussions with current eBay PowerSellers. They're merely suggestions that point out methods and starting points that work for others. You definitely need to test them out and find out which practices work for you — and for the types of items you sell.

Starting the bidding

The most generally accepted theory about starting bids is that starting the bidding too high scares away new bids.

Some sellers begin the bidding at the price they paid for the item, thereby protecting their investment. This is a good tactic, especially if you bought the item at a price far below the current going rate on eBay.

To determine the current going value for your item, I recommend using the completed-auctions search, which I explain in Practice 5. If you know that the item is selling on eBay for a certain price and that there is a demand for it, starting the bidding at a reasonably low level can be a great way to increase bidding and attract prospective bidders to view your auction.

Years of advertising experience can't be wrong about this: If your item is in demand and people are actively buying, start the bidding low. Retail stores have done this for years, with ads that feature prices starting at $9.99 or $14.98. Even television commercials advertising automobiles quote a low starting price. To get the car as shown in the ad (which usually has some ups and extras), you may end up paying twice the quoted price.

When sellers know they have an item that will sell, they begin their bidding as low as a dollar — or even a penny. Because of the eBay *proxy bidding system* (which maintains your highest bid as a secret, increasing it incrementally when you're bid against), it takes more bids (due to the smaller bidding increments) to bring the item up to the final selling price.

The downside is that new bidders who aren't familiar with the system may bid only the minimum required increment each time they bid. This can be frustrating, and they may quit bidding because it might take them several bids to top the current bid placed by someone who is familiar with the proxy bid system. Very few of us remember the proxy increments, so as a refresher, I give you the goods in Table 9-1.

TABLE 9-1: PROXY BIDDING INCREMENTS

Current High Bid	Bid Increment
$.01 to $.99	$0.05
$1.00 to $4.99	$0.25
$5.00 to $24.99	$0.50
$25.00 to $99.99	$1.00
$100.00 to $249.99	$2.50
$250.00 to $499.99	$5.00
$500.00 to $ 999.99	$10.00
$1,000.00 to $2,499.99	$25.00
$2,500.00 to $4,999.99	$50.00
$5,000.00 and up	$100.00

Auction length

Another debatable philosophy is auction timing. People are always asking me how long to run auctions and what's the best day to end an auction. You have to evaluate your item and decide which of the following can become your best practice:

✔ **One-day auction:** Did you just get a load of an item that sells as fast as you put it on the site? Although a Buy It Now feature on any auction can bring great results, a quick sell works only if the item is *hot! hot! hot!* If people are bidding the item up — and they really gotta have it — you may do best by starting the bidding really low and listing it with a one-day format. This way, the bidding may just go up higher than the dollar amount you planned to set as your Buy It Now price.

When you list in a one-day format, your listing goes right to the top of the list. Most people view their searches by auctions ending first in a *listings ending soonest* search. With a one-day format, you can pretty much choose the time of day your item will be at the top.

A one-day auction can be very successful if you have an item that's the hot-ticket-of-the-moment on eBay. I used this format when I sold some TV-show memorabilia. The 24-hour auction opened at midday before the show's final episode, and ended the next day — at a healthy profit!

If you choose a one-day auction format, carefully consider how you set your starting price as well. If your competition starts their auctions at $.99 with a reasonable Buy It Now price, you'll find that bidders foil many of their Buy It Now offers by making token bids. Retaliate by listing the item with a starting bid just a dollar or so below your Buy It Now (and make your Buy It Now at least $.50 below the competition), and you'll find your items will be snapped up quickly.

✔ **Three-day auction:** If (as with the introduction of the iPhone) the item's price will shoot up right after you post it, a three-day auction works just fine. And it's great to attract those last-minute holiday shoppers looking for hard-to-find items. (Or just last-minute desperate buyers who will buy almost anything.)

A three-day auction is good, for the same reasons that a one-day is good — only it's better for the faint of heart and nervous types (like me) because it gives your item more time to sell.

Another good use of a three-day auction is when you already have a seven-day auction up on the site and the bidding is going crazy. You've reached your sales goal by the middle of a seven-day cycle. Once the seven-day auction is in the last couple of days of the listing, put up another listing as a three-day auction.

✔ **Five-day auction:** A five-day auction gives you two days more than a three-day auction and two days less than a seven-day auction. That's about the size of it. If you just want an extended weekend auction or your item is a hot one, use it. Five-day auctions are useful during holiday rushes, when gift buying is the main reason for bidding.

✔ **Seven-day auction:** Tried-and-true advertising theory says that the longer you advertise your item, the more people will see it. On eBay, this means you have more opportunity for people to bid on it. The seven-day auction is a staple for the bulk of eBay vendors. Seven days is long enough to cover weekend browsers and short enough to keep the auction interesting.

✔ **Ten-day auction:** Many veteran eBay sellers swear by the ten-day auction. Sure, eBay charges you an extra 40 cents for the privilege, but the extra three days of exposure (it can encompass two weekends) can easily net you more than a dime a day in profits. This is especially the case when you're selling a rare (I mean *really* rare — not "eBay-rare") item.

A ten-day auction is good for special collectibles or an expensive item that normally doesn't get listed on the site by the hundreds. Putting up a ten-day auction (starting Friday night so you get exposure over two weekends) is a near-perfect way to attract bidders.

Your auction closes exactly one, three, five, seven, or ten days — *to the minute* — after you start the auction. Be careful not to begin your auctions when you're up late at night and can't sleep: You don't want your auction to end at two in the morning when no one else is awake to bid on it. If you can't sleep, prepare your listings ahead of time with the TurboLister program and upload them for future launching when the world is ready to shop.

Knowing what day to end an auction

The specific day you close your auction can also be important. eBay is full of weekend browsers, so including a weekend of browsing in your auction time is a definite plus. Often, auctions that end late Sunday afternoon through Monday close with high bids.

Back when eBay counted its listings by the hundreds (and then the low thousands), it clearly made a difference what day of the week you chose to end an auction. That is, when the number of buyers and sellers on eBay was relatively small, matching your auction time with the bidders' online habits was important. Now that eBay spawns more than 13 million listings a day — with countless buyers and looky-loos visiting the site — you find the eBay netizens looking for bargains at virtually all hours of the day and night. So, for a traditional auction, you can choose almost any ending time and know that you'll still have some bidders.

 You'll have browsers dropping by almost 24 hours a day if you're selling internationally.

The wildcards in the mix are the Buy It Now and fixed-price transactions, which have become wildly popular. Although they don't always follow a daily pattern of sales, they can still follow the preferred auction-ending days you find in this section.

For the test I include in this practice (shown in Figure 9-1), I didn't use the Buy It Now option. My

auctions ended on different days. Here are the historical visits to my listings. You'll see (interestingly) that Saturday and Tuesday were the most active days for my store listings (Figure 9-1) and for my auctions, Sunday (Figure 9-2) — but I didn't end my listings on Sunday. The ViewTracker data has an AE column. The AE column and ratio reflect the number of views when an auction is actually ending. The reasoning behind the ratio of visits and number of auctions ending is based on a common belief that auctions tend to receive a higher number of visits on the day the auction ends. This can skew the data when you're trying to determine which day is best to sell on. As you can see, this is not the case for these particular listings.

4. Most Active Day of the Week (Last 14 Days) GO				
Date	**Visits**	**Graph**	**AE**	**Ratio**
Sunday	126		1	126.0
Monday	67		4	16.8
Tuesday	137		1	137.0
Wednesday	115		0	230.0
Thursday	127		0	254.0
Friday	82		0	164.0
Saturday	137		3	45.7

• **Figure 9-1: Daily tracking for my store listings in the past 14 days.**

4. Most Active Day of the Week (Last 14 Days) GO				
Date	**Visits**	**Graph**	**AE**	**Ratio**
Sunday	59		0	118.0
Monday	25		6	4.2
Tuesday	31		0	62.0
Wednesday	37		0	74.0
Thursday	33		0	66.0
Friday	11		0	22.0
Saturday	26		0	52.0

• **Figure 9-2: Daily tracking for my auctions in the past 14 days.**

Note that this data reflects the type of items I am selling. I have found that the most-visited auction days can easily change depending on what I'm selling — whether golf equipment, model trains, or women's or men's apparel.

To figure out when to end an auction, you need to know when to start it. Figures 9-3, 9-4, and 9-5 are the top preferred timelines for running a sale on eBay.

• **Figure 9-3: A timeline for a 3-day auction.**

• **Figure 9-4: This is 7 days of auction action.**

• **Figure 9-5: A full 10 days of bidding frenzy (if you're lucky).**

You may notice that all these preferred datelines end on a Sunday. Sunday is the top-ranked ending day for auctions by eBay sellers.

I can't list everyone's opinions on the subject — that would probably confuse you anyway — so here are the item-ending days ranked in order from most to least popular:

1. Sunday

2. Monday

3. Thursday

4. Tuesday

5. Wednesday

6. Saturday

7. Friday

Be sure to coordinate these dates with what you sell. Some buyers (say, men who buy golf goods during lunch hour and women who buy collectibles while their husbands are out golfing on weekends) can throw these days a curve.

A definite time *not* to close your auctions? Experience has taught many sellers never to close an auction on a national holiday. Memorial Day, the Fourth of July, and Veteran's Day may be bonanza sales days for brick-and-mortar retail shops, but eBay auction items closing on these days go at bargain prices.

Interesting fact of eBay

Here's an actual screen shot of data from my eBay listings. We used to think that more people checked listings sorted by Items Ending Soonest — but that is no longer the case! Take a look at this chart illustrating some sample data — that is, consistent over months of eBay listings.

5. Most Popular Sorting Methods

#	Sorted by	Visits	%
1.	Newly Listed	2,264	87.7
2.	Ending First	276	10.7
3.	$ Lo -> Hi	24	0.9
4.	$ Hi -> Lo	16	0.6
5.	Dist: Nearest 1st	2	0.1
6.	PayPal First	0	0
7.	PayPal Last	0	0
8.	Current	0	0
9.	Ending Today	0	0
10.	Going, Gone!	0	0
11.	New Today	0	0

People mostly search for items Newly Listed!

Knowing what time to start your auction

The only way to figure out when to end your auction is by planning when to start it. An auction beginning at 12:00 will end at that same time on the ending day. Below in Figure 9-6, you see 14 days of visits to my eBay store. Although 7:00 p.m. comes in a close second, you'll notice that 11:00 a.m. (eBay time) is the winner. I have found this result consistently throughout my research. I'm showing you "store" visits, because I feel they're more neutral — there are no closing times to be seen by the visitor. So, in my experience, 11:00 a.m. to noon is a very strong period for visits — perhaps a good time to end your auction as well?

eBay time is military time in the Pacific time zone. Table 9-2 converts the eBay clock to real time for your time zone. Make a photocopy of this table and keep it by your computer. Even after all these years, it still takes too much time to decipher eBay time

without a printed chart — besides, I hate counting on my fingers . . . . If you want to check out the way eBay time relates to the rest of the world, go to my Web site for an International Time Chart at

www.coolebaytools.com/world_time_zones.html

or (handier still) set up the International Time Chart side of the Cheat Sheet next to your computer.

If you ever need to check your time zone or want to know exactly what time it is in eBay-land you can look for a link on the bottom of many eBay pages: **eBay Official Time**. If you can't find a link, point your browser to

    http://viv.ebay.com/ws/eBayISAPI.
        dll?EbayTime

and you'll see the map pictured in Figure 9-7.

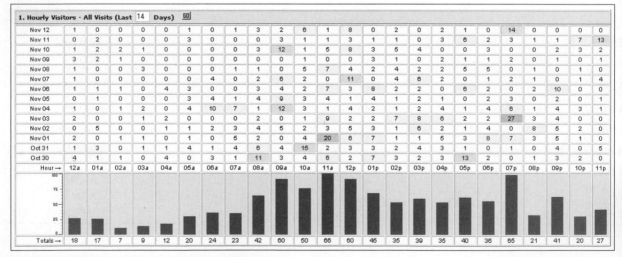

1. Hourly Visitors - All Visits (Last 14 Days) GO

	12a	01a	02a	03a	04a	05a	06a	07a	08a	09a	10a	11a	12p	01p	02p	03p	04p	05p	06p	07p	08p	09p	10p	11p
Nov 12	1	0	0	0	0	1	0	1	3	2	6	1	8	0	2	0	2	1	0	14	0	0	0	0
Nov 11	0	2	0	0	0	3	0	0	0	3	1	1	3	1	1	0	3	6	2	3	1	1	7	13
Nov 10	1	2	2	1	0	0	0	0	3	12	1	5	8	3	5	4	0	0	3	0	0	2	3	2
Nov 09	3	2	1	0	0	0	0	0	0	0	1	0	3	1	0	2	1	1	2	0	1	0	1	
Nov 08	1	0	0	3	0	0	0	1	1	0	5	7	4	2	4	2	2	5	5	0	1	0	1	0
Nov 07	1	0	0	0	0	0	4	0	2	6	2	0	11	0	4	6	2	0	1	2	1	0	1	4
Nov 06	1	1	1	0	4	3	0	0	3	4	2	7	3	8	2	2	0	6	2	0	2	10	0	0
Nov 05	0	1	0	0	0	3	4	1	4	9	3	4	1	4	1	2	1	0	2	3	0	2	0	1
Nov 04	1	0	1	2	0	4	10	7	1	12	3	1	4	2	1	2	4	1	4	6	1	4	3	1
Nov 03	2	0	0	1	2	0	0	0	2	0	1	9	2	2	7	8	6	2	2	27	3	4	0	0
Nov 02	0	5	0	0	1	1	2	3	4	5	2	3	5	3	1	6	2	1	4	0	8	5	2	0
Nov 01	2	0	1	1	0	1	0	5	2	0	4	20	6	7	1	1	5	3	8	7	3	5	1	0
Oct 31	1	3	0	1	1	4	1	4	6	4	15	2	3	2	4	3	1	0	1	0	4	0	5	
Oct 30	4	1	1	0	4	0	3	1	11	3	4	6	2	7	3	2	3	2	0	1	3	2	0	
Hour →	12a	01a	02a	03a	04a	05a	06a	07a	08a	09a	10a	11a	12p	01p	02p	03p	04p	05p	06p	07p	08p	09p	10p	11p
Totals →	18	17	7	9	12	20	24	23	42	60	50	66	60	45	35	39	35	40	36	65	21	41	20	27

• **Figure 9-6:** Fourteen days of visits over 24 hours.

TABLE 9-2: eBay Time versus Continental U.S. Time

eBay Time	Pacific	Mountain	Central	Eastern
0:00	12:00 a.m.	1:00 a.m.	2:00 a.m.	3:00 a.m.
1:00	1:00 a.m.	2:00 a.m.	3:00 a.m.	4:00 a.m.
2:00	2:00 a.m.	3:00 a.m.	4:00 a.m.	5:00 a.m.
3:00	3:00 a.m.	4:00 a.m.	5:00 a.m.	6:00 a.m.
4:00	4:00 a.m.	5:00 a.m.	6:00 a.m.	7:00 a.m.
5:00	5:00 a.m.	6:00 a.m.	7:00 a.m.	8:00 a.m.
6:00	6:00 a.m.	7:00 a.m.	8:00 a.m.	9:00 a.m.
7:00	7:00 a.m.	8:00 a.m.	9:00 a.m.	10:00 a.m.
8:00	8:00 a.m.	9:00 a.m.	10:00 a.m.	11:00 a.m.
9:00	9:00 a.m.	10:00 a.m.	11:00 a.m.	12:00 p.m.
10:00	10:00 a.m.	11:00 a.m.	12:00 p.m.	1:00 p.m.
11:00	11:00 a.m.	12:00 p.m.	1:00 p.m.	2:00 p.m.
12:00	12:00 p.m.	1:00 p.m.	2:00 p.m.	3:00 p.m.
13:00	1:00 p.m.	2:00 p.m.	3:00 p.m.	4:00 p.m.
14:00	2:00 p.m.	3:00 p.m.	4:00 p.m.	5:00 p.m.
15:00	3:00 p.m.	4:00 p.m.	5:00 p.m.	6:00 p.m.
16:00	4:00 p.m.	5:00 p.m.	6:00 p.m.	7:00 p.m.
17:00	5:00 p.m.	6:00 p.m.	7:00 p.m.	8:00 p.m.
18:00	6:00 p.m.	7:00 p.m.	8:00 p.m.	9:00 p.m.
19:00	7:00 p.m.	8:00 p.m.	9:00 p.m.	10:00 p.m.
20:00	8:00 p.m.	9:00 p.m.	10:00 p.m.	11:00 p.m.
21:00	9:00 p.m.	10:00 p.m.	11:00 p.m.	12:00 a.m.
22:00	10:00 p.m.	11:00 p.m.	12:00 a.m.	1:00 a.m.
23:00	11:00 p.m.	12:00 a.m.	1:00 a.m.	2:00 a.m.

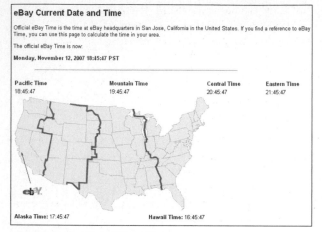

• **Figure 9-7: eBay Official Time.**

Here's the consensus of the some *experts* in order of ending-time preference (these are shown in eBay time; check the table for a translation):

1. 18:00 to 22:00

2. 21:00 to 0:00

3. 15:00 to 18:00

4. 13:00 to 16:00

Here are the worst times to end an auction:

1. 2:00 to 6:00

2. 0:00 to 3:00

This information should give you some good ideas for your own auction sales.

Doing Your Own Research with Sellathon

Good-quality research can make the difference in whether a business endeavor is a success or a failure. I strongly advocate doing at least the minimal research on any item's eBay availability and current selling price. Call it a practical necessity.

I also recommend using certain advanced counters (those that break down Web page visits to hours and days, rather than showing only totals), because such tools tell you more than the number of people who click your page — that number alone doesn't tell you much. Wouldn't it be nice to know, not only how many people visited your listing, but what page sent them there and what city they come from? Wouldn't it be nice to have more data about the people who visit your listings?

The problem with gathering this kind of information is that the coding and programming involved is probably beyond the skill set of even the top-level eBay sellers. After all, they're merchants, not computer programmers. That's why this technique tells you about an online service — ViewTracker — that gives you all the research you can use.

You get the info just by putting a small bit of code (which ViewTracker supplies) into your listings. Every time someone visits your auctions, the code you've embedded sends your online account definitive information about your visitor — in real time.

Best of all, this information — while important for your sales efforts — remains noninvasive for your potential customers. For example, you may find out the timeslots and keywords used by your listing visitors, but you find out nothing that compromises their identities.

What you get from Sellathon ViewTracker

ViewTracker from Sellathon answers the most popular questions I'm asked by eBay sellers. Before ViewTracker, when trying to figure out the exact time and day to end an auction, you had to do a considerable amount of research by running test auctions on the eBay site. Now you can follow the "body clocks" of your buyers and find out when they search for your type of item.

You will also find out which keywords the browser was using when they came to your listing. This information is crucial when writing titles — and planning keyword campaigns. By applying the information from ViewTracker, you can change tactics to help your little business grow into a big one. You'll be able to customize your items to match your very own eBay market.

 Setting up your account is painless. After you give your contact information to Sellathon (and make up a new User ID and password for the site), you will be presented with a small amount of code to add to your listing's description. It's that easy.

Checking out your data on Sellathon

When you first log onto ViewTracker, you'll be presented with your General (combined items) page. Here you'll see a couple of statistics. Keep in mind that ViewTracker constantly tracks your items in real time, so the data may change by the minute as you're changing screens within the program!

After you log in to your account, you see a mini-graph at the top of every page. This shows you a quick graphic snapshot of your last 24 hours total up-to-the-minute visit counts.

You'll also have folders that will have your live and expired auctions. You can click links to get general information on all your auctions, or click the folder to view information on individual items. You can get data on all your items — whether consolidated or as individual information for each listing.

There's a whole lot more to this amazing service — and since this isn't a commercial, I suggest you go to the site and check out the free trial. For the free trial, go to www.sellathon.com/coolebaytools.

Setting Shipping Costs That Pay

Buyers who visit the eBay site are bargain shoppers, and they look for the lowest possible prices for their items in the eBay search engine. They're also becoming more cognizant about the "hidden" expense buried in the item's shipping and handling fees.

When you set your shipping fees, you must take into account every expense involved in the packing and shipping area of your business. Your shipping area can become a losing proposition if you don't work out these figures every so often.

Too many eBay sellers — unquestionably out of greed — have increased shipping prices to outrageous amounts. I'll bet those sellers think they've found a cute way to shave a couple of cents off their Final Value fees (after all, Final Value fees aren't charged on shipping costs). But when the shipping fee is half of (or even equal to) the item cost, a prospective bidder may think twice about placing a bid. It seems that eBay has smartened up on this practice as well; they have gone so far as to alter the search engine options to allow a price plus shipping sort. This sort can also be affected by eBay's Shipping Calculator, discussed further on.

 When buyers search for an item on eBay, remember that they can use the drop-down menu that appears at the top-right of the search results. This menu allows shoppers to reorganize search results by various parameters. One such parameter is *price plus shipping cost*. This search option returns results in price order (from lowest to highest) but also includes the shipping amount in the total. Using this feature allows savvy shoppers to see through the "low item price, high shipping price" seller's come-on. So keep in mind that overstating shipping costs can show up even on an initial search — and establish your shipping charges accordingly.

 If the item you're selling is big and/or the buyer wants it fast, he or she may feel more comfortable about paying higher shipping fees.

Business is business, and when you're on eBay to make a profit, every penny counts. In this practice, you find out how to evaluate all the costs involved with packing and shipping the items you sell. Also, you see how to use the tools at your disposal — such as eBay's Shipping Calculator — to make the best decisions about how to charge your buyers for your shipping expenses.

Figuring the Hidden Shipping Costs

When calculating shipping costs, don't assume you have to cover just the cost of your postage. You also have per-item costs for boxes, padded mailers, shipping tape, labels, and pickup or service fees from your carriers. Now and again, you may even pay the college kid across the street five bucks to schlep your boxes for you. Expenses show up in the strangest places.

In addition to adding up the packing and shipping supplies, you need to amortize the monthly fees from any online postage-printing services. (See Practice 28 for more info about these services.) When you occasionally pay for a pickup from the carrier, you have to add that expense to the shipping charges as well. The following list runs down some of the expenses involved:

Be sure to check out Practice 29 to find sources for deals on the various shipping products you need.

✔ **Padded mailers.** Select an average-size padded mailer that works for several types of items you sell. Selecting an average size for all your products works well because everything (including shipping supplies) is cheaper when you buy in quantity. Even if a few of your items could fit in the next-size-down mailers, buying the bigger size by the case gives you a considerable discount. Why keep five different sizes of mailers in

stock in large quantities if you don't have to? If you don't use all of the bigger ones, you can always sell them. And besides, padded envelopes don't go bad.

Don't be misled by packaging suppliers' claims that their mailers cost only __¢ each. They *usually* don't include their shipping costs in these price "estimates." Add the shipping you'll have to pay to the cost of the packaging supplies you're buying. Then divide by the quantity purchased to get your cost per item.

When you price out your cost-per-piece, be sure to include (as part of your cost) what you have to pay to get the item shipped to you. The prices shown here were taken off the eBay site during this writing. So, if you purchase your mailers — say #4s (9 ½" × 14 ½") — by the hundred, they usually cost you $.40 each (or in one source I found — only $.31). If you buy a case of 500, they have an average cost of $.28 for each envelope. By buying in quantity, you can save $.12 per mailing envelope! The more business you do, the more significant the savings.

✔ **Packing peanuts.** The inedible foam kind. I must admit that storing all those packing peanuts is a real drag. (See the upcoming tip for a handy storage idea.) Here's another place where buying in bulk (by the cubic foot) equates to huge savings. These figures, for example include shipping cost:

4.5 cubic feet for $11.99 = $2.66 per cu. ft.

10 cubic feet for $21.98 = $2.20 per cu. ft.

20 cubic feet for $43.96 = $2.20 per cu. ft.

Actually, 10 cubic feet turns out to be the most economical deal — that's because of the big pocketbook pinch that shipping adds to the equation. eBay sellers who sell packing peanuts offer them for *half* what they cost when you purchase them from a brick-and-mortar retailer. (That's because a store you can actually walk into has to use up precious, dollar-costing square footage to store these babies, which means a higher cost to you.)

In one of my other eBay books, I share my solution to peanut storage, and I've been asked to include it here as well. Here it is (in a nutshell): Take some drawstring-type trash bags. Fill them fully with packing peanuts, then tie the drawstring. Screw some cup hooks into the rafters of your garage and hang the bags from the rafters. You can store a *big* bunch of peanuts there! *Be sure to recycle!*

✔ **Packing tape.** Packing tape is a real hidden cost of shipping. You need a stock of clear packing tape; not only to secure packages, but to sometimes affix labels. The common size for a roll is 2 inches wide by 110 feet long. The following average eBay prices *include* shipping:

6 rolls = $16.95 = $2.83 per roll

12 rolls = $26.96 = $2.25 per roll

36-roll case = $49.85 = $1.38 per roll

Again, compare prices before buying.

✔ **Boxes.** Price out boxes in quantity orders. I won't take you through the various costs of boxes because *hundreds* of sizes are available. Shop eBay (the shipping costs will kill you unless you're located next door to the seller), and check out www.uline.com for boxes at reasonable prices. Uline.com ships from six regional hubs, which allows them to offer a reasonable delivery price. For our example, let's just say a typical box will cost $.47 each.

✔ **G&A (general and administrative) costs.** For the uninitiated (translation: you never had to do budgets at a large corporation), G&A represents the costs incurred in running a company. But the principle is familiar: Time is money. For example, the time it takes you to research the costs of mailers, tapes, and boxes on eBay is costing you money. The time it takes for you to drive to the post office or bundle up your items and prepare them for shipping — time costs you money. We won't actually put a figure on this just now,

but it's something you need to think about — especially if you ship very delicate items every other day. In effect, that's time wasted. You could be finding new sources of merchandise with the time. It costs you money that you might have earned.

✔ **Online postage service.** If you're paying around $10 a month for the convenience of buying and printing online postage, you have to assume that's an expense, too. If you ship 100 packages a month, that amortizes to $.10 per package.

 If you're questioning whether you need an online postage service, here's my two cents: Being able to hand your packages (even International ones with customs forms) to the postal carrier still beats standing in line at the post office.

When you add together expenses from this list, you have the cost for mailing out a padded envelope cushioned with packing peanuts, as in Table 10-1.

TABLE 10-1: SAMPLE SHIPPING COSTS PER SINGLE PACKAGE

Item	Estimated Cost per Shipment
Padded mailer	$ .38
Peanuts	.09
Tape	.03
Mailing label	.04
Postage service	.10
TOTAL	**$1.27 per package — *not* including postage!**

Before you even put postage on the package, you could possibly be spending $1.27 — not including your time. (Excuse me while I go to my eBay listings and raise my shipping charges!)

If you're shipping many packages a month, read Practice 36 on how to use QuickBooks to easily and simply see your exact average per package costs.

Using a Shipping Calculator in Your Listings

If you put a flat shipping fee on some larger items, you may be costing yourself money. Make everything fair for the buyer (and for you) — use eBay's free Shipping Calculator to post clear shipping charges for your items.

When listing an item for sale on eBay, you come to the area where you need to input your payment-and-shipping information. You have the option of using a flat rate from a drop-down menu (as in Figure 10-1) where you simply input your flat shipping charges. These appear in a box at the bottom of your item description.

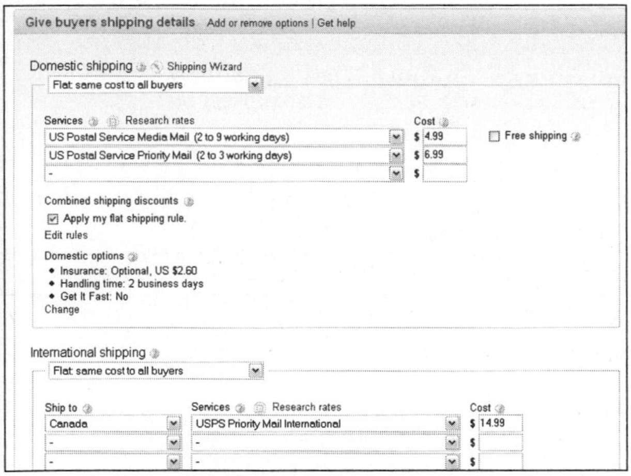

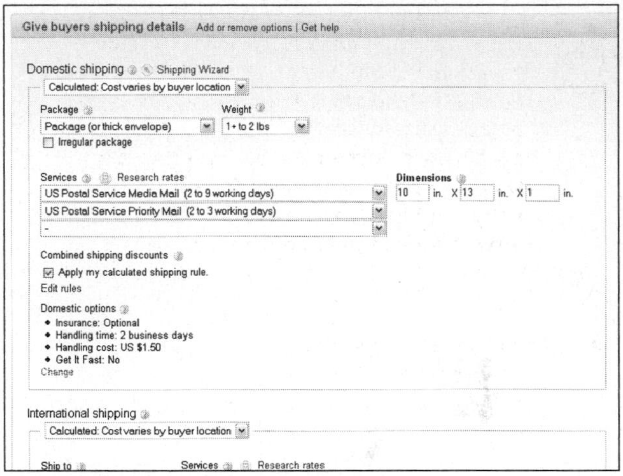

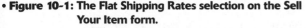

• **Figure 10-2: Calculated Shipping Rates form.**

2. Select your package weight and size from the related drop-down lists, as shown in Figure 10-3.

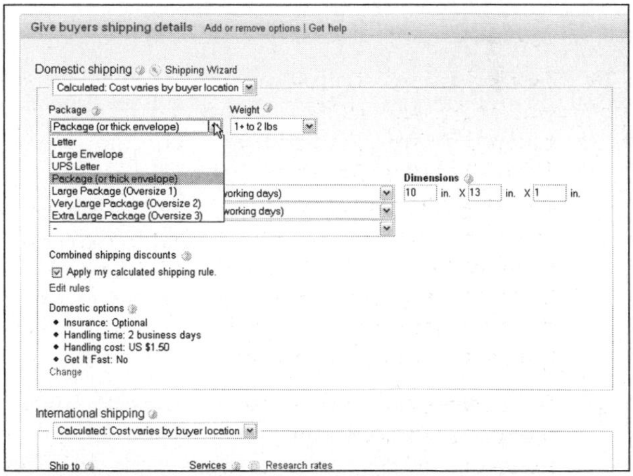

• **Figure 10-1: The Flat Shipping Rates selection on the Sell Your Item form.**

You also have another option for figuring shipping charges on the items you list on eBay. To have eBay calculate the charges for you when your buyer supplies his or her postal/ZIP code, follow these steps as you input listing information:

1. Click the drop-down menu to select Calculated Shipping Rates.

The form shown in Figure 10-2 appears.

• **Figure 10-3: The Package Size drop-down menu.**

3. Select a carrier service from the Services drop-down list.

Figure 10-4 shows the choices available for Domestic shipping in this drop-down list.

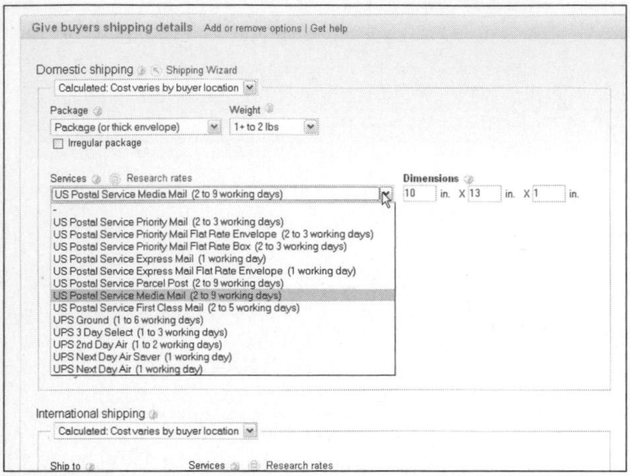

• **Figure 10-4: Selecting the shipping service.**

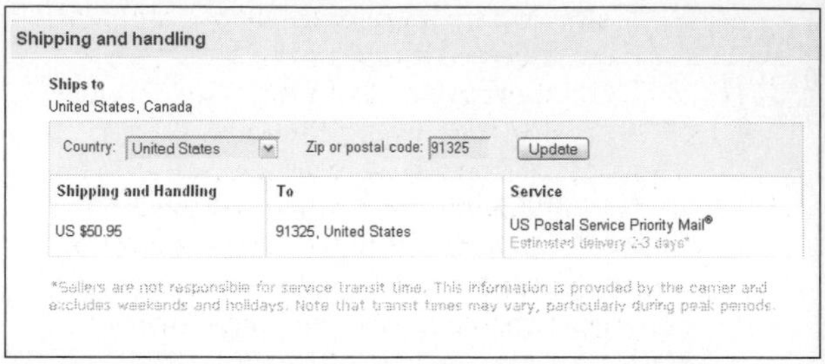

• **Figure 10-5: The Shipping Calculator in an auction.**

After bidders sign in to eBay, their eBay accounts' registered ZIP codes become part of the service. Then, when they perform a search, they can see all calculated shipping costs in the search results options.

4. **Type the rough dimensions of your package in the indicated box.**

5. **Type your packaging fees in the Packaging & Handling Fee box.**

▶ When adding your packaging and handling charges, don't worry that the buyers will see these individual fees. eBay combines this amount with the actual shipper costs and shows the total as one shipping price.

▶ If you selected the U.S. Postal Service as your carrier, be sure to add the cost of a delivery confirmation for items other than Priority Mail (if you use one) when you figure your packing and handling fee.

6. **Select the appropriate options in the Shipping Insurance and Sales Tax drop-down lists.**

If you require the buyer to pay for insurance, or even if it's optional, be sure to indicate it. eBay's calculator will give the buyer the actual insurance cost based on the final bid.

After you've input all your information, you can forget about it; eBay takes over. Figure 10-5 shows the results calculated from a buyer's registered ZIP code.

You can check out the fees for different shipping services by using the full eBay Shipping Calculator located at

```
http://cgi3.ebay.com/aw-cgi/eBayISAPI.
dll?emitsellershippingcalculator
```

and shown in Figure 10-6. This tool shows you all the shipping costs so that you can decide to ship with either the U.S. Postal Service or UPS.

• **Figure 10-6: The full Shipping Calculator.**

Before setting shipping costs for my products, I always test my packages from a California ZIP code (because that's where I live) to a ZIP code in New York. Doing this gives me an estimate for Zone 8, which is the most expensive option (by distance) when shipping in the U.S. You can accomplish this same test for the items you sell by testing sample package weights to the zone farthest from where you ship.

Practice 11

Marketing Your Items to Grow Sales

In This Practice

- ✔ Getting Google search on the case
- ✔ Feeding other engines and comparison sites
- ✔ Adding AdWords for good measure
- ✔ Linking through your own special eBay pages

In the early days of the Web, making money was all about making your site *sticky* — that is, able to attract people and keep them hanging around for a while. Stickiness happens when you give buyers a direct route to your items so they can buy, buy, buy — and this is still your goal; hopefully every visitor will buy something. To achieve this goal, you take advantage of promotions, affiliate programs, the eBay About Me page, search-engine optimization (SEO), and more. Those tools are still in place — and you can put them all to good use.

Now the Web is in a new incarnation — Web 2.0. Today's Web is more about interaction, getting sites involved with other sites by syndication through RSS feeds. Sites like Nextag, PriceGrabber.com, Shopping.com, and even Google have become places for people to interact with thousands of sites at once.

If you find the theory behind these mega-sites confusing, think about it like this: When most people want to book an airline flight, they go to a site such as Orbitz or Expedia (which access the databases of most major airlines) to seek out low prices. They find the flight and price they want and buy it right there (rather than going to the individual airline's site). The airlines syndicate their stock of seats for sale to these sites. You can do the same with the items you have for sale.

In this practice, I introduce you to the tools and tricks that grab buyers' attention, which gives you the short version of Web optimization. It's just enough to make you dangerous (to your competition, that is).

Catching Attention on Google

Have you ever *Googled* (a new verb meaning to search the Google engine for something) your eBay Store? I did; I searched a portion of my store name (Fabulous Finds) and included the word *eBay* in the search parameters. Figure 11-1 shows you the results. Google your store; is it listed?

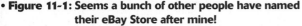

• **Figure 11-1: Seems a bunch of other people have named their eBay Store after mine!**

If it isn't, you're missing out on a huge opportunity for free promotion. Google runs *spiders* (just picture the way a spider runs — swiftly and all over the place). These are automated robots (with the silly-sounding name *Googlebots*) that scour the Internet monthly, looking for data to make part of the Google index.

Thousands of sites are added to the Google index every time their spiders crawl the Web — and you *do* know that because your eBay Store has a unique URL, it's considered a Web site, right? That's opportunity knocking. Google also takes feeds as advertising from independent sites (eBay being one) to promote items for sale.

How about your own Web site? Is it listed? If, for some unknown reason, it isn't listed, go to www.google.com/addurl.html, as pictured in Figure 11-2 and take care of that important detail.

• **Figure 11-2: Get your free shot at the big time.**

When you get to this page, follow these steps:

1. **Type your Web site or eBay Store URL in the URL text box.**

   To make sure you have the complete, correct URL, just click the store red-tag icon next to your eBay User ID to get to your store. When I go to my eBay Store, the URL http://stores.ebay.com/Marsha-Colliers-Fabulous-Finds appears in the browser address line. The URL you see there is the URL you should use in your e-mail and printed propaganda to promote your store. Copy and paste the URL in the address line of your browser into the URL text box.

2. **If you want, type a comment describing your store merchandise in the Comment text box.**

3. **If you want, type the squiggly letters that appear in the Optional section into the box provided.**

   This distinguishes you as an individual instead of an automated software robot.

4. **Click Add URL.**

There are no guarantees here, but odds are you'll find your little shop popping up on Google searches within a few weeks.

Optimizing for search-engine success

The preceding step list gives you instructions on how to get a "natural" listing in a search engine (Google), but getting a prime position in the listing takes a bit of finesse. Having a good Web site isn't enough; you've got to take some extra steps to real success in search engines.

1. **Keyword phrases or *keyphrases*.** In this book, I talk about keywords (see Practice 18). Pick ten keyphrases that describe your products. Be as specific as you can. Each phrase should be at least two words — for example, cashmere scarf or eBay books. Think like a shopper when you select these phrases. Consider using the Google AdWords keyword tool at

   adwords.google.com/select/KeywordToolExternal

(continued)

as in the figure shown here. You can type in your Web site's URL and Google will suggest keyphrases for you.

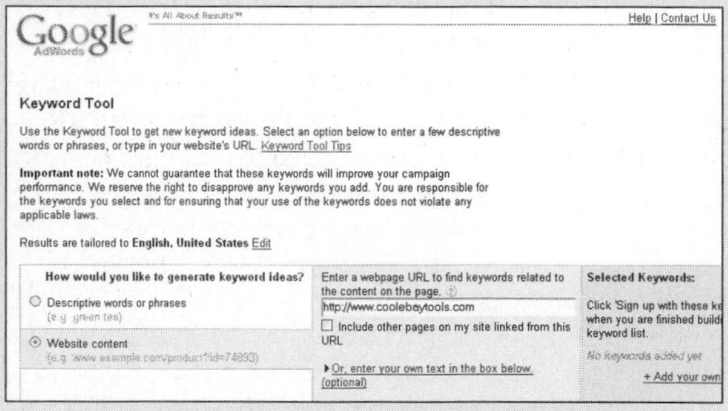

2. **Content is king.** Use the keyphrases you came up with to insert content on your pages. Use the exact wording and repeat the phrases throughout the page if possible (this increases your relevancy). Don't just repeat the phrases; work them into your text naturally.

3. **Update your page titles.** Use the keyphrases (where applicable) in your page titles. Make the page title descriptive, but short.

4. **Take advantage of metatags.** *Metatags* are short paragraphs, hidden in your HTML code, that describe your pages. The description metatag is recognized by some search-engine *bots* (another term for software robots) and is also used by many search engines when listing a site on a search-results page. Be sure to include as many of your keyphrases as you can without sounding incoherent. Metatags used to be the gold standard for search-engine optimization, today they're not as important as *content*.

5. **Don't use spurious keyword terms.** Repeating the same words over and over constitutes cheating with keywords. The bots are wise to that trick. The same tip-off occurs if keywords that crop up on a site are unrelated to the site or its product. Many search engines entirely ban sites that try such tricks.

Setting Up an eBay Store Listing RSS Feed

There are many online services that will accept feeds from your eBay store or Web site. A "feed"

will list your items for sale on another Web site. (Often, you have to pay for *click-throughs* — which are usually not too expensive — but if they result in a sale, it's money in the bank.) You can even set up another page on the Web incorporating your feed. The RSS feeds that eBay provides look something like Figure 11-3 — a bunch of HTML code all nicely set up for someone's RSS-reader software to display.

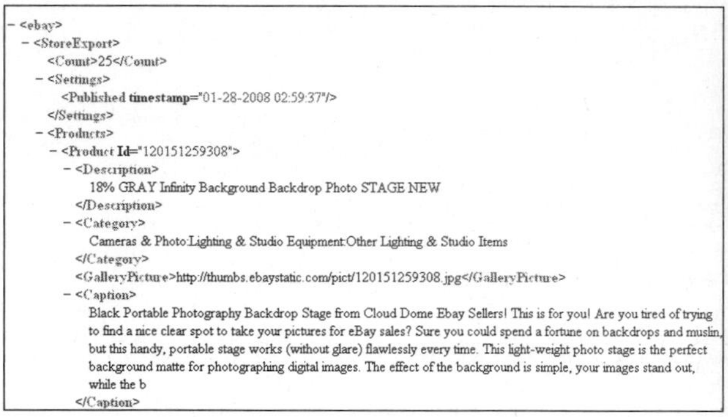

• **Figure 11-3: A portion of my eBay Store's RSS feed.**

eBay will provide this file with a little help from you. Here's the drill:

1. **Go to your My eBay page.**

2. **Find the Marketing Tools link in the eBay Views sidebar link box and click it.**

   You arrive at the Marketing Tools Summary page shown in Figure 11-4.

3. **Click Manage in the Listing Feeds area.**

   Your Listing Feeds management page appears, as shown in Figure 11-5.

4. **Select the Activate Your Store Inventory Listings via RSS radio button.**

   After you activate your listings, an RSS tag appears in your store footer.

5. **Select the Make a File of Your Store Inventory Listings Available radio button to export your listings to third-party search engines and product-comparison sites.**

Your HTML code file is now available for you to use with product search engines and comparison sites at the URL shown.

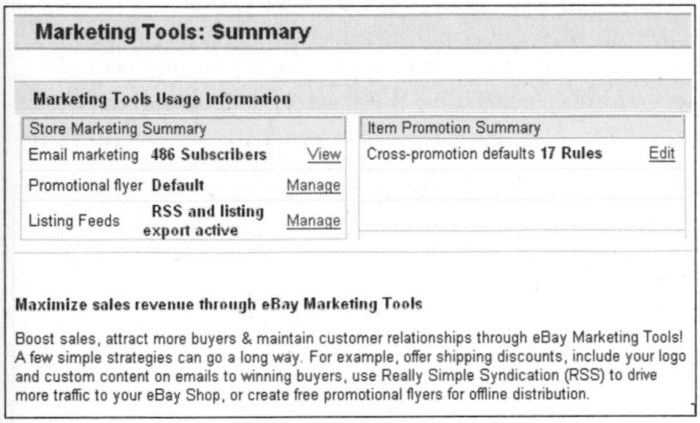

• **Figure 11-4: Your Marketing Tools control panel.**

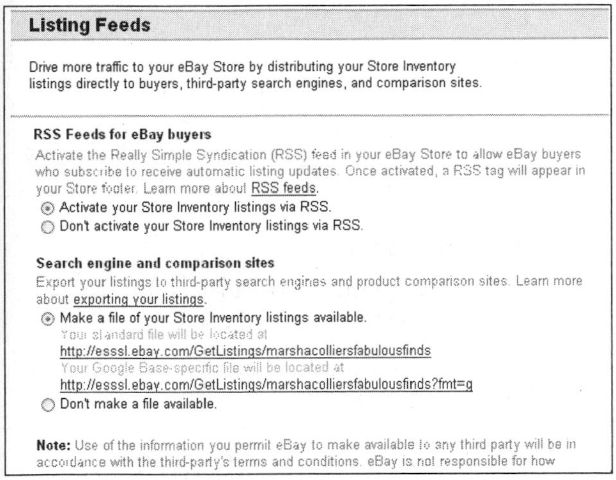

• **Figure 11-5: Here's where the magic begins.**

Listing Your Store Feed on Google Base

When you have your RSS file ready, it's not going to make money for you if it just sits there. Find a place to get your items listed. I send mine to Google Base and so should you.

Google Base is a data feed that allows your individual listings (not just your store) to become searchable on Google. This service won't cost you a penny.

To take advantage of Google's eBay Store Connector, you need to sign up for a Google account. You can get a quality e-mail address with them too — so just sign up for Google Mail and you become a Google account holder. If you don't want the e-mail, just go to www.google.com and sign up.

Once you have a Google account, go to the Store Connector at

> www.google.com/base/storeconnector/
> index.html

Click the box that says Download The Google Base Store Connector and install it.

You've got your file set up, so just open the Store Connector software and you'll see the screen like the one in Figure 11-6.

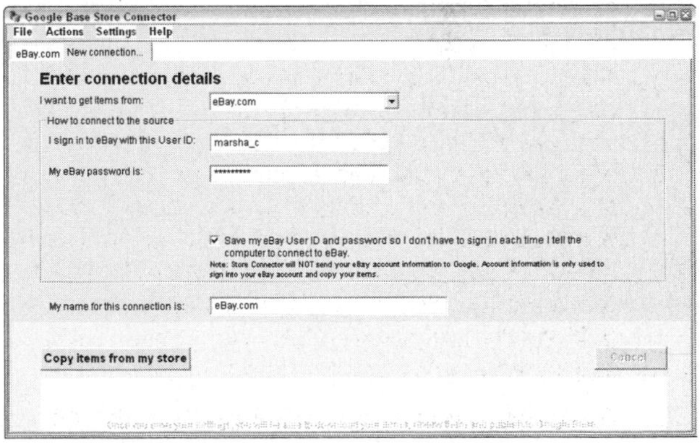

• **Figure 11-6: The Store Connector is ready to connect you.**

With the Store Connector open, follow these steps:

1. **Select eBay.com for the drop-down menu.**

2. **Type in your User ID and password on the appropriate lines.**

Your eBay account information is used solely to retrieve your store's RSS file that's waiting for Google.

3. **Click the Copy Items From My Store Box.**

Voilá: The new tab on your software appears, show-ing your eBay store categories and how many items have been uploaded, as in Figure 11-7.

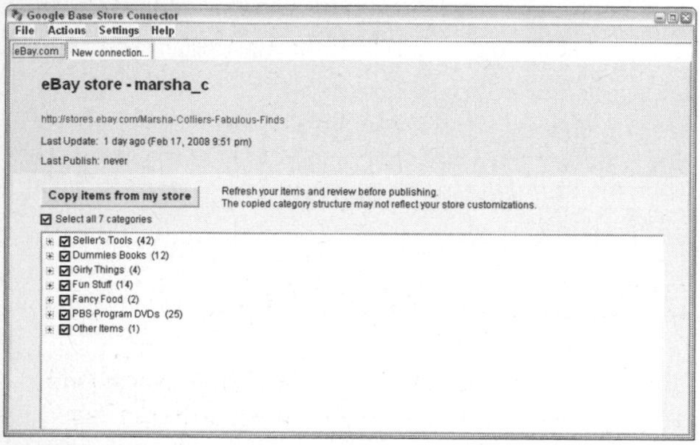

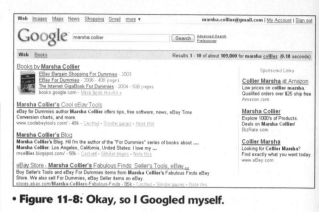

• **Figure 11-7: Your store categories and upload tally show on the new tab.**

As your store merchandise changes, you can repeat this procedure to keep Google up to date.

Get Found in a Hurry with AdWords

Being a regular user of the Google index, I began to notice small ads along the right side of my search screens, under a headline called Sponsored Links. I figured those must be expensive links from high-dollar operations — until I found out the truth. If you take a look at the results of a Google search in Figure 11-8, you'll see my little ad on the right.

People use Google more than 200 million times a day. Google AdWords allow you to create these prof-itable little ads. You choose keywords to let Google know where to place your ads. Certainly you can come up with some relevant keywords to promote your eBay Store! (Check out Practice 18 for tips on choosing the right keywords.)

• **Figure 11-8: Okay, so I Googled myself.**

The coolest part of the AdWords deal is that you have to pay for the ad only when someone clicks it. Wanna know more? Go over to www.adwords.com. Once you're there, you can go over the details and set up your own campaign.

For your campaign, there are a few things to keep in mind:

✔ **Keywords and keyword phrases:** Come up with a list of keywords that would best describe your merchandise. Google helps you estimate, based on current search data, how often your selected keyword will come up every day. You can also estimate your daily cost based on the current number of clicks on that word. (That can be a shocking number. Don't worry, not everyone who sees your ad will click it — but if they did, eeyow!)

✔ **CPC (cost per click):** You determine how much you'll pay each time someone clicks your key-words. You can pay as little as $.05 or as much as $50 a click. The dollar amount you place on your clicks determines how often your ad appears.

✔ **CTR (click-through rate):** This statistic reflects how many people click your ad when they see it. If your CTR falls below .5 percent after 1,000 impressions, AdWords may slow down, or even discontinue, your ad views. When one of your keywords isn't passing muster, it will show up on your reports as Moderate or less.

Without showing my keywords, Figure 11-9 shows you a month's worth of keyword analysis for my account. You can see clearly that some keywords are doing their jobs and others aren't. (To keep my account current, I evaluate my CTR every month and delete the laggards.)

✔ **Daily budget:** You can set a cap on how many dollars you'll spend per day. The more business you do, the more necessary this is; if you have some really hot keywords, you could spend thousands on clicks!

Status	Clicks	Impr.	CTR ▼	Avg. CPC	Cost	Avg. Pos
	657	37,770	1.7%	$0.08	$46.21	3.7
	272	726,644	0.0%	$0.08	$19.10	3.1
Strong	34	111	30.6%	$0.05	$1.70	1.0
Strong	13	256	5.0%	$0.09	$1.10	1.2
Strong	22	434	5.0%	$0.09	$1.89	5.1
Strong	221	9,712	2.2%	$0.08	$17.61	4.2
Strong	40	1,853	2.1%	$0.06	$2.12	1.2
Strong	106	6,138	1.7%	$0.06	$5.79	1.3
Strong	156	10,423	1.4%	$0.07	$10.87	1.5
Strong	28	3,199	0.8%	$0.08	$2.13	3.4
Strong	5	649	0.7%	$0.06	$0.28	1.9
Moderate	9	1,191	0.7%	$0.10	$0.84	14.2
Strong	23	3,247	0.7%	$0.09	$1.88	7.1
Moderate	0	161	0.0%	-	-	6.4
Moderate	0	158	0.0%	-	-	33.9
Moderate	0	99	0.0%	-	-	103.1

• **Figure 11-9: An AdWords keyword-analysis report.**

Setting up your AdWords account will take a while and some thinking. So wait until your mind is clear (Saturday morning?), sit down at the AdWords site with a cup of coffee, and expect to take a while.

There are a few tricks to writing that tiny pay-per-click ad. To serve you best, your ad should

✔ **Emphasize benefits, ask a question, or arouse curiosity.** If you have a common marketing tagline, be sure to include it to build your brand.

✔ **Be specific about what you're offering,** so you don't get a lot of clicks from people who are looking for something different than what you have to offer. (Remember, you're paying for each click, whether it turns into a sale or not.)

✔ **Include your keywords:** They will appear in bold, which will be an added encouragement for people to click.

eBay's About Me Page

The About Me page is a really fun and helpful tool on eBay — and it's free to every registered eBay user. Having an About Me page shows the community you're jumping in with both feet. Prospective customers can use your About Me page to get to know a little more about you — to get a sense of your personality and your dedication. You can use your About Me page as a tool to direct customers to your eBay Store (or to your own Web site — About Me is the only place on eBay where it's legal to post an off-eBay commerce Web site).

eBay members like to check out both sellers and buyers on the site. By learning about your potential trading partner, you get information — and accurate information is the key to preventing fraud. From an eBay member's About Me page, you can see just how involved the person is in the eBay business world.

Deal or no deal

The About Me page can also be a deal-maker — or a deal-breaker. Once (for example) I was looking around eBay for some extra-long printer cables, and found several sellers selling just what I wanted. One of the lower-priced sellers had a low feedback rating — only because he was new at eBay. But he had an About Me page, so I clicked. I found out that the seller was a computer technician by trade and that he and his son made these computer cables together as a family business at home in the evenings.

(continued)

> The money they made went to pay for their father-son trips to see their favorite baseball team play. What a great family enterprise! Better yet, he guaranteed the cables. As you might have guessed, I bought the cables, and we *both* got positive feedback.

You can tell whether someone else has an About Me page because you'll see a small icon with a blue lowercase *m* and a red lowercase *e*.

Putting together your About Me page takes no time at all. Most of the time you spend will be in the planning. The page can be as simple or as complex as you want. You may use one of eBay's templates as presented, or you may gussy up the page with lots of pictures and varied text using HTML. (See Practice 17 for the basics on formatting with HTML.)

Setting up the page

There are several things you must think about ahead of time:

- ✔ **Title:** Come up with a title for your page. It can be as simple as a welcome greeting.

- ✔ **Subtitle:** Decide on a few words that go below your page title and elaborate on your page theme.

- ✔ **Introductory paragraph:** Structure this paragraph to tell a little about you and your hobbies or interests. You can also talk about the items you sell on eBay, but most of all, it should reflect your personality.

> In the paragraphs of the About Me page, you can use HTML to add images or fancy text. The titles, however, are standard; they won't permit HTML coding.

- ✔ **Second subtitle and paragraph:** Elaborate on your interests and your business on eBay. Add more information. Pictures are good, too!

- ✔ **eBay activity:** Decide what you'd like to show on the page — like how many of your most recent feedback comments — and whether you'd like to show your current listings.

> Don't get carried away with showing your last 100 feedback messages; doing so takes up too much space. Display either 10 or 25 and leave it at that. If visitors want to know more about your feedback rating, they can click your feedback number. (After all, they clicked your Me icon to get here, and that's right next to your feedback number.)

- ✔ **Web site links:** Think of some of your favorite Web sites; also include yours or a friend's (ask first). You may legally put these links on your page.

If you've been an advanced user on eBay for a while, consider adding the following to your existing About Me page:

- ✔ **Your logo:** If you've designed a logo for your eBay business, be sure to put it on the page.

- ✔ **Returns policy:** Outline your standard returns policy on the page for your customers.

- ✔ **Shipping policy:** Explain how you ship and when you ship. Offer discounts on shipping for multiple purchases through your eBay Store.

- ✔ **Searchable index to your eBay Store:** Let your customers search your store by such specifics as apparel size, brand name, or item. You can accomplish this by HTML coding.

- ✔ **Payment methods:** Let the customer know what payment methods you accept.

> When you have an eBay Store, your About Me page is also the About the Store page. Your eBay Store's graphic header will appear at the top of your About Me page.

Using little-known, eBay-unique HTML tags

It's not a highly publicized deal, but you can use some special *unique-to-eBay* HTML codes that give your About Me page a custom look. Some of these codes can be combined with others (such as those for bold and color). Play around with them and see what you come up with!

Table 11-1 gives you the secret codes (sorry, no decoder rings) and shows you what they can do.

TABLE 11-1: EBAY HTML TAGS

Tag	What It Does
<eBayUserID>	Displays your User ID and real-time feedback rating
<eBayUserID BOLD>	Displays your User ID and feedback rating in boldface
<eBayUserID NOLINK>	Displays your User ID with no clickable link (useful if you plan to change your ID soon)
<eBayUserID NOFEEDBACK>	Displays your User ID with no feedback number after it
<eBayUserID BOLD NOFEEDBACK>	Combines two of the above tags into one
<eBayFeedback>	Shows your up-to-the-minute feedback comments
<eBayFeedback COLOR="red">	Changes the color of the second line on your feedback-comment table to red
<eBayFeedback TABLEWIDTH="75%">	Changes the width of your feedback-comment table as a percentage of the allowed space (the default value is 90%)
<eBayItemList>	Automatically inserts a list of the items you currently have up for sale

Tag	What It Does
<eBayItemList BIDS>	Displays everything you're currently bidding on
<eBayTime>	Inserts the official eBay time into your text
<eBayMemberSince>	Inputs the exact date and time of your initial eBay registration

eBay My World

eBay's foray into the world of Web 2.0 is eBay My World. Believe it or not, keywords and phrases count for a lot here, too! eBay My World is new, but every Web page counts for getting buyers to your listings, so you just can't ignore it. Your My World page, as well as your eBay Store, gets listed on the major search engines. I found mine on Google, MSN, and Yahoo. Figure 11-10 shows my My World page.

• **Figure 11-10: My very own World.**

To set up your own My World page, click your user ID anywhere it appears next to your feedback rating. It's a very simple process of selecting your template, colors, and what information you'd like eBay to feed onto your page.

Ideally, your page should have lots of links to your listings. I suggest you select the option to show ten. That way, if someone is searching those keywords, your page can come up high in the search. Also, be sure to put in a featured item, which is ideally an item that you regularly stock and (hopefully) one that makes you a good profit on each sale.

Your listings should, as this project takes off, raise your search rankings.

 I mentioned Sellathon in Practice 5 as a way of checking out how your item listings are pulling in shoppers on eBay. Using this tool, I've been noticing that the number of visitors to my listings coming from my My World page has been increasing steadily. I like that.

12

Making the eBay Store Decision

Once you've started selling successfully on eBay and you're earnest in your commitment to running a business online, it's time to open your eBay Store. Many new sellers make the mistake of opening a store first, find their sales abysmal, and give up. Opening your store too soon can be an expensive and disheartening mistake. You need to know the ropes first. You need to have a decent number of transactions under your belt so you know what to expect. By the time you reach PowerSeller status, you have the experience — but you still need the caution.

Making the decision to open an eBay Store can expand your business when planned properly. The more that savvy buyers learn about the eBay Stores, the more popular they become. The more popular they become, the more people buy from them. Simple. An eBay Store provides you with your own little corner of eBay in which you can leverage your good relationships with your customers to promote your auctions — and sell directly to those loyal customers. But having an eBay Store is not a total solution or a one-way ticket to easy street.

The purpose of expanding your eBay business is to make more money, not to start losing money. Big businesses expand in order to make more money, even though their costs may increase. There's *always* risk involved in *any* business venture, but with experience on the site and what you learn in this book, hopefully you can minimize that risk. In this practice, I lead you through the process of opening and running an eBay Store. With plenty of insight from my years as PowerSeller, I show you how to get started with your store and how to use it for the best benefit. Your eBay Store is your first step into the world of full-blown e-commerce.

Getting Grounded First

I hear from people who open eBay Stores but are not successful in moving merchandise. Why? Because running an eBay Store takes an extra level of effort. The more energy you invest in your eBay business, the more work you have to do. Simple.

No matter how many "money-back guaran-tees" you receive from online spammers promising magical success on eBay, the only magic that *works* is putting your nose (and shoulder) to the grindstone and exerting the effort necessary to bring customers to your store.

eBay wants you to succeed as well. Although I'm sure they like getting the monthly fee for the store, they'd much rather see your sales grow. After all, the more you sell, the more eBay earns in Final Value Fees.

If you're just beginning on eBay, the best advice I can give you is to hold off on opening an eBay Store until your feedback rating is over 100. There is no substitute for experience. Participating in transactions on eBay is a natural teacher because you'll see mistakes that sellers make when they sell to you. You'll get e-mails from sellers that are plain unfriendly, and you'll have a true understanding of how quality customer service will help you build your business. You'll also learn from your own mistakes and be able to provide better service to your customers.

Planning the "Opening"

So you think it's time to open a store, eh? If you feel it in your gut and you're ready to take the leap, here's what you need to know. eBay has very few requirements when it comes to opening an eBay Store:

- ✔ **Registered user:** You need to have an eBay seller's account with your credit card on file.

- ✔ **Feedback rating:** You must have a Feedback rating of 20 or more and be ID verified or have a PayPal account in good standing.

It doesn't get much easier than that! Personally, I like to add these additional prerequisites to back you up for success:

- ✔ **PayPal account:** You need to have a Business (account under a company or group name) or Premier (personally owned) PayPal account to accept credit cards. Accepting credit cards is a necessity for building sales, and PayPal is inte-grated directly into the site, as well as being widely accepted by buyers.

  Be sure you understand how a PayPal account works so you can decide on the types of pay-ments you will accept — and from which coun-tries you intend to do business. Check out Practice 37 for the scoop on PayPal accounts.

- ✔ **Sales experience:** Having selling (and buying) experience over and above the 20 transactions required by eBay is a big plus. The best teacher (aside from my books) is the school of hard knocks.

- ✔ **Merchandise:** Opening an eBay Store with ten items of which you have only one each isn't a good idea. You need to have enough merchan-dise to support consistent sales in your store.

- ✔ **Devotion:** You need to have the time to check into your eBay business *at least* once a day, and the time to handle shipping the purchased mer-chandise in a prompt manner.

 The items listed as store inventory will not come up in a regular eBay search. New buyers have only two ways to find your store inven-tory: Clicking the Stores link and searching for items on the Store Hub page or clicking the Inventory link from one of your auction pages to see what else you have on sale.

Ways your store items will show up in main eBay search

- ✔ When 30 or fewer Auction and Fixed Price results are found

- ✔ When the "All items including Store Inventory" or "Store Inventory items only" check box in the Search Options box is checked

- ✔ If your search returns no Auctions or Fixed Price items, then up to 30 Store Inventory items will be shown

Choosing between store types

Different real estate has different costs. Just as opening a store on Rodeo Drive in Beverly Hills, California, will cost more than opening a store in Anamoose, North Dakota, opening your eBay Store can also incur varying startup costs. But these cost differences don't relate to physical location. The old real estate adage "location, location, location" counts only in real estate — when you're on eBay, you have the excellent location needed to get new customers.

All eBay Stores are on a level playing field. You can be right up there with the big guys and compete. The only cost differential is the type of store you wish to open. All stores are equally searchable from the eBay Stores hub page, as pictured in Figure 12-1.

• Figure 12-1: The eBay Stores landing page.

In Practice 13, I show you how to best take advantage of the store features. All eBay stores share these features:

✔ **Listings:** All your eBay listings, whether auction, fixed price, or store inventory, will appear in your eBay Store.

✔ **Custom URL:** Your eBay Store has its own Internet address that you can use in links in promotional material — even to promote your store on the Internet.

✔ **Unlimited product pages:** As many items as you choose to list can fill as many pages as they require. No limit!

✔ **Store search:** When customers visit your eBay Store, they can search within your listings for their desired items — with your own personal search engine.

✔ **Custom categories:** Invent your own set of store categories — up to 300 of them — to cover the various types of items that you sell.

✔ **E-mail marketing:** Send out newsletters and promotional e-mails to your customers.

✔ **Cross-promotions:** Specify which additional items are displayed on your Item page, as well as on the Bid Confirmation and Purchase Confirmation page, for each of your items on the regular eBay site.

✔ **Store referral credit:** Get a 75% rebate on Final Value Fees when you refer customers to buy from your store via printed flyers, e-mails, and other Web sites.

✔ **Vacation hold:** Put your listings on hold or insert text into your listings at will to alert customers when you're away.

✔ **Picture Manager:** Store images for your listings on eBay's servers at no extra charge.

✔ **Markdown Manager:** With a click of your mouse, put any or all your store items "on sale."

✔ **Traffic reports:** Analyze your store traffic to improve your merchandising and listing strategies.

Although you'll have to pay a small fee for each listing, eBay Store rental is available on three levels:

✔ **Basic Store:** For $15.95 a month, you get your own eBay Store with all the benefits.

✔ **Featured Store:** You get all the benefits of a Basic Store, plus a link to your store from the store category page and at random intervals on the eBay Stores hub page (refer to Figure 12-1). You also get more advanced sales reports. This type of store will set you back $49.95 per month.

✔ **Anchor Store:** This is a top-of-the-line store on eBay. For $299.95 a month, your store logo takes turns with other logos as part of the display on the home hub page of eBay stores. Your logo also appears at random intervals on eBay's home page. When prospective buyers are browsing eBay Store categories, your logo shows up at the top of the pages.

 There is no limit to the number of items you put up for sale in the Basic Store. An Anchor Store can have as few or as many items as the Basic Store.

For the independent seller, a Basic Store will do the trick. In fact, many high-level PowerSellers find that the Basic eBay Store fulfills their needs. Table 12-1 shows you *most* of the added benefits of each level.

TABLE 12-1: EBAY STORES TIERS FEES AND BENEFITS

Feature	Basic Store	Premium Store	Anchor Store
Monthly subscription fee	$15.95	$49.95	$299.95
Store home page and unlimited product pages	•	•	•
Custom pages	5 pages	10 pages	15 pages
Customized Web address	•	•	•
Promotion boxes	•	•	•
Store categories	300	300	300
Custom store header	•	•	•
eBay header reduction		•	•
FREE sales management tools	Selling Manager ($4.99/month value)	Selling Manager Pro ($15.99/month value)	Selling Manager Pro ($15.99/month value)
Markdown Manager	250 Listings/day	2,500 Listings/day	5,000 Listings/day
Vacation hold	•	•	•
Picture Manager	1 MB free	1 MB free and $5 off subscription	1 GB free/free subscription
Store logo appears next to your store name in listings	•	•	•
Listings show up in eBay Stores gateway search and browse results	•	•	•
Store name appears in "Shop eBay Stores" on search results	Occasionally	Sometimes	Frequently
Rotating promotional placement on eBay Stores gateway		Text link at center of page	Store logo at top of page
Listing frame	•	•	•
E-mail marketing	5,000 e-mails/month	7,500 e-mails/month	10,000 e-mails/month
Search engine keyword management	•	•	•

Feature	Basic Store	Premium Store	Anchor Store
RSS listing feeds	•	•	•
Track Your Success	Basic	Premium	Anchor
Marketplace research		Research Basic $9.99/mo value	Research Pro Reg. $24.99/mo value

Knowing the fee structure

There are other fees involved (are you surprised?) over your basic monthly subscription. Stores also carry listing fees, options fees, and Final Value Fees, as shown in Tables 12-2, 12-3, and 12-4.

TABLE 12-2: STORE INVENTORY LISTING FEES

Starting or Reserve Price	30 Days	Good Until Cancelled
$1.00 – $24.99	$0.03	$0.03 / 30 days
$25.00 – $199.99	$0.05	$0.05 / 30 days
> $200.00	$0.10	$0.10 / 30 days

 Listing your items on a good-until-cancelled basis may be a tempting way to automate your listings — and it's a good strategy. Remember, though, that once someone makes a purchase from an item's listing, you can no longer make changes — you can only update inventory. If you have a new picture or new ideas for a title or description, you must close that listing and relist the item with the new information. But heck, you can do that for only 5¢!

TABLE 12-3: STORE INVENTORY LISTING UPGRADES

Upgrade	Cost per 30 Days of Listing Duration
Gallery	$.00 — FREE!
Item Subtitle	$.02
Listing Designer	$.10 (same as auctions)
Bold	$1.00 (same as auctions)
Highlight	$5.00 (same as auctions)
Border	$3.00 (same as auctions)
Featured Plus	$19.95 (same as auctions)

TABLE 12-4: STORE FINAL VALUE FEES

Final Item Price	Final Value Fee
$.01 to $25.00	12% of the closing value
$25.01 to $100.00	12% on the first $25, plus 8% of the closing value balance ($.01 to $75.00)
$100.01 to $1,000.00	12% on the first $25, plus 8% on the next $75, plus 4% of the closing value balance ($.01 to $900).
$1,000 and up	12% on the first $25, plus 8% on the next $75, plus 4% on the next $900, plus another 2% on the closing value balance over $1,000

Store Final Value Fees are the same as the Final Value Fees for eBay auctions. For a more detailed description of how to calculate fees and set profitable price points, see Practice 8.

 When someone visits your eBay Store, there's no way they'll know whether it's a Basic, Featured, or Anchor Store. The design of your store is up to you — you can make it as fancy as you wish.

Save 75 percent on your Store Final Value Fees!

Yes! The honchos at eBay are really smart. By promoting your eBay Store on your Web site and linking to your eBay Store, you can save 75 percent of your Final Value Fees on the items you sell though the referral link. It's a win-win situation. You draw people to your eBay Store, where you can have a more robust layout and features and save on fees — and eBay gets more visitors coming to the site!

(continued)

In order to get the referral bonus, you must set up a special link. The link consists of your eBay Store URL, and some code. Here's my referral link with the referral code in bold-face text:

```
http://stores.ebay.com/marshacolliers
       fabulousfinds?refid=store
```

This code can also be used in promotional e-mail that you send out. The only tricky thing is that buyers have to purchase the item during the same browser session as when they enter your store.

But it's definitely worth a try! Check out the figure included here to see a part of one of my eBay invoices; it shows how the savings can stack up!

Payments & Credits

▸ **Transaction Fee Credits**

Date (PDT)	Title	Item	Fee Type	Amount (USD)
Nov 4 17:43:25	eBay Live 1st Bobblehead For Dummies Man Pin Pins NIP 7165022237 Final price: $3.50 (Store)	7165022237	Store Referral Credit	-$0.26
Nov 12 23:13:02	Museum Putty QUAKE HOLD Wax Quakehold Earthquake LARGE 120150648326 Final price: $6.75 (Store)	120150648326	Store Referral Credit	-$0.51
Nov 22 11:59:55	Organic Catnip 9" Christmas Candy Cane Cat Toy FREE Bag Relisting item: 120177608554.	120187489307	Insertion Fee	-$0.40
Nov 24 08:11:33	20" Cloud Dome PHOTO BOX LIGHT CUBE Tent Lighting Kit 120148377392 Final price: $39.95 (Store)	120148377392	Store Referral Credit	-$2.66

Setting Up Your Store

If you're up to the task of opening a store, read on to find out about the things you need to have ready *before* you open your eBay Store.

It's best to sit down during some uninterrupted quiet time to plan your store. Opening a store properly involves providing more detailed information (such as the name and description of your store) — and writing it out first really helps you to gather your thoughts. Also, think about the look and feel your store will present to your buyers. A little up-front work on color and visual appeal can help ensure that the buyer's experience portrays your personality and style, as well as your customer-conscious business sense.

Naming and describing your store

Have you thought of a good name for your store? Your store name doesn't have to match your eBay User ID, but they're more recognizable if they relate to each other. You can use your company name, your business name, or a name that describes your business.

I recommend that you use the same name for your eBay store that you plan to use in all your online businesses. By doing so, you'll begin to create an identity (or, as the pros call it, a *brand*) that customers will come to recognize and trust.

After thinking up a great name, move on to considering how to describe your store. The importance of this description is huge. When people search eBay Stores and descriptions, the keyword information you put here is referenced. Also, if the store header contains your description (as in the Classic style themes available for your store), search engines such as Google and Yahoo! will look in this description for the keywords they use to classify and list your store.

Counting characters the easy way

Because you have only 300 characters to use to describe your store, I recommend that you type out this information in advance, using Microsoft Word. Use its handy Word Count feature to count the characters in your text when you're looking to fit it into areas that allow only a limited character count. Here's how:

1. Type out your idea of the text you'd like to use.

2. Highlight the text.

3. Click Tools⇨Word Count.

   Your total count will be found in the line *Characters (with spaces)*.

As long as you're in Word, use the spell checker before copying and committing your text to the eBay Store Content page.

Deciding on color and visual elements

While you're setting up your store, eBay provides some elegant color and graphics themes. You can change the color scheme or layout later, so until you have time to go hog-wild and design a custom masterpiece, choose one of the 14 clearly organized layouts, either predesigned or with easily customizable themes. Don't select something overly bright and vibrant; you want something that's easy on the eyes and more conducive to a comfortable selling environment.

Since not everyone is an HTML color expert, eBay graciously offers quite a few pretested color combinations that you can use for your store. You also have the option of selecting your own hexadecimal colors. Huh? Yes, that's what I said. eBay shows you teeny boxes on a color chart that includes the hexadecimal numbers associated with the available colors.

If the teeny boxes on the color chart don't give you enough of a taste of the colors, you can go to my Web site `www.coolebaytools.com` and find a link in the Tools area to a very large sampling of hundreds of colors, including their hexadecimal numbers.

In addition to appealing color, the use of graphic elements can enhance the look of your eBay Store. If you use one of eBay's prefab graphics, people shopping your eBay Store will know that you aren't serious enough about your business to design a simple and basic logo.

I've had many years of experience in advertising and marketing, and I must tell you that a custom look will beat out clip art any day. Your store is special — put forth the effort to make it shine.

If you have a graphics program, design a graphic with your store's name. Start with something simple; you can always change it later when you have more time. Save the image as a GIF or a JPG, and upload it to the site where you host your images (your own Web site, your ISP, or a hosting service).

A bunch of talented graphic artists make a living selling custom Web graphics on eBay. If you aren't comfortable designing your own, search eBay for *Web banner* or *banner design*. Graphic banners on eBay sell for about $10 to $20 — certainly worth the price in the time you'll save.

Once your store is rolling, you can look for a company that specializes (and is experienced) in store design and marketing refinement — like eBay Certified Provider AsWas. You can find them at `www.aswas.com`.

Getting your store started

To open a store, go to the eBay home page and click the Stores link in the central navigation bar for eBay Stores (it's under the search box, as shown in Figure 12-2). You can also go there directly by typing the following URL:

```
http://stores.ebay.com
```

Although eBay may change the step-by-step procedure for opening a store, you'll still need to have all the information in the Setting Up Your Store Content area pages.

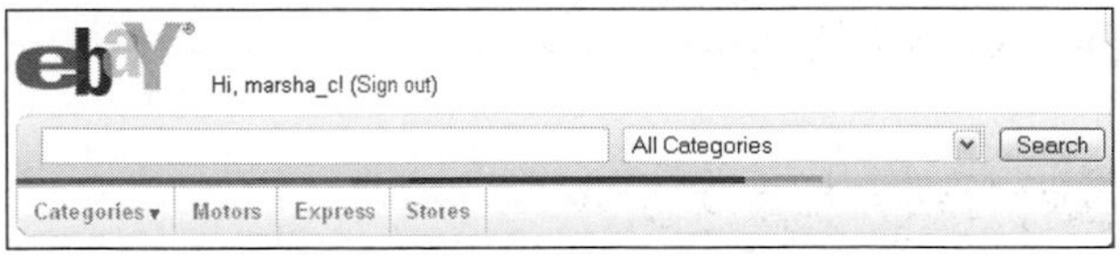

• **Figure 12-2:** Click the eBay Stores link from the eBay home page.

Now follow these steps to get your store up and going on eBay:

1. Click the Open a Store link on the right of the eBay Stores home page.

2. From the resulting page, which describes the store requirements and subscription levels, click Open a Store Now.

3. Choose a store theme.

Click the drop-down box to select a color combination by name. If you want to view the colors before selecting them (an excellent idea), click the link on this page that says `Preview Colors Below`.

Or to choose your own hexadecimal colors, click the little color box next to the text boxes here, and get a teeny color chart. If you roll your mouse pointer over the teeny boxes, you'll see the HTML hexadecimal numbers for that color.

 You have the option of selecting a store theme that doesn't require you to insert a custom logo or banner — but I highly recommend against it. You need to establish a unifying brand for your online business.

4. **Click Continue.**

5. **Type your new store's name.**

You've decided on a store name, right? Your eBay store name can't exceed thirty-five characters. Before you type it, double-check that you aren't infringing on anyone's copyrights or trademarks. You also can't use any permutation of eBay trademarks in your store's name.

6. **Type a short description of your store.**

When I say short, I mean *short*. The paragraph you're reading is 315 characters, and you have only *300* characters to give a whiz-bang, electric description of your store and merchandise. You can't use HTML coding to doll up the description, and you can't use links. Just the facts please, and a little bit of dazzle.

7. **Select a graphic to jazz up the look of your store.**

You can use one of eBay's clip-art-style banners or create a custom banner sized at 310 × 90 pixels. If you use one of eBay's graphics, you must promise (hand over heart) that you won't keep it there for long. (Refer to the earlier section, "Deciding on color and visual elements," for info on designing your own graphics — or hiring someone to do it.)

8. **Click Continue.**

Now you're getting somewhere. Now you should have an idea of what your store will look like. Now you are about to open an eBay storefront (drum roll, please).

9. **Sign up for the Basic Store ($15.95 a month), and click the Start My Subscription Now button.**

Your store is now live on the Internet with nothing up for sale — yet.

10. **Click the supplied link to get in the trenches and customize your store further.**

After your store is set up, listing a store item is the same procedure as listing an auction — save for a few differences:

- On the item listing form, you indicate that you are listing a Store Inventory item rather than an auction or a fixed-price listing.

- You also indicate the quantity of the items you have in stock that you're putting up for sale.

- Aside from indicating which eBay category you want your item to be listed in, you need to indicate up to two custom categories from your own store.

- In the shipping area, you indicate the additional shipping cost per item, should a customer want to purchase more than one.

If you're wondering in which category your store will be listed on the eBay Stores home page, it's all up to you. eBay checks the items as you list them in the standard eBay category format. For example, if you have six books listed in the Books: Fiction and Nonfiction category and five items in the Cameras & Photo category, you'll be in the listings for *both* those categories. Your custom store categories (outlined in the next section) will be used to classify items *only in your store*.

Running Your Store

As part of your store subscription, your My eBay selling area is replaced with eBay's Selling Manager. Selling Manager gives you easy access to customize your store at any time by going to the Manage My Store box, at the lower-right of your Selling Manager summary page (shown in Figure 12-3).

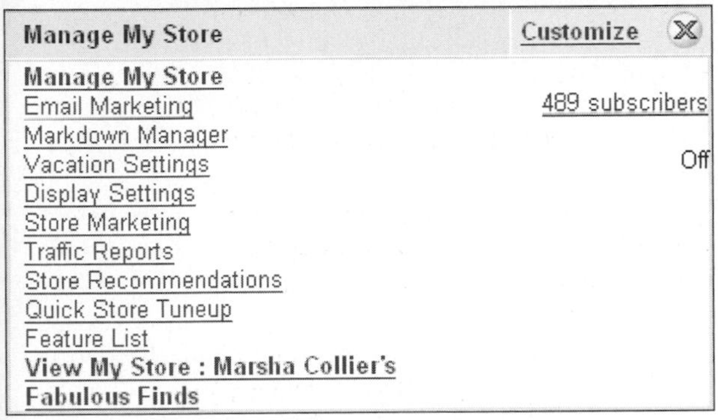

Manage My Store
Customize
Manage My Store
Email Marketing
489 subscribers
Markdown Manager
Vacation Settings
Off
Display Settings
Store Marketing
Traffic Reports
Store Recommendations
Quick Store Tuneup
Feature List
View My Store : Marsha Collier's Fabulous Finds

• **Figure 12-3: Here's where you can perform all the necessary tasks for running your store.**

Modifying to define your store and inform your customer

Here are a just few of the tasks you should consider revisiting:

- **Store design:** You can always go back here to change the name of your store or the theme of your pages. You can also change the way your items are displayed: Gallery view (as in Figure 12-4) or List view. Neither view is inherently better, but I like the Gallery view because it shows the thumbnail Gallery pictures of my items.

  You should also select the order in which your items will sort; highest-priced first, lowest-priced first, items ending first, or newly listed first. I like ending first as my sort, so buyers can get the chance to swoop in on items closing soon.

- **Custom pages:** Most successful eBay sellers have (at the very least) a store-policies page. Figure 12-5 shows you the one for my store. When you set up a policies page, eBay supplies you with a choice of layouts. Just click the Create New Page link to select the template you want to use. Don't freak out if you don't know HTML; eBay helps you out with an easy-to-use HTML generator, as in the Sell Your Item form.

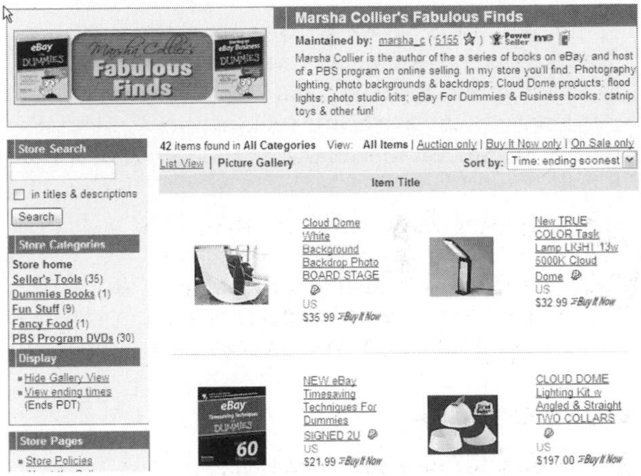

Marsha Collier's Fabulous Finds
Fabulous Finds
Store Search
Search
Store Categories
Store home
Display
Store Pages
Item Title

• **Figure 12-4: My eBay store in Gallery view.**

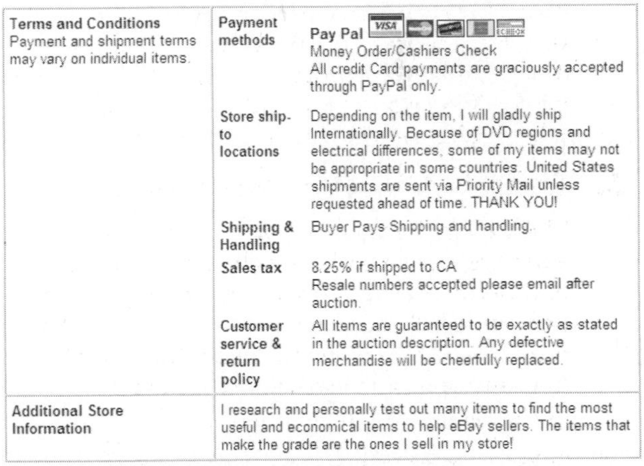

Terms and Conditions Payment and shipment terms may vary on individual items.	Payment methods	Pay Pal Money Order/Cashiers Check All credit Card payments are graciously accepted through PayPal only.
	Store ship-to locations	Depending on the item, I will gladly ship Internationally. Because of DVD regions and electrical differences, some of my items may not be appropriate in some countries. United States shipments are sent via Priority Mail unless requested ahead of time. THANK YOU!
	Shipping & Handling	Buyer Pays Shipping and handling.
	Sales tax	8.25% if shipped to CA Resale numbers accepted please email after auction.
	Customer service & return policy	All items are guaranteed to be exactly as stated in the auction description. Any defective merchandise will be cheerfully replaced.
Additional Store Information		I research and personally test out many items to find the most useful and economical items to help eBay sellers. The items that make the grade are the ones I sell in my store!

• **Figure 12-5: My eBay store-policies page.**

Following are some important policies to include:

- **Indicate to what locations you'll ship.** If you choose to sell to the entire world, you'll be smart to indicate this here.
- **Specify the sales tax you plan to collect.** If your state doesn't require you to collect sales tax, leave this area blank. If it does require sales tax, select your state and indicate the

proper sales tax. Most states won't require you to collect sales tax unless the sale is shipped to your home state. Check the links in Practice 43 to verify your state's sales-tax regulations.

▶ **State your customer service and return policy.** Fill in the information regarding how you handle refunds, exchanges, and so on. If you're a member of SquareTrade (see Practice 32) or BuySAFE, mention here that you subscribe to its policies. Be sure to include whatever additional store information you think is pertinent.

You can also set up a custom home page for your store (as noted in the next section), but it's not a popular option. Most sellers feel it's best to let your visitors go right to the listings of what you're selling.

✔ **Custom categories:** Here's where you really make your store your own. You may name up to three hundred custom categories that relate to the varied items you sell in your store.

✔ **Promotion boxes:** Set up some promotion boxes and change them every month or so to keep your store's look fresh. Select items for promotion that work well with the particular selling season.

✔ **Search-engine keywords:** Check out this area to see the keywords that eBay forwards to the major Web-shopping and search feeds. If you think there are better keywords, be sure to add them.

Designing a custom home page for your store

If you want your eBay Store to be totally customized and you're comfortable with writing HTML, you can design a custom home page for your store in this area.

If you don't want a custom home page, just check the box that says No, do not include a custom home page. Don't feel bad if you don't want to devote the time and effort into designing a custom page. What the heck, I opted not to. I would rather err on the side of caution — my HTML talent really isn't up to snuff. I'll let my items do the talking!

When you finish with these steps, press the button that says Save Changes and Publish. Your new store should be ready for action within the hour.

Technique 13

Taking Advantage of eBay Stores Marketing

Selling is all about marketing, and marketing is all about promoting. eBay provides you with some awesome tools to promote your items. Face it; if you sell more, you make more money — and so does eBay. It's to eBay's benefit to help you become a retailing mogul on the site. And eBay isn't naïve — making it easy for you to drive sales to eBay also makes it less likely that you'll spend tons of time selling from your own retail Web site. Many successful PowerSellers make hundreds of thousands of dollars a year selling merchandise exclusively on the eBay site. The tools for promoting your goods are easy to use, and not all eBay sellers know how to use them or where to find them. In this practice, I help turn you into a marketing-savvy seller by turning you on to the tools that come gratis — with your eBay Store.

To get to all the bells and whistles that eBay provides for sellers with eBay Stores, find the Manage My Store link on the Selling Manager page. Click it, and you'll see the marketing tools mentioned in this practice — and any more that eBay adds as time wears on. I explain my favorite tools found here, but feel free to explore more of them. They can only do one thing for you: increase your bottom line.

Another important link for storeowners is pages.ebay.com/storefronts/latestnews.html; clicking this link takes you to the latest news about those soon-to-be-implemented tools that eBay gurus have up their sleeves.

eBay Cross-Promotions

A very slick promotional tool is the cross-promotion. Every time prospective buyers view an item for sale on eBay, they see a vertically scrollable filmstrip featuring up to 12 other items that the seller currently offers for sale (as shown in Figure 13-1).

• **Figure 13-1: eBay cross-promotion in one of my auctions.**

A different filmstrip-with-items appears after the bidder bids on an item or makes a purchase. A smart PowerSeller with an eBay Store will have preselected the items you see when viewing or bidding on an item. So, for all you clever PowerSellers, simply click the Cross Promotion Link under Item Promotions, and you'll end up on the page where you can specify the items your shoppers will see in the cross-promotion filmstrip.

Smart cross-promoting

Cross-promoting can work to the *nth* degree for you if you think about what buyers want. If you're selling a man's size Large shirt and you have ties or similar shirts in the same size, why not list those items in the cross-promotions area? Promoting a jackhammer along with the shirt, on the other hand, may be a bit more of a stretch. And you might be slipping even farther from reality if you chose to promote an eye-makeup kit along with the man's shirt (provided you aren't marketing to glam-rockers). Get it? Promote items that relate to each other, and catch the prospective buyer's eye.

You can also change your promotions if you have a hot item that appeals to everyone. You can switch that item into one of the boxes by visiting the cross-promotions area.

Setting up cross-promotions

To match up items for cross-promotion, find the Manage My Store links on the Selling Manager page. Or if you subscribe to Selling Manager Pro, find the link on the left side of the page and click Marketing Tools. On the resulting page, click the Cross Promotion link, and you'll come to the Main Controls page (as shown in Figure 13-2).

Hello, marsha c (5384 ★) 📷

Cross-Promotion: Summary	
Cross-Promotion	
Defaults	18
Settings	

• **Figure 13-2: Command central for your eBay cross-promotions.**

Click Manage so you can see your defaults — if you haven't set these up, eBay will have assigned them randomly (not such a good thing). Figure 13-3 shows the resulting defaults page from my eBay listings.

Cross-Promotion: Defaults

By default, these rules determine which of your items are selected for cross-promotions.
Note: If an item matches more than one rule, only the rule appearing highest in the list will determine the cross-promotion rules.

When someone views an item	When someone bids on or wins an item

Create new rule

When someone views an item:	Promote items:
Store category: **Dummies Books**	Store category: **Seller's Tools**
Store category: **Fancy Food**	Store category: **Fun Stuff**
Store category: **Girly Things**	Store category: **Fun Stuff**
Store category: **Other**	Store category: **Other**
Store category: **Seller's Tools**	Store category: **Seller's Tools**

• **Figure 13-3: My default cross-promotion category referrals.**

By clicking the Edit button next to each category on this page, you can select which of your individual complementary store category items you'd like to appear when someone views, bids on, or buys from one of your listings.

The changes take effect almost immediately, so this is an important marketing tool that helps you present the right items and trigger additional purchases from the people who view your listings.

Using a Markdown Manager

Everybody loves a sale. I love a sale! When I'm doing a little window shopping on eBay, the items that have the small *sale* icon (or the *"Percent Off"* icon) always grab me just a little harder. You know how crummy you feel when you think you've found a deal and then get to the item listing, only to see the dreaded Reserve Not Met sign? Well, seeing the sale icons works the opposite way — it puts the buyer in a happy mood and ready to buy. The sale sign I saw one day while browsing on eBay even prompted me into buying a new sofa for my family room — what was I thinking? I was thinking I'd get a pretty good deal — and I did!

From the PowerSeller's point of view, there are many reasons to hold a sale:

- ✔ To raise cash to buy new merchandise.

- ✔ To get rid of items that have cluttered up your store way too long. (Your clue should be that when you start dusting some of your items, it's time to move them out!)

- ✔ To change the type of merchandise you're dealing into a different type or a competing line.

- ✔ To stimulate sales by giving customers a reason to buy from YOU.

If you have any of the above reasons, go to those Marketing Tools and click Markdown Manager. You'll come to the page, as in Figure 13-4, where you find a Create Sale button.

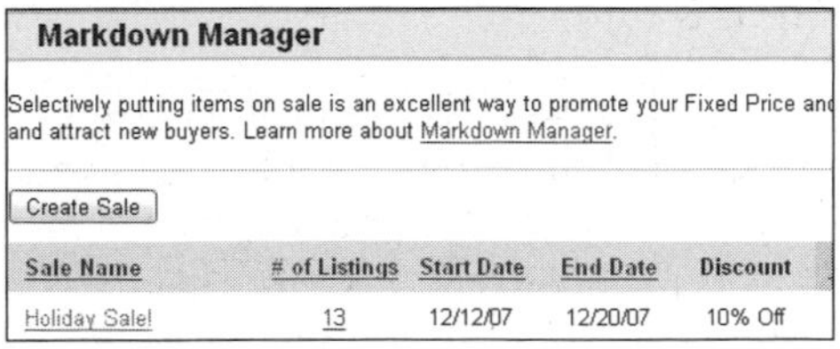

• **Figure 13-4: Click Create Sale to, er, create a sale.**

Clicking the Create Sale button brings you to the Markdown Manager: Create Your Sale page (Figure 13-5).

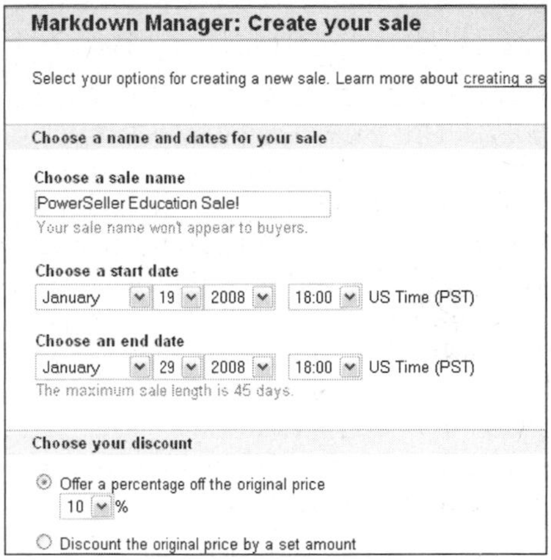

• **Figure 13-5: Okay, NOW create the sale.**

On this page, you will be asked to

- ✔ **Give your sale a name**. The name shows up only in an e-mail splash that eBay prompts you to send out at the end of the form. The name of the sale does not appear on item pages.

- ✔ **Select the time frame for your sale**. You can run a sale up to 45 days.

- ✔ **Name your discount**. You can choose to

  - ▶ Offer a percentage discount off the original price by selecting the percentage from the supplied drop-down menu.

  - ▶ Discount the original price by a set amount. For this option, you can type in an exact dollar amount that will apply to all listings selected for your sale.

- ✔ **Choose your listings**. You have to figure out what you want to put on sale. So you can

  - ▶ Add all listings from a particular store category. You select your store category from a drop-down menu pre-populated with your personal store categories.

▶ Add all active Store Inventory listings.

▶ Add all Fixed Price listings.

▶ Select Items Individually. I like this option because it allows you to pick and choose what you want to offer a deal on. When you select Individual item, you're brought to a page that has all your items. Just click the check box next to the item. When you're through, click Save.

✔ **Promote your sale.** Your next decision is whether you want to promote your sale to those who have selected you as a favorite seller and are interested in receiving e-mails from you. Why not do this? It always results in at least a couple of sales for me. You should note that, as required by federal law, eBay will include your physical mailing address in the footer of the e-mails.

You're done! Just click the Create Your Sale button at the end of the page and instantly you see a form (see Figure 13-6) that shows your sale as scheduled.

• **Figure 13-6:** My sale is scheduled to run.

If you've chosen to promote your sale, at the moment your sale starts, eBay sends out an e-mail like the one shown in Figure 13-7, which comes from the PowerSeller Education sale I created (refer to Figure 13-6).

Figure 13-7: That big Sale sign on the promotional e-mail makes the prospective buyer sit up and take notice.

E-Mail Marketing

When you become someone's Favorite Seller and you're added to their Favorites page, people can also opt to receive your newsletter and sale list. These people are your customers, and eBay encourages you to reach out to them through e-mail marketing.

 According to eBay's Terms of Service, you are not allowed to e-mail buyers after your transaction with them is completed. Heed, heed. If you ignore that rule, don't be surprised if they report you to eBay security. Then eBay will (at the very least) send you a nasty e-mail. After enough violations, you can be removed from selling on the site.

Depending on your store tier (Basic, Premium, or Anchor), you are allowed to send a finite number of e-mails per month for free. Table 13-1 shows the limits — and the costs that you incur for sending additional e-mails.

TABLE 13-1: E-MAIL MARKETING BY STORE TIER

Store Level	Monthly Free E-mails	Cost per E-mail Sent Over Allocation
Basic Store	5000 e-mails	$0.01 per e-mail
Premium Store	7500 e-mails	$0.01 per e-mail
Anchor Store	10000 e-mails	$0.01 per e-mail

To create an e-mail for your store newsletter campaign:

1. **Go to your My eBay page.**

2. **Click the Marketing Tools link in the left navigation pane.**

3. **On the resulting page, click the Email Marketing link in the left navigation pane.**

    The Email Marketing page appears.

Click the Create Email button, and you'll be transported to a page — pictured in Figure 13-8 — that helps you to do just that.

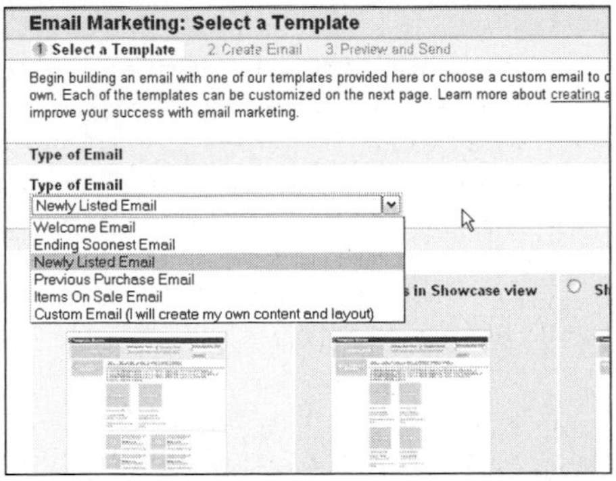

Email Marketing: Select a Template

1. Select a Template 2. Create Email 3. Preview and Send

Begin building an email with one of our templates provided here or choose a custom email to c own. Each of the templates can be customized on the next page. Learn more about creating a improve your success with email marketing.

Type of Email

Type of Email

Newly Listed Email

Welcome Email
Ending Soonest Email
Newly Listed Email
Previous Purchase Email
Items On Sale Email
Custom Email (I will create my own content and layout)

in Showcase view

• **Figure 13-8: Simple steps to professional marketing e-mails.**

It's a simple, step-by-step process, as follows:

1. **Select your type of e-mail from a drop-down menu.**

Your choices are

▶ **Welcome Email:** To welcome new users to your list.

▶ **Ending Soonest Email:** An e-mail featuring your items that are Ending Soon.

▶ **Newly Listed Email:** Features items you've newly listed.

▶ **Previous Purchase Email:** An e-mail to those who have shopped with you before.

▶ **Items on Sale Email:** This puzzles me. You have the option to send this e-mail when you're creating your sale — so why would you do it here?

▶ **Custom Email:** I like this one, because I like to send out newsletter-type e-mails.

> Don't get carried away sending out constant e-mails. You'll find people opting to get off (rather than on) your list if you're constantly hammering on them to buy something. So if you can send out newsletter-type, useful e-mails about the products you sell, people will be more inclined to open and read them.

2. **Choose one of the template layouts from the five solid options that eBay gives you.**

    You can also do a custom one, but if you're not proficient in HTML, no need to strain your brain: The standard templates are excellent and will do the job.

3. **Click Continue.**

    You arrive at a page where you're hand-held through the process of deciding what to include in your e-mail.

Composing your perfect e-mail is a simple process — and you can take as long as you want. Give it a try once, just to test the waters, and you'll see how effective this e-mail marketing can be to boost your sales.

Vacation Settings

I use Vacation Settings whenever I plan to be away from my office for more that a couple of days. This way, you can alert buyers that shipping may be delayed — or (alternatively) you can remove all your store listings from the site for the time span you indicate that you'll be away.

Click the Vacation Settings link and turn your settings on or off. Figure 13-9 gives you a quick look at the page. It even allows you to insert text that announces your time away on your store's home page.

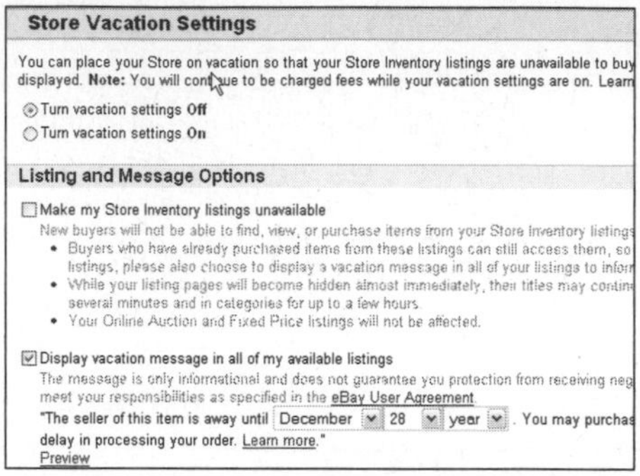

Store Vacation Settings

You can place your Store on vacation so that your Store Inventory listings are unavailable to buy displayed. **Note:** You will continue to be charged fees while your vacation settings are on. Learn

◉ Turn vacation settings Off
○ Turn vacation settings On

Listing and Message Options

☐ Make my Store Inventory listings unavailable
New buyers will not be able to find, view, or purchase items from your Store Inventory listings
   • Buyers who have already purchased items from these listings can still access them, so listings, please also choose to display a vacation message in all of your listings to inform
   • While your listing pages will become hidden almost immediately, their titles may contin several minutes and in categories for up to a few hours.
   • Your Online Auction and Fixed Price listings will not be affected.

☑ Display vacation message in all of my available listings
The message is only informational and does not guarantee you protection from receiving neg meet your responsibilities as specified in the eBay User Agreement
"The seller of this item is away until [December ▾] [28 ▾] [year ▾]. You may purchas delay in processing your order. Learn more."
Preview

• **Figure 13-9: My oft-used Vacation Settings page.**

Practice 14

Becoming an eBay Trading Assistant

What is an eBay Trading Assistant? Simply, eBay Trading Assistants sell merchandise for people who have stuff to sell but no motivation to learn about eBay. They also charge a commission. They also can make some serious cash. An official-sounding definition is that a Trading Assistant sells items on consignment for those who are not familiar with the eBay site or are simply too lazy to learn the ropes. Several companies have sold franchises for this type of business. A few national franchisers (for example, iSold It) have opened up across the country with retail locations accepting consignment merchandise from the general public to sell on eBay. By becoming an official Trading Assistant, you don't have to buy a franchise and can compete on your own with the big boys in your own area.

The best part is that if you are already running your eBay business out of your home, from a garage, or from a low-rent industrial office, you're a step ahead of the big guys who have to pay high rents in fancy neighborhoods to get their "drop in" business. These chains also have to hire people who are familiar with setting up auctions on eBay — aren't you already set up for that?

eBay helps individual Trading Assistants with many business practices. Most important, you're listed in a searchable directory with other eBay selling professionals for all the world to find at www.eBay.com/tahub.

Becoming a Trading Assistant

The first thing to take into consideration before becoming a Trading Assistant is to be sure you're familiar with the eBay site, know the rules and regulations and — most of all — are experienced in selling items at a profit. To be a successful Trading Assistant, you need to be savvy about how to research items on eBay and also know how to parlay keywords into winning auction titles. You also have to act pretty quick-on-your-feet to become an instant expert on many different types of merchandise. (Your expertise, of course, will come from researching the items on eBay.) The Trading Assistant directory appears on the eBay site at www.eBay.com/tahub, as shown in Figure 14-1. From the directory page, potential customers can click a link to search for a Trading Assistant to sell their items by ZIP code, telephone area code, or by country. I just ran a search and at this moment there seem to be no Trading Assistants in Jamaica or the Bahamas (either of which might be a nice place to do business from)!

• **Figure 14-1: The Trading Assistants main page.**

This page is promoted on the eBay site to new users and in eBay Promotions. Being listed in the directory (see Figure 14-2) search will help your customers find you.

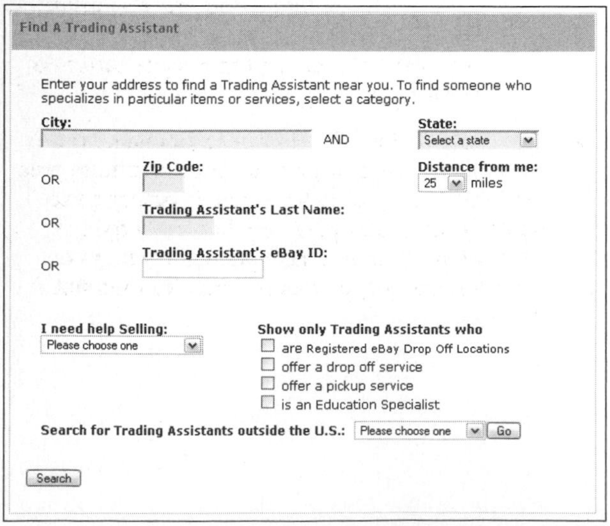

• **Figure 14-2: The Trading Assistants search area.**

Meeting the requirements

eBay makes it very clear that whether you fulfill the requirements for Trading Assistant or not, being a Trading Assistant is a privilege. If eBay receives complaints about your services, they have the right to remove you from the Trading Assistant directory. eBay's basic requirements are

- ✓ **Listings:** You must have sold at least ten items per month within the previous three months.

- ✓ **Feedback rating:** You must have a minimum rating of 100 or higher, while maintaining a minimum of 98 percent positive comments.

If you have a retail location, you can opt to become a Registered Drop Off Location (REDOL). Drop Off Locations receive priority listings in the directory and have a special icon next to their ID. If you want to open a Drop Off Location, your basic requirements are

- ✓ **Storefront:** You must offer a staffed drop-off location with regular hours.

- ✓ **Sales:** Have eBay sales of at least 10 items in the prior 3 months.

- ✓ **Feedback rating:** You must have a minimum rating of 100 or higher, while maintaining a minimum of 98 percent positive comments.

- ✓ **Insurance:** You must maintain all insurance coverage required by state or federal law. In addition, you must procure comprehensive general liability insurance covering your retail location(s) and activities on an occurrence basis with a combined single limit for bodily injury, death, or property damage of not less than $1,000,000. You must also carry a $25,000 bond to protect your sellers' checks.

The requirements for REDOLs are considerably more complex than for the basic Trading Assistant program. Please visit `http://ebaytrading assistant.com/index.php?page=userAgreement s&type=redol` to read the current User Agreement.

. . . and the responsibilities

As a Trading Assistant, you will acquire merchandise and sell it on eBay on consignment. You will also be responsible for

- ✔ **Consulting with consignors about their items.**

- ✔ **Researching the value of the item.** Many non-eBay users may have unreasonable expectations of the price their items will sell for. It's your duty to check this out beforehand and explain the realities to them.

- ✔ **Coordinating the listing.** Take digital photos and write a complete and accurate description of the item.

- ✔ **Keeping a close accounting of fees and money collection.**

That doesn't sound like much in the way of responsibilities, but you need to get some things together before you sign up.

 Becoming a Trading Assistant does not make you an employee, agent, or independent contractor of eBay. You should be careful to refer to yourself as an independent business.

Putting your best face forward

When you sign up as a Trading Assistant, you have to fill out a form describing your business to prospective customers. Think through the things you have to say before posting them. The information on this form works like an ad for you. Here are the things you have to put on your Trading Assistant listing page:

- ✔ **Personal Information:** This includes your eBay User ID, your real name, address, and languages spoken.

- ✔ **Category Specialty:** If you specialize in a particular category, be sure to mention it. You may indicate up to three eBay home page categories.

- ✔ **Service Description:** In this area, you can say as little or as much as you like about your eBay experience and the services you provide. Remember that the more you communicate in advance, the more successful you'll be.

  Here is a sample Service Description:

  I've been active on the site since 1996 and am an eBay PowerSeller. I specialize in selling all types of eBay items and am particularly familiar with the fashion category. I can handle large numbers of listings. Please contact me so we can discuss your particular needs and time availability.

  I can visit your home within 15 miles from my place of business to inventory the items. I will list, ship, and provide you with an itemized list of all items sold, with the sale price and my fees.

- ✔ **Policy Description:** Ensure that the consignees understand your policies. A sample description looks like this:

  I will list your items for two listing cycles, spread up to 30 days. If items do not sell, they will be returned to you. Items must be in my possession to be submitted to eBay unless prior contractual arrangements are made in advance. I handle all correspondence and shipping. A consignment contract is required. I also do independent consulting specializing in Internet auctions and their application to your business.

- ✔ **Fee Description:** This is where you need to do some research. Search your own telephone area code on the Trading Assistant directory page and see what other fees are being charged in your area. After you have an idea of what you want to charge, you can put that information here.

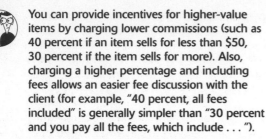

You can provide incentives for higher-value items by charging lower commissions (such as 40 percent if an item sells for less than $50, 30 percent if the item sells for more). Also, charging a higher percentage and including fees allows an easier fee discussion with the client (for example, "40 percent, all fees included" is generally simpler than "30 percent and you pay all the fees, which include . . . ").

Many Trading Assistants also use transaction fees for listing with a reserve price (knowing, for example, that the item probably won't sell because the consignor doesn't have a fair guess at market valuation).

When you've decided everything you need to list, click the link on the Trading Assistant homepage that says `Become a Trading Assistant`. Fill out the forms, and just like magic, you've become a Trading Assistant!

You may not use the term "Auction" or "Auctioneer" in your Trading Assistant business name, signage, and marketing materials unless you are a licensed auctioneer.

Promoting Your Business

When I was working in the newspaper advertising business, we had a saying about someone who opened a new store: If all the advertising they do is their Grand Opening ad and nothing after, it won't be long before you'll see the Going-Out-of-Business Sale ad.

The same is true with your Trading Assistant business. Although you may not go out of business if you don't promote it, you'll probably have no business at all if you don't keep it visible.

Adding the Trading Assistant logo to your eBay listings

Your best customers may come from among all those people who see your existing items while they're browsing eBay. Why not show all viewers that you're a Trading Assistant? Put the Trading Assistant logo into your listings, as shown in Figure 14-3. Then, when prospective customers click the link, they're sent to your Trading Assistant Information page (just as if they searched you out in the directory).

• **Figure 14-3:** The eBay Trading Assistant logo.

Insert the Trading Assistant logo when your regular eBay business is slow, and take it out when you're overly busy. That way you can control the amount of work you have coming in.

To add the link to your listings, you have to use a little HTML. Don't panic, though — I supply the code for you right here. To get the code for your personal Trading Assistant link, follow these steps:

1. Find out your Trading Assistant number.

Go to your listing in the directory. Take a look at the top of your Internet browser, and you see your Trading Assistant number (this is also your eBay account number) at the end of that Web page's URL. The Web address looks like this:

```
http://contact.ebay.com/aw-cgi/
    eBayISAPI.dll?ShowMemberToMember
    Details&member=000000
```

In this example, your number would be 000000.

2. Add code to your listing description.

Add the following HTML code at the end of your listing description (be sure to replace 000000 with your own eBay number):

```
< <p align="center"><img src=
"http://pics.ebaystatic.com/aw/
pics/logos/logoUS_R_TA_RGB_
141x106.jpg" alt="I am a Trading
Assistant on eBay" width="141"
height="106" border="0"
longdesc="TA Logo" /></a></p>

<p align="center" class="style3"><a
href="http://ebaytrading
assistant.com/directory/index.
php?page=profile&ebayID=000000"
target="_blank">I am a Trading
Assistant - I can sell your
stuff on eBay!</a></p>
```

After you insert this code in your listings, a link and button appear in your eBay sales (refer to Figure 14-3 to see what they look like).

"American households have approximately $2,200 worth of unused items"

In 2004, eBay worked with the famous AC Neilsen Company to do a survey of just what people had lying around the house — unused! The quote above gives you the answer. If households had that much in 2004, can you imagine the value of the junk in everyone's home now? The figure below shows what the survey found in the various categories.

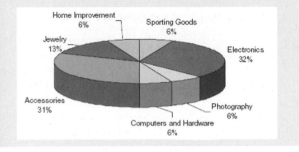

Posting flyers

eBay has designed a nifty flyer that you can customize and print out on your own printer. Put it up at the supermarket, the car wash, the cleaner — anywhere and everywhere flyers are allowed.

Even if you don't see flyers in a retail location, ask the owner of the business if you can put one up — maybe even offer a discount to the business owner for selling their items on eBay in exchange!

eBay has collateral material available to all Trading Assistants. The material is in Adobe Acrobat format so you can easily customize them with your own business information. The flyer/poster, shown in Figure 14-4, is a pretty slick marketing piece that you can distribute in your service area.

• **Figure 14-4: The Trading Assistants flyer.**

Putting the logo on your Web site

You can promote your business on your Web site and on your eBay About Me page. You can find a special promo logo in the Trading Assistant's hub, as shown in Figure 14-5. Just save it to your computer in JPG format and make it a part of your pages, providing you follow all the rules outlined in the Trading Assistant Style guide.

• **Figure 14-5: The Trading Assistant logo is a .JPG graphic.**

Compete with the Big Guys

Don't worry about the competition! You may hear about the many brick-and-mortar eBay consignment stores that are opening up. As a matter of fact, a company sells franchises for this business — for up to $15,000! But consider: You already know how to sell on eBay, so why would you need a franchise? Use your good sense (and positive feedback) to build your own eBay consignment store.

Following are some of the chains that sell goods on eBay for consumers:

✔ AuctionDrop, www.auctiondrop.com

✔ iSold It, www.i-soldit.com

✔ Instant Auctions, www.InstantAuctions.net

These retail locations have a much higher cost of doing business than you have if you just work from your home. They need to be open for set hours during the day, and have several employees on duty at all times. Many of these stores won't accept an item worth less than $75 — and there's still a lot of profit left for you in the under-$75 item.

Table 14-1 shows an average range for fees charged by consignment chain stores, as of this writing (although as with cars — your mileage may vary).

TABLE 14-1: AVERAGE CONSIGNMENT CHAIN FEES

Sold Price	Fee Percentage
up to $200	35–38%
$201 to $500	30–35%
over $500	20%

In addition to these fees in the table, these chain stores (of course) also charge for all eBay and PayPal fees. There's also a charge of $5.00 minimum commission per item. Check out these sites regularly so you can keep up with the competition in your own area.

What do you charge for all your work? I can't give you a stock answer for that one. Many sellers charge a flat fee for photographing, listing, and shipping; that fee ranges from $5–$10, plus as much as a 30-percent commission on the final auction total (to absorb the eBay fees). Other sellers base their fees solely on the final sale amount, and charge on a sliding scale — beginning at 50 percent of the total sale, less eBay and payment service fees. You must decide how much you think you can make on an item.

Table 14-2 will give you some ideas based on the input I've received from some successful eBay consignment sellers. (These percentages may be in addition to the listing fee and gallery charges.)

TABLE 14-2: SAMPLE PROGRESSIVE COMMISSION SCHEDULE

Final Value	Your Commission
Under $50	40%
$50.01 to $150.00	35% of the amount over $50
$150.01 to $250.00	30% of the amount over $150
$251.00 to $500.00	25% of the amount over $500
$501.00 to $1000.00	20% of the amount over $500
Over $1000	15%

Remember that you can always choose to charge a flat commission if that works best in your area. Check out the eBay Trading Assistants in your area to see what they charge.

If you're really interested in starting a retail location, there's a new company, started by some old eBay pros. They've decided to help eBay sellers to start their own Trading Post drop-off stores — but this is different from the others: There are no franchise fees to get set up; you just pay them a royalty on what you sell. Check out their plan at

www.esavz.com

Handling Your Business Professionally

Handling merchandise that's not yours takes a healthy sense of responsibility, and how you conduct your business can demonstrate to your customers that you're a responsible person. You need to present a professional appearance when you meet your clients, and you should have a professional attitude in your dealings.

Being professional also means anticipating possible problems. In addition to being very clear about financial issues with your clients (especially fees and the *realistic* selling value of your clients' merchandise), you may want to consider getting additional insurance to cover merchandise you're holding in your home.

You may also want to consider designing a few forms to reinforce your clients' understanding that this is your business and that you know it well. For example, forms like these are pretty standard:

- **Inventory form:** This form lists the entire inventory you receive from the client and should include as detailed a description of the item as your client can supply. Also, include the minimum amount (if any) the client will accept for the item — this will be your reserve price if necessary.

- **Sales agreement:** Professional Trading Assistants have their clients sign a sales contract. Read on for some good suggestions about what to put in your contract. You may want to have a lawyer look at your contract before you use it.

The following information was graciously supplied by one of eBay's successful Trading Assistants. It includes passages from a Trading Assistant contract, which cover many things that you might overlook when you put together your own contract. This, of course, is not a full agreement, but it provides some of the salient points.

Be sure to include an explanation of the consignment process:

- The Consignor will bring item(s) to the Seller, who, upon both parties signing this contract, will take possession of the items for the duration of the auction.

- Acceptance of any item consigned will be at the Seller's sole discretion.

- The Seller will inspect the item(s) for quality, and clean if necessary (a fee may apply).

- The Seller will take quality photographs and write an accurate description of the item(s).

- The Seller will research eBay for similar items to ensure proper pricing.

- The Seller will start the auction(s) and handle all aspects of the sale, including correspondence with bidders.

✔ The Seller will collect payment from the winning bidder ("Buyer") at the end of the auction, and will ship the item(s) in a timely manner, once the funds have cleared.

✔ The Seller will follow up the sale by contacting the Buyer to make sure the Buyer is satisfied with the transaction.

✔ Once the Seller and Buyer are satisfied with the transaction, payment will be made to the Consignor.

✔ The Seller will keep the Consignor aware of the auction progress by telephone or e-mail, and by supplying the Consignor the auction number(s) to track the item(s).

✔ The Seller will return unsold item(s) to the Consignor upon payment of outstanding fees.

It's also a good idea to provide the consignor with a statement of items sold, summarizing the total purchase price, all fees, and the amount the consignor receives.

✔ **Outline your fees:** "The Consignor will be billed the actual rates and fees as incurred for all services, to include the Seller's *00%* Commission. Any services or upgrades requested by the Consignor will carry the exact fee and will be deducted from payment, or after three (3) failed auction listings, will be due to the Seller payable in cash. If the auction sells, these fees will be subtracted from the winning bid before the Consignor receives payment."

Be sure to include a copy of current eBay fees: listing, options, reserves, PayPal fee, and Final Value Fees.

✔ **Outline the terms of your commission:** "The Seller's commission for this service is a percentage based on the auction's winning bid. If the auction does not sell, the Consignor is only responsible to pay the applicable insertion and reserve-price auction fees. An Unsold Reserve fee of *$0.00* will be due to the Seller for a reserve-price auction that does not sell."

✔ **Be sure you don't guarantee the item will sell.** "If an item does not sell, the Seller will re-list it two additional times. The Seller may contact the Consignor to discuss combining individual items into lots to attract buyers. The Consignor's verbal consent, or e-mail consent, will be documented in the Consignor's file and will serve as a revision to this contract. After a third unsuccessful listing, the Consignor will be billed for the fees associated with all three auctions, plus a $5.00 surcharge. Items will be returned to Consignor upon payment of those fees. Items not claimed within 14 days from the end of the final listing will become the property of the Seller."

✔ **Protect yourself and your eBay reputation:** "The Consignor of said item(s) consents to the sale of said item(s) based on the terms described in this agreement. The Consignor also attests that said item(s) are fully owned by the Consignor and are not stolen, borrowed, misrepresented, bogus, etc."

You might also mention that you will only sell the item if eBay policies allow the item to be sold:

"The Seller will do everything possible to secure the safety of the Consignor's item(s), however, the Seller is not responsible for any damage to the item, including fire, theft, flood, accidental damage or breakage, and acts of God. The Consignor releases the Seller of any such responsibility for any unforeseen or accidental damage."

You may want to protect yourself additionally, because reputation on eBay is paramount. You can place a small business rider on your homeowner's insurance that covers merchandise in your home valued at up to (say) $5,000. It's an inexpensive addition to your policy — *definitely* worth looking into.

✔ **Ending a sale prematurely:** "If such an instance arises that the Consignor demands the item(s) to be pulled, the Consignor will pay a cancellation fee of $75. Items will not be surrendered to Consignor until this fee is paid in cash."

✔ **Protect yourself from possible shill bidding:** An important line you should add protects you from possible shill bidding. How about something like this:

"The Consignor also agrees not to place a bid on an auction that the Seller has listed for the Consignor (hereafter "Shill Bid") on eBay, nor to arrange for a Shill Bid to be made on the behalf of the Consignor by a third party. If the Consignor or an agent of the Consignor submits a Shill Bid on an auction listed by the Seller, the Consignor agrees to pay all fees, commissions, and penalties associated with that auction, plus a $75.00 fine, and the Seller may refuse to grant auction services to the Consignor in the future."

 Again, because we're talking about a legally binding document here, I *strongly* suggest that you get professional advice before putting together your own contract or agreement.

Practice 15

Your Web Site: Expanding Beyond eBay

In This Practice

- ✔ Starting with a no-cost or low-cost Web site

- ✔ Expanding into a more professional site

- ✔ Establishing your own online domain

Once you've got the hang of selling on eBay and are successfully running an eBay store, you can start to look into producing an additional revenue stream on other Web sites. With the experience you gain selling on eBay, you can start your own little (hopefully not "little" for long) Web site. Items you sell from your own Web site will not have the eBay fees incurred, so even if you're paying a reasonable monthly fee for the site, profits will land in your pocket.

Your eBay store is important to your business, but it doesn't replace a wider-ranging e-commerce Web site. You should establish your own presence on the Web. And although you should link to your site from your My eBay page, don't miss out on the rest of the Internet dollars out there.

Consider these results: According to a study by the Graphics, Visualization, and Usability Center, nearly three-quarters of all U.S. households have Internet access, and more than 85 percent of users say they find new businesses through Internet search engines. Statistics don't lie (well, okay, they can be misleading, but not in this case): You need to be on the Web.

It seems that everyone these days has a blog or a My Space or Facebook page. The Web has so many sites with pictures of people's dogs and kids that I assume you have some sort of Web presence off eBay.

You can start small and start for free. Yes, the space for a Web site comes *free* from your ISP (I even have one with embarrassing family pictures). A site like this can become the practice site for your business. Take down pictures of the baby and install the eBay widgets instead. (Check out the Cheat Sheet in the front of the book for more info.)

 Web sites that succeed are about content, not just about what you can buy from them. This means you're going to have to do a little bit of work to add articles (available from feed services at low or no cost) to engage your visitors with your site.

Setting Up a Web Presence at No Cost

Although I love the word *free*, in real life it seems nothing is *really* free. In practical terms, *free* generally means something won't cost you too *much* money — but may cost you a bit more in time. When your site is free, you can't have your own direct URL (Universal Resource Locator) or domain name. Most likely, a free Web site has an address such as one of the following:

```
home.earthlink.net/membername
home.socal.rr.com/membername
members.aol.com/membername
```

Having some kind of independent site — even as a subset of your ISP's domain — at least gives you experience in site setup. (Facebook and My Space don't count here.) When you're ready to jump in for real with your own direct URL and domain name, you can always use your free site as an extension of your main business site.

Discovering free space online

When you signed up for Internet access, you had to sign on with an Internet service provider (ISP), which means you probably have your own Web space. Take a look at Table 15-1, where I compare some popular ISPs and online portals.

TABLE 15-1: ISPs AND PORTALS THAT GIVE YOU FREE WEB SPACE

ISP	Number of E-Mail Addresses	Total Space per Account
America Online (AOL)*	7	2 MB per e-mail address (14 MB)
Earthlink	8	10 MB
AT&T World Net	6	25 MB per e-mail address (150 MB)
Road Runner	5	5 MB, with $.99 per extra MB per month
MSN*	1	3 MB
Yahoo! GeoCities*	1	15 MB

*Yahoo! GeoCities, AOL, and MSN aren't ISPs, but each is a reliable online community that gives each member online Web space. Membership is free. Extra megabyte space is available for purchase.

Most ISPs allow you to have more than one e-mail address per account. Each e-mail address is entitled to a certain amount of free Web space. Through the use of *hyperlinks* (small pieces of HTML code that, when clicked, route the clicker from one place to another on the page or on another Web site), you can combine all the free Web space from each e-mail address into one giant Web site.

If America Online (AOL) is your e-mail service, you may already know that AOL often has issues regarding its users getting e-mail from the rest of the Internet. You can't afford to run a business in an area that has e-mail issues. Your AOL account gives each of your seven screen names 2 MB of online storage space. You can best utilize this space by using it to store images for eBay, not to run a business site. Each screen name, at 2 MB, can store fifty 40K images.

Many ISPs have their own page-builder (HTML-generating) program that's free to their users.

Creating a free personal home page

Poke around your ISP's home page for a Community or Your Web Space link. For example, after poking around the Road Runner ISP's home page (www.rr.com), I found and clicked the Member Services link, which led me to a page offering various options. I finally found a Personal Home Page link, which took me to a page that could walk me through setting up my own home page. After agreeing to the terms of service, I simply logged on and then set up my home page. If you're having trouble locating the proper place to access your pages, Table 15-2 gives you some links.

TABLE 15-2: LINKS TO FREE WEB PAGES

ISP	URL
AT&T	home.att.net/announce/
Earthlink	www.earthlink.net/ membercenter/benefits/ Webspace/?e15=PSP_Start: Page_1_FreeWebspace
Road Runner	home-admin.rr.com
AOL	hometown.aol.com
Yahoo! Geo Cities	geocities.yahoo.com
MSN	groups.msn.com

Save 75% of eBay Final Value Fees

Even if you're not ready to set up a full-on store, you can link to your eBay auctions. If a customer goes to eBay and buys one of your eBay store items from a link on your site, eBay will credit you 75 percent of the Final Value Fees in the transaction. To get all the details on how to qualify, go to

pages.ebay.com/help/specialtysites/
referral-credit-steps.html

Finding Web Space at a Reasonable Cost

If you've been using the Internet for any length of time, you've been bombarded by hosting offers through your daily spam. A *Web-hosting company* houses your Web site code and doles out your pages and images electronically to your Web page's visitors.

 If you take advantage of PayPal's free Pay Now (or Buy It Now) buttons or Shopping Cart, you can turn a basic-level hosted site into a full-on e-commerce store without paying additional fees to your hosting company. The PayPal tools are easily inserted into your pages with a snippet of code provided by PayPal — and they don't require any extras from the hosting company. See Practice 38 for more information on incorporating PayPal tools into your Web site.

Before deciding to spend good money on a Web-hosting company, check it out thoroughly. Go to that company's site to find a list of features offered. If you still have questions after perusing the Web site, look for a toll-free number to call. You won't find any feedback ratings of the sort you find on eBay, but the following are a few questions to ask (and don't hang up until you're satisfied with the answers):

✔ **How long has the company been in business?** You don't want a Web host that has been in business only a few months and operates out of the owner's basement. Deal with a company that's been around the Internet for a while and knows what it's doing. Is the company's Web site professional-looking? Does the company look like it has enough money to stay in business?

✔ **Who are some of the company's other clients?** Poke around to see whether you can find links to sites of other clients. Take a look at who else is doing business with the hosting service and analyze the sites. Do the pages and links come up quickly? Do all the images appear in a timely manner? Web sites that load quickly are a good sign.

✔ **What is the downtime-to-uptime ratio?** Does the Web host guarantee *uptime* (the span of time its servers stay operational without going down and denying access to your site)? Expecting a 99-percent-uptime guarantee is not unreasonable; you're open for business — your Web host needs to keep it that way.

✔ **Does the hosting service offer intuitive tools to build your site?** There's nothing worse than signing up with a hosting company, getting the e-mail that says you're set up, and suddenly wondering, *What do I do now?* Low price may mean few features. Look for templates or, ideally, some sort of site-builder application on the site.

✔ **Does the company offer toll-free technical support?** When something goes wrong with your Web site, you need it corrected immediately. You must be able to reach tech support quickly without hanging around on the phone for hours. Does the Web host have a technical-support area on its Web site where you can troubleshoot your own problems (in the middle of the night)?

 Whenever you're deciding on any kind of provider for your business, take a moment to call the provider's tech-support (*not* sales) department with a question about its services. Take note of how long you had to hold and how courteous the techs were. Before plunking down your hard-earned money, you should be sure that the provider's customer service claims aren't merely claims.

✔ **What's the policy on shopping carts?** In time, you're probably going to need a shopping cart interface on your site. Does your provider charge extra for that? If so, how much? In the beginning, a convenient and professional-looking way to sell items on your site is to set up a PayPal Shopping Cart or PayPal Pay Now (or Buy Now) buttons. When you're running your business full-time, however, a shopping cart or a way to accept credit cards is a must.

✔ **Are there any hidden fees?** Does the hosting company charge exorbitant fees for setup or an extra fee for reporting statistics? And will you see increasing charges if your bandwidth suddenly increases?

✔ **How often will the Web host back up your site?** No matter how redundant a host's servers are, a disaster may strike and you need to know that your Web site won't vaporize. *Redundancy* (having multiple copies of your content) is the safety net for your site. Ask how many power backups a company has for the main system.

Table 15-3 provides a comparison of some host-service costs. In the rest of this section, I fill in details about the four Web-hosting companies listed in the table. Make sure you check out each company's Web site, however, to get the most current information.

TABLE 15-3: COMPARING ENTRY-LEVEL HOSTING COSTS

Feature	ReadyHosting.com (readyhosting.com/ readyhosting/)	Web.com (Web.com/ Websites/DoItYourself Websites.aspx)	eBay Pro Stores (www.prostores.com)	Yahoo! Web Hosting (smallbusiness. yahoo.com/ Webhosting/ hostingfeatures.php)
Monthly plan cost	$66.00 year	$11.95	$29.95 +.5% Transaction Fee	$11.95
Yearly contract	Yes	No	3 month	
Disk space storage	100GB	5GB	5GB	Unlimited
Data transfer/month	1000GB	20GB	50GB	Unlimited
24/7 Toll-free tech support	No	Yes	Yes	Yes
E-mail aliases	Unlimited	30	50	1,000

Don't be fooled by ridiculously high quotes on storage space or data transfer (marketing ploys by hosting companies). Most small-business Web sites can operate well and still fit into 100 MB of disk storage. That means in one GB, you can (technically) have ten Web sites.

Web-site best practices

As I said before, setting up your site as a "store" may be tempting, but Web users are way too wise to be lured into boring Web sites. Content is king on the Web, and your site will need some. As you create your site, make sure it's attractive, readable, efficient, and easy to navigate. Regardless of whether you create a site yourself or have someone do it for you, keep the following best practices in mind:

✔ **Design for appeal.** Use an attractive, professional-looking design. Your site reflects directly on your business.

✔ **Make photos bolster your image.** Not only can photos help visitors see your products and services, but they can help reflect your company's culture, your staff, and other aspects of your business. Photos can be warm and familiar, conservative and businesslike, or fun and trendy, depending on your desired image.

✔ **Keep your words under control.** Avoid using way too much text (unless your site is a blog or informational). People are turned off by text-heavy sites, so get to the point.

✔ **Engineer fast-loading pages.** In particular, avoid high-resolution pictures, which take a long time to load, and stay away from animated introduction pages. Pages created with Adobe Flash (a Web-authoring tool that provides text-animation effects) can be distracting or even problematic to load. Display your home page as quickly as possible.

✔ **Remember the three-click rule.** It should take visitors no more than three clicks to get to the information they're looking for.

✔ **Don't include a counter on your site.** Counters tend to look unprofessional, so invite interaction in other ways.

✔ **Test your site on a dial-up line.** There are still many people out there using dial-up connections, which are slower.

Also, be sure to personalize your site. Customers who shop with small companies prefer the sort of personal relationship they don't find with larger companies. Include personalized information about your business, such as your history, your commitment to the community, staff bios, and so on. This will create more of a bond with customers when they see you're serious about doing business — and are not just there to take money. (A word to the wise: The personal touch is fine, but keep it relevant to the business.)

Going with the Web Site Pros

The reason I'm going to talk about hosting companies is to give you an idea of what you can expect when you do business with a Web hosting firm. I've had my Web site with Yahoo Geocities (family) and Web.com (business) since the nineties. Hosting companies go in and out of business and tend to eat up smaller companies, so I'm lucky to have landed with professional firms.

Looking at Web.com's offerings

My `coolebaytools.com` Web site is hosted at Web.com; a major player in the hosting arena. It's a big company with big, sophisticated equipment, and it hosts a bunch of the big guys on its servers. As of this writing, Web.com hosts sites for more than 250,000 small and medium-sized businesses. Seems good enough for me. I'm using Web.com as an example of what you should expect from a full-service Web host.

While working with Web.com, I've found it's easier than I thought to maintain my Web site. The basic hosting plan includes a simple-to-use SiteBuilder tool (shown in Figure 15-1). The tool gives me easy-to-understand instructions for how to build and maintain my Web site.

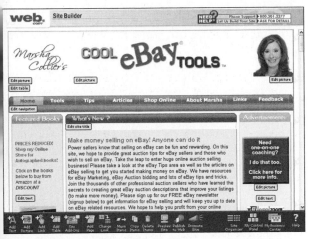

• **Figure 15-1: Editing my site in Web.com's SiteBuilder online software.**

As a new user, you have access to thousands of design template combinations, customizable starter content, and dynamic features such as interactive maps, blogs, and RSS feeds. Web.com gives you everything you need to build a Web site that engages visitors and keeps them coming back.

I like to manage my own site, or contract with a reasonably priced Web designer who can update my site for me. By using automated tools like SiteBuilder, I find it's really worth my time to do the maintenance myself once I set up the site.

Web.com offers many tools with its basic package (as of this writing):

- ✔ Step-by-step design tool
- ✔ Over 30,000 design and page-layout combinations
- ✔ Starter content so you don't have to create copy from scratch
- ✔ Picture galleries, which add multiple viewing options to store and display different types of photos, keeping business and family photos separate
- ✔ Image, stock photography, and clip-art library of 5,000+ images

- ✔ Interactive maps and driving directions from Microsoft MapPoint
- ✔ Site map
- ✔ HTML support for referencing images, files, JavaScript, media players, and plug-ins from any service provider
- ✔ Blogging tools
- ✔ PayPal Buy Now buttons (so you don't have to worry about any coding)
- ✔ Business Forms Builder for e-mail newsletter signups, customer surveys, and lead capture forms
- ✔ Guestbooks
- ✔ News Feeds powered by Moreover, which lets you post timely, dynamic news content to your site from third party sources
- ✔ RSS Feed Support, which lets you select and publish any type of frequently updated content such as blog entries, news headlines or podcasts
- ✔ Loan and mortgage calculators
- ✔ Real-time local weather viewer from Weather.com
- ✔ Support for audio, video, and Flash files
- ✔ Customer Access Management, which lets you password-protect Web pages

Not a bad deal for $11.95 a month. Be sure the company you choose has similar offerings.

In Practice 11, I talk about the importance of marketing your site, and Web.com helps me there, too. Google AdWords and Yahoo! Search Marketing credits — along with instructions on how best to take advantage of these services — made a great deal of difference in enabling me to promote my site.

 Sometimes a little hand-holding is what you need, and having the benefit of 24/7 technical support fulfills that need. Somehow I'm never working on my Web site during normal business hours, so knowing that I can call someone in the middle of the night is a blessing: Be sure the company you choose has this service.

Considering Yahoo! Web-site services

Yahoo! is trying to do a little bit of everything these days. I'm never sure which direction it's going. Yahoo! took over GeoCities (one of the original free Web-site hosts) a few years back, so my family Web site became a free Yahoo! site. Considering that I have a free site, I must admit that the services that Yahoo! offers have been top-drawer, disproving the notion that you get *only* what you pay for. But then again, I'm not running a business from the site; it's just a bunch of family pictures.

When you subscribe to one of Yahoo!'s Web-hosting plans, you can download the free SiteBuilder software, which allows you to be up and running with the basic site quickly. Thank goodness you don't have to know any HTML to use it. The download includes access to more than 300 stock templates that you can customize any way you want.

If you're looking for a complete store solution, you can subscribe to a do-it-yourself, e-commerce, full-featured site for $39.95 a month. This site includes product-merchandising templates, order-management systems, and more business goodies. Check out the Yahoo! offerings at

```
smallbusiness.yahoo.com
```

Naming Your Web Site

What to name the Web site? It's almost as much of a dilemma as deciding on your eBay User ID or eBay Store name. If you don't have an existing company name that you want to use, why not use the same name as your eBay Store? Register that name and lock it up now so you can keep your brand forever.

Name your site with a word that identifies what you do, what you sell, or who you are. And be sure you like the name; once you begin operating and establishing a reputation under it, you'll have that name 20 years from now when you're still selling online! (I know — it should only happen!)

A few Web sites offer wizards to help you decide your domain name. A particularly intuitive one can be found at the following:

```
www.namesarecheap.com/wizard.shtml
```

In a small, Web-based form, you input your primary business type and keywords that describe your business. The wizard then displays a large number of options and also lets you know whether the options are available. Very convenient.

Domain parking

Suppose you've come up with a brilliant name for your site and you get really big and famous. Then someone else uses your Web site's name but registers it as a .net — while yours is a .com. To avoid this situation, make sure you register *both* domains (.com and .net) and park them with your registrar — and you may as well do the same with the .org domain while you're at it. That way, any permutations of your domain will point to your active Web site. For example, `www.ebay.net` and `ebay.org` are registered to (guess who?) ebay.com. You can check the owner of any domain name at any of the Web-hosting or registrar sites.

Registering Your Domain Name

Talk about your junk e-mail. I get daily e-mails advising me to `Lose 40 pounds in 40 days`, accept `credit cards now`, and of course `REGISTER MY NAME NOW`! This last scam seems to be geared toward obtaining my e-mail address for other junk-mail lists rather than trying to help me register my Web site. (Spam, scams, and other junk are dangerous to your business. You may want to take a little refresher spin through Practices 32 and 33 for ways to fight them.)

Choosing an appropriate *registrar* (the company that handles the registering of your site name) is as important as choosing the right Web host. You must remember that the Internet is still a little like the Wild West, and that the online equivalent of the James Gang might be waiting to relieve you of your hard-earned cash. One of the ways to protect your-self is to understand how the registry works (knowl-edge *is* power), so read on.

Before you decide on a registrar for your domain name, take a minute to see whether the registrar is accredited by ICANN (Internet Corporation for Assigned Names and Numbers — the international governing body for domain names) or is reselling for an official ICANN-accredited registrar. (You'll have to ask who your chosen company registers with.) The Accredited Registrar Directory is updated con-stantly, so check the following for the most recent list:

www.internic.com/regist.html

Making your personal information private

ICANN requires every registrar to maintain a publicly accessible whois database displaying all contact information for all domain names registered. Interested parties (or fraudsters) can find out the name, street address, e-mail address, and phone number of the owner of the site by running a *whois* search on the domain name. You can run a whois search by going to www.whois.net and typing the domain name in question.

This information can be useful to spammers who spoof your e-mail address as their return address to cloak their identity, identity thieves, stalkers, and just about anyone up to no good. To see the difference between private and public registrations, run a whois search on my Web site, www.coolebaytools.com, which is private, and www.ebay.com, which is public.

Registrars such as Network Solutions offer private registra-tion for an additional $9 a year. Check to see whether your registrar offers this service.

You'll usually get a substantial discount from the more expensive registrars when you regis-ter your domain name for multiple years — a good idea if you plan on staying in business. Also, if you register your name through your hosting service, you may save big money! The only drawback is that your prepaid registra-tion might go out the window if you choose to change hosting companies.

If you're registering a new domain name but already have a site set up with your ISP, you need a feature called *URL forwarding* or *Web-address forwarding*. This feature directs any hits to your new domain name from your existing long URL address.

Some registrars offer a URL-forwarding ser-vice, but watch out for hidden surprises. A free offer of this service may mean that the registrar intends to smack a big, fat banner at the bottom of your home page.

Your registrar should also have some available tech support. Trying to troubleshoot DNS issues is a job for those who know what they're doing! Remember, sometimes you get what you pay for — but it helps to know what you're paying for.

Practice 16

Giving Back to Nonprofits through Giving Works

In This Practice

- Finding out about eBay Giving Works
- Shopping for charity
- Raising money for your favorite charity

By shopping eBay's Giving Works, buyers have more fun buying unique things, and the money goes to charity. Many charitable organizations are selling their wares on eBay to raise money for their fine work.

eBay has partnered with MissionFish, an organization based in Washington, D.C., that has been raising money through online auctions since 2000. A forward-thinking, great group of people founded this company with the purpose of doing good for others. Now, MissionFish is a service with the Points of Light Foundation and operates its Web site at www.missionfish.org.

MissionFish functions as the hub for nonprofit organizations selling on eBay. The service qualifies the organizations by verifying their eligibility before they can begin to raise money online with eBay. Aside from verification, MissionFish also provides other service and support activities including donation collection and disbursement, tax receipting, and online contribution tracking.

You can get some very rare and unusual items through Giving Works, like the annual NBC Today Show Green Room autograph book. This one-of-a-kind book has signatures and notes from the famous guests of the Today show. Following are some other super-hot items that have been up for sale:

- **Lunch with Warren Buffett,** offered yearly and raising **2 million dollars** for the Glide Foundation.

- **Three celebrity-signed Harley-Davidson motorcycles** featured on the Tonight Show with Jay Leno raised a total of **$1.7M** — one of the motorcycles raised **$800,100** for the Red Cross Tsunami Relief effort, and is the highest-selling charity item to date.

- **The Dalai Lama's personal 1966 Land Rover 88 Station Wagon.** The winner of this auction also received a three-day Buddhism study session with the Dalai Lama in India and a meeting with actress Sharon Stone at The Missing Peace Art Exhibit show — dinner included. This auction raised huge money for the nonprofit.

✔ **A golf foursome with Tiger Woods** raised $425,000 for the Tiger Woods Foundation.

When buyers come to the site for these very special offerings, they get in the habit of looking for sellers who also sell items for charity. Through eBay's Giving Works, you can donate a percentage of one (or all) of your items to charity. This puts your listings in the Giving Works category, giving them additional visibility. Get it? Do some good — and get some good advertising for your business!

Sellers who wish to raise money can pick a nonprofit from the certified list of over 12,000 nonprofit groups — and designate a percentage of the proceeds (from 10 to 100 percent) to donate — when they list an item on eBay. These items will appear in the search results with a "charity auction" icon. When you go to the item page, you'll see the name of the nonprofit, some information about it, and the percentage of the final bid that the seller is donating. You can search eBay for your favorite nonprofits by name.

When charities receive donations of merchandise rather than cash, the merchandise is called *gifts-in-kind*. Many manufacturers donate excess inventory to charities for a full-value tax deduction. The charity can either use the merchandise in their charitable works or sell the items to raise money. (You mean you've *never* shopped at the Salvation Army store?) In the past, charities had to rent retail locations to turn their gifts-in-kind into cash. Now they've got eBay; and eBay supplies the Giving Works area for all qualified charities.

Buyers find the charitable listings by clicking the Giving Works link — or by clicking one of the graphic promotions on the eBay home page. Figure 16-1 shows you the Giving Works main page on eBay. Should such things as link names or locations change at eBay (and they often do), you can always access the eBay nonprofit area directly at

www.ebay.com/givingworks

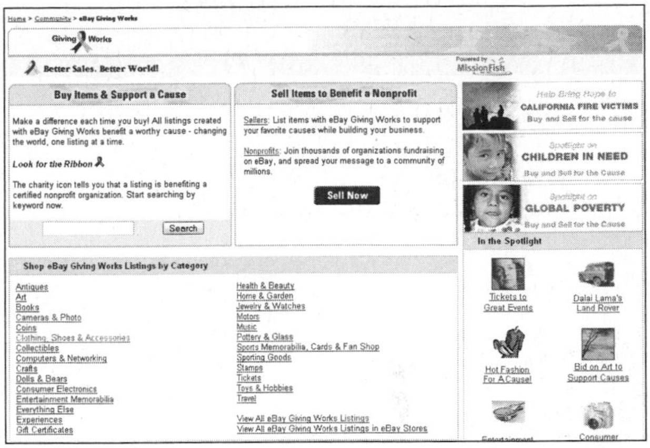

• **Figure 16-1: Here's where people can find listings for charity, or you can start your own charitable auction.**

eBay themes the year to feature various types of organizations on the Giving Works home page (although all nonprofits are featured continually). In 2007, the featured themes were

Theme	Time Period
Heart Health	January/February
Supporting the Arts	February/March
Saving the Environment (Earth Day)	April/May
Helping Animals	June/July
Empowerment through Entrepreneurship	June
Education	August/September
Breast Cancer Awareness	October
Children in Need	November/December
Global Poverty	November
AIDS Awareness	December

When a catastrophe occurs, MissionFish puts up links to help victims of specific disasters. Figure 16-2 shows you the hub page to help those facing adversity from the 2007 California wildfires.

• **Figure 16-2: Donate a portion of your item for sale to help those less fortunate.**

Whenever you list an item for charity, your listing appears with the GivingWorks blue-and-yellow-ribbon icon next to the title. Also, at the top of your description, is a further description of your charitable donation. Take a look at Figure 16-3 to see the MissionFish information in a listing.

• **Figure 16-3: eBay GivingWorks Charitable donation information in a live auction.**

Raising Money for the Little Guys

If you're currently an eBay seller, and you'd like to sell some items to benefit a nonprofit, eBay will do most of the work for you. You must select a non-profit from the directory (shown in Figure 16-4) and

you can contribute from 10 percent to 100 percent of the final bid at the end of the auction.

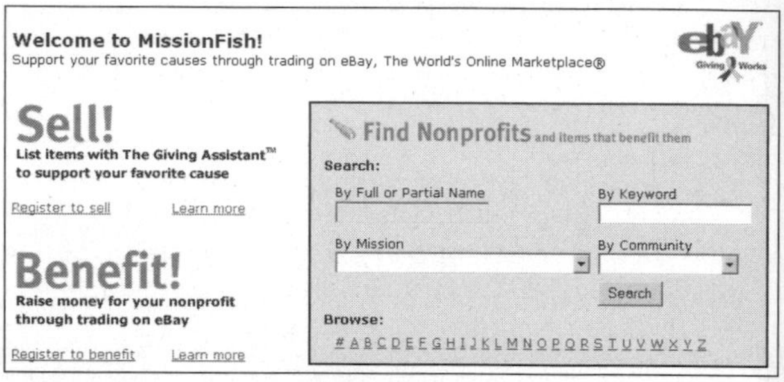

• **Figure 16-4: The nonprofit directory.**

After an item is sold, it's your job to collect the money from the buyer and to ship the item. You'll receive an e-mail confirming the dollar amount of the final sales price and the percentage that you agreed to donate. After you verify these figures, MissionFish charges your credit card for that amount.

MissionFish sends your donation to the nonprofit, and you receive a receipt for your contribution.

To participate in the program, you must register at MissionFish. Go to the Web site at

```
www.missionfish.org
```

and click the Seller Registration link.

1. **Type your eBay User ID and password and click Continue.**

   After MissionFish confirms that you are registered at eBay, you proceed to the next page (a SLL secure connection), which is populated with your mailing address from eBay's records.

2. **Check over your information and correct it if necessary.**

3. **Type your credit-card information.**

   This information is used to send the money to your selected nonprofit when your auction is over.

4. **Create a MissionFish user ID and password for accessing your information at MissionFish. (I used my eBay User ID.)**

To sell on eBay Giving Works, you must do the following:

- Register with MissionFish and maintain an account in good standing.

- Agree to donate to at least 10 percent of the final sale price or $5 — whichever is greater — to a certified organization in the nonprofit directory, if the item sells. **Note:** The $5 minimum donation requirement does not apply to nonprofits selling items on their own behalf as a Direct Seller.

And, yes, eBay does credit your listing and final value fees to the percentage that you donate to charity. Table 16-1 shows you an example when a seller lists an item on eBay and elects to donate 20 percent of the final sale price to a nonprofit.

TABLE 16-1: EBAY CREDITED FEES IN A 20% DONATED AUCTION

Description	Amount
Starting price	$10.00
Insertion Fee	$0.60
Final sale price	$100.00
Final Value Fee	$3.75
Total selling fees	$4.34
Insertion Fee credit to seller: 20% × $0.60	($0.12)
Final Value Fee credit to seller: 20% × $3.75	($.75)

Now you're ready to sell. To see if your chosen nonprofit is listed in the directory, type in its name (or keywords relating to the charity). You can also find a nonprofit by browsing through the alphabetic directory.

Select your nonprofit, and listing your item is the same as listing any other item on eBay — only this time you'll have a Giving Works gold-and-blue ribbon next to your item title (indicating to the eBay community that your auction is for a nonprofit).

Raising Money for Your Small Nonprofit

Are you involved in a charitable organization that you'd like to raise money for? If you think your organization is too small, think again. Perhaps you just want to sell an item to benefit your favorite charity; you can do that, too. If you're a larger charity and you don't think you have enough people to handle the sales, eBay has a program that can help you! The formal Giving Works area was launched in November 2003, and within the first month had signed up over 2000 nonprofits. eBay ran charity auctions prior to the launching of Giving Works, but these auctions were mostly for high-profile organizations with an IRS 501 (c) (3) designation.

eBay Giving Works is now open to any IRS-approved nonprofit, which could include your high school band booster club, local volunteer fire fighters, or cat-rescue organization.

If you are involved in a small organization that's not listed in the Giving Works directory, it's easy for you to become listed. And after your organization appears in the directory, any eBay member can select it to receive auction proceeds.

 Whenever an eBay member chooses your nonprofit for an auction, you have the opportunity to accept or decline the beneficial listing.

From the MissionFish home page, click the For Non-Profits link. From there you may register your organization to participate. You must have a few things ready, including a fax machine to get the required documentation to MissionFish:

✔ Contact Information (in case they need to call you).

✔ The nonprofit's Federal Employees Number (EIN).

✔ A copy of the logo in GIF or JPG format, with a maximum size of 50 KB.

✔ Your prepared Mission Statement in about 40 words (512 characters maximum).

✔ A copy of your nonprofit status letter.

✔ A voided organization check with authorized signature (to verify your banking information for deposits).

✔ Web-site information. If you have a Web site, supply the URL, so that a link can be made from beneficial eBay listings to your Web site.

✔ Acceptance setting. You'll have to indicate what's best for you:

▶ **Accept all, don't notify me.** This means that anytime anyone selects you as a benefiting nonprofit, the item will go up for sale on eBay without prior authorization from you. You will still be able to view all items you are benefiting from in your MissionFish account.

▶ **Notify me, one-day auto accept.** You'll be notified by e-mail every time someone wants to list an item for you. If you don't approve or disapprove within one business day, the listing will go live automatically.

▶ **Notify me, one-day auto decline.** You'll receive an e-mail notifying you of someone's intent. If you don't approve or decline within one business day, the item will be declined automatically.

Check out Table 16-2 for the timeline of activities for running a Giving Works auction on eBay.

TABLE 16-2: TIMELINE FOR A GIVING WORKS AUCTION

Action	Time Interval
Nonprofit accepts or declines item	1 business day after the item is listed (1 to 3 days is the usual reality)
Listing on eBay	3, 5, 7, or 10 days, depending on the selling format
Seller pays donation	1 to 7 days after listing ends
Donation is automatically collected	2nd Monday after listing ends (from 8 to 13 days)
Refund request period	Until the end of the month when the listing ends, plus one month and 15 days
Donation delivered to the nonprofit; tax receipt available to the seller	End of the month when the listing ends, plus one month, plus 20 days.

Planning a big auction?

If you're with a charitable organization and you'd like to plan a really big auction, you may not want to handle all the details yourself. You want to get the highest prices for your items, and when the bidding gets into the thousands per item, getting help from someone who knows the ropes can really help.

Kompolt & Company, an auction management agency founded by two marketing wizards, Jenny Kompolt and Melissa James, runs some of the top auctions on eBay for nonprofits. They've run charitable auctions for The Today Show, The Grammys, Lifetime Television, British Airways, Bon Jovi, and Britney Spears (just to drop a few names). Their client list is a who's who in the giving community.

Kompolt & Company handles everything for the charity including registration, pricing strategies, photography, custom design of the listing pages (as well as the About Me page), bidder pre-qualification (payment assurance and protection against bogus or fraudulent bidding), payment collection and item fulfillment, and full closing reports and analysis.

Check out the Web site at www.kompolt.com.

Browsing and Buying

Suppose you enjoy shopping and would like to buy items from a charity. (I do this all the time.) Your first stop should be the eBay Home page where you scroll down through the long list of categories to the Giving Works link at the bottom. The URL is `givingworks.ebay.com` or `www.ebay.com/givingworks`.

To browse all items being sold to benefit nonprofits, click the link View All eBay Giving Works Listings. There will also be nonprofit items listed in eBay Stores, so to view these click the link View All eBay Giving Works Listings in eBay Stores.

You may also search Giving Works items with the Search box offered on the page — although I find that browsing charity auctions is more fun — you just might find something you didn't even know you needed!

Part III

Build Better Listings

The 5th Wave   By Rich Tennant

I've never seen an eBay listing so alive with colorful images.

Oo—look! Stare long enough at the product thumbnails and a 3-D image of a bird in flight pops out.

Practice 17

Creating Listings That Sell with HTML

I must admit, the very thought of using HTML used to terrify me (pinky-swear you won't tell anyone else). HTML. Doesn't it sound so very high-tech and geeklike? But HTML isn't all that scary once you realize that it's just a fancy name for HyperText Markup Language, a pretty easy-to-use language for creating online content. All you need to know is the markup part. HTML uses tags to mark up pages to include elements such as text and graphics in a way that Web browsers understand. A Web browser sees the tags and knows how to display the document (that is, the Web page) on-screen. HTML also makes possible the whole work of links. When you click a link, you jump to another place: another Web page, document, or file, for example.

Many eBay sellers somehow think that putting dancing bunnies, flaming fireworks, and background music in their auctions will bring in more bids. Unfortunately, that's pretty far from the truth. (But video on demand can be a good thing.) People go to your auctions to find information and get a great deal on something they want, not to marvel at your creative work. They need to see the facts, placed cleanly and neatly on the page.

 The addition of music to your auction may cause another problem: an extremely s-l-o-o-o-o-w page load for those on slower connections. If loading your page takes too long, it's a proven fact that the majority of customers will click back and go to another listing.

So what should you do to attract buyers? I spent most of my career in the advertising business, and the byword of good advertising is, "Keep it simple!" An organized and well-written selling description will outsell dancing bears and pictures of your children every time.

That's why HTML is now my friend — you can create a professional look for your sales through the use of varied typefaces, type sizes, and colors. I show you how to create templates using an HTML generator. But using the generator without understanding the commands is akin to using a language translator without speaking a word of the language — you're never really sure that what's coming out is correct, or confident you know how to make minor tweaks yourself. In this practice, I help you understand what HTML commands are all about, and I encourage you to consider enhancing your listings with HTML as part of your standard selling practices.

Using eBay's Built-in Editor

Practice 18 lays out the essentials of building a winning item description; here's where we get down to the basics of dolling up that description for eBay. If you don't want to monkey around with HTML (not just yet, anyway), you can use the standard way of inputting your text — which is (blessedly) much like using a word processor. Figure 17-1 shows you the standard input area.

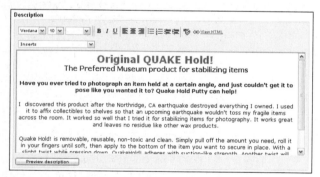

• **Figure 17-1: Dolling up a listing here is as simple as using a word processor.**

For those not familiar with the boxes, bars, and menus, let me list them here (from left to right):

- **Font Name:** This is a drop-down menu that will change the typeface of the text on your screen. Merely highlight your text to select the text you want to change, and then use your cursor to select the typeface of your choice from the drop-down menu. You have choices of Arial, Arial Black, Comic Sans, Courier, Georgia, Impact, Times, Trebuchet MS, and Verdana.

 The Verdana font was designed especially for legibility on computer screens.

- **Size:** Here's another drop-down menu that allows you to select the size of your type. The numbers in the drop-down menu indicate the type's point size. The higher the number, the larger the text.

- **Color:** Want some fiery red text? Here's your chance! You can change your highlighted text to Black, Blue, Brown, Red, or Green.

- **B:** Stands for **Bold face**. Highlighting your text and clicking the B changes your type from regular text to bold.

- **I:** I is for *italic*. You want to slant the text in part of a sentence for effect? Just highlight your text and click here.

- **Flush Left:** When you want your text to align to the left, just highlight it and click the simulated left-aligned text.

- **Centered Text:** Sometimes text looks best centered (especially when your picture is a horizontally based rectangle). Highlighting the text and clicking here centers your text perfectly.

- **Flush Right:** Sometimes the most effective look is to align your text to the right side of the page. Just click here and voilà!

- **Numbered List:** Highlight a group of paragraphs and click here for a nicely ordered, numbered list.

- **Bulleted List:** We use this one a great deal for listing an item's features. Highlight (just as in the numbered list) and eBay's magic will produce a cleanly ordered, bulleted list like the one you're reading now.

- **Move Right:** This pushbutton command moves the entire selected paragraph of text to the right of the text box.

- **Move Left:** Surprise! Clicking here will move your block of text to the left (but you knew that).

- **Inserts:** Here's a drop-down menu (shown in Figure 17-2) that helps you insert certain preassigned pieces of text that you create and save for later use, for example, a standard paragraph of information for international buyers.

✔ **Create Links:** Be careful here. eBay's policies say that you cannot link to outside Web sites that sell your item. Here you can put in three different types of links:

▶ Links to another item on eBay

▶ Links to a page in your store

▶ Links to a search of your eBay store

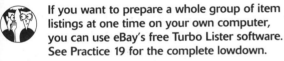

After you create a link using eBay's system, you can choose to save it to use again.

✔ **Spell Checker:** Hallelujah! Here sellers can check the spelling in their listings before going live. What I can't understand is why there are still plenty of misspellings in eBay listings. Be sure to use this feature — *and* check your work carefully! (A word to the wise: Try reading it out loud to catch some of the embarrassing typos that spell checkers can miss.)

• **Figure 17-2:** Look how easy it is to create an insert for your description page!

✔ **Help**. The question-mark button permits you to access eBay's help menu for this form.

If you want to prepare a whole group of item listings at one time on your own computer, you can use eBay's free Turbo Lister software. See Practice 19 for the complete lowdown.

Getting Started with Basic HTML

When you want to make your listings stand out a bit, you could use one of eBay's graphic themes. (Remember that doing so will add 10 more cents to your listing fee.) You could insert your own graphics into your listing, however, and it wouldn't cost you a penny more.

But even if you use one of eBay's lovely graphic designs, you would still need to format your text. That's where your HTML coding comes in.

You can also use HTML to insert multiple pictures into your descriptions to promote your item even better. This won't cost you a penny extra, and you can still use eBay's Pictures Services' one free photo for your top-of-listing picture. The magic code for this feature is

```
<img src="http://www.yourchosen
server.com/picturename.jpg">
```

Be sure to input the proper address where your image is stored — along with the proper image file name. If you want to insert two pictures, one below the other, use the same code, but put a break <br> in between the two image lines of code. See the section "Inserting additional photos in your listings for free," later in this practice.

What HTML can do

Take a look at Figure 17-3; it contains a listing description typed in the Notepad program that you'll find in Windows Accessories.

```
infiniti.txt - Notepad
File  Edit  Search  Help
Portable Photography Backdrop Stage from Cloud Dome
Ebay Sellers! This is for you! Are you tired of trying
to find a nice clear spot to take your pictures for eBay
sales? Sure you could spend a fortune on backdrops and
muslin, but this handy, portable stage works (without
glare) flawlessly every time. This is the most versatile
product that I've found for tabletop photography.
The Infiniti Board is white textured, washable and
scratch proof. It can be used flat or curved; the height
and curve are adjustable with the attached locking
cords. The total size is 19 inches wide by 28 inches
long.
I am the author of "eBay for Dummies" and I scour the
country looking for new reasonably priced tools for the
eBay seller. Check my feedback to see that customer
service is the byword of my eBay Business. Winning
bidder to pay calculated Priority Mail (2 to 3 day)
shipping based on distance. Please use the eBay Shipping
Calculator below. Type your zip code in the box below to
determine your shipping rate. If time is not of the
essence, please email and we will quote a lower FedEx
Ground shipping rate. Please submit payment within a
week of winning the auction. Credit cards graciously
accepted through PayPal.
This item is NOT being drop-shipped by another party. We
have these in stock and will ship immediately - directly
to you!
GET IT QUICKLY! I ship via 2 - 3 day Priority Mail.
GOOD LUCK ON EBAY, HAPPY HOLIDAYS!
Click below to...
Visit my ebay Store for low prices on handy seller tools
and Cloud Dome Products
```

• **Figure 17-3:** Raw auction text in Notepad.

If I add some appropriate HTML coding from Table 17-1 (later in this practice) to the file, the auction page will look a whole lot different, as shown in Figure 17-4.

Pretty cool, huh?

How HTML works

HTML uses a series of codes to indicate the specifics of display to a browser — such as when text should be bold or italic, or when text is actually a link. Brackets are used to indicate commands: What's within them is an instruction to the browser, rather than actual text that should appear on your page.

In the example that follows, the b and I in brackets indicate that text between them should be formatted **bold** and *italic*. Notice that there is both a start formatting and end formatting indication (<b> starts bold formatting and </b> ends it). Here's one example:

✔ HTML start and end tags:

   <b><i></i></b>

✔ The same tags with text between them:

   <b><i>eBay tools</i></b>

✔ The resulting text on your page:

   eBay tools

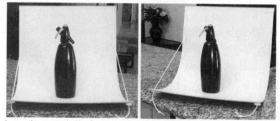

Portable Photography Backdrop Stage from Cloud Dome

Ebay Sellers! This is for you! Are you tired of trying to find a nice clear spot to take your pictures for eBay sales? Sure you could spend a fortune on backdrops and muslin, but this handy, portable stage works (without glare) flawlessly every time. This is the most versatile product that I've found for tabletop photography.

The Infiniti Board is white textured, washable and scratch proof. It can be used flat or curved; the height and curve are adjustable with the attached locking cords. The total size is 19 inches wide by 28 inches long.

I scour the country looking for new reasonably priced tools for the eBay seller. Check my feedback to see that customer service is the byword of my eBay Business. Winning bidder to pay calculated Priority Mail (2 to 3 day) shipping based on distance. Please use the eBay Shipping Calculator below. Type your zip code in the box below to determine your shipping rate. If time is not of the essence, please email and we will quote a lower FedEx Ground shipping rate. Please submit payment within a week of winning the auction. Credit cards graciously accepted through PayPal.

This item is NOT being drop-shipped by another party. We have these in stock and will ship immediately - directly to you!

GET IT QUICKLY! I ship via 2 - 3 day Priority Mail.

Click below to...
Visit my ebay Store for low prices on handy seller tools and Cloud Dome Products

• **Figure 17-4:** Auction description dolled up with HTML.

See? Using such commands you can set up text on a page to be formatted in bold, begin a new paragraph, fall into a list format, and so on.

 Table 17-1 lists many of the common HTML tags to get you started.

A few things to keep in mind about HTML:

✔ Don't worry about placing a return at the end of a line. You must use a command to go to the next line; pressing Enter on your keyboard has no effect on what the page looks like.

✔ It's not necessary to put the paragraph command at the beginning and at the end of the paragraph. This is one command that doesn't need a close. Just put the <p> command where you want the breaking space to be.

 It's a good idea to get into the habit of closing *all* commands, so you should put a </p> at the end of the paragraph. (This meets XHTML standards, which is prudent.)

✔ The same principle applies for a horizontal rule, <hr>. Just place the command where you want the line and it will appear. In the changing world of XHTML, it is preferred to close all commands. A shortcut for opening and closing in one (for a horizontal rule) would be <hr/> (the / before the closing bracket simply means that the command "closes itself."

✔ Most HTML coding commands have a clearly marked beginning and end. The beginning code is in < > and to end the formatting, you must repeat the code — only this time with a slash </ >.

✔ Because people have different fonts set up on their computers, they may not have the ultimately trendy font you want to display. Be sure to list (as in the code shown here) alternate fonts for your text. If you don't, different browsers may substitute other fonts that might look really bizarre on some readers' pages!

If you'd like to see how HTML looks, I've placed an auction description here and put the HTML code in bold so it's easier to spot:

```
<center><font face='VERDANA,
   HELVETICA,ARIAL' color='crimson'
   size=5>
<B>Portable Photography Backdrop
   Stage<BR>from Cloud Dome</B>
</font></center>
<center><font
   face='verdana,arial,helvetica,sans
   serif' color='Black' size=4>
Ebay Sellers! This is for you! Are
   you tired of trying to find a nice
   clear spot to take your pictures
   for eBay sales? Sure you could
   spend a fortune on backdrops and
```

```
muslin, but this handy, portable
   stage works (without glare) flaw-
   lessly every time. This is the most
   versatile product that I've found
   for tabletop photography. </font>
<BR><center><font
   face='verdana,arial,helvetica,sans
   serif' color='Black' size=2>
The Infiniti Board is white textured,
   washable and scratch proof. It can
   be used flat or curved; the height
   and curve are adjustable with the
   attached locking cords. The total
   size is 19 inches wide by 28 inches
   long. <P>
<img src="http://www.collierad.com/
   whiteboard.jpg">
<font
   face='verdana,arial,helvetica,sans
   serif' color='Black' size=2>
   <center>
I scour the country looking for new
   reasonably priced tools for the
   eBay seller. Check my feedback to
   see that customer service is the
   byword of my eBay Business. Winning
   bidder to pay calculated Priority
   Mail (2 to 3 day) shipping based on
   distance. Please use the eBay
   Shipping Calculator below. Type
   your zip code in the box below to
   determine your shipping rate. If
   time is not of the essence, please
   e-mail and we will quote a lower
   FedEx Ground shipping rate. Please
   submit payment within a week of
   winning the auction. Credit cards
   graciously accepted through
   PayPal.<br>
<b>This item is NOT being drop-
   shipped by another party. We have
   these in stock and will ship imme-
   diately - directly to
   you!<BR></font>
<font
   face="verdana,arial,helvetica,sans
   serif" color="crimson" size=2><I>
GET IT QUICKLY! I ship via 2 - 3 day
   Priority Mail.</b> </I></font><P>
<I><font face="verdana,arial,hel-
   vetica,sans serif" color='Black'
   size=3><p>
Click below to... <BR>
```

```
<A HREF= http://cgi6.ebay.com/ws/
    eBayISAPI.dll?ViewSellersOtherItems
    &include=0&userid=marsha_c&sort=
    3&rows=50&since=-1&rd=1 target=_
    blank>
Visit my eBay Store <B><I>for
    low prices </I></B>on handy
    seller tools and Cloud Dome
    Products</a></b></font></center>
```

 Note that the HTML code shown here is bold-faced to help you spot it, but it's not necessary to bold HTML code when you *use* it.

Safe and simple formatting

One of the simplest tricks that can make things easy when you're adding HTML commands to your text is to put each command on a separate line. When a Web browser interprets a page that includes HTML commands, it ignores which lines they're on, and doesn't bother to display any extra blank lines or spaces. That means you can write your HTML so it makes the best possible sense to you and still *works*. The following code, for example, will be interpreted and displayed as shown in Figure 17-5:

```
<font size="+1">
It doesn't matter whether your text
    is
all
on
one
line, or if you have  some    extra
    spaces or
```

blank lines

```
in your text, it will all be format-
    ted
properly when the HTML commands are
    interpreted
and displayed by a web browser.
</font>
<p>
To make it easier on yourself, put
    each opening and
closing HTML tag on a
<strong>
separate
</strong>
line.
</p>
```

 Want to save your sanity — and maybe keep from pulling your hair out later when you discover formatting that doesn't end where you thought it did? Always enter the closing tag when you enter the opening tag, and just put your text between 'em. That way you avoid forgetting to close the tag later.

Uh-oh. I just said that extra blank spaces won't be displayed. What if you *want* more than one space at a time — that is, how do you create an area of "white space" in your description? Don't panic; there is a special HTML command that accomplishes this feat: the *non-breaking space*. To get one, just insert   in your text for each space you want to include: will force the display of five blank spaces in a row.

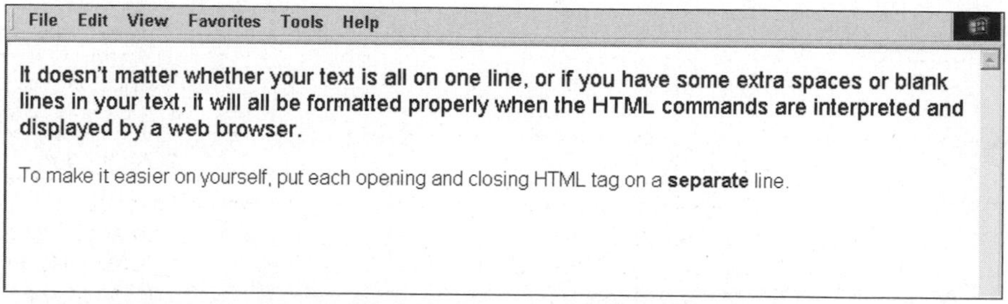

```
File  Edit  View  Favorites  Tools  Help
```

It doesn't matter whether your text is all on one line, or if you have some extra spaces or blank lines in your text, it will all be formatted properly when the HTML commands are interpreted and displayed by a web browser.

To make it easier on yourself, put each opening and closing HTML tag on a **separate** line.

• **Figure 17-5:** Formatted description from unformatted text and HTML commands, saved in Notepad and opened in the browser.

The non-breaking space comes in handy in several other ways. For instance, if you have two or more words that should stay together, no matter what, the   can make it happen. Here are some examples of how to use this command to keep words from being separated:

Los Angeles, CA - Los Angeles, CA

March 4, 2008 - March 4, 2008

4:00 PM - 4:00 PM

 Though some browsers recognize and interpret the non-breaking-space command without the semicolon (;) character at the end, not all browsers do. Be sure to include that semicolon; otherwise the actual characters   will be displayed instead of any space at all, making your text messy.

The non-breaking-space command stands alone; no need for angle brackets or a corresponding closing tag.

TABLE 17-1: BASIC HTML CODES

Text Code	How to Use It	What It Does
`<b></b>`	`<b>eBay tools</b>`	**eBay tools** (bold type)
`<I></I>`	`<I>eBay tools</I>`	*eBay tools* (italic type)
`<b><I></I></b>`	`<b><i>eBay tools</b></i>`	***eBay tools*** (bold and italic type)
`<font color=red></font>`	`<font color=red>ebay tools</font>`	Selected text appears in red. (This book is in black and white so you can't see it.)
`<font size=+1></font>`	`<font size=+3>eBay</font> tools`	eBay tools (font size normal +1 through 4, increases size *x* times)
` `	`eBay tools`	eBay tools (inserts line break)
`<p>`	`eBay<p>tools`	eBay tools (inserts paragraph space)
`<hr>`	`cool eBay<hr>tools`	cool eBay ───── tools (inserts horizontal rule)
`<h1><h1>`	`<h1>eBay tools</h1>`	eBay tools (converts text to headline size)

Code for Lists	How to Use It	What It Does

`<ul><li>`
`</ul>`
	`<ul><li>I accept`
	`<li>PayPal`
	`<li>Money Orders`
	`<li>Checks</ul>`
		I accept
		· PayPal
		· Money Orders
		· Checks

(continued)

TABLE 17-1 *(continued)*

Code For Lists	How to Use It	What It Does

`<ol><li>`
`<ol>`
	`<ol><li>I accept`
	`<li>PayPal`
	`<li>Money Orders`
	`<li>Checks</ol>`
		I accept
		1. PayPal
		2. Money Orders
		3. Checks

Linking (Hyperlink) Code	How to Use It	What It Does
`<img src>`	`<img src="http://www.yourwebsite.` `com/imagename.jpg">`	Inserts an image from your server into the description text

`<A HREF= >`	`<A HREF= http://www.yourwebsite.`
	`com/shippinginfo.htm>Click Here`
	`for shipping info</A>`
		When selected text is clicked (in this instance, *Click here for shipping info*), the user's browser goes to the page you indicate in the URL

`TARGET=_BLANK`	`<A HREF= http://www.yourwebsite.` `com/shippinginfo.htm TARGET=_BLANK>`	When inserted at the end of a hyperlink, it opens the page in a separate browser window

Table Code	How to Use It	What It Does
`<table border>`	`<table border=4>`	Puts a border around your table at a width of 4 pixels

`<table>`
`</table>`
	`<table>`
	`sample text`
	`</table>`
		The table command must surround *every* table

`<tr></tr>`	`<tr><td>text</td><td>text</td>`	Table row `<tr>` must be used with `<td>`
`<td></td>`	`</tr><tr><td>text</td><td>text</td>` `</tr>`	Table data to end and open new boxes. text text text text

Adding Structure and Visual Interest

You want shoppers to read your carefully crafted item description, but catching their attention with a picture of your item can't hurt. Have you ever noticed how some people manage to have a photo on the right or left side of their descriptions? It's really not that difficult to do. It just involves a little HTML code added to the listing, using something called *tables*.

Arranging with tables

In this example, an HTML table contains a picture that shows up on the left side of the description, as in Figure 17-6. (By the way, when the actual auction ran on eBay, with the kind cooperation of the people on *The View*, we raised over $1,000 for UNICEF!)

All you fans of *The View*, this is your chance to own a coffee cup autographed by all four stars of the show. The proceeds from this auction will be donated to UNICEF. The winner will be announced on ABC's *The View* TV show on Monday. We'll be checking this auction live on the show on Wednesday, April 23rd, 2003 with Marsha Collier, the author of *"eBay for Dummies"*.

Shipping will be via Priority Mail. Credit cards are accepted through PayPal.

• **Figure 17-6:** An auction using tables with the picture on the left.

The HTML code for this description goes like this (where the `<tr>` and `<td>` codes make up the table format):

```
<table align=center cellpadding=
   8 width='80%' border=7 cellspacing=
   0 bgcolor='White'>
<tr><td>
<center><font face='VERDANA,
   HELVETICA,ARIAL' color='crimson'
   size=5>
<B>"The View"<br>Cast
   Autographed<br>Coffee
   Mug</B></font><P>
<img width=250
   src='http://images.auctionworks.com
   /viewmug.jpg'>
</td>
<td>
<center><font face='verdana,
   helvetica,arial' color='crimson'
   size=3>
<b><i>Signed by</i><br><b>Joy
   Behar<br>Star Jones<br>Barbara
   Walters<br>Meredith Vieira</b>
</font><p>
<font
   face='verdana,arial,helvetica,sans
   serif' color='Black' size=2>
```

```
<B>All you fans of <i>The View</i>,
   this is your chance to own a coffee
   cup autographed by all four stars
   of the show. The proceeds from this
   auction will be donated to UNICEF.
   The winner will be announced on
   ABC's <i>The View</i> TV show on
   Monday. We'll be checking this auc-
   tion live on the show on Wednesday,
   April 23rd, 2003 with Marsha
   Collier, the author of <i>"eBay For
   Dummies"</i></B>.</font><P>
<font face='verdana,arial,helvetica,
   sans serif' color='Black' size=1>
Shipping will be via Priority Mail.
   Credit cards are accepted through
   PayPal. </font>
</center></td></tr></table>
```

Inserting additional photos in your listings for free

Many eBay sellers pay too much in fees by paying an additional $.15 for each image they put in their listings. Remember that every penny counts! Although Practice 25 goes into photo-hosting in depth, I want to put this code in this Practice — so you'll have it twice. To put one photo into your description, put the following text into the HTML view:

```
<img src="http://www.yourisp.com/
   yourimage.jpg" />
```

To put two images, one on top of the other, the code would look like this:

```
<img src="http://www.yourisp.com/
   yourimage.jpg" /><br>
<img src="http://www.yourisp.com/
   yourimage.jpg" />
```

Remember to insert your hosting ISP and your image name in the appropriate spots. For information on how to upload your images to a server, see Practice 25.

Creating Your Own HTML Templates

When you're ready to take on HTML in earnest, it really helps to have a few listing description templates all set up and ready to go. This is what the big guys, those top sellers on eBay, do (granted, some do a better job than others). Although it's fun to play around with using different graphics as you sell on eBay — and I must admit, I've seen some cute ones — having a standard look to your ads establishes you as a serious, professional PowerSeller. After all, how often does eBay change its look? (Okay, maybe that's a bad example if you wish that answer were *never*.) The answer is *not too often*. The colors and the basic look remain the same because this is eBay's very valuable brand.

What might go into a template? Well, you can insert your logo within your description, or add links to your Me page or your store, for example. Look at it this way: Your template can become your "brand."

Many auction-management services offer pre-designed templates for your descriptions, but they often charge a lot of money for their services. Alternatively, you can put together your own template and update it occasionally.

Some HTML editors can be overwhelming and hard to learn. What to do? I like to use eBay's Turbo Lister. Not only does it have a great built-in HTML editor, it also allows you to design your ads and save the templates to your own computer. Practice 19 teaches you the fine points of Turbo Lister.

Also, on my Web site, I offer a quick and easy HTML generator that you can download and use. It will give you an easy template that you can customize with your own touches. It takes only a little extra HTML knowledge to make the template your own.

The free ad tool is located on my Web site at

www.coolebaytools.com

When you land on my homepage, click the link in the navigation bar labeled Cool Free Ad Tool. You jump to my very cool instant-template page, shown in Figure 17-7.

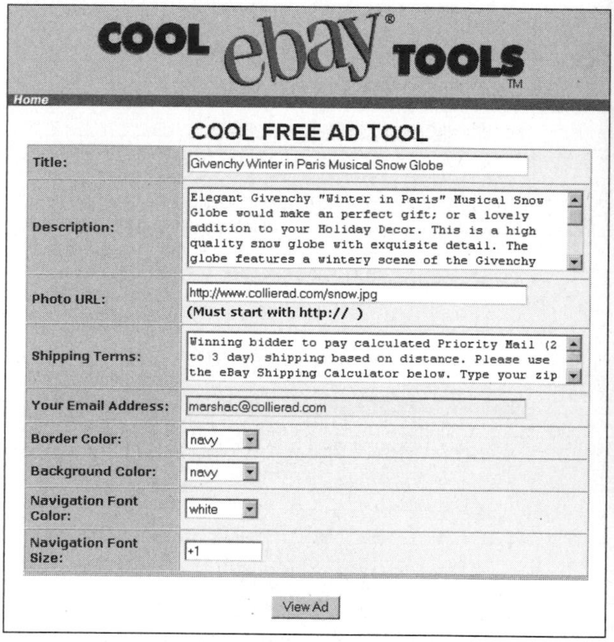

• **Figure 17-7: The Cool eBay Tools ad tool.**

To set up a quick eBay template using this tool, follow these steps:

1. **In the Title box, type the headline for your description.**

2. **In the Description box, enter a description.**

   You can copy and paste prewritten text from Notepad or a word-processing program, or just write your copy text as you go along.

3. **In the Photo URL box, enter the URL of your image.**

4. In the Shipping terms box, type in pertinent information. (If you don't want to include it, you don't have to.)

5. Enter the e-mail address that you use for eBay.

The address is used to put code in your description for an *E-mail for Questions* link. We do not keep your e-mail information (for oh, so many good reasons — and we figure you know 'em).

6. Select the border and background colors from the drop-down menus.

7. Click View Ad.

On the page that appears, you see how your new auction description looks (as in Figure 17-8).

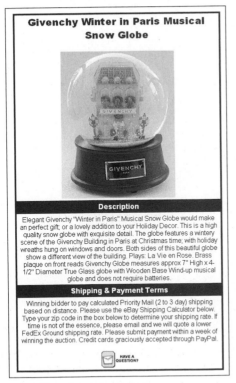

• **Figure 17-8: Your instant eBay ad.**

Scroll down and you see a box containing the auction-description HTML code. (See Figure 17-9.)

> **Copy & Paste the following code into the auction's description box:**
>
> ```
> <CENTER><table border="3" bordercolor="navy"
> cellspacing="0" cellpadding="0" width="500"
> bgcolor="#ffffff"><tr><td colspan="3"
> bgcolor="#ffffff"><center><font face="arial black"
> color="navy" size="+2">Givenchy Winter in Paris
> Musical Snow Globe </font><br><br><table border="0"
> width="500" bordercolor="#000000" cellspacing="0"
> cellpadding="5"><tr><td width=500 align="center"><img
> src="http://www.collierad.com/snowglobe.jpg"
> hspace="0" vspace="0" border="0"></td></tr> <tr><td
> align=center bgcolor="navy"><font color="white"
> size="+1"
> face="arial"><b>Description</b></font></td></tr><tr><td
>  align=center><font face="arial">Elegant
> ```

• **Figure 17-9: HTML coding for your auction.**

Your code can be copied and pasted directly into the eBay description area of the Sell Your Item form (or any eBay listing tool).

 I recommend saving the template you create in Window's Notepad, so you can have it available as a text file. That way, you can open it up at any time and simply change the description.

You can also use your template to practice HTML and develop more complex listings. Just save the text file as `filename.htm` and then open it up in your Internet browser to check out your work. By checking the View Source option (as in Figure 17-10), you can reopen the file in Notepad, make your edits, and reopen it again. Keep in mind you can always add more HTML codes to your auction description, or even add another picture.

Today eBay, tomorrow the planet.

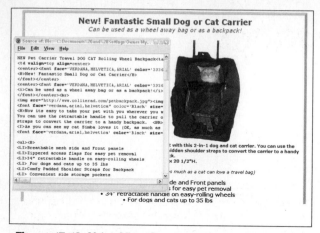

• **Figure 17-10:** Using View Source to save your template.

Practice 18

Writing Effective Listings

Why is it that some eBay sellers are successful while others can't seem to move their similar items? I get e-mails every week from sellers who just can't figure out why their listings aren't generating sales. For some reason, they're not moving items as quickly as they feel they should. And they sense that other sellers are highly successful despite those sellers' confusing and overly graphic ads.

This quandary sets the stage for the advice in this practice. Your item listings become your face to the buyers, and your auctions reflect your image. When you walk into a retail store; the décor projects an image. A visit to K-Mart (with the Blue Light special blaring from above) will give you an entirely different feeling from the one you get when you stroll into Nordstrom (when you're lulled into shopping paradise by the music of a pianist at a grand piano). This is your listings' goal: *to make prospective customers feel comfortable spending their money with you.*

Creating Unique, Eye-Catching Listings

As a seller, you may be tempted to adopt the selling style of other people whom you perceive as successful (imitation is the sincerest form of flattery?). But have you done the research to see whether the "professional" you're tempted to emulate is truly a "success"? Heck, even the pros have been known to do it; in my early days on eBay I tried copying the style of a seller who listed hundreds of items a day. (Hey, learn by doing.) But no matter how I tried, no dice — until I did a little homework and figured out that there was more to this seller than met the eye.

Sometimes the only way to know the real story is to do some online research. I looked at the completed listings from the "big-time" seller — and found that only about 1 in 20 of the listings resulted in the item being sold. So how on earth could this person be such a huge success on eBay? Here's the scoop:

✔ **Quantity does matter:** The seller listed hundreds of items per day, and whatever sold, sold. If it didn't sell on eBay, the item then came up for sale in the seller's retail location.

✔ **Service fees make money, too:** This seller was an *eBay Trading Assistant* (a seller who sells items on eBay for those who choose not to sell their own) — and charged clients a minimum fee to cover the time and expenses for every item listed. Those fees mount up.

 Research — whether it's for an item you plan on selling or buying, or for just about any situation you face on eBay — is your number-one tool for success. If you think that a certain seller is a whiz-bang success, confirm (or challenge) your suspicions by taking a look at that seller's completed listings.

As sellers, you need to concentrate on what works best for our own style of listings and the type of items you sell. Learning from other sellers can be helpful, but copying the look of someone else's listings is really a waste of time (not to mention unfair to the person who worked hard to develop his or her own branded templates).

Oddly enough, whether you sell auto parts or designer dresses, the basic rules for successful listings are the same. You may choose different colors for your descriptive text depending on whether you're an automotive seller or a fashion peddler, but what this practice tells you about the structure and content of your listing still applies.

 A successful listing gives prospective buyers the right information — in a pleasing manner that entices them to either place a bid or click the Buy It Now button. And you need a catchy title to lure the buyers' eyes up front so they get to your winning description. It's as simple as that!

Writing a Title That Sells

Your title is (next to your Gallery image) the most important way to draw people to your listing. eBay buyers are search-engine-driven — they find most of their items by typing selected keywords into the search box and clicking the Search button. Those keywords should be all your title consists of. No fancy prose. No silly words that people won't search for. Treat your titles with respect. Titles are not advertising, they are tools for the eBay search engine. If your title reflects what prospective buyers want, they'll click your listing to find out more.

 Many eBay sellers use comments in their titles — but I say, "Don't." While teaching classes at eBay University, I've polled the students and have still to find anyone who searches for these words: Nice, LQQK, Must See, Great, WOW, or Cool.

Here are a few examples of eBay's worst title words:

✔ L@@K

✔ Nice

✔ WOW

✔ Fantastic

✔ stunning

✔ RARE

Do yourself a favor — *never* include these words in your title. No one searches for them — ever! (For that matter, nobody's looking for "!!!!!!" in the title, either. Can't think why . . .)

 If you've finished writing your item title and you have spaces left over, *please* fight the urge to pepper it with exclamation points and asterisks. No matter how gung-ho you are about your item, the eBay search engine may overlook your item if the title is encrusted with meaningless ****, $$$$, and !!!! symbols. If bidders do see your title, they may become annoyed by all that virtual shrillness and ignore them!!!!!!!! (See what I mean?)

Take a look at some actual item titles and think about how you could improve them:

- MS65 PCI FULL STRUCK 1921 MORGAN DOLLAR NICE!

- GARLIQUE, All Natural, 60 Tablets, WOW!!

- VINTAGE SET PORCELIAN ROSES**LQQK**NR**

- GREAT Fendi purse Must see!!!!

- COOL! *BLACK ONYX* silver pendant

There is plenty of room in these titles to list colors, types, sizes, and more descriptive nouns that would make better use of the space. ***Bottom line:*** Use as many *keywords* as the title will allow.

Avoid ALL CAPITAL titles

The reason scribes of long ago invented upper- and lowercase letters was that they made phrases and sentences easier to read. When titles appear in all capitals, they are not interpreted as quickly by prospective buyers when their eyes dance over a search result or page.

A very distracting habit of even successful sellers is overdoing capital letters. To buyers, seeing everything in caps is LIKE SEEING A CRAZED SALESMAN SCREAMING AT THEM TO BUY NOW! Using all caps online is considered *shouting* — it's annoying and tough on the eyes. Use capitalization SPARINGLY, and only to finesse a particular point or name.

Take a look at Figure 18-1. I did a search on the useless eBay keyword *stunning*. Notice how the titles all in capitals are the most difficult to read in the results. It's easy to see that in a page loaded with hundreds of listings, those in upper- and lowercase text combined are easier to read.

☐	STUNNING SIGNED PHOTO PRINT OF BRUCE SPRINGSTEEN	ℙ $6.00	-
☐	~~ NICE & GORGEOUS 22K GOLD STUNNING EARRING ~~	ℙ $0.01	-
☐	BEAUTIFUL & GORGEOUS 22K GOLD STUNNING PENDANT	ℙ $0.01	-
☐	Stunning 6-7mm white freshwater pearl bracelet bangle	ℙ $9.99	-
☐	GORGEOUS STUNNING 22K GOLD TRADITION BRACELET	ℙ $0.01	-
☐	Exclusive stunning official Vatican large photo book	ℙ $90.00	-
☐	.012ct SI Stunning White Genuine Loose Diamond Round	ℙ $0.99	1

• **Figure 18-1: Some *stunning*-ly unsuccessful listings.**

Using uppercase letters for a few, select words in your title is okay. Take a look at the titles listed here; decide for yourself which ones make effective use of capital letters:

- NIB Cloud Dome White Photo Background PORTABLE BOARD STAGE

- Rare LOU GEHRIG Authentic Signed 1934 baseball card NR

✔ HIGH RELIEF 1921 PEACE DOLLAR PCGS MS65 NR

✔ NEW NFL Bobblehead BRIAN URLACHER Chicago Bears Limited Edition

✔ NEW Ladies Black Wool Kenneth Cole Skirt $79 Size 8 NR

✔ BEAUTIFUL VINTAGE 23" ARMAND MARSEILLE DOLL

Look for keywords that pay off

Hands down, the most valuable real estate on eBay is the 55-character title of your item. The majority of buyers do title searches, and that's where your item must come up to if it's going to be sold!

Here are some ideas to help you fill in the keywords in your item title:

✔ **Use the most common name for the item.** If there's room, list the alternate name For example, say salt *shaker* — and if there's room, add *cellar*.

✔ **If the item *is* actually rare or hard to find, okay, mention that.** But instead of the word *RARE* (so overused it's practically invisible), include the acronyms (OOAK, OOP, or HTF) that eBay users have come to rely on. (No, they aren't cartoon noises; Table 18-1 in the next section lists what they mean.)

✔ **Mention the item's condition and whether it's new or old.** When applicable (as with gently used items), include the item's age or date of manufacture.

✔ **Mention the item's special qualities,** such as its style (for a handbag), model (for a camera), or edition (for a book).

✔ **Include brand names,** if those names are significant. If you're selling a for-real Tiffany lamp, you want people to know it!

✔ **State the size of the item or other descriptive information,** such as color or material content.

Many savvy eBay sellers go to a special link, `http://data.terapeak.com/title builder`, free from Terapeak. Terapeak has great subscription services (see Practice 5 for more information on them), but they also offer a free service called Title Builder. It will help you select keywords for your item's title — based on current successful eBay sales. Figure 18-2 shows Title Builder at work when putting together a title for a camera lens.

Keyword:	Listings:	Avg. Price:	Avg. Shipping:	Max Price:	Min Price:	eBay:
Lens	85	$7.31	$3.06	$16.95	$0.99	View
For	49	$7.39	$3.05	$27.95	$0.99	View
Snap-on	25	$7.95	$3.24	$14.95	$4.99	View
Mm	24	$8.41	$3.23	$14.95	$4.99	View
Replacement	21	$8.27	$3.10	$14.95	$4.99	View
Rear	18	$6.12	$2.68	$14.00	$0.99	View
Body	17	$5.12	$2.37	$9.95	$0.99	View
62mm	10	$6.43	$2.70	$9.50	$3.99	View
58mm	10	$5.64	$2.75	$12.00	$1.49	View
77mm	9	$10.64	$2.80	$16.95	$4.99	View
Front	9	$5.77	$2.16	$12.00	$1.49	View
52mm	9	$5.42	$2.52	$7.50	$1.90	View
Brand	9	$4.44	$2.00	$12.00	$1.49	View
72mm	8	$10.47	$2.80	$13.95	$9.95	View

• **Figure 18-2:** The tool shows which keywords brought the highest price as you build your own title.

This particular secret is especially handy for PowerSellers: Another subscription service, View Tracker by Sellathon (you can get 30 days free by scrolling down on this page: `www.sellathon.com/?af=0-186`) will let you review your listings — once you've input a snippet of HTML into your description — to let you know which keywords in your titles are performing best for you. Take a look at Figure 18-3 for my current keywords. Notice also how important those keywords are: For approximately 500 listings tracked, buyers searched with Titles only over 98 percent of the time.

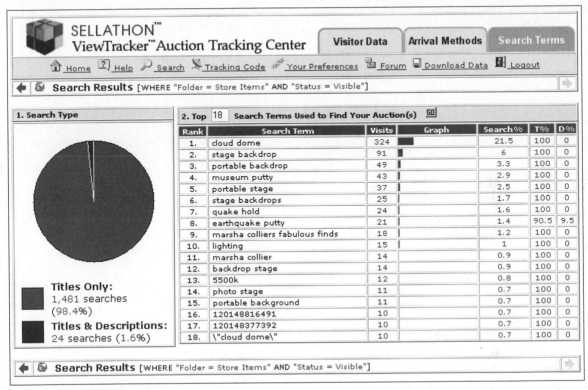

SELLATHON™
ViewTracker™ Auction Tracking Center

Visitor Data | **Arrival Methods** | **Search Terms**

⌂ Home | ? Help | 🔍 Search | ✗ Tracking Code | ✏ Your Preferences | 📑 Forum | 💾 Download Data | Logout

Search Results [WHERE "Folder = Store Items" AND "Status = Visible"]

1. Search Type

2. Top 18 Search Terms Used to Find Your Auction(s)

Rank	Search Term	Visits	Graph	Search%	T%	D%
1.	cloud dome	324		21.5	100	0
2.	stage backdrop	91		6	100	0
3.	portable backdrop	49		3.3	100	0
4.	museum putty	43		2.9	100	0
5.	portable stage	37		2.5	100	0
6.	stage backdrops	25		1.7	100	0
7.	quake hold	24		1.6	100	0
8.	earthquake putty	21		1.4	90.5	9.5
9.	marsha colliers fabulous finds	18		1.2	100	0
10.	lighting	15		1	100	0
11.	marsha collier	14		0.9	100	0
12.	backdrop stage	14		0.9	100	0
13.	5500k	12		0.8	100	0
14.	photo stage	11		0.7	100	0
15.	portable background	11		0.7	100	0
16.	120148816491	10		0.7	100	0
17.	120148377392	10		0.7	100	0
18.	\"cloud dome\"	10		0.7	100	0

Titles Only:
1,481 searches
(98.4%)

Titles & Descriptions:
24 searches (1.6%)

Search Results [WHERE "Folder = Store Items" AND "Status = Visible"]

• **Figure 18-3:** Keywords most searched in my listings.

eBay lingo at a glance

Here's a crash course in eBay lingo that can help bring you up to speed on attracting buyers to your auction. Table 18-1 summarizes some abbreviations used frequently in eBay listings; they can do wonders to jump-start your title.

Also, a generous smattering of acronyms that abbreviate item characteristics are part of the eBay business experience. As eBay has grown, so has this specialized lingo. Members use these acronyms as shortcuts to describe their merchandise.

So here, as promised, is Table 18-1: a handy list of common acronyms and related phrases used to describe items on eBay. (***Hint:*** *Mint* means "may as well be brand new," not "cool chocolate treat attached.")

Normally you can rely on eBay slang to get your point across, but make sure that you mean it *and that you're using it accurately.* Don't label something MIB (Mint in Box) when it looks like it's been Mashed in Box by a meat grinder. (You'll find more abbreviations on my Web site at `www.coolebay tools.com`.)

Use the spell checker to verify your titling! It bears repeating: Check and recheck your spelling. Savvy buyers use the eBay search engine to find merchandise; if the name of your item is spelled wrong, the search engine can't find it. In addition, poor spelling and incomprehensible grammar reflect badly on you. If you're in competition with another seller, the buyer is likelier to trust the seller *hoo nose gud speling.*

TABLE 18-1   **A QUICK LIST OF EBAY ACRONYMS**

eBay Code	What It Abbreviates	What It Means
MIB. NIB	Mint in Box or New in Box	The item is in the original box, in great shape, and just the way you'd expect to find it in a store.
MIMB	Mint in Mint Box	The box has never been opened and looks like it just left the factory. Usually for collectible items that need to be in their boxes to command top dollar.
MOC	Mint on Card	The item is mounted on its original display card, attached with the original fastenings, in store-new condition.
CIB	Cartridge/Instructions/Box	Refers to video games sold in their original boxes with instructions. All three items are included.
FE	First edition	First edition of a book.
NRFB	Never Removed from Box	Just what it says, as in "bought but never opened."
COA	Certificate of Authenticity	Documentation that vouches for the genuineness of an item, often accompanying (say) an autograph or painting.
OEM	Original Equipment Manufacture	You're selling the item and all the equipment that originally came with it, but you don't have the original box, owner's manual, or instructions.
NBW	Never Been Worn	New apparel items that may have been sitting around in someone's closet for awhile — but have never been worn.
OOAK	One of a Kind	You are selling the only one in existence!
NR	No Reserve Price	You can set a *reserve price* when you begin your auction. If bids don't meet the reserve, you don't have to sell. Many buyers are leery of reserve prices because they're after a more obvious bargain. If you're not listing a reserve price for your item, let bidders know.
NOS	New Old Stock	New merchandise that may be retired, discontinued, or no longer sold in retail outlets.
NWT	New with Tags	An item, possibly apparel, is in new condition with the tags from the manufacturer still affixed.
HTF, OOP	Hard to Find, Out of Print	Out of print, only a few ever made, or people grabbed up all there were. (HTF doesn't mean you spent a week looking for it in the attic.)

Add information with a subtitle

eBay allows you to buy an additional 55-character subtitle, which will appear under your item title in a search or in a category browse. The fee for this extra promotion is 50 cents; in a few circumstances, it may be worth your while. Any text you input will *really* make your item stand out in the crowd — but (you knew there would be a *but,* didn't you?) these additional characters don't come up in a title search.

So if you have the same words in your subtitle as in your description, the words will be found either way with a title and description search. The benefit to having the subtitle is how it makes your listing stand out when users browse or look up your item during searches.

Copywriting, eBay-Style

A fabulous description goes a long way to upping your bottom line. Those aforementioned big guys don't leave any details out of their descriptions, so why should you? Don't think Hemingway here; think *infomercial*. Figure 18-4 shows a listing with a great description — and yours can be magnificent. All you have to do is click in the Description text box of the Sell Your Item form and start typing — glancing at this book now and then for sage guidance, of course.

Make your description complete

Here's a list of suggestions for writing an effective item description:

- **List the item's benefits.** Give the buyer a reason to buy your item and be enthusiastic when you list all the reasons everyone should bid on it. Unlike the listing's title, your description is where you can use as much space as you want. Be precise: tell how big the item is, what color, what kind of fabric, what design, and so on. Also, mention any alternative uses for the item — perhaps those pantyhose can also be used for straining yogurt?

- **Include the negative.** Don't hide the truth of your item's condition. Trying to conceal flaws costs you in the long run — in terms of (for openers) returned items, bad feedback, or (at very worst) a fraud investigation.

If the item has a scratch, a nick, a dent, a crack, a ding, a tear, a rip, missing pieces, replacement parts, faded color, dirty smudges, or a bad smell (especially if cleaning might damage the item), mention it in the description. If your item has been overhauled, rebuilt, repainted, or hot-rodded, say so. You don't want the buyer to flip out because you weren't truthful about imperfections or modifications.

- **Promote your other listings.** The pros always do a little cross-promotion, and it works. When the hosts on the morning news tell you to tune in for something special, they're trying to prevent you from turning to the competition. So, a word to the wise: If you're selling photography equipment *and* cat toys, be sure to point to *both* store categories.

- **While you're at it, promote yourself, too.** As you build your feedback rating, point out your terrific track record to potential bidders. Add statements like "I'm great to deal with. Check out my feedback." You can even take it a step farther by inviting prospective bidders to your About Me page (where you may also include a link to your personal Web site if you have one).

- **Spell out pre-sale details.** Occasionally, sellers offer an item as a *pre-sell* or *pre-sale* — an item that the seller doesn't yet have in stock but expects to. If you're offering this kind of item, be sure to spell out all the details in the description.

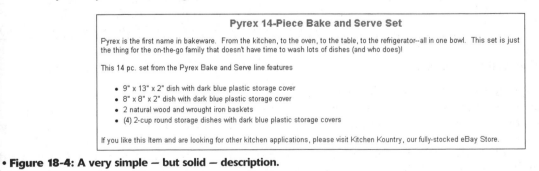

• Figure 18-4: A very simple — but solid — description.

eBay policy (and Federal Trade Commission law) states that you must ship a pre-sale item within 30 days of receiving payment, so be sure you will have the item within that time span. Also don't forget to include the actual shipping date. And don't forget that putting up an item for sale *without actually having it in hand* is a practice fraught with risk. The item you are expecting may not arrive in time, or it may arrive damaged. We've heard too many sad tales of sellers who got caught in this situation — and had to go out and purchase an item at retail for a buyer in order to preserve their feedback.

- **Invite questions**. Make the buyer comfortable with the idea of e-mailing you with a question. Some sellers seem way too busy (or full of themselves) in their text to make you want to ask a question. Remember, customer service is the key to high bids.

- **Wish your potential bidders well.** Communication is the key to a good transaction, and you can set the tone for your auction and post-auction exchanges by including some simple phrases that show your friendly side. Always end your description by wishing bidders good luck, inviting potential bidders to e-mail you with questions, and offering the option of providing additional photos of the item if you have them.

As with stores that hang up signs saying "No shirt, no shoes, no service," eBay members can refuse to do business with other members. You have the right to be selective (within reason and the law, of course) about whom

you want as a prospective buyer for your item. The listing is yours, and you can protect your investment any way you want. However, you can't discriminate or break any state or federal laws in your description.

If you've had bad experiences with certain members of the eBay community, you may block them as bidders from your business. Just don't be rude and negative. There's no faster way to turn off a bidder than by having more warnings and rules than you have description. Take a look at Figure 18-5 for a listing that doesn't exactly exude customer service.

Keep it positive

I'm sure many of us have run across listings that are overrun with negativity. What sells your item (aside from clear and complete information) is a positive tone throughout your description. Here are some examples of listings that come across as hostile:

- DO NOT BID ON MY ITEM UNLESS YOU UNDERSTAND AND FOLLOW MY STRICT POLICIES!

- If you have a less-than-10 feedback rating, do not bid — it will be cancelled.

- I will only send one e-mail requesting your information. If you don't respond, the item will be relisted and I will leave negative feedback!

- If the bidder does not contact me within three days of winning the auction, the item will be relisted and negative feedback will be given.

- WE WILL FILE NON-PAYING BIDDING ALERTS ON ALL DEADBEAT CUSTOMERS.

Description

DO NOT BID IF YOU DO NOT AGREE TO THESE TERMS!!!!!!!! IF YOU HAVE LESS THAN 10 POSITIVE FEEDBACKS, EMAIL ME FIRST!

PLEASE READ LISTING VERY CLOSELY BEFORE YOU BID! PAYMENT WITHIN THREE DAYS OF AUCTION. PAYPAL ONLY. DO NOT BID IF YOU DO NOT INTEND TO PAY. PLEASE KEEP EBAY SAFE FOR THE HONEST EBAYERS!!! US ONLY. DO NOT BID ON THIS AUCTION IF YOU HAVE LESS THAN 10 POSITIVE FEEDACKS!! CHECK OUT MY OTHER AUCTIONS!

• **Figure 18-5: Is this any way to start your description? Is that any way to attract new customers?**

I'm sure when you read those comments, you felt a bit queasy. Although there may be a reason for the seller to make those remarks, the way they're phrased makes the reader uncomfortable.

Try to use a nice tone when listing your sales requirements. That way, your verbiage won't set up what could (otherwise) be a positive transaction as an adversarial deal!

 Make your policies show up in smaller letters — I don't mean teeny-tiny, but smaller. This will get the practical message across without becoming overbearing.

Get the right perspective

Following these tips will go a long way to helping you raise your bottom line. Patti "Louise" Ruby (my tech editor on this book — and my coauthor on *eBay Listings That Sell For Dummies*) and I have two unique perspectives for enhancing an item description. They are always worth remembering:

- ✔ **Remember what your English teacher taught you.** Make your description like a woman's skirt: Long enough to cover the subject but short enough to keep it interesting.

- ✔ **Write your description as if you didn't have a picture.** Use words to draw a mental image of your item. That way, your prospective buyer will know what the item looks like if the photo server fails and the image doesn't show up. ("Electric guitar" just doesn't say much if what you're selling is a "near-mint Fender Stratocaster, American Deluxe Series, maple neck, abalone inlays, Transparent Crimson finish, gold hardware, in original plush-lined hardshell case.")

Remember these pearls of wisdom next time you write up a listing.

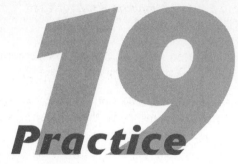

Practice 19

Listing Made Easy with Turbo Lister

In This Practice

- ✔ Organizing and tracking sale items
- ✔ Staying current with automatic updates
- ✔ Listing quicker with built-in templates

Okay, not much in this world is *free*, but eBay offers you a *free*, convenient tool you can use to list your items for sale: Turbo Lister. It's powerful software that provides a professional capability (and look) to the listings of medium-to-large-size eBay sellers. Turbo Lister helps you organize your items for sale, design listings, and upload them easily. It also facilitates future relisting by saving your initial item input and enabling you to create folders for organized storage. Your items disappear from Turbo Lister only if you delete them. As a PowerSeller, you reap the benefits of a consistent, professional look *and* a sustainable database of your items when you incorporate Turbo Lister into your listing practices.

Although you can find other services and software for listing on eBay at no cost, the reason I recommend using Turbo Lister is that it is eBay's own. There's no waiting for third-party programmers to update their software, so there's no associated risk of error or delay in listing your items when you want.

 Although you get the Turbo Lister program free, you're still responsible for any fees you incur by listing an item on the site.

Turbo Lister is robust software with the following features:

- ✔ **Self Updates.** Turbo Lister automatically updates itself regularly from the eBay site, and includes any new eBay enhancements so your listings always take advantage of eBay's latest features.

 Whenever you start the program and it finishes loading, it immediately checks with the eBay server for updates. Waiting for this update can be a bit tedious (especially if the servers are busy), so if you plan to list your items at a particular time, open Turbo Lister with a few minutes to spare.

- ✔ **HTML Templates.** Pre-designed HTML templates are built into the program's Listing Designer. If you use one of eBay's multitude of colorful themes or layouts, you'll be charged an additional $.10 on top of your listing fees. (To use these templates for free, see the upcoming InsiderSecret icon.) You can use a provided template or a template of your own design (without extra charge) to jumpstart your ad design. Simply paste it into the HTML view. You can even use templates from other sources, as long as they are in HTML format.

✔ **WYSIWYG Interface.** If you choose to design your own ads from scratch, you can do it with Turbo Lister's easy-to-use WYSIWYG (What You See Is What You Get) layout designer.

✔ **Bulk Listing Tool.** Prepare your listings whenever you have the time (say, the middle of the night when you can't sleep, or when an order comes in that you're not ready to list yet). When you're ready to launch a group of listings (or just one of them), transfer them to the upload area, and, well, upload them.

✔ **Item Preview.** You can preview your listings to be sure they will look just as you want them to before you upload them to eBay.

✔ **All Item Listing Capabilities** without being online. By using Turbo Lister (with its constant auto-upgrading), you will not sacrifice any of the features available to you when you list on the site using the Sell Your Item form.

In this practice, you'll have an inside look at how Turbo Lister works. Then, when you download the software, you can get up to speed quickly.

 Using Listing Designer can be a quick way to put a little pizzazz in your listings, but at ten cents a listing, it can take a big chunk of your bottom line over time. But if you subscribe to Selling Manager Pro (as I recommend), you pay no fees to use these templates.

Checking the Minimum Requirements

Though the Turbo Lister software is definitely useful, you have to decide whether it's really for you.

The first thing to check is whether your computer meets Turbo Lister's minimum requirements.

✔ Your computer must be a PC, not a Mac (sorry, Apple fans) running the Windows 2000, XP, or Vista operating system.

✔ The processor must be at least a Pentium II. The faster your processor, the better.

✔ You must have at least 128 MB of RAM (and that's a bare minimum).

 The more RAM you have, the better — and faster — things work.

✔ You should have at least 250 MB of free space on your hard drive to run the installation.

✔ Your monitor settings must be at least 800 × 600 resolution and 256 colors (8-bit). Keep in mind that the software interface looks a lot better with 16-bit color and 1024 × 768 resolution. All new monitors today have this capability, so you should be just fine here.

✔ Microsoft Internet Explorer should be version 5.5 or later.

 To check your version of Internet Explorer with the browser open, click the Help menu (shown in Figure 19-1). Click the About Internet Explorer command (Figure 19-2); on the top line, your Internet Explorer version number is listed.

• **Figure 19-1: Checking your version number.**

• **Figure 19-2: Now you know! In this example, I've got version 7.0.5730.11.**

Downloading Turbo Lister

If, for some reason, you can't use the DVD that came with this book, you can go to eBay to download the software. At the bottom of the eBay home page, you'll see a group of links like the ones shown in Figure 19-3. Click the handy Downloads link to display the eBay Downloads page (or go directly to `pages.ebay.com/turbo_lister`).

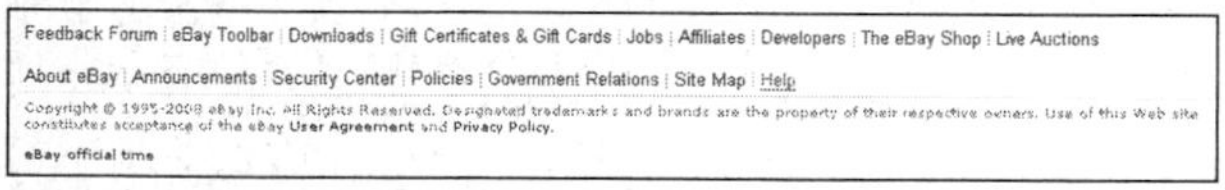

Feedback Forum | eBay Toolbar | Downloads | Gift Certificates & Gift Cards | Jobs | Affiliates | Developers | The eBay Shop | Live Auctions

About eBay | Announcements | Security Center | Policies | Government Relations | Site Map | Help

Copyright © 1995-2008 eBay Inc. All Rights Reserved. Designated trademarks and brands are the property of their respective owners. Use of this Web site constitutes acceptance of the eBay User Agreement and Privacy Policy.

eBay official time

• **Figure 19-3: eBay's valuable base-of-the-home-page navigation links.**

Now, to download Turbo Lister, follow these steps:

1. **Scroll down the eBay Downloads page to locate and click Turbo Lister link.**

The Turbo Lister hub page appears.

2. **Click the Download Now button.**

The requirements for using Turbo Lister appear below this button.

3. **Click the Turbo Lister Web Setup link.**

The Windows Security Warning appears (shown in Figure 19-4), cautioning that you're about to download something foreign to your computer.

4. **Click Yes.**

Clicking Yes downloads Turbo Lister. Clicking No doesn't. Just trust me (and eBay) and click Yes.

From this point on, installation is automatic until — voilà! You've got Turbo Lister on your computer!

Note that this procedure first downloads a small setup version of the program that checks your computer for preinstalled files. When that task is done, Turbo Lister checks back with the mothership and automatically downloads any files it needs.

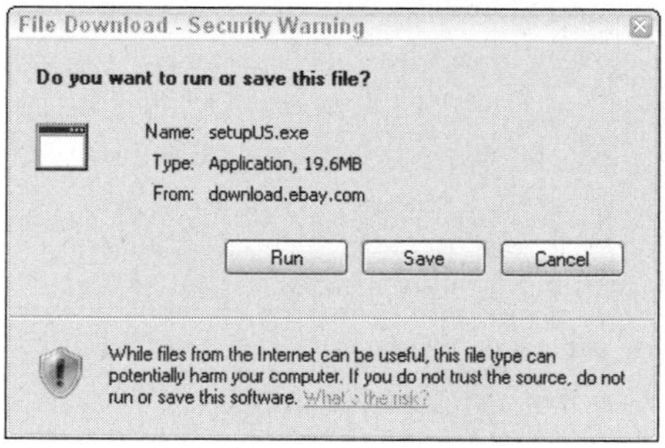

• **Figure 19-4: The Windows Security warning.**

Firing Up Turbo Lister

After you've installed the program, you'll see a new icon on your desktop; it's a little green man juggling magic pixie dust over his head. This is the icon for Turbo Lister. Double-click it, and you'll see the Turbo Lister Introduction screen shown in Figure 19-5. This will pop up every time you open the program and give you a handy little tip — if you like reading the tips, just click Next and you can read another.

If don't like seeing your tip-o-the-day every day, you can simply disable it (keep it from opening) by removing the check next to the box labeled Show Tips at Startup, and then click Done. The little green man's tip screen will be forever banished.

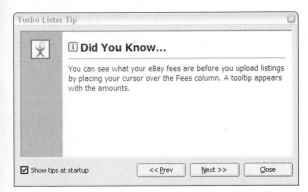

• **Figure 19-5: The useful Turbo Lister tip screen.**

When the program is open, the first thing you do is set up a new Turbo Lister file, as follows:

1. **Select that option from the opening splash, and click Next.**

2. **Type your eBay User ID and password in the blanks and click Next.**

   Turbo Lister now wants to connect back to eBay to retrieve your eBay account information. Make sure your Internet connection is live.

3. **After you check for a live Internet connection, click the Connect Now button.**

   In a minute or so, a small window opens with your eBay registration information (your name, address, and registered e-mail address). The last text block on the page offers you the option of listing locally.

4. **Click the down arrow in the corner of the last text box, and choose the eBay region within your metropolitan area, if there is one.**

   Your item will be searchable within your region of the United States.

5. **Click Finish, and the program fires up.**

Preparing the eBay Listing

When you have the powerful Turbo Lister tool ready to go to work for you, you can prepare hundreds of

eBay listings in advance — and, with one click of the mouse, launch them on eBay. You can also select a scheduling format that makes your listings upload and start at a particular time and date. (Find more on scheduling in the section, "Uploading items to eBay," later in this practice.)

This example lists an auction using these steps:

1. **Click the New button (the one with the Sun symbol) in the upper-left corner.**

   From the drop-down menu click *Create New Item*. The Create a New Item page appears, as shown in Figure 19-6. This is where you decide the type of listing you want and can enter title and subtitle if you like. You'll notice that most of the information requested is identical to the eBay Sell Your Item form.

• **Figure 19-6: The main Turbo Lister screen ready for action.**

> If you want to prepare your listings without Turbo Lister open, you can write your titles and descriptions before you even go into the program. You can type them into Notepad or Word, and then copy and paste them into the Turbo Lister form, adding the HTML tags after the text is inserted.

2. **Enter the title in the Item Title Box.**

If you want to use a subtitle, type that in as well. Subtitles are handy for adding selling points that accompany your title in search results. (Entering a subtitle for your listing adds an additional $.50 charge.)

3. **Select your category by clicking the Select button.**

You are presented with a screen that lists all eBay categories in a hierarchal format. The main categories are listed with a plus sign next to them. When you find your main category, click the plus sign, and subcategories are displayed, as shown in Figure 19-7. To drop even lower into the world of nether-categories, keep clicking plus signs next to subcategories. You know you've hit the bottom rung of the category ladder when you see only a minus sign.

 After you've used the program for a while, a list of your recently used categories will be accessible from a drop-down menu in the Category box.

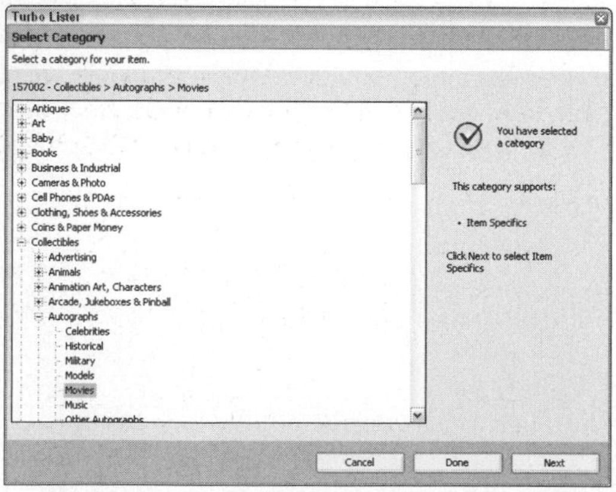

• **Figure 19-7: Select your category from the ample list.**

4. **If you have an eBay Store, select a category for the item in your store from the Store Category drop-down menu.**

Open the drop-down menu (shown in Figure 19-8) by clicking the small arrow on the right. Then click the category you want to use and watch it jump into the selection area.

This drop-down menu is automatically populated from your eBay Store when eBay updates your Turbo Lister installation.

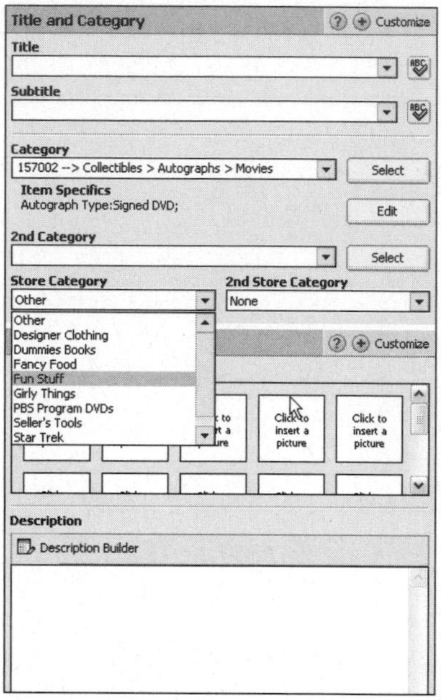

• **Figure 19-8: Select your eBay Store Category from the drop-down list.**

5. **Add your picture for Gallery and your description.**

This feature works the same as the Gallery feature on eBay's Sell Your Item form. Click the picture frame to evoke a menu to upload a picture from your computer.

If you host your pictures for eBay on an outside site to save money, click the Customize box next to Pictures and Description. Change the option from eBay Picture Services to Self-hosted pictures. This will change Turbo Lister to ask for URLs for your pictures. Just Click Picture URLs and type in the full URL (including the http://). Then, if you're online, click back to Pictures and you'll see a tiny thumbnail of your picture in a frame.

After you add your picture, it's time to start your description.

Designing your listing

If you're an HTML whiz, you can just type (or copy and paste from another program) your text into the Description Builder box. If you're like the bulk of eBay sellers, make it easy on yourself by clicking the words *Description Builder* to open a simple-to-use template designer, as shown in Figure 19-9. (Notice that the picture I loaded is already in the template form at the bottom.)

Turbo Lister
Listing Designer
Use Designer
$ fee applies
Themes
Layout
Picture Show
Other Tasks
Change photo hosting
Set default description
Help for this page
Enter Your Description
Help
Design View
HTML View
Preview
Times New Roman
3 (12 pt)
Inserts
100%
This item has a picture included in the description
Cancel
Save

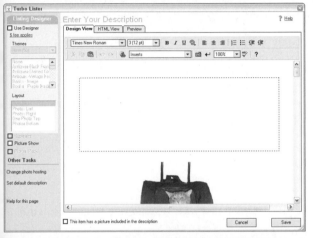

• **Figure 19-9: Turbo Lister's simple Description Builder tool.**

When it comes to designing your listing, you've got several options. Take a look at the Listing Designer templates on the left side of the screen. Click the Use Designer check box and the dazzling array of template names will go from gray (inactive) to black (active). (Having to activate the templates keeps you from accidentally using them without realizing you're spending ten cents.) Click a template and be dazzled by its glory. eBay makes it a snap to design your item listing — all with a few easy features:

- **Templates and Themes:** I'm sure you've seen eBay listings with very nice graphics in the borders. These come from eBay's easy-to-use theme templates listed at the left of the screen. You may select any of these colorful templates to doll up your listing. Keep in mind, though, that eBay charges you an additional $.10 to use one of these themes in your listing. You don't have to use any of the themes (just click None when you reach this screen).

Themes make the listing look pretty, but they may draw attention away from the selling strength of your pictures. Remember, it's your good description and a quality photo that will sell your item.

- **Layout:** You may select from several Layouts: Standard, Photos Left, Photos Right, One Photo Top, Photos Bottom, or Slide Show if you want to take advantage of eBay's Slide Show option.

When you use eBay Picture Services, the first picture is free. By using your first free picture, you can have a great-looking header picture at the top of your listing page. Additional pictures are 15 cents; a Picture Pack of one to six photos will cost you the princely sum of 75 cents.

- **WYSIWYG HTML Design Form:** You can base your ad on this very easy-to-use design form and come up with a listing that looks similar to the one shown in Figure 19-10. It has a toolbar very similar to the formatting toolbar in Microsoft Word (see Figure 19-11), so the buttons should be familiar. There's even a command to insert a Web link or online stored photo into your description (see Figure 19-12) by typing in the URL of the photo.

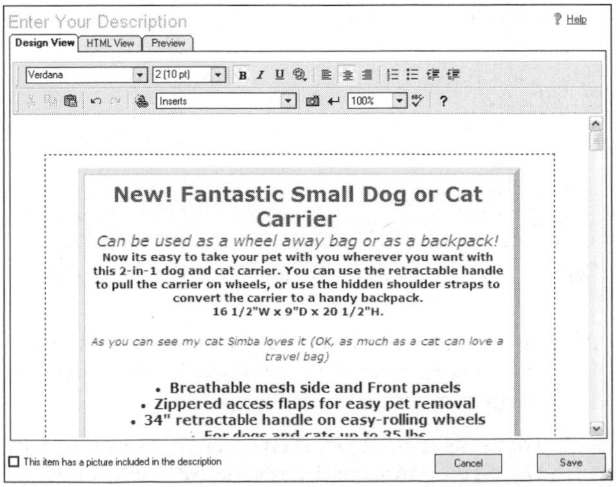

Enter Your Description
Help
Design View
HTML View
Preview
Verdana
2 (10 pt)
Inserts
100%
New! Fantastic Small Dog or Cat Carrier
Can be used as a wheel away bag or as a backpack!
Now its easy to take your pet with you wherever you want with this 2-in-1 dog and cat carrier. You can use the retractable handle to pull the carrier on wheels, or use the hidden shoulder straps to convert the carrier to a handy backpack.
16 1/2"W x 9"D x 20 1/2"H.
As you can see my cat Simba loves it (OK, as much as a cat can love a travel bag)
• Breathable mesh side and Front panels
• Zippered access flaps for easy pet removal
• 34" retractable handle on easy-rolling wheels
This item has a picture included in the description
Cancel
Save

• **Figure 19-10: The Design Your Listing page in Design View.**

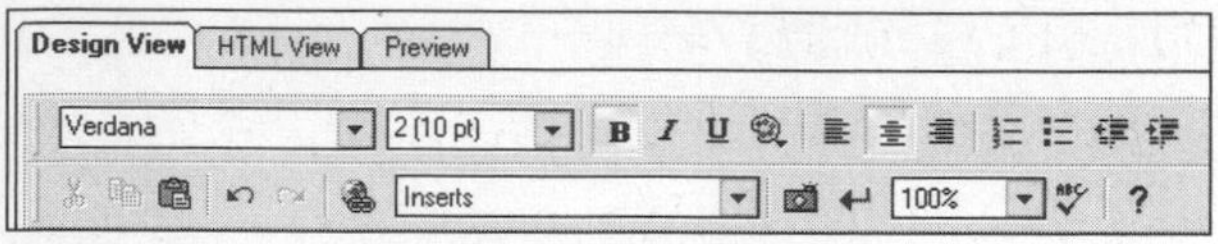

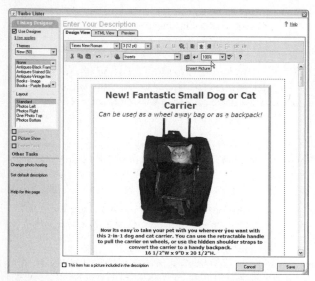

• **Figure 19-11: The HTML design toolbar.**

• **Figure 19-12: Inserting a photo in the description area.**

✔ **HTML View:** If you have a smattering of HTML knowledge, you may want to display the HTML view and edit your listing design from there. You can also insert your hosted images by entering supplementary coding into the HTML view. (See Practice 17 for additional information about coding and on inserting your pictures into the description area.) Also, if you have your own predesigned template, just copy and paste the HTML for the template into the HTML view box.

 At any time during the design process, click the Preview tab to see what your listing looks like.

 Be sure to add your Gallery picture using eBay's Picture Services so you can have the free header picture. Just click one of the boxes entitled *Click to Insert Picture*, select any picture on your computer's hard drive (or type in

the URL as described in the previous section), and the image will upload with your listing to eBay. When your picture appears in the Turbo Lister box, you're good to go.

Getting down to specifics

Now it's time to get all the little details into your listing. How many days do you want the listing to run? You must add your shipping and payment information, and more. You do all this on the left side of the Turbo Lister screen.

Much of this information is filled in for you by eBay, based on your listing defaults. You can edit the information pertaining to an option such as Payment Methods and Ship To Location by clicking the Edit or Options button in the appropriate box. Note that on this page, each format option has an Edit button. Clicking the Edit button opens a small box where you may add text or change defaults. After you make your changes, click OK. The new information appears in the appropriate box.

 Save time by saving repetitive text as the default. When you come to a box such as Payment Instructions or Payment Methods, and you want this exact information to appear in all your listings, click the Save for Future Listings check box to save this information as your default. You can always change the info on a case-by-case basis when listing another item.

Once you've filled out all the information in each of the Format Specifics areas, click Save, and you return to the main Turbo Lister screen.

Organizing your listings

Once you've put together a few listings, your Turbo Lister Item Inventory begins to look something like Figure 19-13.

 If you click and move the scroll bar at the bottom of your Inventory, the view scrolls to show you all the data that is stored for each listing.

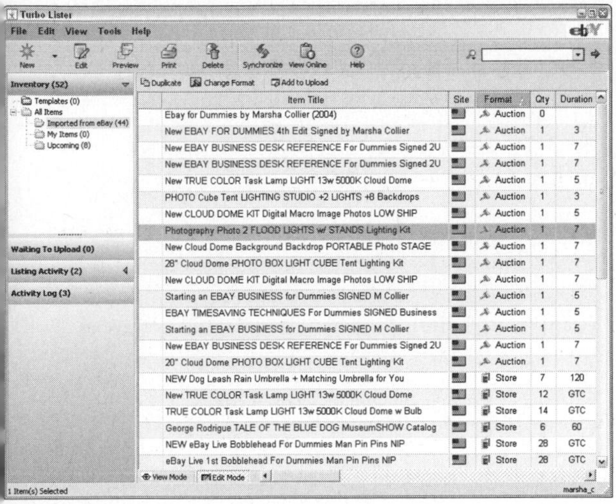

• **Figure 19-13: Turbo Lister Item Inventory.**

Note that you can add folders to the folder list on the left to save inventories for different categories of items.

Here's how to create a folder and move items into it:

1. **Click the New button (the one with the sun) and select the command to create a new folder.**

2. **Give your new folder a name and click OK.**

   The folder now appears in a folder list on the left side of the screen.

3. **Highlight a listing and drag it to your new folder.**

   You can save time if you press and hold the Control or the Shift key while selecting multiple items. Then you drag them to the folder all at once.

You now have the option of looking at your items in an All Items view (which includes those you have inserted into folders), or organized in categories (which you do by double-clicking to open the various folders).

Uploading items to eBay

Here's how you upload the items you see on Turbo Lister's Item Inventory tab:

1. **In the Item Inventory list, highlight the item you want to upload and click the Add to Upload button at the top of the list.**

   This copies your item to the Upload tab.

2. **If you want to schedule a listing to upload at a later date or time, click Schedule to Start On and choose a date and time after clicking the Add to Upload button.**

    You're charged an additional $.10 fee for any item you choose to schedule for a delayed listing.

3. **To double-check on your fees before listings (always a good idea), click the Calculate Fees button.**

   After a little pause, your screen will refresh and you can use the bottom scroll bar to see the fees you'll be charged.

   When you've populated your Waiting to Upload list, you can view it by clicking the tab, which looks similar to Figure 19-14.

• **Figure 19-14: Just waitin' around is what they're doing.**

4. **On the Waiting to Upload tab, click Upload All to send your items to eBay immediately.**

Instantly your items will be live on the site!

Practice
20

Managing Your Business with Professional Tools

In This Practice

✔ Managing your auctions through eBay

✔ Using Selling Manager and Pro

✔ Using e-mail effectively

✔ Checking out auction-management services

When you get to the point of running 20 or so listings a week (with an over-50 percent sell-through rate), I highly recommend that you start using a management tool. At this level of activity, eBay's Selling Manager will suit your needs nicely. But when your eBay business begins to push 60 or 70 listings a week, I even more highly recommend that you get additional help in the form of an auction-management service or software — Selling Manager Pro helps PowerSellers, too.

 Whether you use an online service or software installed on your own computer is a personal decision. You may find it easier to use an online system because you can log on to your selling information at any time — from any computer. But if you have a slow Internet connection or pay usage fees by the hour, managing your eBay business online can become impractical.

Most desktop-based software packages have features that enable you to do your work on your desktop computer and then upload (or download) your data when you go online. If your business doesn't actually *need* multiple locations to work from, and you run your eBay business from a single computer in your office, you may feel more comfortable with a desktop-based software product.

In either case, if your business has reached a level that demands an auction-management tool, congratulations! I want to save you some time finding the service or software that's right for you. In this practice, I outline some of the specific tasks that you can expect an auction-management product to provide. Since I'm a big fan of using eBay's Selling Manager, I go into that program in depth.

Choosing Your Auction-Management Tools

There's a huge difference between auction-*listing* software and sites, and auction-*management* products. If you just need help organizing your listings, then auction-listing software such as eBay's Turbo Lister (see Practice 19) may just do the trick. Combine that with eBay's Selling

Manager (a *management* program) and your eBay business will be humming along just fine.

When your business activity level increases and you turn to an auction-management solution for your eBay business, plan to look for certain standard features when you evaluate software and services. Also, consider what *information*-management features you currently have, courtesy of your bookkeeping program. You have the data there, regardless of whether you use it in a management solution.

 Never choose auction-management tools solely by price. Go to the various Web sites and take a look at everything they offer for the price stated. You may find a particular service that charges a bit more may just be worth it because of all the extra tools it offers — even if you don't need every tool just yet.

Looking for the essential features

Here are some of the must-have features to look for when you evaluate the offerings of auction-management services and products:

✔ **Image hosting:** Some Web sites dazzle you with high-megabyte storage numbers. Keep one thing in mind. If your average eBay image is around 40 KB (that's kilobytes, not megabytes) then in a 5MB storage space you could store around 128 pictures. In a 100MB storage space, you could hold around 2,500 images.

Unless you're a big-time seller, you really don't need that much space. Your eBay images should be archived on your own computer (how about in a folder called eBay Images?). Images for current listings should be on the hosted site only while the transaction is in progress. When the buyer has the item and all is well, you can remove the item image from the remote server.

 All eBay store sellers get 1 MB of storage for free, but check out Practice 25, where I talk about free image hosting. You most likely already have free image hosting on your ISP's Web site.

✔ **Designing listings:** The basis of most of these products is a good listing function. You'll be able to select from supplied templates or be able to design your own and store them for future use. An important feature now coming into use is a spell checker. There's nothing worse than a misspelling in a listing!

✔ **Uploading listings:** Most of these products have a feature that launches a group of listings to eBay all at once. They may also allow you to schedule auctions to get underway at a prescribed time.

You can also expect to be able to put together your listings at your leisure offline and upload them to your service. The service usually archives your past listings so you can relist at any time.

Many services also offer *bulk relisting* (relisting many items at once).

✔ **E-mail management:** Expect to have access to sample e-mail letters (templates) that you can customize with your own look and feel. The services will also offer auto-generated end-of-auction, payment-received, and/or shipping e-mail service.

✔ **Feedback automation:** Post feedback in bulk to a number of your completed listings, or leave predesigned feedback one by one. Some products support automatic feedback when a buyer leaves you a positive message.

✔ **Sales reports:** Some services (even the least expensive) offer you some sort of sales analysis. Be sure to take into account how much you really need these; base your estimate on data that you may already receive from QuickBooks, PayPal, and eBay Stores.

Exploring the advanced features

Depending upon the type of business you run, you may need some of the more advanced features offered by management products:

✔ **Inventory tools:** Management products may allow you to create inventory records for your different products, permitting you to click a quantity of items at a time to automatically list. When an item is sold, it is automatically deducted from your inventory.

✔ **Sales-tax tracking and invoicing:** With full management, you can expect your sales tax to be calculated into your invoices, and complete line-item invoices to be sent automatically. Multiple items, when purchased by the same buyer, will be combined.

✔ **Consignment tracking:** If you are a Trading Assistant, be sure to look for a product that enables you to separately track the merchandise you sell for different clients. You should also be able to produce reports of consignment sale by customer.

✔ **Shipping:** Most of the services will give you the option to print your packing lists and shipping labels directly from the product. Some of the larger services integrate with the major shippers, allowing you to ship directly from within the software.

Table 20-1 gives you the dollars and cents of subscribing to various online and offline services. To put together these tables, I disregarded lower subscription levels where companies offered only listing products. These are the lowest prices for products that are truly management tools.

Now that you've heard how the big guys think, let's start small. Many eBay sellers sell part-time.

TABLE 20-1: REPRESENTATIVE AUCTION MANAGEMENT

Name	URL	Prices Start at	Number of Closings	Image Hosting?
AAA Seller	http://www.aaaseller.com/fees.asp	$9.95/month	Unlimited	YES 50 MB
Andale	cms.vendio.com/corp/pricing_corp.html	$10.95/month	40	YES 3 MB
Auction Wizard 2000	www.auctionwizard2000.com/Compare.htm	$75 first year $50 renewal	Unlimited	NO
Auctiva	www.auctiva.com	FREE	Unlimited	YES Unlimited
ChannelAdvisor MarketplaceAdvisor	www.channeladvisor.com/products/marketplace advisor/mpa_fees.html	$29.95/month plus 2% final value on auctions ($.20 min)	Unlimited	YES 100 MB
eBay Selling Manager	pages.ebay.com/selling_manager/	$4.99/month FREE with Basic Store	Unlimited	NO 1 MB with Basic Store
eBay Selling Manager Pro	pages.ebay.com/selling_manager_pro/	$15.99/month FREE with High Tier stores	Unlimited	NO
eLister (for MAC)	www.blackmagik.com/elister.html	$19.95 for 3 months	Unlimited	NO
InkFrog	www.inkfrog.com/pricing.php	$9.95/month	Unlimited	YES 300 MB
Shooting Star	www.foodogsoftware.com	$120.00 first year $60.00 renewal	Unlimited	NO
Meridian	www.noblespirit.com/products-pricing.html	$9.95/month	25 (Sold Auction only)	YES Unlimited

Observing the progress of their auctions is part of the fun, and also serious business when they rely on the money they earn from auctions as a regular source of income. Using eBay's tools — such as the Selling page of My eBay, Selling Manager, and Selling Manager Pro — can help the part-time (and even full-time) seller keep track of all the transactions they're juggling on eBay.

 Selling Manager Pro adds many additional options for post-auction management, bulk e-mail and inventory — all of which are perfect for enhancing PowerSeller practices.

Using My eBay to Manage Your Listings

Start managing your listings with baby steps (the best way to start) by visiting the Selling tab of My eBay. For the newbie seller (and even a small PowerSeller who sells a low number of high-priced items), the tools on the Items I'm Selling page work great. They're simple and get right to the point.

 A PowerSeller with fewer listings can use the Items I'm Selling page in combination with Turbo Lister for uploading listings, and these should be sufficient for managing those listings.

For example, Figure 20-1 shows the Items I'm Selling page of My eBay. This feature alone gives you quite a bit of information you can use to track your auctions as they happen.

 The Items I'm Selling page uses a color code that helps you see right away what's going on. If the current price listed for an auction appears in green, a bid has been placed on the item. If it's red, there have been no bids. Fixed-price listings (including store inventory items) show up in black.

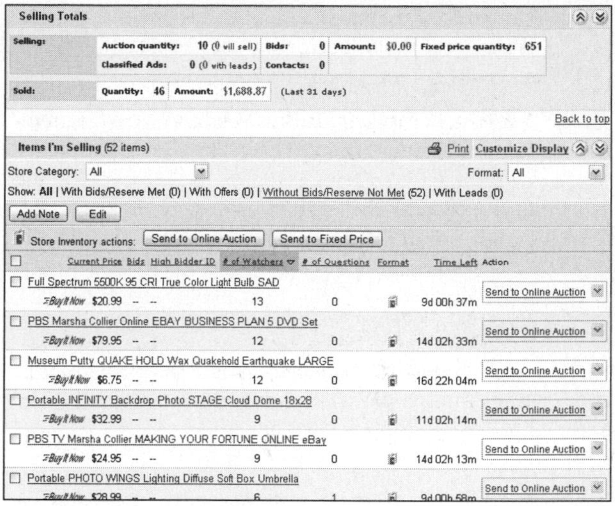

• **Figure 20-1:** The Items I'm Selling page.

Tracking active listings

On the Items I'm Selling page, you can view details for your active listings — you can customize the display by clicking the link you want to customize, including these:

- **Links for listings.** Each listing has clickable links you can use to go instantly to an item page.

- **Item Number.** Just in case you need an item number to contact a bidder or send auction information to a friend, you'll find the item number here.

- **Current Price.** This may be the starting price of your item (if you have no bids) or the current price, based on bids received.

- **Reserve Price.** This is a very handy feature that reminds you of the reserve price you've set on an item. There's nowhere else to check this; if you forget to write it down when you're listing the auction, you can still find it here.

- **Quantity Available.** Here's where you can see how many of this item are still available for purchase on the site. As you can see in Figure 20-1, when an eBay Store item is listed, this feature shows you how many are left and the original quantity you listed.

✔ **# of Bids.** When you see that the price is rising on an item, check out this column to see how many bids have been placed to date.

✔ **# of Watchers.** The number of people who have selected your item and put it in their My eBay Watch lists.

✔ **# of Questions.** If you have customer questions pending, they will show up here.

✔ **Start Date.** This is the date the listing was posted on eBay.

✔ **Time Left.** In this column, you can check how much time is left (to the minute) in your listing.

✔ **Drop-down Action Menu.** The drop-down action menu has links that perform different actions, depending on whether the listing is a store or an auction item.

Store Items will have most of these options:

✔ **Send to Online Auction.** Click here if you'd like to send one of your items out of the store and into an auction listing.

✔ **Send to Fixed Price.** Here you can send an item to a fixed-price listing.

✔ **Respond.** If there are questions pending you can click here to respond.

✔ **Sell Similar.** List a similar item, using the exact same template as that of the item listed.

✔ **Revise.** As long as you have no sales, you can make a change in your listing.

✔ **Add To Description.** If you've sold items from your listing, you may only add to your description; you may not make changes to the core of the listing.

✔ **End Item.** If the dog ate it, click here.

✔ **Mark As Answered.** If you answered questions elsewhere, as in direct e-mail or from My Messages, it still may show up here. Click to make them go away.

Auction listings have similar links that have the same definitions as listed here: Sell Similar, Search in Want It Now, Revise, Add To Description, and End

Item. It's a much more limited selection of options than for the store items.

If you don't see all the options from the preceding bullet points on your My eBay Selling page, click the Customize link in the upper-right corner to be able to view the data you want to track.

If you have an eBay Store, the Selling Totals tally won't include revenue for store items that have sold. If you have an eBay Store, I strongly recommend using Selling Manager (hey, it comes *free* with your store!).

Checking sold items

There's also an area where your sold items appear, called (coincidentally) Items I've Sold. When the selling cycle is over and someone has purchased an item, it shows up here.

And, alas, the unsold items

Sob. Sadly, there's an area that lists items that just didn't pique the interest of eBay shoppers — at least this week. (Remember, there's always another selling day on eBay.) From here, for up to 30 days, you can click the Relist link to relist an item on the site.

If your unsold item sells on the second (repeat) listing, eBay refunds your listing fee for the originally unsold item if the second listing is successful.

Ramping Up with Selling Manager

Once the selling bug has bitten you, it's a natural transition to go from listing a few items a month to 50 or more. That means, dear reader, that you are now officially running an eBay business. Congratulations!

There's a good side *and* a bad side to this. The good is that you're making considerably more cash than you did before hooking up with eBay. The bad? It's time to start investing in some tools to keep your business professional.

The first tool I recommend to smooth your transition (as you're juggling more listings) is Selling Manager. This program makes the process of running eBay auctions and sales consistent.

Practice 19 tells you about eBay's *free* Turbo Lister program (it gets your items on the site without having to go through the slow, sometimes-torturous Sell Your Item form). As with Turbo Lister, Selling Manager is a suite of tools for managing your selling business from any computer (as long as it has an Internet connection). eBay gives you 30 days to try out the service for free, thereafter charging you $4.99 per month. (Believe me, the time that Selling Manager will save you is well worth the fee.)

 I've run well over 60 auctions in a single month, successfully managing them with Selling Manager Pro. I use it, along with PayPal's tools and QuickBooks. This approach provides a professional solution for my medium-size eBay business.

Getting a first glimpse of Selling Manager

To sign up for the Selling Manager program, follow these steps:

1. **Click the Site Map link below the eBay Navigation Bar at the top of every eBay page.**

2. **In the second column of the Site Map, under the Selling Tools heading, click the link for Selling Manager.**

3. **Read the information on the Selling Manager hub page and click the Subscribe Now link.**

You're now subscribed. If you continue using Selling Manager, eBay will add the additional $4.99 fee to your monthly bill (unless you have a basic eBay Store). eBay will automatically populate Selling Manager for you with your information from the My eBay Selling tab. The Selling tab will change to Selling Manager when it's all set up.

With Selling Manager, you can click the tab to view a summary of all your auction activities. Figure 20-2 shows a portion of my current Selling Manager Pro Summary page. Note that the Summary pages look the same; the differences between the Standard and Pro editions are embedded in the links.

• **Figure 20-2: My Selling Manager Pro Summary page.**

The Summary page lists at-a-glance statistics so I can see what's going on with my sales quickly, at any time — from any computer. This page also includes links to other pages in the Selling Manager tool. Please note that it would take an entire book to outline all the tools that are part of Selling Manager and Selling Manager Pro. I highly recommend that you go to this page on eBay for the lowdown:

```
pages.ebay.com/selling_manager/
   comparison.html
```

There you can look at the comparison chart to see just how much you can do with Selling Manager.

If you plan to exceed 50 transactions a month, consider using Selling Manager Pro (it has bulk feedback and bulk invoice-printing features that save you time and trouble) or a third-party solution.

Reviewing scheduled listings

The Scheduled Listings link on the Summary page takes you to any auction, fixed-price, or store listing you've sent to eBay through Turbo Lister (or listed on the Sell Your Item page) and scheduled for a later starting date or time. You can also view these pending listings through links on the Summary page that narrow them down to *Listings starting within the next hour* and *Listings starting within the next day*.

When you enter the Scheduled Listings area by clicking a pending listing link from the Summary page, you can go directly to that listing, as shown in Figure 20-3. If you want to promote your listing-to-be in a banner ad — or create a link to it from elsewhere on the Internet — you can do so using the URL of the pending listing.

 Just in case you're planning a big getaway, you can schedule a maximum of 3,000 listings and up to three weeks in advance.

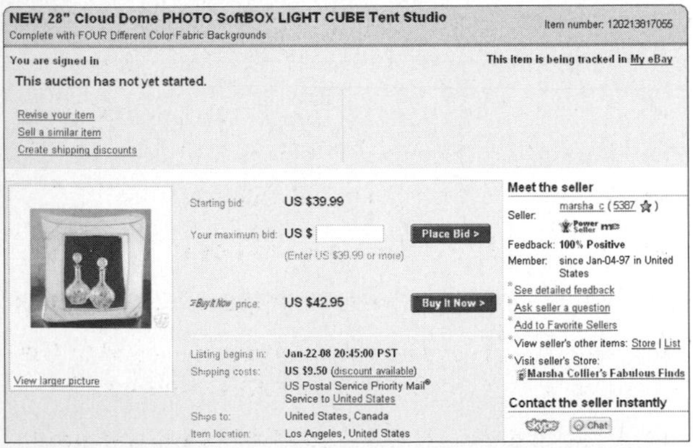

• **Figure 20-3: What an auction looks like before it starts.**

From the pending listing's page, you can confirm all information about the sale, as well as make any changes to the listing or to the scheduling time.

Observing active listings

Click the Active Listings link on the Summary page, and you can observe the bidding action just as you can from the My eBay Items I'm Selling page. The color-coding that indicates bidding activity is the same as on the My eBay Items I'm Selling page, and your listings are accessible with a click of your mouse.

You have the option to show only auctions, store listings, or fixed-price items on the Active Listings page. You can also search your own listings by keyword or item number.

> For more about active listings, visit the Summary page, which includes links to items ending within the hour and those ending within the next 24 hours.

Looking at the status of sold listings

The Sold Listings feature (which you get to by clicking its link on the Summary page) is where Selling Manager really shines. You'll find quite a few links that organize your sold items, including these:

- **Awaiting Payment:** This is where items that have been won or bought are listed before a payment is made.

- **Awaiting Payment, Items that Are Eligible for Non-Paying Bidder Alerts:** Items that are awaiting payment are listed when they become eligible for you to file a Non-Paying Bidder Alert. This happens when 7 days have passed without a payment being received.

- **Paid and Ready to Ship:** If you input the fact that a buyer has sent payment, or if the buyer pays via PayPal, the transaction automatically moves to this category.

- **Paid and Ready for Feedback:** Once an item is paid for, a reference to it appears here so you can keep track of the feedback you need to leave.

- **Paid and Shipped:** These are (you guessed it) items for which the buyer has paid, and you've indicated on the transaction record that you shipped the item.

✔ **Unpaid and Eligible for Final Value Fee Credit:** This is the sad category where buyers from the Non-Paying Bidder column go if, after all your attempts to get action, they have not responded and sent payment. (If they don't cough up within 10 days after you file a Non-Paying Bidder Alert, the listing moves to this category automatically.)

Accessing archived listings

From the Archived Listings link, you can access completed transactions that closed within the last three months. You can also download this information to your computer. There are good sales records here; download them and keep them.

Selling Manager Pro File Management Center

The File Management Center link — on the left side of the Summary page (waaay at the bottom) — is a powerful link that takes you to a page with links to your sales reports as in Figure 20-4. These links enable you to export your sales history by item as a Microsoft Excel–compatible file and download it to your computer. (Read the next section, "Sales Reports Plus," for a bunch more information on other reports you can get — and how you get them.)

You can download the following reports and items using the File Management Center:

✔ Item Listing templates

✔ Product Inventory templates

✔ Upload Results file

✔ Inventory Reports

✔ Active Listings

✔ Awaiting Payment

✔ Paid Awaiting to Ship

✔ Sold and Unsold Items

✔ Archived Items

✔ All Sold and Archived

✔ Inventory Products

• **Figure 20-4: Selling Manager Pro's File Management Center.**

Your eBay sales reports include important information about your transactions and download in a spreadsheet format. Here is some of the information you can expect to find in the reports you download:

✔ **Sales Record Number:** This is the number assigned to the transaction by Selling Manager for identification purposes.

✔ **User ID:** The eBay User ID of the person who purchased the item from you.

✔ **Buyer Zip:** The buyer's ZIP code.

✔ **State:** The state the buyer resides in.

✔ **Buyer Country:** The country your buyer lives in.

✔ **Item Number:** The eBay number assigned to the item when you listed it for sale on the site.

✔ **Item Title:** The title of the listing as it appeared on eBay.

✔ **Quantity:** The number of items purchased in the transaction.

✔ **Sale Price:** The final selling price of the item.

✔ **Shipping Amount:** The amount you charged for shipping the item.

✔ **Insurance:** If the buyer paid insurance, it will be listed next to the sales record.

✔ **State Sales Tax:** If you've set up Selling Manager to calculate sales tax for your in-state sales, and sales tax was applied to the item when it was sold, that amount is listed here.

✔ **Total Price:** This is the GSA (Gross Sales Amount) for the transaction.

✔ **Payment Method:** The method of payment used by the buyer. This is inserted automatically if the item is paid through PayPal or you insert it manually (if paid by another method).

✔ **Sale Date:** The date the sale transaction occurred on eBay.

✔ **Checkout:** The date of checkout. This is usually the same as the transaction date.

✔ **Paid on Date:** The date the buyer paid for the item.

✔ **Shipped on Date:** The ship date you entered in Selling Manager.

✔ **Feedback Left:** Indicates whether you left feedback for the buyer by a Yes or No in this column.

✔ **Feedback Received:** The feedback rating (Positive, Negative, or Neutral) left for you by the buyer.

✔ **Notes to Yourself**: If you input any personal notes regarding the transaction in the Sales Record, they appear here.

Notice that there is no column reflecting the eBay fees you paid for listing and selling the item. You'll find those in Sales Reports Plus (see the upcoming section).When you're just starting out as a PowerSeller, the Selling Manager Pro's reporting functions can help you identify profitable items and find the direction for your business. But beware — delving into too many reports may make your eyes glaze over and cause you to second-guess everything you do.

It's a good idea to create a directory on your computer with a name such as eBay Sales. In this directory, you can store all the reports you download from eBay, PayPal, or any other online service. Be sure to include this directory when you perform regular data backups.

After the file is downloaded, you see a confirmation with your new filename. Now you can open the new file in your spreadsheet program, and it will look very similar to Figure 20-5.

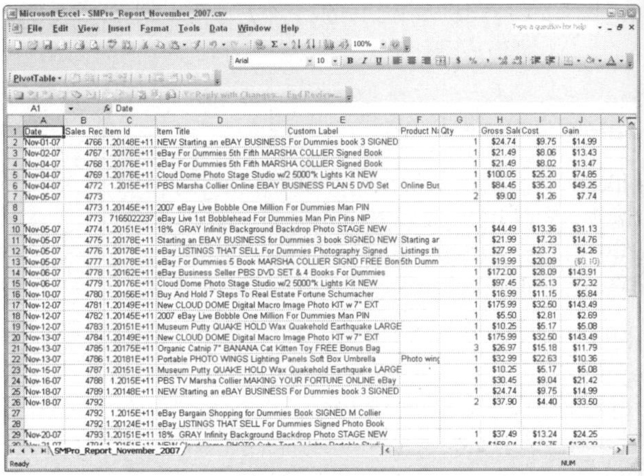

• **Figure 20-5: An SMPro sales report.**

Customizing a Works or Excel spreadsheet

With simple spreadsheet commands, you can customize the look of your report. For example, if the column for Buyer Country is unnecessary for your records (you ship only within the United States, so that information isn't useful), you can delete the column.

To delete the wasted space, follow these steps:

1. Highlight the column by clicking the column letter.

2. Choose Edit⇨Delete.

Voilà! The offending column is no more.

The spreadsheet generated by Selling Manager is easy to use because the columns are totaled for you. There's even an area for eBay Listing Fees and Credits. With all this information, you can see your total sales at a glance.

You can perform all spreadsheet tasks mentioned here in similar fashion in either Microsoft Works or Excel.

Reviewing Selling Manager reports can reveal good information, such what's selling and what isn't. But these reports aren't a complete picture of your business. Don't make major changes in your selling plan because of something you read in a report until you're absolutely sure something isn't (or is!) working.

Sales Reports Plus

I like eBay's Sales Reports Plus because it gives you the opportunity to keep all your hard-line selling information in one place. It also allows you to download the reports to archive for your business records.

Reports, reports, reports; when you're active in the eBay selling community, you're deluged with reports. Reports are grand because they give you an idea of where your business is at any point in time. But the key to getting some *value* out of all these reports is knowing which reports are important to you — based on your levels of online selling.

These reports differ from the File Management Center reports considerably. While the File Management reports give you accounting data, your Sales Reports Plus reports give you an idea of sales trends by showing you sales ratios and data.

Here's the information you get:

- ✔ **Total Items Sold**
- ✔ **Total Sales Amount for the Month:** Pretty self-explanatory, huh?
- ✔ **Auction Data:** Total sales with month-to-month sales growth data including
  - ▶ Ended listings
  - ▶ Ended items
  - ▶ Sold items
  - ▶ Sold items %
  - ▶ Average sale price per item
  - ▶ Total buyers
  - ▶ Total unique buyers

- ▶ Repeat buyers %

- ✔ **Fees:** Total Net eBay and PayPal fees.

This secret is very important (take this seriously — it may be the most valuable piece of information in this book). Take my advice and click the link on the Fees area to change the view from Summary to Details! The Details view gives you the most pertinent data that any seller needs, specifically, your net eBay and PayPal fees *as a percentage of your total sales*.

Take a look at Figure 20-6 to see just what you get when you choose to view the Fees in detail. Add all the fees together and you've got an instant snapshot of how well your business is doing — how much "rent" you're paying to stay alive in the marketplace. Watch this percentage like a hawk (you can compare three months of data on the report) and you'll always know if you're listing too much without selling — and whether your expenses are too high for your sales.

```
Fees (Definitions)
Show: Summary | Details

eBay
  Fees
       Insertion fees
       Listing feature fees
       Final value fees
       Subscription fees
  Subtotal
  Credits
       Store referral credits
       Other credits
  Subtotal
  Net eBay fees
  Net eBay fees as % of sales
PayPal
  Fees
  Credits
  Net PayPal fees
  Net PayPal fees as % sales
eBay & PayPal
  Net eBay & PayPal fees
```

• **Figure 20-6: The most important data in all your reports is right here.**

Setting up cross-promotions

If you have an eBay Store, you may notice that the Cross-Promotions area of the page has a great many links. Here is where you can set up a *merchandising bar* that shows selected additional items you have up for sale on each item page when it's viewed by the prospective buyer.

I have extra links in this area because I have an eBay Store; when you have an eBay Store, you can control which items go into the merchandising bar that appears below the description of your items. (You can see a sample merchandising bar in Figure 20-7 and find out more about cross-promotions in Practice 13.)

• **Figure 20-7:** Seller's merchandising bar that appears at the bottom of all item listings.

Auto-sending invoices from Selling Manager

One of my favorite features of eBay's pay-by-the-month program, Selling Manager, is that I can follow the progress of my sales from the Selling Manager Summary page.

When an item has been won or paid for via PayPal, you can click the appropriate link to see it in the list. Figure 20-8 shows my Sold Listings: Paid & Waiting To Ship area in Selling Manager.

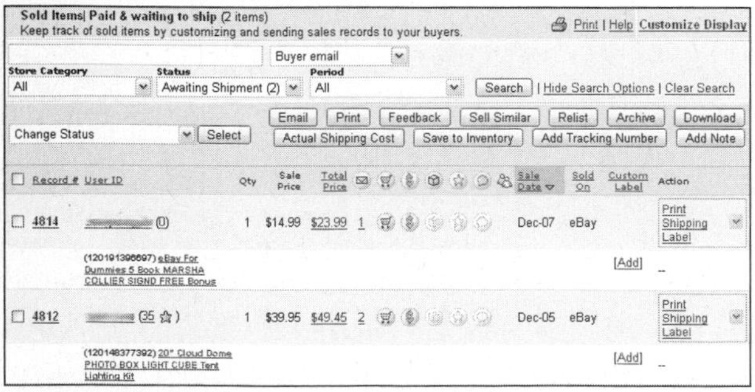

• **Figure 20-8:** Sold! And ready to ship.

Notice the record number next to the winner's e-mail address. To send the lucky buyer an e-mail, follow these steps:

1. **Click the record number and you're sent to the Transaction Details record for that sale.**

When you get there, you see the items sold to that buyer. (If the buyer has made more than one purchase, you see this notation and can click to combine the purchases in the Transaction Details record.)

2. **Click the button that says E-Mail Buyer (see Figure 20-9).**

3. **Select the appropriate e-mail to send.**

You can personalize the e-mail further by altering the Selling Manager–supplied templates (if you choose) before you send it.

4. **When you're ready for the e-mail to go, click Send.**

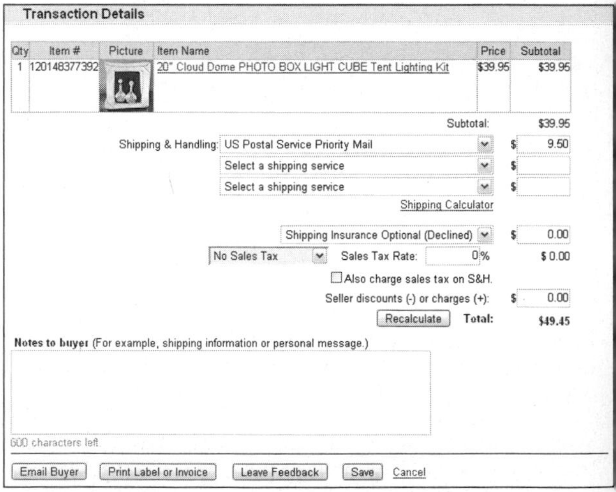

• **Figure 20-9:** Item summary and the E-Mail Buyer link.

Selling Manager's customizable templates

Selling Manager has seven e-mail templates that you can customize with minimum fuss. As shown in the figure included here, these templates allow you to add Auto Text features; eBay's server fills in the proper information for that particular transaction.

Edit Email Template

Any changes you make to this template will apply to all Winning buyer notification email you send to your buyers.
Tip: Use Email Marketing to create and send emails to promote your items to customers.

Custom Header

☑ Include my eBay Store logo in the header

☐ Include this message in the header (no HTML)

Characters left: 350

Message Details

Personalize your message by inserting automatic text (autotext) such as buyer name, item number, etc. See all available autotext.

Subject
Good news! eBay item #[ITEM#] [TITLE]

Message
Thank you for winning on my eBay item. Buyers tend to go unrecognized on eBay a little too often, so I want you to know that your purchase is very much appreciated. If I can be of any assistance to you, please let me know. While this first email is being generated automatically, I do welcome one-on-one contact with you. Simply send a reply to this mail and I'll answer your inquiries directly.

I am serious about my business and I look forward to the opportunity to serve you. I'd also like to invite you to check out our other items available on eBay.

marsha_c

Marsha Collier
Author, eBay for Dummies" and
"Starting an eBay Business for Dummies"

Payment Information

☑ Include the [Pay Now] button and accepted payment methods

Cross-Promotions

☑ Include my default cross-promotion in this email

[Save] Preview | Reset to default | Cancel

First you select the template you'd like to edit. Notice the drop-down menu that provides tools to edit any of the eBay-supplied templates.

When a winner buys an item, I have a preformatted Winning Buyer Notification letter I created from a template; if the winner pays immediately via PayPal, I also have a payment-received e-mail to use.

Practice 21

Shooting Quality Product Photos

In This Practice

- Knowing your camera
- Making digital magic
- Outfitting your photo studio

Success in your eBay sales not only depends on the quality of your descriptions, it depends equally on having high-quality photos. Producing those high-quality photos doesn't always mean spending buckets of money on high-end equipment — though you'll have to spring for the photography products that do the job for a reasonable outlay of cash. The first and foremost item of importance is your camera. In this practice, I talk about the basics — your camera and studio — and show how you can get a reasonably priced but fully functional photography setup that supports your eBay business practices.

Choosing a Camera and Making It Work

Your digital camera is the heart of your eBay operation (okay, maybe your computer is the heart, but give me a little leeway here). Without quality photos, your listings end up blah and unattractive. You need alluring pictures to catch the eye of the buyer.

Your pictures tell the story of your item, and if the item looks off-color or out of focus, odds are it won't seem as appealing to your prospective customers. Retailers — those who know you're an eBay seller — will play on your goal of taking appealing photos. And if they think you're not savvy about digital cameras, they may steer you toward an omnifunctional, complex (and did I mention, *pricey?*) model. Reading this chapter sets you straight and helps you save time and money when you choose and use your digital camera. The decision's not that hard; don't let an overzealous salesperson talk you into spending unnecessary bucks. You can buy a simple camera that allows minor adjustments, and you accomplish the rest of the photography magic with the proper setup.

Deciding how much to spend for what features

Thinking about your target price and how much you want to spend is nice; in theory. If you're anything like me, once you're faced with an array of cameras (which amazingly tend to look all the same — even after first glance) you start to get picky and look for the one with the most horsepower — or options in this case. Remember that for eBay photography, more horsepower is purely unnecessary. If you'd *like* to spend $500 on a camera, you may — but you'll be using only a fraction of that camera's abilities for your eBay pictures. You can find a perfectly suitable camera for your online photography needs for around $100. You can use a high-dollar camera for family photos, but the most basic model is all you need for eBay.

Soon-to-be-big-time sellers, just starting out in an eBay business (with no experience on the site), seem compelled to go out and buy the most expensive digital camera with scads of megapixels (more about those in a minute). Maybe that's a macho thing — but realistically, it's overkill. For eBay images, there are a few important (and some merely desirable) features to look for when you're shopping for a digital camera. Here's the short list:

- **Optical versus digital zoom:** *Zoom* is the feature you need to get close-ups when you photograph smaller or more detailed items in the macro setting (say, the fine inlay on that guitar you're selling).

  - ▶ *Digital zoom* is the latest hocus-pocus from the camera industry. It simulates what happens when you shoot moving pictures with a camcorder and zoom in, enlarging a picture in much the same way as image-editing software: It centers the focus over half the focal plane (the camera's focusing area), and uses software mimicry (interpolation) to enlarge the picture — which may make your image slightly fuzzy.

  - ▶ *Optical zoom,* on the other hand, harkens back to the fine lenses used in traditional photography. No software tricks here, just old-fashioned glass and light: Optical zoom is produced through magnification from the camera's lens, using the camera's internal lens optics to produce a vivid picture.

Professional photographers spend big bucks on lenses, and the zoom lens is one of the most important of those. If you've used a regular single-lens reflex camera, you might find it useful to note that a 3x optical zoom on a digital camera gives you results equivalent to what you'd get from a 35mm to 105mm zoom lens.

My advice is to select a camera with the highest optical-zoom value you can afford. Figure 21-1 shows you one place to look for the optical zoom.

- **Megapixels:** A *megapixel* is a unit of measurement that tells you how high the resolution is. When the number of pixels is equal to or greater than 1 million, it's more convenient to write the number in megapixels. For example, multiply the active horizontal by active vertical pixels in a full computer display (1280 × 1024) and you get 1,310,720 pixels — basically a 1.3-megapixel image.

The more megapixels, the more detailed your image will be. Your images can be enlarged without losing precious detail. Fun, but not always practical for eBay image photography; you *don't* need 'em (mega-megapixels, that is).

 If you use a high-resolution, multi-megapixel image on eBay, you risk having it look huge on your listing page (taking up the entire screen), or having the file size be so huge (pixel-bloated) that the image could take several minutes to load. No point in showing a high-res image to customers who have already moved on.

For online use, all you need from a camera is 800 × 600 pixels (even 640 × 480 will work) because the average computer display is incapable of taking advantage of more pixels.

- **Power supply:** When you're picking out your camera, be sure to check into the length of time the camera's battery will hold a charge. The last thing you want is to run out of juice at the wrong moment. Even though you may adore having a huge LCD on the back of the camera for image preview, those things burn power like there's no tomorrow! Consider the following:

  - ▶ Look for a camera battery with at *least* three hours of photo-taking time.

  - ▶ Keep a spare battery on hand.

  - ▶ Invest in a charger and rechargeable lithium ion batteries.

• **Figure 21-1: The camera company shows you the zoom rating.**

I recommend that you get rechargeable backup batteries for all your cameras. These batteries last a long time and are worth the investment.

✔ **Memory storage:** Many cameras have up to 10 MB of internal memory. This means you can store up to that amount, without using any external removable storage media. You retrieve images held in memory with a hard-wired connection to your computer. Most cameras also have removable media where they can store photos you take. (Check out Practice 25 where I describe the various sorts of storage media available.)

✔ **Tripod mount:** Have you ever had a camera hanging around your neck while you're trying to repackage some eBay merchandise that you've just photographed? Or perhaps you've set down the camera for a minute and then can't find it? Avoid this hassle by using a tripod to hold your camera. Tripods also help you avoid the blurry pictures that result from a shaky grip on the camera. To use a tripod, you need a *tripod mount*, the little screw hole that you see at the bottom of some cameras. (An upcoming section,

"Adding on Other Valuable Equipment," gives you some ideas on tripod features to look for.)

✔ **Macro-setting capability or threading for a lens adapter:** These features will come in handy if you plan to photograph coins, jewelry, or small, detailed items. A camera's *macro setting* enables you to get in really close to items while keeping them in focus. Usually the macro mode can focus as close as 1 inch and as far away as 10 inches. A small flower icon in the camera's menu normally signifies the macro setting. A threaded lens mount is an alternative that enables you to screw in different types of lenses to give the camera macro-focus capability.

 The average camera's *focal length* (focus range) is from 3 feet to infinity. If your camera says its macro-focus range is set at 5.1 inches, it means you can't focus it clearly on an object any closer than 5.1 inches. Macro pictures require a steady hand; any vibration can blur your image. Some of the newest hot-shot, high-dollar cameras have a feature called *image stabilization,* which automatically compensates for the shakiest of hands.

✔ **White-balance setting:** Most eBay digital photographers set the camera's white balance to Auto and hope for the best. Look for a camera that allows you to *adjust* the white balance. (This can be a bit tricky, so I show you how to make this adjustment later in the practice.) Keep in mind that different manufacturers use different presets. The list of options can include settings for incandescent lights, twilight, fluorescent lights, outdoor, indoor, or shade. All these lighting situations have different color temperatures. It's worthwhile to take the time to play with the various white-balance settings of your camera in the different places where you normally photograph eBay merchandise.

While you're experimenting with your camera's white balance, always take notes on the settings you use; that way you can identify which ones give you the truest colors in your digital images.

At the end of the day, I recommend that you buy a brand-name camera. I still use an ancient Sony Mavica FD92 mounted to a Cloud Dome (an apparatus that diffuses light) for jewelry and coin pictures. Also, I keep an old Nikon CoolPix 3200 around for shooting images of . . . well . . . just about everything else. It turns out that my Sony Mavica DSC-H1 is far, far too much camera for eBay images. (The FD92 may be outdated, but it has all the bells and whistles needed for eBay photos — that is, not too many.)

Linking to a video in your listing to demonstrate a product can really help an obscure product sell. (Check out my eBay listings for Quake Hold.) I have been shooting some video for some of my listings, too, using a digital-media camera that takes still pictures (nice macro) as well as videos so I don't have to switch cameras. It's a Sanyo Xacti VPC-CG65. It's fun to use in and out of the eBay photo studio!

When budget is also a factor in the purchase decision (and when isn't it?), savvy eBay shoppers find deals on lower-resolution cameras (3 megapixels or less). Because much of the world's population is upgrading to mucho-megapixel cameras, the displaced — but still perfectly good — low-resolution cameras show up for sale on eBay for a pittance. (I bet you could find a camera that fits your needs right now on eBay for considerably less than $100.) You can be right there to snap up the deals! And remember that many professional camera stores also sell "outdated" equipment.

Checking out the camera parts

Strangely (or not so strangely), digital cameras are pretty much the same from manufacturer to manufacturer. Take a look at Figure 21-2, which shows you two of my cameras. Notice that several gizmos on the cameras seem to be the same — whether the camera is a Nikon or a Sony.

Many of the buttons are self-explanatory (*Shutter button = push here to take picture*), while others are a bit more esoteric. Figure 21-2 shows a sampling.

Most digital cameras have the following dials and switches:

✔ **Zoom toggle:** These two buttons, generally placed toward the top of the camera (as shown in Figure 21-3), function very simply: Press one side and the camera zooms in (the view gets closer); press the other side, and the camera zooms out (the view gets farther away).

✔ **Optical viewfinder:** Just as on a trusty old (and I mean old) Brownie camera, you have the option of viewing your subject in the classic way — through a viewfinder — instead of using the LCD screen. If you've ever tried to look at an LCD screen in sunny, bright conditions, you'll know the value of alternative viewing. LCDs are rendered pretty useless in the sun; they just aren't bright enough for accurate viewing.

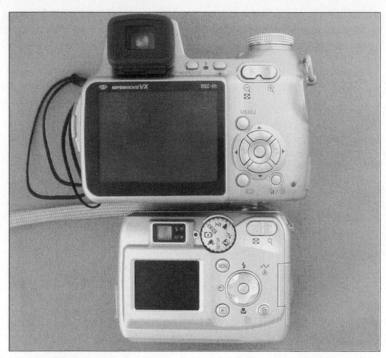

• **Figure 21-2:** Check out the similarity between these two cameras' gizmos and buttons.

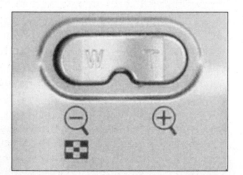

• **Figure 21-3:** The zoom toggle works pretty intuitively.

✔ **Mode dial:** Here's a look (in Figure 21-4) at a magically quick tool that enhances your control over your camera. You can choose from a plethora of settings that make your camera do technical magic — for example, Portrait mode for taking pictures of your dog and Fireworks mode for taking images of (duh) fireworks displays at night — although (sadly) very little of

this fun stuff is useful for eBay purposes (where generally you just set your camera on auto and shoot). Have fun with the various modes when you take your trusty camera out for a walk — or on vacation!

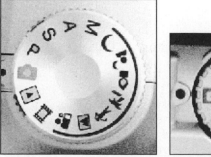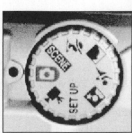

• **Figure 21-4:** Here's a look at Sony and Nikon mode-dial features. Check out the subtle differences.

✔ **Control button:** The control button (sometimes more than one) is usually a quick toggle for five basic functions. Pressing in the center usually finalizes your selection from among these:

  ▶ **Flash control:** Here you click to force the flash to go off (whether or not the camera thinks it should) or to turn off the flash. Having that kind of say-so is often useful when you're trying not to wash out details with too much light.

  ▶ **Macro photography:** You can only zoom into your item so far with the toggle buttons, but when you push this button to set the Macro mode, you may be able (depending on your camera) to zoom in your focus as close as a couple of inches — accurately!

  ▶ **Self-timer:** Yawn. Use this when you have the camera set on a tripod and want to jump into the image with your spouse before the shutter goes off.

  ▶ **Image review:** Shows you the last image you shot, putting it in the LCD screen for quality review.

  ▶ **Menu selectors:** Thought you caught us stumped, eh? Well, yeah, there are only *four* buttons or directions on this control — but then there are the menus. When you select the Setup mode from the Mode dial (or another button on your camera that might say *Menu*), you can use these buttons to make selections and go up or down the menus.

The magical white-balance setting(s)

I know, I know, you don't have a good picture unless it's in focus. I'll give you that. But in my experience, focus isn't the biggest issue that eBay photographers face. Often a photographed item is masked with too much shadow or washed out by too much light. The complexity of producing accurate colors in your photos can easily become the more dreaded issue.

Never fear! Practice 22 shows you how you can control color reproduction in special situations. But before diving into that topic, consider this:

You can turn to one simple-to-set control — White Balance — to improve color right away. The good news is that most digital cameras have this control.

White balance is sort of the digital equivalent of a good laundry detergent — it makes sure your whites stay white instead of turning yellow — and that helps keep the other colors vibrant. Table 21-1 outlines how different types of lighting will affect your images.

TABLE 21-1: IMAGE COLOR AS AFFECTED BY LIGHT

Type of Light	Results During Exposure
Daylight	Turns out white (about the best you can get)
Cloudy	Sets a blue/gray cast on everything
Fluorescent light	Tinges everything a nasty bluish
Incandescent bulb	Casts the entire photo in reddish-yellowish ickyness

Most top-name cameras will have a setting to cover all the lighting situations listed in Table 21-1. These settings work very well, but you have to remember to set up your camera for each shooting session. (You can find the instructions for making these settings in your camera's manual, or online.) I've had success with all modes except Incandescent. That yellow cast from regular lighting is a bear to get rid of.

 Instead of using regular light bulbs in your lights, I suggest counteracting the "incandescent yellows" by using a full-spectrum white-light bulb (such as the GE Reveal) or a halogen-type bulb. Also, Daylight Balanced or True Color bulbs are a quick shortcut to true color rendition.

Your camera may also have an "auto" (automatic) White Balance (WB) setting. This setting will work *sometimes* — when you have perfectly balanced lighting for your items (sadly, I can't claim that positive experience). If you really want best results, set the white balance manually. It's usually as easy as pressing the right button so the camera's computer can view the ambient lighting and make its own adjustments.

Outfitting Your Studio

A bad workman blames his tools — I've certainly heard that time and again. Coincidentally, blaming the tools is also a common phenomenon amongst eBay sellers who just can't get a decent photo. Personally, I feel the problem stems from laziness on two fronts. Some sellers don't take enough time to get the picture quality that's necessary to display their items. Nor do they take the time to set up their pictures properly before shooting — for example, shooting a picture of a crystal vase against a white backdrop (versus a black one) makes the vase blend totally into the background and prevents the viewer from seeing any details.

Simple, small things, such as props and backdrops, can help you build a good informal photo studio. But don't go nuts thinking that you need to outfit your studio all at once — that's an ongoing venture (at least it is for me — I add items continually) over many years. A well-stocked studio for shooting online photos stays current with the latest "tricks of the trade."

Storing your studio equipment

I realize that the entire population of eBay sellers may not have as much room as I do for an eBay photo studio. At least that used to be the case. I used to have an entire room set up just for prepping the merchandise and shooting the pictures. Now most of that room is filled with shelves of merchandise for eBay — but (oops) that's a different business practice!

 Most sellers don't have a lot of space for a permanent studio — so making efficient use of the space you have is the name of the game. At the very least, keep all the supplies for your eBay photo studio in a few boxes that you can conveniently access at a moment's notice (no,

that *doesn't* mean stored in the rafters of the garage). That way, when you want to start shooting pictures in the dining room, you can pull out whatever you need from your prepackaged boxes.

Many photography and lighting products sold on eBay come with their own storage boxes, so stowing these items is fairly easy. I suggest that you package your portable photo studio into several labeled boxes, broken down in the following manner:

- Lighting and tripods
- Cloud Dome
- Lighting panels and/or tents
- Props (backgrounds, risers)
- Cleaning supplies
- Apparel kit (items you use only when you photograph clothing)

 If, due to lack of space, you wind up having to shoot on a usually cluttered kitchen counter or desktop (where you've shoved aside your paperwork and/or cat food), be sure to acquire and use an inexpensive *photo stage*, which (no surprise) you can easily find for sale on eBay.

Quality equipment breeds quality photos

At the outset, I want you to know that I'm as cost-conscious as anyone. In this practice, I list some items that would help you prepare your online photo studio for almost any eventuality. But let's not be chintzy about it. Many other current books suggest that you put together temporary studio props out of cardboard and light filters out of cut pieces of shower curtain. If you're serious about your online business, skip the duct-tape solutions.

There are good reasons to purchase substantial, quality products for your photo studio:

- **Durability:** Products designed for a photo studio (even if they are entry-level and not top-dollar) are less likely to get crumpled and trashed.

✔ **Suitability:** Products made for a real photo studio are probably made so they won't catch on fire from your lights (a significant benefit). Not a bad idea to look for a fire-resistant style.

✔ **Resale value:** Studio equipment maintains its value while you use it. Although this may be the least important reason to furnish your studio with quality products, if you decide that this business isn't for you, you can always resell your photo studio equipment to someone else.

In general, don't buy everything all at once! The exception is, of course, that rare deal you might find on complete kits — or if you buy a whole used photo studio from another seller who may be retiring from the online selling game (although I can't imagine who might consider retiring)!

Picking out basic equipment

Besides a camera, an effective photo studio needs several basic pieces of lighting and background equipment — fortunately, they're pretty straightforward and aren't that hard to find. If you're selling particular types of merchandise, you may need, say, a mannequin to display clothing or an easel to display artwork. If you sell a variety of items, then you can use all such extras you can lay your hands on. I admit to being a bit of a gadget freak, so my photo studio seems to sprout new ones all the time — gadgets like Cloud Domes, tripods, light wings — to make photo-taking easier.

 Be sure to double-check with your tax person, but in most cases, the money you spend for photo-studio equipment becomes a write-off for your profitable eBay business.

There are really only two things you can't do without — besides your camera — in your photo studio:

✔ **Lights:** You need a floodlight with a reflector — and something to hold the light in place — either a clamp or a traditional light stand. No need to spend big bucks here, although it's best to use lights designed specifically for photography

(lights made to illuminate a garage for nighttime automotive work aren't quite what you need).

You can also use a small tabletop true-light lamp for illuminating smaller items. Be sure your bulb is rated at about 5000 K, where *K* stands for *Kelvin*, a measurement of light's color temperature. See the sidebar, "Checking out the Kelvin (K) rating" for more on this aspect of lighting.

✔ **Backgrounds/backdrops:** Here's where you use your imagination. A backdrop can be almost any solid-color surface (whether painted or draped) that provides a contrasting background for your image photography. Remember, your goal is to show the product — not lay out a museum piece. The only thing you want a picture of is your item; a clean, solid surface behind it makes the item easy to see but doesn't call attention to itself. Here are some suggestions:

▶ Backgrounds come in many shapes and sizes. You can get paper, fabric, or use a portable plastic photo stage for smallish items.

▶ In professional photo-talk, *seamless* is a large roll of 3-foot (and wider) paper that comes in various colors and is suspended and draped behind the model and over the floor so the model seems to be floating in infinity — and is instantly the center of attention. Photographers also drape seamless over tabletop shots, or use fabrics such as muslin instead.

 I recommend using wrinkle-free backdrops in neutral colors — such as white, light gray, "natural," and black — for photographing your merchandise. That way, the color of the paper or fabric doesn't clash with or distract from your items.

For taking a picture anywhere, indoors or out, a portable photo stage is a valuable tool. It's made of a textured plastic made to be set in a curved shape; the stage rests on any surface and permits you to take a clean picture without any extraneous stuff in the background. You can use a photo stage to achieve an infinity look by curving the background under the item, as shown in Figure 21-5. Best of all, you can store it flat on a bookshelf until you need it next.

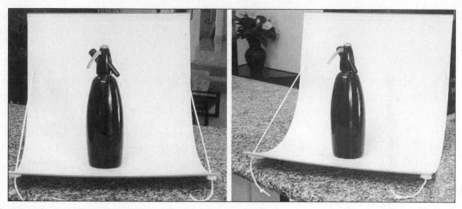

• **Figure 21-5: An item being photographed on an infinity background.**

Checking out the Kelvin (K) rating

You can get some good buys in true-color light bulbs on eBay. Such lights usually have a Kelvin rating of 5,000 or higher. *Kelvin* (K) is the standard unit used to measure color temperature, or the degree of warmth or coolness of a light source. Higher Kelvin temperature produces a fuller color spectrum in the light. The higher the K, the bluer — or cooler — the light appears. The lower the K, the more red light is present, and the warmer the lamp appears. Take a look at the following chart. It gives the various Kelvin ratings for common everyday light sources.

Kelvin Temperature Rating (Degrees)	Light Source
1200 K	Candlelight
2680 K	40W incandescent lamp
3000 K	Studio lamps
3200 K	Sunrise/sunset
3400 K	Tungsten lamp
5000 K	Electronic flash and standard daylight (also designated by the symbol D50, which stands for "Daylight 5000 K")
5500 K	Midday sun

Kelvin Temperature Rating (Degrees)	Light Source
7000 K	Lightly overcast sky
8000 K	Hazy sky

 The industry standard for a "Daylight Balanced" rating is between 5000 and 6500 Kelvin.

Checking out some common setups

Take a look at Figures 21-6 through 21-8. They show you several of my photo setups — and as you can see, I'm about ready to photograph nearly anything that comes my way.

The original home photo studio (shown in Figure 21-6) is a super beginner's setup. It has a black backdrop, a white backdrop (pictured), and can be set up anywhere in the house. These days I also use the Cloud Dome (a light-diffusing device — not pictured) for specialty photos such as macro jewelry shots.

Figure 21-7 shows another option: a pure white photo cube, lit with either small clamp lights (shown) or with tall floodlights. A photo cube works well for finely detailed and collectible objects — as well as any other object that will fit in it. Using a translucent white fabric cube, you can fully illuminate your item without glare, harsh shadows, or detail burnout!

In Figure 21-8, you can see how to change a photo setup to accommodate large items by placing Photo Wings light panels on tall *floodlights* (regular lights inside hemispherical aluminum reflectors, mounted on adjustable stands). With a setup like this, you can get close to the same effect as you get when using a Cloud Cube on a table — but for much larger items! Traditionally photographers used expensive, umbrella-like reflectors for this purpose — but the umbrellas required special mounts for the light stands, and the Photo Wings attach simply with Velcro.

• **Figure 21-6: My original eBay photo setup.**

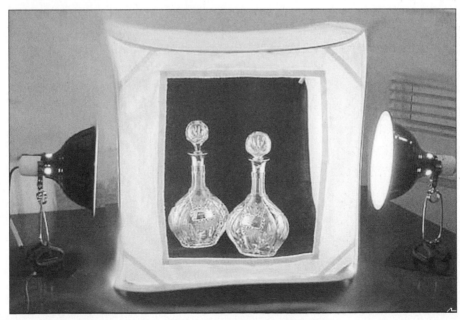

• **Figure 21-7: Using a photo cube on a dining-room table to photograph antiques.**

• **Figure 21-8:** Floodlights illuminating Midge the Mannequin, star of many an auction.

Adding on Other Valuable Equipment

The basics are great, but (as with any venture worth doing right), there will always be things you can add to your arsenal of tools to improve your pictures. I'm constantly adding new stuff (most recently, my new set of risers — gotta love those gadgets). Every professional has a special bag of tricks, and you might find that the tools in this section are more than you thought you'd need for photographing your items.

A Tripod

A *tripod* is an extendable aluminum stand that holds your camera. Look for one that has a quick release so that if you want to take the camera off the tripod for a close-up, you don't have to unscrew it from the base and then screw it back on for the next picture.

The legs should extend to your desired height, lock in place with clamp-type locks, and have a crank-controlled, geared center column so you can move your camera up and down for different shots. Most tripods also have a panning head for shooting from different angles. You can purchase a tripod from a camera store, or on eBay for as little as $25.

Power supplies

If you've ever used digital cameras, you know that they can suck the life out of batteries faster than sugar going through a five-year-old. A reliable, consistent power supply is a must. You can keep the power flowing in a couple of ways:

- ✔ **Rechargeable batteries:** Many specialists on eBay sell rechargeable batteries and chargers. Choose quality Ni-MH (nickel metal hydride) batteries because this kind, unlike Ni-Cad (nickel cadmium) batteries, has no memory effect. That means you don't have to totally discharge them.

- ✔ **Lithium-ion batteries:** Lithium batteries are the longest-lasting and lightest batteries available, but they're also expensive. Or at least they were. Then some smart cookie figured out a way to put two batteries into one unit; considerably cutting the price. This new battery can average 650 photos before you have to change it. The CR-V3 is a new kind of battery that takes the place of two standard AA batteries. It is also available in a rechargeable form, thereby extending the life even further (and reducing your battery budget significantly).

Props — for example, a mannequin

To take good photos, you need some props. Although you may think it strange that a line item in your accounting program will read *props,* they do qualify as a business expense. (Okay, you can put it under *photography expenses* — *props* just sounds so Hollywood!)

How often have you seen some clothing on eBay from a quality manufacturer, but just couldn't bring yourself to bid more than $10 because it looked like it had been dragged behind a car and then hung on a hanger before it was photographed? Could you see how the fabric would hang on a body? Of course not. But take a look at Figure 21-9 — *that* dress looks simply fantastic, darling!

![Figure 21-9 photo of mannequin in a dress]

• **Figure 21-9:** Midge the Mannequin, modeling for a successful eBay sale.

If you're selling clothing, you'd better photograph it on a mannequin. If you don't want to dive right in and buy a mannequin, at least get a body form to wear the outfit. Just search eBay for *mannequin* to find hundreds of hollow forms selling for less than $20. If you sell children's clothing, get a child's mannequin form as well. The same goes for men's clothes. If worst comes to worst, find a friend to model the clothes. There's just no excuse for hanger-displayed merchandise in your auctions.

I got my mannequin (Midge) at a department store's liquidation sale here in Los Angeles. I paid $25 for her. Her face is a little creepy (so I often crop her head out of the photos), but she has a great body — and everything she wears sells at a profit. Many stores upgrade their mannequins every few years or so. If you know people who work at a retail store, ask when they plan to sell their old mannequins; you may be able to pick one up at a reasonable price.

Display stands, risers, and more

Jewelry doesn't photograph well on a human being. Most people's hands and necks aren't exactly works of art (that's why there are professional "hand models" and such). Your item will look a lot better when you display it on a stand or a velvet pad.

If you're selling a necklace, display it on a necklace stand (or photograph it flat using a Cloud Dome — the ultimate light-gadget for jewelry — see Practice 22). I bought my necklace-display stand from a manufacturer but had to wait several months to receive it. Apparently, this type of quality display stand is made to order, so a more economical way (in both time and money!) to search for a stand is — you guessed it — on eBay. (You'll get it sooner and probably cheaper.)

Risers can be almost anything stairlike that you use to prop up your item to make it more attractive in a picture. If your riser isn't all that attractive, put it under the cloth you use as a background. Keep a collection of risers and propping materials in your photo area so they're always close at hand.

You wouldn't believe what the back of some professional photo setups look like. Photographers and photo stylists think resourcefully when it comes to making the merchandise look good — from the *front* of the picture, anyway! Throughout years of working with professional photographers, I've seen the most creative things used to prop up items for photography:

- **Bottles of mercury or (better yet) sand:** Mercury is a heavy liquid metal. A photographer I once worked with used little bottles of this stuff to prop up small boxes and other items in a picture. But mercury is a poison, so I suggest you do your propping up with small bottles (prescription bottles work well) filled with *sand*.

- **Museum Gel or Quake Hold:** These two products are invaluable when you want to hold small objects like jewelry at unnatural angles for a photograph. (They're like beeswax and clay, but cleaner.) Quake Hold is used by the leading museums in earthquake territory to keep valuable artifacts from careening off the table when the inevitable earthquake occurs. The clear version, Museum Gel, is often difficult to remove from items; I recommend using Quake Hold instead for your eBay items.

  A single packet of Quake Hold (that much will last you nearly forever) is only about $6. Although plain old clay is a cheaper alternative, it can leave grease spots on paper and fabrics.

- **un-du or GooGone:** If your items have stickers or sticker residue on them, the gunk is bound to show up in the picture — and your customers won't be too thrilled with sticker goo on their items. Squirt a little of these products on the sticker area and use the included scraper to remove the sticky stuff and bring back the shine.

- **WD-40:** Clean your item's plastic or cellophane with WD-40 (no kidding); unbelievably, it takes off any icky smudges. Just spray a tiny bit on a paper towel, and use the paper towel to polish the plastic surface. Don't spray right on the article — it's an oily mixture and you don't want accidental stains on the surrounding cardboard.

 Almost any cleaning solution can help your items (sometimes even a little 409), but use these chemicals with care so you don't damage — or destroy — the item while cleaning it.

- **Kneaded-rubber art eraser:** Keep one around to clean off small dirt smudges on paper items. Use it just the way you did in school: rub, rub, rub and then brush off the dirt.

- **Clothespins and duct tape:** (You know . . . the stuff that holds the universe together.) These multipurpose items are used in many photo shoots in some of the strangest places. For example, if your mannequin is a few sizes too small for the dress you want to photograph, don't pad the mannequin; simply fold over the dress in the back and clamp the excess material with a metal clamp or a bunch of clothespins. You can also use a small piece of non-sticky, non-glossy gaffer's tape to hold the fabric taut.

Practice 22

Photographing Specialty Items

Wouldn't it be great if every item you needed to photograph would fit in a small place and use the same light setup? As an eBay PowerSeller, you have a challenge: Often the items you put up for sale are different in size, shape, and materials — and they don't appear the same under the lights. You have to make special accommodations when you photograph certain types of items.

It's especially a drag for the seller whose eBay career involves selling anything and everything. This type of seller (sigh) needs a bit more knowledge (and a few more tools) to keep ahead of the competitors who sell exclusively in each category. In this practice, I go over a few of the photo tricks of the trade.

I've been selling on eBay since 1996 — and thought I was pretty good at showing off and selling my wares. But when I purchased a small lot of Morgan silver dollars to resell, I figured I'd just take a standard digital picture and sell away. Oops, not so fast. Coins are small, and the detail that remains on the coins is what brings a higher price. The first pictures I took bore only the slightest resemblance to the actual coins. Not only were the details either enhanced or fuzzy, but also the pictures made the beautiful silver coins look gold! Yikes — this would never do!

My next challenge was to photograph some stunning silver- and gold-tone costume jewelry. The setup — with its perfect positioning, beautiful lighting, and black velvet jewelry pads — looked exquisite, certain to bring a high price. The pictures *should* have been perfect. But NO: Silver looked gold, and gold looked silver. What's the deal?

The deal is lighting — specifically, the need for ambient lighting. In my past life, I worked with fashion and catalog photographers who took pictures of jewelry. I remember working in a darkened room while the photographer used an elaborate photo setup within a silk tent — the kind that produced the sparkling images you see in ads. It's a slam dunk that most of us won't be able to recreate the experts' silk tents, minimalist lighting, and multiple light flashes per exposure — but we can still set up for some great-looking images that do justice to our wares. That's why this practice shows you how to diffuse your lighting — and how to take advantage of the ambient light you have at home.

Low-Cost Photography Tricks for Jewelry and Coins

The first time you figure out that there must be a "trick" to photography is when you try to photograph coins or jewelry for online sale. The novice photographer is, for the most part, totally floored in this situation. And because they don't know the trick, several things become apparent right away:

- ✔ It's almost impossible to photograph any form of metal in its native color — silver looks gold — and gold looks silver.

- ✔ It's impossible to photograph the patina (finish) of any metal accurately.

- ✔ Gems lose their sparkle and often look muddy. Pearls often go flat white.

- ✔ Detail in coins may be too strong or too faint to show up to best advantage.

- ✔ The photos may have horrendous shadows.

In a nutshell, there's the short list of why this type of photography challenges even seasoned eBay photographers. So this practice offers a few fixes, ranging from the most economical (and unfortunately *still* the most difficult), to the expensive. At that end of the spectrum, you wind up investing in a serious piece of equipment — but at least the equipment will last you forever.

Take the pictures outdoors

I know this is going to sound kind of hokey, but most "necessity is the mother of invention" solutions *are* hokey, so bear with me. Here are the prehistoric-and-cheap-outdoor-photo-studio details:

1. **Go outside in bright sunlight with your item and a white piece of poster board to use as your background.**

2. **Arrange your items on the poster board so they're ready to photograph.**

3. **Position an old white sheet or cheap curtain sheers purchased at a discount store (the thinner, the better) between your item setup and the sun.**

In this setup, the sunlight has to travel through the sheet or curtain, which cuts down on direct sunshine, diffuses the light, and cuts out harsh shadows. You can have a friend hold the sheet or sheers for you, but if you don't have a friend to help out, tie the sheet to something stable and drape it over your shoulder (yes, I've actually done this — pitiful as it may seem); then *hold really still* while the shutter clicks.

4. **Turn off your camera's flash and take the picture in the self-created ambient light that illuminates your item.**

With any luck, you'll find that the thin-old-white-fabric is a fast, cheap way to filter the sunlight and reduce the glare and shadows. This system really does work, but I guarantee after doing it long enough, you're gonna want to upgrade! See the section "Going Pro with the Cloud Dome" later in this practice for my recommendation on a professional-quality upgrade.

Scanning the small stuff

I know that it's hard to believe, but beginners and pros alike often scan their items on a scanner — and get good images! Scanning an item is far faster than taking the time to set up, take the picture, and download it to your computer. I scan a good many of my paper items (and more) in the All-In-One that sits on my desk. The All-In-One is a copier, fax, scanner, and part-time printer — and I purchased it for about $150.

 I used to capture all my coin and jewelry images by scanning but found that I was spending a bit too much time in an image-editing program to get 'em to look right. And spending too much time is a no-no for a PowerSeller. So check the time you take for scanning and editing against the time you need for shooting and downloading. Then choose the quickest way that maintains the desired picture quality.

I still use the scanner now and then — mainly because it's easy! If my item fits on the scanner, it's no contest — I'll try to scan it first rather than taking a picture.

Figure 22-1 shows you a quick and easy scan of a very expensive gold metal belt. It's amazing how well the image turned out. (It looks even better in color.)

• **Figure 22-1:** You can even clearly read the manufacturer's hallmark.

• **Figure 22-2:** A 2004 United States Proof Set clearly still encased in plastic

Next is a picture from auctions by Cardking4 on eBay. Figure 22-2 shows a proof set of coins that are encased in plastic (which is why they look a tad hazy). If you took the picture with proper lighting it would still be a nightmare — considering the mount of glare you'd get off of the plastic case!

Figure 22-3 shows a scanned image of coins in a paper holder — I think this scan illustrates the coins adequately!

• **Figure 22-3:** A scan of vintage American coins.

Here are the steps you need to follow for scanning:

1. **Clean your scanner glass.**

   Magnified on a scanner, nothing looks grosser than a hair or an icky piece of dust.

2. **Cover your now-clean scanner glass with a plastic page protector from the office supply store.**

   Any piece of crystal-clear plastic will do — the point is to not scratch up the glass.

3. **For jewelry, use a jeweler's cloth to polish the piece to it most shining glory.**

    Please leave the coins alone — no polishing — cleaning only brings down the value!

4. **Arrange your jewelry or coins on the scanner (over the plastic protector).**

5. **Before you bring down the lid, place a small object on the glass so as to wedge the scanner in an open position so the cover doesn't squish your layout.**

6. **Lay a background over your item and the scanner lid to prevent light from leaking in around the side.**

I know this seems like a huge hassle, but it really isn't. You'll get some perfectly good images to use in your listings. And although scanning works well, you still may have problems in getting the right colors. So if you're in the coin or jewelry business in earnest, it's time to climb up to the next step.

Going Pro with the Cloud Dome

Ambient light — light that occurs naturally — is the best light for photographing many types of items (especially those shiny items). Problems start when you use a flash or floodlighting alone (without a Cloud Dome) for pictures of metallic objects. Common lighting problems that affect the quality of your photographs include shiny spots from reflections (off walls and ceilings), washed-out areas from the glare of the lights, and loss of proper color.

Enter the Cloud Dome to offer your at-home photos the ability to take advantage of natural, ambient light. The Cloud Dome looks like a giant bowl that you place upside-down over the object you want to photograph. This bowl evenly diffuses ambient room light over the surface area of the object. This way, you can produce quality digital images in average room lighting — and avoid troublemaking flash or floodlights.

 A fellow eBay University instructor introduced me to the Cloud Dome, and I've found it an amazing tool. You can purchase the Cloud Dome and its accessories at many professional camera shops, from the Web site at www.clouddome.com, or (you guessed it) discounted on eBay.

Shooting pictures with the Cloud Dome

The Cloud Dome looks like a giant inverted salad bowl with a camera mount attached. Figure 22-4 shows a Cloud Dome being set up to photograph jewelry. Follow these steps to take a picture with the dome:

1. **Attach your camera to the Cloud Dome's mount with the lens positioned so it peers into the hole at the top of the dome.**

2. **Place your item on top of a contrasting background.**

   See "Tips for taking Cloud Dome pictures" later in this chapter for ideas on choosing a background.

3. **Place the dome with camera attached over your item.**

4. **Check the item's position through your camera's viewfinder or LCD screen.**

   If it's not in the center, center it. If you feel you still need added lighting to bring out a highlight, position another lamp outside the dome.

5. **Focus your camera and shoot the picture.**

• **Figure 22-4:** Taking a picture with the Cloud Dome.

Many items benefit from being photographed through a Cloud Dome, especially:

- ✔ **Jewelry:** Taking pictures with the Dome keeps the gold color gold and the silver color silver. Also, using the Cloud Dome helps your camera pick up details such as engraving and the metal surrounding cloisonné work. It also gives pearls their unique luster and soft reflection, as in Figure 22-5. Much of the detail that the Cloud Dome helps capture can be washed out when you apply enough light to take the picture without it.

• **Figure 22-5:** A pair of lustrous pearl earrings.

- ✔ **Gems and stones:** You can capture some beautiful pictures of gems and stones with the Cloud Dome. You may want to focus a floodlight or lamp on the outside of the dome for extra sparkle. Take a look at Figure 22-6: On the top is a lovely ruby-slippers pin photographed under the Cloud Dome. On the bottom is the same pin, taken without the dome — notice the glare.

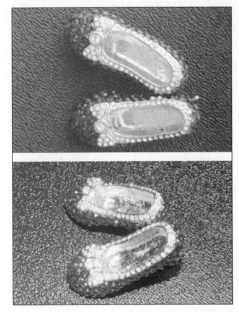

• **Figure 22-6:** Notice the benefit of using ambient light.

- ✔ **Coins and stamps:** The Cloud Dome allows you to hold the camera steady for extreme close-ups — and when you photograph coins, it helps you leave out any coloration that is not on the coins. For small detailed items such as coins and stamps, the Cloud Dome helps you achieve sharp focus and true color.

Photographing slabbed, graded coins can be difficult. Figures 22-7 and 22-8 show you slabbed quarters that were up for sale on eBay. One was shot in a Cloud Dome, and one wasn't. One sold for $15.99, and the other sold for $34.99. Can you guess which is which?

• **Figures 22-7 and 22-8: A quarter made clearer by shooting with a Cloud Dome.**

✔ **Holographic or metallic-accented items:** If you've ever tried to photograph collector cards, you know that the metal accents glare and the holograms are impossible to capture.

Also, the glossy coatings confuse the camera's light sensors, causing overexposed highlights. Check out the before-and-after images in Figure 22-9 and see how clear the hologram on the credit card appears after shooting through the Cloud Dome.

• **Figure 22-9: A hologram, before and after.**

✔ **Reflective objects:** Items such as silverware or even computer chips reflect a lot of light when lit properly for photos. The Cloud Dome diffuses that light so the pictures become clear. Check out the before and after in Figure 22-10.

• **Figure 22-10: Computer chips, before and after shooting with the Cloud Dome.**

Tips for taking Cloud Dome pictures

Surprisingly, there's very little learning curve to using a Cloud Dome. (Hey, how about those simple steps in the preceding section? The curve doesn't get much flatter than that.) What may take you more time is discovering the tips and tricks that help you achieve professional-looking results. Not to worry: Reading this section will kick-start your discovery process. While that's going on, here are a few things to keep in mind when taking photos with the Cloud Dome:

✔ **Focus:** Due to the focus limitations of many digital cameras, I found it best to use the Cloud Dome with the extension collar (often sold along with the Dome), which allows you to put your camera 17 inches away from the item you're photographing on a flat surface.

✔ **Close-ups:** When attempting *macro* (extreme close-up) photography, the Cloud Dome holds your camera still while shooting the picture. If

you prefer, after you've centered your item, stand away and use your camera's self-timer to take the picture.

✔ **Fine upstanding items:** If your item is vertical and doesn't lend itself to being photographed flat, use the optional angled extension from Cloud Dome, which allows you to shoot the item from an angle instead from the top. An angled collar is also sold separately, or in a package deal with a Cloud Dome.

✔ **Keeping background where it belongs:** When selecting a background for your item, choose a contrasting background that reflects the light properly for your item. Make it a solid color — white is always safe — and you can use black to add dramatic highlights.

 The background can mean a lot when taking pictures. A light (white) background can trick your camera's light meter into thinking the item to be photographed is very light — the reverse can occur with a dark background. If you're very adept at using your camera, you'll be able to get the item centered in the camera's focal plane — that way the light will read properly. Professionals often use an 18 percent gray card to set up a light meter for their pictures. Alternatively, you can use an 18 percent gray background (or photo stage) to easily balance out the lighting in your pictures.

Selling Fashion through Pictures

A simple truth of eBay: Nothing gets fewer bids than a photograph of a pair of jeans (or a dress) folded up on a table (or hanging on a hanger). In Figure 22-11, look at the Gallery thumbnails. Notice which jeans look desirable and which do not. There's proof positive in the bidding, too.

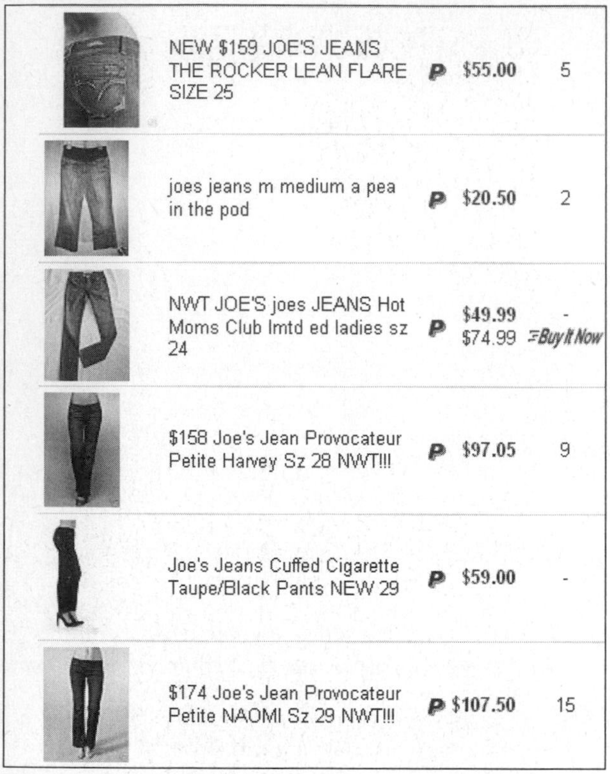

	NEW $159 JOE'S JEANS THE ROCKER LEAN FLARE SIZE 25	𝒫 $55.00	5
	joes jeans m medium a pea in the pod	𝒫 $20.50	2
	NWT JOE'S joes JEANS Hot Moms Club lmtd ed ladies sz 24	𝒫 $49.99 $74.99	- *=Buy It Now*
	$158 Joe's Jean Provocateur Petite Harvey Sz 28 NWT!!!	𝒫 $97.05	9
	Joe's Jeans Cuffed Cigarette Taupe/Black Pants NEW 29	𝒫 $59.00	-
	$174 Joe's Jean Provocateur Petite NAOMI Sz 29 NWT!!!	𝒫 $107.50	15

• **Figure 22-11: Searching for jeans on eBay. It seems a good title goes a long with a good picture to get high bids.**

Photographing fashion *right* takes a little time, but the right tools make the project easier. Here's a list of some of the items you'll need when photographing clothing.

➤ **Mannequin body double:** You don't want to deal with supermodels and their requirements for non-fat, sugar-free vanilla lattes, so you have to find someone who will model the garments and not give you any grief.

You can purchase full-body mannequins on eBay for under $100. I bought mine from a local store that was updating their mannequins. Major department stores often liquidate their display merchandise in auctions, so keep your eyes peeled in your local newspaper for auctions of store fixtures.

Keep in mind that you needn't spend a mint on a brand-new model. If your mannequin is used and has a few paint chips — so what?

Following are some less expensive alternatives to a mannequin:

➤ **Molded body form:** Before you decide to jump in with both feet, you might want to try using a *hanging* body form. No, it isn't a gruesome movie prop; it's a molded torso that has a hanger at the top. You can find molded styrene forms on eBay for as little as $20. If you decide to stay in the apparel-vending business, you can always upgrade to a full-size mannequin.

➤ **Dressmaker's adjustable form:** You can also use a dressmaker's form to model your eBay clothing. The best part about using these is that you can adjust the size of the body to fit your clothing. You can often find new or good-condition used ones on eBay for around $50.

➤ **Photo floodlights:** To light your merchandise when ambient light just doesn't cut it (midwinter blahs, anyone?), you'll do best to invest in some floodlights — and to prevent glare you could use some diffusing elements. You don't have to spend a mint, but (as you'll see when you start taking pictures), the little flash on your camera just can't bring out the really good parts of your apparel. Floodlights can be on stands or can be the type you clamp on the edge of a door (very convenient — and they don't take up a lot of storage space).

You can also use desk-size, true-light task lamps. They are sold on eBay quite reasonably; a pair can make an excellent countertop lighting solution.

 When using floodlights, you may want to prevent the flash on your camera from going off altogether when you take pictures of clothes; too much light coming from the front will wash out the detail in the fabric.

✔ **Clothespins (or metal clamps):** To fit your clothing on the mannequin, use clothespins to take up any slack in the garment (be sure to place the clothespins where the camera won't see them). Before you think I'm crazy, I'll have you know that clothespins were used in almost every apparel photo that I've participated in. Think about it: The clothing you're selling will come in different sizes and may not always hang right on your mannequin.

Accessories: Using light cubes, panels, and umbrellas

A super advantage of using photo accessories such as light cubes, panels, and umbrellas is that you can get the benefit of true-color white light without using special bulbs. When you shine a light through a high-quality, pure-white fabric, it changes the quality of the light and you get a near-perfect picture — often the first time. Below, you can see a light cube in action. Depending on what I'm shooting, I use different backgrounds in the cube. I find that white or light gray is best for most items, and black (inside the cube) is good for making glass and crystal stand out.

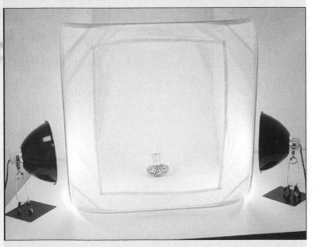

Floodlights can often be *too* bright and burn out detail in large items. Direct lighting can often produce some really nasty, unwanted shadows. But if you attach light-diffusing panels (Photo Wings) to your floodlights, you have a cheap, safe way to spread your light around just right. Here you can see a floodlight outfitted with these inexpensive panels.

Umbrella-style diffusers are the true professional solution for diffusing light, but they're expensive. By and large, you can simulate them well enough by using the panels, the light cube, or even by attaching a temporary 12-inch-by-12-inch *diffusion-gel filter* (available at your photo dealer, or on eBay for a few dollars) to your floodlight. Nothing fancy needed; clothespins work fine. You can also diffuse the light with a piece of translucent shower-curtain plastic — but be careful not to get it too close to your lights, especially if you're using special bulbs that throw off a lot of heat. You don't want to burn down the house when you're taking a picture!

Remember, good lighting is the key to good pictures — and *consistent* good lighting can save you time. After you've set up your lighting — if at all possible — *leave it alone* until you finish a large group of pictures. Setting up once and taking pictures of similar-size items can make your image assembly line move much faster!

Cleaning and pressing essentials

Before you photograph your clothing items, make sure each one imparts the image you want your buyers to see. For example, remove any loose threads and lint that may have accumulated on the fabric.

Have the following items handy to help you with the cleaning and pressing chores:

- ✔ **Garment rack:** When you unpack your merchandise from the carton it was shipped in, the items can look pretty ragged. Hanging the merchandise on a portable garment rack keeps it fresh-looking so it looks great when you get ready to ship.

- ✔ **Steamer:** Retail stores, clothing manufacturers, and drycleaners all use steamers. Why? Because steaming the garment with a steam wand is kinder to the fabric and takes wrinkles out in a hurry. Steam penetrates the fabric (not crushing it, as does ironing) and seems to make the fabric look better than before.

Steaming garments is a breeze. Steaming is also five times *faster* than ironing — and not as backbreaking — which is why it's truly the professional's choice.

A handheld travel steamer will work well enough if you're selling only one or two apparel items a month — and that's fine for beginners, but the extra time needed can add up. While a professional-style steamer gets a garment done in a minute or two, you might have to work on the same garment with a travel steamer for 15 minutes to get usable results. If you're thinking about selling any significant quantity of clothes on eBay, then a professional-style, roll-base steamer is what you should look for. I use a Jiffy Steamer that I've had for quite a while. (I even bought it on eBay and got a great deal.) It's the same kind they use in retail stores, only slightly smaller.

Steaming hot tips

Keep these tips in mind when steaming the clothes you sell on eBay:

- ✔ Always keep the steam head in an upright position so the condensation inside the hose drains back into the steamer (or it could run down your arm).

- ✔ Run the steam head lightly down the fabric.

- ✔ Don't let the steam head come directly in contact with velvet or silk; otherwise you may spot the fabric.

- ✔ Steam velvet (or any fabric with a pile) from the reverse side.

- ✔ Hang pants by the cuff when steaming.

- ✔ Heavy fabrics may respond better to steaming from the *underside* of the fabric.

- ✔ When you're through steaming your clothes for eBay, try steaming your mattresses and furniture. Steaming has been proven to kill a majority of dust mites and their accompanying nastiness.

✔ **Dryel:** This is a popular, reasonably priced, home-dry-cleaning product you use in your dryer. Dryel can be used with almost any type of garment (be sure to double-check the packaging before you use it). After going through a Dryel treatment, clothes come out of the dryer sweet and clean. The starter kit even comes with a spot remover. You can buy Dryel at your local supermarket.

According to eBay rules, *all* used clothing must be cleaned before it's sold on the site. Even if the vintage garment you have up for sale is clean, it can always benefit by a roll in the dryer with Dryel. New garments, too, benefit; Dryel removes any smells that have clung to the garment during its travels. I use this product on every apparel item before I ship it out.

✔ **Spot cleaners:** I recommend that you use spot cleaners *only* if you know what you're doing. Some really great ones out there will remove a small spot, but you'd best practice on items that you're *not* selling first.

Turning Cars into Dollars

Cars can do more than burn gas and look cool — they can also turn into quite a few dollars. During the last part of 2006, eBay sellers sold 2 million passenger vehicles. Is that enough to make *you* want to sell a vehicle? I would think so, but photographing cars for eBay auctions is a bit . . . involved. Typically a successful vehicle auction shows at least 10 pictures of the vehicle, including photos showing

✔ All four sides of the car

✔ Driver's-side interior through open door

✔ Passenger's-side interior with open door

✔ Driver's side from the back seat

✔ Close-up of the dashboard

✔ Back-seat from the front seat

✔ Tires and fenders (all four)

✔ All documentation that comes with the car

✔ The engine

Pictures in your listings make a huge difference. Be sure to treat your picture-taking as the serious enterprise that it is. Once you've got our methods perfected, you should be whizzing through your shoots — taking only minutes for each listing! That's music to a Power Seller's ears.

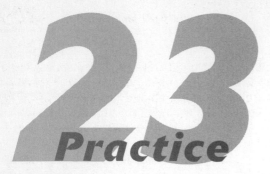

Getting Your Photos Web-Ready

Practice

In This Practice

- ✔ Getting the photo file size right
- ✔ Identifying the necessary edits
- ✔ Choosing a handy image-editing tool
- ✔ Cleaning up images in Fast Photos

You may hear all kinds of myths — such as "more is better" — regarding images for eBay, and personally, I refuse to perpetrate any more. Because you already know how to take a reasonable picture of your product (provided, of course, you've read the how-to information from the preceding practices in this part), I use this practice to show you how fast you can get the photos you take — or the scans you make — spruced up for eBay.

 No eBay seller should spend hours playing with and perfecting images for eBay listings (although some do). One pass through a simple image-editing software program gets any reasonable picture Internet-ready.

Here's a checklist of tried-and-true techniques for preparing elegant, fat-free, fast-loading images to display on eBay:

- ✔ **Set your image resolution at 72 pixels per inch.** You can do this with the settings for your scanner. Although 72 ppi may seem a low resolution, it merely nibbles computer memory, shows up fast on a buyer's screen (even over a dial-up connection), and looks great on eBay.

- ✔ **When you're using a digital camera, set its resolution to no higher than the 800×600 format.** That's custom-made for a VGA monitor. You can always crop the picture if it's too large. You can even save the image at 640×480. It will display well on eBay but take up less space — so you can add more pictures!

- ✔ **Make the finished image no larger than 480 pixels wide.** When you size your picture in your image software, it's best to keep it no larger than 300×300 pixels or 4 inches square on a monitor set for 600×800 resolution (or 3.5×3.5 inches on the more commonly used 1280×1024 resolution). These dimensions are big enough for people to see the image without squinting, and the details of your item show up nicely.

- ✔ **Crop any unnecessary areas of the photo.** Show only your item; everything else is a waste.

- ✔ **Use your software to darken or change the photo's contrast.** When the image looks good on your computer screen, the image also looks good on your eBay auction page.

✔ **Save your image as a .JPG file.** When you finish editing your picture, save it as a .JPG. (To do this, follow the instructions that come with your software.) .JPG is the best format for eBay; it compresses information into a small file that loads fast and reproduces nicely on the Internet.

✔ **Check the total file size of your image.** After you save the image, make sure it takes up no more disk space than about 40 KB (if it's too much bigger than that, see if you can crop judiciously — or compress your JPG to reduce total size). That way, eBay users will see the image appear on-screen in a reasonable amount of time.

Size Really Does Matter

So many sellers ignore the impact of image size — but it's one of the most crucial issues in eBay photography. Keep your file size small — that's right, in this case, size *does* matter, and small is beautiful. Limiting your image's file size means you don't bog down the prospective buyer's computer loading time when trying to view your item page (especially if you use multiple pictures in the item description).

Why? It's simple mathematics: The larger your item's image files, the longer the viewer's browser takes to load the listing page. Most eBay users will click back out of a listing to avoid a long page load. You're looking for eyes on your items — you don't want to turn away the curious!

 There are a few utilities on the Internet that you can use to measure how fast your page loads a completed listing. Just search Google.com for *page load timer,* and you should come up with a few services. One we tried out was at www.numion.com/Stopwatch. When you're viewing your listing, just copy its URL from the address line at the top of the browser into the timer page. Click *Start Stop Watch* and the program will load your requested page and tell you how long that loading takes. But realize that, in this instance, the listing is loading at *your* computer's speed.

Pathetically, the United States (maybe because our country is so big?) lags behind the rest of the world in its percentage of broadband users. Without going into a political discussion of the high costs here in the U.S., let's just say that over 50 percent of users still dial up. *Dialing up* (if you broadband folks can remember back that far) means excruciatingly slow page loads.

Viewing Images on a Monitor

To get a better idea of the size for the images you use online, remember that no matter which camera setting you choose, your image should be designed to be viewed on a monitor. Low resolution is just fine because the average computer monitor just isn't an HDTV.

 Don't confuse a printer's dots-per-inch (dpi) with a monitor's pixels-per-inch (ppi). They are two different things. Computer monitors measure resolution in pixels (tiny squares of on-screen light) per inch. The average monitor can only produce 72 pixels per inch (some upper-end models can produce 96 pixels and better). This means that regardless of your vision, if an image exceeds 72-pixel resolution, *you won't be able to tell by looking at the monitor.* (The average printer can produce 600 dpi or better.) All you get for your effort is a huge file that takes forever to load.

The average monitor-resolution settings (in pixels) are

✔ 640 horizontal×480 vertical (VGA)

✔ 800×600 (Super VGA)

✔ 1024×768 (XVGA)

These settings determine the number of pixels that can be viewed on the screen. No matter how large your monitor is (whether 15, 17, or even 21 inches), it shows only as many pixels as you determine in its settings. On larger screens, the pixels just get larger — and make your pictures fuzzy. That's why most people with larger screens set their monitors for a higher resolution.

The popular viewing resolutions for monitors are:

- ✔ 640×480 or 800×600 pixels for 15-inch monitors

- ✔ 800×600 or 1024×768 pixels for 17-inch monitors

- ✔ 1024×768 or 1152×864 pixels for 19-inch monitors

 Remember that scanned images are measured in dpi (dots per inch). The average monitor displays scanned images at 72 dpi. Do not confuse this with pixel size.

Just keep in mind that when you design pictures for your eBay items, you must design for the lowest common denominator. There are still many people using MSNTV (which used to be WebTV), and their screen resolution is fixed at pre-HD television resolution: 544×372. Also consider that over 50 percent of the United States Internet population still hooks up with a dial-up connection; they're not very likely to be using high-end monitors with high resolutions.

 Since higher resolutions make screen images smaller, many users prefer to keep their screens at the 800×600 size for eye comfort during the time they spend on the computer. They don't want to squint!

Read the upcoming section "Accommodating your customers' viewing space," where I give you an idea how the different-size images look on various screens.

If you choose to use eBay's Picture Services

Using eBay's Picture Services (for the free image) is a good idea. It's the only way to get a picture of your item at the top of the listing near the title. And if you use eBay's Picture Services for all your eBay items, setting your image size is not a huge deal. eBay Picture Services apply a compression algorithm that will force your pictures into eBay's prescribed size — and, odds are, they'll look fuzzy when forced into high compression (squeezing the pixels to the prescribed size).

 The more compression put into computer images, the less sharp they appear. So why not set your images to a monitor-friendly size in a software program before uploading them?

Accommodating your customers' viewing space

The higher the resolution of an image, the sharper it is within its patch of precious on-screen space. But all monitors are not created equal. If you choose a resolution that's too high, some of your customers' monitors will have to use too much screen space to show your image, or won't be able to show it at all.

Many of us like to keep up with the latest technology, and so we upgrade to at least 19-inch display screens. But we might forget that many computer users still have 15-inch monitors — with an actual display area no more than 12 inches wide by 9 inches high. This scrunches up the area available for displaying the images in your eBay listings and Web images.

Here's how all those resolution and pixel numbers affect what your customer actually sees for an (eBay recommended) image size of 400×300 (that's pixels, of course, not inches):

- ✔ **On a 15×12-inch screen set at its lowest resolution (640×480 pixels),** the image would show up as 9.375 inches wide and 7.5 inches tall — and take up approximately ⅔ of the height and width of the screen.

- ✔ **On the same monitor set at the highest resolution (1280×1024),** the image would appear approximately 4.7 inches wide and 3.5 inches tall, about ⅓ of the height and width of the screen.

That's a big difference! Check out Table 23-1 to find out how much of the available screen space a 400×300-pixel image covers at different resolutions.

TABLE 23-1: DISPLAY SIZES (WIDTH×HEIGHT) FOR A 400×300-PIXEL IMAGE

Screen Area in Pixels	On a 19-Inch Monitor		On a 15-Inch Monitor	
	Image Size	Required Display Area	Image Size	Required Display Area
640×480	9.4"×7.5"	62.5%×62.5%	7.5"×5.6"	62.5%×62.5%
800×600	7.5"×6"	50%×50%	6"×4.5"	50%×50%
1024×768	5.9"×4.7"	40%×40%	4.7"×3.5"	40%×40%
1280×1024	4.7"×3.5"	31%×29%		

So what happens when the images you want to put on-screen are too big? Even more of the display space is used! Table 23-2 shows what happens on a 19-inch monitor when the image's pixel size increases by 50 percent in both directions — making the image 600 × 450 pixels. As you establish your image-sizing practices, think about how much screen real estate you're asking your shoppers for.

TABLE 23-2: DISPLAY SIZES (WIDTH×HEIGHT) FOR A
600×450-PIXEL IMAGE ON A 19-INCH MONITOR

Screen Area in Pixels	Image Size	Required Display Area
640×480	14.1"×11.25"	94%×94%
800×600	11.25"×9"	75%×75%
1024×768	8.8"×7"	59%×59%
1280×1024	7"× 5.3"	47%×44%

More than you ever wanted to know about dpi, ppi, pixels, resolutions...

If you read avidly about digital images and printers (and who doesn't?), you see the terms *dpi* (dots per inch) and *ppi* (pixels per inch) bandied about. Trade secret: These measurements actually have no effect on the size of the images displayed on your computer screen. Instead, they're all about how sharply the details show up. The dpi specification is normally used only when referring to printers; it describes how many dots of ink (per inch) can be printed on a page.

A *dot* is an actual, tiny drop of ink; a *pixel* is the electronic equivalent — a lit-up "dot" in an on-screen image. If you look closely at a printed image, you can usually see the individual dots that make up a picture. Your eyes usually ignore individual dots and smooth them together.

An image displayed on a computer screen is completely different than one printed on a piece of paper, for more than the obvious reason. An image on a piece of paper is the size that it is, forever and ever. An image on a computer screen, however, can be many different sizes, depending on the display settings of the screen. A 19-inch monitor screen — like a 19-inch television — is measured on the diagonal from corner to corner. The actual display area is approximately 15 inches wide by 12 inches high. However, the size of the screen is only one part of how text and images are displayed. The *resolution,* or degree of sharpness of displayed text or images, also comes into play.

By tweaking the number of pixels used to create an on-screen image, you can give the image its best possible look on the widest range of monitors. So finding the highest possible resolution (that still lets the image load quickly) means paying some attention to computer hardware. You define resolution for a 19-inch monitor, for example, by making settings through the computer's operating system; these tell the monitor to display Web pages at resolutions ranging from 640×480 pixels (lower) to 1280×1024 pixels (higher). What these measurements mean, in essence, is how large and how clear your image can be. At lowest resolution, an image is made up of 640 pixels (or dots) spread from left to right across the screen, and 480 pixels from top to bottom. The highest resolution uses 1280 pixels left to right, and 1024 top to bottom. Okay, please stop yawning; wrestling with screen resolution is how you get images that are right-sized for your eBay listings.

Sizing (and Resizing) Your Pictures

Whether you use a digital camera or a scanner, you may often find that the picture you end up with is too big to use with your eBay listing. The image might take up too much of your computer screen because it has too many *pixels* (the dots that make up the picture). Or the image file might take up 500 K — or more! — and take an eon to load. (It's recommended that you keep the size of your eBay image files around 40 to 50 K instead.) If you notice one of these problems, then you probably have both. And to correct either problem (screen-hogging or file bloat), you need to resize the image.

Most digital cameras and scanners come with an image-processing program. We encourage you to learn how to use the basic features of this program; it has what you need for cleaning up your pictures before you use them in your listings. The most useful functions help you *crop* and *resize* pictures that are too big:

✔ **Cropping** is trimming off unnecessary areas around the edges of a picture. For example, if you have a picture of a lamp that you are selling, but discover your daughter peeking in on the left side of the picture, you'll want to remove that little "extra" from your image before using it in your listing.

✔ **Resizing** is making a big image smaller — or vice versa — so you can see what it is but still have room for everything else on-screen. Although digital pictures are rarely too small, re-taking a too-tiny picture is our usual recommendation. You probably want to resize your picture if it is larger than 400×300 pixels (the recommended size for an image on eBay).

 When the program shrinks a picture by resizing, it simply removes pixels to bring the image down to the new size. If the original size is 800×600 and the new size is 400×300, every other pixel is discarded. Such arbitrary pixel discarding may not leave you with the best-looking image.

✔ *Resampling*, if your image-processing program has this function, is a better choice than resizing. When a picture is resampled, rather than simply removing pixels at random, the computer actually analyzes the surrounding pixels and determines which pixel is the more logical one to remove. This selective process retains the closest reproduction of the original image for a crisper, clearer result.

 Every time you save a picture in JPEG format, it's compressed all over again, in order to make the final size of the file as small as possible without losing much of the clarity of the image. Be careful when editing pictures that you intend to save in this format. If you save an image multiple times, each save takes away just a little of the sharp edges in the picture; eventually the image quality gets sketchy and muddy.

 For sharpest clarity, try this formula: When resizing or resampling your photos, make the new size evenly divisible into the old. For example, if your original image is 1200 pixels by 900 pixels, a good size for the resized image would be 400 pixels by 300 pixels. This will result in exactly 1 in every 3 pixels being kept for the new, smaller image. If you select a new size of 500×375, 1 pixel will be kept for each 2.4 pixels in the original image, resulting in rougher edges throughout.

Pursuing Other Image Improvements

Suppose you just took a bunch of pictures for your new eBay items, using camera settings between 640×480 and 1024×768. (Those are common low-resolution digital camera settings.) Now you need to get these pictures snazzed up to give your items the best possible image (and get you the best possible price).

The process for fixing your pictures is twofold: (1) knowing which common edits improve your pictures' appearance on eBay and then (2) doing them. The next sections show you the quick path through the process.

Knowing what image elements to edit

Surprise — pictures don't always come out of the camera in perfect form. There are a few tweaks you can make to bring them into perfection range:

- ✔ **Cropping.** Sometimes there's a little too much background and not enough product. Don't waste precious bandwidth on extraneous pixels. To crop your image means to cut away the part of the picture that is unnecessary.

- ✔ **Alter the size.** Reduce or increase the size or shape of the image.

- ✔ **Change the orientation.** Rotate the image left or right; flip it horizontally or vertically.

- ✔ **Brightness and Contrast.** These two functions usually work together in most photo programs. By giving your picture more brightness, it (duh) makes the picture look brighter. Raising contrast brings out detail; lowering it dulls the difference between light and dark.

- ✔ **Sharpen.** If your camera was not perfectly in focus when you took the picture, applying a photo-editing program's sharpening feature can help. Be careful not to sharpen too much, or it can destroy the smoothness of the image.

If your images need any more help than the above alterations, it's probably easier (and faster) just to retake the picture.

Choosing an image-editing tool

eBay sellers use a wide array of image-editing software. As a matter of fact, some listing software has built-in mini-editing capabilities. Choosing software for your images is like choosing an office chair: What's right for some people is dreadful for others.

When you buy a digital camera, it will no doubt arrive with a CD that includes some variation of image-editing software. Give it a try. If it works well for you, keep it. If not, check out the two options we mention farther on in this chapter.

 Every image-editing software program has its own system requirements and capabilities. Study the software that comes with your camera or scanner. If you feel that the program is too complicated (or doesn't give you the editing tools you need), investigate some of the other popular programs. I use Fast Photos (discussed below). You can get some excellent shareware (software that you can try before you buy) at www.tucows.com and www.shareware.com.

 Just because a program is elaborate (and pricey) doesn't always mean it's *better* for your purposes. I used to be happy using Adobe Photoshop, but it's a large, expensive program — and it's overkill for eBay images. Stay tuned for two simple, low-cost solutions: Fast Photos and eBay's own Enhanced Photo Services.

Quick touch-up and FTP in Fast Photos

If budget is a consideration (and it should be in any business), you might be happy giving Fast Photos by Pixby Software a try. It's a simple, all-in-one photo-editing program designed especially for e-commerce and eBay sellers. The developer of the software knew exactly what capabilities online sellers need for their images — and included just those — nothing else: cropping, JPEG compression, sharpening, resizing, enhancing, rotating, and adding watermark text and borders.

The software is a PC application that runs on Windows Vista, XP, or 2000. Install a *free* trial from the CD at the back of this book or visit their Web site at

www.pixby.com/marshacollier

Fast Photos is an *all-in-one* tool for eBay sellers because it not only allows you to touch up your images quickly, but also has a built-in FTP program so you can upload your images to a hosting service immediately after editing them.

Editing an image for eBay in Fast Photos is simple:

1. **Open the program.**

2. **Click Browse and find the directory containing your image.**

    This location can be a media card (a Memory Stick, a CompactFlash card, Secure Digital card), or an area on your hard drive that you've set aside for storing your images.

3. **Once you've found the photo, click it, and then click the Add to Tray button (near the top of the screen).**

    Before you can settle on the correct image to edit, you have to get a good look at it, right? Figure 23-1 shows the selection process that puts it on-screen.

• **Figure 23-1: Selecting a photo for editing in Fast Photos.**

4. **Choose Edit.**

5. **Click to perform any of the following tasks. (the editing screen is shown in Figure 23-2):**

▶ **Rotate:** If you've shot your picture sideways or upside down, you can rotate it here.

▶ **Crop:** In crop mode, a gray rectangle appears with corner dots. Click a corner dot, drag the rectangle until it closes in on your item. If you want to adjust your cropping area, click and drag an edge or corner handle to adjust the rectangle's size. When you're satisfied with the cropping, double-click Apply. Poof! It crops itself and appears at your new size.

▶ **Enhance:** Brighten, darken, increase or decrease the contrast, and work with image gamma (how it appears on a monitor) and color. If you feel that the color of your image isn't vibrant enough or is too dark, adjust the brightness and contrast. Just move the sliders to the left or to the right: increasing or decreasing these values. The image in the main window will change as you perform your alterations, so you know what your image will look like before you save your changes. When you're happy with the image results, feel free to click Apply.

Don't worry, everything you do is visible on-screen — and can be undone if you mess up.

▶ **Resize:** You can resize your image to the standard eBay sizes or make the image a custom size.

▶ **Sharpen:** Is your image a little fuzzy? Click here to bring out the details. You can apply three different strengths of sharpening to your pictures.

▶ **Add border:** If you want a border or a drop shadow on your image, you can apply it here.

▶ **Add text:** Type your user ID so you can *watermark* your images (add distinctive text in a see-through font that can help dissuade those who might try to use your images as their own).

▶ **JPEG compress:** By moving a sliding bar, you can compress the image as much as you dare. The more you compress, the less detailed the image will be. Find a workable balance between clear detail and compact file size.

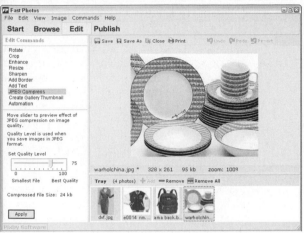

• **Figure 23-2:** Here we're compressing the size of the file after cropping.

▶ **Create gallery thumbnail:** You can create a perfect 192×192 thumbnail of your image on a white background for use in the gallery.

6. To save the changes you've made to your image, click Save As, give your file a name, and press Enter.

Now you can upload your newly edited image to the Web. Those steps are just as fast:

1. Choose Publish (on the toolbar).

2. Go to the Publish screen and click the Add button under the FTP accounts box.

This is the procedure for adding (setting up) an FTP account for uploading. The box shown in Figure 23-3 appears.

 Not to brag, but we can send 5 MB worth of pictures to our ISP for free! Check to see what your ISP offers. (Also, check out auctiva.com in Practice 25 — they host images for free.)

3. Input the data required for your FTP server and click OK.

Your image is ready to upload.

4. Highlight the image(s) you want to upload and then click the Publish button.

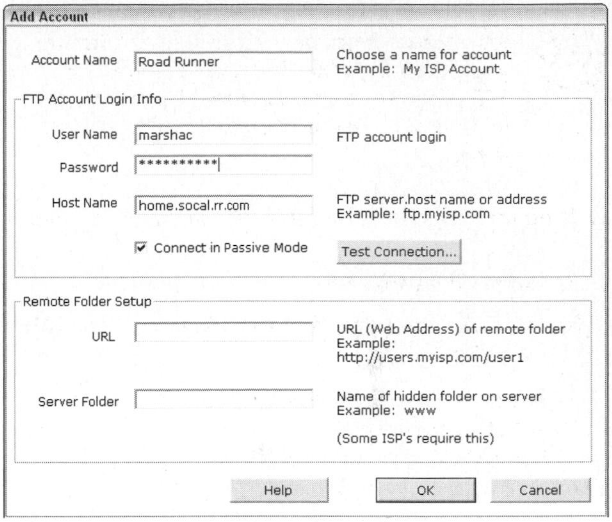

• **Figure 23-3:** Here's where to fill in the form with your FTP information.

You can upload your images to the Web space individually or in a batch — with the same single mouse click. Once an image is uploaded, you'll see the word *done* appear in the status box at the top of the page. (Notice that it showed up after we uploaded the image in Figure 23-4.) You also see the URL suffix to call up the picture from your Web space.

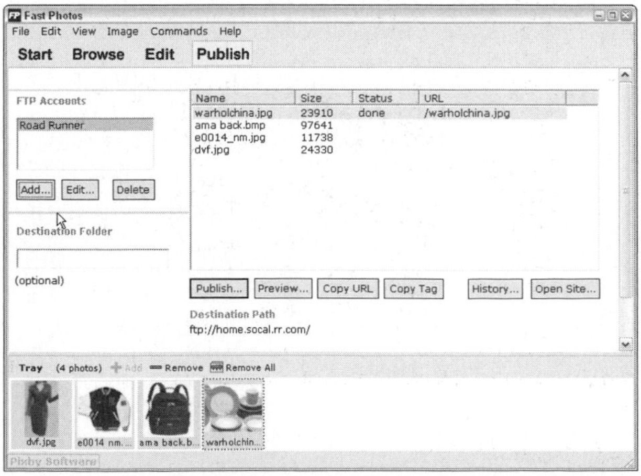

• **Figure 23-4:** Here we've successfully uploaded a picture to our ISP Web space for use in an auction.

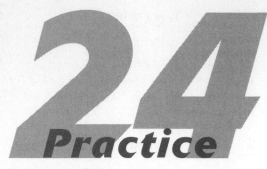

Using Item Images Effectively

Practice 24

In This Practice

- When one image is not enough
- Deciding what image goes where
- Positioning images for impact
- Checking out eBay's Picture Services

Taking great item photos and editing them to perfection are both important PowerSeller practices. But using your well thought out creations appropriately to sell your items gets you another step closer to counting the money. In this practice, I tell you how to choose and use images to save you time and build more interest with your prospective bidders.

Embedding Images in Your Listing for Free

eBay gives you the ability to add pictures to your listings, but if you have a place to host your own images (Practice 25 tells you how — and where — to host), you can embed one or more images directly in your listing — and without paying any additional fees!

An image can be embedded anywhere within your listing with the help of the *img* (Image) HTML tag. This is one of those tags that stands alone — no need for a closing tag (the / just before the ending > is a signal that the tag closes itself).

```
<img src="http://www.yourisp.com/yourimage.jpg"/>
```

Check out Practice 17 for more information about using HTML to spice up your listings.

Selling up with multiple pictures

Selling items online is, without a doubt, much different from selling the same merchandise in a brick-and-mortar storefront. One major difference is that your customer can't pick up the item to view it more closely, or to look at the bottom or inside. But here's the next best thing: to offer potential buyers a look at multiple pictures of your item.

Take a main picture that shows the entire item, but also take pictures of the back, sides, top, and bottom. Close-up photos can also be important.

Here are some item-specific examples for secondary images; if you are selling

- ✔ **A painting:** Take a close-up picture of the artist's signature besides the picture of the actual painting. Apply this concept to any artwork you have for sale, including pottery, sculpture, prints — or signed first-edition books.

- ✔ **Silver:** If the silver piece has a maker's mark, take a close-up of the mark itself. Take another close-up of any dings or damage.

- ✔ **A designer dress:** Make sure to take an additional close-up of the tag that shows size, fabric content — even laundering instructions!

As with other aspects of your listing, put yourself in the position of a potential buyer. What parts of the item for sale would you like to see in detail?

 Make sure that the entire surface of the item is visible in your picture(s). If you zoom in too close on the item and leave out some of the edges, your buyer might think you're hiding something.

With multiple pictures of your merchandise, placement of the images in your description can become simpler or, for that matter, more complex depending on the size of the images. If the pictures all have similar widths, stacking them along the left or right side of your description might be the most appropriate placement — just be sure to place the appropriate text for each image right next to it.

Choosing a main or dominant photo

So you've followed my instructions and taken multiple pictures of your item — there will be one that stands out as the main (dominant) photo. This image might be an overall picture of the item or a close-up of its most important element.

Emphasize this main photo in your listing. If you use eBay Picture Services, this picture will be the first picture your customers encounter — thus it's the one to display at the top of the listing. When you design the layout of your description, place this picture prominently — for example, centered at the top — so it's the first element seen by your customer when viewing the listing.

Selecting the Gallery image

When you list an item for sale on eBay, you have the option of a Gallery image. The Gallery image is a thumbnail photo, automatically created by eBay, of a specific photo you designate when creating your item listing. The Gallery image helps your selling efforts as follows:

- ✔ **By showing up in search results:** The Gallery image appears to the left of your listing title in search and category results — and, by virtue of this location, gives potential customers an additional incentive to choose your listing to view the item in more detail.

- ✔ **By simulating a catalog entry:** If you have an eBay Store, the Gallery image appears to the left of the item title on your Store category pages, which gives customers an experience similar to catalog shopping.

The Gallery image is a useful marketing tool that provides greater visibility for your merchandise. Choosing the correct photo for the Gallery image can have a significant effect on its value as a marketing device — and can help you get the biggest bang for your buck when you use this feature.

 Don't automatically select the main picture of your item as the Gallery image; that particular photo might be completely ineffective when reduced to eBay's standard thumbnail size (80 pixels wide by 60 pixels high as of this writing). Do choose an image that will be easy to view and will catch your potential customer's eye *when reduced*.

Placing your pictures for maximum effect

Although it isn't the most important aspect of your description, the picture of the item you're selling is a big part of the first impression it makes. No surprise that the position your pictures take within a description can make a huge difference in ease of viewing the information about the item. Keep the following in mind:

✔ **If the item image is wider than it is tall,** centering the picture above the text describing the item is appropriate.

✔ **If the item image is taller than it is wide,** placing it on the left (or right) side of the description text is better.

Placing your images according to these general guidelines helps to keep the image and the description together on-screen when your customer views your listing. See Figure 24-1 for an example of both placements.

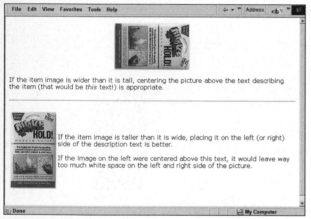

Figure 24-1: Proper placement of figures with the descriptive text.

If your image is just about as wide as it is tall, then placement of the picture with respect to the text isn't as crucial. You just want to avoid forcing your customer to scroll up and down too much to view both image and text.

 Always use the one-free-picture option that stores an image with your item listing on eBay. This image can be the same one you embed in your description, or a different

image. This way, if eBay is having problems displaying pictures stored on its server, odds are that your own picture-hosting service won't be having the same problems at the same time (and vice versa). Thus an image of the item you're selling is always available.

Using eBay's Enhanced Picture Services

Free tools — that actually work. How nice is that? eBay's Picture Services are now far more than a fancy FTP program. Using the current version, you can upload your images and perform minor editing right on your screen without any additional software.

 You can use eBay Enhanced Picture Services only if you're using Microsoft Internet Explorer Web browser (version 5 or later) with Microsoft Windows (Windows 98SE or later). So if you use Mozilla Firefox (like I do), you have to fire up a second browser to take advantage of this free tool.

 The Enhanced Picture Services are great for quick one-off items and for beginners — but if you're selling many items on eBay, especially over the long term, you might want to invest in a more robust image-editing program such as Fast Photos.

The Sell Your Item form is where you find the area that requests your images. Click the tab for enhanced Picture Services. If you've never used this feature before, you may have to download a small program.

To use this wonderful tool, follow these steps.

1. **Click the small Add Picture button.**

Doing so opens Picture Services with three tabs: Basic, Enhanced and Self Hosting, as in Figure 24-2. You want the Enhanced tab.

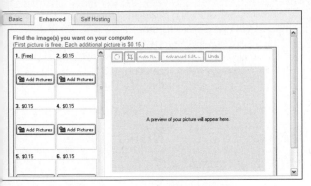

Figure 24-2: Selecting a picture for uploading.

2. **Click an Add Picture button to (duh) load a picture.**

Doing so opens a directory on your computer. Point the window to the directory (see Figure 24-3) in which your photo resides on your computer.

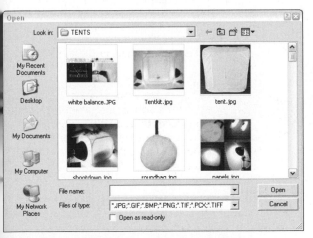

Figure 24-3: Your directory appears on-screen.

3. **When you've selected the picture you want, click Open.**

The name of the file appears in the filename box and the image appears in the main preview screen, as in Figure 24-4.

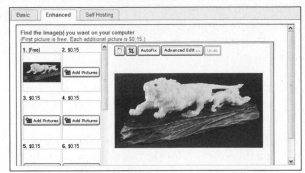

Figure 24-4: My lovely lion figurine picture is ready for editing.

4. **Apply the appropriate controls to your picture, as follows:**

▶ You can click the little circle if you want to rotate your image (as in Figure 24-5).

Figure 24-5: Rotating the image.

▶ To crop your picture, click the crop marks. You can now drag the corners inward or outward to make your picture its best size for eBay (as in Figure 24-6).

▶ You can use AutoFix to let eBay's server decide what's best for your picture — but we don't recommend it. For more satisfying results, click the Advanced Edit button (as in Figure 24-7) so you have control over the changes made to your images.

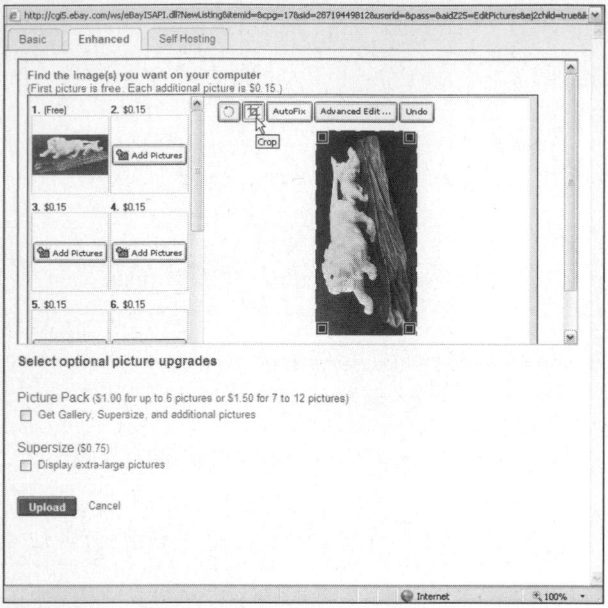

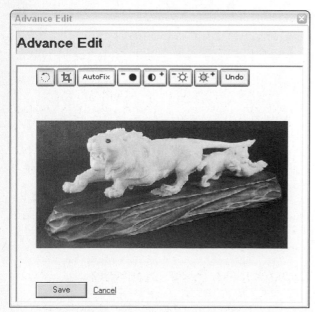

Figure 24-6: Cropping an image on eBay.

▶ In Advanced Edit mode, you can adjust contrast and brightness, along with the previously mentioned features. Thankfully, there is also the Undo button, to whisk away any overaggressive changes you may have made to your image.

4. When you've made all your changes, click Continue in the Sell Your Item form.

Your image is uploaded to eBay's server for use in your listing.

> The purpose of an eBay listing is to sell your stuff, and this book's mission is to help demystify eBay listing practices. I'm not trying to set you up to buy fancy software or to fill your head with pages upon pages of technobabble that will keep you awake all night. My job is not to make you feel bad if you can't remember what an f-stop is or remember the numeric coding for the color red (though of course you *can* worry about all that if you need another hobby). This is the simple deal. Explained this way, there's not much mystery, is there?

Figure 24-7: Clicking Advanced Edit opens your image in a new smaller screen.

25 Practice

Storing Photos Where Your Listings Can Find Them

In Practice 24, I showed you how to upload your pictures, using eBay Picture Services. I don't think you should abandon that habit, as the picture you upload via eBay is the one that ends up on the top of your listing. Most listings can make good use of more than one photo in the description. That's why you'll need the information in this practice.

Some of you may find this information to be a bit basic, but it's here so you can pass it along to your employees or even ad a refresher for you!

You see, two of the most common questions I hear are these:

> "How do I get my pictures up on eBay?"
>
> and
>
> "How do I get my pictures out of my camera?"

So if you've ever asked yourself those questions, look to this practice for the answers. Not only do I guide you step by step — until you're an expert at uploading your pictures to eBay — but I also advise you on best practices for storing and safeguarding any pictures you take.

A good way to start developing your picture-handling skills is by understanding how your camera stores its images. And then you'll recognize that storing your images in the camera is a waste of precious picture-taking space. But never fear; this practice shows you how to get those pictures out of your camera, store them on your computer, and safeguard your artistry with regular appropriate backups.

Finding the Pictures in Your Camera

Digital cameras can store your images on various types of removable media. The industry refers to these media types as removable *flash media*. Why, you ask? I hear that the *flash* part has something to do with how quickly the media can be erased, but I advise you to just hum along and go with it. To recap the media types, you can find Smart Digital,

Secure Digital, Memory Sticks, Compact Flash, and DVDs all used in digital cameras. And you also discover that the storage media come in lots of sizes — all the way up to 4 GB (gigabytes) of storage space!

Your camera's manufacturer decides which media type your camera takes, but the size of the storage space you choose is up to you. Most new cameras also have an internal memory where they can store images. So you've got plenty of ways to store pictures and three ways to retrieve them. We go over your options, one by one.

 Your camera names your images in a random manner — and in a language that makes sense only to your camera. The language dubs your images with names like *MVC-015F.jpg* or *DSCN0237.jpg*, and odds are that those strange names will make recognizing your images of choice difficult (to say the least). So getting the images onto your computer where you can view them — and rename them as something more sensible — becomes quite important. See the sidebar "Image names do matter" (later in this practice) for some image-naming ideas.

Retrieving images from your camera's memory

Surprisingly, some digital cameras can even store your pictures without removable media! I've been known to be a bit ditzy at times and I bought a new Nikon digital camera and started snapping away happily until I realized that I hadn't inserted a memory card! Yikes, did I lose all my images? Nope, most of the newer cameras have their own internal memory that can hold many images in temporary storage. (This memory is also useful when you want to do some in-camera photo editing.)

You can transfer images held in your camera's internal memory to your computer through a direct cable connection. In some cases, the camera has a docking station (as is the case with the Nikon Cool-Station or the Kodak EasyShare).

Kodak has been the leader in offering cameras that depend on a docking station to retrieve the images (see Figure 25-1). With its cameras, Kodak includes its own EasyShare software, which makes downloading and editing images in one place über-easy. The camera dock connects to your computer and allows you to download pictures with the push of a button. Once the images are on your computer, you can edit and rename them easily.

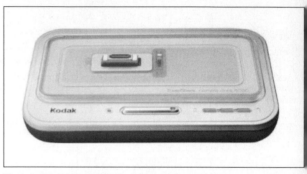

Figure 25-1: Kodak's docking station allows you to snap on the camera and download your images quickly.

Older digital cameras come with a cable that connects directly to your computer's USB port. When you connect your camera and computer via the cable, your computer treats the camera as if it were a hard drive. You can then pull up a folder window and download the images as if you were copying files from one drive to another.

Whether you're hard-wired, using a docking station, or a flash memory card (see farther on for the complete lowdown on memory cards), the process of getting the pictures from the media to your computer is about the same. On my PC running Windows XP, the process goes something like this:

1. **Right-click in your computer's My Pictures folder and select New⇨Folder from the resulting menu.**

2. **Type a logical name for your new folder (something like eBay Items) when prompted, and then click OK.**

3. Plug your camera's cable into the computer's USB port or plug the memory card into the appropriate port on your computer.

If you're lucky, your computer has the ports in a convenient location. After you make the connection, your computer should confirm that a new device is attached to your computer and will ask what you'd like to do, as shown in Figure 25-2.

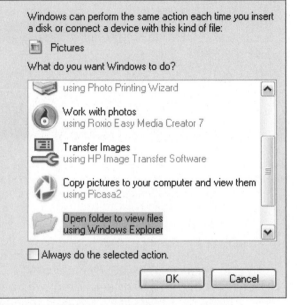

Figure 25-2: When you connect a new device (say, a camera or media card), your computer asks what you want it to do.

4. Click a folder which selects your camera as a device. When you do this you see the memory folder in your camera (the name depends on the kind of camera you have); select the option to open the folder and view the pictures.

When you select this option, your computer can access the memory in your camera. So you can see the pictures, and not just filenames, be sure to select the View Thumbnails option in your system's View menu.

5. When you see the memory folder in your camera (the folder's name depends on the type of camera you have), select the option to Open Folder and View Files.

 I prefer to view the files as thumbnails in a folder before doing anything to them — and suggest this strategy for preparing to transfer your image files. Not only is it a good way to organize, but it's also handy for selecting the best shots before downloading.

6. Click individual files, Ctrl+click to select multiple files, or Ctrl+A to select all files in the folder.

7. Drag the selected file or files over to the My Camera (or whatever you've named your eBay picture folder) folder on your computer.

Alternatively, you can right-click and choose Copy from the resulting menu to copy all the highlighted files. Then right-click your My Camera folder and choose Paste. In either case, the image files will be copied to your computer.

 You can create subfolders in your My Camera folder to store images from different photo shoots. You can also have separate folders — with names like *Jewelry, Shoes,* and *Collectibles* — for storing your sales items by category.

Types of Flash media

Many cameras have up to 10 MB of internal memory. This means you can store up to that amount, without using any external removable storage media. (Most cameras also have removable media.)

Your computer may have the appropriate slots to insert and read the media (just like a mini-drive) but you may need an external media reader if your computer isn't so outfitted. Consider it to be a teeny disk drive for the little cards. You insert the media into the media reader to transfer the data into your computer. You can buy a new USB card reader on eBay for as little as $5.00. Here's a list of the removable storage media currently available:

- ✔ **CompactFlash memory card:** This is a small medium, slightly smaller than a matchbook. There are also readers for a laptop's PCMCIA slot. CompactFlash cards come in different sizes and hold from 16 MB to 4 GB worth of memory capacity.

- ✔ **Secure digital card:** An amazing little piece of technology in a postage-stamp size (it's the smallest card in Figure 25-3), it's one the most durable. The small media is encased in plastic, as is the CompactFlash card and the Memory Stick. It also uses metal connector contacts rather than pins and plugs like other cards, making it less prone to damage. These cards can be set to hold up to 4 GB, but more commonly hold 256 to 512 MB.

- ✔ **SmartMedia cards:** A SmartMedia card is slightly smaller than a Compact Flash card but is very thin and has no plastic outer case. It is only used in a few brands of digital cameras (such as Olympus). SmartMedia cards come in different data sizes from 8MB to 128MB.

- ✔ **Memory stick:** A tiny media card is about the size of piece of chewing gum and as long as an AA battery. The Memory Stick is a Sony device and is used in most Sony products. Memory Sticks now hold as much as 2 GB of memory. One of the great things about a Memory Stick is that you can use it in numerous devices besides cameras, including PCs and video recorders.

- ✔ **Mini CD, CD/RW, and DVD:** These mini optical discs hold tons of images for eBay, as much as 185 MB worth. You can read them right in your computer's CD or DVD reader. If you look at the disc platter of your computer's CD or DVD drive, you'll notice a smaller round indentation. This is to hold the mini-disc format.

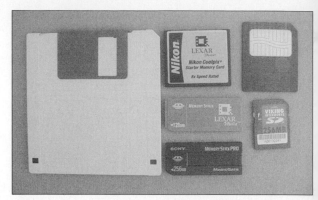

Figure 25-3: There's quite a variety of digital media available to store your images.

- ✔ **Micro Secure Digital card.** This is the very teeniest incarnation in mini storage. It is so small that computers need to use an adapter (as in Figure 25-4) that mimics a regular secure digital card. They are very popular in cell phone cameras — and wherever space is at a premium. (The Micro Secure digital card is so small — it's about the size of my pinky's nail — that mounting it takes a bit of concentration.)

Figure 25-4: The new Micro Secure digital card next to an adapter that fits computers' Secure Digital card ports.

You may find that you use more than one type of medium with your digital camera. And because you can record any type of digital data on these removable media, you may find other uses for them. For example, when I want to back up files or move larger files to my laptop, out of laziness (now where's my flash drive?) I copy them onto one of my Sony Memory Sticks in my desktop computer, and then I plug the stick into the port on my laptop and copy the file.

Mounting the Flash-media card

To retrieve the digital pictures from your Flash media, you first need to find the media in your camera. Think back to where you found a tiny trapdoor in your camera — the one you opened when you put the media card in the camera in the first place. When you've scratched your head a few times and found the trapdoor, open it and remove the media card, as shown in Figure 25-5.

Figure 25-5: Removing a teeny-tiny 256MB card from my camera.

When you pull out the camera's media card, you've got a handful of pictures in a tiny piece of plastic. What to do now? If your computer doesn't have a bay of media card readers, you may need to go out and buy a media reader. A *media reader* is a small, portable device that sports slots for many types of

flash media. If you need to buy one, we recommend that you get a media reader that reads as many different media types as possible. That way, when something goes wrong (you *know* it will) and the new camera you have to buy uses a different media, your media reader can still have you covered.

After you find a place to stick the card that will permit your computer to read it, stick it there, and a small window — similar to the one shown in Figure 25-2 — should pop up. You can follow the same procedure to extract files from the camera's media card as you would for getting pictures from the camera's memory (see the section "Retrieving images from your camera's memory," earlier in this practice). Unless your camera comes with some fancy downloading software, the procedure to copy images onto your computer works the same in either case.

Removing the media

No, you don't just yank the camera's media card out of your computer when you're through copying over the files (although I must admit to doing so several times myself, until I figured out why that isn't a good idea).

 If you don't follow your computer's unmounting procedure, it's very possible that you can mung up the files on your media card so the pictures residing on it become unreadable! That is (need we say) potentially a very, very, bad thing to happen. You never know when you might need a backup copy of an image — which you won't have *until* you back up your images elsewhere (for example, on a CD).

For Windows XP users, it's best to look in the lower-right corner of your taskbar at the bottom of your screen to find a small icon with a left-pointing arrow. If you don't see this Safely Remove Hardware icon, click the chevron-shaped icon to reveal your hidden icons. When you see the right one, follow these steps:

1. **Right-click the Safely Remove Hardware icon.**

A small list appears.

2. **Click to highlight the media you want to remove.**

Your computer may chug and grind a bit, and soon a bubble appears to let you know that it's okay to remove your flash media.

3. **Remove the media from your computer's slot and insert it back in your camera's little trap door.**

Image names do matter

After you get your digital images onto your computer, you might want to take a quick look at them and then name them appropriately. You can also use this quick-look time to delete the truly crappy pictures with those random, letter-and-number-based nightmare names *before* you rename the keepers. Go to the folder that holds your images, and if you're using Windows XP, choose View⇨Filmstrip to get a display as shown in the sidebar figure.

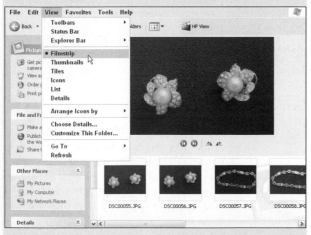

Viewing your images in the filmstrip mode gives you a good idea of how they came out.

Going with a *For Dummies* philosophy of naming subfolders with the category of the items in it, I usually name images so that I know exactly what the image portrays, without having to open it. For example, I might name the image shown above *pearl_cz_earrings.jpg*.

Here's an important thing to keep in mind: Some file-naming conventions apply specifically to files that will be used on the Internet. Although your computer (MAC or

PC) may permit other naming options, the interoperable nature of the Internet requires these rules:

- ✔ Use only letters, numbers, underscore (_), and hyphen (-) as characters in filenames.

- ✔ Leave no spaces between characters.

- ✔ Use mostly lowercase letters; uppercase letters may be used to distinguish words, for example, *STBirthdayPartyDVD.jpg*.

- ✔ When separating words, use the underscore mark (_), as in *green_earring.jpg*.

- ✔ Use a period (.) only to separate the extension from the rest of the filename, as in *dome.jpg*.

- ✔ Use a maximum of 16 characters when naming an image.

Uploading Your Images to a Server

Often, people look at uploading their pictures to their own (non-eBay) Web spaces as a major mystery. Many users are still convinced that they have to pay for an image-hosting service — but that's rarely the case these days.

 I highly recommend that your first move (for getting your images onto a listing) be to take advantage of the one free picture from eBay's Picture Services. First, it's available at no charge; second, Picture Services offers many other benefits. Practice 24 shows you how to upload an image with eBay's Picture Services, and even how to edit your image a bit.

To use multiple images in a listing (and avoid paying eBay to do so), you will need to upload your images to a server somewhere on the Internet. By doing so, your images will have an address, or URL, which you insert into your HTML coding or on eBay's Sell Your Item form. This address allows the eBay Web site to display the picture in your listings. To get such an address for your pictures, you have several options:

✔ **Your ISP (Internet service provider):** All the big ISPs — AOL, AT&T, Road Runner, and EarthLink — give you space to store your Internet stuff. You're already paying a monthly fee to an ISP, and you can park pictures there at no extra charge.

✔ **An image-hosting Web site:** Web sites that specialize in hosting pictures are popping up all over the Internet. Some charge a small fee; others are free. The upside here is that these specialized sites (such as auctiva.com and inkfrog.com) usually have uploading software built in, which makes them extremely easy to use.

✔ **Your server:** If you have your own server (those of you who do know who you are), you can store those images in your own home base.

Many ISPs give you a minimum of 5 MB (that's megabytes) of space to put a personal home page up on the Internet. You can usually store your images for your eBay sales there — unless your provider has some strict rules about not doing that (it's a good idea to check first).

 I highly recommend a Web site at www. auctiva.com. **They have free image hosting and lots of tools for sellers — all free!**

Obtaining an FTP program

Internet providers may supply you with an image upload area, but they may require you to use File Transfer Protocol (FTP) to upload your images. If so, you may want to locate an FTP program to help you manage this process.

You may be able to find a free or shareware (requiring a small fee) FTP program on various Web sites. But wait, I use an alternate Internet browser called Firefox from Mozilla. It's a great Web browser, used by many Internet professionals because it is generally more stable and less apt to crash like the competition — also it is a bit more secure. It also has an add-on

called FireFTP. An FTP program that's built right into the browser! Best of all? Both Firefox and FireFTP are free for anyone to download. Just go to www. mozilla.com/en-US as pictured in Figure 25-6 below.

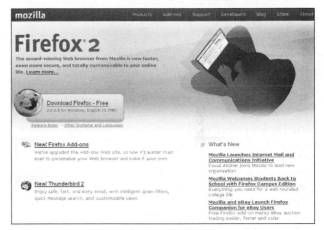

Figure 25-6: The Firefox and FireFTP download page.

 Before you upload a picture, your image must be ready to go and Internet ready. See Practice 23 for details.

Uploading to an ISP server

Now I show you how to upload pictures using FireFTP. Most FTP software programs work in a similar fashion, but FireFTP really simplifies the entire process. After you have installed the program on the Firefox browser, open it by clicking the Tools link at the top of the browser and select FireFTP. Before you attempt an upload, go to your ISP's home page area to get any specific FTP addresses. Follow these steps to upload a file to any server:

1. **Click the Manage Account link⇨New to set up the information for uploading to your ISP or server.**

   The Account Manager shown in Figure 25-7 appears.

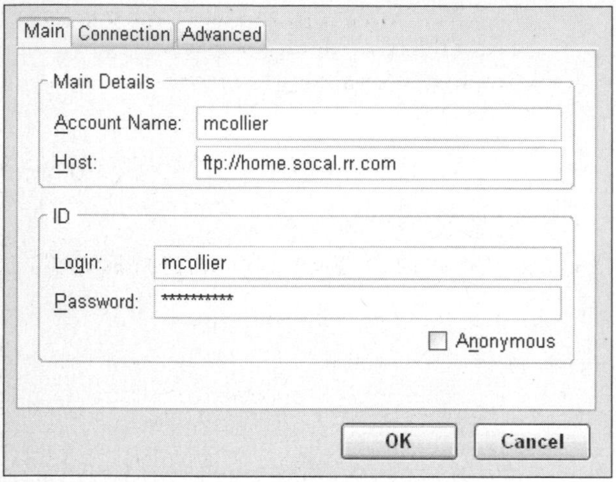

Figure 25-7: The Account Manager in FireFTP showing the setup for a Road Runner ISP account.

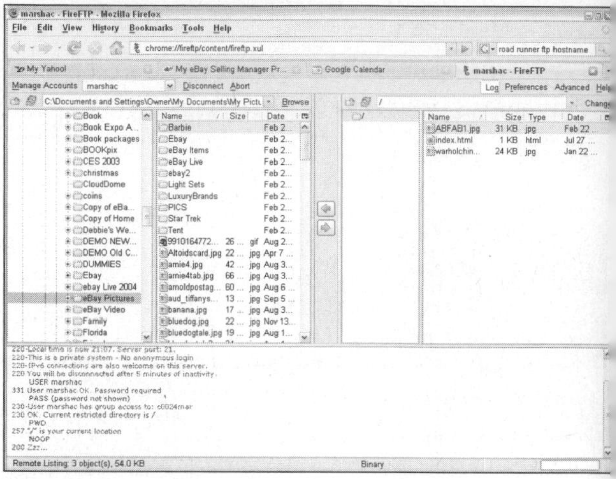

Figure 25-8: Logged in and ready to upload.

2. **Type in the information you got from your ISP (FTP address, user name, and password)**

Click OK. You've just set up your FTP transfer account.

3. **On the FireFTP main screen click the word *Connect* next to the Account name that appeared after you set up your FTP account.**

On the left side of the screen you will see your computer (with searchable directories, as in Figure 25-8) and on the right the contents (if any) from your ISP home page server.

4. **Specify the file you want to upload by clicking on it to highlight it.**

5. **Click the green arrow that points to the Web server directory**

Voilá! Your file is now up on the server, ready to be inserted in your eBay listing. Repeat this procedure to get all the files you want to use for eBay sales on the server.

6. **When you're done uploading all your files, click Disconnect and close FireFTP.**

Uploading to AOL

AOL handles image uploads a bit differently from other ISPs. (But those of you on AOL knew that already.) Many people love AOL because it provides an easy, step-by-step interface. As you probably imagine, uploading pictures is handled in that same AOL style.

To upload pictures to AOL, follow these steps:

1. **Sign on to your AOL account.**

2. **Display the FTP area of AOL in one of two ways:**

For users of AOL 5.0: Select Keywords and type **my ftp space** in the text line and click Go.

For users of later versions of AOL: Search Keywords by typing **my ftp space** in the text line (as in Figure 25-9). On the next page, click *members ftp space*. Then double-click *members.aol.com*.

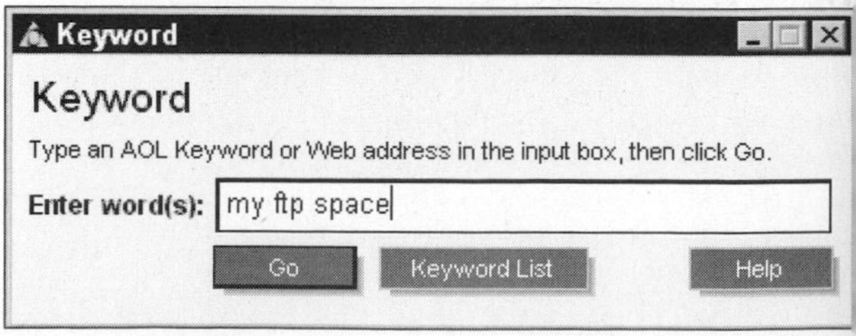

Figure 25-9: Going to your AOL FTP space.

3. Click the bar that says *See My FTP Space*, as in Figure 25-10.

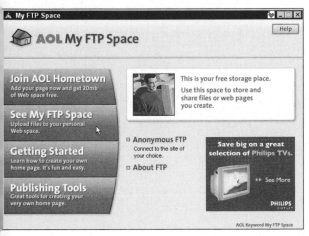

Figure 25-10: Selecting your FTP Space.

Magically you're sent to your AOL storage area.

4. Click the Upload Box to upload a file, as in Figure 25-11.

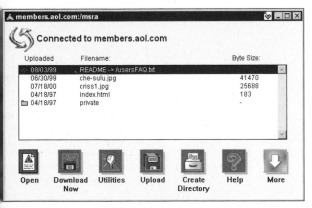

Figure 25-11: Your FTP Control area.

A box appears; it's where you name the file for upload, and it's called *remote file.*

5. Enter a name for your picture in the Remote Filename box (as in Figure 25-12), in all-lowercase letters, using no more than eight characters.

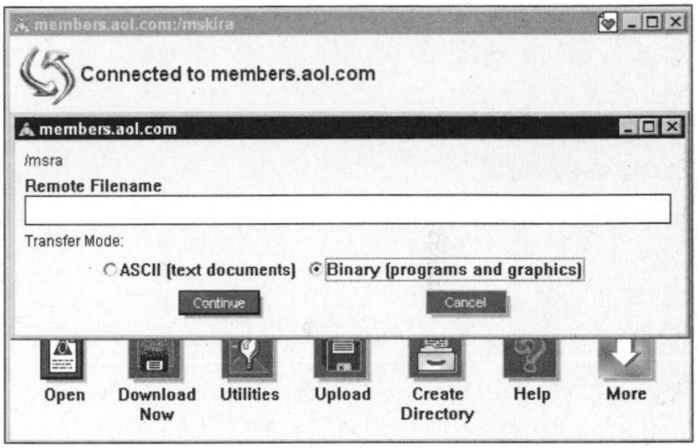

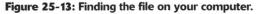

Figure 25-12: Giving your file a name for AOL.

6. When the name is entered, click Continue.

A window opens so you can locate the file on your computer, as shown in Figure 25-13.

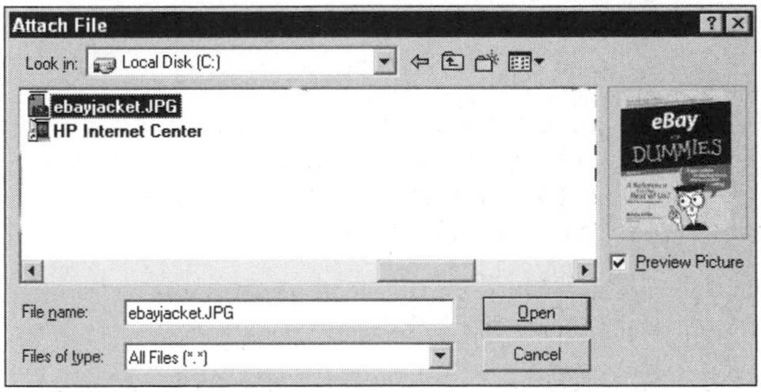

Figure 25-13: Finding the file on your computer.

7. **When you find the file, click its filename and then click Open.**

Your file will now whiz though the wires to the server at AOL, as shown in Figure 25-14.

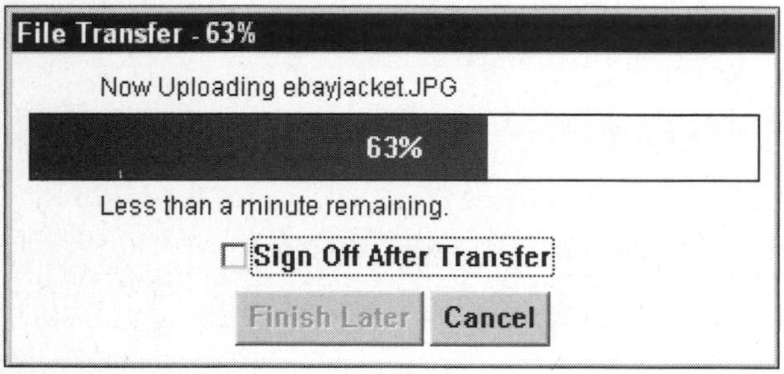

```
File Transfer - 63%
      Now Uploading ebayjacket.JPG
                        63%
      Less than a minute remaining.
        Sign Off After Transfer
          Finish Later    Cancel
```

Figure 25-14: The file is on its way!

8. **Double-check to make sure your file arrived safely.**

Type its URL in your browser this way, and then press Enter:

```
http://members.aol.com/your
  screenname/picturename.jpg
```

 This is also the URL you use when you insert the picture into your eBay item description, as in

```
<img src= http://members.aol.com/
  yourscreenname/picturename.jpg>
```

26 Practice

Giving Unsold Items a Second Chance

A s a full-time or part-time career, selling on eBay can be rewarding and frustrating — all in the same day. You'll find a product that sells like hot dogs in a baseball stadium for months (rewarding), and then, all of a sudden, no one is buying it (frustrating). It's times like these that try sellers' souls . . . or patience.

Many sellers sell unique, one-of-a-kind items, but the majority of sellers stock multiple quantities of many items. After getting some eBay experience under your belt, you're bound to find several items that you're comfortable selling. In addition, if you follow my suggestions in Practice 6, you'll buy multiples (dozens? cases? pallets?) of the items at a seriously discounted price. But when you have all these items lying around the garage, your goal is to get them quickly into buyers' hands at a profit.

 I know several sellers who have bought items in such bulk that they're stocked with the item to sell one a week for the next few years! That's a good thing only if the product is a staple item that will always have a market on eBay.

In Practice 12, I talk about opening an eBay Store. But in addition to your own store, you need to be running auctions on the eBay core site. Why? Auctions are the key to drawing buyers into your store. And stores are not only added potential sales, but they're also a distinct marketing tool for your personal eBay brand.

If you don't have an eBay Store and plan to sell the items one at a time through auctions, you don't want to reinvent the wheel for each sale. Relisting your items efficiently will save you time and aggravation, which makes doing so an effective business practice. So, in this practice, I show you methods for giving your unsold items a second chance (or your similar items a first chance).

Selling Similar after a Sale

Reward time — your new-age yoga pad with built-in DVD player sold! Considering you have three dozen more to sell, the quicker you can get that item back up on the site, the sooner you'll have the opportunity to connect with the next customer.

When bidders lose an auction on eBay, one of the first things they do is search for somebody offering the same item. The sooner you get an item relisted, the sooner a disappointed underbidder will find your listing. Of course, relisting the item also makes it available to other interested bidders who may not have bid on the item before because the bidding went out of their league.

When you offer an item for bidding and it reaches well beyond your target price, why not offer another one? True, this will slow (or possibly end) further bidding on the first item, but if you've exceeded your target price and there are folks out there hot for your item — sell it to them now! That kind of initiative is what eBay is all about.

If you've had more than one bidder on your auction, why not make a Second Chance offer? You can find the details on this money-making tool in the section "Making a Second Chance Offer," later in this practice.

When you want to relist a recently sold item (because you have more to sell), be sure to use the *Sell Similar* option. The *Relist* item option is what you want to use when an item hasn't sold and you want the opportunity to have your listing fees refunded when it sells during the second listing. eBay gives you only two sales cycles to get a refund — so if you're relisting for the third time, use the Sell Similar link to start the item in a new selling cycle in eBay's master computers. If (heaven forbid) the item doesn't sell upon the third listing cycle — which you have started through the Sell Similar option — the fourth relist will allow you to get the listing fee refund if it sells. Get it? Even sales cycle: Relist. Odd-number sales cycle: Sell Similar.

Figure 26-1 shows you the Sell Similar link on a sold item page.

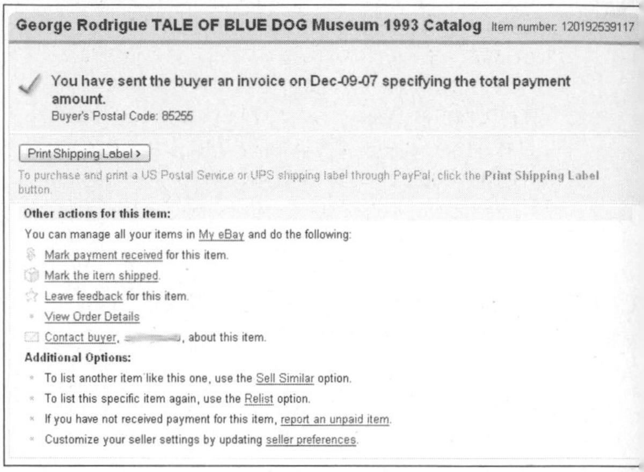

• **Figure 26-1: Have another to sell? Click Sell Similar.**

Relisting When It Doesn't Sell

Drat! Your Dansk China Maribo dinner plate didn't sell. Don't take it personally. It's not that someone out there doesn't love you. It doesn't mean that you merchandise is trash. It's just that this particular week no one was looking to fill their place setting with Maribo plates (go figure).

eBay shoppers shop with no discernible pattern; don't waste your time trying to figure them out. There are too many of them from too many parts of the world. During a specific week, no one may want your item at a certain price, and then the next week you may sell five or six. Unpredictable sales happen all the time.

If you don't have your items listed on the eBay site, your goods will stay on your shelves and get dusty. If you list your items regularly, someone will buy them and send you money. Find something that will sell now!

Often, when relisting, you need to make adjustments. For instance, there's always a chance that you're off-base on your title. Or perhaps the keywords in your title aren't drawing people to your listing. To help you figure out whether it's you or just the market, try running a search for other, similar items — is anyone buying? If you find no bidding activity (perhaps you're selling bikinis in winter?), then perhaps that item needs to be retired from the eBay marketplace for a while.

Consider some other variables that factor into whether your items sell:

- ✔ **Starting price:** Are similar items selling on the site with a lower starting price? Perhaps your starting price is too high.

- ✔ **Shipping costs:** Is your competition charging lower shipping fees? To the buyer, lower is better.

If you can comfortably lower your starting price or shipping fees, do so. If not, wait until other sellers run out of the item. *Then* put yours up for auction — you may just get more bidding action if you are one of the few (versus one of the many) sellers offering the same item.

Here's an example: In Figure 26-2, I'm going to relist an item that didn't sell buy clicking the Relist button.

More than once, I've purchased cases of a particular item right along with a bunch of other eBay sellers. They desperately dumped their items on the site, without paying any attention to the competition. I waited — and got my target price for the item the following season.

Also, it's best to be first if you can. If an item hasn't been offered on the site for a while, the first few sellers who list the item often get the highest prices.

 eBay is a supply-and-demand marketplace. If the supply exceeds the demand, prices go down. If you have an item that sells as fast as you can list it, prices go up.

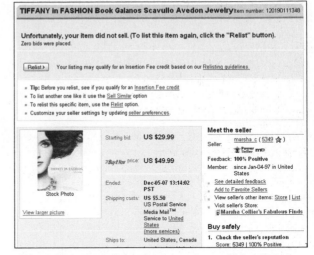

• **Figure 26-2: Two clicks of my mouse, and it's relisted (with a new title).**

Mechanizing Your Relisting

eBay gives you so many ways to relist (or Sell Similar) an item that it's almost dizzying. There are efficient ways and ways that will waste your time. Because this book is all about establishing business practices worthy of PowerSellers, I say just concern yourselves with the speedy ways.

Figure 26-1 shows you the seller's version of a sold item (only the seller sees this when they are signed in), which includes a link to relist. If you always relist using this link on each item's page, you'll have to go to the page for every item you want to relist to find the corresponding link. To save time, get off the auction page and go to My eBay page or Selling Manager. These tools were designed to make relisting fast.

Relisting from your My eBay page

Your My eBay page has lots of handy features. Best of all, it has all your sold and unsold items in one convenient area. It's so much easier to see all your sold or unsold items at once!

Figure 26-3 shows My eBay displaying the Items I've Sold area. (The Unsold Items area is farther down on the My eBay Selling tab and has similar columns of information.) Notice the drop-down menu next to every item. Click the menu and select Relist. If you click the Relist link for an item, a Sell Your Item page appears, fully filled in. You can then make any changes you want — or not!

• **Figure 26-3:** Items I've Sold on the My eBay page, showing the drop-down menu.

What's so very convenient about this method is that all your sold (or unsold) listings appear in one place. You can just go down the list and quickly relist items.

Relisting from Selling Manager

Wouldn't it be even better if you could select a whole bunch of items at once and list them all together? Step up to Selling Manager for a one-click relisting option. I really like Selling Manager as a tool for the mid-sized eBay seller (even a PowerSeller), and this bulk-relisting option is just one of this program's many excellent features.

You can access items that have sold, logically enough, from the Sold Items area (pictured in Figure 26-4). Relisting is done with a click of the mouse! (On the other hand, if you haven't been so lucky lately, you can look at your unsold items in the Unsold Items area.)

To relist an item through Selling Manager, follow these steps:

1. **Go to the Sold or Unsold Listings by clicking the appropriate link in the My eBay Views box on the left of the page.**

2. **Once you're on the page, select an item to relist by selecting the check box next to its record number.**

   You may select any or all of the items listed on the page.

3. **Once you have selected all the items that you want to relist, click the Relist (or Sell Similar) button.**

   The Relist Multiple Items page appears. This page is titled Relist Multiple Items whether you're relisting or selling similar.

4. **Review all the items listed (along with the fees being charged) and submit the items by clicking the Submit Listing button.**

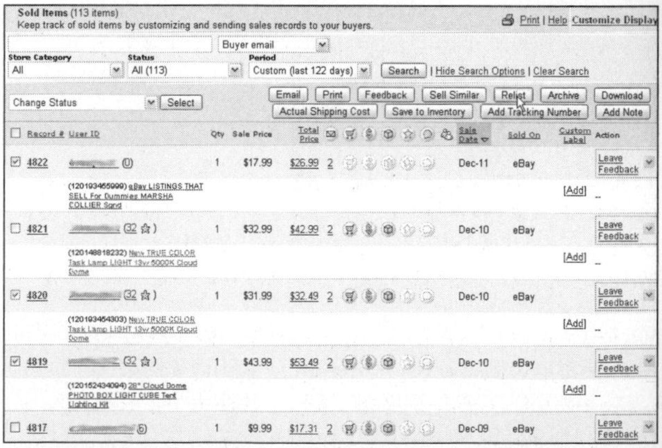

• **Figure 26-4:** A portion of my Sold Listings in Selling Manager.

Figure 26-5 shows a portion of the Relist Multiple Items page that displays the details of each of your items. If you proceed, the items are relisted exactly as you had them listed before. On the bottom of this page, eBay gives you a recap of all relisting fees.

Relist Multiple Items: Review & Submit

Step 1: Review your listings

Please review your listings and fees and then click the **Submit Listings** button below. To remove an item, click the "Remove item" link.

▶ **PayPal is now turned on for all your listings.**
You have opted to turn on PayPal for all of your listings. If you would like to turn off this preference, please edit your payment preferences.

Item #120177591050 - Starting an EBAY BUSINESS for Dummies 3 book SIGNED NEW	✗ Remove item

Main Category

Books : Nonfiction Books (# 378)

Pictures & Details

Duration	7 days
Quantity	1
Optional Features	Gallery
Fees	Insertion ($0.60); Gallery ($0.35)	**Total Fees: $0.95**

Item #120193455999 - eBay LISTINGS THAT SELL For Dummies MARSHA COLLIER Sgnd PHOTOGRAPHY & HTML for Higher Sales SIGNED by Author	✗ Remove item

Main Category

Books : Nonfiction Books (# 378)

Pictures & Details

Duration	7 days
Quantity	1
Optional Features	Gallery
Fees	Insertion ($0.60); BIN Fee ($0.10), Value Pack ($0.65)	**Total Fees: $1.35**

• **Figure 26-5:** Relisting several items at once from Selling Manager.

Making a Second Chance Offer

When you have multiples of an item and your final bid amount exceeded your target price, you can feel free to make offers to underbidders to buy the same item for their high bid. You can also make a Second Chance Offer if the winning bidder doesn't come through with the payment.

These are perfectly eBay-legal ways to make a second sale. Best of all? eBay doesn't charge you a second listing fee for your offer. You just pay a Final Value fee if the bidder accepts your offer.

You can make Second Chance Offers to as many of the underbidders as you wish. The underbidder has a prescribed time period — 1, 3, 5, or 7 days — to take you up on the offer or pass. You can make Second Chance Offers on your item for up to 60 days.

You do not necessarily have to make an offer to an underbidder if you are not comfortable with that person's feedback. It's up to you to decide to which bidders you make offers.

The link to make a Second Chance Offer (similar to the one shown in Figure 26-6) appears on the My eBay page or in Selling Manager only when an auction has more than one bidder.

Second Chance Offer

Original item number:	3580553775
Title:	eBay TIPS for Dummies AUTHOR SIGNED 2003
Duration:	3 days ▼

Select who will receive your offer

Below is a list of eBay users who did not win your item. Remember: The number of eBay users you select can't be more than the number of items you have.

Select	User ID	Buy It Now price
☐		$10.00
☐	8	$8.50

Note: Users who have chosen not to receive Second Chance Offers or who have already been sent one will not appear above.

Receive a copy of your Second Chance Offer

☐ Send me a copy at: mcollier1@
Change my email address

[‹ Back] [Review ›]

• **Figure 26-6:** The decision-making page for making a Second Chance Offer.

Once you've made your Second Chance Offer, the underbidder will receive an e-mail, as shown in Figure 26-7.

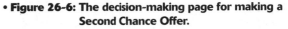

eBay sent this message to Marsha Collier (marsha_c). Your registered name is included to show this message originated from eBay. Learn more.

Lucky you. Here's a second chance to buy the item you recently lost.

You can be sure a Second Chance Offer is legitimate when you see it in My Messages with the subject line, "You have a second chance offer". If it is not, it's fake. Do not respond to the sender or complete the transaction. Outside of eBay offers may be fraudulent and not covered by buyer protection programs. Learn more

Lucky you, Susan! The seller has offered you a second chance to buy this item. The second time can be a charm.

George Rodrigue TALE OF BLUE DOG Museum 1993 Catalog
Current price:	$25.00
Buy It Now price:	$25.00 = Buy It Now
Shipping:	$5.99
Expiration Time:	Dec-12-07 20:24:12 PST
Message from seller:	I have one more of these catalogs if you would still like to buy it for your high bid. Happy Holidays!
Seller:	marsha_c (5347 ☆)
	100.0% Positive Feedback
	Member since Jan-04-97 in United States

View Item | Ask Seller A Question

• **Figure 26-7:** The official eBay e-mail sent to the buyer for your Second Chance Offer.

Relisting from Your "Item Did Not Sell" Notices

When an item doesn't sell, eBay sends you an e-mail notice, as you can see in Figure 26-8. Whenever I got one of these notices, I used to take it as a personal defeat. But then I realized that the e-mails have an excellent purpose — and possibly the largest Relist Now button I've ever seen. Click there, and you can relist immediately.

• **Figure 26-8:** eBay's "Your Item Did Not Sell" e-mail.

Part IV

Become a Model Seller

The 5th Wave   By Rich Tennant

@RICHTENNANT

SOVIET Memorabilia

"The bids are coming in, all right, but where are we going to find a shipping crate for an attack submarine?"

Practice 27

Choosing the Best Shipper for Your Type of Business

One decision about your eBay business that *seems* easy is selecting the right shipper — but actually it's one of the more difficult choices, at least if you care about your buyers. Shipping can make or break your customer service. Whoever delivers the package to the buyer is a virtual extension of your company.

Professional labels, clean boxes, nifty packing peanuts — those are the things you control. But safe and timely delivery falls into the hands of complete strangers. Once the package leaves your door, it's no longer under your control — yet somehow the buyer blames you for the tardiness or sloppiness of the shipping. Your bottom line isn't the shipper's concern, and no matter how many refunds you get for missed delivery schedules, it won't help when you have one irate customer after another. Simple equation: Irate customers = lousy eBay feedback.

So, what's a seller to do? Do you use the shipper that other sellers rave about? Perhaps opt for convenience over low price? After you decide on a shipper, how often do you re-evaluate its services?

 Did you know that the big two — United Parcel Service and Federal Express — raise their rates every year? The United States Postal Service raises its rates too, but the difference is that the media makes a lot more noise (it's in the newspapers and on the TV news) every time a postage stamp goes up by 1 cent. (Hey, *that's* traditional!)

It's easy to go on the Internet or talk to friends and hear horror stories about any of the main shippers. The bottom line is, which one works best for you?

Meeting Your Front Line

Who constitutes your eBay business front line? My shipping front line is Scooter from UPS; Tim the Post Office carrier, and Jorge who picks up for FedEx Ground. I know the front-line guys because they make my eBay business run smoothly — or not. If we have a good relationship, they don't leave deliveries outside under a bush, and make a point to deliver packages to a neighbor if I'm not home. When they pick up my sundry packages with a smile and give me a light-hearted, "They're sure buying things on eBay, aren't they?," I know these guys are on my *front line*. I always respond with a smile and a bit of friendly chitchat (as time permits).

Your front line is what makes your business run smoothly.

Wait — are you telling me that you don't get person-alized service from your courier? Not from any of them? Have you ever taken a moment to chat with your delivery person? When you personalize a busi-ness relationship, you become more than a street address, you become . . .well . . . a *person*. When you're no longer a number, you become a fellow human being with needs and wants. Believe it or not, people want to make other people happy, even when they feel grumpy. (I'll bet your eBay activities leave you grumpy sometimes, too!)

Your front line can help you by watching out for your packages. They can be sure that your packages go into the bin that leaves immediately, versus the one that sits till the end of the day.

I leave a signal when there are packages to be picked up, and (mostly) every one is picked up. When my thoughtful USPS letter carrier delivers a big box, he brings it to the back door near my office so I don't have to drag it through the front door and across the house. The FedEx guy puts the huge boxes next to the garage door — just because the word *service* isn't a formal part of their company name doesn't mean they won't provide any.

Of course, your front line can go on vacation — or (heaven forbid) have a sick day. On one day, I was the victim of what I refer to as a "dump and run" from a substitute driver (see Figure 27-1). He dumped stacks of large boxes on my front doorstep — practically blocking access to the door — and didn't even ring the bell!

Try building a relationship with your shipping front line. If you can — some couriers move too fast to even ring the bell. But if you can catch them, try inviting them to company holiday parties (they usu-ally won't show but will appreciate the invitation), and offer them a cool drink on a hot summer day. The result? Your shipping can be the easiest part of your business.

You can imagine what happens when you have a good front line — and I've got one. On a day when I had a lot coming in, they had to call in the reserves — and I got *two* trucks for the price of one!

• **Figure 27-1: He dumped, ran, and didn't even ring the bell.**

Location, Location, Location

What happens if you have to drop off your packages for shipment? It's important to consider where the closest local drop-off point for your carrier is.

Each of the major carriers has a search feature on its Web site to find the nearest drop-off location. You input your address or ZIP code, and the feature tells you the locations closest to you.

To get the nearest location lowdown quickly, go to the following sites:

- **FedEx:** www.fedex.com/us/dropoff

- **USPS:** www.usps.com/locator/welcome.htm

- **UPS:** www.ups.com/dropoff

Remember that when you go to a drop-off location, it is invariably at the height of rush hour traffic. Take this into consideration and plan your time accordingly. From where I live, a half-mile drive can take anywhere from 5 to 20 minutes — depending on the route I take and the amount of traffic at the time.

Be sure to read the details about each location online. There may be different fees involved in dropping off packages. Some locations may accept certain types of packages and not others. Read the fine print.

Compare the Costs

The general consensus is that a particular method of shipping is cheaper for large items and another is cheaper for small packages. Each method has its own personal peculiarities.

- **USPS.** Priority Mail knocks the heck out of the competition, until your package exceeds five pounds. eBay sellers who neglect to use USPS for shipping small packages can't be competitive. Also, USPS now gives a discount when you print your postage from an authorized online service or a specifically authorized third-party postage vendor (like endicia.com).

- **FedEx Home Delivery.** Generally cheaper than UPS, and eBay sellers report less damage to their packages.

- **UPS.** The most expensive out there for most packages — but hey, it's so easy to print those labels out of your PayPal account. Charging the extra to your buyers will only cut your sales in the long run.

While writing this chapter, I tested several of the free shipping calculators on the Internet. They're fast, they're free . . . and they all came up with different prices for the same package, going to the same location. It seems that FedEx and UPS have some difficult-to-figure *Fuel Charges* and *Residential Surcharges*. If you want a price quote, be sure to go to the Web site of your selected courier.

Take a look at Table 27-1 — compare the pricing for certain types of packages. Know that there are extras to consider for some services, so become familiar with the variations and hidden costs. The FedEx costs below include additional fees. If you print your USPS postage online, Delivery Confirmation is free.

TABLE 27-1: SAMPLE COSTS FOR RESIDENTIAL DELIVERY PACKAGES (NEW YORK CITY TO LOS ANGELES)

Weight	FedEx Home Delivery 3 – 5 Days	UPS Ground 1 – 6 Days	USPS Priority Mail Electronic Rate 2 – 3 Days	USPS Priority Mail Flat Rate Envelope Electronic Rate
13 ounces	7. 47	9.95	3.21 (First Class Mail)	
1 pound	7.47	9.95	4.75	4.75
2 pounds	8. 29	11.14	7.96	4.75
5 pounds	9.87	13.45	16.21 (flat rate box 9.30/ 12.50)	4.75
10 pounds	12.28	16.97	26.59 (flat rate box 9.30/ 12.50)	4.75

Table 27-1 should get you thinking about your carrier. It's very revealing. Even more revealing is when you realize that the USPS charges a fractional amount more for 2-to-3-day Priority Mail for small packages.

Shipping with the U.S. Postal Service

I'm a big fan of the U.S. Postal Service (USPS). Just ask my wonderful letter (or multiple-parcel) carrier, Tim. I use the Post Office for the bulk of my eBay sales because it's cost effective and convenient. In my over-10-years of selling items on eBay, they've never lost a package.

The Post Office has worked hard to keep up with the competition in the parcel business by offering many online features and custom pickup. USPS also offers many classes of service that top out with a maximum weight of 70 pounds. Table 27-2 shows services that are most popular with eBay sellers.

TABLE 27-2: CLASSES OF USPS SERVICE MOST USED BY EBAY E-TAILERS

Service	Time to Cross the Country	What You Can Ship
First Class	Three days	First Class mail can be used to mail anything, as long as it doesn't weigh much. You can send a letter, large envelope, or a small package. Maximum weight is 13 ounces.
Priority Mail	Two days	Priority Mail is just First Class mail on steroids (for heavier items). They have those flat rate free boxes, too.
Parcel Post	Eight days	Parcel Post is only slightly cheaper (and much slower) than Priority Mail.
Media Mail	Eight Days	Media Mail is the least expensive way to mail heavy items. The only caveat is that you can use Media Mail to ship only books, film, manuscripts, printed music, printed test materials, sound recordings, scripts, and computer-recorded media such as CD-ROMs and diskettes (remember those?).

Before taking any of the transit times I've mentioned (say from Los Angeles to New York) to heart, be sure to get a calculation from the Post Office Web site (which you'll find at `postcalc.usps.gov`). When you calculate postage, the Post Office will indicate expected transit times for your packages.

Understanding USPS charges

The Postal Service levies additional charges for some often-used services, including these:

- **Pickup:** If you have a postal license through an online service (see the section "Getting free package pickup from the Post Office," later in this practice), the Post Office offers free pickup. You have to give your packages to your carrier at the time of your regular delivery, or schedule a pickup on the USPS site. If you need a pickup at a special time, there is a fee.

- **Insurance:** This guarantees that you're covered if your package doesn't arrive safely and will reimburse you up to the value you declare when purchasing the insurance as long as you can document the amount. There is a maximum of $5,000. If your package gets lost or severely mangled in shipping, the Postal Service will, after a thorough investigation (see Practice 30), pay your claim. Fees start at $1.65 for packages up to $50, and $2.05 for packages up to $100. It continues to ratchet up for each $100 of insured value. (For discount information and tips on insurance, see Practice 30.)

- **Delivery Confirmation:** Delivery Confirmation provides you with proof of delivery or attempted delivery. You can get it free when you print your Priority Mail package postage online. Parcel Post or First Class Mail adds $.18 online. If you want to go to the Post Office, purchasing Delivery Confirmations can cost as high as $.65 for Priority Mail. You get a tracking number that you can check online at

  www.usps.com/shipping/trackand confirm.htm

  You can also verify a package's delivery by calling a toll-free number, 800-222-1811.

Getting free Delivery Confirmations

If you aren't shipping a great many items each week, you can get free Delivery Confirmations by visiting a secure area of the Post Office Web site at https://sss-Web.usps.com/cns/landing.do. Here you can generate a custom barcode mailing label with an e/Delivery Confirmation number for Priority Mail packages. You can print these labels directly from your inkjet or laser printer, and then simply tape the label to your package.

If you're in business and need to keep records of your shipping (dates, weights, and confirmation numbers), this method may be the way to go. The Post Office site, although free, prints out a label only once. If you want to keep records, you'll have to enter the information separately into a spreadsheet or a text file.

You can also get free Delivery Confirmation for Priority Mail packages if you subscribe to an online shipping service, as described in Practice 28.

Getting free package pickup from the Post Office

Because most package services charge for pickup, the Post Office decided to one-up them. If you have a postal license and print your own postage from an online service, the Post Office will pick up your packages free. For free pickup, you must have your packages ready for your regular carrier's stop. For more information visit

http://carrierpickup.usps.com/cgi-bin/ WebObjects/CarrierPickup.woa

to arrange for your packages to be picked up (see Figure 27-2).

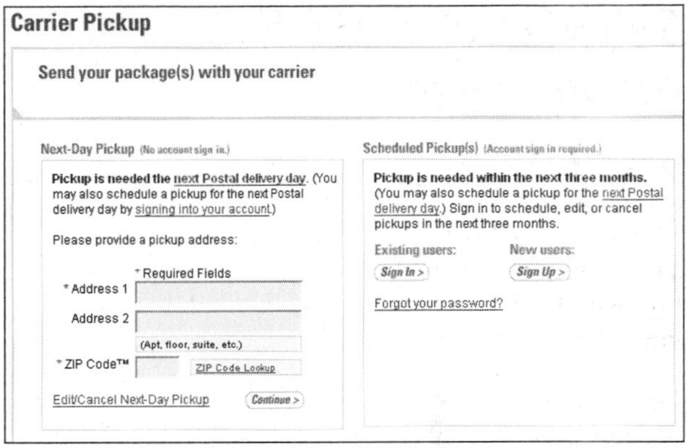

• **Figure 27-2:** Just put in your request for pickup by your letter carrier the day prior to your pickup day.

Shipping with United Parcel Service

Around the turn of the previous century (in 1907 to be exact), an enterprising 19-year-old figured he could make some money delivering pizzas for the local Italian restaurant. Just kidding about the pizzas. Actually James (Jim) Casey borrowed $100 from a friend to buy some used bicycles and began the American Messenger Company to run errands, send messages (no fax machines or IM!), deliver packages, and (you guessed it) carry trays of food from local restaurants to off-site patrons in Seattle, Washington. And from American Messenger's 6-foot-by-17-foot headquarters in a basement beneath his uncle's tavern, Jim helped The Little Parcel Service That Could grow into the Jolly Brown Giant we know as UPS.

Many eBay sellers just love using UPS. They think of it as the ultimate way to ship their packages. But as I note earlier in this practice, the right shipper for one seller may not be the best for another. For example, since the USPS has converted to the cost by mileage/weight formula, you may find (based on your location and the buyer's location) that the U.S. Postal Service may be more economical.

So while you make your shipping decisions, use the handy tables and other information in this practice to make the most of the services that UPS offers.

Using UPS today

Today's UPS is a $30 billion company focusing on enabling commerce around the world. Every day UPS delivers over 13.3 million packages and documents — I'm sure much of which represents eBay transactions.

UPS (along with the USPS) has hooked up with eBay, and you can access their information through the eBay site. To visit the eBay/UPS Shipping Center, visit `pages.eBay.com/ups/home.html`.

 You have choices for how you set up shipping arrangements, and you can pick the way that saves you the most time. If you take a look at Practice 37, you can find out how to ship through USPS or UPS directly from your PayPal account. You can also access shipping information through your My eBay Selling tab, Items I've Sold area as in Figure 27-3. Clicking the Print Shipping Label button in the item's row takes you to the PayPal shipping area.

Items I've Sold (1-25 of 33 items)								Print Customize Display
Show: **All** | Awaiting Payment (0) | Awaiting Shipment (1) | Awaiting Feedback (12)						Period: Last 31 days		
Remove Add Note Print Shipping Labels Add Tracking Number							Undo Remove: Select an option	
☐ Buyer ID		Qty	Sale Price	Total Price	Format	Sold Date	Sold On	Action
☐	1	$14.99	$23.99		Dec-07	eBay	Print Shipping Label	

• **Figure 27-3:** My eBay Items I've Sold page with a Print Shipping Label button.

Timing your shipments

If you're thinking about using UPS, you'd do yourself a favor by becoming familiar with the company's different classes of service — and what those classes mean to your customers in shipping days — as listed in Table 27-3.

TABLE 27-3: CLASSES OF UPS SERVICE MOST USED BY EBAY E-TAILERS

Service	Time to Cross the Country
UPS 2nd Day Air	Two business days
3 Day Select	Three business days
UPS Ground	Seven business days

UPS considers neither Saturday nor Sunday to be delivery days. So when your package is quoted for a five-day delivery, and the five days cross over a weekend, add two days to the delivery schedule. (The USPS and FedEx Ground deliver on Saturday — but FedEx won't deliver on Monday.)

Checking out the varied UPS rates

UPS has several different rate levels that depend on the type of account you have with them.

 The UPS charges charged through PayPal are based on "occasional" shippers (the "on demand" rate) shipping to home addresses. If you're shipping a lot of merchandise via UPS, you could have your packages picked up, and it might cost you less in the long run.

When you ship via UPS and wonder how to get the best rates, you've got quite a conundrum. In 2008, UPS basically charges small-time shippers three different rates:

- ✔ **Retail Rate:** This is the rate you pay when you go to the UPS Customer Center and they create the label for you. It's the most expensive, and with the eBay/PayPal solution, you can save yourself some bucks by printing your own label and dropping the packages at the Customer Center.

- ✔ **On Demand:** The charges you see on eBay/PayPal shipping are these rates. They are really made for the occasional shipper.

✔ **Daily Rate:** When you have arranged a daily pickup through UPS. This is when you get to make friends with the folks in brown shorts, and as an added benefit, you pay the lowest possible rates.

Package pickup costs a bundle

If you don't have a regular daily pickup UPS account, you're going to have to pay for package pick-up; $4 per package! You could set up a daily pickup account and maybe save some money. You do have to pay for that pickup service, and you have to do the math. The fees are on a sliding scale based on the amount of "postage" you use in a week.

Getting It There with FedEx

Unlike the warm and fuzzy story of the beginnings of UPS, Federal Express was the brainchild of a rich kid. (Somewhat reminiscent of those touching apocryphal stories you hear about a few top-ranked eBay sellers from moneyed backgrounds, who had lots of cash and connections before they ever came to eBay and met with immediate success.)

Yep, in 1965 — while an undergraduate at prestigious Yale University — Frederick Smith wrote a term paper about current air carriers' freight-forwarding side-business. Smith thought this a very uneconomical way to ship freight, and proposed that a freight-only carrier would do a better job for less money. Fast-forward to 1971. After serving in the military, Smith bought controlling interest in Arkansas Aviation Sales. He felt the need for even faster delivery than in days past, and worked to fill the void in the second- and next-day delivery services. Federal Express was born and officially launched in 1973, with 14 planes housed at the Memphis International Airport. On the first night of operation, Federal Express delivered 186 packages to 25 U.S. cities from Rochester, New York, to Miami, Florida.

Saving by shipping with FedEx Ground

FedEx Ground is the service that delivers to businesses; for delivering to homes (most eBay buyers), you'll use a service called FedEx Home Delivery. FedEx can save you a considerable amount of money over UPS in most cases. Perhaps it's not as convenient to ship with FedEx as it is to use the PayPal shipping area, but the savings just might be worth your while.

Here are a few time- and money-saving facts about shipping with FedEx that you should know.

✔ **Saturday delivery:** FedEx Ground will deliver to residences on Tuesdays through Saturdays at no extra charge.

✔ **Delivery until 8:00 p.m.:** If your customers work for a living and can't make it home to babysit deliveries, FedEx Ground will deliver until 8:00 p.m.

✔ **Guaranteed delivery time**: FedEx guarantees one to five delivery days to every address in the United States, and three to seven days to Canada and Puerto Rico.

✔ **Printing labels online:** Through the FedEx Web site, you can print bar-coded labels on plain paper and place them in the FedEx-provided clear envelopes that stick to your packages.

✔ **Many drop-off locations:** After printing your label, you can drop off your packages at any FedEx counter, many private postal stores, or at your local Kinko's (now owned by FedEx).

✔ **Lower pickup costs:** FedEx Ground charges less for their pickup service (read on).

Signing up with FedEx

You sign up for an account only once; there's no cost and it only takes a few minutes. This is a two-step process. You've first got to sign up for a Web-site login, and then sign up for an actual, for-real FedEx account. When you have a fedex.com login and account, you'll be able to ship your items quickly from your own private FedEx Web space.

To get a FedEx account and be able to ship right away:

1. Go to www.fedex.com/us.

2. **On the left side of the screen, click the link to FedEx Ground.**

   The FedEx Ground page appears.

3. **From the FedEx Ground page, click the Ship tab (first tab at the top).**

   You land at the login page. If you've previously signed up for an account with a password and User ID, you can login immediately here.

4. **If you're signing up for a new account, click the link that says "Sign Up Now!"**

5. **On the resulting registration page, type in the following information:**

   ► **User ID:** Make up an ID you'll remember. (I tried my eBay User ID and it was already taken — I guess they have lots of customers.)

   ► **Password:** Come up with a password you'll remember.

   ► **Password Reminder:** Input your password reminder question and answer. This way, if you ever forget your password (or have to prove your identity to FedEx), you'll have your mind-jogger.

   ► **Contact Information:** This includes the usual — your name, (optional) company name, address, city, state, e-mail address, and phone number.

   ► **Agree to Terms of Use:** If you want to ship via FedEx, you must agree to their terms. You may click the link provided if you want some really boring legalese to read. When you've decided to play by their rules, press the bar that says I Accept.

6. **On the next page, there's some more legalese in the form of FedEx's License Agreement.**

7. **When you're through reading that (I'm sure you'll read every word), click Yes, indicating that you accept the Agreement.**

8. **When asked whether you want to set up a FedEx account, follow the prompts and input your credit card information.**

   You're presented with your very own nine-digit FedEx Account number.

9. **Click Start Using FedEx Ship Manager to ship now, or log in later when you're ready to ship.**

Saving more by paying with American Express

If you have an American Express Business Credit Card (which also allows you access to the American Express Open Network), you can save even more on your FedEx shipments!

✔ **Save 5 percent** of ALL FedEx Ground Shipments when you fill out your forms online.

✔ **Save 10 percent to 20 percent** on your FedEx Express shipments.

To be sure your American Express card is officially linked so you get the discount, call the Fedex/Open Network desk at 1-800-231-8636.

As a member of the Open Network, you can also save money on other business needs.

Shipping your packages Online

Perhaps one day we'll actually be able to beam our products to the buyers (kinda like Scotty in *Star Trek*). Meanwhile, "shipping online" merely means filling out the forms and printing them out.

To ship your item on the FedEx Web site, just go to the online Ship Manager by pressing the Ship tab on the navigation bar. You'll be presented with a simple, all-in-one online waybill, somewhat like the kind you're used to filling out by hand.

Copy and paste addresses from your PayPal account by highlighting the text you want to copy and pressing Ctrl+C. Paste in the text by placing your cursor in the area you want to fill and pressing Ctrl+V.

When you're filling out the form, note some important entries:

✔ **Service Type:** Be sure to use the FedEx Home Delivery option from the drop-down menu if you're shipping to a residence.

✔ **Dimensions:** Be sure that you know the proper dimensions for the package you're sending.

If you sell repeat items in your eBay business, why not measure the boxes ahead of time and keep a list near your computer so you'll know the size? For example: *Light kit 14 x 12 x 26.*

✔ **FedEx ShipAlert:** Select the e-mail option to send the buyer (and yourself — at up to three e-mail addresses) a notice that the package was shipped. Add a personal message so that the e-mail won't have a cold, automated feel to it.

Once you've filled out the form, you can press the button at the bottom to get a courtesy rate. This will give you a rate estimate (not including any special discounts) on your shipment.

When shipping with FedEx online, if your package is valued over $100 and you use U-PIC for your insurance (a private insurance company, see Practice 30), put $0 in the Declared Value box. Make note of the package on an insurance log and submit it to U-PIC. (FedEx will charge you 50 cents per $100 in value, and U-PIC will charge you only 15 cents per $100.)

Practice 28

Automating Your Shipping Chores

In This Practice

- Avoiding trips to the Post Office
- Printing postage and labels on PayPal
- Using third-party services

Waaay back in August of 1999, the United States Postal Service announced a brand-new service: Information-Based Indicia (IBI). Targeted at the SOHO (small office/home office) market, IBI is USPS-certified postage that you can print on envelopes and sticker labels right from your PC. Sellers on eBay and elsewhere on the Internet — whether they're selling from home or from a huge office — are all printing their own postage. Not only is printing postage quicker than sticking stamps on a package, but the result looks way more professional.

I'm a savvy consumer and businesswoman. I don't believe in paying for extras, nor do I believe in being a victim of hidden charges. The online-postage arena — while providing helpful tools that make running your eBay business easier — is fraught with bargains, deals, and introductory offers. (Usually the free postage offered in these deals only comes after the 30-day trial period.) I urge you to read these offers carefully so that you know what you're getting yourself into: Evaluate how much it will cost you to start and to maintain an ongoing relationship with any online-postage-service company. Although you may initially get some free hardware and pay a low introductory rate, the fine print might tell you that you have agreed to pay unreasonably high prices six months down the line. I always double-check pricing before getting into anything, and I urge you to adopt this same strategy as part of your business practices.

Your old pal the United States Postal Service has Web tools that enable you to print postage and delivery confirmations online. One caveat: This is a no-frills online service, and often you get what you pay for. Keep in mind that you can't print the labels on a label printer. You must print to standard size 8½×11 paper or label sheets. For more details, go to www.usps.com/clicknship.

The Benefits of Online Postage Service

If you're asking yourself why I haven't included a world-famous, popular postage meter service in this book, you have a good question.

Purchasing and printing online postage is just about the *de facto* standard in the online selling industry. Postage meters not only eat up your profits in fees, but the ink is *sooo* expensive. Inkjet ink is expensive enough (I know I don't have to tell *you* that), so if you're going to print your labels on paper, try to use a laser. (That's another reason why I love my Zebra label printer. No ink! It's thermal and prints over and over without ever needing a refill.)

 Printing labels from your printer and taping them on can be convenient until you start sending out a bunch of packages at a time — then cutting the paper and taping the label gets to be a bit too time-consuming. I highly recommend that you do yourself a favor and get a label printer. Yes, they can be expensive, but you can find some great deals on eBay. I bought my heavy-duty, professional Eltron Zebra 2844 thermal label printer on eBay for one-fourth the retail price. (Search eBay for *zebra 2844*.) It's saved me countless hours. Dymo also makes a very good label printer for beginners.

Printing your USPS postage the 21st-century way makes life a lot simpler with these features:

- **Average a 3.5 percent discount on Priority Mail** when you use electronic postage for your packages.

- **Online postage purchases:** With a click of your mouse, you can purchase postage instantly using your credit card or by direct debit from your checking account.

- **Hidden postage:** A stealth indicia (also known as the postage-paid indicia) is an awesome tool for the eBay seller. By using this feature, your customer will not see the exact amount of postage that you paid. This allows you to add reasonable shipping and handling costs to your invoice and not inflame the buyers' ire when they see final costs on the label.

- **Free delivery confirmations on Priority Mail:** Delivery confirmations may be printed for First Class, Parcel Post, and Media Mail. Priority Mail delivery confirmation is free (that's right — no more $.65 or $.75 each) when you print postage

online. See Table 28-1 for more confirmation discounts.

- **Address validation:** Before printing any postage, the server contacts the USPS database of every valid mailing address in the United States and verifies the address you're sending to. This Address Matching System (AMS) is updated monthly.

- **ZIP-code check and completion:** The software runs a check on your addresses and corrects any ZIP-code errors you've made. Also, it adds the extra four digits to your addressee's ZIP code — a nifty feature that helps ensure swift delivery while freeing you from the hassle of having to look up those extra digits.

- **International postage discounts:** When printing postage for your international mailings online, you automatically get the following discounts:

  - 10 percent on Global Express Guaranteed (1- to 3-day delivery)

  - 8 percent on Express Mail International (3- to 5-day service)

  - 5 percent on Priority Mail International

- **Carrier-ready packages:** Once you've used the online services, you have all your mail ready to go. No more socializing (or standing around stewing) in Post Office lines!

TABLE 28-1: ELECTRONIC POSTAGE DISCOUNTS AND RETAIL COUNTER (AT THE POST OFFICE) RATES

Class of Postage	Retail Counter Rate	Electronic Rate
Delivery Confirmation First Class Packages*	$.75	$.18
Delivery Confirmation Priority Mail	$.65	$.00
Delivery Confirmation Package Services	$.75	$.18
Signature Confirmation (all classes)**	$2.10	$1.75

* To qualify for Delivery Confirmation on a First Class price of mail, the package must be greater than 3/4" at its thickest point.

** PayPal requires that all items valued over $250 have a Signature Confirmation in order to be covered by the Seller Protection Program.

As you can see, the benefits hugely outweigh any possible service costs. The major players that cater to online sellers are PayPal.com, Endicia.com, and Stamps.com.

Shipping Directly through PayPal

I consider PayPal to be *de rigueur* (a *must have*, to all you non-French speakers) for all eBay PowerSellers. By using PayPal, a seller can streamline the buyer's shopping experience, making it simple to buy, click, and pay. Those out in the eBay world who try PayPal for the first time find using the service to be a life-changing experience.

 Along with all its time-saving tools for the seller, PayPal now offers online shipping services through the United States Postal Service (USPS) or UPS at no extra charge. Shipping through PayPal is especially helpful for those who don't ship many packages per week because there's no need to use additional software or sign up with an additional service.

This practice shows you how to take advantage of this incredibly convenient system.

Because a rose has thorns . . .

It all seems so simple, right? Ahh, well, as they say, there are no free lunches. Although PayPal shipping seems incredibly easy — seeing as how it's integrated directly into your payment system — there are a few caveats. Although PayPal USPS postage printing is convenient, at this time, you'll find some drawbacks:

✔ **Paying for postage:** The PayPal postage system can make your bookkeeping a nightmare for your business. That's because PayPal withdraws the postage amounts directly from your PayPal account balance. This is problematic for keeping your books in balance: Your final deposits won't match your posted eBay or Web sales.

 You can make the bookkeeping end of the shipping process work more efficiently by posting your PayPal sales to your bookkeeping program and withdrawing your money (from your PayPal account to your business bank account) prior to processing your shipping. Then you simply charge your shipping to a credit card — which makes it easier to balance your books at month's end. Unfortunately, this two-part process can eat up a lot of precious time. Many sellers only post their sales and withdraw once a week.

✔ **Label-printing issues:** When you're shipping more than 20 packages a month, using a label printer to print your postage is incredibly convenient (saves time and effort) and gives you a more professional-looking result. But if you use a label printer for your PayPal postage printing, PayPal requires that you set it as the default printer in your computer's operating system.

If you comply with that requirement, everything you try to print from your computer will go to your label printer unless you change the printer every time you wish to print something that isn't a label. Continually changing the default printer is problematic for some people and a waste of time for others. Fortunately, if you're using one of the online postage services I talk about in the upcoming section "Opting for Third-Party Software and Service," this isn't an issue.

✔ **Measuring each package:** PayPal postage printing requires that you type in the length, width, and thickness of every package you ship in order to print your label. All that typing is truly laborious (I did it once and never will again). When you use one of the third-party services, there's no need to input package size unless you're mailing an oversize package. Plus, because you're working on a server over the Internet, all your work can be lost if there's a glitch in the connection.

 Perhaps you have to input your package dimensions on PayPal (and not on the third-party services) for a good reason. When you use third-party software, you apply for a USPS mailing permit that makes you a *known mailer*. (A known mailer uses a mailing permit imprint as an indication of postage payment.) Then the USPS can scan the permit codes on the package and see exactly who sent it. When you print postage through PayPal, PayPal is the known mailer.

✔ **Online-only connection:** If you're using third-party software, you type your mailing information into a program that lives in your own computer rather than hanging out remotely somewhere on the Internet. That way you have your data handy; in the online-only scenario, a momentary glitch in an upload or download can lose you all your data.

Establishing shipping preferences

When you get those wonderful e-mails from PayPal that let you know someone has made a payment, it's a great feeling. But it's also your notice that you've got to ship out our merchandise really soon. When you're ready to deal with shipping, it's very simple to sign on to your PayPal account and handle it right on the site.

Before you attempt to use PayPal shipping, you can really save some time if you go to your preferences by clicking your PayPal account's Profile link. Click the Shipping Preferences link in the Selling Preferences area, and you'll see a form like the one in Figure 28-1. Fill it in with your shipping information (printing preferences, UPS account information, default shipper). Once this is done, your PayPal shipping will be all set up and ready to go.

After you set up your Shipping Preferences, go back to your PayPal Overview page. In Figure 28-2, you see my PayPal Overview page, and it's clear that I have to ship some items pronto.

• **Figure 28-1:** PayPal's Shipping Preferences page.

• **Figure 28-2:** After signing in, you can see which items need shipping.

If you have more than one package to ship, you may select PayPal's MultiOrder Shipping process to print your labels along with a manifest for your carrier to scan when he or she picks up the packages.

First, I'll withdraw my PayPal balance into my bank account, so that I can put my postage expense on a credit card. Then I'll begin the shipping process, as follows:

1. **Click the Print Shipping Label button in the item's row.**

2. **Choose which method of shipping you'd like to use: U.S. Postal Service or UPS.**

I hope that you already decided which shipping method to use *before* you came to PayPal. You had to specify a shipping amount in your auction, and it would be a tad awkward (and possibly costly) to switch shippers now. If you need help deciding which shipper to use, please check out Practice 27 of this book.

Shipping with the USPS

If you plan to use the ever-popular United States Postal Service (USPS), printing your postage and label through PayPal gives you a free Delivery Confirmation with Priority Mail. A Delivery Confirmation is also available for Media Mail, Parcel Post, and First Class Mail for a minimal charge. Since I've chosen the USPS as the primary shipper in my preferences, the USPS form (see Figure 28-3) comes next. At the top of the page (not pictured) your mailing address and the ship-to address are listed.

After you confirm that this information is correct, fill out the details of the form, including

✔ **Service Type:** Choose the level of mailing service you want for your package from this drop-down list. Priority Mail is usually the standard.

✔ **Package Size:** From this drop-down menu, select the type of package you're sending. To decide which packaging to select, keep the following in mind:

▶ **Package/Thick Envelope:** Your package or envelope qualifies for this status if the combined length and girth are no more than 84 inches.

▶ **Large Package:** Your package is a Large Package when it is larger than the dimensions of the previous category, but doesn't exceed 108 inches (130 inches for Parcel Post) in combined length and girth.

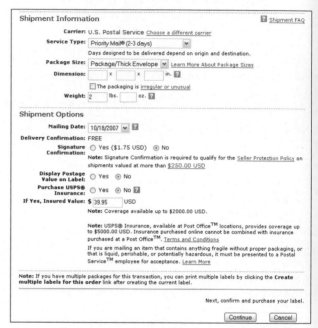

• **Figure 28-3: Confirming the details of your shipment.**

▶ **USPS Flat Rate Envelope:** These handy Express and Priority Mail envelopes are available free from the USPS. (See Practice 29 for information on how to get them delivered to your door.) You can ship whatever fits into the envelopes at a flat rate, no matter how much the package weighs.

If you really stuff your flat rate envelopes, you can always reinforce your envelope with clear shipping tape — I do! Some eBay experts may disagree, but here's the straight info right from the Postal Service:

"When mailing at the Priority Mail or Express Mail flat rate, the contents of the flat-rate envelope must be confined within the envelope with the adhesive provided on the flap as the primary means of closure. The flap must be able to close and adhere to the envelope. Tape may be applied to reinforce the envelope provided the design of the envelope is not enlarged by any means."

- **Weight:** Here you enter the weight of your package. (You may use your bathroom scale; or better yet, buy a digital postage scale on eBay.)

- **Delivery Confirmation:** Confirmation is free with Priority Mail.

- **Signature Confirmation:** Signature confirmation provides you a signature and date of delivery, and is available for many levels of service. If you'd like a signature confirmation for your package, it will add to the postage cost. You can request Proof of Delivery online or on the phone.

- **Display Value of Postage on Label:** If you'd prefer not to show the actual amount of the postage on the label, do not check this box. That way, whatever handling fees you charge your customer are transparent.

- **E-mail Message to Buyer:** Bring customer service to the fore! Type in a nice note letting customers know you appreciate their business. This might also be a good place to ask them to e-mail you immediately if there are any problems with the item when it arrives. (A good defense against knee-jerk negative feedback.)

- **Item(s) Being Shipped to Your Buyer:** The item number and name of the item you are shipping appears here.

If you've finished filling in the form and everything looks okay, complete the USPS shipping process with these steps:

1. Click Continue.

The USPS Shipping Confirmation page appears. On the Shipping Confirmation page, all the information from the previous page is listed.

2. If you've made a mistake on any entry, click Edit Shipment Details, or cancel the transaction by clicking Cancel.

3. Click Pay and Continue if everything looks okay.

Your PayPal account is charged for the postage amount and a new window opens to allow you to print postage on your printer. You have the option of printing a sample label, which is a good idea if you want to make sure that your printer and all the connections are working properly.

4. After you print the sample and you're happy with the results, print the label by clicking Print Label.

You can now request a pickup from the Post Office by clicking the Request Pickup link that takes you directly to the USPS site. You can request a pickup for the next business day. Or, if you're shipping the same day, you can tape a note to your mailbox asking your letter carrier to ring your bell and pick up your boxes.

Shipping with UPS

Shippers such as UPS charge different rates based on how often you use their services (see Practice 10 for this breakdown).

 If you're shipping many packages (more than five) a week, it might be best if you printed your labels directly from the UPS site. All PayPal UPS shipments are charged the occasional-shipper rate. If you use UPS just once in a while, the PayPal method will work perfectly for you.

If you've selected UPS as your shipper on the PayPal Shipping preference page, you'll arrive at a page with these choices:

- **UPS Account:** You can open a new UPS account immediately online, or, if you have an existing UPS account number, you may type it in this field.

  To open a new account, you'll have to verify your company data (it's already entered here from your PayPal account information) and let UPS know approximately how many packages you ship per week.

- **Shipping Payment Information:** You also have to indicate whether you'd like to pay for your shipping with your PayPal account, or you'd like the shipping billed to your existing UPS account.

When you're through with these choices, finish the shipping process with these steps:

1. **Click Continue.**

2. **If any information on the resulting confirmation page is wrong, press Edit to go back and fix the erroneous entries.**

3. **When all the information on the confirmation page is correct, click Continue.**

4. **Read the UPS Shipping Agreement (if you're opening a new account), and**

   - ▶ If you agree, click I Agree.

   - ▶ If you don't, click I Decline. Then you can go back and ship via the USPS.

Now you're ready to print a label. Fill out the requested information and proceed in the same manner as for USPS shipping, which I described in the preceding section.

When your label has printed, you may elect to go back to your PayPal Overview page, as shown in Figure 28-4. The items you've selected to ship will include a Check Shipment link, and the charges for your shipment will appear in your history log. You may click the Check Shipment link at any time after you've shipped your item to track the package's progress and confirm delivery.

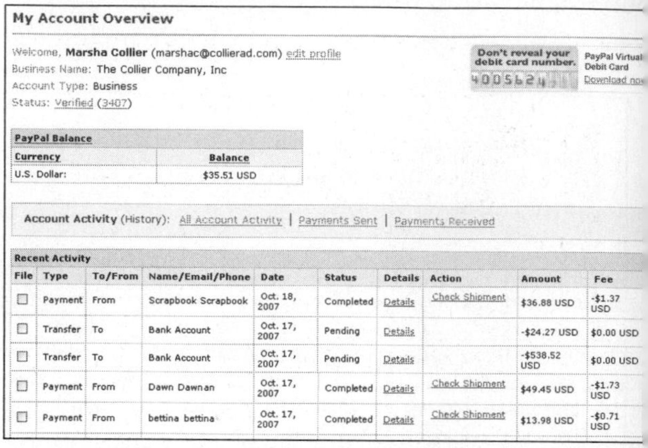

• **Figure 28-4: Your PayPal Overview page after shipping.**

Opting for Third-Party Software and Service

In the early days of online commerce, I had to scour the Internet to find places to conveniently print my shipping postage. My previous books listed each service individually, but in this practice, I concentrate on advantages of chosen services that can save you time and money. There are many choices; your choice of service is a personal preference. You'll find that online postage labels have a unique look. Figure 28-5 shows you a typical online 4×6 postage label printed from Endicia's DAZzle software.

Endicia.com

At the beginning of PC graphics in the early 1990s, I attended a cutting-edge industry trade show. I had a successful graphics and advertising business, so I was interested in the latest and greatest innovations to bring my business off the light table and onto my computer. In a smallish booth were a couple of guys peddling new software to enable artists to design direct-mail pieces from the desktop. Wow! What an nnovation! Their inexpensive software even let you produce your own bar codes for the Post Office. I fell in love with that software and used it throughout my graphics career.

• **Figure 28-5:** A custom label, instantly printed on my thermal printer.

Today's Endicia Internet Postage is based on DAZzle, their award-winning mailpiece-design tool that lets you design envelopes, postcards, and labels with color graphics, logos, pictures, text messages, and rubber stamps. You can print your mailing label with postage and delivery confirmation on anything from plain paper (tape it on with clear tape) to fancy 4×6 labels in a label printer from their extensive list of label templates.

DAZzle software is also available for Mac users — who have generally been unjustly ignored by most vendors in this online e-commerce world.

DAZzle, combined with their patented Dial-A-Zip, became the basis for today's version of the software (see Figure 28-6), which is distributed to all Endicia.com customers. There isn't a more robust mailing program on the market.

• **Figure 28-6:** DAZzle, the label-and-design software that comes with Endicia.com services, printing its custom Priority Mail International label.

Their service also makes International mailings a breeze. From Anniston, Alabama to Bulawayo, Zimbabwe, the DAZzle software not only prints postage but also lists all your shipping options and applicable rates. For international mailing, it will also advise you as to any prohibitions (for example, no prison-made goods can be mailed to Botswana), restrictions, necessary customs forms, and areas served within the country.

One of the things I love about Endicia is that you can highlight the buyer's name and address from an e-mail or from your PayPal history, click Copy, and the data is automatically transferred to the DAZzle software in the address field area. No pasting required!

You may find this feature on other services, but I checked this out — the others license the technology from Endicia, who developed it!

Endicia offers other services that complement their mailing program, including the following:

- **Insurance options:** Endicia offers private (third-party) package insurance, and also supports U-PIC (one of the first private package insurers catering to online sellers). The insurance cost is charged to you automatically — or, in the case of U-PIC, you can send your monthly insurance logs electronically to U-PIC (a service that's integrated into the DAZzle software). That way, there's no need to print insurance logs to mail.

- **First-class stamps:** If you send out envelopes (you know, for paying bills, sending birthday cards) you may always be scrounging for stamps. Endicia has the answer to this as well, with their InstaPostage product. Users of their services can download this software from the Endicia Web site and print their own first class postage stamps on their printer (or as I do — from a small Dymo label printer). Figure 28-7 shows you the InstaPostage software on my computer.

- **Auction-management support:** If you're using an auction-management service or software, Endicia integrates directly with the most popular: Channel Advisor, Andale, Blackthorne, and more. Visit www.endicia.com/Developers/IntegratedPartners/ for the current list.

All the features just listed come with Endicia's standard plan. The premium plan adds customizable e-mail, enhanced online transaction reports and statistics, business reply mail, return-shipping labels (prepaid so your customer won't have to pay for the return), and stealth indicias (for more about those, check out the sidebar "What's a stealth indicia?" near the end of this practice).

With all this, you'd think the service would be expensive, but it's not. The standard plan is $9.95 a month, and the premium plan is $15.95 a month. For a free 60-day trial *only for my readers*, enter the code **MC083** when you sign up for the standard 30-day trial, check out the CD at the back of the book, or go to

www.endicia.com/coolebaytools

• **Figure 28-7:** InstaPostage software, ready to print on an 8 1/2 by 11-inch sheet of postage labels on my inkjet printer.

Stamps.com

Stamps.com purchased 31 Internet postage patents from e-stamp, making its services a combination of the best of both sites. (I was a big fan of e-stamp, but they discontinued their online postage service late in 2000.) Many eBay sellers moved their postage business over to Stamps.com, which is shown in Figure 28-8.

• **Figure 28-8: The Stamps.com home page.**

Stamps.com works with software that you probably use every day, integrating itself into many programs — for example, Microsoft Word, Outlook, and Office, Corel WordPerfect, Palm Desktop, and Quicken.

Stamps.com offers all the standard features of an online postage service, and purchasing postage is as easy as going to www.stamps.com and clicking your mouse. With Stamps.com, you don't *need* any extra fancy equipment, although most introductory deals come with a free 5-pound-maximum scale. The scale also functions without connecting it to your computer. Serious users should get a better-quality postage scale from a seller on eBay or through an office-supply store.

To find the Stamps.com introductory deal of the month, visit its Web site. The service charges a flat rate of $15.99 per month. The site regularly offers sign-up bonuses that include as much as $25 free postage. (The free postage may only be available to you once you've passed the free trial period — be sure to check if this is important to you).

 Because Office Depot, Staples, and OfficeMax delivers any order more than $50 free the next day, it's a great place to get paper and labels. Better buys on scales, though, can be found on eBay, especially if you search *postage scale*. I'm using a super-small, 13-pound-maximum scale I bought on eBay for only $29.95, complete with a five-year warranty.

Figuring out the best solution for your business

Before deciding which service is the one for you, check out the current fees and features offered by each. Following are some of the specialized features you might want to look for:

✔ **Mac compatibility:** If you use a Mac in your daily business, you need to be sure that your postage vendor has easy-to-use Mac-compatible software that has all the features the service offers on the PC platform. Endicia is the service with Mac-compatible features.

✔ **Print customs forms for international mail:** Printing postage for international mail isn't enough. You must be able to print the associated customs forms that go with each package and their particular level of service.

✔ **Mailpiece design:** It's nice to be able to add your own logo or even slightly customize a label (within postal guidelines).

✔ **Use your printer to print envelopes:** If your printer allows it, you can even print logo-designed envelopes along with bar-coded addresses, your return address, and postage. This saves quite a bit in label costs.

✔ **Third-party insurance:** Save time and money using a private postal insurance company (get the lowdown on this money saver in Practice 30). Software that automatically integrates this feature is worth its weight in gold.

✔ **Integrated package tracking:** It's nice to have all your shipping data in one place and a sophisticated mail-ing system will allow you to simply click a button or link to discover whether your package has been delivered.

✔ **Hard-drive records of shipping:** Software that permits you to keep your shipping records on your computer is important. That way, you can check records even if the server on the Internet is down.

Posting third-party tracking information on PayPal

If you use a third-party software to print your postage, PayPal allows you to input the tracking information on the site even if you've printed your delivery confirmations with postage elsewhere. Just click the Details link for the transaction, and then click the *Add Tracking Info* link that appears. Input the tracking or delivery confirmation information from USPS, UPS, or another shipping company on the resulting page, as shown in Figure 28-9, and PayPal sends an e-mail to your buyer with that information.

• **Figure 28-9: Input your tracking information and PayPal sends an e-mail to your buyer.**

The information you added appears in both the record of your PayPal transaction (as shown in Figure 28-10) and the buyer's account, in the transaction list. You can check whether the package has progressed by clicking the Check Shipment link on the transaction list.

• **Figure 28-10: The tracking information becomes part of the sales record on PayPal.**

PayPal shipping services work great when you're just starting out in your eBay business, but once you get rolling, you need a mailing service that includes e-mail and recordkeeping, such as Endicia or Stamps.com. When you process your shipping (UPS or USPS) through PayPal, the shipping amount is deducted from your PayPal (sales revenue) balance. This is an important issue.

What's a stealth indicia?

Have you ever wondered why, when you receive a package from UPS or FedEx, you can't see how much the service charged for the shipping the way you can with postage stamps? Well, that's called a "stealth" indicia.

Certain levels of electronic postage are permitted by the U.S. Postal Service to print postage labels without the postage amount. It's a very handy feature that allows you the privacy of adding handling charges without freaking out the recipient.

Mechanizing Your Shipping

Okay, I'm not talking about moving giant mailing machines into your home office; I'm just talking about using a label printer. There are several quality brands of label printers on the market. Two of the most popular sold on eBay are the Zebra 2844 and the Dymo LabelWriter.

 If you're interested in investing in one of these handy label printers, be sure to look for one on eBay. You can often get them at a hefty discount off of retail price.

When using an online postage service, you simply cut and paste the address of your buyer from the PayPal payment confirmation e-mail into the postage software. When the address is in the program, you can print the postage and Delivery Confirmation directly to a label that you peel off and place directly on the package. No taping, no muss, or fuss.

I have received packages from several of eBay's largest sellers only to get handwritten mailing labels, or my address cut out from the PayPal payment-confirmation e-mail printed on a piece of paper. Wow, real businesslike, huh? This is not a good way to impress your customers with your professionalism.

The investment in a label printer saves you time and money, and pays for itself in short order. When you use a "mechanized" setup, you'll never want to print labels on plain paper again.

U.S. postage at a big discount!

I just had to share this with you! Look at the figure in this sidebar. It's a picture of an envelope that I recently received on an eBay purchase. I had to e-mail the seller to find out how and why she used so many stamps.

It seems the seller is a collector of U.S. postage. She checks out eBay auctions and buys deals on old sheets of mint-state stamps. U.S. stamps, no matter how old, are always good, so she buys these stamps at discount and uses them on her eBay packages.

Of course, she *also* says that when she brings her packages to the Post Office, all the clerks scatter to take a break!

Practice 29

Getting Your Item There in One Piece

In This Practice

- Packing the package safely
- Picking the right envelope for your item
- Understanding the types of mailing envelopes
- Getting deals on boxes

The most common area where online sellers drop the time-and-money ball is in shipping. I buy hundreds of items from sites all over the Internet, and have seen it all when it comes to packing, padding, and shipping.

I've received triple-packed unbreakable plastic items, swathed in yards of plain (heavyweight) newsprint sheets. I've seen money thrown out the window by e-tailers who use incorrect packing materials (bubble wrap on books?), which are expensive for the seller and often increase the package's shipping cost due to its final weight.

 The packing materials you use for your shipments can either make or break your bottom line in the shipping income/expense column of your business reports.

Many online sellers remark, "The buyer pays shipping, so what do I care what it costs? I pass on all those expenses to my buyers." Well, yes and no. Not only do buyers judge your services by giving you stars in your Detailed Seller Ratings (DSRs), but prudent packing can also be a boon to your business. Hey, in the constant competition with other sellers on the site, having lower shipping costs can often make the difference between a sale and no sale. This difference becomes obvious with eBay's new Price Plus Shipping Cost search option because buyers can find out the total amount of the purchase (including shipping) when performing a search. Also, when you're one of several people who have the same item for sale on eBay — with a minuscule difference in the item's selling price — having reasonable shipping charges can really tip the scale in favor of your auction. If you haven't read Practice 10, I suggest that you do; that practice talks about calculating the costs of shipping your items.

Pay attention to packing. It's expensive only if you don't know what you're doing. It's wise to compare shipping materials, know where you can save money, and recognize where saving money isn't prudent. You can ship your items in quality packing, keep your items safe (and, as a result, your buyers happy), and still make a dollar or so on each item for your handling fees. Remember that using recycled products is free.

Use only as much packing material as necessary to get the item where it's going and have it arrive intact. This saves time, money, and space.

Using Void Fill

Nope! *Void fill* is not a new drug to prevent hunger pangs when dieting — it's the industry term for the stuff you use to fill up space in shipping boxes to keep items from rolling in transit. (It's really the modern-day term for the old-fashioned word *dunnage*.)

There are many forms of void fill, and the best kind to use really depends on the item that you're shipping. Here are the most popular types and a description of their plusses and minuses.

Air-filled packing pillows

I first found out about these nifty little pillows when I received books from a major online bookseller. (See Figure 29-1.) When I looked into purchasing the pillows, I was disappointed to find out that they are made on-site in the shipping department by a rather expensive machine that injects air into pre-manufactured continuous tubing and then produces pillows of the desired size. Sadly, my shipping department (a table in the garage) was not big enough for this machine, and my shipping budget couldn't absorb the price of the equipment.

If you're looking for an extra income, why not buy your own air-pillow machine? It can be as small as a tabletop unit; you can manufacture those pillows for your own shipping — and sell bags of air on eBay for extra profit! After you have the machine installed (and paid for), producing these pillows is very cost-effective. But if you don't want to make that investment, you'll be glad to hear that buying air-filled packing pillows from sellers on eBay is quite economical, mainly because the manufacturing and shipping costs are low. What these folks are essentially shipping you is 99 percent air (something the Post Office hasn't yet figured out how to charge for).

• **Figure 29-1: Delicate items can be shipped in a box within a box, padded with cheap air pillows.**

To find sellers, search eBay for *air pillows* in the Business and Industrial category.

eBay shipping supply e-tailers make their livings selling packing materials to other sellers online. Their overhead is much lower than that of any retail outlet. Even after paying shipping to get the bubble wrap, air pillows, or packing peanuts to your door, you still save money *and* time. Most of these sellers ship the same day they get your order.

Air-filled packing pillows are perfect for filling in the area around smaller boxed items that you want to double-box. They're also handy if you have breakables that you've pre-wrapped in bubble wrap; just use the pillows to fill out the box. They're crush-proof and can support about 150 pounds of weight without a blowout.

Ten bags of Styrofoam peanuts can weigh 31.7 lbs. It takes only 10 pounds of air pillows to fill the same volume!

Plentiful packing peanuts

Every serious eBay seller has to have a stock of packing peanuts. They're handy for padding Tyvek® envelopes, filling boxes so that items don't shift around, and filling collectible milk bottles so they look full when you sell them on eBay.

Packing peanuts seem to multiply in dark areas. I know, because in all my time on eBay, I've had to buy some only once. That's probably because I buy almost everything online, and everything I buy arrives packed in peanut stuffing — so I never run out. (By the way, bags of peanuts make great bumpers in the garage.)

For functionality, foam packing peanuts are the granddaddy of all void filler. When properly placed in a box, they fill every nook and cranny and cushion your shipment to make it virtually indestructible. The key is to not go short in the land of plenty — use plenty of peanuts and make sure there are no vacant air spaces in your box. An extra bonus: They're cheap, and if you recycle them, they don't hurt the environment.

Figure 29-2 shows you how eBay sellers ship packing peanuts in very big bags!

• **Figure 29-2: Gary (eBay seller) Gatorpack waits for his mail pickup.**

Bubble wrapping by the roll

Bubble wrap (or *air cellular packaging material*) is *de rigueur* shipping material. Not only is it fun to play with, but it protects your items in shipping like nothing else! Bubble wrap is made up of air-filled cushions of polyethylene. It's supplied in rolls of different widths and lengths (see Figure 29-3). It really shines for those who wrap very delicate, breakable items.

• **Figure 29-3: Different sizes of bubble wrap.**

When you're wrapping an item with bubble wrap, wrap it tightly one way and then the other, then affix some packing tape to make your item an impenetrable ball. Bubble wrap is reasonably priced and adds next to no weight to your packages.

 When you purchase bubble wrap, be sure you buy the perforated, (tear-off) kind. Cutting a giant roll of bubble wrap with a box cutter can be a potentially dangerous proposition.

Bubble wrap not only comes in different widths, but you may have noticed that it comes in different thicknesses as well:

✔ **³⁄₁₆ inch thick (small):** Perfect for inner wrap of delicate breakables — then finish off with a layer of large wrap.

✔ **½ inch thick (large):** I use this for just about anything; it keeps things from rattling around and protects items from shock.

Plain old rolls of white newsprint

In the right shipping situation, plain white newsprint is fantastic. It's cheap and easy to store. The bad news? It's heavy — and sellers often use too many sheets to wrap the items they pack. It can be the perfect packing material when you are using the Flat Rate boxes from the U. S. Post Office — because there's no weight limitation on the box.

eBay sellers dealing in glass, china, and breakable knick-knacks often use newsprint to wrap each piece before placing it in a box full of packing peanuts.

If you feel that newsprint will be just thing to pack with, I suggest you buy it by the roll and use a table-mounted roll cutter to cut the exact size you need. (This is the kind of thing you may have seen in old-style butcher shops and delis.) This setup helps you to avoid using too much paper.

Bargains on newsprint can be found (where else?) on eBay. Just search for *newsprint rolls*. Hopefully you'll find a seller close to you so the shipping won't take a large chunk out of your budget.

Enveloping Your Items with Bubbles

Many eBay sellers miss the boat completely when they ship all their items in boxes, just because they're free from the Post Office. When you get into serious selling, using padded envelopes will cut your shipping costs and your items will still arrive safe and sound.

 Items sent in envelopes can be sent via First Class mail as long as they weigh 13 ounces or less.

Thankfully, the envelope makers of the world have united to manufacture their envelopes in standard sizes. Figure 29-4 gives you an idea what these look like.

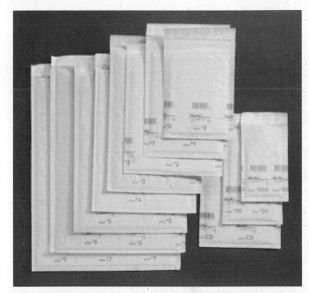

• **Figure 29-4: A variety of bubble envelopes in standard sizes from eBay seller, grasup.**

Not only are there different sizes, but someone actually gave some thought to making these envelopes so that they fit certain items. Take a look at Table 29-1 for a listing of standard envelope sizes and their uses.

TABLE 29-1: STANDARD BUBBLE-PADDED MAILER SIZES

Size	Measurements	Suggested Items
#000	4"×8"	Collector trading cards, jewelry, computer diskettes, coins
#00	5"×10"	Postcards, paper ephemera
#0	6"×10"	CDs, DVDs, Xbox or PS2 games
#1	7 ¼"×12"	Cardboard-sleeve VHS tapes, jewel-cased CDs and DVDs
#2	8 ½"×12"	Clamshell VHS tapes
#3	8 ½"×14 ½"	Toys, clothing, stuffed animals

(continued)

TABLE 29-1 *(continued)*

Size	Measurements	Suggested Items
#4	9 ½"×14 ½"	Small books, trade paperbacks
#5	10 ½"×16"	Hardcover books
#6	12 ½"×19"	Clothing, soft boxed items
#7	14 ¼"×20"	Much larger packaged items, framed items, and plaques

Mailing envelopes come made of many types of materials. Some are sturdier than others. Here's what many eBay sellers use:

- **Polyvinyl envelopes:** If you've ever ordered clothing or bedding from any of the television-shopping clubs, this is what they came in. Polyvinyl envelopes are lightweight, puncture- and tear-resistant, and light as a feather. They are the most durable envelopes available. Who says you have to ship in boxes?

- **Tyvek envelopes:** You know those really cool indestructible white envelopes you get from the Post Office or FedEx? They're made of DuPont Tyvek. It isn't made of paper, it's spun-bonded olefin fiber. It's got all the benefits of vinyl envelopes and more. Tyvek breathes (allows air to reach your product) and has a higher strength-to-weight ratio than other envelope materials. (That ratio business means it's very strong, yet feather-light.)

- **Bubble-padded mailers:** This is the type of envelope most often used by eBay sellers. The envelopes are lined with small bubbles (very similar to bubble wrap). They're great for shipping a variety of items. Bubble-lined mailers come in different materials; the pros and cons of each are

  - *Plain paper bubble mailers* are the cheapest possible way to go, but can be damaged in the mail if you ship heavy items in them. The perfect way to get around that is to wrap some cheap clear packing tape once around the envelope in each direction.

  - *Vinyl bubble mailers* aren't very expensive and are a super-protective way to ship. They're 15 percent lighter than paper bubble mailers and are water-resistant.

 If you're buying bubble mailers in quantity (100 or more), check out a new vendor that I discovered: www.royalmailers.com. Their prices are the cheapest around because they manufacture the envelopes they sell. They have offered my readers a *10 percent discount* on your order, and will give you *free shipping*! Just use the code *COOLEBAYTOOLS* when you place your order and the discount will be applied! (You can use this discount more than once — for as many orders as you wish.)

Getting It Boxed

Boxes come in thousands of sizes. The more variety you have in your inventory, the handier that is.

Buying in bulk

If you've been buying shipping boxes from brick-and-mortar office supply stores, you're paying a lot for the convenience. Yes, they do deliver — but so do the companies who do nothing but manufacture boxes. And these guys offer terrific discounts if you buy 100 at a time.

Check your local phone book and look up Boxes, Manufacturers. If you're a legitimate business, they will be happy to sell to you if you buy in quantity. I buy mine (for items that don't fit in Priority Mail boxes) online from a box manufacturer at www.uline.com. They ship from six different hubs in the United States; one happens to be right near me. (So that keeps the shipping costs — and transit time — down.)

Buying boxes on eBay

If you want smaller quantities of boxes, say ten at a time, look for eBay sellers offering various sizes of boxes on the site. Just use your search tricks and search shipping (box,boxes).

Free Priority Mail boxes

Yes, you savvy sellers out there, I know that many of you already know you can get free boxes from the Post Office to ship your Priority Mail packages. But every day I meet more sellers who don't know about this incredible way to save money. So here's the deal . . . you can get *free* Priority Mail shipping supplies direct from the United States Postal Service.

Type in the URL for the Post Office Web site at shop.usps.com, and you'll find yourself in the Postal Store. Click the link for *For Mailing/Shipping*. Then, on the next page, when you select Priority Mail, you can order boxes in a multitude of different sizes (as shown in Figure 29-5) — as well as Priority Mail packing tape and several sizes of Priority Mail envelopes at no charge. You have to order the boxes in lots of 25 (some in quantities of 10), but have no fear: Your regular letter carrier will deliver the boxes to your home! It's free and easy to order. Table 29-2 shows you the different sizes of available shipping items.

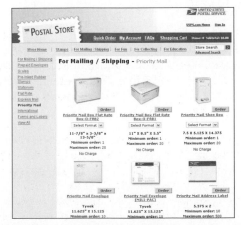

• **Figure 29-5: Your postage fees include a bonus when you ship via Priority Mail.**

 In the USPS Shipping Zone of the eBay Shipping Center, you can order five sizes of free Priority Mail boxes that have the eBay logo on them (see Figure 29-6). If this is something you really want, go ahead and order, but the consensus of many

PowerSellers is that the eBay logo on the *outside* of the box is just an invitation to thieves. (What looks more interesting than a box that says "eBay" sitting alone in front of someone's door?) Why tempt fate? Get the standard USPS issue free boxes — they don't look quite as inviting.

• **Figure 29-6: Special eBay branded Priority Mailboxes for free!**

TABLE 29-2: FREE PRIORITY MAIL PACKAGING

Size	Description	Minimum Quantity
8 ⅝"×5 ⅜"×1 ⅝"	Small video box 10965	25
9 ¼"×6 ¼"×2"	Large video box 1096LX	10
7 ⁹⁄₁₆"×5 ⁷⁄₁₆"×1 ⅜"	Electronic media box	10
11 ¼"×14"×2 ¼"	Medium 1097	10
12 ½"×15 ½"×3"	Large 1095	10
12 ⅛"×13 ⅜"×2 ¾"	Medium 1092	10
6"×38"	Triangle tube 14F	10
6"×25"	Triangle tube 1098S	10
7"×7"×6"	Small square cube BOX4	25
12"×12"×8"	Square cube BOX7	25
11 ⅞"×3 ⅜"×13 ⅝"	Flat-rate rectangle box FRB2	20

(continued)

TABLE 29-2 (continued)

Size	Description	Minimum Quantity
11"×8 ½"×5 ½"	Flat-rate cube box FRB1	20
12"×12"×5½"	Large flat-rate box	20
7 ½"×5 ⅛"×14 ⅜"	Shoe box	10
11 ⅝"×15 ⅛"	Tyvek envelope EP14	10
6"×10"	Cardboard envelope 14B	10
12 ½"×9 ½"	Flat-rate cardboard envelope 14-F	10
5"×10"	Cardboard window envelope	1

What happens when you put a new item up for sale and someone buys it immediately, but you have no clean box to ship it in? If the item comes in a sturdy, shippable box, you're somewhat safe. However the Post Office won't always accept boxes that are overprinted with manufacturer's pictures and promotional info. Get some tan-color shipping tape, and cover most of the box. It will make the package look somewhat like a plain brown box. You can label it and off it goes.

If the item didn't come in its own box, you can always do some box begging at your local shopping center for a box of appropriate size (just be sure you get one in clean, fresh-smelling condition).

Practice 30

Understanding the Limitations of Package Insurance

Selling on eBay requires you to become an expert on shipping. I try to give you all the information you need in my books, but the rules change from time to time, so you need to stay updated. Shipping a few items or shipping a hundred items is all the same when it comes to insurance. Are you going to offer your buyers insurance against damage or loss? Bottom line: Whether you offer insurance or not, you (the seller) are ultimately responsible for getting the product to the buyer. The lost-in-the-mail excuse doesn't cut the mustard, and having a Delivery Confirmation number doesn't guarantee anything either.

You may *think* that it's the buyer's responsibility to pay for insurance. If they don't, you say, it's their hard luck if the package doesn't arrive. This is far from the truth; a buyer who does not receive an item that she's paid for can legitimately file a fraud report against you. Buyers can also have the payment removed from your PayPal account if you have no physical proof that you've shipped the item, and you have no defense against this.

 For PayPal to protect you under their Seller Protection Policy (by not yanking out your money when a buyer screams "fraud"), you must have proof that the package was delivered. A Delivery Confirmation that has been scanned on delivery will provide that proof. Occasionally, however, the letter carrier neglects to scan the item and there is no proof of your package arriving. This is why PayPal requires that any package valued over $250 be sent with a Signature Confirmation (USPS Confirmation Signature Required: $2.50 fee; UPS Delivery Confirmation: $1.50 per package). Signed proof is rarely questioned.

You need to realize that the responsibility for delivering the goods you sell is in your PowerSelling hands. So, offering insurance to your buyers is good business, and including insurance with every shipment over a certain value is excellent business. This practice speaks to the various ways you can insure your packages — and stay within a reasonable budget.

Even the best insurance won't protect you against shoddy packing practices. If you end up with a damaged shipment because *somebody* threw a couple of crystal goblets in a box with a few pieces of paper, odds are the shipper won't pay off on the claim. (Major carriers request to see the package before they pay.) Follow safe shipping practices; see Practices 27, 28, and 29 for more info.

Self-Insuring Your Items

Self-insuring by collecting a handling fee from buyers is a way to reduce your insurance costs by maintaining an adequate reserve fund. By maintaining a personal reserve fund, you're allowing yourself to acquire — that is, assume — some of your risk. Doing so means you can immediately reduce your current insurance costs, keep your premium rates down, and release extra funds to purchase insurance as needed.

You take the risks and use money out of your reserve fund if (or *when*) a shipping-related loss occurs. Relying on self-insurance demands that you be especially careful about packing your items to prevent damage — and be sure to purchase Delivery Confirmations when using the Postal Service.

 eBay policy is pretty specific about what kind of insurance you can charge for:

> *Sellers offering insurance may only charge the actual fee for insurance. No additional amount may be added, such as "self-insurance". Sellers who do not use a licensed 3rd party insurance company may not require buyers to purchase insurance. This is a violation of state law.*

So the way to build your reserve fund is to bump up your shipping-and-handling fee to cover yourself in any calamity. Tack an additional $1 onto every item's postage amount as part of your handling fee. The more items you sell and ship, the more that little dollar-per-item profit builds up — and gives you a fund that you can use to cover the rare instance of a damaged or missing item.

 Savvy self-insurers usually do not ever self-insure items of high value. If you sell mostly lower-priced items (under $50) and decide to self-insure, consider making an exception when you do occasionally sell an expensive item. Bite the bullet and pay for the shipping insurance; doing so could save you money and hassle in the long run.

No "Insurance" through the Major Carriers

Although all the major shippers offer extended liability coverage (for a fee) as an option, remember that they are in the shipping business (duh), *not* in the insurance business. Processing claims for the inevitable damaged-during-shipping event is a dirty, annoying — but necessary — sideline to their package-transit business.

The major carriers, other than the United States Postal Service (who offers insurance), cover all shipments automatically (and at no extra charge) for the first $100 of package value. By the way, the *package value* of an item sold on eBay is the final bid (or Buy It Now) amount. Of course, you can always buy additional package liability coverage for your shipped items. Should a package get lost or damaged, making a claim opens an entirely new can of worms. (Read on for the scoop about the procedures for filing claims with the major carriers.)

 Although you may see optional extra coverage referred to (in the eBay world) as *insurance*, the major commercial carriers (including UPS and FedEx) do not call this *insurance* — it is clearly called something else: "Declared Coverage." These companies want to be very careful *not* to call it insurance.

n its current statement (at the time of writing) regarding declared value and the limits of liability, FedEx indicates that it does not provide insurance coverage — and that associated loss in excess of a package's declared value passes to the shipper (that's you) or to an insurance carrier (provided you've purchased insurance from one). Any shipper who doesn't want to assume the risk of a loss that could exceed the declared value should get appropriate insurance coverage, purchasing a policy from an agent or company that does provide that kind of insurance.

So if you think you pay the fees for items in excess of $100, you're safe, right? You may not be. A perusal of Federal Express' ground tariffs shows that if you're selling certain items and you wish to insure them for over $100 — you might be out of luck! (I wish you could've seen my face when I read the FedEx Ground Tariff that excludes just about every item that many eBay sellers sell.) The FedEx liability on any packages that include the following items is *limited to a maximum declared value of $100*:

- ✔ Artwork of any kind — including paintings, photographs, prints, vases, sculpture, collector's items, and statues.

- ✔ "Any commodity that by its inherent nature is particularly susceptible to damage or the market value of which is particularly variable or difficult to ascertain."

- ✔ Antiques, coins, tableware, sports cards, souvenirs, and memorabilia. "Collector's coins and stamps may not be shipped."

- ✔ Glassware, china, crystal mirrors, ceramics, porcelains, or any other commodity with similarly fragile qualities.

- ✔ Plasma screens.

- ✔ Jewelry — even costume jewelry — mounted gems, or jewelry made of precious metal.

- ✔ Furs.

- ✔ Precious metals in any form (hey, no shipping those gold bars you sold).

- ✔ Any type of negotiable or transferable cash equivalent (for example, stocks, bonds, non-collectible postage stamps, checks, money orders, gift cards, and so on). You get the idea.

- ✔ Musical instruments that are more than 20 years old, or personalized.

What exactly is left? To examine their policy in full, go to www.fedex.com/us/services/terms/intl.html#liabilitylimits and read the gory details yourself.

UPS states a similar policy and indicates that a declared value in excess of $100 does not grant the shipper insurance. And as with FedEx, shippers who specifically want any form of insurance to cover a package valued at over $100.00 must purchase it from a third party.

So, in essence, the seller is responsible to be sure to pay all additional fees for declared values of over $100.00. You're also responsible for proving that the item shipped is worth over $100.00. No matter how much "extra coverage" you buy — unless you can prove the specific value, you won't get reimbursed in case of a loss.

Table 30-1 shows you what the major carriers charge for their liability.

TABLE 30-1: DECLARED VALUE RATES FOR COMMERCIAL CARRIERS

Shipper	Shipper Rate
USPS	$1.65 for $0.01 – $50.00 value
	$2.05 for $50.01 – $100.00 value
	$2.45 for $100.01 – $200.00 value
	$4.60 for $200.01 – $300.00 value
	$4.60 and $.90 per $100 over $300.00 (or fraction thereof)
UPS	$1.80 minimum for $100.01 to $300.00 (after first $100.00 of value) plus $.60 per each $100.00 (or part of $100.00) up to $50,000.00

(continued)

TABLE 30-1 *(continued)*

Shipper	Shipper Rate
FedEx Ground	$0.55 per $100 (after first $100 of value)
Airborne Express (now part of DHL)	$0.70 per $100 (after first $100 of value)
DHL@Home	$0.70 per $100 (after first $100 of value)

Getting Third-Party Shipping Insurance

Since it seems that getting true insurance from anyone other than the U.S. Postal Service just isn't happening, the small package shipper can get his or her own third-party insurance. And shippers have been taking measures to insure what they're shipping for a long time (as outlined in the sidebar "Brokers not baristas . . . ").

 The point of the Lloyd's of London story in the "Brokers not baristas" sidebar is that your business can have a separate insurance policy to cover your eBay shipments. Depending on quantity and type of goods you ship, such insurance could ultimately save you thousands of dollars per year.

Brokers not baristas . . .

Some smart person, long, long ago, came up with the idea of privately insuring freight as it traveled over long distances. As early as 1688, Edward Lloyd became known in business circles as the guy who knew all about shipping. His small coffeehouse became the hub where ships' captains, merchants, and rich men went to get the facts about lost ships and salvage cargo.

A merchant wanting to insure cargo being sent out on a ship would show up at Lloyd's coffeehouse looking for a broker to get a policy. The broker would solicit many wealthy individuals to pool their resources so that each took just a portion of the risk. Mr. Lloyd ran his business from the coffeehouse until his death in 1713, and the brokers who started with Lloyd formalized the business that is

now the famous Lloyd's of London. The company currently insures much more than shipments — movie stars' body parts, singers' voices, and just about anything that one might wish to insure.

If you think that printing your own postage is slick, you're gonna love Universal Parcel Insurance Coverage (U-PIC), a service that automates the post-office-insurance hassle. U-PIC has been in the package insurance business since 1989, mainly insuring packages for large shippers. U-PIC has expanded its business to the online auction arena, and you can insure packages that you send through USPS, UPS, FedEx, and other major carriers.

Recognizing U-PIC advantages

If you use U-PIC insurance on USPS-shipped packages, you can save as much as 80 percent on insurance rates. And, when you use U-PIC with other major carriers, you can stop adding extra declared value fees for your shipments. Here are some great features of the U-PIC service:

- ✔ **No time wasted standing in line at the Post Office:** The U-PIC service is integrated into online shipping solutions such as endicia.com.

- ✔ **Quick payments on claims:** When you do have a claim, U-PIC pays it within seven days of receiving all required documents from the carrier.

 As with any insurance policy, assume that if you have many claims against your packages, you can be dropped from the service. (This thought only gives me more impetus to package my items properly — I never want to be banished to the counter lines again!)

- ✔ **Blanket approval:** U-PIC is approved by all major carriers. And turnabout is fair play: All carriers covered must be on the U-PIC approved carrier listing.

- ✔ **Cost savings:** Again, depending on the quantity and type of items you ship, using U-PIC may save you between 65 and 90 percent on your insurance-related costs. Table 30-2 shows the company's current rates. International coverage is available for all carriers listed in the table, as well as for approved air carriers.

The U-PIC service also enables you to print your postage through an online postage service — and, if you have just a few packages, give them directly to your USPS mail carrier. (You don't have to stand in line to get your insurance form stamped.) If you have a ton of boxes, you'll still need to drive them to the Post Office and shove them over the counter, but here's the bottom line: No waiting in line, no hassle!

Applying for a U-PIC policy

Fortunately, you can apply for a U-PIC policy with a minimum of hassle.

To apply for your own U-PIC policy — with no charge to apply and no minimum premium — go directly to the application on their Web site at http://delta.u-pic.com/Apply/rtp.aspx. **Tell 'em Marsha sent ya!**

On the U-PIC Request to Provide (RTP) form shown in Figure 30-1, you must answer questions about who you are, how many packages you send, and how many insurance claims you've filed in the past two years.

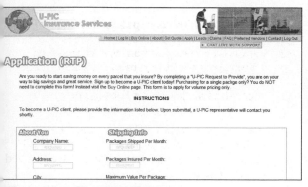

Figure 30-1: The U-PIC RTP form.

After you fill out the online form and agree to the policy (Evidence of Insurance), a U-PIC representative will contact you within 48 hours. The representative will answer your questions and help you decide which of their programs will work best for your eBay business. (I tell you about the cost for a standard shipper program in the next section.) Depending on volume, your other options include the following:

- ✔ **Occasional-shipper program:** Works well for the person who ships one to five packages per month. You can pay for your insurance online using a credit card, but the rates are not as attractive as those for the standard program.

- ✔ **Offline standard program:** Serves eBay businesspeople who ship a large number of packages per month. At the end of each shipping month, you generate an insurance report and use it to calculate your premium (which you can pay by check or through PayPal). You can get a discount when shipping online with the Post Office when you use a Delivery Confirmation.

Comparing U-PIC rates

Your U-PIC sales representative will explain to you exactly how to declare value with U-PIC based on your present shipping practices. At the end of each shipping month (under a standard shipping program), you fax, e-mail, or snail-mail your shipping reports to U-PIC. (If you use the endicia.com postage service, they send the reports electronically to U-PIC.)

Because you're paying for private insurance, U-PIC suggests that you include in the package a copy of your insurance policy (or, at the very least, a note explaining that you have an insurance policy covering your shipments) so your buyer doesn't think you're overcharging (which makes some folks a bit cranky).

TABLE 30-2: U-PIC STANDARD RATES

Shipper	U-PIC Rate
UPS	$0.20 per $100
FedEx	$0.20 per $100
USPS	$0.55 per $100 with Delivery Confirmation
DHL	$0.20 per $100
LTL Freight	$0.50 per $100

Table 30-2 outlines the U-PIC standard rates that apply when you ship with major carriers, and Table 30-3 compares U-PIC and USPS insurance rates. UPS charges $.60 per $100.00 package value (after the initial $100.00) with a $1.80 minimum, but U-PIC charges only $.20 per $100.00 of UPS shipment value. FedEx charges $.60 per $100.00 value with a $1.80 minimum. By using U-PIC, you can insure your FedEx packages for $.20 per $100.00 value.

TABLE 30-3: USPS AND U-PIC DOMESTIC INSURANCE COVERAGE RATE COMPARISON

Coverage	USPS	U-PIC Standard	U-PIC with USPS Delivery Confirmation
$.01 to $50.00	$1.10	$.75	$.50
$50.01 to $100	$2.00	$.75	$.50
$100.01 to $200.00	$3.00	$1.50	$1.00
$200.01 to $300.00	$4.00	$2.25	$1.50
$300.01 to $400.00	$5.00	$3.00	$2.00

 U-PIC will also insure international shipments. The cost to insure international USPS parcels is only $1.20 per $100.00, with no deductible.

If you're a high-volume shipper, you can negotiate an even lower rate with U-PIC. To reach U-PIC, call toll-free at 800-955-4623 or visit their Web site at www.u-pic.com.

Doing Everything Possible to Avoid Filing a Claim

Lost packages have been the bane of all carriers since they started accepting packages for delivery. The Post Office has been dealing this problem since it opened the Dead Letter Office in 1825.

The Postal Service's Dead Letter Office employees (I'll call them DLOs) are the only people legally permitted to open lost mail. When an address label gets smooshed, torn, wet, or otherwise illegible enough that the box can't be delivered, it finds its way into the hands of the DLOs, who open the package with the hope of finding enough information to get it to the rightful owner.

 Make sure that you always include a packing slip — like the kind you print from Selling Manager or My eBay — inside your packages. The packing slip should have both your address and the buyer's so that if the label is illegible, the packing slip will identify the owner and the package can be delivered.

And regardless of the carrier you use, having the buyer's address correct on the label is critical to begin with. The following ideas and practices will help you create accurate shipping labels:

✔ **Cut and paste the buyer's address:** The safest way to correct addressing is to cut and paste the buyer's address information from an e-mail or the PayPal payment confirmation or download. If your buyer's address shows as unconfirmed through PayPal, send a quick e-mail to your buyer to verify. People do make mistakes, even when writing their own addresses.

✔ **Don't depend on the carrier to correct an address:** No carrier is really going to tell you whether the address you have is incorrect. To test my theory, I've deliberately typed nonexistent addresses into the Post Office, UPS, and

FedEx forms. The carrier's forms didn't correct a thing. The only time I've had inaccurate addresses corrected is when I used endicia.com's DAZzle software (find more about DAZzle in Practice 28).

✔ **Use software or online services to check your buyer's address:** It's good business practice to confirm the viability of an address before you send your item. Through Dial-A-ZIP, software such as DAZzle (from endicia.com) corrects most common addressing errors such as misspelled city or street names. If you have a question about a ZIP code, you can check it at the Post Office Web site at `www.usps.com/zip4`.

 If you have the Google toolbar or go to `www.google.com,` you can type in any UPS, Post Office, or FedEx tracking number and find the current tracking information from the carrier's Web site. Just copy and paste the tracking number into the Google search box and start your search. You'll come to a page that presents a link for tracking packages — with your number and carrier showing. Click the link and you end up at the carrier's site with all the current tracking information. Nice!

Making a Claim When Shipments Go Awry

If you've been selling or buying on eBay for a length of time, odds are you've been involved with making a claim for lost or damaged packages. The process is often grueling — with all the paperwork that's involved — and the decision of the carrier is final. If you don't agree with the carrier, you could try small claims court. But realize that you'll lose around a day of work — and, in court, you'll face all the legalese you find in the teeny-tiny print on the carrier's Terms of Service.

I understand the hassles because I've had to make several claims myself. One claim that I actually won several years ago, after much haggling, was for

(please don't judge me here) a framed original-wardrobe uniform tunic from the *Star Trek* series — autographed by Leonard Nimoy. I'd like to help you avoid similar unpleasant experiences, or at least make them less unpleasant.

But if you do a lot of shipping, you'll inevitably be faced with making a claim. I first tell you about the U.S. Postal Service because their claim process is more stringent than that of the other carriers. With any carrier, you need to gather the same type of backup information before making a claim.

 Here's something to keep in mind when you're thinking about filing a claim. When you purchase insurance from a carrier, only the content of the package is insured. The shipping carrier doesn't seem to care whether an item's packaging gets destroyed. I've heard that many a claim for damaged packaging has been denied on collectibles where mint-condition packaging is just as important as the item being perfect. If a Barbie doll was shipped, only the safe intact arrival of the doll seems to matter, not the special collector's box surrounding it.

Making a claim with the Post Office

Making a claim with the Post Office: Oh man, talk about a hassle. But making a claim with *any* carrier isn't a bowl of cherries on any day! Before making a claim with the USPS, check to make sure your package was actually covered by Postal Insurance purchased at the time of mailing. If you use private insurance instead, you don't make a claim to the Post Office.

If an item has Postal Insurance and arrives at the buyer's door damaged, you may immediately make a claim with the Post Office. When a package is lost in transit, the Post Office puts some time constraints on your making a claim: You must wait a minimum of 30 days after the mailing date before you make the claim.

There's always a question as to who makes the claim:

- ✔ **Damaged or loss of contents:** Either the seller or the buyer can make the claim.

- ✔ **Complete loss:** When a package never turns up after 30 days and it's officially MIA, the seller must be the one to file a claim.

Gathering the tools and supporting info

First you go to the Post Office to get a copy of *PS Form 1000, Domestic Claim or Registered Mail* inquiry — or just download the form at `www.usps.com/forms/_pdf/ps1000.pdf`. Fill out the form with all the details required.

 Be sure to bring your backup information. To make a damage claim, you must produce evidence of insurance. This can be either of the following documents:

- ▶ **Original Mailing Receipt:** The receipt that was stamped at the Post Office counter when the item was mailed.

- ▶ **Original box or wrapper:** This must show the addresses of both the sender and the recipient, along with whatever tags or stamps the Post Office put on the package to say it's insured.

 If only the box or wrapper is presented as proof of insurance, the Post Office will likely limit the claim to $100.

You must also produce evidence showing the value of the item *when it was mailed*. Here's a quick list of documents accepted by the Post Office for damage claims (be prepared for them to ask for more thorough proof):

- ✔ Sales receipt or descriptive invoice.

- ✔ Copy of your cancelled check or money order receipt.

- ✔ Picture and description of a similar item from a catalog if your receipt isn't available.

- ✔ A letter from the seller stating the value of the item.

- ✔ Your own description of the item. Include date and time the item was purchased and whether it is new or vintage.

For missing packages, you (the seller) need a letter from the buyer (dated 30 days after the package was mailed) stating that they never received the package.

If your buyer is too cranky to cooperate, go to the Post Office where you mailed the package. Ask for a written statement that there is no record of the delivery being made. Postal employees can look up the insurance or Delivery Confirmation numbers to find whether the delivery took place, but the Post Office will charge you $6.60 for their efforts. That amount will be reimbursed if the Post Office pays your claim and doesn't locate your package under a bale of hay in Indiana.

If all goes well and your claim is deemed legit, you should get your payment within 30 days. If you don't hear from the Post Office within 45 days (maybe the payment got lost in the mail?), you have to submit a duplicate claim using the original claim number.

 Note to self (and to you): Always make a copy of any form you give to the government.

Making your claim online

Using a new service from the Post Office, you can file a claim for domestic insurance purchased online for packages valued up to $500, either through Click-N-Ship or eBay. Just go to

```
www.usps.com/insuranceclaims/
online.htm
```

nd have the following information available:

- ✔ The insurance tag number
- ✔ Your Click-N-Ship transaction number or eBay listing number
- ✔ Proof of Value and Proof of Damage

adly, even though this process is automated, dam-ged items (including the mailing box and packing naterials) must still be brought to the Post Office fter you submit your online claim.

Filing a claim with UPS

Vhoa! The stories of filing claims with UPS are leg-ndary. Almost any eBay seller can tell you quite a tory. I must admit that making a claim with UPS is a ;ood deal easier than making a claim with the Post)ffice. At least, once your damage claim is filed and .ccepted, you get a check within five days.

'or damaged packages, UPS recently streamlined he process as well, although the buyer must make he claim. You *can* (if you really want to) call 1-800-'ICK-UPS (cute, eh?) to file your claim. The better lea is to go directly to the online reporting form at

```
www.ups.com/content/us/en/resources/
    service/tracking/claims.html
```

3e sure you make your report to UPS within 48 ours of delivery.

)n the online claim form, you'll be asked to input all nformation about the package and the damage. UPS eems to be very familiar with its own handiwork; ou get to select a particular type of damage from a nenu.

.fter you've filled out and submitted the form, just it on your haunches and wait for the UPS claims lepartment to contact you.

 I recommend that you print your form after filling it out so you can keep all reference information for the claim in one place.

After the buyer makes the claim, UPS sends a Damage/Loss Notification Letter form to the seller. The seller must fill out the form to state the item's value and attach supporting documentation. The form can then be faxed back to UPS for final verification.

 Save the damaged item and all the packaging that it came in. UPS may send an inspector out to look at the package before approving a claim.

If a UPS shipment appears to be lost, the seller must call UPS to request a package tracer. If UPS is unable to prove delivery, the claim is paid.

Filing a claim with FedEx

Filing a claim with FedEx is similar to the UPS proce-dure, except FedEx gives you a little more leeway as to time. Instead of the 48-hours-after-delivery dead-line, you have 15 business days to make your claim. (This extra time sure helps out when a package is delivered to your house while you're out of town.) FedEx processes all Concealed Loss and Damage claims within five to seven days after receiving all the paperwork and information.

As with UPS, keep all packaging, including the car-ton, along with the item in case FedEx wants to come and inspect the damage.

You can make your FedEx claim in a couple of ways:

- ✔ **By fax:** You can download a PDF claim form with instructions at

  ```
  www.fedex.com/us/customer/claims/
      Claims.pdf
  ```

  Fill out the form and fax it to the number on the form.

- ✔ **Online:** Fill out the online claim form on a secure server at https://www.fedex.com/us/claimsonline.

To file a claim online, you must have a FedEx login to begin your claim. If you file your claim online, you'll still have to mail or fax in your supporting documentation. When you file online, you can also choose to receive e-mail updates from FedEx regarding your claim (good idea!).

 The claim payment will be sent to the seller, so it's up to the seller to make restitution with the buyer. As soon as the claim is approved, a refund should be made.

Making a claim with U-PIC

Making a claim with U-PIC is a far more civilized process. Remember: You've been approved for an insurance policy with them. You're not just some stranger coming in with a broken lamp.

To place a claim with U-PIC on a shipment, you must do so no sooner than 30 days after the date of mailing, and you must supply the following:

- ✔ A signed letter, stating the loss or damage from the consignee

- ✔ A copy of the monthly insurance report you turned in to U-PIC reflecting the insured value

- ✔ A completed U-PIC claim form (one claim form per claim)

- ✔ A copy of the original invoice or the end-of-auction form

Practice 31

Handling the Inevitable: Returns

Selling on eBay — especially as a PowerSeller — equates to making money. When you're making money, one of the last things you want to think about is taking returns on a product you've sold. But the customer's occasional need to return an item is an integral part of the retail model. You have to decide whether you'll accept returns on your sales — and whether you do is entirely up to you.

That said, one of the ways to keep making money on eBay is to have happy customers who do not leave you negative feedback and who return to buy additional merchandise from you. Even neutral feedback can leave a pain in your gut when you read it. So, you ask, what is the way to be sure that all customers are happy? Sellers who have high feedback ratings bend over backward to make their customers happy — and sometimes making a customer happy means accepting a return.

Personally? I hate taking returns. Arrgh, there's not much more to ruin my day than an e-mail from a customer who wants to return an item. I always try to accommodate my buyers, and the way I save myself grief is to have a clear return policy that's stated on my listings.

Establishing a Clear Return Policy

Setting the parameters of your sale upfront is a good policy for all retailers — no matter how much they sell or where. Interestingly, several states — including California, eBay's home state — have laws regarding giving refunds for returned merchandise. The law in California assumes that consumers have the expectation for a store to refund, credit, or exchange an item. Consumers also expect to have to produce proof of purchase, and feel they should be able to return an item within (at least) seven days.

If retailers in California have a policy that differs from the standard expectations of the consumer, they must conspicuously display their policy in the store. If the store accepts no returns, management must post the policy near the cash register (at the very least). If a retailer has additional conditions related to accepting returns, these must also be posted in a conspicuous manner. Although it's not the law, the same good business practice belongs on eBay.

 Please, please, *please* use eBay's return policy form on the Sell Your Item page. Lots of sellers load up the description area with paragraphs full of rules and regulations. But remember that eBay provides a place to put your return policy — so put it there (for one thing, that's where your buyers will look for it). The description area is the place to describe your item. (Describe. Tell people about the *item*, not about the policy.)

You don't *have* to take returns — so, if you don't, indicate that's the case. Use the Sell Your Item form's Return Information area — just don't put a check mark in the *Returns Accepted* box. But remember, unless you're selling specialty items like jewelry, buyers may be more willing to buy if they do have the option to return.

Filling Out eBay's Return Policy Form

To use eBay's return policy form (shown in Figure 31-1), you have several options. Select the various options by using the drop-down menus that appear after you select the *Returns Accepted* check box.

✔ **Item must be returned within**. This is where you give the customer the information as to how fast you want the item returned.

▶ **3 days**. Three days is not really giving the customers a fair chance, but many sellers use this as an option to dissuade buyers from using the item and then returning. It's also often used when the seller really doesn't want to take returns and three days doesn't give the buyer enough time to fully test the item.

▶ **7 days.** This is a fair and reasonable time to give a customer to return an item.

▶ **14 days**. If you're feeling generous, and don't want the item back right away to resell, you can give 14 days. But keep in mind that merchandise on the Internet can go stale — and the buying surge (or is that *splurge*?) for your particular item may disappear.

▶ **30 days.** This option is usually given by regular dealers who can return the merchandise to the manufacturer for a refund (see the next section "Considering Your Policy Options").

✔ **Refund will be given as**. Decide ahead of time just how you plan to refund to the customer.

▶ **Exchange.** They can exchange the item for another item in your store.

▶ **Merchandise credit.** When the item is returned, you e-mail (or snail mail) the buyer a credit slip that they may use in your store in the future.

▶ **Money back**. Yuck. Gotta hate this option!

✔ **Return-policy details.** This is the most important part of all. You put text here that is specific to your own business. (In the next section, I go over some of the options that eBay forgot and you need to include.)

Return policy

☐ Returns Accepted

Item must be returned within

Refund will be given as

Return policy details

Although I want you to be happy with your purchase, I've found that
catnip toys are pretty gross once a cat has played with them. So for
that reason, I cannot accept returns.
THANK YOU

Note: 500 character limit

Figure 31-1: eBay's Return Policy listing information from the Sell Item form.

Considering Your Policy Options

When you're setting your return policy, you have a lot more to consider as to how you'll handle your customer's needs. Consider the circumstances I present in the following sections.

Dealing with defective merchandise

What happens if you send something out, it isn't damaged in shipping, but it's simply not functional? Certain sellers, especially liquidators (who know that a certain amount of their merchandise could be defective), use some of the terms defined in the upcoming bullets. Some phrases can put potential buyers on alert, and they may not be willing to bid as much as you'd like for the item. Common phrases that are relevant to possibly non-working merchandise are

✔ **As-is-where-is**. An item sold *as-is-where-is* means that it has no implied warranty of any sort. The seller very possibly doesn't know whether the item works.

✔ **Guaranteed not to be DOA**. The seller guarantees that the item will work when it arrives at the buyer's door.

✔ **Satisfaction guaranteed.** Sellers using this term usually buy direct from a manufacturer who has a similar policy. Also, if your markup is big enough on an item you stock, it may be worth

your while to take back an item if not doing so means the buyer will leave you negative feedback.

PayPal's Buyer Protection Plan will take a buyer's word that an item is "not as described" and refund their money anyway (and yank the payment from your PayPal account). In this case, the buyer may not even return the item. You'd be out the item and your money. It behooves you — not only for customer-service reasons but for the PayPal chargeback policy — to take back returns when something is questionable.

When customers have a change of heart

Customers can change their minds, too. I'm not very forgiving in this case. After all, I write a good description, I pack and ship exactly what the buyer orders in a timely, safe manner — and then the customers have the nerve to change their minds? Sheesh. This situation is annoying, inconvenient, and expensive — and I personally don't accept returned items when customers merely change their minds. In your policy, you may want to state that you will take back items (except in the case of defective units) only if the item is:

✔ **In new condition.** You'd be shocked at the number of people who will buy clothing on eBay and wear it to an event — then attempt to return it to the seller. Believe me, you *can* tell whether an item has been worn, even if the tags are artfully put back on the item with a tag puncher.

✔ **Still sealed or in an unopened box.** Media, such as DVDs and CDs, came from the manufacturer sealed in clear plastic. Once that clear plastic is removed from the item, it can't be resold as new. Toys and games often can never be put back into their original packaging after the item is removed. In this case, too, you can't get as much for the item as when it was in the original packaging.

Some very unscrupulous buyers (okay, thieves) will buy a collectible item from an eBay seller and attempt to return a counterfeit in its place. They're hoping the seller is too busy to notice when the item is unpacked. They will get their refund and the seller will then (if he or she isn't paying attention) sell the counterfeit to another buyer. The thieves may also have a broken item at home, buy a duplicate in perfect condition from you, and attempt to return the broken one instead.

A fellow seller I knew was caught up in this wrong-item-returned scam. Together, we devised a plan to outwit the buyer. On eBay, you can buy an ultraviolet-sensitive pen. This pen can put a small mark on an item that is invisible to the naked eye. When the item is returned to you, all you have to do is pass a small UV light over the item and you'll know whether it's yours. These pens sell for under $10 each, and make a worthwhile investment for any eBay seller.

Factoring in the cost of shipping

Another thing to consider is shipping costs. The buyer paid for shipping to their location. You need to state whether you will pay for shipping of the item back to you — and then the shipping costs for re-shipping another item back to the customer. Whew. Personally, unless the item is defective and I choose to accept a return, I do not pay all that extra shipping. With shipping costs as high as they are, shipping something three times can cost more than your item.

Relieving the pain with a restocking fee

To take away some of the pain involved when accepting a return, some retailers apply other conditions, such as restocking fees, to merchandise exchanges. I like the restocking-fee concept. It pays you back a little extra for your time and effort when taking a return. Sellers usually charge a recalcitrant buyer 15 percent of the selling cost as a restocking fee to take back the item. I have seen sellers go as

low as 5 percent; I've also seen restocking fees as high as 20 percent.

Some sellers do a good job of outlining their return policies; take a look at the examples in Figures 31-2 through 31-4.

Return policy	
Item must be returned within:	7 Days
Refund will be given as:	Money Back
Return policy details:	SATISFACTION GUARANTEED! Your original purchase price will be fully refunded if the item is returned in its original condition within 7 days (buyer pays all shipping costs). Please note that, except in cases of damage, items signed to a specific person cannot be returned.

• **Figure 31-2: 100% Satisfaction Guarantee (with a small caveat).**

Return policy	
Item must be returned within:	7 Days
Refund will be given as:	Exchange
Return policy details:	All items are guaranteed to be in working order exactly as described. We cannot accept returns for other reasons. Defective items are always replaced

• **Figure 31-3: We'll take it back if it's broken.**

Return policy	
Item must be returned within:	7 Days
Refund will be given as:	Money Back
Return policy details:	To receive a full refund of your purchase price less shipping costs, this product must be returned at your cost no later than 7 days after you receive it.
	Item is subject to a 15% restocking fee if it is returned without defect, or the reason for return is not the fault of the Seller. In the case of defect or our error, no restocking fee is charged.

• **Figure 31-4: Return it within 7 days at your own expense and we'll charge you 15% to take it back (I like this option).**

Items You Might Not Want to Take Back

Despite the fact that many brick-and-mortar retailers have big signs posted that the health department prevents returns on some items, this may not be the case. I searched the Internet archives and couldn't find actual laws. Supposedly, some state health departments require that swimwear and underwear be tried on over underwear, but again — I couldn't find the laws.

Local health departments may possibly have ordinances, but retailers generally still take back any item returned to them. Interestingly, in 1916, according to a story in the *New York Times,* stores banned returns on children's wear because of the polio epidemic — but the health department refused to make an official ban. The Health Department, at that time, felt that it would be an extraordinary financial burden to enforce the law. As I said, these "laws" may all be apocryphal.

At any rate, there are items you may not want to take back — it's important to mention this in your return policy.

- **Pet toys**. Animals gnaw on pet toys in their mouths to play with them. I would say that you wouldn't want to accept a pet toy back unless it's in "unused" condition.

- **Underwear, intimate apparel, and bathing suits.** I searched eBay and (surprisingly) some sellers do accept returns for these items. Again, due to "hygienic" reasons, it's perfectly acceptable not to accept returns for these items.

- **"Adult" toys.** Whatever the real hygienic issues, you might not want to accept returns on such personal items when (and if) you sell them. Same goes for antique intimate gear like merkins and codpieces.

- **Wigs.** Here's another hygiene issue. My mother didn't even like me trying on hats in a store.

- **Personalized items.** After an item has been personalized with a monogram or dedication, it's almost impossible to find another buyer for the item, and the seller would take a huge loss upon accepting a return.

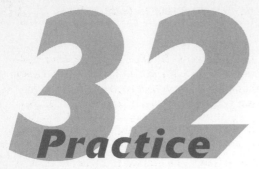

Practice 32

Steering Clear of Fraud

Transactions can go wrong. Horribly wrong. Sometimes the buyer doesn't read the description, or they don't see the chip out of the corner of the antique vase in your picture. Those are the simple ones. Perhaps the item functioned properly before you shipped it (because, as a careful seller, you tested it before you shipped), and it arrives at the buyer's door in a non-functioning state. Worse yet? The buyer didn't buy insurance and the item was destroyed en route. I discuss accepting returns in Practice 31, but this practice addresses what to do when the unthinkable happens and you're accused of fraud.

Fraud is a horrible word. But buyers throw it around all the time. It could be a case of an innocent mistake on the seller's part, but some buyers (especially those new to eBay) don't give the seller a chance to make good and scream "Fraud!"

In the real world, buyers are protected from real fraud. As a PowerSeller, you may come face to face with circumstances that, according to the Federal Trade Commission, do constitute fraud. I encourage you to establish consistent business practices that steer you away from any situation resembling the following:

✔ **Untimely shipping:** Did you know that the Federal Trade Commission, in its Prompt Delivery rules, says that you must ship your newly sold item *within 30 days of the close of the auction or sale?* If you don't, the buyer must give you permission to delay shipment further — or you must refund the buyer's money.

✔ **Failure to disclose complete and accurate information:** Also, according to the Federal Trade Commission, a seller perpetrates a fraud by failing to disclose all relevant information on an item or by sending an item that fails to match the description used to sell it.

Find additional information about buyer protection under the law at http://www.ftc.gov/bcp/conline/pubs/alerts/intbalrt.shtm

Save yourself potential grief by presenting accurate, complete information in your listings. If there could be any question about the authenticity or condition of your item, be sure to include photos of the item from all sides!

Recognizing Problematic Transactions

Meanwhile, buyers and sellers also need to beware of these other illegal scams that go on in the eBay world . . .

- **Shill bidding:** Confederates of a seller may place ultrahigh bids on an item, thereby forcing buyers to bid even more if they want the item. This practice tricks buyers into paying much more than they would in an honest, open marketplace.

- **Bid siphoning:** While bidding on a legitimate item, a buyer may receive an e-mail offering him or her the item at a lower price. These messages are sent by unscrupulous scammers, and usually come with a very legitimate-sounding (or not) story about why they're selling this item so cheap. Don't be greedy; the biggest hogs get slaughtered. If you offer to sell the item off-site, you are in violation of eBay policies.

  Buyers may also receive an e-mail asking for payment from someone other than the seller. Such a request shows an e-mail address that's different from the address associated with the item won.

- **Bid shielding:** A buyer places a very high bid on an item, and at the very last possible moment, retracts the bid, and places another (lower) bid under a different User ID. eBay policy fights this cheat by not allowing retractions when only 12 hours remain in an auction, even if the item is not bid up to the appropriate selling amount before time runs out.

- **Online escrow fraud:** The seller puts a high-ticket item up for sale online at a very reasonable price. To protect the buyer (they say), the buyer "must" use a particular online escrow service. After the dupe — guess who — makes the purchase, the seller sends the buyer a link to the "preferred" (fake) online escrow service. The buyer sends the money, the seller keeps the money and disappears, and the buyer never gets the goods. Touch-and-go escrow services are a growing problem; a scammer can set up a bogus "escrow" Web site in a couple of hours and make the whole thing look legit.

- **Money-wire fraud:** Buyers should avoid transacting business with a seller who requires them to wire money via Western Union or other sources. The seller can pick up the money anywhere and disappear, leaving buyers with no further way to find the seller.

Communicating to Combat Fraud

If you're doing your job as a seller, you should be checking out the competition — for example, by shopping on eBay to see how the competition "does it." Looking at the scene from a buyer's point of view, you can see all kinds of shenanigans that go on at the eBay site.

When an item arrives "not as described," the first feeling that crops up when you know you've been ripped off — right after outrage — is embarrassment. *(Ack! How could I have been so stupid?)* Feeling foolish often triggers an urge to cover up the blunder — just what an unscrupulous seller is counting on. So head 'em off at the outset: If you see a possible violation shaping up before a buyer gets sucked in, you do have a few places to turn to. You *can* stop fraud before it occurs.

Reporting questionable items on eBay

Suppose you see an item that perks up your scam-radar — say, an auction that has lots of bids but all the bidders have no or little feedback. Or you see your bids instantly raised by another bidder, check that bidder's history, and find out whether that person does the same thing in other auctions *but never wins*.

The first thing you must do is report the item in question to eBay. The sooner you report it, the better. If the eBay security folks don't receive notice till a few minutes before the listing is over, they may not be able to protect an eBay member caught in a scam.

1. If the issue is with a particular item, click the *Report This Item* link at the bottom of the item page.

You come to the Listing Violations reporting page, as in Figure 32-1.

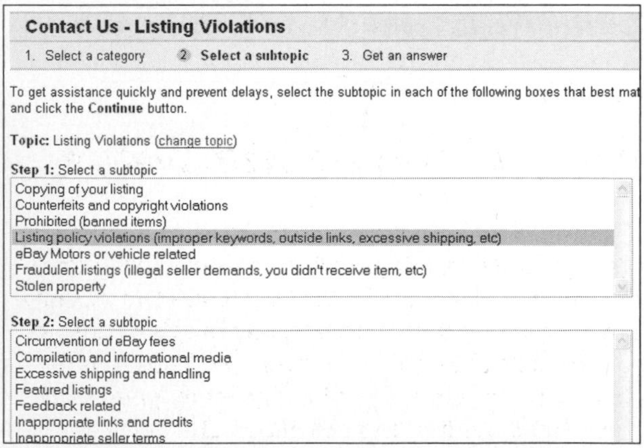

• **Figure 32-1: The Listing Violations reporting form.**

2. Begin at the top of the form and select the appropriate choices in each box to complete the form.

When you make a choice in the top box, a corresponding group of responses appears in the second box, and then the third — all based on your choices.

3. Click Continue.

Another Contact Us page appears and offers you several clickable options to read more about eBay's policy on the violations.

4. Click the E-mail link to send your report to Customer Service.

5. On the resulting e-mail form, type the item number(s), the Seller's User ID, the User IDs of the suspected shill accounts, and a description of your concerns.

By default, you do not receive a copy of the e-mail report. If you want a copy, click the check mark in the appropriate box.

6. Click the Send E-mail button to file your report.

In addition to a copy of your e-mail report, you receive another e-mail with a confirmation that eBay will look into the issue, as in Figure 32-2.

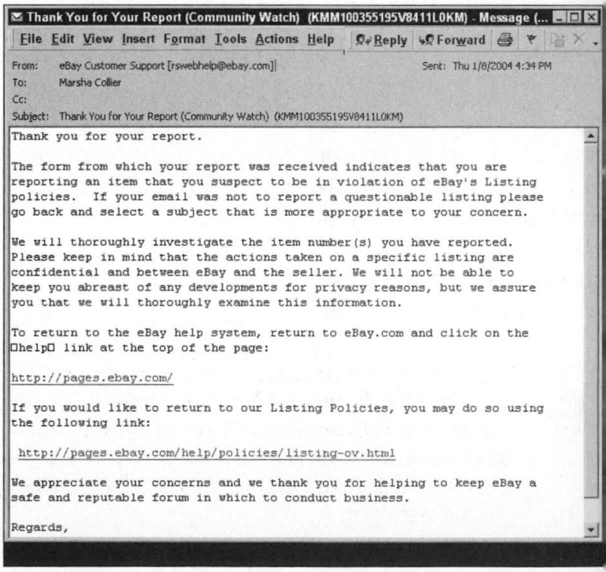

• **Figure 32-2: eBay Reporting Confirmation e-mail.**

If the issue is not tied directly to a listing (such as a problem with spam), you can go directly to the eBay Security Center, shown in Figure 32-3. You can get there by clicking the link that appears at the bottom of all eBay pages or by going to

        pages.ebay.com/securitycenter

In the Security Center, you can find out about the current eBay rules (and any changes), and you get access to a Contact Us link on the lower-left side of the page.

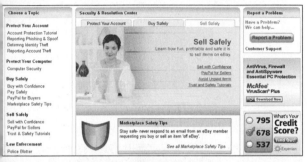

• **Figure 32-3: The eBay Security Center.**

After you file your report and receive your confirmation, don't feel disheartened if eBay doesn't contact you with an update on the investigation. As the confirmation e-mail states, privacy reasons prevent eBay from updating you. The only way you can be sure that the bad-deed-doer was stopped is to revisit the auction in a few hours.

 If you revisit the problem item you reported and the eBay listing police haven't ended the listing, it doesn't mean the investigation is over. As with most crime dramas, eBay has to build a case before going full-force after a suspected fraudster.

Staying available for buyer contact

To be on the up-and-up while transacting business on eBay (and to keep others honest, too), make sure that you

✔ **Have your current phone number on file:** If a buyer can't reach you, you're in violation of the eBay regs and you *can* be disciplined.

✔ **Have your current e-mail address on file:** If your buyer continually gets e-mail bounced back from your e-mail address, you could get in big trouble.

✔ **Report all underage buyers:** If you suspect that a buyer in one of your transactions is underage (eBay requires that all users be over 18), eBay may close the account. Underage buyers may be using their parents' credit card without permission, or perhaps even a stolen card, for registration.

✔ **Verify e-mail purportedly coming from an eBay employee:** If someone e-mails you claiming to work for eBay, be sure to check it out before replying. When eBay employees conduct personal business on the site, company policy requires that they use a personal, non-company e-mail address for user registration. If you suspect someone is impersonating an eBay employee for harmful purposes, contact the Security Center.

Filing an Unpaid Item Notice

If there's one thing that just isn't tolerated on eBay, it's *unpaid items*. eBay reminds all potential buyers, before they place a bid, that "If you are the winning buyer, you will enter into a legally binding contract to purchase the item from the seller." You'd think that was clear enough, but sadly, many people out there think bidding and buying on eBay is just a game. If you see a high bidder on your auction who has very low (or even negative) feedback rating, dropping a line reiterating eBay policy never hurts.

How you, as a seller, communicate with the high bidder is also important. Many times a well-written, congenial, businesslike e-mail can cajole the basically good person into sending payment.

I've been selling and buying on eBay for more than 11 years. During that time, out of about 7,000 transactions, I've had to file only about 20 Unpaid Item alerts (see the steps a bit later in this section). I think that nonpaying buyers tend to bid on certain types of items. After you've seen some unpaid items, you'll get an idea of which items to stay away from. My items? A gas-powered scooter, DVDs, a video game, and some Beanie Babies. Serious collector or business items have never been an issue.

 To reduce the number of nonpaying buyers, eBay has established that all eBay users are indefinitely suspended if they have too many nonpaying buyer disputes filed against them. An *indefinite suspension* is a suspension of members' privileges to use the eBay site for more than 60 days, with no definite reinstatement date. If users attempt to re-register at eBay and use the system under new IDs, they risk being referred to the United States Attorney's Office for the Northern District of California for criminal prosecution.

Before filing an Unpaid Item dispute, give the winner a second chance to send payment. If you still don't receive payment, follow these steps to recoup your Final Value fees and be eligible for the nonpaying-buyer relist credit:

1. **As soon as you have a winner, contact him or her.**

2. **If you don't hear from the winner within seven days of the auction's end time, file an Unpaid Item report:**

   a. Go to the My eBay Views area on the My eBay page. Under Selling, click the Item's I've Sold link.

   b. Click the Report an Unpaid Item link next in the drop-down menu to the listing in question.

   You'll see a form similar to the one in Figure 32-4.

   c. Click Continue to file the dispute.

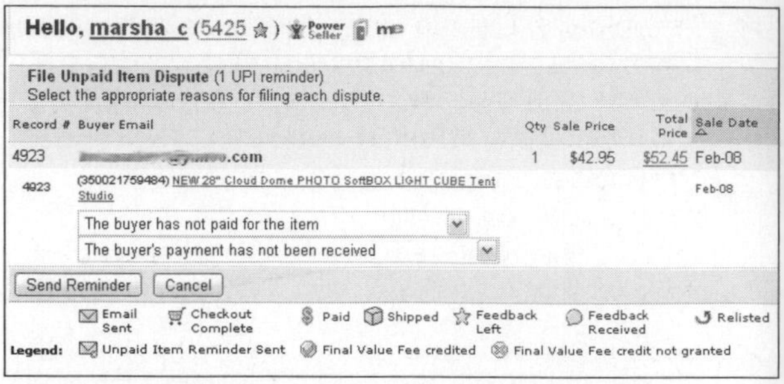

• **Figure 32-4: Starting an Unpaid Item dispute.**

If you still don't hear from or receive money from your high bidder, it's time to swing into action by filing an alert.

You must file the alert no earlier than 7 days and no later than 45 days after the auction has ended.

Follow these steps to file an Unpaid Item report:

1. **In the My eBay Views area of the My eBay page, click the Dispute Console link.**

   Alternatively, go to the following address:

   `http://rebulk.ebay.com/ws/`
   `   eBayISAPI.dll?CreateDispute`

2. **Check the Dispute Console to select the transaction that is eligible for filing.**

   eBay sends the buyer an e-mail, and the buyer has the right to respond in the dispute-management process.

Eight days after filing an Unpaid Item report, you may close the dispute and apply for a final-value-fee credit in the Dispute Console. At this point, eBay offers several options. To close the dispute, you must select one of the below:

✔ **We've completed the transaction and we're both satisfied**. You received your payment and you're ready to ship! The buyer will not receive an undeserved Unpaid Item strike.

✔ **We've agreed not to complete the transaction.** If you feel sorry for the buyer or believe their tale of woe as to how they cannot possibly buy your item, you can select this option. The buyer won't get a strike on his or her permanent record, and you will receive a final-value-fee credit. (The item is eligible for the standard relist credit.)

✔ **I no longer wish to communicate with or wait for the buyer.** You've had it — either no response or no payment. The buyer receives their well-deserved Unpaid Item strike and you get your final-value-fee credit. (This item is eligible for a relist credit.)

You must file for your final-value-fee credit within 60 days of the transaction's close.

Don't forget! When you file for your final-value-fee credit, you also have the option of blocking that buyer from participating in your future sales.

If you work things out with the winner, you may remove the Unpaid Item strike within 90 days of the close of the listing. eBay sends an e-mail to notify the winner that the strike has been removed at your request. You'll find the link to remove the warning at your Dispute Console:

1. Go to the My eBay page. Scroll down the My eBay Views to the Dispute Console link and click it.

2. On the Dispute Console page, next to the dispute in question, select Cancel the Unpaid Item Strike for This Dispute from the drop-down menu.

3. Click Confirm to remove the Unpaid Item strike.

An e-mail is sent to the buyer, letting the buyer know that the strike has been removed and his or her reputation is clear.

In the case of Multiple Item listings or eBay Store items, you may file an Unpaid Item report only *once* per listing. You may file against as many buyers as necessary in that one alert, but you can't go back and file more strikes later. You may remove an Unpaid Item strike at any time. (Now, there's a really good reason *not* to use the Good-Till-Cancelled option automatically for Store listings.)

If an Unpaid Item buyer leaves you a negative feedback, and you've filed the report, the negative feedback will be removed. The comment will remain in your records, but you can easily respond to the feedback so future buyers will be aware of the transgression.

SquareTrade to the Rescue

Threats of suing each other, filing fraud charges, and screaming back and forth don't really accomplish anything when you're in the middle of a dispute at eBay. Back in the olden days of eBay, when you weren't able to respond to feedback, users threw negative feedback back and forth willy-nilly, which resulted in some vile flame wars.

You can handle such a contretemps in eBay's Dispute Console, or you can take it off eBay and go to SquareTrade. When you're selling regularly at eBay, you will undoubtedly run into a disgruntled buyer or two. SquareTrade, a Web-based dispute-resolution company, waits in the wings to pull you out of the most difficult situations. SquareTrade pioneered large-scale online dispute resolution — and has helped consumers and merchants mediate resolutions to more than 2 million e-commerce disputes across 120 countries in 5 languages.

Should you find yourself in an inexorably difficult situation with one of your buyers, and you'd like to take the quest for resolution up a notch, go to the following page, shown in Figure 32-5:

```
http://www.squaretrade.com/cnt/jsp/
    odr/overview_odr.jsp?marketplace_
    name=ebay
```

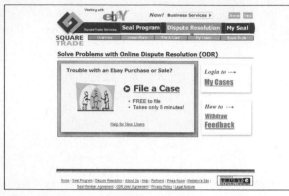

• **Figure 32-5: Let SquareTrade handle your dispute.**

Online dispute resolution

Online dispute resolution (ODR) is a fast, private, and convenient way to resolve your auction disputes — and it's *free*. Both you and the buyer work together through the SquareTrade Web-based system. ODR works whether your transaction is in the United States or another country.

The SquareTrade Web-based negotiation tool is automated, and you and the other party get to communicate on neutral ground. When (and if) the buyer responds, the two of you can work out the situation online and without human interaction. If you're unable to reach a solution, then it's time to move on to professional mediation (see the following section).

SquareTrade states that problems are usually solved in 10 to 14 days and 85 percent of all their cases are resolved without going to mediation. The process will run a quicker course if both people in the transaction are at their computers and answer e-mail during the day.

Participation in ODR is voluntary. If a buyer is set on defrauding you, he or she probably isn't going to engage in a resolution process. If you get no response to your ODR, report your situation to the Security Center.

Professional mediation

If push comes to shove — and in auction disputes it certainly may — you might have to resort to professional mediation. A *mediator,* who is neither a lawyer nor a judge but an impartial professional, works with both parties to bring the situation to a convivial (or at least workable) conclusion. This service is available for a reasonable fee of $29.95 per issue.

If both parties participating in dispute resolution agree to mediation, each party communicates only with the assigned mediator, who communicates with both parties through the same *case page*. Your case page shows only your communications with the mediator; the other party sees only his or hers. The mediator reviews both sides of the story to find a mutually acceptable solution to the problem — trying to understand the interests, perspectives, and preferred solutions of both parties, and to help both parties understand each other's positions.

The mediator is there to disperse the highly charged emotions commonly associated with disputes, and recommends a resolution only if both parties agree to have the mediator do so. By using the mediation service, you do not lose your right to go to court if things aren't worked out.

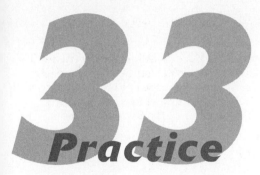

Keep Your E-Mailbox Free of Scams and Junk

E-mail spam is no longer merely an annoyance. In the past, the biggest thing we worried about was having our computers contract a virus or a Trojan horse from opening an infected e-mail. We still have that to worry about, but now, certain nasty e-mail scams actually pose a danger to our personal financial well-being. Identity fraud is the fastest-growing white-collar crime — and spam is one of its most common tools.

To put even more of the fear into you, here is a scary statistic: Identity-theft complaints to the Federal Trade Commission (FTC) made up a whopping 32 percent of the total number of complaints the agency received in 2007. The FTC reports that 27.3 million Americans have been victims of identity theft from 2001 through 2006, including 9.9 million people in 2006 alone. According to the FTC, identity-theft losses to businesses and financial institutions in 2006 totaled nearly $48 billion — and consumer victims reported $5 billion in out-of-pocket expenses. How do these identity theft crimes break down?

- Credit-card fraud: 23 percent
- Utilities/phone fraud: 18 percent
- Employment fraud: 14 percent
- Bank fraud: 13 percent

The risk doesn't end with this list. At one time, a massive hue and cry arose over how shopping on the Internet (especially eBay) was the source of the most fraud in the United States. In 2007, online shopping slipped down the list considerably. Take a look at Table 33-1 to see a ranking of consumer complaints to the FTC.

TABLE 33-1: FEDERAL TRADE COMMISSION TOP CONSUMER COMPLAINTS IN 2007

Rank	Category	Number of Complaints	Percent
1	Identity Theft	258,427	32%
2	Shop-at-Home/Catalog Sales	62,811	8%
3	Internet Services	42,266	5%
4	Foreign Money Offers	32,868	4%
5	Prizes/Sweepstakes and Lotteries	32,162	4%
6	Computer Equipment and Software	27,036	3%
7	Internet Auctions	24,376	3%
8	Health Care	16,097	2%
9	Travel, Vacations, and Timeshare	14,903	2%
10	Advance-Fee Loans and Credit Protection/Repair	14,342	2%
11	Investments	13,705	2%
12	Magazines and Buyers Clubs	12,970	2%
13	Business Opps and Work-at-Home Plans	11,362	1%
14	Real Estate (Not Timeshare)	9,475	1%
15	Office Supplies and Services	9,211	1%
16	Telephone Services	8,155	1%
17	Employ Agencies/Job Counsel/Overseas Work	5,932	1%
18	Debt Management/Credit Counseling	3,442	<1%
19	Multi-Level Mktg/ Pyramids/Chain Letters	3,092	<1%
20	Charitable Solicitations	1,843	<1%

Those are some scary figures. Falling victim to identity theft can start with something as simple as clicking a link in an e-mail that *supposedly* came from your bank. Check out Figure 33-1 for an example of an e-mail that contains a false message urging you to click the link and offer up personal information.

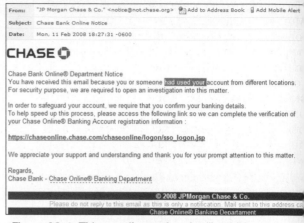

• **Figure 33-1: This e-mail says that the "bank" is investigating and needs my help.**

Dealing with Spam

Spam started out as an annoyance, but these days it's downright sinister. Each day I have to allow about five minutes clearing the spam out of my e-mail inbox. It used to take up to a half hour, considering that I flip on my computer and am greeted by close to 200 e-mails every day. It used to be a terrifying time when I clicked my Send/Receive button in Outlook. I never knew what would be coming down the pike, or wires. Check out the section "Finding spam before it finds you" later in this practice to see how I've cut my spam-scanning time!

Spam is insidious. Hopefully, we all have the latest in antispam software, but I've found that antispam software often causes me to lose e-mail that I need (because it seems that the word "eBay" is a favorite among spammers). These programs, because of my liberal use of the word *eBay*, often bounce the newsletter I send out to my readers from my Web site. Sometimes I do a spot-check with occasional readers, and they say they want the newsletter — the problem is that their spam protection refuses it. There's not much I can do!

I want *news* on eBay — but I don't want to get those make-a-fortune-on-eBay e-mails. Nor do I want to help out those pretending to speak for dear Mrs.

Harriet Mutambara, the wife of late Dr. (chief) Daniel Mutambara, who was murdered last year in June by forces loyal to President Robert Mugabe. It seems her family lost millions in Zimbabwe to a scammer in the government, and the late Dr. M. wanted me (of course — who else?) to help him get his secret stash of "Eleven million, five hundred thousand united state Dollars." She was going to give me 20 percent just for helping her — how thoughtful! Uh-huh. (In case you didn't know, this e-mail is part of what the FBI calls the *Nigerian e-mail scam* — also called the *419 scam* — named after the specific part of the African Penal Code that this crime violates.)

For the record, I'm also very comfortable with my investments; the size of my body parts; where I purchase my prescriptions (I don't want to buy drugs from some stranger over the Internet); and I don't need another mortgage.

Some scams aren't so amusing. They're the ones who pretend to be from eBay, PayPal, Citibank, and others, and try to bilk you out of your personal information. I show you a foolproof way to recognize them as well.

It's Phishing with a P

Phishing, pronounced just like "fishing" with an *F,* is growing in popularity as a scamming technique. Unscrupulous individuals try to take advantage of innocent folks like you and me by posing as legitimate financial entities to get personal, financial, and other security information from you. Their goal is to steal you blind (until they get caught — which they hope they won't because they figure you don't go over your bills all the time — you just pay them).

PayPal (which we all use) is one of the largest online financial institutions. Almost anyone who's purchased online (or who will purchase online at some point) will more than likely establish and use a PayPal account.

Popular PayPal e-mail scams seem to grow almost daily — and many involve *spoofing* (making a fake message or Web site look the part by adding fake

logos). Beware of these — and others — that arrive in your inbox asking you to click a link and log in for any number of "reasons." The folks at the real PayPal won't ask you to send personal information via e-mail; they know it's not a secure medium — and so should you.

 When you receive any e-mail that claims to be from PayPal (or from eBay, for that matter), *do not click any link in the e-mail*. Go directly to the Web site in your browser and log in by typing the URL. You then will have a secure connection starting with *https* instead of the regular *http*. When you get one of these e-mails, help out PayPal security by forwarding it to `spoof@paypal.com`. With your next keystroke, delete the e-mail.

 When you forward a spam or phishing e-mail for inspection, don't click that *Forward* button. If you do that, you lose all the header information that reveals exactly where the e-mail has been sent from. Instead, send the e-mail as an attachment, so all the incriminating data will be intact — but be very careful not to click anything in the original message.

Keep in mind that PayPal — or any other financial institution — will *never* ask (in an e-mail) for you to produce the following:

- Driver's license numbers
- Banking account numbers
- Credit card numbers
- Social security numbers

Also, you'll *never* be asked to download "special" programs to solve the fake problem. Scammers often disguise a virus or Trojan Horse as a "helpful" program such as

- Something to "fix" your account
- Something that gives you access to new features

. . . or they promise to send you those goodies and then just make off with your personal information.

In this practice, I show you how spammers get your e-mail address. Even if you never give it out, they have ways of getting it from you. So I hope to sharpen up your savvy about which e-mails you open, which ones you don't touch — and how to fight back.

Keeping Your E-Mail Address Quiet

Have you ever signed up for anything on the Internet? Before you signed up, did you check to see whether the site had a posted Privacy Policy page? If you're like a lot of us, you probably didn't. When you type your name in a box on an Internet site that has no spam or privacy policy, you're basically giving your privacy away, because you're considered an "opt in" customer. *Opt in* means you asked to be on a list, and the site that now has your e-mail address can sell it to spammers.

Take a look at Figure 33-2. It's a portion of an ad that should really scare you. It's an eBay auction for a CD containing 140,000,000 opt-in e-mail addresses. Yes, and you can buy all 14-million potential suckers for only $5.

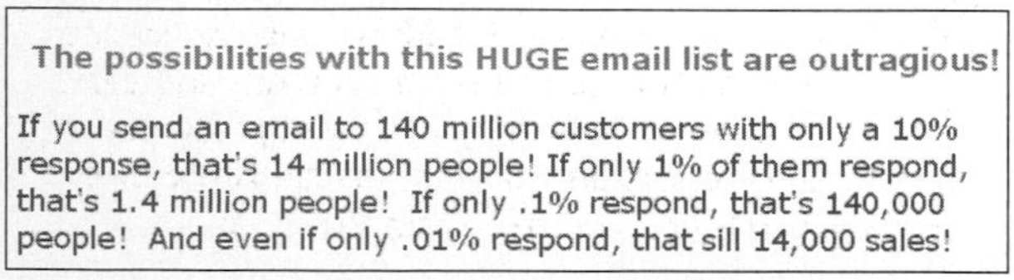

> **The possibilities with this HUGE email list are outragious!**
>
> If you send an email to 140 million customers with only a 10% response, that's 14 million people! If only 1% of them respond, that's 1.4 million people! If only .1% respond, that's 140,000 people! And even if only .01% respond, that sill 14,000 sales!

• **Figure 33-2:** A tempting offer to violate people's privacy.

Just opening your e-mail can give you away as well. Spammers will often (as you can tell by some of the To addresses) make up return e-mail addresses to mask their true location. If you open and view their e-mail, the e-mail sends a notice to the spammer's server and then they know that your e-mail address is valid. This can be masked in the HTML to occur when the e-mail consists of merely a picture — when it goes back to grab the picture for your e-mail, it reports your e-mail address is good.

How easy is it to forge the sender in an e-mail?

I used to think that you had to be some weird kind of computer geek or programmer (sorry, Patti) to be able to fake the return address on an e-mail. It's as easy as opening up the Tools tab on your Microsoft Outlook program. Click Tools and then click E-mail Accounts. You'll come to a page where you can view or change existing e-mail accounts. On the next page, just select the account you want to forge — and voila! You can change the sender and return e-mail address for the next outgoing e-mails. Sad, eh?

Recognizing Spam

I guess this isn't rocket science. Much of the spam and phishing e-mails you get can be recognized by the subject line. I used to check my e-mail once I downloaded it to my computer. That's a pretty dangerous procedure, though, considering that some e-mails do their job without your even having to respond.

Some dead giveaways are subject lines like:

"Verify your account."

"If you don't respond within 48 hours, your account will be closed."

"Click the link below to gain access to your account."

HTML-formatted messages often have links or forms that are hidden by a graphic, such as a picture. The links that you are urged to click may contain all or part of a real company's name and are usually "masked," meaning that the link takes you to an address different from where you expect to be going, usually a fraudulent Web site.

Finding spam before it finds you

Now I'm using a program called MailWasher Pro. When I flip on my computer in the morning, I open MailWasher and see the giant barrage of trash in my mailbox, as in Figure 33-3.

Delete	Bounce	Blackli	Status	Size	From	Subject	Sen	To	Attac
✔	✔	✔	Possible	2.7KB	dale halverson (astyllan@mail.bulgaria.com)	Cgllesiotv Re: Your H_y_d_r_0_c_0_d_0_	15 Mar	hans da	none
			Normal	4.3KB	Gordon Boucher (yipe23@tourspain.es)	Fw: Fw: Upt0 50% off on Prescr1pt1on DF	15 Mar	marshac	none
			Normal	3.0KB	Raphael Swanson (vgplqvj44@wanadoo.fr)	Re:crewel INdian generic Citratemorgen	15 Mar	marshac	none
			Normal	3.2KB	tiana peele (peele8384@proxad.net)	Fwd: Full Meds Here. Fwd: Xanlalx ~ Vali	15 Mar	marshac	yes
			Normal	3.6KB	pqplykgvntzh@mail2rusty.com	Start saving now	15 Mar	marshac	none
			Normal	3.2KB	alysha rosenberg (jp.rosenberg@interbusiness	Fwd: Have Pills x/ana/x < Valiu/m/ % vl6	14 Mar	dummier	yes
			Normal	2.2KB	Trina Garrison (umedriband@velnet.co.uk)	The NEW ISSUE STOCK I was telling yo	14 Mar	marshac	none
			Normal	3.9KB	apjfbpb@attglobal.net	Re: ti Over Due wj Account	14 Mar	marshac	none
			Normal	3.3KB	Jeffery Haskins (jefferyhaskinsh@translate.ru	Spring time!	14 Mar	marshac	none
			Normal	8.0KB	velma_ewing@yahoo.com	You Will Enjoy This	14 Mar	breeders	yes
			Normal	2.2KB	Lavonne N. Bingham (lbinghamcw@tvh.be)	06-Refinance as low as 2.90%	14 Mar	dummier	none
			Normal	2.9KB	roniemvalofbo@baguda.com	dummies Boost Your Cable Modem Speec	14 Mar	Yvette D	none
			Normal	5.8KB	Viola Cantu (jsavcxy@yahoo.com)		14 Mar	marshac	none
			Normal	5.7KB	chun-she (came@t-online.de)	Íñåoéòå ñåéåá			
			Normal	4.4KB	reports-headers (reports-response@habeas.c	[habeas.com #240754] AutoReply: Spam	14 Mar	marshac	none
			Normal	7.6KB	apxbdnfp@germany.net	Be All You Can Be.d k o	14 Mar	dummier	none
			Normal	4.3KB	Leigh Callahan (jvl505bl@150mail.com)	Re: Get it in the convenience of your hom	14 Mar	marshac	none
✔	✔	✔	Possible	4.2KB	Jarvis Sykes (sbyi9cz@aloha.net)	unhappy about the size of your love tool.	14 Mar	marshac	yes
			Normal	2.7KB	rudy cato (gc7347@telesp.net.br)	Many On Stocks. Fwd: Vcod1n > X/A/N/	14 Mar	marshac	yes
			Normal	2.5KB	houston.christian@yahoo.com	With this simple patch I became bigger an	10 Mar	marshac	none

• **Figure 33-3: MailWasher (the Free version).**

MailWasher lists your e-mail directly from your ISP's server. It does NOT download the e-mail to your computer. By using MailWasher, you can delete the offending e-mails from your mailbox, and then bring only the ones you want into your e-mail program.

As you can see from the figure, I can find out all the following:

- ✔ **Who sent the e-mail:** I'm not really acquainted with Lavonne N. Bingham (note that her e-mail address ends in .be — that's Belgium). I'm also not familiar with Viola Cantu, who strangely has *jsavcxy* as her e-mail ID at Yahoo!. Not to mention my buddy, Chun-she (otherwise known as carrie@t-online.de). Hmmm, Germany? Nope. Don't know anyone there either.

- ✔ **E-mail subject:** Just in case Chun-she really does know me, she should also know that I don't read Cyrillic — and, as the subject line looks like *Ilocemume cemuhap,* I'm pretty sure I can delete that one. And although Velma sent me an e-mail letting me know how much I'd enjoy something, I'm really too busy to enjoy anything offered by a total stranger just now, so I guess I'll delete that e-mail, too.

- ✔ **To:** Notice that the To line can be a definite tip-off. If someone has e-mailed to a name other than my own or to an e-mail box at my Web site (with news about mortgages), I can fairly assume that the e-mail wasn't sent by someone I know. For example, one e-mail was sent to Yvette. I have no Yvette at this e-mail address! There are no dummies here either.

- ✔ **Attachments:** Yes or none. If there's an attachment from someone I don't know, I delete the entire e-mail. As a matter of fact, I delete most e-mails with attachments. If friends want to send me something, they can always resend if I delete it accidentally (or on purpose).

MailWasher allows you to put check marks next to suspect e-mails. You can merely delete them, or you can bounce them back to whence they came (note my caveat in the "Fighting Back!" section later in the practice) and blacklist them (so they'll always be marked for deletion if they e-mail you again).

My e-mail program is set to get e-mail from the server only when I ask it to — so after I delete all the spam, I can click Send/Receive and feel considerably safer.

 Also, I use the MailWasher Pro version, which can scan more than one e-mail account. If you have just one e-mail address, you can try the free version for one e-mail account and see whether you like it before paying $29.95 for the Pro version. You can download the free version at www.mailwasher.net.

Checking out nefarious e-mail

What's this? It seems I've gotten an e-mail from PayPal. They say my account needs to be renewed. Oh my! I certainly don't want to lose my PayPal account, so I'd better click the link and give them the information they need. (They wish. Fakers.)

Or how about an e-mail "from PayPal" that says:

> We recently reviewed your account and suspect that your PayPal account may have been accessed by an unauthorized third party. Protecting the security of your account and of the PayPal network is our primary concern. Therefore, as a preventative measure, we have temporarily limited access to sensitive PayPal account features.

> Click below in order to regain access to your account:

STOP RIGHT THERE!

Responding to such e-mails is tantamount to giving away your information to a stranger. Let me give you a set of steps for double-checking these e-mails instead:

1. **Open the e-mail, as I have in Figure 33-4.**

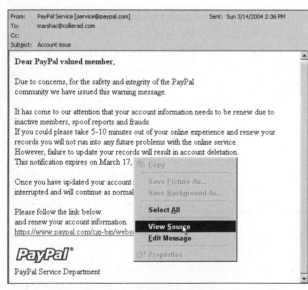

• **Figure 33-4: Checking to View Source on an e-mail.**

2. **Right-click and choose the option to View Source from the pop-up menu.**

The Notepad program opens on your computer, and you see the e-mail message as HTML text.

3. **Scroll to the bottom of the Notepad window.**

In this example, I go to the line that says `Please follow the link below...` followed by a URL, as shown in Figure 33-5.

```
<br>Please follow the link below <br>
<i></i> and
renew your account information.
<br><a
href="http://66.223.44.203/cgi/index.htm"onMouseOver="status
='https://www.paypal.com/cgi-bin/webscr?cmd=login-run';
return true"
onMouseOut="status='';return
true">https://www.paypal.com/cgi-bin/webscr?cmd=login-run</a
>
```

• **Figure 33-5: The HTML coding for the link URL address.**

Take a good, long look at the figure. You'll see the link to the URL in the e-mail.

4. **When you find the URL in the message, look just before it in the source code to see where the link is being redirected.**

Figure 33-5 shows that the link in my message redirects to `http://66.223.44.203/cgi/index.htm` — not to the PayPal secure URL!

When I click the link, I come to an *exact duplicate* of the PayPal Log In page — or is it? A quick glance at the Address bar of my browser confirms I've been misdirected, as shown in Figure 33-6. If I were at PayPal, the URL address would read

```
https://www.paypal.com/cgi-bin/
webscr?cmd=_login-run
```

(Note that the real PayPal URL begins with `https`, not an `http` URL; the `s` in `https` stands for *secure*.)

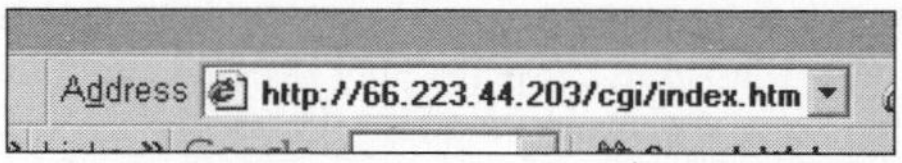

Address ⊜ http://66.223.44.203/cgi/index.htm ▾

• **Figure 33-6: My address bar with the misdirected URL.**

You can use the right-click and View Source trick on any HTML e-mail, and HTML e-mail is what fraudsters use to hide the misdirected address.

If you still question whether your PayPal or eBay account has a problem, close the e-mail and go directly to the site and log in at the real URL. If there is a problem with your account, believe me, they'll let you know after you properly log in.

Preventing Identity Theft with LifeLock

Since we've already established that identity theft is the fastest growing white-collar crime in America, we need to find a way to combat it. I signed up with a company called LifeLock. Unlike other services, LifeLock specializes in the *prevention* of identity theft (rather than the reporting of it after the damage is done). With LifeLock, a member has the assurance that the service is protecting personal and/or business information. In addition, LifeLock is the industry's only identity theft solution that is willing to protect its customers' identity with a $1 million service guarantee.

How does it work? Among other things, LifeLock contacts credit bureaus on your behalf to set up — and automatically renew — fraud alerts with the major credit bureaus on a regular basis. If anyone tries to access your account or establish new credit under your name, vendors are automatically alerted and the request is thoroughly researched before any such access is granted. LifeLock maintains these fraud alerts as long as you are a customer. Another aspect of the service removes members' names from pre-approved credit card offers and junk-mail lists. (My letter carrier is very happy about this — my daily paper mail was cut by two-thirds!)

The fraud alert prevents anyone from getting credit using your personal information. If a credit request is made, you are personally contacted before the credit is granted. If they can't contact you, then the credit is denied (and something really bad happens to the person impersonating you). Find out more information on this service that's become an important, permanent part of my standard business expenses by going to www.lifelock.com.

Fighting Back!

You can do quite a bit to help stop the flood of unwanted messages. Spam and fraud come in many forms and eventually, if things keep going the way they do, cleaning spam might become a full-time proposition.

Follow these general rules to deal with and minimize the spam you receive:

- **Don't validate your e-mail address for spammers.** Have you ever clicked the link at the bottom of some spam you've received to have your name "removed" from their list? I have — at least I used to — until I found out that's the gold standard for spammers to collect valid e-mail addresses! If you respond to the spam in any way, shape, or form, they know they have found a valid address — and watch the spam to your mailbox increase!

  Never, I repeat, *never* click one of those links again.

  When signing up for some sort of newsletter with an organization you're new to or unsure of, be sure to use an anonymous Yahoo! or Hotmail address. It's easy enough to sign up for one, and if spammers get hold of that address, they will not be privy to your private address.

- **Don't even open obvious spam.** No matter how curious you are about enlarging certain parts of your anatomy, don't even open the e-mails — some viruses get launched that way. But in any case, don't respond. You're only encouraging the vicious cycle.

- **Do report spammers.** Several legitimate Web sites take spam reports and forward them to the appropriate authorities. Don't bother trying to forward the spam to the sender's ISP. These days they're mostly forged with aliases, and all you'll do is succeed in clogging up the e-mail system. You can report spammers at the following sites:

▶ **Federal Trade Commission:** Yes, your tax dollars are at work. You can forward spam to uce@ftc.gov, where it will become available for law enforcement (especially in the case of e-mail trying to get your personal information).

▶ **The Anti-Phishing Working Group.** This volunteer organization is building a repository of phishing-scam e-mails and Web sites to help people identify them — and avoid being scammed in the future. Send your suspicious e-mail as an attachment to report phishing@antiphishing.org.

Practice 34

Securing Your Accounts

How safe do you feel with all your online accounts? I know when I really think about all the financial data I have on the Web — technically accessible to anyone — I get a little queasy. In the preceding practice, I discuss spam, including the most dangerous of all spam — the *phishing* e-mail. It's a kind of e-mail that tries to get you to reveal your passwords and important data about your accounts. I get these e-mails regularly and try to never click the links in e-mails that say they lead to "secure" sites. But just when I think I'm careful (and lulled into complacency), an e-mail comes along containing a link that I click. When I soon realize that I've almost logged on to a fake financial site, the panic sets in.

Yep, I've done it — been caught by a phishing e-mail, that is. Should this same thing happen to you, the best course of action is to immediately log out and close your browser window. As fast as you can, open a new window, type in the legitimate Web site URL — whether it be PayPal, your bank or your investment advisor — and log in again. Change your password and your heart will stop feeling like it's about to jump out of your chest.

You've seen the commercials on TV poking fun at the very real problem of identity theft. If you ask around your circle of friends, no doubt you'll find someone who knows someone who's been in this pickle. It can take years to undo the damage caused by identity theft, so a better plan is to stay vigilant and protect yourself from becoming a victim. In addition to recognizing and thwarting phishing e-mails (see Practice 33 for the full story), you can institute some other easy practices for helping protect yourself against identity theft. Perhaps most importantly, you have to set clever passwords to secure your accounts.

In this practice, I give you tips for selecting good passwords and safeguarding other personal security information. I also show you the sort of passwords to stay away from and what to do if (heaven forbid!) your personal information is compromised.

Always make sure your wireless network is as secure as possible. I recommend using WPA rather than WEP, since WEP can be hacked by a junior high school student. Someone can pull up to the curb in front of your house, pick up your signal, log your keystrokes, get your passwords, and drive away before you know it. When was the last time you changed your passwords? I mean the whole enchilada: eBay, PayPal, your online bank account?

Changing Passwords Religiously

Hey, I'm not the keeper of the shoulds, but you *should* change your critical passwords every 60 days — rain or shine. It's not just me saying that. It's all the security experts who know this kind of stuff.

For example, if you suspect something has gone awry with your e-mail (say, you're getting a lot of bounced e-mails that you never sent), you may just be a victim of someone spoofing your e-mail address as a spam return address. This happens a lot. As a matter of fact, it seems someone is posing as me roughly once a month. These people don't actually have your e-mail passwords (they perform this trickery through software), but changing your main password is always a good idea.

 The world is full of bad-deed-doers just waiting to get their hands on your precious personal information. Password theft can lead to your bank account being emptied, your credit cards being pushed to the max, and worst of all, someone out there posing as you . . . who *isn't* you (and in the worst ways).

Here's what to do:

✔ **Change your personal e-mail account password with your ISP:** Go to your ISP's home page (for example www.earthlink.net) and look for an area called Member Center or something similar. In the Member Center, access your personal account information — probably through a link

called something like My Account. You should be able to change your password there.

✔ **Change the e-mail account password on your home computer:** Don't forget to change the password on your computer's e-mail software as well (Outlook, Eudora, and the like) so you can continue to download your e-mail from the server.

Reporting and Fixing Possibly Hijacked Accounts

If someone gets hold of your personal information, the most important thing to do is report it immediately. On eBay, if you see any items that aren't yours on the Items I'm Bidding On or the Items I'm Selling areas of your My eBay page, it's time to make a report — and *fast!*

Maybe you suspect that something hinky is going on with your eBay account because *you* never placed a bid on the Britney Spears parenting guidebook (did you?). And you can't imagine that your spouse did either (but double-check just to be sure). It may even be that you discover your private information has been compromised when you suddenly can't log in to your eBay or PayPal account. If this happens on eBay, follow these steps to request a new password:

1. **Go to the eBay Sign In page.**

Don't type your password. You just tried that and it didn't work.

2. **Click the Forgot Your Password link, as shown in Figure 34-1.**

Doing this takes you to the appropriate place:

```
http://cgi3.ebay.com/aw-cgi/
    eBayISAPI.dll?ForgotYourPassword
    Show
```

3. **On the next page type in your eBay User ID and click continue.**

Those silly security questions that you answered when you registered for eBay become very important now.

Already an eBay user?

eBay members, sign in to save time for bidding, selling, and other activities.

eBay User ID

marsha_c

Forgot your User ID?

Password

Forgot your password?

[Sign In Securely >]

☐ Keep me signed in on this computer for one day, unless I sign out.

💡 Account protection tips
   Be sure the Web site address you see above starts with https://signin.ebay.com/

• **Figure 34-1:** The Forgot My Password link on the Sign In page.

4. **Answer the security question you see on the page, type in your registered phone number and ZIP code, and click Continue.**

eBay produces a screen that resembles Figure 34-2, and then sends you an e-mail with instructions for resetting your password.

Forgot Your Password: Confirmation Step

You're almost done

An email has been sent to the email address you have on file in My eBay

To complete the process of changing your password:

1. Check your email account.
2. Click the link or button in the email.

• **Figure 34-2:** Confirmation that eBay will send an e-mail.

5. **When the e-mail arrives, follow the steps and change your password.**

If you *don't* get eBay's e-mail telling you how to change your password, that means some fraudster may have changed the contact information in your eBay account. See the sidebar "Stay calm, take action!" for instructions on what to do.

Take a look at Figure 34-3. At the bottom of the e-mail, it indicates which IP address requested

the change. This is a good indicator (I told you that you're tracked on the Internet) as to who made the request.

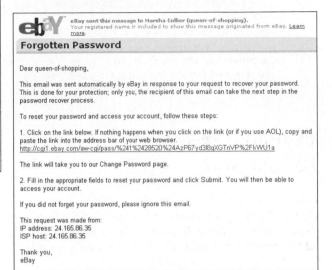

eBay sent this message to Marsha Collier (queen-of-shopping).
Your registered name is included to show this message originated from eBay. Learn more.

Forgotten Password

Dear queen-of-shopping,

This email was sent automatically by eBay in response to your request to recover your password. This is done for your protection; only you, the recipient of this email can take the next step in the password recover process.

To reset your password and access your account, follow these steps:

1. Click on the link below. If nothing happens when you click on the link (or if you use AOL), copy and paste the link into the address bar of your web browser.
http://cgi1.ebay.com/aw-cgi/pass/%241%2428520%24AzP67yd3l8gXGTnVP%2FkWU1a

The link will take you to our Change Password page.

2. Fill in the appropriate fields to reset your password and click Submit. You will then be able to access your account.

If you did not forget your password, please ignore this email.

This request was made from:
IP address: 24.165.86.35
ISP host: 24.165.86.35

Thank you,
eBay

• **Figure 34-3:** The e-mail sent from eBay.

6. **If all goes well and you can change your password, go to the link pictured in Figure 34-4 to change your secret question.**

When you get to the page, just click the Edit link next to your secret question and make the change.

Hello, queen-of-shopping (3)   Review It Now
                                          Read user reviews.

Personal Information

Account Information

Account type	Not Specified	Edit
User ID	queen-of-shopping	Edit
Password	********	Edit
Secret question	What is the name of your favorite restaurant?	Edit
About Me page	--	Edit

Email and Contact Information

Registered email address	r____a@aol.com	Edit
Registered name and address		Edit
	United States	
Mobile phone number for SMS alerts	None	Add
Instant Messenger IM alert provider	None	Add

• **Figure 34-4:** Your My eBay, My Account; Preferences; Personal Information page with all the security links.

Stay calm, take action!

If you can't seem to get a new password for your eBay account, and you're unsuccessful at finding a Live Help link (Hint: it usually resides on eBay's Home page in the upper-right corner), there's still hope. If you can't find the Live Help Link, remain calm, follow these steps, and take notes as you go:

1. **Go to any eBay page, scroll all the way to the bottom, and click the Security Center link shown in the following figure.**

   | About eBay | Announcements | Security Center | eBay Toolbar | Policies | Government Relations | Site Map | Help |

   Copyright © 1995-2008 eBay Inc. All Rights Reserved. Designated trademarks and brands are the property of their res Web site constitutes acceptance of the eBay User Agreement and Privacy Policy.

2. **On the left side of the resulting *Report a Problem* Page, you will see a bunch of links under the heading "Choose a Topic."**

   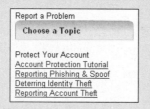

   Report a Problem
   Choose a Topic

   Protect Your Account
   Account Protection Tutorial
   Reporting Phishing & Spoof
   Deterring Identity Theft
   Reporting Account Theft

3. **Click the link that reads Reporting Account Theft.**

4. **Scroll to the bottom of the page, and you will find a handy, Live Help link.**

   Be sure to temporarily disable any pop-up blocker you may have.

   Contact Customer Support
   👁 Live help - Chat online with a Customer Support representative.

 If you have installed pop-up blockers on your computer, disable them before you access eBay's Live Help. Once your Live Help session is finished, re-enable the blocker to be sure your computer is protected from pop-ups, ads, and spyware.

Choosing a Good Secret Question

If you read the harrowing procedure in the "Stay calm, take action!" sidebar, you know that having someone sabotage your eBay account is something you never want to go through. But if your secret question is easy to figure out, a hacker can find it even easier to wreak havoc on your account.

 Your password is only as secure as the secret question, so *don't relate your password and secret question to each other in any way*. For example, do not make your secret question a clue to your password — and *especially* don't make your password answer the secret question. Better yet, think of your secret question as a completely separate, auxiliary security device for your account.

Figure 34-5 shows eBay's Change Secret Question and Answer page, which you can access from your My eBay Preferences; Personal Information page. It shows several suggested questions.

Home> My eBay> **Change Secret Question**
Change Secret Question

Select a new secret question, provide the answer. Then click the **Change Secret Question** button below. If you ever forget your password in the future, eBay will ask you about this information before allowing you to change your password.

Secret question   Secret answer
Pick a suggested question...
Pick a suggested question...
What street did you grow up on?
What is your mother's maiden name?
What is the name of your first school?
What is your pet's name?
What is your father's middle name?
What is your school's mascot?

• **Figure 34-5:** Change Secret Question page.

Here are some tips for setting a secure secret question:

✔ **Never use your mother's maiden name.** That is most likely the *secret* that your bank uses as your challenge question. (They usually ask when you open the account.) So that is definitely out — you don't want to give *anybody* that word.

✔ **Select a question and provide a creative answer.**

   ▶ **What is your pet's name?** Give an answer like Ralph the Rhino or Graak the Pterodactyl or something *creative*. Don't give your actual pet's name (or species). Anyone who knows you is likely to know your pet's name.

▶ **What street did you grow up on?** Name an unusual landmark from your hometown. Don't use a street name.

▶ **What is the name of your first school?** Make up a good one — perhaps Elementary Penguin Academy? School of Hard Knox?

 It should go without saying, but what the heck: Don't use any of the sample passwords or questions / answers shown here. It's safe to say that lots of people will be reading this book, and anything seen by lots of people isn't secret. (I know you know that, but still . . .)

▶ **What is your father's middle name?** Make up a goodie or skip it.

▶ **What is your school's mascot?** There's a lot of creativity that can go on here. How about *Red-and-white-striped zebra? Pink elephant?*

Your bylaws for selecting answers to a secret question are two: Be creative *and* be sure you remember the darned thing!

Setting a Hard-to-Crack Password

Poorly chosen passwords are the number-one loophole for hackers. If you think that hackers are just a small group of hypercaffeinated teenagers, think again. It's now also the domain of small- and big-time crooks who hack into an account, spend a few thousand dollars that belong to someone else, and move on.

I searched Google for hacking software and came up with over two million matches. Many of these Web sites offer an arsenal of free hacking tools. They also provide step-by-step instructions for beginners on how to crack passwords. The Internet can be its own worst enemy.

Any password can be cracked by the right person in a matter of seconds. Your goal is to set a password that takes too much of the hackers' time. With the number of available users on eBay or PayPal, odds are they'll go to the next potential victim's password rather than spending many minutes (or even hours) trying to crack yours.

Here are some industrial-strength tips for setting a secure password.

✔ **Number of characters:** Compose your password with more than eight characters.

✔ **Case sensitivity:** Since passwords are case-sensitive, take advantage of the feature. Mix lower- and uppercase in your passwords.

✔ **Letters and numbers:** Combine letters and numbers to make your passwords harder to crack. Y0u g3t the d4ift?

✔ **Proper words:** Don't use proper words. Think of the title of your favorite book. Make your password the first two letters of each word with numbers in the middle (*not* sequential).

Stay smart: Don't make it easy!

Any beginning hacker (or tech-smart teenager) can figure out your password if it falls into the following categories. Don't use 'em! They are pathetically easy!

✔ **The obvious:** The word *Password*. D'oh!

✔ **Birthdays:** Don't use your birthday, your friend's birthday, or John F. Kennedy's birthday. Not only are these dates common knowledge, but so is this truism: *A series of numbers is easy to crack.*

✔ **Names:** Don't use your first name, last name, your dog's name, or anyone's name. Again, it's common knowledge and easy to find out. (Most people know my dog's name; it's been in many of my books!)

✔ **Contact numbers:** Social Security (if they get hold of *that* one — watch out!), phone numbers, your e-mail address, or street address (got a White Pages? So do they . . .).

(continued)

✔ **Any of the lousy passwords in Table 34-1:** These have been gleaned from the millions of password dictionaries available from hackers. Note that this is *not a complete list* by any means; there are thousands of common (lousy) passwords, and unprintable ones are more common than you may think. If you really care to scare yourself, Google the phrase *common passwords*.

• **Figure 34-6:** PayPal and eBay Security key.

eBay and PayPal Hyper-Security Practice

VeriSign, previously known as the worldwide clearinghouse for credit cards and cash, has developed a new technology. VeriSign Unified Authentication provides two-factor authentication credentials through a one-time password token.

PayPal and eBay have embraced this technology through a new device, aptly named the PayPal Security Key, which looks like a small pager. Once you get your Security Key (picture in Figure 34-6), you need to register it on your eBay or PayPal account. Once registered, it generates a new — and different — security code *every time you log in* to your PayPal or eBay account. Just enter the security code displayed on the device's small screen after you enter your user name and password, and you're in.

Can anyone else pick this number up from your wireless network? Possibly. But the key code changes every 30 seconds, so even if someone does get the code, it will be invalid 30 seconds later.

If you're like me, the first question you have is: What if I lose the Security Key? You can still log in to your PayPal account if you can't find your Security Key (or break it). Before you can log in, though, PayPal will ask you questions to confirm your account ownership.

The device is available for $5 from PayPal. If you'd like your own Security Key, visit the Security Key area of PayPal at www.paypal.com/securitykey. This technology will surely catch on with other financial sites, and technically, the device could handle codes from other companies. But only time will tell how this technology will progress.

TABLE 34-1: LOUSY (EASILY CRACKED AND MOST FREQUENTLY USED) PASSWORDS

!@#$%	!@#$%^&	!@#$%^&*(	0	0000	00000000	0007	007	01234
12345	02468	24680	1	1101	111	11111	111111	1234
123456	1234qwer	123abc	123go	12	131313	212	310	2003
2004	54321	654321	888888	a	aaa	abc	abc123	action
absolut	access	admin	admin123	access	administrator	alpha	asdf	animal
biteme	computer	eBay	enable	foobar	home	internet	login	letmein
monkey	mypass	myspace	myspace1	link	lust	money	private	sexy
snoopy	mypc	owner	pass	password	passwrd	papa	peace	penny
pepsi	qwerty	secret	superman	temp	temp123	test	test123	whatever
whatnot	winter	windows	xp	xxx	yoda	mypc123	powerseller	(*your first name*)

Interesting note: On a search of a German dating site, Bruce Schneider (a security expert) found that 123456 works 1.4% of the time and that 2.5% of all passwords begin with 1234.

35
Practice

Communicating with Your Buyers

One of the best parts of running an eBay or online business is that you rarely have to deal with customers. I mean, you don't have to go face-to-face (or worse, toe-to-toe) with another human being. The majority of your communication goes through e-mail, and your remaining comments see life through your feedback and Skype.

Your e-mails are your ongoing contact with your prospective customers and buyers. Skype has become an excellent tool for the same reason — using Skype is like having your own toll-free number. Your customers can reach you with a click of the mouse button. (Very 21st century.) Later in the practice, I show you more about Skype and how it works. First, I concentrate on the importance of *Feedback* — you always see it capitalized on eBay — and how it affects your bottom line.

Feedback: Graceful Reviews

eBay's success is largely due to the community's participation in a Feedback system. How else could strangers feel comfortable sending their hard-earned money to a stranger halfway around the world? In 1996, eBay's founder, Pierre Omidyar, proposed the Feedback system to eBay's six-month-old community. After personally ending up in the middle of a few member squabbles, he felt that the community could police itself by leaving comments after transactions. "Give praise where it is due; make complaints where appropriate," he posted on the eBay message board — and so it began.

Every eBay member, when buying an item from another member, should provide a comment and fill in the DSR (Detailed Seller Ratings) form. If you don't participate, you're really not completing your transaction. Leaving Feedback on eBay is the last bit of paperwork you do to close a deal.

2008 Feedback overhaul

eBay caused a major upheaval in 2008 when they made major changes to the Feedback system. For the first time, sellers could no longer leave negative Feedback for buyers. There were other changes, too:

1. All repeat customer positive Feedback will count towards the seller's Feedback total.

   A buyer may now leave more than one Feedback entry as long as they are spaced as one per week.

2. Feedback that's more than 12-months old no longer counts towards your eBay Feedback percentage.

3. Negative or neutral Feedback entry will be removed if it was left by a buyer who didn't respond to the Unpaid Item (UPI) process.

4. Once a member is suspended from eBay, any negative and neutral Feedback entries they've left for sellers will be removed.

5. There is a three-day waiting period before a buyer can leave negative or neutral Feedback for sellers who have an established track record.

6. All Feedback must be left within 60 days of listing end.

When a prospective buyer clicks on the Feedback number next to your name, they see your full report card. My current one is in Figure 35-1.

Here are some guidelines for participating in the Feedback system:

- You may leave Feedback for up to 60 days after a transaction is complete.

- Remember: After you leave Feedback, it cannot be retracted — you are responsible for what you've put there, and have to live with its contents for eternity (unless you're suspended from the site — Feedback from suspended members will be removed).

- Keep your Feedback businesslike and don't make personal comments.

- Do unto others as you would have them do unto you: If you have a problem, try to work it out with the other party via e-mail or phone before leaving negative Feedback.

Feedback Profile

marsha_c (5425 ☆) 🏆 Power Seller me 🔲   Contact member | View items for sale | View seller's Store | More options ▾
Member since Jan-04-97 in United States

Feedback Score:	**5425**
Positive Feedback:	**100%**
Members who left a positive:	5425
Members who left a negative:	0
All positive Feedback:	6648
Find out what these numbers mean	

Recent Feedback Ratings (last 12 months) ⑦

	1 month	6 months	12 months
⊕ Positive	46	248	454
⊙ Neutral	0	0	1
⊖ Negative	0	0	0

Detailed Seller Ratings (since May 2007) ⑦

Criteria	Average rating	Number of ratings
Item as described	★★★★★	213
Communication	★★★★★	213
Shipping time	★★★★★	213
Shipping and handling charges	★★★★☆	211

• **Figure 35-1: An eBay member's Feedback Profile.**

Using the Feedback Forum

At the bottom of almost every eBay page, there is a group of links. Click the one that reads Feedback Forum, and you'll be beamed to eBay's Feedback Mecca, as shown in Figure 35-2.

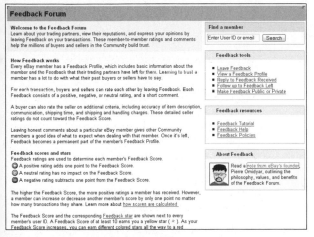

• **Figure 35-2: eBay's Feedback Forum.**

From this page, you can accomplish many Feedback-related tasks:

- ✔ **Find a Member:** Typing in a User ID (or a portion of the ID if you're not exactly sure what the ID is) and clicking Search will bring you to the Find a Member page (see Figure 35-3). Here you see all permutations of the user ID you typed, and you can (hopefully) figure out from here who the community member is you're looking for.

- ✔ **Leave Feedback:** This leads you to a very handy and efficient tool. If you click the Leave Feedback link, you are taken to a page (or pages) that list all your outstanding transactions for the past 60 days. You may leave Feedback for many transactions at once from this area.

- ✔ **View a Feedback Profile:** By clicking this link, you go through the Find a Member form (as noted in the first bullet) to find the member whose Profile you want to view. (Using this

method is not quite as efficient as clicking the Feedback number next to a user's name when you're looking at a transaction.)

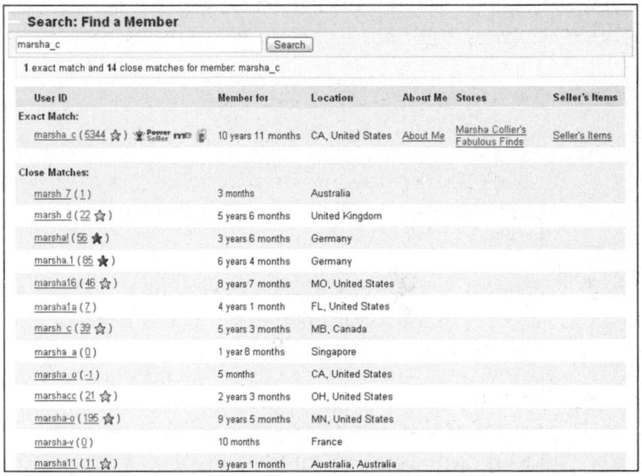

• **Figure 35-3: Searching for member marsha_c (me).**

- ✔ **Reply to Feedback Received:** Here's a link that's worth its weight in gold! You can also find a similar link at the bottom of your Member Profile Feedback page. If you receive Feedback that you feel requires a comment from you — especially neutral or negative comments — click here to locate the transaction (see the list in Figure 35-4) and leave your side of the story.

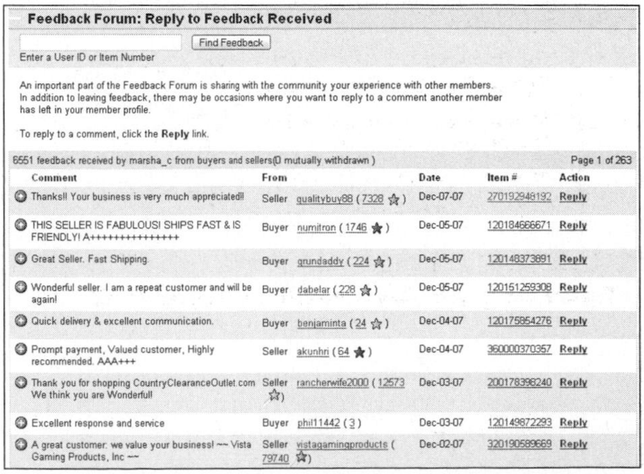

• **Figure 35-4: Review and respond to Feedback here.**

To respond to Feedback, follow these steps:

1. **On your Feedback Forum Review and Respond page, click the link labeled Respond (it's next to the transaction number).**

2. **On the page that appears, enter your response.**

3. **Click the Submit button.**

You can now see your response in your Feedback Profile.

✔ **Follow Up to Feedback Left:** This link enables you to follow up on comments you have made about a buyer. This is very useful if you have left Feedback prior to the completion of the transaction and have a change of heart.

If, as a buyer, you've left a neutral or negative comment prematurely, this is a way to smooth things over (but only somewhat — remember that your negative Feedback becomes part of the other person's permanent record and affects his or her Feedback percentage).

 If you prematurely left a positive comment and the transaction went haywire, you can leave a negative follow-up comment here.

✔ **Make Feedback Public or Private:** From here you can make a setting to hide your Feedback record from other eBay users, but *this is not a good idea.* If people can't see your rating, they may not want to do business with you. Also, hiding your Feedback generally lowers the bids you get on your items. Prospective buyers want to see your Feedback!

If you're trying to overcome some bad Feedback comments by hiding your Feedback, you'll be stymied. When you hide Feedback, a lousy Feedback percentage will haunt you on your transaction pages. What's even worse is that sellers who hide their Feedback are *no longer permitted to sell on the site.* A far better idea is to participate in more transactions and get lots more Feedback of the positive kind!

Posting Feedback from Selling Manager

As you can tell if you've read any other part of this book, I'm a big fan of eBay's Selling Manager tool. It essentially condenses your eBay business into one central command point. After you hear from your trading partner that all is well, you can quickly leave Feedback from your Selling Manager Summary page (see Figure 35-5).

Here's how to send Feedback from Selling Manager:

1. **Click the Sold Listings: Paid and Shipped and Waiting to Give Feedback link.**

You arrive at the transaction list of items waiting for Feedback.

2. **Scroll down to find the transaction you want to leave Feedback on.**

3. **Click the record number next to the listing.**

The Sales Record page appears.

Sold (last 90 days)		Customize ⊠
	Sales	# of Listings
All	$3,848.70	**110**
Awaiting Payment	$0.00	**0**
Buyers eligible for combined purchases		0
Awaiting Shipment	$119.42	**5**
Paid and waiting to give Feedback		20
Paid and Shipped	$3,729.28	**105**
Shipped and waiting to give Feedback		15
Dispute Console	$0.00	**0**
Eligible for Unpaid Item dispute		0
Disputes awaiting your response		0
Eligible for Final Value Fee credit		0
Items not received or not as described		0

• **Figure 35-5:** My Selling Manager Sold item summary.

4. Scroll down to the action links below the transaction information and click the Leave Feedback button.

5. Select an appropriate comment from your stored entries (as shown in Figure 35-6), or feel free to type in a new one.

6. Click the Leave Feedback button.

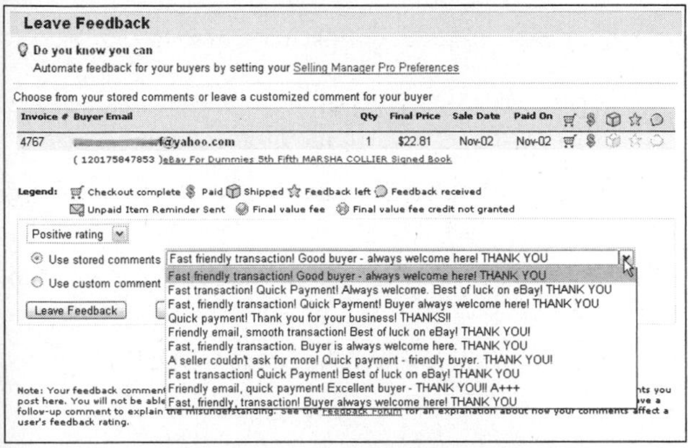

• **Figure 35-6: Selecting an appropriate Feedback comment from Selling Manager.**

Entering Feedback from My eBay

On your My eBay Items I've Sold page (as in Figure 35-7), you can see now-ended transactions from up to 30 days ago. If you're not using Selling Manager, you can easily follow up on your Feedback duties here as well.

You can click the Leave Feedback link for the transaction you want to work with. You'll be brought to the official Leave Feedback page, shown in Figure 35-8.

The other person's User ID will already be filled in, as will the transaction number.

• **Figure 35-7: My eBay Items I've Sold page, with Leave Feedback links in the drop-down boxes.**

• **Figure 35-8: The Leave Feedback form.**

To leave Feedback via this link, follow these steps:

1. Click the radio button next to the Rating you want to leave (as a seller you can leave only positive — but you can still make your thoughts known in your comment).

If you were a buyer in a transaction, DSR star ratings will show up at this point (as in Figure 35-9). These are anonymous ratings that can't be traced back to the buyer who left them. I'm showing you these so you can become familiar with what buyers see when they leave their Feedback for you.

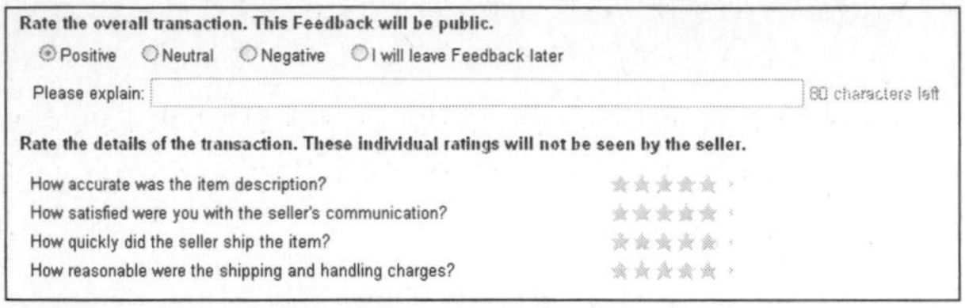

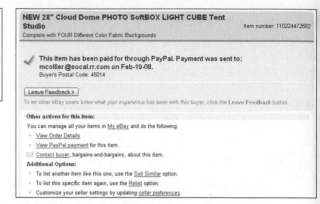

• **Figure 35-9: The buyer's additional leverage on Feedback to the seller.**

2. **Enter your Feedback in the Comment field.**

   Your comment may not exceed 80 characters.

3. **Click the Leave Feedback button.**

 From the buyers' perspective, the most important reason to leave Detailed Seller Ratings (stars) is that through the star rating, you can give future buyers more information. If you feel the item really wasn't up to the description — or if shipping costs were unconscionable — you can telegraph your feelings here. Most eBay users are intimidated about leaving a Negative Feedback because once you leave a negative (and the other person has not already left you a Feedback), you open yourself to receiving a nasty comment from the seller.

Leaving Feedback from an end-of-transaction e-mail

You got an e-mail when the transaction ended, and whether you noticed it or not, it contained a link to the item. This link can take you to the item for up to 90 days! Because you save this e-mail until the transaction is complete, you can use it to leave Feedback just prior to deleting the e-mail.

Here's how to leave Feedback from your e-mail:

1. **Sign in to eBay.**

2. **Click the link on the e-mail to go to the transaction page, as pictured in Figure 35-10.**

• **Figure 35-10: The seller information on a closed transaction page.**

3. **Click the Leave Feedback link to begin the process of leaving Feedback for the other party.**

E-Mailing with Style

Thank goodness, somebody submitted a winning bid on one of your items in an auction. It's a good feeling. When I get those end-of-transaction e-mails from eBay, I whisper a silent "oh, yeah." I then hold my breath to see if the buyer will go directly to PayPal and make the payment. Usually that's what happens. More and more buyers are getting savvy about paying immediately after winning an item.

New buyers, and those who buy or win multiple items from you (my favorite kind of buyer) usually wait to hear from you regarding payment and shipping. Many newbies feel more comfortable hearing from you and knowing who they're doing business with. Also, in the case of multiple purchases, you have to recalculate the postage. The sooner you contact the buyer, the sooner you get your payment.

Notifying winners

eBay sends out an end-of-transaction e-mail to both the buyer and the seller. The e-mail is informative to the seller and, hopefully, a welcome e-mail for the buyer.

Figure 35-11 shows you a typical, "yippee, you won" e-mail. It is brightly colored and joyful, probably designed to evoke some strong level of excitement in the buyer. Note that in the winner's e-mail, there is a Pay Now button for the buyer to pay via PayPal.

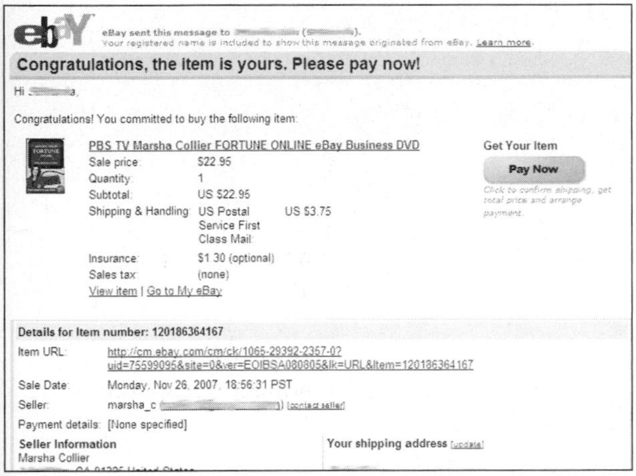

• **Figure 35-11:** Lucky you! You're a winner!

Both e-mails have similar information; the one to the buyer will have the link to pay now. The seller's e-mail will have a link to create an invoice. Either of these linked forms include

✔ Item Title

✔ Item Number

✔ The Final Bid or Buy It Now price

✔ Quantity

✔ Seller's/Buyer's User ID

✔ Buyer's Details (first initial, last name, city, state, and ZIP code)

✔ Seller/Buyer's e-mail addresses

✔ A bunch of links:

➤ The View Item link is good for up to 90 days. (Note that this e-mail is the only place you get this link, and unless you subscribe to eBay's Selling Manager, you'd better keep hold of it.) Sold items remain on your My eBay page for

30 days, but the items disappear from the eBay search engine within two weeks.

➤ A buyer's button to Pay Now to get the money into the seller's pocket (or PayPal account).

➤ eBay Help

➤ Go to My eBay

That's a lot of information, and I'll bet the average user just glances over it and either deletes it (bad idea) or files it in a special folder in his or her e-mail program. You can create extra folders in your e-mail program, drag all sold items to an eBay Sales folder and all purchased items to an eBay Buy folder, delete the e-mails when you finish the transaction, and then leave the Feedback.

If you think that relying on eBay's notification is good enough, it's time to rethink your customer-service policy. An e-mail to the buyer at this point is important. Customer contact is the key to a good transaction.

 If the buyer sprints directly to PayPal and sends you some money to pay for a purchase — a different e-mail is required. Thank them for their payment and let them know when the item will ship (see the upcoming section, "Thanks for the money!").

One of the benefits of Selling Manager Pro is that it can be set up to send your customer e-mails out automatically. I have mine configured to thank every customer the moment they have bought an item. It's not filled with ridiculous rules and regulations; it's filled with sincere thank-yous for doing business with me. Pleasing my customer is my #1 priority (after collecting their money).

Reinforcing a positive experience

I know you're happy that the customer bought your item, and you know you're happy. Now's the time to let the customer know just how darned tickled you are that this person spent hard-earned money with you.

Time to send out a thank-you (and-please-pay-me) e-mail. This is a quasi-invoice and informational note. What should go in it? Well, try to keep in mind what your mother said — always say *please* and *thank you*. After thanking the buyer for purchasing your goods, be sure to cover the following points (this is where the please part comes in):

✔ **Item name.** Lest they forget what they purchased from you.

✔ **Payment terms.** Let the buyer know what forms of payment you will accept and how long you intend to wait for your money.

✔ **Payment Address.** Be sure to tell them where you want the money sent.

✔ **PayPal link.** Inserting a PayPal link in your e-mail is a snap — and may pay off in some rapid payments.

✔ **Return Policy.** Will you accept returns? Under what circumstances? It's OK if you won't accept returns, but be sure that you had that information in your item description *before* the purchase was made.

✔ **Reminder to print the e-mail and enclose it with payment.** Veteran eBay sellers can all tell you stories about the money order that arrived with no item number, no return address, no e-mail address — basically no clue as to what the payment was for.

✔ **Store pitch.** If you have an eBay Store, mention it here. If not, just be sure to tell your buyers you are happy to have them as customers and you look forward to serving them again.

✔ **Feedback pitch.** Most PowerSellers that I know include a small pitch at the closing of the e-mail that asks buyers to leave Feedback on eBay, which will encourage future sales.

 Remind your customers to e-mail you immediately if there is a problem when the order arrives. Stress how you want them to be happy with their purchases. That may stave

off some of the knee-jerk negatives that beginners tend to leave when an item arrives cracked. (They shoulda bought insurance — and it helps to *require* insurance on very fragile items. For more about insurance, see Practice 30.)

That ought to do it. Including this information will make your newbie buyer or old-time veteran feel at home doing business with you.

Thanks for the money!

Sometimes you have to beg for payment. On the other hand, when some blessed buyer pays immediately through PayPal, it's time to show your gratitude. Now's the time to send the old thanks-for-the-money e-mail. This message doesn't have to be very long. Make it short and sweet and to the point. Be sure to tell the customer these four essentials:

✔ Thanks for the purchase and swift payment.

✔ When the item will ship.

✔ That the business is appreciated.

✔ When you intend to leave Feedback. (I leave Feedback *only* when the transaction is complete — when the buyer has received the item and is happy with the transaction.)

Sending Out Invoices

Invoices look very professional. On the other hand, they can be kind of cold and impersonal. PayPal or eBay will send out invoices automatically for you, but (thankfully) you can customize them.

PayPal invoicing

To set up your PayPal account to send out invoices automatically when an item is purchased, follow these steps:

1. Go to www.PayPal.com **and log on to your account.**

2. **Click the Auction Tools tab.**

3. **Scroll down to the heading Receiving and Managing Payments and click the End of Auction E-mail link.**

The PayPal Winning Buyer Notification Registration page, as pictured in Figure 35-12, appears.

End of Auction Email

How It Works

eBay automatically sends an End of Auction email to your winning buyers, informing them they've won your item and enabling them to pay you. You can customize this email for listings which offer PayPal as a payment method.

To customize your End of Auction emails, sign up and enter the information below or select an existing account.

eBay User ID: [marsha_c (eBay) ▾]   Add

Your preference to customize End of Auction emails is currently **On.**

Select your preference to customize End of Auction emails:
◉ On ○ Off

Customize End of Auction Email
The email always includes item information, your payment instructions from the listing, as well as a **Pay Now** button. Create your custom message below. Use the AutoText drop-down menu to insert personalized information (such the buyer's User ID). If you sell internationally, be sure to add information about international shipping, handling, and insurance charges.

Customize Your Email Message
AutoText   Sample Email
[Buyer User ID ▾] [Insert]

AutoText glossary   See message examples

Thank you very much for your purchase.
Your business is appreciated.

For more information on my shipping,
insurance, and other policies, or if you
would like to pay for this item with a
method other than PayPal, please see this
item listing for details.

• **Figure 35-12: PayPal's End of Auction E-mail controls.**

4. **Select the eBay User ID you have registered with PayPal from the appropriate field.**

If you have more than one eBay User ID registered with PayPal, all are listed in a drop-down box in this field. Choose one.

5. **Customize your message.**

The blank text box allows you to enter up to 2,000 characters of a personal message. There's plenty of room to fill in all the niceties, so lather it on. Remember, without the personal touch, this is just a cold invoice when it comes to the buyer. It's up to you to make it nice!

6. **If you have a logo you use on your Web site or eBay Store, enter the URL that will display it, so it appears at the top of your invoice.**

You can also use this method to select any image you'd like to appear on your invoice. The image must be 310×90 pixels in size, 10KB or smaller, and in a GIF, JPG, or PNG format.

There's also a link in the logo area that you can click to test whether your logo appears correctly. If the logo appears in the pop-up window, then everything is fine. If not, double-check the URL.

7. **From your registered e-mail addresses, choose the one you want to appear as the return address on the invoice.**

Again, if you have more than one address registered, you select the correct one from the drop-down list.

8. **Select the Send a Copy to Me check box if you want to receive copies of all the invoices that PayPal sends out for you.**

FYI, getting these copies may get very old fast. But give it a whirl for a while so you can see what your buyers see.

9. **Click the Submit button at the bottom of the page.**

You're notified that the invoicing service will commence sometime within the next 24 hours.

eBay invoicing

eBay also allows you to send out invoices for your items, but they're not sent out automatically (as they are by PayPal). For eBay invoices, you have a couple of options:

- **From the item page:** Invoices can be sent directly from the item page. You see the Send Invoice bar only if you are signed in to eBay when you visit the auction. Once you've sent the invoice, the transaction will appear (as in Figure 35-13) until the item is paid for.

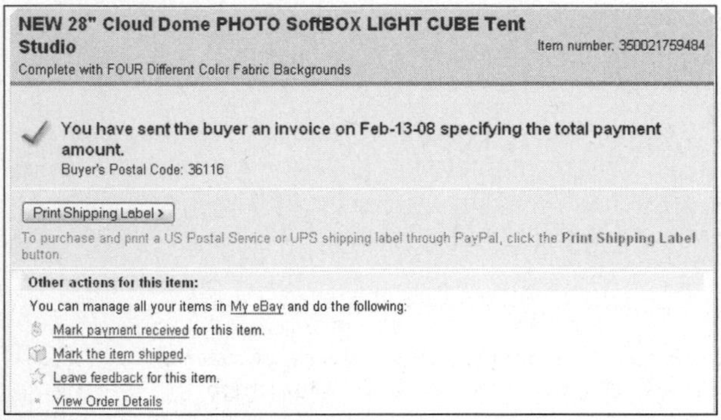

NEW 28" Cloud Dome PHOTO SoftBOX LIGHT CUBE Tent Studio
Item number: 350021759484
Complete with FOUR Different Color Fabric Backgrounds
You have sent the buyer an invoice on Feb-13-08 specifying the total payment amount.
Buyer's Postal Code: 36116
Print Shipping Label >
To purchase and print a US Postal Service or UPS shipping label through PayPal, click the Print Shipping Label button.
Other actions for this item:
You can manage all your items in My eBay and do the following:
Mark payment received for this item.
Mark the item shipped.
Leave feedback for this item.
View Order Details

Figure 35-13: I've sent an invoice — let's hope they send the money.

- **From My eBay:** Go to My eBay, Items I've Sold page, as shown in Figure 35-14. If the winner did not pay for the item immediately through PayPal, you'll see a Send Invoice button in the Next Step/ Status column.

1 $119.99 $129.84 Feb-09 eBay Sell Similar
5 DVD & eBay Business For Dummies/Timesaving Technique (120161698500)
1 $42.95 -- Feb-08
Print
Print Shipping Label
Mark As Payment Received
Mark As Shipped
Leave Feedback
View Order Details
Contact Buyer
Send Invoice
Sell Similar
Relist
NEW 28" Cloud Dome PHOTO SoftBOX LIGHT CUBE Tent Studio
1 $39.59 $52.36 Feb-05
28" Cloud Dome PHOTO BOX LIGHT CUBE Tent Lighting Kit
1 $6.75 $10.25 Feb-05
Museum Putty QUAKE HOLD Wax Quakehold Earthquake LARGE (120150648326)
1 $18.99 $24.74 Feb-03 eBay Leave Feedback
Starting an EBAY BUSINESS for Dummies 3 book SIGNED NEW (350021514522)
3 $20.25 $26.42 Feb-02 eBay Sell Similar

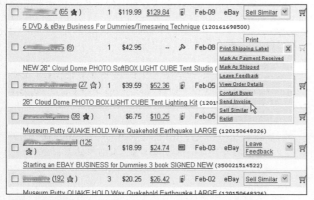

Figure 35-14: My eBay status on Items I've Sold.

After you click the button to send an invoice, you see a page with the auction details. The buyer's User ID, ZIP code, and editable details are displayed. You may also enter a personal message and further payment instructions here. You are allowed up to 500 characters.

If the shipping amount hasn't been filled in (due to multiple purchases or calculated shipping), you can calculate it easily enough.

1. **Click the teeny calculator button next to the Shipping and Handling box.**

   A version of the eBay shipping calculator opens.

2. **Type in the buyer's ZIP code, and click calculate.**

   A postal quote based on your shipping location appears.

3. **Enter the calculated shipping amount in the Shipping and Handling box.**

Chatting with Skype

Skype is eBay's foray into the world of real, person-to-person communication. Skype allows you to make calls from your computer — without cost (yes, you need a microphone and speakers at the very least) to other people who have the Skype software installed on their computers — and dirt-cheap to landlines and cell phones around the world. If you haven't tried it, you really must.

I love Skype because where else can I call my family in the UK for about 2.1 cents per minute? I can call my friends anywhere in the United States — without burning up my cell-phone minutes. I can also call one of my eBay or Web-site customers when there's an issue to be attended to — without any extra cost! The Skype software is available for a free download at `www.skype.com`; installed on your computer, it looks something like Figure 35-15.

• **Figure 35-15: My Skype software in action.**

TABLE 35-1: SKYPE FEATURES AND CHARGES

Feature	Charge
Skype-to-Skype calls	Free
Transfer calls to people on Skype	Free
Video calls	Free
Instant messaging and group chats	Free
Conference calls with up to nine people	Free
Forward calls to people on Skype	Free
Call phones and mobiles	From $ 0.021 per minute
Receive calls from phones and cell phones	$18 for 3 months or $60 for a year
*SkypeIn	$18 for 3 months or $60 for a year
*Send and receive voicemails	$6 for 3 months or $20 for a year
*Skype To Go number	Only as part of Skype Pro.
Forward calls to phones	From $ 0.021 per minute
Send SMS messages	In the US $0.112
*Transfer calls to phones and cell phones	From $ 0.021 per minute

Available only in the Skype Pro package

Skype also allows you to forward your calls to your cell phone, office, or home phone number (or all three) for the same 2.1 cents per minute. You can simply answer whichever phone line you want.

Skype has a few charges, but they include a lot for free; see Table 35-1 to get an idea.

You might check the Skype site for current rates and description of the services. Here are details on a few of their unique offerings:

✔ **SkypeIn**. Get your own personal online telephone number. Available in 20 countries, you can get a number through Skype and use it as your own office line.

✔ **Skype To Go number**. This is a local number assigned to your mobile phone; it allows you to call an international number at your local rates. This feature is available only with Skype Pro.

✔ **Skype Pro.** You get Voicemail, Skype to Go, Call Transfer, Free U.S. and Canada calls, and a 60 percent discount on a SkypeIn number.

I can see you now saying how you don't want to be tied to your computer 24/7 and would rather not pay for forwarding (me, too). Skype has a few solutions for this. There are (for example) Skype phones! I like the ones made by Netgear because they're very stylish and work incredibly well. I have used two types. One type of Skype phone runs on your Wi-Fi network signal and the other is a dual-phone that carries Skype as well as your regular home phone line.

Figure 35-16 shows you the Skype phone I use. It allows me to use any of my Skype contacts that are online for free, or to call any land line or cell phone. I use the Skype line for my long-distance calls. After dialing a number, you can choose whether to place the call through the Skype network or from your home phone line. So simple and easy. It's replaced my other cordless phones at home (you can have up to four handsets).

The best thing about the dual line phone is that it operates on DECT technology. (I was always having problems getting a signal through my house). DECT (Digital Enhanced Cordless Telecommunications) cordless phone technology uses 1.8/1.9 GHz band, which avoids interfering with WiFi networks. DECT cordless phones provide long-range, clear voice quality, and advanced digital features.

You can also use Skype to exchange instant messages with your customers. You can set up this option on the Sell Your Item form on the first page, as pictured in Figure 35-17.

• **Figure 35-16: The Netgear Skype dual line phone.**

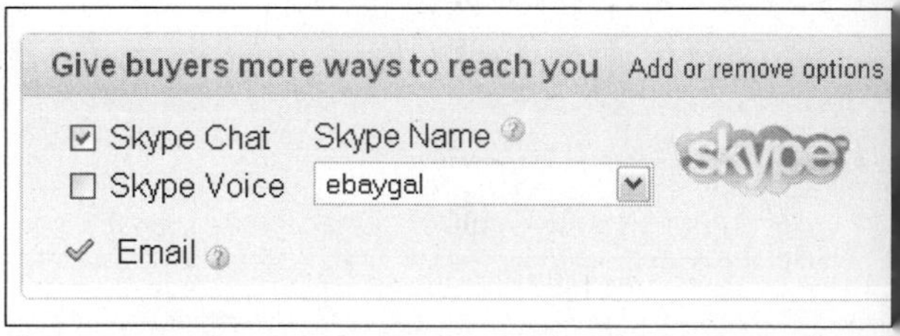

• **Figure 35-17: Setting up "Skype Me" in my auction.**

To use this option in your eBay listings, just click the box indicating whether you'd like to accept Skype chat only (on your computer) or Skype calls on your Skype phone (for free) or forwarded to another line at the standard 2.1 cents per minute. Figure 35-18 shows you how these instant contact options look in the Meet The Seller area of my listing, and there you go! Excuse me . . . a question is coming in (see Figure 35-19)!

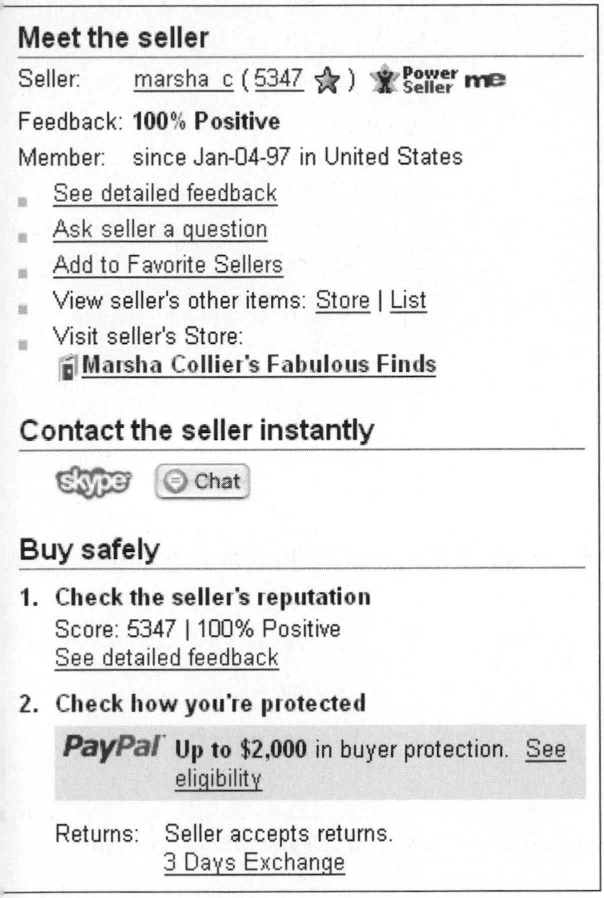

Meet the seller
Seller: marsha_c (5347) Power Seller me
Feedback: 100% Positive
Member: since Jan-04-97 in United States
See detailed feedback
Ask seller a question
Add to Favorite Sellers
View seller's other items: Store | List
Visit seller's Store:
Marsha Collier's Fabulous Finds
Contact the seller instantly
skype
Chat
Buy safely
1. Check the seller's reputation
Score: 5347 | 100% Positive
See detailed feedback
2. Check how you're protected
PayPal Up to $2,000 in buyer protection. See eligibility
Returns: Seller accepts returns.
3 Days Exchange

• **Figure 35-18: Just click *Chat* and I'm on the line.**

Mallie Prytherch (This user has not shared his/her details with y...
Add
Send
More
Options
Bookmark
Show messages from: This conversation | Today | This week | Last 30 days | Beginning
Mallie Prytherch says: 4:50:34 PM
Hello. I have a question about one of your eBay listings and wonder if you would be kind enough to help me.
Marsha Collier says: 4:51:03 PM
Yes, which listing please? Thank you for contacting me.
Mallie Prytherch says: 4:51:18 PM
The eBay listing # is 120193458502
4:51:49 PM
I was wondering what the shipping to Albrightsville, PA zip code 18210 is.
Mallie Prytherch
Menu
Add more people to this chat!
Emoticons
Videos
Set Font
Hold on, I'll check
Marsha Collier
Personalise »
Online
History on

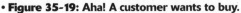

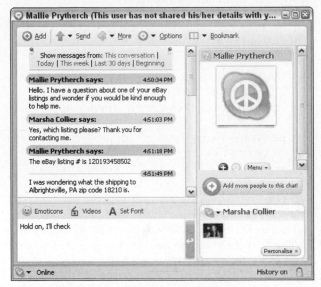

• **Figure 35-19: Aha! A customer wants to buy.**

Part V

Manage Your Business

The 5th Wave   By Rich Tennant

"Oh, we're doing just great. Philip and I are selling decorative jelly jars on eBay. I run the auctions and Philip sort of controls the inventory."

36 Practice

Keeping the Books

Once you have a lot of online business coming in, you've got to face the fact that you need to keep your books in a professional manner. You'll know when the time has come, but it's best to start good bookkeeping practices when your business is still small. I get lots of e-mails from people who have questions about how to keep their books straight. (Incidentally, although I don't always have time to keep up with answering all my e-mail, rest assured that I at least *read* every message.)

These sellers are confused by the myriad of products and services vying for the eBay PowerSeller's dollar. Many of these products and services claim to do everything, and that running a business on eBay is impossible without them — as if they were all an eBay seller needed to achieve success . . . but that's not quite right. As much as auction management services do for the seller — and they can do some amazing things — they can't maintain your books in the proper bookkeeping form.

 With the advent of e-commerce, many aspects of the business world updated and changed to keep pace with the speed of the Internet. One thing that didn't change, however, is the need for methodical, rock-solid bookkeeping. Why can't you do your bookkeeping *your* way? Because the United States Tax Code demands that businesses adhere to some tried-and-true accounting procedures.

It's all well and good to manage your sales data in spreadsheets, note pads, and homemade ledgers. (I keep my PayPal monthly sales in spreadsheets, but only as backup and customer-list documentation.) Just realize that you're making more work for yourself in the long run. Keeping your books in ways that are easy for you to understand doesn't preclude the necessity of maintaining your books in the proper format.

The government wants your records to follow GAAP (Generally Accepted Accounting Principles), and using a leading software program like QuickBooks will help you meet this requirement.

Dealing with a Professional

Have you ever wondered why big businesses have CFOs (Chief Financial Officers), Vice Presidents of Finance, CPAs (Certified Public Accountants), and bookkeepers? It's because keeping the books is the backbone of a company's business.

Do you have a professional going over your books at least once a year? You really should. A paid professional experienced in business knows what to do when it comes to your taxes. The complexity of the tax code means not just any paid preparer will suffice when it comes to preparing your business taxes.

 Should you use tax-prep software in a box? Now I'm not going to say that preparing your own taxes is a bad idea, it's just foolhardy when you have a business. You need the advice of someone who is an expert in the field. There are too many variations, twists, and turns in the tax code for businesses. Your software program can't ask you all the important questions that relate to your specific type of business.

Here's a list of possible people who can prepare your tax returns.

✔ **Tax Preparer (or Consultant):** This is the person you visit at the local we-file-for-you tax office. Did you know that a tax preparer could be anybody? There is no licensing involved. H&R Block hires as many as 100,000 seasonal workers as tax preparers each year. Where do these people come from? I'm sure that some are experts at the tax code, but the sheer number of tax preparers and the lack of regulation can make using a *we-file-for-you* tax office a risky proposition for business people who want to minimize their tax liability.

 A United States General Accounting Office report estimated that over 2 million American citizens overpaid their taxes because they claimed the standard deduction when it would have been more beneficial to itemize. Half of

those taxpayers used paid preparers who clearly were not cognizant of the full tax law as it applied to their individual cases. Scary, huh?

✔ **Volunteer IRS Certified Preparers:** From February 1 through April 15, the AARP (American Association of Retired Persons) does an outstanding job of assembling nearly 32,000 volunteer tax preparers to serve the needs of low- to middle-income taxpayers (special attention going to seniors) through their Tax-Aide program. Their goal is to maximize legal deductions and credits, resulting in "tangible economic benefits" for their clients. These volunteers have to study, take a test, and become *certified by the IRS* before they can lend their services to the cause.

In 2003, AARP volunteers served a total of 1.85 million seniors in the United States. My mother was a retired corporate comptroller, and she volunteered in this program for many years. (She was disappointed when she made her lowest score on the IRS test — 94 percent!) AARP volunteers staff over 8,500 sites around the United States, and you can find out if there's one near you. Go to

```
https://locator.aarp.org/vmis/
    sites/tax_aide_locator.jsp
```

or call 1-888-AARP-NOW (1-888-227-7669) and select Tax-Aide Information.

✔ **Public Accountant:** A Public Accountant or PA, must complete educational, testing, and experience requirements and obtain a state license. PAs must take an annual update course to maintain their status.

✔ **Enrolled Agent:** Often called "one of the best-kept secrets in accounting," an Enrolled Agent is federally licensed by the IRS. (CPAs and attorneys are state-licensed.) EAs must pass an extensive annual test on tax law and tax preparation every year to maintain their status. (They also have to pass annual background checks.) Enrolled Agents are authorized to appear in place of a taxpayer before the IRS.

Many EAs are former IRS employees. To find an Enrolled Agent near you, go to the Web site www.naea.org and enter the Taxpayer's area.

✔ **Certified Public Accountant:** A Certified Public Accountant (CPA) must complete rigorous testing and experience requirements as prescribed by the state in which they practice. Most states require that CPAs obtain a state license.

CPAs are accountants. They specialize in record keeping and reporting financial matters. Their important position is to act as an advisor regarding financial decisions for both individuals and businesses. CPAs must take an annual update course to maintain their status.

Commercials for tax preparers often claim that they will stand behind your tax return preparation in case of an audit. Think about that. Of course they can stand by the return preparation, because it's done in a computer. Besides, during an audit, the IRS is interested mostly in the data that was used to prepare the return: the data that you supply. *You* are responsible for the data and no preparer will "stand behind" what you supply.

Keeping Your Books Accurately

When you meet with one of the professionals discussed in the previous section, that person expects you to bring a complete and accurate set of books. To prepare accurate books, you either need a bookkeeper (who will use accounting software), or you can learn how to use professional accounting software yourself.

Don't be mortified; you *can* do this. Lots of people who use bookkeeping software successfully today knew nothing about bookkeeping before they set up their own accounts. I'm one of them.

My tutor, helping me every step of the way, was *QuickBooks For Dummies* by Stephen Nelson, CPA.

I met Stephen a couple of years ago. He's just as funny and smart in person as he appears in his writing. I highly recommend his books to help you with learning the program.

I highly recommend QuickBooks from Intuit for your eBay business accounting because it's tailored for business. At the end of each year, I hand my CPA a copy of my QuickBooks backup, along with the printed reports he requires. Most professionals use and accept data from QuickBooks.

When your business gets so busy that you have no time to post your bookkeeping, you can always hire a part-time bookkeeper to come in and do your posting for you.

Using QuickBooks in your eBay business

QuickBooks offers several versions, from the basics to enterprise solutions tailored to different types of businesses. QuickBooks Simple Start and QuickBooks Pro have a few significant differences. QuickBooks Pro adds job costing and expensing features, payroll, and the ability to keep track of your inventory through your sales receipts and purchases (making it a sound upgrade for eBay PowerSellers).

QuickBooks Simple Start, which you find on the CD at the back of the book, does a darn good job, too. So check out the comparison at quickbooks.intuit.com and see which version is best for you. I use (and highly recommend) QuickBooks Pro, and that's the version I describe in the rest of this section.

Aside from the professional reasons to use QuickBooks, there's another, more basic reason: The program can give you up-to-the-minute reports about the status of your eBay business and keep track of everything in the background — including payroll and sales-tax liability.

Here are a few things (among many others) that I really like about using QuickBooks to streamline an online business:

✔ **Inventory Reports:** As you purchase inventory, aside from deducting the money from your checking account and expensing your merchandise account, QuickBooks adds the purchased merchandise to your inventory. Every time you sell an item, QuickBooks deducts the item from your inventory. QuickBooks has many other reporting features for your inventory, as well as end-of-year reporting for taxes.

Figure 36-1 shows you a part of an inventory report that I pulled out of the program today. You can see how valuable the data is. With a click of my mouse, I can see how much I have left in stock and the average number that I've sold per week.

The Collier Company, Inc.
Inventory Stock Status by Item
October through December 2007

	Item Description	Reorder Pt	On Hand	Sales/Week
Inventory				
5550 Bulb	Full SPectrum Bulb		-5	0.8
STBP	Stephen Tobolowsky DVD		18	0.2
PBS				
Online Business	Your Online Business Plan		4	0.8
MYFOL	Making Your Fortune Online		-18	0.6
PBS - Other			0	0
Total PBS			-14	1.4
Calendar	Fraggle Rock		-9	0
20" Tent	20" Photo Tent		14	1.8
28" Tent	28" Photo Tent		37	2.4
Angled Collar	Cloud Dome Angled Collar		23	0
Black Infiniti	Black Infiniti Board		14	0.2
Book Sales				
BIZ 3	▶ Starting an eBay Business 3rd Edition		0	0.9 ◀
5th	eBay For Dummies 5th edition		23	0.6
Santa Shops	Santa Shops on eBay		8	0
Listings That Sell	eBay Listings That Sell		-4	0.3
Desk Reference	eBay Business Desk Reference		14	0.4
Shopping book	eBay Bargain Shopping for Dummies		126	0.1
Timesaving	eBay Timsaving Techniques For Dum...		3	0.1
Tips booklet	eBay Tips for Dummies Booklet		73	0
4th Dummies	eBay For Dummies 4th Edition		-3	0
Biz 2nd	Starting an eBay Business 2nd Edition		15	0
Business Book Sales	Starting an eBay Business for Dumm...		-10	0

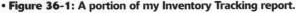

• Figure 36-1: A portion of my Inventory Tracking report.

✔ **Sales Tax Tracking:** Depending on how the program is set up (based on your own state sales tax laws), you can request a report that has all your taxable and non-taxable sales. The report calculates the amount of sales tax you owe. You can print out this report for backup information on your sales-tax payments to your state.

✔ **Payroll:** Whether you use the online payroll service to prepare your payroll or input the deductions yourself, QuickBooks posts the appropriate withholdings to their own accounts.

When it comes time to pay your employees' withholding taxes, QuickBooks can generate the federal reporting form (all filled in) for submitting with your payment.

✔ **Sales Reports:** QuickBooks gives you a plethora of reports with which you can analyze your sales professionally. One of my favorite reports is the *Sales by Item Summary*. This report gives you the information below for every inventoried item you sell in whatever time period you choose:

▶ Quantity sold

▶ Total dollar amount sold

▶ Percentage of sales represented by each individual item

▶ The average price the item sold for

▶ COGS (cost of goods sold) by item

▶ Average cost of goods sold by total sales per item

▶ Gross profit margin in dollar amounts

▶ Gross profit margin expressed as percentages

 Depending on how you post your transactions, you can analyze your eBay sales, Web-site sales, and/or brick-and-mortar sales individually or together. You can also select any date range for your reports.

Posting sales in QuickBooks the easy way

Some online auction-management services integrate with QuickBooks. This integration means your individual transactions can be downloaded into the QuickBooks program, setting a up a new customer for each of your sales.

Although this process is quick and easy, inputting each sale as a new customer will cause your database to get huge quickly. QuickBooks is a very large program to begin with, and if you're going to use it (and update it) for several years, the database will become even larger.

f you've ever worked with large files, you know that he larger the data file, the more chance there is for he data to become corrupt. That's the last thing ou want. Besides, QuickBooks will max out with ver 14,000 customers — a very doable number fter several years on eBay.

 To keep track of your customers, you can use an additional copy of your PayPal monthly report and combine it with your cash-sales summary into an Excel spreadsheet (you can also use Microsoft Works) to build this important data.

n the upcoming sidebar, I show you a procedure I eveloped to process my PayPal sales. I've run it ast several accountants and QuickBooks experts, nd it's gotten rave reviews. I'm sharing it with you ecause I want you to be able to run your business moothly.

Using QuickBooks the "Collier" way

Rather than posting an invoice in my QuickBooks software for every customer (for those very few customers who need formal invoices), I can print them out on demand from eBay's Selling Manager; I input my sales into a customer Sales Receipt as shown in the sidebar figure. Whenever I make a PayPal deposit into my business checking account, which is every few days depending on how busy sales are, I post my sales into QuickBooks. This way, the total of the Sales Receipt equals the exact amount of my PayPal deposit. (If you've ever tried to reconcile your PayPal deposits with your sales and your checking account, you know how frustrating it can be.)

In my QuickBooks account, PayPal is the customer. It makes no difference who bought what, it just matters what item is sold (to deduct from inventory) and for how much (to post to my financial data).

The program gives you the flexibility to customize forms, so the figure given here shows my customized sales receipt for PayPal sales. PayPal is a taxable customer when sales are made in the State of California, and the appropriate sales tax is applied automatically.

Here are the things I have added to customize the form:

✔ **PayPal Fees:** I have set up PayPal fees as a credit against sales. (In the figure, you can see they are applied as a negative.) This helps to match the total amount of the Sales Receipt to my PayPal deposit. It also gives me a discount line in my sales reports that tracks my total paid PayPal fees. This also appears in my Costs of Goods Sold area of my financial statements.

In case you're wondering about eBay fees, they have their own line in my chart of Accounts. I charge eBay fees to my company credit card. When the credit card expenses are posted, I post the eBay expense to the eBay fees account which appears in the Costs of Goods Sold in my financial reports. (Later on, I show you how to set up QuickBooks for eBay, and I include a suggested chart of expense and income accounts.)

✔ **State:** I type in the two-letter state abbreviation of the shipping location with each item. This serves as backup information for my State Board of Equalization (the California sales tax board) and also allows me to run reports on what has sold in which states.

✔ **Date:** The date at the top of the Sales Receipt is the posting date. The date in the product posting indicates the date the PayPal payment was posted.

(continued)

✔ **Class:** Every item posted in QuickBooks can be part of a Class to make data easier for you to isolate certain types of transactions. I have set up two classes of PayPal sales: California sales and out-of-state sales. The California sales are classified as Taxable, and the Out-of-State sales as Non-taxable. QuickBooks calculates the tax liability automatically.

✔ **Tax Classification:** When I type the first two letters into the class area (OU for out of state, and CA for in-state sales), the tax line changes automatically to Tax or Non-Tax. QuickBooks would do this regardless of whether I show this field in the Sales Receipt; by having it appear, I get a secondary mental reminder to post the taxable Class properly.

By inputting my eBay sales data in this way, I streamline the process in several ways. I post data to only one program once. From this Sales Receipt, I get updated inventory reports, accurate Sales Tax data, accurate expense and income tracking, and easy reconciling of my checking account.

QuickBooks chart of accounts

After you've successfully set up your business in QuickBooks, the program presents a chart of accounts. Think of the *chart of accounts* as an organization system, such as file folders. It keeps all related data in the proper area. When you write a check to pay a bill, it deducts the amount from your checking account, reduces your accounts payable, and perhaps increases your asset or expense accounts.

You have a choice of giving each account a number. These numbers, a kind of bookkeeping shorthand, are standardized throughout bookkeeping. Believe it or not, everybody in the industry seems to know what number goes with what item. (To keep things less confusing, I like to use titles as well as numbers.)

Learning about COGS

No, no, I'm not talking about Cogswell's Cogs (the competitor to George Jetson's employer, Spacely Space Sprockets); I'm talking about Cost of Goods Sold. It's a special type of expense, and often varies depending on the type of business. The general definition of COGS reflects the cost of purchasing raw materials and manufacturing finished products. Some accountants look at it slightly differently in an eBay business: encompassing credit card (PayPal) fees, eBay fees, and shipping costs, making it include all direct costs of products sold and shipped to customers.

I like it this way, because in the financial profit-and-loss statement, QuickBooks lists COGS ahead of other expense accounts. This gives me a snapshot view of the sales profitability of my eBay business — without clouding things by including telephone, payroll, travel, and all the other expenses that affect the gross profits.

To customize your chart of accounts, follow these steps:

1. **Choose Edit⇨Preferences.**

2. **Click the Accounting icon (on the left).**

3. **Click the Company preferences tab and indicate that you'd like to use account numbers.**

   An editable chart of accounts appears. Because QuickBooks doesn't assign account numbers by default, you'll need to edit the chart to create them.

4. **Go through your QuickBooks chart of accounts and add any missing categories.**

   You may not need all these categories, and you can always add more later. In Table 36-1, I show you a chart of accounts that a CPA wrote for an eBay business, and I also include this table on the CD at the back of the book. Take a look at Figure 36-2 — it shows you a portion of the Chart of Accounts for my business; you can see how I've adapted this in Table 36-1.

QuickBooks on the Web

If you want to handle everything on the Web, use QuickBooks online service. The online QuickBooks program offers fewer features than the home version, but if your accounting needs are simple, it may be a solution for you. Before you decide, however, consider that while your accounting needs may be simple now, they may not be so simple later.

Intuit charges $19.95 a month for the service, which is comparable to buying the QuickBooks Pro version. The online version also requires you to have a broadband connection to the Internet so you're always online (dial-up connections need not apply). The online edition doesn't include integrated payroll, purchase orders, online banking, and bill payments.

Chart of Accounts		
Name	$	Type
1010 · CASH IN BANK		Bank
1100 · Accounts Receivable		Accounts Receivable
2120 · Payroll Asset		Other Current Asset
1120 · Inventory Asset		Other Current Asset
1150 · Advances to Officers		Other Current Asset
1200 · Est. Franchise Tax		Other Current Asset
1300 · Fed Inc Tax Refund		Other Current Asset
1400 · Inventory		Other Current Asset
1499 · Undeposited Funds		Other Current Asset
1410 · Furniture & Equipment		Other Asset
1420 · Trucks		Other Asset
1510 · Acc. Depreciation		Other Asset
2020 · A/P Account		Accounts Payable
2030 · Loan from M Collier		Other Current Liabi…
2080 · Sales Tax Payable		Other Current Liabi…
2090 · SalesTax Payable-Other		Other Current Liabi…
2100 · Payroll Liabilities		Other Current Liabi…
1110 · Retained Earnings		Equity
3000 · Open Bal Equity		Equity
3910 · Capitol Stock		Equity
3930 · Addt. Paid In Capitol		Equity
3950 · Ret. Earnings		Equity
4010 · Sales		Income
4021 · eBay Sales		Income
4030 · Shipping Income		Income
4020 · Consulting		Income
4080 · Newsletter Advertising		Income
4099 · Royalty, Auction Advisor DVDs		Income
4100 · Book Income Royalties		Income
4100a · Santa Shops Royalties		Income
4109a · 5th eBay FD		Income
4109 · eBay Listings That Sell		Income
4108 · eBay Business AIO		Income
4107 · Starting a Business 2nd Edition		Income
4106 · Timesaving Techniques		Income
4105 · 4th eBay For Dummies		Income
4104 · eBay Bargain Shopping		Income
4101 · Ebay for Dummies 2nd Edition		Income
4102 · Starting an eBay Business FD		Income
4103 · Dummies 3rd		Income
4110 · Reimbursed Expenses		Income
5301 · eBay Costs		Cost of Goods Sold

• **Figure 36-2: A portion of my Chart of Accounts.**

TABLE 36-1: eBay Business Chart of Accounts

Account Number	Account Name	What It Represents
1001	Checking	All revenue deposited here and all checks drawn upon this account
1002	Money market account	Company savings account
1100	Accounts receivable	For customers to whom you extend credit
1201	Merchandise	COGS: Charge to cost of sales as used, or take periodic inventories and adjust at that time
1202	Shipping supplies	Boxes, tape, labels, and so forth; charge these to cost as used or take an inventory at the end of the period and adjust to cost of sales
1401	Office furniture and equipment	Desk, computer, telephone
1402	Shipping equipment	Scales, tape dispensers

(continued)

TABLE 36-1 *(continued)*

Account Number	Account Name	What It Represents
1403	Vehicles	Your vehicle if it's owned by the company
1501	Accumulated depreciation	For your accountant's use
1601	Deposits	Security deposits on leases
2001	Accounts payable	Amounts owed for the stuff you sell, or charged expenses
2100	Payroll liabilities	Taxes deducted from employees' checks and taxes paid by company on employee earnings
2200	Sales tax payable	Sales tax collected at time of sale and owed to the state
2501	Equipment loans	Money borrowed to buy a computer or other equipment
2502	Auto loans	When you get that hot new van for visiting your consignment clients
3000	Owner's capital	Your opening balance
3902	Owner's draw	Your withdrawals for the current year
4001	Merchandise sales	Revenue from sales of your products
4002	Shipping and handling	Paid by the customer
4009	Returns	Total dollar amount of returned merchandise
4101	Interest income	From your investments
4201	Other income	Income not otherwise classified
5001	Merchandise purchases	All the merchandise you buy for eBay; you'll probably use subaccounts for individual items
5002	Freight in	Freight and shipping charges you pay for your inventory, not for shipments to customers
5003	Shipping	COGS: Shipping to your customers: USPS, FedEx, UPS, and so on
5004	Shipping supplies	COGS: Boxes, labels, tape, bubble pack
6110	Automobile expense	When you use your car for work
6111	Gas and oil	Filling up the tank!
6112	Repairs	When your business owns the car
6120	Bank service charges	Monthly service charges, NSF charges, and so forth
6140	Contributions	Charity
6142	Data services	Do you have an outside firm processing your payroll?
6143	Internet service provider	What you pay to your Internet provider
6144	Web-site hosting fees	Fees paid to your hosting company
6150	Depreciation expense	For your accountant's use

Account Number	Account Name	What It Represents
5151	eBay fees	COGS: What you pay eBay every time you list and item and make a sale
5152	Discounts	Fees you're charged for using eBay and accepting credit card payments; deducted from your revenue and reported to you on your eBay statement
5153	Other auction-site fees	COGS: You may want to set up subcategories for each site where you do business, such as Yahoo! or Amazon.com
5156	PayPal fees	COGS: Processing fees paid to PayPal
5158	Credit card merchant account fees	COGS: If you have a separate merchant account, post those fees here
5160	Dues	If you join an organization that charges membership fees (relating to your business)
5161	Magazines and periodicals	Books and magazines that help you run and expand your business
5170	Equipment rental	Postage meter, occasional van
5180	Insurance	Policies that cover your merchandise or your office
5185	Liability insurance	Insurance that covers you if (for example) someone slips and falls at your place of business (can also be put under Insurance)
5190	Disability Insurance	Insurance that will pay you if you become temporarily or permanently disabled and can't perform your work
5191	Health insurance	If provided for yourself, you may be required to provide it to employees
5200	Interest expense	Credit interest and interest on loans
5220	Loan interest	When you borrow from the bank
5230	Licenses and permits	State and city licenses
5240	Miscellaneous	Whatever doesn't go anyplace else
5250	Postage and delivery	Stamps used in your regular business
5251	Endicia.com fees	COGS: Fees for your eBay business postage service
5260	Printing	Your business cards, correspondence stationery, and so on
5265	Filing fees	Fees paid to file legal documents
5270	Professional fees	Fees paid to consultants
5280	Legal fees	If you have to pay a lawyer
5650	Accounting and bookkeeping	Bookkeeper, CAP, or EA
5290	Rent	Office, warehouse, and so on

(continued)

TABLE 36-1 *(continued)*

Account Number	Account Name	What It Represents
6300	Repairs	Can be the major category for the following subcategories
6310	Building repairs	Repairs to the building where you operate your business
6320	Computer repairs	What you pay the person who sets up your wireless network
6330	Equipment repairs	When the copier or phone needs fixing
6340	Telephone	Regular telephone, FAX lines
6350	Travel and entertainment	Business-related travel, business meals
6360	Entertainment	When you take eBay's CEO out to dinner to benefit your eBay business
6370	Meals	Meals while traveling for your business
6390	Utilities	Major heading for the following subcategories
6391	Electricity and gas	Electricity and gas
6392	Water	Water
6560	Payroll expenses	Wages paid to others
6770	Supplies	Office supplies
6772	Computer	Computer and supplies
6780	Marketing	Advertising or promotional items you purchase to give away
6790	Office	Miscellaneous office expenses, such as bottled-water delivery
6820	Taxes	Major category for the following subcategories
6830	Federal	Federal taxes
6840	Local	Local taxes
6850	Property	Property taxes
6860	State	State taxes

Practice 37

Working with PayPal to Increase Your Bottom Line

If you're in the business of selling a product, you have to take credit cards, plain and simple. When you want to pay for something yourself, don't you often opt to pay with a credit card — even if the price of the item you want is a dollar or so more? Online shoppers loathe sending money orders (or even checks) to strangers these days. The protection a consumer gets from the credit card companies has been emblazoned on our brains by constant advertising. We equate using a credit card with safety. That's where PayPal comes in.

If you want more sales and higher bids, you need to make PayPal your first payment option.

 If you've read any of my books, you know I've been a huge fan of PayPal from the beginning. PayPal is one of the safest and least expensive ways for a vendor to accept money over the Internet. For a small retailer, PayPal fees can be much more cost-effective than a credit card merchant account (as I explain in the next section).

Understanding How PayPal Works

Joining PayPal is just the beginning. It doesn't give $10 bonuses for sign-ups any more, but the benefits far outweigh any fees charged to sellers. Also, there's no charge to send money to anyone. But if you plan on selling on eBay in earnest, you should know that as of 2008, all new eBay sellers, and sellers who sell items in high customer complaint categories must offer PayPal as a payment option. On the bright side? PowerSellers have unlimited protection coverage on their transactions (whether the buyer's shipping address is confirmed or not) and in many markets around the world.

 Before planning on a free ride from PayPal, always double-check the PayPal Web site (www.PayPal.com) for any changes in fees and policies.

You may have up to eight e-mail addresses registered with a PayPal account. Note, however, that you may not register an e-mail address if it's already registered with another PayPal account.

A little history

In the early days of eBay, a typical online auction was a scary place. You could send a check to your trading partner, but the wait for the product could be interminable. There was very little feedback in the beginning, so you couldn't separate the good sellers from the bad. The most widely accepted form of payment was a money order. Somehow, we weren't afraid, in our small (but growing) community, to send money orders to strangers. Heck, some sellers even shipped the merchandise *before* the payment was received! Things were a lot simpler, if riskier, in the old days.

A company called x.com came up with a convenient credit card service for online sellers. (They even gave you a $10 bonus to sign up.) The early eBay (née AuctionWeb) crowd signed up for this service quickly. x.com soon became the most widely used payment service on the Internet — the first mover-and-shaker in online, person-to-person payments.

The emerging eBay countered, acquiring a company called Billpoint during spring 1999 in hopes of launching its own payment service (in a partnership with Wells Fargo). In a disaster of bad timing, the service was not available to eBay members until the second quarter of 2000. Meanwhile, newcomer PayPal (x.com reborn with a new name) was growing by leaps and bounds — and quietly taking over the market.

PayPal went public in February 2002 to an encouraging Wall Street. The feud between PayPal and Billpoint heated up. The number of customers who signed up with Billpoint couldn't keep pace with the numbers joining PayPal. PayPal posted a profit, while Billpoint was losing millions every year.

In July 2002, eBay bit the bullet and acquired the massive PayPal in a deal valued at $1.5 billion. Billpoint was then simply phased out of the site.

Getting payments through PayPal

Your buyer can fund the money they send you via PayPal in several ways:

- **Instant Transfer:** Sending money this way means the money will be immediately credited to the recipient's account. That person can then transfer the money to his or her personal bank account without delay. Any buyer who wants to send a transfer must have a credit or debit card registered with PayPal as a backup for the funds — just in case the buyer's bank denies the transfer. It's like writing a very secure check — without exposing any personal information (such as a checking-account number) to another party.

- **eCheck:** Sending an eCheck isn't as "instant" as an Instant Transfer. As with writing a check from your checking account, it can take up to four days for the eCheck to clear. You don't need a backup source of funds when you use eCheck.

- **PayPal balance:** If someone has sent you money through PayPal — or if you've sold something on eBay and your buyer has paid you through PayPal — you will have an amount deposited to your PayPal account. This balance will first be applied to any purchases you make. Once there is no cash balance left in your account, *then* you can choose to pay by credit card. It's simplest to keep your books balanced if you withdraw any PayPal balance to your business checking account before you make a purchase.

- **Credit Card:** Charge it! Putting your PayPal purchases on a credit card is a good idea. Not only are you protected by PayPal, but your credit-card company also backs you up in the case of fraud.

You can register multiple credit cards on your PayPal account, and select a different one for different types of purchases. That way you can place any personal purchases on one credit card account and business purchases on another. It makes end-of-year bookkeeping a whole lot easier!

When you add a credit card to PayPal, you may be may be charged an Expanded Use enrollment fee. PayPal charges your credit card a small amount to prove that the credit card is really yours. A unique, randomly generated four-digit Expanded Use number is posted next to the charge. When you see the charge (it's quickest to check your online statement) go to

```
https://www.paypal.com/MEM-NUMBER
```

and type in the four-digit number. Your new card will be registered. Once you send out a payment through PayPal, the fee (just a few cents) is credited back to your PayPal account.

Figuring out the payment types

PayPal also breaks types of payments into categories based on what you're paying for. You can pay for almost anything in the world on the PayPal system (as long as the recipient has an e-mail address).

After signing into their PayPal account, customers click the Send Money tab and have several ways to send money through PayPal:

- ✔ **eBay Items:** When your buyers pay for an eBay item they bought from you, they simply click through from the item page. Each item number (along with each buyer's eBay User ID) appears automatically on the record so the payment will integrate directly with the seller's statements.

- ✔ **Goods:** Buyers can use this option when they need to send money to anyone in the world for goods purchased anywhere other than in an online auction. As an eBay PowerSeller, you can use the option when someone wants to purchase additional items from your Web site, or if a repeat customer e-mails you and says she wants to order additional items.

- ✔ **Service/Other:** You can also make a payment for a service performed for you or your business, such as Web design, bookkeeping, psychic readings, or whatever.

✔ **Cash Advance:** Use this when you need to send money to your kid in college (or pay back your roommate for saving you from great embarrassment when you left your wallet at home on a double date).

 When using the Cash Advance feature, consider using a payment method other than your credit card to avoid possible credit card fees for a cash advance.

Comprehending PayPal's Accounts

PayPal has three different types of accounts to accommodate everyone from the casual seller to the professional business.

PayPal Personal Account

When you begin your career with PayPal, you may want to sign up for a Personal Account. With this basic account from PayPal, you can send and receive money for free. Should you wish to occasionally receive a credit or debit card payment, you're limited to a prescribed number of credit card payments received per year; each is assessed a transaction fee. The current transaction fee for Personal accounts is 4.9% + $0.30 USD (limit of five transactions per 12-month period) for domestic or U.S. transactions. To view your current limit, log in to your Personal Account and click the View Limits link. After you reach your yearly limit, PayPal requires that you upgrade to a Premier or Business account.

A Personal Account also has a receiving limit on payments. This amount is established by PayPal at the time you open the account, and that figure is reset monthly. Your receiving limit is for Goods and eBay items, any other money sent to you (say, a little cash from Mom) doesn't count toward the total.

PayPal Personal Accounts are for one person only and not for a business. You cannot have a joint Personal Account, either.

Business and Premier Accounts

The PayPal professional seller accounts allow you to accept credit (and debit) card payments, get a debit card, and participate in PayPal's high-yield money-market fund. A Premier Account can be held in an individual's name (although it may still be for a business); a Business Account is held in a business name and allows multiple login names.

You can use the features of a Premier or full-on Business Account to:

- Send money

- Request money

- Use PayPal's Auction Tools

- Make Web-site payments

- Use your name or a corporate name, DBA, or Sole Proprietor name

- Accept unlimited credit or debit card payments

- Apply your own Payment Receiving Preferences

- Accept payments for subscriptions

- Accept mass payments

- Download monthly statements

- Allow multi-user access (for Business accounts)

- Download advanced transaction logs

After you reach these account levels, you'll have access to a toll-free customer service phone number as well as all the PayPal tools I discuss in the other practices (for example, the Buy Now buttons, Shopping cart, and so on in Practice 38).

There is a fee levied on all money you receive through PayPal at these levels, but the costs are reasonable. (Just ask anyone with a brick-and-mortar business that accepts credit cards.)

 All U.S. Premier and Business accounts that receive more than $2,000 a month in payments through PayPal have an additional requirement: Holders of such accounts must supply PayPal with additional information about their businesses.

PayPal has two levels of rates, a Merchant Rate and a Standard Rate. When you open your account, you will be charged the Standard Rate. When your sales grow and you've been receiving over $1,000 per month through PayPal for three consecutive months, you can apply for a Merchant Rate as shown in Table 37-1.

TABLE 37-1: PAYPAL TRANSACTION FEES

Monthly Sales	Price per transaction
$0 to $3000.00	2.9 percent + $.30
$3,000.01 to $10,000.00	2.5 percent + $.30
$10,000.01 to $100,000.00	2.2 percent + $.30
More than $100,000.00	1.9 percent + $.30

The numbers in Table 37-1 do not apply when you use Virtual Terminal or Website Payments Pro. For information on these services, check out Practice 38.

In Table 37-2 you can see how the PayPal fees stack up in foreign currencies.

TABLE 37-2: PAYPAL INTERNATIONAL CURRENCY TRANSACTION FEES

Payment Currency	Merchant Rate	Standard Rate
U.S. Dollars	2.2 percent + $.30 US	2.9 percent + $.30 US
Canadian Dollars	2.7 percent + $.55 CA	3.4 percent + $.55 CA
Euros	2.7 percent + €.35	3.4 percent + €.35

Payment Currency	Merchant Rate	Standard Rate
Pounds Sterling	2.7 percent + £.20	3.4 percent + £.20
Yen	2.7 percent + ¥40	3.4 percent + ¥40

 If you receive a payment from a buyer in another country, your payment will have an additional fee. The monies in will convert at the current exchange rate and an additional 2.5% fee is levied.

38 Practice

Payment Options for Your Web Site

In This Practice

- Discovering all the merchant options

- Integrating PayPal Web-site services

- Getting an additional merchant account

Yᴏᴜ already know that I'm a huge fan of PayPal. Allowing customers to pay with credit cards can boost the sales of any online business by as much as 30 percent. I suspect that percentage is actually higher because a definite trust issue takes over once buyers are comfortable paying for online purchases with credit cards. I won't buy from an eBay seller if I can't pay with a credit card — and I'm not alone.

According to what I've read on the Internet, businesses can lose up to 80 percent of impulse buys if they don't accept credit cards. Many eBay purchases *are* impulse buys. You know how it goes. You start to search on eBay, then look for something else; then find an item you want to buy so you check the seller's store . . . and that leads to an unplanned impulse buy.

Breaking down the ways people pay for Internet purchases clearly demonstrates that credit cards are the key to successful online sales:

- Credit card online: 85%

- Check mailed: 10%

- Credit card via phone: 2%

- Credit card via mail: 1%

- Other method: 2%

If you think that PayPal is only for your eBay sales, think again! Before eBay purchased PayPal, approximately 15 percent of PayPal's revenues came from online gaming (read: gambling!). Since eBay took over in late 2002, PayPal no longer draws revenue from this sketchy area. And there's good news for us; today PayPal offers tools that you can use to process PayPal payments on your own personal or business Web sites.

Aside from your eBay auctions and Store, you can sell directly from your own Web site or from your AOL page. In time, as your business grows outside eBay to your own Web site, you'll find that using PayPal as your payment provider is a great deal. You pay the same transaction fees — to PayPal only — for processing your credit-card sales.

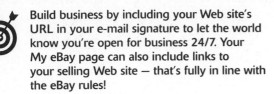

Build business by including your Web site's URL in your e-mail signature to let the world know you're open for business 24/7. Your My eBay page can also include links to your selling Web site — that's fully in line with the eBay rules!

In this practice, you discover how to make your own Web site an extra revenue builder. Remember, any sale you make from your own Web site involves no eBay fees — which means extra income for you.

Making the PayPal Payment Option Available on Your Site

Once you get a few items in your garage or business location that you stock in quantity, you've got the makings of your own online store. Don't let the thought of this creep you out. You *can* do this! PayPal has some solid options that *don't* require the assistance of a Web professional.

The first step for having your own online store (after you've set up an eBay Store, of course) is to create your Web site and get it running. After you do so, adding Buy Now buttons that link your site to PayPal is the most basic way to enable sales through PayPal from your site. These buttons are easy to insert — you don't have to be a rocket scientist to create the links — because PayPal makes this process almost automatic.

PayPal charges no fee to use these buttons other than their standard processing fees levied when someone buys an item. All you need is a Verified PayPal Premier or Business account.

Finding your way to PayPal Merchant Services

PayPal offers many ways to integrate its tools into your site, and you can find them in the Merchants area of the PayPal site:

1. Log on to your PayPal account.

2. Click the Merchant Services Tab on the main navigation bar.

    You'll arrive at the Merchant Services page where you can have your choice of options to integrate PayPal into your Web site, as shown in Figure 38-1.

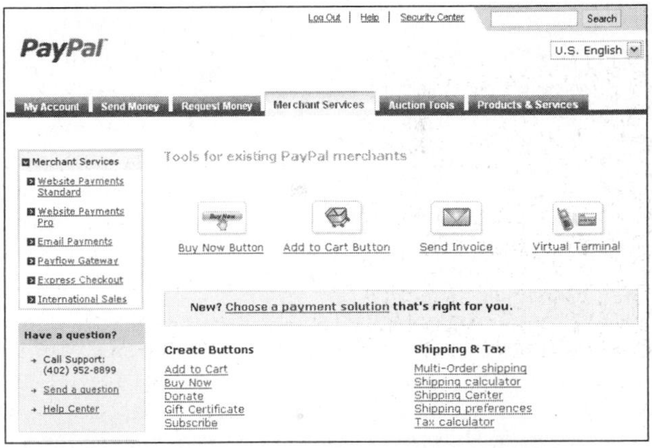

• **Figure 38-1: The PayPal Merchant Services page.**

What I'm about to show you is the easiest way to increase your revenues. Your Web site is the key to selling, and PayPal is the graphite that eases your way. On the Merchant Services page, you'll see several opportunities to easily work your site into a tree that grows business (and seems to grow money). These tools range from quite simple to more involved; the next sections describe them for you.

Incorporating Buy Now buttons

I must confess that I've relied on the Buy Now button for too long; it's just way too convenient. This button allows you to insert the graphic of your choice (six versions, as shown in Figure 38-2) directly into your page. If you like to get your hands into the code that makes it all happen, later on, I give it to you — but for now, check out PayPal's widget for an instant, no-coding-required Buy Now button.

• **Figure 38-2: The six basic Buy Now Button options.**

The Buy Now button integrates your site with PayPal, enabling buyers to purchase your item with a click of the mouse button — as in a page from my Web site, shown in Figure 38-3.

• **Figure 38-3: Click here and buy it NOW!**

When the buyer clicks the Buy Now button, a confirmation page appears; there the buyer can click through to a direct payment-by-PayPal experience. You may be surprised to know that often the folks who click that button are fairly new buyers to the online scene — and that this will be their first payment sent using PayPal.

To build your Buy Now button using PayPal's ultra-handy widget, follow these steps:

1. **Click the Buy Now Button link on the Merchant Services page.**

You'll arrive at the Buy Now buttons customization form.

2. **Type in a name for your item.**

Give your item a short name to appear on the Confirmation page. This name is not like an eBay Title, which must be optimized for keywords, but instead, needs to concisely identify your item.

3. **Optionally, assign an item number to your product.**

If you use *SKUs* (Stock Keeping Unit numbers — an identification number assigned to each item you have in stock) you can use them here. Also, if you keep track of your inventory by *UPCs* (Universal Product Codes) and *ISBNs* (International Standard Book Number, for media), you can input them here. If you don't, no worries. Just skip this step; it's optional.

4. **Fill in the next box with the item's selling price.**

Be sure to select your currency from the drop-down list below the Selling Price box (the defaults is U.S. dollars).

5. **Optionally, type in the weight of the item in its package ready to mail.**

Inserting the packaged item weight enables you to offer calculated shipping charges for your item. You may find that a flat rate is more convenient when you use the Buy Now buttons. Calculating shipping charges is not required; so as long as your item isn't huge, you can skip this step.

6. **Select your choice for a Buy Now button by clicking the radio button to its left.**

If you have your own "custom" Buy Now button that you choose to use, you can click the link to insert it into the code.

7. **Decide on whether you want to encrypt your button.**

If you choose to encrypt your buttons for security's sake, you won't be able to use option fields, edit the HTML, or create e-mail links. PayPal promises to release a new version of the tool soon, which will allow you to encrypt buttons while still keeping these dynamic options. For now, if you have no intention of customizing the buying experience, I recommend that you choose to encrypt. Personally, I don't; instead, I simply edit one bit of code and insert it into my various items for sale.

8. **Select how you want your shipping calculated.**

If you have a flat shipping rate for each item, type that number in the box. If you want the items calculated by weight, set up your shipping options in your Profile and click that box.

 If you have items that cannot be shipped in the same box, you may want to use the flat-rate option. Otherwise you may end up not assigning enough money to ship to a customer who orders more than one item.

9. **Indicate you how want to apply sales tax.**

You can type in a flat amount, but if you sell from within the United States, odds are you don't need to charge sales tax to all buyers. But to be on the safe side, check the sales-tax information in Practice 43 one more time. Then (again) go to your Profile and indicate which states need to be charged sales tax. (Usually, those will be only the states you're selling from — the ones from which you ship.)

10. **Choose to Create Button or Add Options.**

For a better buyer experience, select Add Options.

Adding options to your Buy Now button truly makes your Web site look professional. You can set up such important functions as these:

▶ **Adding option fields.** If your item has variations, such as color or size, your buyers will be able to make the selections that fit their orders.

▶ **Customizing the payment pages.** Enables you to design your own page or customize the standard PayPal page with your Web site's logo.

▶ **Customizing the buyer experience.** Assigns a special page on your Web site for the customer to return to after completing payment. According to PayPal policy, the return page must let buyers know that the payment has

been made, the transaction has been completed, and details of the payment transaction will follow in an e-mail.

Now you can set up two kinds of pages:

▶ **Payment Landing Page**: If you want your customers to land on a specific page after they've made a payment — for example, setting up a thank-you page on your Web site is a nice idea — you enter that URL here. The page also has links to take the buyer back to your Web site.

▶ **Cancel Transaction Page:** If you want to include a page to which people are taken if they cancel the transaction before completing it, you can insert that address here. If you don't specify a page, they will land at a PayPal Web page.

▶ **Transferring payment data.** Allows you to receive notice once a payment has been made.

▶ **Offering PayPal Account (Optional).** Allows buyers who are new to PayPal to sign up and pay you (a very important option).

▶ **Soliciting a contact telephone number**. Requires buyers to supply their telephone numbers so you can contact them about their purchases.

Expanding with Add To Cart buttons

When you have many items to sell, expanding your site with Add to Cart buttons makes the shopping experience even easier. It works just like the cart in the supermarket (without the wobbly wheel): Buyers can push their virtual carts through your Web site and use the shopping-cart buttons to add items one by one.

As a result, you end up with one (hopefully large) order. The easy-to-use Add to Cart button (see Figure 38-4) encourages customers to buy more — and allows them to review the shopping cart before they finalize payment.

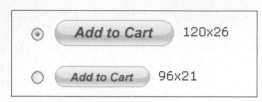

• **Figure 38-4:** The fairly boring Add to Cart buttons. I'd prefer a picture of a little shopping cart (but that's me).

To set up your cart buttons, the procedure is strikingly similar to creating Buy Now buttons. The selections and options are the same. Click the Add to Cart Button link (see Figure 38-5) and you're on your way.

• **Figure 38-5:** Click the Add to Cart Button link to get started.

PayPal's Virtual Terminal

If your eBay business is bringing in more than $10,000 a month, PayPal's Virtual Terminal merchant service may be for you. PayPal's Virtual Terminal sets you up to accept credit cards — not only through PayPal, but also on the phone from a supplied credit card. It's the big time. It's the same as having a *merchant account* (explained in the upcoming section "Having a Merchant Account"), except PayPal (instead of the bank or clearinghouse) is your payment provider.

You don't run into contracts or minimums when using this Virtual Terminal service — use it as much or as little as you wish. Costs for using the Virtual Terminal (a monthly service fee plus transaction charges, shown in Table 38-1) are surprisingly cheaper than the costs involved with a merchant account.

 With PayPal's Virtual Terminal service, you have unlimited transactions and do not have a minimum or maximum (as you do with a merchant account).

TABLE 38-1: FEES FOR PAYPAL VIRTUAL TERMINAL

Monthly Sales	Per Transaction	Per Month
$0.00 - $3,000.00	3.1% + $0.30	$30.00
$3,000.01- $10,000.00	2.7% + $0.30	$30.00
>$10,000.00	2.4% + $0.30	$30.00

That's it — there are no other fees involved. You must contact PayPal to set up the online interface should you wish to make the jump to this service.

 Direct Payment and Virtual Terminal transactions are not covered by PayPal's seller-protection policies and programs.

Having a Merchant Account

Before you decide whether to get an independent Merchant Account, I recommend looking at the costs carefully. Using PayPal's Virtual Terminal keeps all your payment services in one place. As an eBay merchant, you'll still be receiving payments through PayPal, and receiving payments from an additional provider may make your business far more complex than necessary. I regularly get e-mails begging me to set up my own Merchant Account, and each one offers lower fees than the last. But such fees are often hard to calculate — and even harder to compare. Charges are buried in the small print. Even those who advertise low fees often don't deliver. Be sure to look at the entire picture before you sign a long-term contract.

The best place to begin looking for a merchant account may be your own bank. Your bank knows you, your credit history, and your business reputation, and has a vested interest in the success of your business. If, for whatever reason, your credit isn't up to snuff, I recommend building good credit before pursuing a merchant account; as your business grows, your credit rating is your feedback to the offline world.

f your bank doesn't offer merchant accounts for nternet-based businesses, find a broker to evaluate your credit history and hook you up with a bank that fits your needs and business style. (An easier option may be to join Costco, as detailed in the following section.) These brokers make their money from your application fee, from a finder's fee at the bank that you finally choose, or from both.

After you get a bank, you'll be connected to a *processor* (a clearinghouse for transactions). Your bank merely handles the banking; the clearinghouse is on the other end of your Internet connection when you're processing transactions, checking whether the credit card you're taking is valid — in particular, making sure it's not stolen or maxed out.

The next step is setting up your *gateway,* the software (ICVerify or PCAuthorize, for example) with which you transmit charges to the clearinghouse. Some gateways use HTML Web sites and take the transactions directly on Web-based forms (Cybercash or VeriFone, among others). Web-based gateways connect your Web forms to credit-card processing in real time.

Checking out the cost of merchant accounts

In Table 38-2, I highlight various *possible* costs associated with setting up and maintaining a merchant account. Remember that not all merchant accounts will pass on these charges. Some may charge just a few such fees; others may take a whole bunch of little snipes at your wallet.

TABLE 38-2: *POSSIBLE* INTERNET MERCHANT ACCOUNT FEES

Fee	Average Amount
Setup fee	$25–$250
Monthly processing fee to bank	2.5% (1.5%–5%)
Fee per transaction	$.20–$.50
Processor's fee per transaction	$.35–$.50
Internet discount rate	2%–4%
Monthly statement fees	$9–$15
Monthly minimum processing fee	$15–$30
Gateway processing monthly fee	$20–$40
Application fees	$50–$500
Software purchase	$350–$1000
Software lease	$25 per month
Chargeback fee	$15

In the following list, I define some of the fees listed in Table 38-2:

- **Setup fee:** A one-time cost that you pay to your bank or your broker.

- **Discount rate:** A percentage of the transaction amount (a discount from your earnings that goes to the bank), taken off the top along with the transaction fee before the money is deposited into your account.

- **Address Verification Service (AVS):** A separate processing service that cross-checks your customers' credit-card numbers with their mailing addresses. (This is already part of PayPal's services.)

- **Transaction fee:** A per-transaction fee paid to the bank or to your gateway; the fee pays for the network.

- **Gateway or processing fee:** Your fee that's paid to the Internet gateway for processing credit cards in real time.

✔ **Application fee:** A one-time fee that goes to the broker (or perhaps to the bank).

✔ **Monthly minimum processing fee:** If your bank's cut of your purchases doesn't add up to this amount, the bank takes it anyway. For example, if your bank charges a minimum monthly fee of $20, and you don't hit $20 in fees because your sales aren't high enough, the bank charges you the difference.

Costco member's credit-card processing

You can indeed get true discount credit-card processing — a one-stop merchant account and gateway in one! With a Costco membership, not only can you buy a case of giant-size cans of tuna fish, but you can also obtain a reasonably priced way to handle a merchant account through the Nova Network.

Costco has gotten together with Nova Information Systems, one of the nation's largest processors of credit card transactions, to offer Costco executive members a Internet credit-card processing service at a discount. (See Table 38-3 for a list of associated fees.) Costco executive membership brings the cost of a Costco membership up from $45 to $100, but you get the benefit of receiving 2 percent back for most purchases (not including tobacco, gas, food, and some other items).

TABLE 38-3: FEES FOR COSTCO INTERNET CREDIT-CARD PROCESSING

Fee	Amount
Discount rate per mail order/Internet transaction to Nova	1.99%
Per-transaction fee to Nova	$ .27
Monthly Fee	$4.95
Application Fee	$25.00
Nova monthly fees minimum	$20.00

Keep these few things in mind about the fees shown in Table 38-3:

✔ You will need a gateway to use this service, whether in the form of software or a paid relationship with a gateway service.

✔ Rates for American Express cards, debit cards, and corporate purchasing cards may vary.

✔ Both the Monthly Fee and the Application Fee are waived for Costco Executive Members.

To get any Internet commerce account, you should already have the following:

✔ Products and pricing

✔ A return and refund policy in place

✔ An active customer service phone number

✔ Posted delivery methods and shipment time

✔ A privacy policy stating that you will not share your customers' information with another entity

✔ A registered domain in your name or your business name

✔ A secure order page with https and lock icon

To apply for a merchant account through Costco, follow these steps:

1. **Go to** www.costco.com **and click the Services link at the top of the home page.**

2. **On the resulting page, scroll to the Services for your Business area and click the link for Merchant Credit Card Processing.**

3. **Read the information and, if all sounds good, click the Apply Now link.**

4. **On the resulting application page, enter your Costco Executive Membership number and fill out and submit the secure form.**

Filling out the form online speeds up the application process. After sending your form, you'll receive a full application package via two-day air. A Costco representative will also contact you by telephone. For further information or to apply by phone, call Costco Member Services at 800-551-0951 and mention promotion code 83500.

PayPal Coding — Creating Your Buttons and Cart

To install a shopping cart on your site for multiple items, it's often easier to just put this code into a Notepad window and edit it individually for each item you want to sell.

Here's the code you can use and edit to create a Shopping Cart button (in the example I used my book *eBay For Dummies,* you'd put your item name in that area). To use the button given here for multiple items, you need to edit the values for three variables:

- Item_name
- Item_number
- Amount

```
< form name="_xclick" target="paypal"
   action="https://www.paypal.com"
   method="post">
   <input type="hidden" name="cmd"
   value="_cart">
   <input type="hidden" name="business"
   value="me@mybusiness.com">
   <input type="hidden"
   name="currency_code" value="USD">
   <input type="hidden"
   name="item_name" value="eBay For
   Dummies">
   <input type="hidden" name="amount"
   value="18.99">
   <input type="image"
   src="http://www.paypal.com/en_US/i/
   btn/btn_cart_LG.gif" border="0"
   name="submit" alt="Make payments
   with PayPal - it's fast, free and
   secure!">
   <input type="hidden" name="add"
   value="1">
</form>
```

To set up your View Cart button (for people to use when they're ready to check out), this code will do it:

```
< form name="_xclick" target="paypal"
   action="https://www.paypal.com/us/c
   gi-bin/webscr" method="post">
   <input type="hidden" name="cmd"
   value="_cart">
   <input type="hidden" name="business"
   value="me@mybusiness.com">
   <input type="image"
   src="https://www.paypal.com/en_US/i
   /btn/view_cart_new.gif" border="0"
   name="submit" alt="Make payments
   with PayPal - it's fast, free and
   secure!">
   <input type="hidden" name="display"
   value="1">
</form>
```

Adding a PayPal Buy Now Button to Your AOL Hometown Page

The procedure for adding a payment button for AOL users is pretty easy. And what's better than making money from your own free Web page!

Here's how to insert your button:

1. **Sign in to your AOL Hometown account.**

2. **Click the Edit My Pages link.**

3. **Select the page to which you want to add the Buy Now button.**

4. **Click the Insert button on the toolbar.**

5. **Select Advanced HTML.**

   A dialog box appears; here's where you put your HTML code.

6. **Copy the HTML code generated by the button factory (or your own homemade coding, as I show you in the previous section), and paste it into the text box.**

7. **Click Save.**

   You can type the URL into the browser to have it go test your page.

Practice 39

It's All About PayPal Protection

In This Practice

✔ Understanding PayPal Protection Plans

✔ Protecting the seller

✔ Protecting the buyer

It seems that the longer I write about eBay and e-commerce, the louder a recurring theme seems to sound: *Protection*. The more we do business in the cyber-world, the more protection we need to keep our privacy safe: to keep us safe from scammers and to see that our hard-earned money remains in our pockets. (See Practice 33 for information on how to avoid identity theft.) This practice is about how PayPal protects the seller and the buyer when using their services for payment processing.

Both buyers and sellers get protection when using PayPal — and PowerSellers deal with both sides of that equation. So the first order of business is to see how sellers are protected in transactions done through PayPal.

PayPal Seller Protection

PayPal wants to protect sellers, so they will continue to process their payments through the system. It's a simple fact of business — keeping your customers safe helps keep your business safe. To PayPal, the Seller is the customer. Of course, you also have some protection against unwarranted claims made on your eBay sales; it's called Seller Protection. (More about that in a minute.)

To check out the buyers, PayPal confirms through AVS (Address Verification Service) that the buyer's credit card billing address matches the shipping address; PayPal gives you the option not to accept payments from buyers whose addresses don't match. Under certain circumstances, PayPal offers Seller protection against spurious *chargebacks* (the credit-card equivalent of what happens when a check bounces; see the sidebar "Understanding the chargeback" later in this practice). Here's the list of possible situations:

✔ **Credit-card chargebacks from fraudulent card use**. If payment is made with a stolen or fake credit card and PayPal processes the payment, you will not be held responsible.

✔ **Credit-card chargebacks for false claims of non-delivery.** If a buyer takes delivery and then complains to his or her credit-card company that you didn't send the item and the company refunds the money to the customer, you won't have to pay the company. PayPal will let you keep your money — provided you can prove delivery (see below).

✔ **Buyer complaints for false claims of non-delivery.** Whining to PayPal that (for example) the nonexistent kid next door took the package won't do would-be scammers any good if your transaction is covered.

What doesn't it cover?

✔ **"Significantly Not as Described" chargeback claims.** When a buyer receives your item and decides what you sent isn't what they thought they bought. (A word to the wise: You'd better send what you pictured.)

✔ **Transactions to some International buyers.** You're not covered for international transactions to some markets. To see a current list of countries covered, visit the PayPal site.

To be protected under the standard protection program, a seller must fulfill a few requirements. Here's the list:

PayPal no longer holds PowerSellers to the confirmed address rule. Any item sold on eBay can be sent to any address in the PayPal system. For PowerSellers, *any* address from PayPal is considered a confirmed address.

✔ **You must have a verified business or premier account:** You must have an upper-level PayPal account to be covered.

✔ **You must ship to a confirmed address:** You must ship to the buyer's address exactly what you displayed on the transaction details page, The payment must indicated as Seller Protection Policy Eligible on the Transaction Detail page.

✔ **You must ship within 7 days:** The item must leave your place of business within 7 days of receiving payment.

✔ **You must accept single payment from a single account:** You must have accepted one payment from one PayPal account to pay for the purchase. (No multiple-account payments are allowed for an item).

✔ **You must ship tangible goods:** Seller protection is not available for services, digital goods (e-books, software, music), and other electronically delivered items.

✔ **You must provide proof of shipping:** You need to provide reasonable proof-of-shipment that can be tracked online. The transaction-details page must show that you shipped the item to the buyer's address. A delivery confirmation suffices for items valued up to $250.

If you use an automated shipping solution other than PayPal, you also just copy and paste the delivery-confirmation numbers onto the PayPal page. PayPal will send an e-mail to the buyer with the information for their records.

For items worth $250.00 or more (£150.00 or more for the U.K.), you must have a signature from the recipient as proof of receipt. If the item was paid in a currency other than U.S. dollars, the amounts shown in Table 39-1 apply.

TABLE 39-1: SIGNATURE RECEIPT REQUIREMENTS BY COUNTRY

Country	Value Requiring Receipt
Canadian Dollars	$325.00 CAD
Euros	€200.00 EUR
British Pounds	£150.00 GBP
Japanese Yen	¥28000.00 JPY
Australian Dollars	$350.00 AUD

(continued)

TABLE 39-1 *(continued)*

Country	Value Requiring Receipt
Swiss Francs	330.00 CHF
Norwegian Kroner	1,600.00 NOK
Swedish Kronor	2,000.00 SEK
Danish Kroner	1,500.00 DKK
Polish Zlotych	800.00 PLN
Hungarian Forint	55000.00 huf
Czech Koruna	6,000.00 CZK
Singapore Dollars	$400.00 SGD
Hong Kong Dollars	$2,000.00 HKD
New Zealand Dollars	$380.00 NZD

✔ **You must not impose surcharges:** Imposing a surcharge on the buyer is against eBay policy anyway.

✔ **You must cooperate with the complaint investigation:** If a complaint is filed, you must provide complete information about the transaction within from the time specified by PayPal.

 If PayPal is required by the buyer's issuing credit-card company to respond immediately to resolve a chargeback situation, you must provide all information within 3 days.

At this writing, Seller Protection is available for PowerSellers for most countries internationally. There are some restrictions, so please check the PayPal site for updates in this policy.

To see whether your transaction is covered under Seller Protection, follow these steps:

1. **In your payment received e-mail from PayPal, click the link titled View the Details of the Transaction.**

2. **Sign in to your PayPal account.**

3. **Scroll down the Transaction Details page to the buyer's shipping address.**

You'll see whether the shipping address is confirmed. (PayPal confirms the address by making sure that the credit card billing address matches the shipping address). If it is, you must ship to that address to be protected.

When your transaction is protected, you won't lose the money should any fraud be involved (such as a stolen credit card or identity hoax). PayPal guarantees the transaction.

 If you receive a PayPal payment that specifies shipping the item to an unconfirmed address, drop the buyer a note and ask about the address. Usually you'll get a reply that makes you feel comfortable, and you'll ship. Remember that you will not be covered under Seller Protection if you ship to an unconfirmed address.

The Seller Protection Policy is limited to the following payout amounts per year for combined eligible Chargebacks and Reversals (note that the combined annual total may not exceed the limit for any one currency):

✔ $5,000.00 USD

✔ $6,500.00 CAD

✔ €4,000.00 EUR

✔ £3,250.00 GBP

The good news? PowerSellers in the United States no longer have the $5,000 limit per year.

 If a buyer initiates a Dispute/Claim and the amount in dispute is greater than $100, PayPal will place the disputed amount (to the extent it remains in the seller's Account) on hold until the Dispute/Claim is resolved. That means the seller can't withdraw this amount while the Dispute/ Claim remains unresolved.

Understanding the chargeback

A buyer who disputes a sale can simply call either PayPal or the issuing credit card company and refuse to pay for the item. If that happens, you lose the sale — and you may not be able to retrieve your merchandise. A payment service or merchant account will then *chargeback* your account — that is, withdraw money out of your account to pay for the item — without contacting you, and without any negotiating. Technically, the buyer has made the purchase *from the payment service* — not from you — and the payment service won't defend you. I've heard of these chargebacks occurring as long as two months after the transaction. And no one is standing at your side, forcing the buyer to ship the merchandise back to you. The credit card companies skew the rules to defend the consumer; as the seller, you have to fend for yourself. You usually have no way to verify that the shipping address is actually the one that the credit card bills go to. So, to add to your problems, the card may actually be stolen.

If the issuing bank resolves a chargeback in the buyer's favor, PayPal charges you $10 if you are found to be at fault — but will waive the fee if you meet all the requirements of the PayPal Seller Protection Policy (as outlined earlier in this practice).

Here's some good news: Major credit card companies are trying to curb online fraud for their merchant accounts. Visa has the new Verified by Visa acceptance, which takes buyers to a Visa screen (through software installed on the merchant's server) and verifies their identities through a Visa-only password. MasterCard uses SET (Secure Electronic Transactions), a similar (and encrypted) transaction-verification scheme. These systems are expected to substantially reduce fraud and chargebacks.

PayPal Buyer Protection

Buyers who pay with PayPal are covered under the terms of its fraud-protection program. Tangible items sold on eBay that can be shipped (and are paid through PayPal) are covered to $200. (Intangibles, such as services, licenses, and other access to digital content — e-books, for example — aren't covered.)

As a buyer who pays for his or her eBay items through PayPal, you can be covered against fraud for up to $2,000. But there's a catch: There are two levels of protection. At the standard level, you're protected up to $200 worth of item value. Some sellers' items (considered "top-tier" sellers) are covered to the full $2,000 worth of value. The amount at which your sales are covered is indicated at the bottom of the Meet the Seller area on each listing page, as in Figure 39-1.

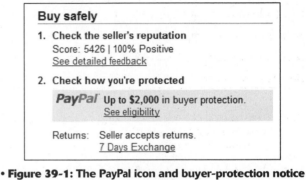

• **Figure 39-1: The PayPal icon and buyer-protection notice in one of my listings.**

In this protection program, *fraud* is loosely defined as non-delivery of items or when you receive an item that's significantly different from the way it was described. Sorry — this doesn't cover you when you're merely disappointed with an item when you open the box.

 When you're browsing eBay, you'll notice that some listings have the PayPal icon that identifies sellers who accept PayPal as payment. Those who don't accept PayPal have no icon.

Following are a few rules for using the buyer-protection system and making claims:

✔ **Number of claims:** You may make only one claim per PayPal payment. (If you pay for multiple items at once, your total claim may not be more than $500.) On a good note, there is no limit on the number of PayPal Buyer Protection claim refunds.

✔ **Timing:** Your claim must be made within 30 days of your PayPal payment.

✔ **Participation:** You must be ready and willing to provide information and documentation to PayPal's Buyer Protection team during the claims process.

 The plan covers only fraud, not damaged packages. The United States Postal Service offers insurance as an option, so I guess this means if your package arrives damaged and isn't insured, the buyer is out of luck and you're going to get some bad feedback unless you make things right. Decide for yourself whether you're willing to take on that risk.

To save you a little time, you can call PayPal, 24/7 at 1-402-935-2050 or 1-402-935-7733. If you have a business or Premier account, you will have a toll-free number on the PayPal contact page once you have logged into your account.

Practice 40

Getting Transaction History from PayPal

Downloading reports from PayPal can save your bacon. After you run a business for a while, you lose some of your "gung-ho." You know what you're supposed to do on a daily basis, but somehow other responsibilities (or maybe even opportunities for fun) get in the way. It's normal. It's what happens. But by downloading reports from PayPal (and backing them up to an external hard drive), you are archiving the actual data that you should have now and will need in the future.

I've been running a home-based business for close to 20 years. Because I came from a corporate background working in the newspaper business, I've always known that recordkeeping is important. Even so, recordkeeping has always been an ongoing bane of my existence. When I began my home-based business, one of my first tasks was to hire a lawyer and a CPA to teach me what I had to do to satisfy the paperwork gods. But even now that I "know" what to do, doing it often falls by the wayside.

Recordkeeping means keeping track of everything: every penny, sou, farthing, or ruble that you spend or take in. Here in the United States (and in most other countries), we have a little thing called taxes. We all have to turn in tax returns of several sorts when we run a business — and they'd better be correct. There may come a day in the near (or hopefully, far) future when we, as online businesspeople, will receive a letter from a state or federal tax agency asking to take a look at our books. This is simply a nice way of saying the dreaded word AUDIT.

 The best defense against an audit is to have backup records. The more records you have proving your business income and expenses, the less painful your audit will be. One excellent piece of information to have at your fingertips is your PayPal history.

Besides meeting tax-reporting requirements, keeping good records helps you stay on top of your business dealings. (See Practice 41 for more about how good recordkeeping — and the resulting reports you get — can help your business succeed.) PayPal helps you with this all-important recordkeeping by providing customizable, downloadable reports on your buying and selling activity.

PayPal's Downloadable Reports

PayPal allows you to customize and download your transaction reports at any time. You might want to consider downloading your reports on a monthly or quarterly basis — as well as generating one big report at the end of the year. You may want to download the reports to coincide with your state sales-tax payments (for backup documentation) or to keep a record of your monthly totals.

You can download reports in several formats. The most flexible of these, however, is a comma-delimited file that can be opened and edited in a spreadsheet program, such as Excel or Microsoft Works.

 If you use a spreadsheet file as your record of customers, you won't bog down a bookkeeping program with hundreds (and eventually thousands) of records of one-time buyers. Even a robust program like QuickBooks will max out at around 14,000 customers!

Starting the Download from PayPal

To get your reports from PayPal, go to www.PayPal.com and log on to your Premier or Business account. After you're logged on, the navigation bar displays various tabs, as shown in Figure 40-1.

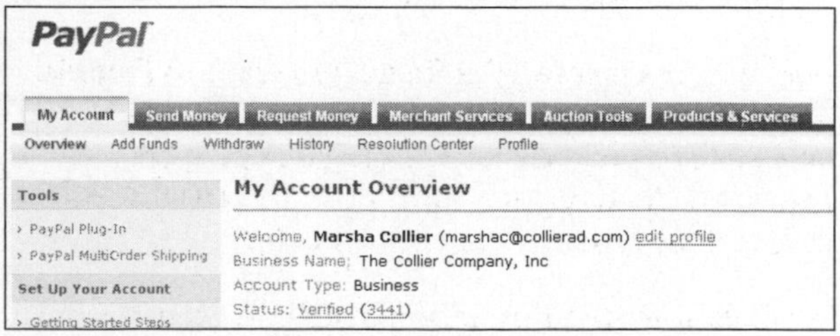

• **Figure 40-1: The PayPal navigation tab bar.**

Now follow these steps:

1. Roll your mouse cursor over the History link below the tabs of the main navigation bar.

2. Click the Download History link from the drop-down menu that appears.

You are now in your Download History area. Here you select the date span for your report, as shown in Figure 40-2.

3. Click the Download History link.

You now land on the Download History page. Before you start clicking, however, consider customizing your reports.

4. If you choose to customize your reports, click the Customize Download Fields link on the right.

I highly recommend customizing because PayPal will give you more data than you really need. (I'm not likely, for example, to care much about the comments the buyer made when the payment was processed.) Remember, however, that Time and PayPal Transaction Number are default fields; you'll receive them regardless.

See the next section for more about your choices.

5. If you decide not to customize, you can skip ahead to the steps in the section "Doing the Actual Download (Finally!)."

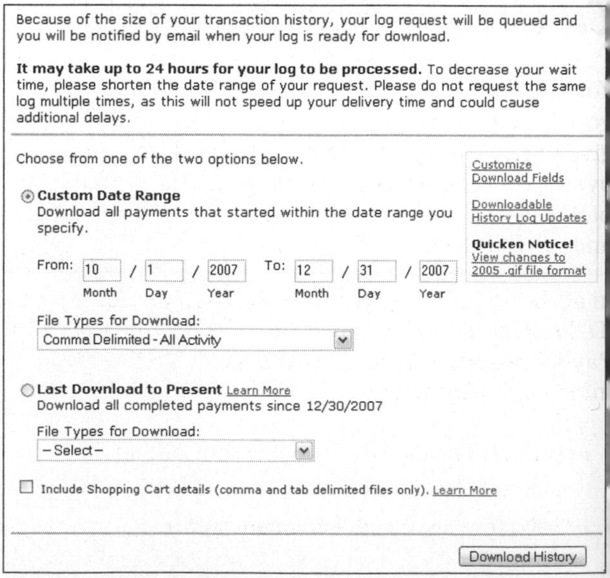

Because of the size of your transaction history, your log request will be queued and you will be notified by email when your log is ready for download.

It may take up to 24 hours for your log to be processed. To decrease your wait time, please shorten the date range of your request. Please do not request the same log multiple times, as this will not speed up your delivery time and could cause additional delays.

Choose from one of the two options below.

⊙ **Custom Date Range**
Download all payments that started within the date range you specify.

From: 10 / 1 / 2007   To: 12 / 31 / 2007
Month Day Year   Month Day Year

File Types for Download:
Comma Delimited - All Activity

○ **Last Download to Present** Learn More
Download all completed payments since 12/30/2007
File Types for Download:
— Select —

☐ Include Shopping Cart details (comma and tab delimited files only). Learn More

Customize Download Fields

Downloadable History Log Updates

Quicken Notice!
View changes to 2005 .qif file format

Download History

• **Figure 40-2: Selecting your history report's date span.**

Accessing monthly, weekly, and daily sales reports

A little-known feature of PayPal is that you can access sales reports if you really need them. Technically, if you input your sales into QuickBooks, you'll be able to pull up those reports directly from your bookkeeping program. Until you're all set up, you can view the reports online — and here's how to get there easily:

1. Roll your mouse cursor over the History link below the tabs.

2. Click the Reports link from the drop-down menu that appears.

You are now in your Business Overview area; below your Weekly Sales Links you'll see a box entitled Reports.

The Weekly Sales links can also give you good information. By clicking the active link for each week, you can pull up a Daily Sales report for each day of the week. The Daily Sales report also has active links that allow you to see your actual daily sales information, including the amount per sale, the buyer's e-mail address and another link — which will take you to the actual transaction.

Customizing Your Download

You may need *all* the information that PayPal gives you. If that's what you want, great. But PayPal can give you information overkill. I suggest you look over the following list of available info so you can pick and choose the fields you want to download and keep in your permanent records.

In addition to Transaction ID, Reference Transaction ID, Receipt ID, and Balance, all your downloadable PayPal reports will contain at least the following information by default:

✔ **Date:** The date each PayPal transaction occurred.

✔ **Time:** The time the payment was made.

✔ **Time Zone:** The time zone used for recording transactions in your PayPal account.

✔ **Name:** The name of the person to whom you sent money or from whom you received money.

✔ **Type:** The type of transaction that occurred: Deposit, Withdrawal, ATM Withdrawal, Payment Sent, Payment Received, and so on.

✔ **Status:** The status of the transaction at the time you download the file (Cleared, Completed, Denied, and so on).

✔ **Gross:** The Gross amount involved in the transaction (before any fees are deducted).

✔ **Fee:** Any PayPal fees charged to the transaction.

✔ **Net:** The net dollar amount of the transaction. (This is the total received, less any PayPal fees.)

✔ **From e-mail:** The e-mail address of the sender.

✔ **To e-mail:** The e-mail address of the recipient.

 If you use different e-mail addresses to classify different types of sales, this can be a good sorting point for your reports. For example, I receive payments for my personal auctions at one e-mail address and payments for my business at another.

PayPal has lots more data that you can have, too. You can set the options listed here separately for your eBay sales and your Web-site sales (where people use your PayPal Buy Now button to make a purchase) as shown in Figure 40-3.

After you've selected the fields you want to include (by selecting the check box next to the desired data), click Save. You find yourself back at the Download History page. Your custom settings will be saved for future report downloads.

If you want more information from one type of sale than from the other, you can set these options appropriately. Here are a few of the options.

✔ **Item ID:** This is that strange combination of letters and numbers that PayPal assigns to each transaction. If the payment is for an eBay auction, the Item ID will be the auction number. Decide whether this is important for your own records. (I don't use it.)

Customize My History Download

Check the boxes next to the fields you want to download. All checked fields will be included in your downloadable log.

Default Fields
Date, Time, Timezone, Name, Type, Status, Currency, Gross, Fee, Net, From Email Address, To Email Address, Transaction ID, Reference Transaction ID, Receipt ID, Balance

PayPal Website Payments
☑ Item ID
☑ Item Title
☑ Invoice Number
☑ Custom Number
☑ Shipping Amount
☑ Insurance Amount
☑ Single Column Shipping Address (Address will be displayed in a single column)
☑ Multi-Column Shipping Address (Address will be displayed in separate columns)
☑ Counter Party Status (Verified vs. Unverified)
☑ Address Status (Confirmed vs. Unconfirmed)
☑ Sales Tax
☑ Option Names and Values
☑ Contact Phone Number

Auction Payments
☑ Item ID
☑ Item Title
☑ Shipping Amount
☑ Insurance Amount
☑ Auction Site
☑ Buyer ID
☑ Item URL
☑ Closing Date
☑ Single Column Shipping Address (Address will be displayed in a single column)
☑ Multi-Column Shipping Address (Address will be displayed in separate columns)
☑ Counter Party Status (Verified vs. Unverified)
☑ Address Status (Confirmed vs. Unconfirmed)
☑ Sales Tax

Other Fields
☑ Subject
☑ Note
☑ Subscription Number
☑ Payment Type
☐ Balance Impact (Any transaction that affects account balance)

[Save] [Cancel]

• **Figure 40-3: Click the boxes on this page to indicate which data you want to show up in your reports.**

✔ **Item Title:** The title of the listing related to the transaction.

✔ **Shipping Amount:** The amount the buyer paid for shipping. It's a good idea to use this field, as it helps you to separate merchandise revenue from shipping revenue.

✔ **Auction Site:** If you're collecting money from other auction sites through PayPal, you might want to include this link so you can sort your sales by auction site.

✔ **Item URL:** The Internet address of the auction or transaction. (For eBay, the URLs are on the site for up to 90 days — here you can go back a year.)

✔ **Closing Date:** The date the transaction closed. The record will always contain the date the payment posted to your PayPal account, whether you indicate closing date here or not.

✔ **Single Column or Multi-Column Shipping Address:** The address to which the item was shipped, displayed in either one column of your spreadsheet or in multiple columns.

I've found the multi-column option to be best for me. It will allow me to sort my sale by state — that gives me a good picture of where my customers come from.

✔ **Counter Party Status (Verified versus Unverified):** A record of whether your buyer was PayPal-Verified.

✔ **Address Status (Confirmed versus Unconfirmed):** Shows whether the address you shipped to was confirmed.

✔ **Sales Tax:** Information about the sales tax you collected.

After you've selected the fields you want to include (by selecting the check box next to the desired data), click Save. You find yourself back at the Download History page. Your custom settings will be saved for future report downloads.

U.S. users read their dates with the month first, the day, and then the year; U.K. users read the day, the month, and then the year. Therefore, if you are a seller in the U.K., your Download History page will look slightly different from the one pictured; your dates will be in DD/MM/YY (day-month-year) format.

Doing the Actual Download (Finally!)

In the Download History page, follow these steps to download a report:

1. **Type in the dates that you'd like to have covered in the downloaded report.**

2. **Select a format for your download from the following:**

   ▶ **Comma-delimited file:** This type of file downloads with the extension .csv. You can easily open a comma-delimited file easily in Microsoft Excel or Microsoft Works. (Microsoft Works doesn't have a direct .csv importer, but the file will open under the All Files (*.*) option as shown in Figure 40-4.)

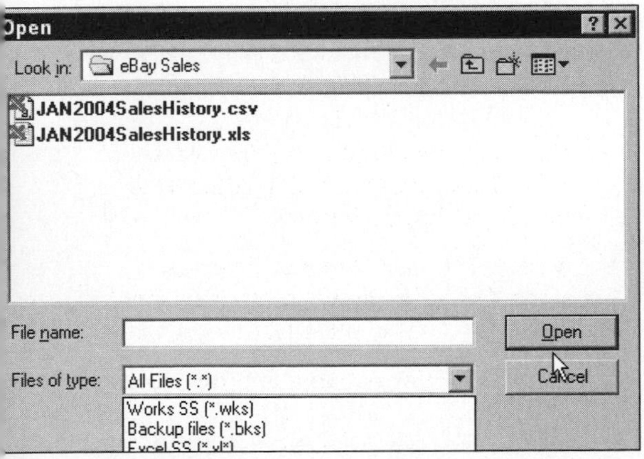

Figure 40-4: Opening a .csv file in Works.

   ▶ **Tab-delimited file:** This file downloads with the extension of .txt. You can open it in a spreadsheet program, or as a text file in Windows Notepad or a word-processing program such as Microsoft Word.

   ▶ **Quicken or QuickBooks file:** You download PayPal reports in the native format, ready to

import into these Intuit bookkeeping programs. Note, however, that importing this way creates a customer for every sale — which will overwhelm QuickBooks in no time. (See Practice 36 for an easier way to handle this issue.)

If you use the Quicken or QuickBooks option, then once these files get imported, they're in your bookkeeping format for good. Maybe that's not such a great idea.

Saving these report files for spreadsheet use gives you more options. You're not limited to using a particular version of a particular program to open your .txt and .csv files. After all, they're universal file types; they can be opened on any PC with basic spreadsheet capabilities.

3. **After you specify dates and format, click the Download History button.**

   If you've asked for a long timeframe (say, a year), get up and make yourself a cup of café Americano. (Or go to bed — PayPal's servers can run slow when many users are ordering their downloads). When you come back, your file will be ready to download.

Saving and Editing Your Reports

When your computer finally is ready to receive the downloaded file (which may take a while — especially if you have a dial-up connection), a window pops up (it looks like the one shown in Figure 40-5).

Click the Save button; in the next screen, select the directory on your computer to which you want to save the file. (I recommend setting up a directory that contains *only* Internet and eBay sales files.)

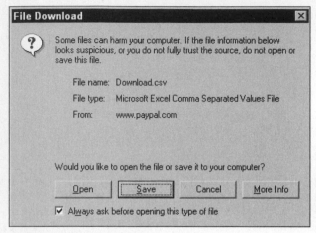

• **Figure 40-5: The Windows File Download window.**

After you save the file, you can open it. Figure 40-6 shows a downloaded history file opened in Microsoft Works. You can now work with your sales history to your heart's content — re-sorting the records, totaling up sales, deleting unnecessary columns, and so on.

This file is now part of your eBay business archive. Should the day ever come that you need to produce it, you have it. (Be sure to back it up, just in case.)

Some CPAs recommend that you keep these files for up to seven years. To be safe, check with your own tax professional (who understands the needs for your particular tax situation) before you throw out or delete any tax records. (I currently have boxes full of receipts, cancelled checks, and such going back over ten years. I promise when this book is done to clear out the backlog.)

	A	B	C	D	E	F	G	H	I	J
1	Date	Time	Zone	Name	Type	Status	Gross	Fee	Net	From Em
2	2/2/2004	11:38:00	PST		Refund	Completed	-13.61	0.6	-13.01	
3	2/1/2004	18:08:28	PST		eBay Payment Receivec	Completed	152.1	-3.65	148.45	
4	2/1/2004	13:03:30	PST		eBay Payment Receivec	Completed	13.23	-0.59	12.64	
5	1/31/2004	18:23:19	PST		Update to Payment Rec	Completed	46.34	...	...	
6	1/31/2004	12:45:31	PST		eBay Payment Receivec	Completed	46.34	-1.32	45.02	
7	1/30/2004	19:46:21	PST		Payment Received	Completed	280	-6.46	273.54	
8	1/30/2004	12:36:17	PST		eBay Payment Sent	Completed	-47.15	0	-47.15	
9	1/30/2004	12:36:17	PST	Credit Card	Charge From Credit Car	Completed	22.78	0	22.78	
10	1/30/2004	12:31:53	PST	Bank Account	Withdraw Funds to a Ba	Completed	-1136.44	0	-1136.44	
11	1/30/2004	12:05:00	PST		eBay Payment Receivec	Completed	78.13	-2.02	76.11	
12	1/30/2004	9:26:55	PST		Web Accept Payment R	Completed	46.5	-1.32	45.18	
13	1/30/2004	8:56:36	PST		Web Accept Payment R	Completed	179	-4.24	174.76	
14	1/30/2004	8:54:42	PST		Web Accept Payment R	Completed	138.5	-3.35	135.15	
15	1/30/2004	6:43:52	PST		eBay Payment Receivec	Completed	18.02	-0.7	17.32	
16	1/29/2004	13:37:16	PST		eBay Payment Receivec	Completed	251.99	-5.84	246.15	
17	1/29/2004	12:07:03	PST		eBay Payment Receivec	Completed	33.19	-1.03	32.16	
18	1/29/2004	4:34:28	PST		eBay Payment Receivec	Refunded	13.61	-0.6	13.01	
19	1/28/2004	23:51:19	PST		Web Accept Payment R	Completed	148.48	-3.57	144.91	
20	1/28/2004	15:29:53	PST		eBay Payment Receivec	Completed	6.87	-0.45	6.42	
21	1/28/2004	15:26:27	PST		eBay Payment Receivec	Completed	6.87	-0.45	6.42	
22	1/28/2004	15:23:31	PST		eBay Payment Receivec	Completed	6.87	-0.45	6.42	
23	1/28/2004	10:59:09	PST		eBay Payment Receivec	Completed	6.5	-0.44	6.06	
24	1/27/2004	10:41:38	PST		Update to Payment Rec	Completed	7	...	...	
25	1/27/2004	10:35:21	PST		Payment Received	Completed	7	-0.45	6.55	
26	1/27/2004	8:54:43	PST		eBay Payment Receivec	Completed	249.99	-5.8	244.19	

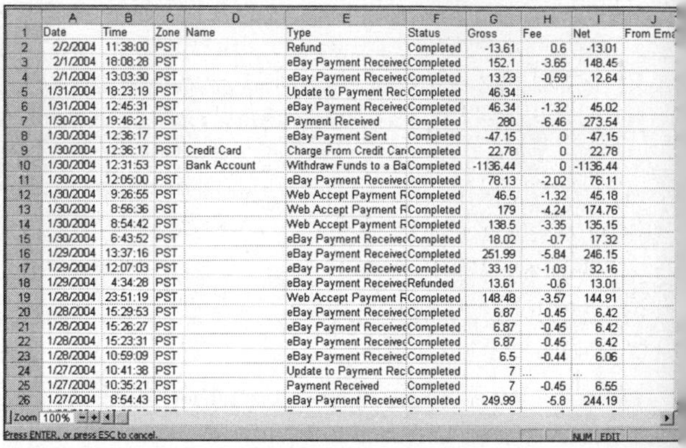

• **Figure 40-6: The downloaded file opened in a spreadsheet program.**

Practice 41

Understanding Your Financial Reports

In This Practice

- Why keep the books?
- Finding a professional
- Regularly posting your sales and inventory info
- Letting your reports talk to you

Truth be told, posting bookkeeping entries is excruciatingly boring. I dislike it more than any other business task, but it's crucial to keeping up with the current status of just "how you're doing." Using a bookkeeping program makes this chore a lot easier — because all you have to do is click a button to generate your sales or tax information. It's a lot less time-consuming than manually going over pages of sales information on a pad of paper. That's why I'm a fan of bookkeeping software — particularly QuickBooks (more about QuickBooks in Practice 36).

If you really want to, I suppose that you *could* use plain ol' paper and pencil to keep your books. If that makes you happy, then go for it — for now — just understand that it definitely won't work for you in the future, especially at the PowerSeller level of doing business. Entering all your information into a software program early on — while your books may still be fairly simple to handle — can save you a lot of time and frustration down the road, when your eBay business has grown beyond your wildest dreams and no amount of paper can keep it all straight and organized.

To manage your business effectively, you must keep track of *all* your expenses — down to the last roll of tape. You need to keep track of your inventory, how much you paid for the items, how much you paid in shipping, and how much you profited from your sales. If you use a van or the family car to pick up or deliver merchandise to the post office (I can load eight of the light kits that I sell on eBay into our car), you should keep track of this mileage as well. When you're running a business, you should account for every penny that goes in and out.

Taking on the Bookkeeping Basics

Bookkeeping has irrefutable standards called GAAP (Generally Accepted Accounting Procedures) that are set by the Financial Accounting Standards Board. It sounds scary to me too, but not to worry: This practice helps get you talking enough of the bookkeeping talk of so your business can walk the walk. For example, *assets, liabilities, owner's equity, income,* and *expenses* are all standard terms used in all forms of accounting to define profit, loss, and the fiscal health of your business.

Every time you process a transaction, two things happen: One account is credited while another receives a debit (kind of like yin and yang). To get more familiar with these terms (and those in the following list), see the definitions in the chart of accounts in Practice 36. Depending on the type of account, the account's balance either increases or decreases.

One account that increases while another decreases is called *double-entry accounting*:

- ✔ When you post an expense, the debit *increases* your expenses and *decreases* your bank account.

- ✔ When you purchase furniture or other assets, it *increases* your asset account and *decreases* your bank account.

- ✔ When you make a sale and make the deposit, it *increases* your bank account and *decreases* your accounts receivable.

- ✔ When you purchase inventory, it *increases* your inventory and *decreases* your bank account.

- ✔ When a portion of a sale includes sales tax, it *decreases* your sales, and *increases* your sales tax account.

Performing double-entry accounting manually can be a bit taxing (no pun intended). A software program, however, adjusts the accounts automatically when you input a transaction.

As a business owner, even if you're a sole proprietor (see Practice 44 for information on business types), you should keep your business books separate from your personal expenses. By isolating your business records from your personal records, you can get a snapshot of what areas of your sales are doing well and which ones aren't carrying their weight. But that isn't the only reason keeping accurate records is smart; there's the IRS to think about too. (In the next section, I explain Uncle Sam's interest in your books.)

 At the end of the year, when you have a professional do your taxes, you'll be a lot happier — and your tax preparation will cost you less — if you've posted your information cleanly and in the proper order. Yet another benefit of bookkeeping software.

Simplifying the Books

Why can't you do your bookkeeping *your* way? Because the United States Tax Code demands that businesses adhere to some tried-and-true accounting procedures. (Practice 36 details my approach to using QuickBooks to tow that line; I like to be safe rather than sorry, and bookkeeping software helps a lot.) Here's a quick list of the accounting practices that are most important for PowerSellers:

- ✔ **Keep your PayPal account for deposits and withdrawals only to your bank account for clarity.** Consider PayPal to be your payment provider, *not* your bank. That way your actual bank records can provide a complete picture of your income and expenses.

- ✔ **Download available reports at least quarterly.** You may never feel like looking at them if you keep your books up on a regular basis, but they are concrete backup information (should you ever need it).

- ✔ **Be sure you've indicated which state you need to collect tax form, so it's charged correctly and automatically on each invoice.** Sales tax is no game. If you don't collect the proper taxes for each transaction, you may end up being personally liable down the road. The tax agencies take a dim view of sellers who don't follow the rules.

- ✔ **Keep on top of changes in state and federal payroll taxes, and make your payments on time.** The Feds have no sense of humor when you tell them you forgot to make a deposit. It's worse yet when you say something like, "Withholding taxes — what's that?"

✔ **Don't pay for business expenses with cash.** Use a credit card for all your business purchases — and pay the balance off each month. By having your expenses all on one card, you'll be able to combine that record with your bank statement to simplify your bookkeeping. (Besides, you can get miles for that "business" buying trip you've been planning.)

Sifting through the Reports

As an owner of a business, you can look forward to having lots (and lots) of reports to evaluate. Of course, you get a boatload of reports from PayPal, eBay, and so on, but the most important reports are those you generate from your bookkeeping program. I use QuickBooks to manage my records, and it keeps several common reports (Balance Sheet, Accounts Payable, P&L, and more) in an easily accessible area.

If you check out the Reports tab of your bookkeeping program, I bet you'll find similar items. Before your eyes glaze over, though, check out this practice for straightforward descriptions of these reports and the information they provide.

 To get your business reports when you need them, you must post your sales receipts regularly and thereby update the figures that represent money in and inventory out. Post your payments (money out) at least weekly, especially on your company credit card — post those transactions the minute you get your statement — and reconcile your checkbook the moment your bank statement arrives.

What do your posting and reconciling tasks get you? The opportunity to hit a button and get a complete picture of your business. From the reports you generate, you find out whether your business is profitable, what products are selling, and whether you're spending too much money in a particular area. Keeping your books up to date allows you to find problems before they become unmanageable.

 If you run your sales and financial reports only quarterly rather than monthly, you might not know if a problem — such as not pricing your items high enough — could be mushrooming out of control.

De-bewildering Your Balance Sheet

Your balance sheet provides the best information on your business. It pulls data from all the other reports and gives you a complete look at your business's financial condition.

Your balance sheet shows all your assets:

✔ **Cash in Bank:** The money in your business bank account.

✔ **Accounts Receivable:** If you've invoiced anyone and not received payment yet, you'll see that amount reflected here.

✔ **Inventory Assets:** This is the value of the merchandise you've purchased for resale but have not yet sold.

✔ **Other Assets:** Things your business owns that aren't your personal possessions — such as office furniture and dedicated vehicles.

✔ **Accumulated Depreciation:** This is deprecation on your assets; the number is either produced by your accounting program or given to you by your accountant.

The balance sheet also (alas) shows your liabilities:

✔ **Accounts Payable:** If you owe any vendors or have money due on unpaid credit cards, it will show up here.

✔ **Sales Tax:** The money you have collected as sales tax (that is due to your state) is a liability.

✔ **Payroll Liabilities:** If you haven't made a bank deposit covering the money you've withdrawn from employees (such as withholding taxes, Social Security, Medicare, and so on), it will show up here.

Your equity shows up in the (literal and figurative) bottom line at the bottom of the statement. It will include your initial investment in your business and the net income total from your Profit & Loss statement.

An important business ratio — the net *working capital ratio* — is drawn from your balance sheet. Subtracting your current liabilities from your current assets gets you the dollar amount of your net working capital. But to get the net working capital ratio, divide your current assets by your current liabilities. Any value over 1.1 means that you have a positive net working capital. If you need a loan from a bank, this is the first figure the loan office will look for.

Tracking your Accounts Payable

When bills come in, post them in your accounting program. This will generate the Accounts Payable report. Accounts Payable is the area that shows how much you owe and when it's due. These are crucial dates and numbers to know so you can be sure to meet your obligations on time.

When you pay an outstanding bill, the bookkeeping program deducts the money from your checking account and marks the bill as paid. That number will no longer appear on this report.

Knowing your sales-tax liability

One of the vendors you'll owe money to is your state. In California, it's the State Board of Equalization. Every time you post an invoice or sales receipt that charges sales tax, that amount shows up automatically in this report. You run this

report on a timeframe determined by the state; you may be required to report monthly, quarterly, or yearly. Also, how often you report may depend on your total in-state sales. Just make sure you match your reporting with your state's requirements for your business.

Analyzing your Profit & Loss Statement

If your tax professional asks for your income statement, he or she is asking for your profit-and-loss statement, or *P&L*. This report lays out clearly every penny you've spent and brought in. You can set these reports in your bookkeeping software to generate by any period of time; usually eBay sellers produce them by calendar month.

A summary P&L (or Profit & Loss Statement) will itemize all your income and expense accounts individually, and total them by category. This way you'll be able to isolate individual areas where you may notice a problem (such as spending too much on shipping expenses).

Please use the following list of income and expense accounts as a guide and not as the gospel. I am not a tax professional, and I suggest that when you set up your own income and (especially) expense accounts, you go over them with a licensed tax expert.

Here's a glimpse of the kinds of accounts and categories you see on a P&L statement:

✔ **Income:** Every dollar you bring in is itemized as income. For many sellers, this can break down into several individual accounts. These figures are automatically generated by your bookkeeping program from the sales receipts you input. The total of all these income areas appears at the bottom of this area as Total Income.

▶ **Sales:** This totals eBay Sales and Shipping income in separate totals. These figures subtotal as Total Sales.

▶ **Commissions:** When selling items on eBay for other (as a Trading Assistant), the income you make you're your photography, setup fees and commissions that is charged to your clients.

▶ **Web-site advertising:** If you are a member of any affiliate programs or have a newsletter that takes advertising, the income you get from such sources will appear here.

▶ **Consulting:** Income from consulting (as a service) or teaching eBay to newbies.

✔ **Costs of Goods Sold (COGS):** This area itemizes by category all the costs involved in your eBay (and/or Web site sales) only. (No business operating expenses — such as your telephone bill — show up here; they're farther down on the report.) Your eBay COGS may subtotal in different accounts, such as

▶ **Merchandise:** The cost of your merchandise that you bought to resell.

▶ **eBay Fees:** Here's where you post your eBay fees from your credit-card statement.

▶ **PayPal Fees:** If you're using QuickBooks to keep your books, the program calculates this figure automatically from your sales receipts (for more on PayPal, see Practice 37; for more on QuickBooks, see Practice 36).

▶ **Shipping Postage:** The totals of the amounts you spend for shipping your eBay items. These also appear here from within your program from your inputting the various expenses when you pay the bills.

▶ **Shipping Supplies:** The costs of the padded mailers, bubble wrap, tapes, and boxes — you get the picture. When those items are paid for, the bookkeeping program inserts the totals here.

▶ **Outside Service Fees:** If you pay for your photo hosting or third-party management tools, those fees appear here.

Cross-reference your Costs of Goods sold to your Sales reports. You've expensed inventory bought — but your merchandise may be sitting idle in your storage area. The COGS report works in concert with others — such as inventory reports (also generated by QuickBooks), sales reports, and P&Ls — to give you a solid picture of where your business is going.

Your Cost of Goods sold will subtotal under the heading Total COGS.

✔ **Gross Profit:** Your bookkeeping program magically does all the calculations, and you will be able to see in a snapshot if your basic eBay business is in good, profitable health. This is the gross profit — *before* you figure in your company expenses (often called G&A — for General and Administrative costs).

Now come your expenses. The totals listed in your individual accounts represent subtotals for your overall business operating expenses, as follows:

✔ **Payroll expenses:** The total amounts you pay your employees.

✔ **Taxes:** Here's where you put the taxes you have paid the regulating agencies so you can run your business, broken out by State and Federal catagories.

✔ **Supplies:** Computer and office supplies. How much paper goes through your printer? Not to mention those inkjet cartridges, pens, computers, telephones, copiers, and various items of network equipment. All those expenses appear here.

✔ **Seminars and Education:** Did you buy this book to educate yourself on your eBay business? It counts. Have you attended a seminar to educate yourself on eBay? Going to eBay Live? Those count too.

✔ **Contract Labor:** This is the money you pay to anyone who is not an employee of your company. If someone *is* an employee, you withhold taxes from that person's paycheck. (For more about that necessity, see Practice 45). This may include an off-site bookkeeper or a company that comes in to clean your office. The federal government has very stringent rules regarding who qualifies as an Independent Contractor. Check the following Web site for the official rules:

```
www.irs.gov/businesses/small/
    article/0,,id=115041,00.html
```

✔ **Automobile expenses:** This is where you post expenses — parking, gas, repairs for an automobile that is used for your eBay business. If you have only one vehicle that you also use for personal transportation, your tax person may have you post a percentage of its use in this area.

✔ **Telephone:** Do you have a separate phone line for your business alone? You should. Phone charges for that line go here. If you don't have a dedicated line, perhaps you use a cell phone exclusively for business? Even a pay-as-you-go phone would work here. Keep in mind, however, that it must be *exclusively* for business use.

✔ **Advertising:** Expenses you incur when running campaigns in Google AdWords or in your eBay banner program.

Your expenses will come to a whopping total at the bottom — and then, at the very bottom of the page, you get to see your net income. This is your bottom-line profit (and yes, that's where the expression comes from). I wish you all a very positive bottom line!

Practice 42

Keeping Your Records and Data Safe

This must be said: Keeping your data safe is just as important as filing your taxes. If the pitfalls of not backing up your computer isn't a tired subject, I don't know what is. Whenever you hear someone talking about their latest computer crash, all they can do is stare blankly into the distance and say, "I lost everything!" I admit, it happened to me — just once. I'm sure that you've also heard this cry from others (if you've not uttered it yourself): "If only I'd backed up my files!"

Even worse than a computer crash, what about a natural disaster? It can happen, you know. When I went to sleep on January 16, 1994, I didn't know that the next day, when I attempted to enter my office, everything would be in shambles. My monitors had flown across the room, filing cabinets turned over, and oh, did I mention the ceiling had collapsed? It seems that my garage office became Ground Zero for the Northridge earthquake. (I want you to picture me shoveling though the mess to find my insurance policies.) This experience taught me some solid lessons about keeping duplicate records and backed-up data copies, preferably in an off-site location.

If the ultimate computer crash (or natural disaster) has happened to you, you have my deepest and most sincere sympathy. It's a horrible thing to go through.

 What's another horrible thing? A tax audit: It can especially make you feel like jumping off a cliff if you've been filing your hard documentation with the shoebox method. (You know, one box for 2005, one for 2006, and so on.) Filing your receipts and backup documentation in an organized, easy-to-find format really can pay off in future savings of time (and nerves). Even if you're not going through a tax audit.

I want to tell you upfront that I don't always practice what I preach. I don't always back up my stuff on time. I have a brand-new box of backup software sitting on the floor next to me, and last year's box of receipts is getting fuller. But in this practice, I'm gonna preach anyway about developing good habits for backing up your computer data and safeguarding the hardcopy documents that you inevitably will have. (I really hope I experience no disasters before I finish writing this book!)

Backing Up Your Data — Just Do It!

I'm not specifically suggesting that you go out and buy backup software (though I think it's a good idea). I *am* suggesting that you back up the eBay transaction records and other data on your computer somehow. Consider the following points when choosing how to back up the data you can't afford to lose:

✔ Regularly back up at least your My Documents folder onto a CD or external hard drive. External hard drives have come way down in price (you can find brand-new external hard drives — 200-gigabyte USB models — for under $100 on eBay), so there's really no excuse not to make some sort of backup.

 I just discovered an automatic online backup service at www..Carbonite,com. Simply install their software on your computer and it will automatically back up your data to Carbonite's online servers. Restoring your data to your computer is just as simple: Just click Restore on the Carbonite Web site. This all comes at a reasonable price of $49.95 a year. They offer a free trial on their site so you can test it out.

✔ Backup software can make your backup chores less *chorelike*. Most such packages have features you can set to run unattended backups automatically, and you don't have to remember anything.

✔ Backup software doesn't have to be expensive either. I just visited one of my favorite shareware sites, www.tucows.com, and searched on the term *backup Windows.* This query returned over 300 matching records!

 If you update to a new computer, you can purchase an inexpensive USB enclosure. This way, you can take your hard drive out of your old computer and after it's installed in the enclosure, it hooks up to your USB port and you can access all of your old data on the new computer.

✔ Consider making monthly (or at least annual) backups of the info from your PayPal account. You can download the data directly from the site and can archive several years' worth on one CD or external hard drive.

Saving Your Business Records

Business records are still mostly paper, and until such time as the entire world is electronic, you'll have some paperwork to store. You can buy manila file folders almost anywhere. A box of 100 costs you less than $10, so expense is no excuse for lack of organization.

If you don't have filing cabinets, office-supply stores sell collapsible cardboard boxes that are the perfect size to hold file folders. You can buy six of these for around $8.

And just what do you need to *file* in your newly organized office? Here are a few important suggestions:

✔ **Equipment receipts and warranties:** You never know when some important piece of your office hardware will go on the fritz, and you'll need the receipt and warranty information so you can get it fixed. Also, the receipts are backup documentation for your bookkeeping program's data.

✔ **Automobile expenses:** Gasoline receipts, parking receipts, repairs: anything and everything to do with your car. You use your car in your eBay business (for example, to deliver packages to the Post Office for shipping), don't you?

✔ **Postal receipts:** Little slips of paper you get that prove you've mailed something from the Post Office. If you use an online postage service, print out a postage report once a month and file it in your filing cabinets or boxes as well.

✔ **Credit-card bills:** Here, in one location, can be documentation on your purchases for your business. Make a folder for each credit card; file every month after you pay the bill and post the data.

✔ **Merchandise receipts:** Merchandise purchased for resale on eBay. Documentation of all the money you spend.

✔ **Licenses and legal stuff:** Important! Keep an active file of anything legal; you will no doubt have to lay hands on this information at the oddest moment. It's reassuring to know where it is!

✔ **Payroll paperwork:** Even if you print your checks and such on the computer, you should organize the state and federal filing information in one place.

✔ **Cancelled checks and bank statements:** These are the only ways to prove you've paid for something.

✔ **Insurance information:** Policies and proposals should all be kept at hand's reach.

'm sure that with a little thinking, you can come up with some more aspects of your business that can benefit from a little more organization. When you need the information quickly and you can find it without breaking a sweat, you'll be glad you kept things organized.

Knowing How Long to Keep Your Paperwork

The possibility that some government organization (city, state, or federal) will want a glance at some of your business documentation, sooner or later, is very real.

The IRS wants you to save anything related to your tax return for three years. But take a look at Table 42-1: The IRS may want backup documentation for up to *six* years. So — for safety's sake — keep things for six years, if only to prove you're innocent.

 Staying on the right side of the law tax-wise is crucial to your business. You may want to skim Practice 43 again to refresh your memory of what to look for and where to find help.

TABLE 42-1: RECORDS THE IRS MAY NEED AND HOW LONG TO KEEP THEM

If You	Keep the Records for
1. Owe additional tax and items 2, 3, and 4 (below) do not apply to you	3 years
2. Do not report income that is more than 25 percent of the gross income shown on your return	6 years
3. File a fraudulent return	Forever
4. Do not file a return	Forever
5. File for credit or refund after you filed your return	3 years after tax was paid
6. File for a loss from worthless securities	7 years

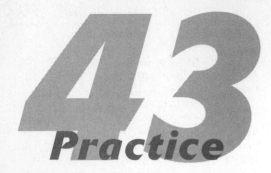

Practice 43

Keeping Up with Your Taxes

In This Practice

✔ Letting eBay help you collect sales tax

✔ Getting ID numbers for your business

✔ Finding out what licenses you need

Every once in a while I get an e-mail from an eBay seller who's been selling on eBay for a couple of years and wants to know, "Do I need to pay taxes?" Do you need to pay taxes? Are you kidding me? By selling online you are *running a business* — no matter how small it may be. That means (among many other things) paying taxes.

If you're earning money or selling anything in the United States, there's a plethora of taxes not only to pay, but also to pay *attention* to. In this practice, I discuss the basic tax information I've learned from professionals. And as I've said before, you need to consult with a tax professional to get the details of your situation properly handled.

At the end of this practice is a state-by-state directory of Web links to tax-related sites for each state. Each of these sites will lead you to the proper place to file for your specific state requirements. In most cases, there are online forms you can fill out to apply for your various permits, licenses, and taxes.

The IRS recognizes that eBay sellers are making money. As a matter of fact, it plans to crack down on those online sellers who avoid their required taxes. It's in the news almost every month. To keep us informed on the changes and regulations, the IRS set up a page on its Web site just for online sellers — aren't we the lucky ones? Just visit www.irs.gov/businesses/small/industries/article/0,,id=163622,00.html every now and again for the latest news on federal regulations.

You not only make money for yourself, but your profits are what supports our state and federal governments. In the words of President Ronald Reagan, "The taxpayer; that's someone who works for the federal government, but doesn't have to take a civil service examination."

In Practice 44, I discuss some of the very costly ways eBay sellers do their business — and how they can save on taxes by just selecting the proper legal identity. So check that out, too; it's all part and parcel of doing business in America.

Isn't selling online just like a garage sale?

In a word, yes it is (actually, that's three words) — but with one big difference: When you sell items at a garage sale, you have generally used them for quite a few years and their value has depreciated. In general, you have paid a great deal more for those items than you sell them for on your front lawn. According to the IRS, losses on personal property are not deductible. Did you ever really sell anything at a garage sale for more than you paid for it? If you did, *technically the profits are taxable*. Just like anything you sell at a profit on eBay.

This is why it is absolutely crucial to save the receipts for items that you sell on eBay. If you can prove that you have bought an item solely to sell on eBay, and that you've sold at a loss, it just might qualify as a business loss. Check with your tax professional to confirm any such potential deductions.

State Sales Tax

It's a fact of life: Most states in the United States charge sales tax on items purchased within their borders. Currently, all states except Alaska, Delaware, Montana, New Hampshire, and Oregon collect sales taxes. Some states have a single rate throughout the state; others charge different sales taxes on a county-by-county basis. Confusing? You bet. This is why it's critical to check out your local requirements through the links provided in Table 43-1.

If your state has a sales tax — a tax paid on items purchased within the state — you need an assigned *sales tax number* (the number you use when you file your sales-tax statement with your state) before you officially sell anything. If sales tax applies, you may have to collect the appropriate sales tax for every sale that ships within the state your business is operating in.

Some states also call this number a *resale certificate* or *seller's permit*. When you want to purchase goods from a wholesaler within your state, you must produce this number (thereby certifying your legitimacy as a seller) so the dealer can sell you the merchandise without charging you sales tax.

 The seller's permit is for business use only; it's not meant for your personal use. Some folks seem to think it's a pretty cool way to buy items they need personally at wholesale cost and avoid paying taxes, but it's way too easy to get caught doing that. The states keep track of all sales of items to resellers who have seller's permits. If the great computer in your state capital tries to match up your vendors' sales with yours, they can easily find a discrepancy. It's not worth the hassle or the penalties and possible fines.

Once you have your permit, eBay makes it easy for you to charge the appropriate sales tax for sales within your state. If you have an office in more than one state, eBay will apply the sales tax to sales in multiple states as you indicate.

To set this up for your eBay business, go to your My eBay (or Selling Manager) summary page and follow these steps:

1. **Using the My eBay Views links on the left side of the page, scroll to the My Account area and click Preferences.**

   You go to the area of eBay where you can adjust the way you do business on the site.

2. **Scroll down the page to the Selling Preferences area where you find the Payments from Buyers box.**

3. **Click the Show link and you'll see a range of options (as in Figure 43-1).**

4. **In the Use Sales Tax Table line, click the Edit link.**

   The next page shows you eBay's Sales Tax table.

5. **In your state's text box, type the appropriate sales tax percentage that you must charge buyers.**

   In Figure 43-2, you see a part of the 50-state table where I typed in the sales tax that's applicable for buyers in my state.

6. **After you type in the tax percentage, scroll to the bottom of the page and click Done.**

Selling Preferences		
Sell Your Item form and listings		Show
Edit your Sell Your Item form preferences and other listing preferences.		
Payment from buyers		Hide
Use checkout	Yes	Edit
Offer PayPal on my listings	Yes	
Display "PayPal Preferred" on my listings	Yes	
Include my items when buyers pay all their sellers at once using PayPal	Yes	
Allow buyers to edit payment totals	Yes	
Use this payment address	See Addresses under My Account.	
Use sales tax table	Yes	Edit
Enable Checkout through your ProStores Web store		Show
Allow buyers to pay for their eBay items in your ProStores Web store.		
Shipping preferences		Show
Offer shipping discounts for combined purchases, edit your UPS and FedEx rate options, and edit your shipping tracking email preferences.		
Promoting Similar Items on eBay Pages and Emails		Show
Promote your items in emails and on item pages.		

• **Figure 43-1: Here you can edit the way buyers buy from you.**

Sales Tax Table		Help

Use the Sales Tax table to enter the tax rate you want to charge for each state. Leave the field blank if you do not charge tax in a specific state. Optionally, you can indicate whether you want to charge sales tax on shipping & handling. Last updated 2007-06-27 17:55:52 PDT

Click the **Save** button when you are done.

State	Sales Tax Rate	Also charge sales tax on S & H
Alabama (AL):	%	☐
Alaska (AK):	%	☐
Arizona (AZ):	%	☐
Arkansas (AR):	%	☐
California (CA):	8.250 %	☐
Colorado (CO):	%	☐
Connecticut (CT):	%	☐
Delaware (DE):	%	☐
District of Columbia (DC):	%	☐
Florida (FL):	%	☐
Georgia (GA):	%	☐
Hawaii (HI):	%	☐
Idaho (ID):	%	☐

• **Figure 43-2: eBay's Sales tax table.**

From now on, when you list an item on eBay, you'll see the reference to charging sales tax in the Sell Your Item form or in Turbo Lister.

The Federation of Tax administrators has a very handy interactive map on its Web site. Just go there and click your state, and another window opens, showing links to your state's tax-form site. Go to

```
www.taxadmin.org/fta/link/forms.html
```

Setting Up with the Federal Government

If you're going to be paying anyone a salary — or even prove you're running a business — you'll need a Federal *employer identification number* (EIN or FEIN), also known as a *Federal tax identification number*. Every business has one. Like a Social Security number for a business, it's a nine-digit number assigned to all businesses for tax filing and reporting purposes. Use this number to identify your business on all government forms. You may also need a similar identification number for your state if your state has a state income tax.

If you have regular employees, you need to file *withholding forms* to collect the necessary taxes that you must send to the state and the IRS on behalf of your employees. You're also expected to deposit those tax dollars with the IRS and your state on the date required, which may vary from business to business. Many enterprises go down because their owners just can't seem to keep their fingers out of withheld taxes, which means that money isn't available to turn in when the taxes are due. (This is another good reason to have a separate bank account for your business.)

No need to dawdle. Might as well get the number while you have the time. Here's why:

✔ There's no charge to get your EIN.

✔ A Federal Employer ID number can be assigned by filing IRS form SS-4. Go to the IRS Web site to apply online at this location:

```
www.irs.gov/businesses/small/
    article/0,,id=102767,00.html
```

✔ State employer ID numbers for taxes may depend on your state's requirements. Visit the following for an overview of the requirements for every state in the country:

```
www.taxadmin.org/fta/forms.ssi
```

City and State Business Licenses

It seems everyone has something to say about your business, doesn't it? Yep, lots of fingers in the pie! When you're part of the business community, your business dealings will have an impact on many more people than just you.

That's why cities and states issue business licenses to home businesses as well as to large corporations. Getting a license at the outset of an ongoing business is better than being forced to pay penalties later.

Table 43-1 is a chart of URLs to individual state's business links. These links should get you all the info you need.

TABLE 43-1: LINKS TO THE INDIVIDUAL STATE'S BUSINESS REQUIREMENTS

State	Link
Alabama	www.ador.state.al.us/licenses/MunBusLic.htm
Alaska	www.dced.state.ak.us/occ/home.htm
Arizona	www.azcommerce.com/BusAsst/SmallBiz/
Arkansas	asbdc.ualr.edu/business-information/1006-business-licenses-taxes-permits.asp
California	www.calgold.ca.gov/
Colorado	www.colorado.gov/colorado-doing-business/get-license-permits.html
Connecticut	www.ct-clic.com/Content/Smart_Start_for_Business.asp
Delaware	https://onestop.delaware.gov/osbrlpublic/Home.jsp
District of Columbia	brc.dc.gov/planning/requirements/requirements.asp
Florida	www.myflorida.com/dbpr/
Georgia	www.sos.state.ga.us/firststop/
Hawaii	hawaii.gov/dcca/areas/breg
Idaho	commerce.idaho.gov/Portals/37/publications/Start.pdf This URL also works: http://www.state.id.us/business/
Illinois	business.illinois.gov/step_by_step_guides.cfm
Indiana	www.in.gov/business_guide.htm
Iowa	www.iowalifechanging.com/business/blic.html
Kansas	www.accesskansas.org/businesscenter/index.html?link=start
Kentucky	sos.ky.gov/business/
Louisiana	www.sec.state.la.us/comm/fss/fss-index.htm The business page here is GeauxBiz.com — no kidding, that's really it!
Maine	www.maine.gov/portal/business/starting.html
Maryland	www.blis.state.md.us/BusinessStartup.aspx

(continued)

TABLE 43-1 *(continued)*

State	Link
Massachusetts	www.dor.state.ma.us/business/doingbus.htm
Michigan	www.michigan.gov/businessstartup
Minnesota	www.deed.state.mn.us/faq/business.htm
Mississippi	www.olemiss.edu/depts/mssbdc/going_intobus.html
Missouri	www.missouribusiness.net/docs/license_registration_checklist.asp
Montana	www.mt.gov/revenue/programsandservices/onestop.asp
Nebraska	https://www.nebraska.gov/osbr/cgi/domestic.cgi?/OSBRApplication/init/init/None
Nevada	http://www.nv.gov/new_DoingBusiness.htm
New Hampshire	www.nh.gov/revenue/business/dra_licenses.htm
New Jersey	www.state.nj.us/njbusiness/starting/
New Mexico	www.rld.state.nm.us/index.html
New York	www.gorr.state.ny.us/Main_GORR_Pages/Business-Permit-Assistance.html
North Carolina	www.nccommerce.com/en/BusinessServices/StartYourBusiness/BusinessLicensesPermits/
North Dakota	www.nd.gov/businessreg/license/index.html
Ohio	www.odod.state.oh.us/onestop/index.cfm
Oklahoma	www.okcommerce.gov/licensing
Oregon	www.filinginoregon.com/business/starting_a_business.htm
Pennsylvania	www.paopenforbusiness.state.pa.us/paofb/site/default.asp
Rhode Island	http://www2.sec.state.ri.us/faststart/
South Carolina	www.scbos.com/Business+Information/License+-+Permits/Default.htm
South Dakota	www.state.sd.us/drr2/newbusiness.htm
Tennessee	www.state.tn.us/ecd/res_guide.htm
Texas	www.business.texasonline.com/?language=eng
Utah	www.utah.gov/business/starting.html
Vermont	www.thinkvermont.com/start/
Virginia	www.dba.state.va.us/licenses/
Washington	www.dol.wa.gov/business/
West Virginia	www.wv.gov/sec.aspx?pgID=1
Wisconsin	www.wisconsin.gov/state/byb/
Wyoming	http://uwadmnweb.uwyo.edu/SBDC/starting.htm

Practice 44

Establish Your Business Type

If you've played around on eBay, had some fun, and made a few dollars, then good for you — enjoy yourself! Once you start making serious money, however, your business is no longer a hobby. Before you know it, it's time to consider some serious issues like business structure, tax planning, and licenses. I say this because when you're concentrating on fulfilling multiple orders and keeping your customers happy, the last thing you need is a G-man breathing down your neck. Worst-case scenario: How about getting audited in December when you haven't been keeping good records all year?

In short, *getting serious* means making some decisions. It means getting licenses that cost something, and possibly, collecting and paying sales tax. I know this sounds like stripping the fun out of doing business on eBay, but taking a bit of time and effort now can save you a ton of trouble later on.

Giving Your Business a Name

Okay, even on eBay, you can't just call your business something like Pharnsworth's Phuzzy Critters, hang out a (virtual) shingle, and start selling plush toys. First you have to let the community know what's up — officially. In most states in the U.S., you can find small liner ads called *fictitious name statements* (in the classified section of the local newspaper) that give the state legal notification of who owns and operates a particular business, as well as what it's called. You have to register a fictitious name statement with your state before you can open a bank account in your business's name. In California, for example, you must file a fictitious name statement within 40 days of the commencement of your business. (Other state laws vary; check the Web sites listed in Practice 43 for more about your state's requirements.) Your statement must also include a physical address where the business is operated — not a mailbox address.

Before you assume registering a name isn't required in your state, be sure to check with your state's business code (I list links to all 50 states in Practice 43). Indiana, for example, requires that a business's assumed name be registered with the Indiana Secretary of State. Yours might have a similar requirement.

In the states requiring publication, your fictitious name statement must be published in an *adjudicated* (officially approved) newspaper for a certain amount of time. Ostensibly, this is to let the community know that a business is starting and who owns it. The newspaper will supply you with a *proof of publication* — a document that confirms you've duly published your fictitious name statement; you keep it in your files as a record of your filing. You generally have to renew the statement after a prescribed number of years.

After you have your proof of publication, you can bring that to the bank and open an account in your business's name, which is a very important step in separating your personal living expenses from those of the business.

Deciding Your Business Structure

I know that this may seem like a leap, but bear with me. You need to decide in what form to set up your business. You're going to have to live with this decision for quite a long time, so I suggest you consult with a tax professional or an attorney who's familiar with your situation. If you don't know such a professional personally, ask around. Getting a personal referral is far better than picking a name blindly from the phone book. You might even get a good referral from another eBay seller in your area.

You have four choices, and each has different tax and legal ramifications. I'll give you the highlights here.

Getting legal documents prepared online

You just *knew* legal services would go online eventually, didn't you? If you're thinking of setting up one of the business formats described in this practice, you might be interested in putting things together online. Real lawyers have put together everything you need at LegalZoom. They handle the preparation of legal documents for business incorporation, partnerships, and lots more — for low prices. This online venture was developed by a group of experienced attorneys, co-founded by Robert Shapiro (yes, *that* Robert Shapiro — of O.J. fame).

To get a discount on your filings, use this link:

```
http://www.legalzoom.com/jump.asp?
iRefer=1817&sURL=/index.html
```

They feature an online law library that can answer many of your questions and help you make informed decisions. Documents are prepared according to how you fill in the online forms. Your responses customize official legal transactions. LegalZoom checks your work, and e-mails your documents to you, or mails them (printed on quality acid-free paper) for your signature.

LegalZoom handled quite a bit of work for me, and I couldn't believe how easy the process was. They had step-by-step instructions and FAQs to handle my silliest questions. I got my paperwork quickly and the entire process was not only inexpensive but painless. I would recommend that you at least do a phone consultation with an attorney or tax expert in your area prior to setting your business' future in granite.

Sole proprietorship

A *sole proprietorship* is the simplest form of business. No other form of business is easier to manage or cheaper to run. A sole proprietorship is the form of business that most business owners use when they're first starting out. Many people often graduate to a more formal business format when bigger money comes in.

Keeping track of all expenses related to your eBay business is crucial, even in a sole proprietorship. (Especially when those expenses act as tax deductions against your profits.) Be sure to check Practice 41 for information on what you need to keep records for.

Here are a few highlights of sole proprietorships:

✔ Profits and expenses of the business appear on the individual's personal tax return.

✔ *Sole proprietors* (the owners of sole proprietorships) are in complete control of the money and are personally liable for paying all taxes.

✔ Some benefits (such as health insurance) are not directly deductible from business income.

✔ You must file a separate form, Schedule SE, for your self-employment tax.

✔ Liability is all on the person owning the business. If you're acting as a Trading Assistant and something seriously goes wrong with an item you've sold for another, you are liable for any damages.

Being in business adds a few expenses, but you can deduct many of those expenses (relating to your business) from your state and federal taxes. A sole proprietorship *can* be run out of your personal checking account (although I don't advise it). The profits of your business are taxed directly as part of your own income tax, and the profits and expenses are reported on Schedule C of your tax package. As a sole proprietor, you're at risk for the business liabilities. All outstanding debts are yours, and you could lose personal assets if you default.

There's also the issue of Uncle Sam. When you're a sole proprietor, you are required to pay a self-employment tax, over and above your regular state and federal taxes. This tax covers the Social Security and Medicare taxes that are normally paid by your employer. Currently, the self-employment tax is 15.3% for the first $97,500 (all net earnings of at least $400 are subject to the Medicare tax of 2.9%). That means the profits you make from your online enterprise get taxed additionally!

 Sadly, many small business owners often pay more in self-employment taxes than they pay in federal income taxes.

You *can* deduct half of your self-employment tax in figuring your adjusted gross income. This deduction affects only your income tax. It does not affect either your net earnings from self-employment or your self-employment tax. Other legal business forms can work around this scourge. For up-to-date data on this tax, visit the IRS Web site page at

```
www.irs.gov/businesses/small/article/
0,,id=98846,00.html
```

On the good side, sole proprietorships are the easiest businesses to dissolve if you choose to end an enterprise.

Partnership

A *partnership* comprises two or more people. It's a slightly more complicated business format, in which everything — profit, decision-making, liability, and so on — is shared between the partners according to terms governed by a partnership agreement.

A partnership should be formed by a written agreement, which is a legal document. Each person in the partnership contributes capital or services; both share in the partnership's profits and losses. The income of a partnership is taxed on both partners, based on the percentage of the business that they own or upon the terms of the written agreement.

 The self-employment tax is applied to each partner in a partnership.

Highlights of partnerships look like this:

✔ The written agreement forming the partnership should outline everything to do with the business:

▶ How to divide the profit and/or loss

▶ Compensation for each partner

▶ Restrictions of authority and spending

▶ How disputes will be settled

▶ What happens if the partnership dissolves

▶ What happens to the partnership in case of death or disability

✔ Profits from the business flow into the partners' personal tax returns, although *a separate tax return must be filed in the partnership's name.*

✔ The partners are personally equally liable for all business debts and product liability.

One more important thing to remember: As a partner, you're jointly and severally responsible for the business liabilities and actions of each person (or all the people) in your partnership, as well as for your own. Again, this is a personal liability arrangement. Each partner is personally open to any lawsuits that come your way through the business.

The partnership has to file an informational return with the IRS and the state, but the profits of the partnership are taxed to the partners on their personal individual returns.

Business decisions must be agreed upon by both partners — and sometimes that can get sticky!

Limited liability company (LLC)

A *limited liability company,* or LLC, is similar to a partnership, but also has many of the characteristics of a corporation. An LLC differs from a partnership mainly in that the liabilities of the company are not passed on to the members (owners). Unless you sign a personal guarantee for debt incurred, the members are responsible only to the total amount they have invested into the company. But all members *do* have liability for the company's taxes.

You'll need to put together an operating agreement, similar to the partnership agreement. This also will help establish which members own what percentage of the company for tax purposes. Most states will require that you file Articles of Organization forms to start this type of business.

An LLC can be taxed like a sole proprietorship, with the profits and losses passed on to the members' personal tax returns. An LLC may opt to pay taxes like a corporation and keep some of the profits in the company, thereby reducing the tax burden to the individual members. Although members pay the LLC's taxes, it must still file Form 1065 with the IRS at the end of the year. This gives the IRS extra data to be sure that the individual members properly report their income.

Here are some vital facts about LLCs:

✔ You are legally liable for the all the debts of the business.

✔ LLC owners may end up paying more taxes than the owners of a corporation would pay. Salaries and profits of an LLC are subject to self-employment taxes

✔ Employees of an LLC who receive fringe benefits — such as insurance, medical reimbursement plans, and parking (for example) — must treat these benefits as taxable income.

✔ If you set up a one-owner LLC, the IRS assumes that you want the LLC treated as a sole proprietorship — the self-employment tax may kick in unless your LLC is set up differently.

 Making a decision on your business format is important and can have considerable impact on your business for years to come. Laws change regularly. I'm not a lawyer or an accountant, so I offer a word to the wise PowerSeller: Please get professional advice before setting your ideas in concrete.

C-Corporation

A corporation has a life of its own; it has its own name and tax return and is a unique and separate entity from the owners. It's chartered by the secretary of state within the state of incorporation (which is usually the state in which you do business).

Federal taxes for corporations presently range from 15 to 35 percent, based on the corporation's net profits.

Setting up a corporation doesn't have to be an expensive venture.

Highlights of a corporation are these:

✔ Shareholders (owners) have limited liability for the corporation's debts. You can lose only the money you invested in the business; your personal property can attach in a few situations — as when (say) you've guaranteed a loan for the business or neglected to deposit your employees' withholding taxes. Check with your attorney for more caveats.

✔ As an officer of a corporation, you are required to report to federal and state agencies.

✔ You pay yourself and your employees a salary and taxes are withheld; therefore, because you are an employee, you pay no self-employment tax.

✔ A corporation can provide corporate retirement and medical plans, as well as greater contribution limits on retirement and life insurance than unincorporated entities can.

✔ You must keep explicit records of expenses and income.

 The tax paid by the corporation is based on *net profits* — that is, whatever profits are left over from paying all day-to-day business expenses; including salaries and benefits.

Employee owners of corporations often use the company to shelter income from being taxed by dividing the income between their personal and corporate tax returns. This is frequently called *income splitting;* it involves setting salaries and bonuses so that any profits left in the company at the end of its tax year will be taxed at only the 15-percent rate.

The state in which you run your business sets up the rules for the corporations operating within its borders. You must apply to the secretary of state of the state in which you want to incorporate. Federal taxes for corporations presently range from 15 to 35 percent (see Table 44-1), and they're generally based on your net profits.

TABLE 44: FEDERAL TAX RATES FOR CORPORATIONS

Taxable Income	Tax Rate
$0–$50,000	15%
$50,001–$75,000	25%
$75,001–$100,000	34%
$100,001–$335,000	39%
$335,001–$10,000,000	34%
$10,000,001–$15,000,000	35%
$15,000,001–$18,333,333	38%
$18,333,334 and more	35%

Running a Smooth Office

In This Practice

- Getting in-office help
- Finding a tax preparer
- Deciding whether to hire people

And you thought that running an eBay business was all about buying, selling, and shipping — plus the occasional bookkeeping. That should be enough — but there's even more. Taxes (as mentioned previously) and government regulations also make running a small business a time-consuming task.

You're gonna need help. Trust me: If you want your business to grow, you're going to have to pay for some outside help.

The downfall of many expanding small businesses is that the hire more and more staff, with the vision of expansion. Bigger business = more revenue. This is not always the case. In my own experience (as well as that of many others), you can hire more people, bring in more sales, and still not make any more profit than you did when you were operating out of your garage with one employee. This is a common scenario. Being tight with spending money and keeping on top of your business are the best ways to gauge your success.

At some point, you have to decide whether you want to expand. You may not be prepared to go to the next step up the ladder, and that's okay. Not everyone wants to be responsible for hundreds of thousands of dollars in monthly expenses. I was there. My home-based marketing business expanded, and I was offered a client list that would have brought me into big money. I honestly didn't have the stomach for all that stress — and declined. It was a good decision.

Finding Help for Your Business

Seems like an easy task, finding people to work for you — but then you think about it. You work from home, so this person will be a part of your extended family. You have personal stuff around and you have to be able to trust everyone who works in that space. Hmmm, running a classified ad doesn't seem so inviting now — does it? (Besides, does the kind of person you want as an employee just sit around reading the classifieds?)

So you need to get creative about where you find them. Here are some possibilities . . .

College students

Is there a university or community college in your area? Many of these institutions have a bulletin board (those used to be tangible things of cork and wood with pushpins, but these days you may have to ferret out a Web site used for the same purpose) where small businesses in the community post available part-time jobs. Why not give the school a call? True, college students need flexibility in their schedules — often they have to work around their classes — but that may just be the perfect scenario for your eBay business.

Senior citizens

In every neighborhood you're going to find some seniors — and if they're healthy retirees, they often have plenty of time on their hands. Get to know them. They may have spent many years in retail or marketing — or have friends who did — and may be Internet-savvy. These people have years of experience that you can benefit from. Ask around. For the online angle, you can try searching on the phrase "senior activities" to find organizations of active seniors in your area, and keep an eye out for local publications that cater to them.

Soccer moms

There's an odd saying that goes, "If you want something done, ask a busy person." Soccer moms are very busy (often doing things they're not enjoying much). Even though it may seem they don't have a moment to spare, they might just be able to find a couple of hours a day for a part-time job. If you luck out, they'll probably surprise you with their enthusiasm — because, truth be told, they may not be getting enough mental stimulation from driving the kids around.

eBay Trading Assistants

Fortunately, eBay helps these folks hang out their shingles. Just visit the eBay Trading Assistant page at `pages.ebay.com/tahub/index.html` and look for experienced eBay sellers in your area. There may be one or two who may not have all their time filled with TA business and may welcome a few paid hours from a fellow seller. If you're already a successful PowerSeller, TAs know they may learn a trick or two from you — and be eager for a part-time gig.

Local Chamber of Commerce

Use Google to find the phone number of your local Chamber of Commerce. Often people looking for jobs will go to the Chamber looking for jobs. It couldn't hurt to join — especially if you have a Trading Assistant business and are looking for excess inventory to liquidate on eBay. Get to know the receptionist and ask that he or she call you when someone who meets your needs checks in.

Of course, this list is just a starting point. Keep your eyes open. Check your church or synagogue, other parents at school, even your extended family. Let the word go forth. You never know where the perfect employee (future office manager?) will come from.

Staying on the Good Side of the Tax Man

Here's a shocker for you: You can't just have folks come in for a couple of hours a day, hand them a check for their work, and off they go. It doesn't work like that. Just as you need licenses for you businesses, you have to handle another small matter: complying with government regulations for employees. There are many resources on the Web, and the IRS Web site at `www.irs.gov` has tons of information. Also check with your tax professional, or even a freelance bookkeeper, and take copious notes on what they tell you. Employee taxes are commonplace, status-quo issues for those in the business world — including PowerSellers.

If you have employees, you are responsible for Federal Income Tax Withholding, Social Security and Medicare taxes, and making sure your practices comply with the Federal Unemployment Tax Act (FUTA). You also need to deposit the income tax withheld, and handle Social Security and Medicare taxes for both employer and employee. You can make your deposits electronically, using the Electronic Federal Tax Payment System (EFTPS), or by taking your deposit and a Federal Tax Deposit Coupon directly to your bank. This coupon is mailed to you from the government once you have an EIN. (For more about the EIN, see Practice 43.) I prefer to go online and make my deposits using the Electronic Federal Tax Payment System.

You can have a freelance bookkeeper handle this for you or do it yourself. I have always done it myself with the help of QuickBooks' Payroll Service. They have two levels of service; the basic service costs around $199 per year, keeps you updated with all the newest rates, rules, and forms — and even does the calculations for you. Check it out at

    payroll.intuit.com/payroll_services/

You have to apply *before* you actually need the online services so the government can mail you all the official paperwork. So pull out your EIN and go to www.eftps.gov to apply to use the online service. Your tax payments will be debited from your business bank account (it works just like an e-check).

United States tax deadlines

Note: Please check with your state government offices for due dates on sales taxes and license fees. (You can find a list of state government Web sites in Practice 43.)

15th of every month: Prior month payroll tax deposit date (if you're on the monthly deposit system)

January 15: Estimated taxes due

January 31: Last day to distribute 1099s and W2s to people you paid during the prior year

January 31: Payroll reports for quarterly period ending 12/31 due

February 28: Last day to send the government copies of your 1099s and W2s

March 15: Calendar year corporation tax due

April 15: Deadline for Individual or Partnership Annual Tax return or deadline to file an extension

April 15: Estimated taxes due

April 30: Payroll reports for period ending 3/31 due

June 15: Estimated taxes due

July 31: Payroll reports for quarterly period ending 6/30 due

September 15: Estimated taxes due

October 31: Payroll reports for quarterly period ending 9/30 due

If the due date falls on a weekend or a federal holiday, then the due date is the first business day after that date.

When you have an employee (part or full time) you have to withhold taxes and keep records. It's a harsh reality, but there it is. Your EIN is your businesses identification number with the government and is used to identify you as a business entity. You may also have to get an employer (or business number from your state. Practice 43 shows you how to get these numbers.

Employee or Contractor?

If you require someone to show up at your office and perform tasks that you set out, that person is an *employee*. I know you've heard of people who come in for a few hours and are paid "under the table." FYI, it's called *under the table* because it's not legal.

A *contractor*, for whom you don't withhold taxes, is someone who performs services for your business that has full control of what will be done, how it will be done and where it will be done. If someone is legitimately an "independent contractor," you must annually file all payments you made to that person — with a 1099 form — to document that you do not have to withhold taxes.

This is serious stuff. The IRS investigates and imposes penalties on companies that treat employees as if they were independent contractors and neglect to withhold taxes. If the IRS determines that your worker is actually an "employee," you may be held personally liable for an amount equal to the taxes that *should* have been withheld.

And no, this stuff isn't simple. In general, the IRS considers 20 factors in determining a worker's status. Meeting just one of the conditions may qualify the worker as an employee. If you still have a problem figuring out the appropriate designation from the guidelines, the IRS will be glad to help (without charge). You can find a Form SS-8 at

```
www.irs.gov/pub/irs-pdf/fss8.pdf
```

Fill out the form and send it to the indicated address; the IRS will let you know whether your worker is an employee or a contractor. (I save time and assume that anyone who works in my office *is* an employee.)

Here's a check list you can use as a guideline for getting a handle on whether a contractor can legally be paid on a 1099.

1. Must the individual take instructions from your management staff regarding when, where, and how work is to be done?

2. Does the individual receive training from your company?

3. Is the success or continuation of your business somewhat dependent on the type of service provided by the individual?

4. Must the individual personally perform the contracted services?

5. Have you hired, supervised, or paid individuals to assist the worker in completing the project stated in the contract?

6. Is there a continuing relationship between your company and the individual?

7. Must the individual work set hours?

8. Is the individual required to work full time at your company?

9. Is the work performed on company premises?

10. Is the individual required to follow a set sequence or routine in the performance of his/her work?

11. Must the individual give you reports regarding his/her work?

12. Is the individual paid by the hour, week, or month?

13. Do you reimburse the individual for business/travel expenses?

14. Do you supply the individual with needed tools or materials?

15. Have you made a significant investment in facilities used by the individual to perform services?

16. Is the individual free from suffering a loss or realizing a profit based on his/her work?

17. Does the individual only perform services for your company?

18. Does the individual limit the availability of his/her services to the general public?

19. Do you have the right to discharge the individual?

20. May the individual terminate his/her services at any time?

As you can see, this is a fairly complex issue. You can get more advice at the IRS Web page, here:

```
www.irs.gov/businesses/small/
  article/0,,id=99921,00.html
```

Practice 46

Bonding Your Business

In This Practice

- ✔ Learning about bonding
- ✔ Bonding your eBay sales
- ✔ Bonding your Web-site sales

In the past, high-dollar transactions on eBay were a bit more complex; the only security a seller could provide for the buyer was to throw in an escrow — an agreement to turn the item over to a third party for safekeeping until the transaction was complete. Escrow is a great way to protect the buyer, but it ties up the seller's money for considerably longer than necessary. The best legitimate company currently for escrow on eBay is `escrow.com`.

Lately there have been many scandals in the online-escrow arena. Fraudsters have put up bogus Web sites, offered expensive items for sale online, and then run the escrow through their bogus sites. Buyers have sent their money (lots of it), thinking everything to be legit — but when the money arrives, the bad guys take down the Web site and make off with the loot.

That happened often enough that escrow got a bad reputation with buyers. As a matter of fact, the issue is so serious that if you go to the escrow.com Web site (at `https://escrow.com/fic/`), you'll find a very helpful zone that gives you the lowdown on recognizing escrow fraud.

There's a viable alternative to escrow, something that will make the customer feel good about spending buckets of money on your site: Bonding. It's all about potato chips, beer, and Monday Night Football. (No, wait, that's *male* bonding . . . just kidding.) The bonding I'm talking about here refers to guaranteeing that a seller will perform *as advertised*.

Bonding isn't just for high-dollar transactions, either. Originally I thought it was, but not so! I've heard from small-time sellers that their total number of bids — and their final selling prices — increased by one third after they bonded *all* their items with the buySAFE seal (even the $5 sales!).

What Bonding Means to a Business

I'm sure you've heard about bonding. In ads on TV maybe you've heard that a contractor is "licensed and bonded." What that amounts to is making a legally binding promise; the *bond* is a legal document guaranteeing that a person or business performing a task will complete his or her part of the deal as promised in the terms of sale.

On large projects in the entertainment or graphic-design business, the person doing the job might be bonded to guarantee that the job will be completed on time. A *bond* warrants that the person (or business) performing the task will complete their part of the deal as contracted.

A bond is not insurance. Insurance assumes that losses will occur. By contrast, bonds are underwritten to protect the buyer from exposure to loss. Bonds achieve this objective by prequalifying prospective sellers on the basis of their credit strength, ability to perform, and character. The bond then *guarantees* that the seller will do what he or she says or the surety will be responsible to repay the buyer or replace the item. The *surety* is a company — usually an insurance or financial-services company — licensed to write bonds and regulated by state insurance departments. The purpose of bonding is to protect buyers from having a problem in the first place.

An eBay Certified Developer, buySAFE, has come up with a traditional bonding plan exclusively for online sellers. buySAFE procures surety bonds through Liberty Mutual, Travelers, and ACE USA.

Online sellers who qualify to bond their transactions through buySAFE's program become "Bonded Sellers." buySAFE and its surety partners back every bonded transaction with a guarantee. Here are the ten points covered by the guarantee, in order (you can also see them online at the buysafe.com Web site):

1. Every Bonded Seller has passed the comprehensive buySAFE Business Inspection process. They are established, trustworthy, and reliable.

2. Buyers will receive what they order as it was shown and described online.

3. The seller's problems will not become the buyer's problems; buyers are protected against unexpected circumstances the seller may experience.

4. Orders will be shipped via the promised shipping method or the specific method the buyer has chosen.

5. The buyer's order will be shipped promptly, on time, as promised.

6. The seller will honor all payment methods offered.

7. The seller will honor any return or refund policies specified.

8. The seller will work with the buyer to resolve any dispute that may arise.

9. There will be no hidden buySAFE costs.

10. If the seller does not honor the terms of sale, buySAFE's surety partners will replace the item or refund the sale price up to $25,000.

Bonding is the only licensed and regulated form of seller guarantee. buySAFE employees are licensed and regulated as the surety's agents in every state.

The bond provides that the bonding company will refund the item sale price or replace the item in the event the seller does not perform as promised in the item listing. Basically a bond guarantees that the seller will perform, period. Bonding your auctions tells your prospective bidders that you care about the buyer, and that you're a professional seller. This assurance can translate easily into more bids and higher final selling prices.

The best part? The seller receives their money through regular channels and doesn't have to ship the item until paid. No waiting around for weeks to get your money (as is the case with an escrow); if you're bonded, you have credentials that save you from languishing at the mercy of the system.

 The bond is available only for buyers and sellers who are residents of the United States and its territories, and does not provide coverage for certain types of losses (such as those arising out of product warranties or guarantees of any kind) or for special, incidental, or consequential damages of any type. The surety bond, backed by financial institutions that serve as buySAFE's trusted partners, covers points 5 through 10 in the 10-Point Guarantee. (Note, however, that other terms, conditions, and exclusions apply.)

The origin of buySAFE

Although he was an experienced eBay buyer, buySAFE founder Steven L. Woda got burned on eBay after buying a handheld computer from an online merchant. "I never received the product, and the seller basically disappeared," he recalls. "I lost all my money, and I thought there has to be a better way!" Inspired by frustration, buySAFE was born. Steve's background in surety-bond underwriting naturally suggested that bonds would provide the ideal protection for buyers and provide a competitive advantage for online sellers.

When buyers see the buySAFE Seal on a seller's item listing, they know they're dealing with one of the best merchants on the internet and that the likelihood of having a problem or needing any post-transaction protection is greatly reduced. This assurance and confidence are what buyers desire *before* making an online purchase. The $25,000 guarantee just helps them understand buySAFE's confidence in the seller's ability to deliver — a very handy hallmark for a PowerSeller to have and display — plus it makes for a nice backup.

When one of your items is bonded, it displays a seal that shows that you've passed the buySAFE Business Inspection. buySAFE essentially gives that seller a third-party stamp of approval by letting them display

the buySAFE Seal (shown in Figure 46-1) on their listings.). Any prospective buyers who click it will see the details of what the seal represents (as shown in Figure 46-2).

• **Figure 46-1:** This item is bonded!

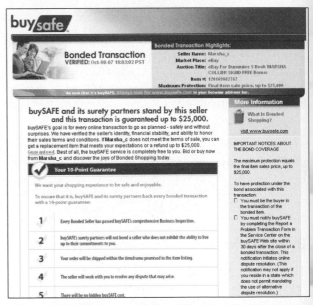

• **Figure 46-2:** Buyers receive confirmation that the exact items they want to buy are fully bonded.

Seller Bonding on eBay

You may be wondering whether it's some sort of big deal to get your items bonded on eBay. Not really. Here's how it works.

You can bond your listings up to a total maximum of a prescribed dollar amount. The total number of bonded listings cannot exceed this figure. Think of the maximum as working like a line of credit; you can only draw against it until you've maxed out your line.

To become bonded, you must meet at least some minimum requirements:

- ✔ A Feedback rating of 100

- ✔ Three months experience selling online

- ✔ Average online sales of $1,000 per month

- ✔ Your business is based in the United States (but not in the state of Hawaii)

If you fulfill those requirements, you then need to fill out a form on the buySAFE Web site, which will ask you for information about yourself and your business. After applying, you undergo a thorough qualification process — which evaluates your online sales experience and reputation, verifies your identity, and analyzes your financial stability. Then you must also legally commit either to honoring their terms of sale or repaying any losses that they cause.

 Yes, you may have great feedback, but bonding is not about the people who are already buying from you — the point is to attract new buyers with a signal that *proves* you're professional and rock-solid.

Bonding items

After you receive approval and know your total bonding amount (based on how you were qualified), you may choose which of your auctions to bond and which not to bond.

The listings you choose to bond cost you 1 percent of the final selling price on the Bonded Merchant Program. You pay nothing in advance, and there are no hidden fees or commitments. You also don't have to pay if a bonded item doesn't sell. With this plan, there's *no* minimum fee either. If the bonded item sells for $3 (shipping, handling fees, and taxes are not included in the bonded total) your fee will be $.03.

Take a look at Figure 46-3 to see my Bonded Seller's page on buySAFE. Here, as a seller, you can see any of your items that aren't yet bonded as well as your total bonding limit, bonds outstanding (bonds on a sold item are kept open for 30 days), and the total of your bonded transactions.

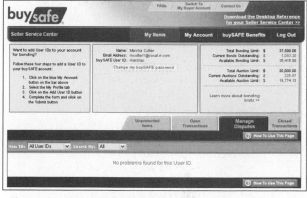

• **Figure 46-3: buySAFE Seller Services area.**

To take a look at your bonded transactions, click the tab to go to that page (as in Figure 46-4). Here you can see any open items with bonds and view any problems that may have arisen.

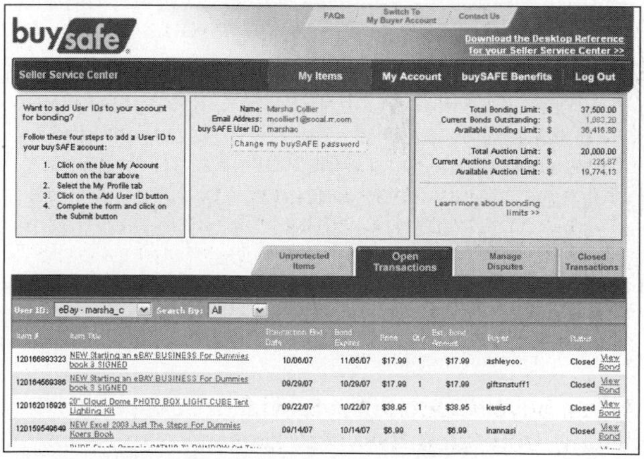

• **Figure 46-4: Your bonded transactions.**

If you click the item title, you can see the details of an open auction, as shown in Figure 46-5.

What happens when something goes wrong?

When a buyer feels slighted in a transaction, that customer is still yours to solve the problem with. If unhappy buyers contact buySAFE, they will be sent directly back to you.

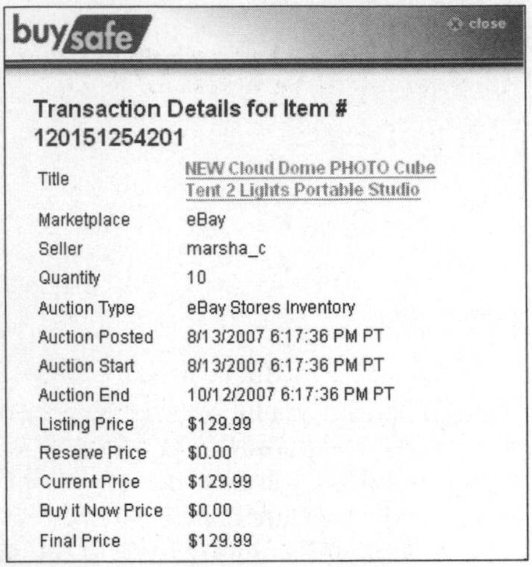

buysafe
close
Transaction Details for Item # 120151254201
Title NEW Cloud Dome PHOTO Cube Tent 2 Lights Portable Studio
Marketplace eBay
Seller marsha_c
Quantity 10
Auction Type eBay Stores Inventory
Auction Posted 8/13/2007 6:17:36 PM PT
Auction Start 8/13/2007 6:17:36 PM PT
Auction End 10/12/2007 6:17:36 PM PT
Listing Price $129.99
Reserve Price $0.00
Current Price $129.99
Buy it Now Price $0.00
Final Price $129.99

• Figure 46-5: Details of an open auction.

If, for some reason, the buyers still insist they need help resolving the issue, they may fill in a Problem Transaction report on the buySAFE Web site, stating the problem and saying what the seller can do to resolve the issue. This will appear on your Seller Services page (Manage Disputes tab); you will see a red button that reads View Problem, indicating a problem. When you log in to your buySAFE seller's account, you will immediately be brought to this page (refer to Figure 46-3).

You can see the buyer's comments when you click the Problem bar.

An e-mail is sent to you, and your response is recorded. If, after two e-mail exchanges pass, nothing has been solved, a professional mediator (a claims representative) joins in to solve the problem.

There is no charge for the mediation. The mediator may contact both the buyer and seller via phone to get both sides of the story. A bond from a surety company, such as The Hartford, has a legal obligation to protect both parties. It *protects the seller from false allegations* and the buyers from losing their money.

If no compromise is made, the mediator will make a binding decision, based on the evidence provided, in favor of one party or the other.

Seller Bonding off of eBay

Once you've been approved as a bonded seller, you can take your seal to many paces on the Web where you're selling — for example, Overstock.com Auctions or TIAS.com — the best of which is your *own* e-commerce Web site! buySAFE provides a special logo you can use on your pages (as in Figure 46-6).

buysafe
certified
INSPECTED & MONITORED
12-07-06
VERIFY

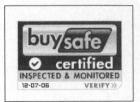

• Figure 46-6: A bonded seller's Web-site logo.

buySAFE will provide you with a small snippet of HTML code that allows you to display the buySAFE Seal wherever you'd like on your site (typically at the top-right corner of the pages for maximum conversion impact). After you've been approved, you receive an e-mail with a user guide that has full instructions on how to maximize your use of buySAFE.

You can have the buyers pay for their individual bonds — purchased through the cart on your Web site and buySAFE will pay you a commission for each bond that's sold! Sweet.

Bonding, as I have said, may be new to the internet, but it's proved successful with many of the sellers who have tried it. If you'd like to give it a whirl, go to

`www.buysafe.com/coolebaytools`

and you'll get an incredibly good introductory offer.

Practice 47

Getting Free with a Home Network

In This Practice

✔ Working from your patio instead of your desk

✔ Figuring out what kind of network you need

✔ Installing your network

Networking is so common among successful companies (and home-based businesses) these days that a business raises eyebrows if it *doesn't* have a network. Not that you should ever adopt a business practice just because everybody *else* is doing it, but . . . they're doing it for some very good reasons that are appropriate for a PowerSeller to consider. These include greater efficiency and higher profits (courtesy of the time you save by using computers most effectively). So that's what this practice is about — giving your PowerSelling a boost with networking.

What is a network? A *network* is a way to connect computers so they can communicate with each other — as if they were one giant computer with different terminals. The best part is that a network enables high-speed sharing of Internet connections, as well as of printers and other peripherals. You can (for example) set up your network to have one computer run bookkeeping, another running a graphics server, and others doing duty as personal PCs for different users. From each networked computer, you can access programs, files, printers, scanners and other hardware on all *other* networked computers.

By networking your home (or eBay office), you'll save time by having the flexibility to work from different rooms or locations. (City dwellers, don't hate me for this . . . those of you still tied to the office, anyway.) You can also list auctions out by the pool (or in your backyard) in summer. (Now, *that's* good working conditions!)

Today's technologies allow you to perform the same miracle that has become such a part of big business . . . on a *home network*. You can connect as many computers as you like, and run your business from anywhere in your home — you can even hook up your laptop from the bedroom if you don't feel like getting out of bed.

The first time I spoke to my editors about putting information in my books about networking, they scoffed at me. Bah! They figured it was a big-business thing; people who worked at home didn't *need* networks (as if networks were solely for the big companies with lots of cubicles). The more I spoke to the eBay community, though, the more I saw the need for networks — especially among PowerSellers — and the more people asked me about them.

I started writing about eBay in 1999, and now it's 2008. A lot of technology has washed under the bridge, and many advances have been made. Setting up a network in 1999 meant spending hours (maybe days) changing settings, testing, and checking computers; and it involved a lot of cursing. That was if you were lucky enough to finally get it right. Otherwise — as in the case of most home users (including me) — you'd give up and take the whole thing as a loss and go on with your life. (I used the old fashioned "sneaker-net": putting files on a high-density disk and walking them over to the other computer where I wanted to work on them).

Lucky for us non-techie types, today's versions of Windows are considerably more home-network-friendly than the earlier versions. Also, more pleasant modes of networking (other than having miles of Ethernet cables going around the walls of your house) came to the fore. Networking technology is more convenient and affordable — and makes a lot more sense for the home-based PowerSeller — these days.

Variations of a Home Network

You basically have a choice of three types of home networks: Ethernet, powerline, and wireless. See Table 47-1 for a quick rundown of some pros and cons of each.

TABLE 47-1: TYPES OF NETWORKS AND THEIR PROS AND CONS

Type	Pros	Cons
Traditional Ethernet*	Fast, cheap, and easy to set up.	Computers and printers must be hardwired; cables run everywhere.
Powerline	Fast; your home is already prewired with outlets.	Electrical interference may degrade the signal.
Wireless network**	Pretty fast; wireless (no ugly cords to deal with).	Expensive; some flavors may not be reliable because of interference from home electrical devices.

Connects computers with high-quality cable over a maximum of 328 feet of cabling.

**Several types of wireless are available. (See "Going Wireless" later in this practice.)*

The wireless network is pretty much today's *de-facto* standard. They are so easy to set up that practically anyone can do it. However, some wireless signals may experience interference because the network runs with the same 2.4GHz technology as some home wireless telephones (and even microwave ovens).

That said, all networks need the following two devices:

- ✔ **Router:** A router allows you to share a single Internet IP address among multiple computers. A router does exactly what its name implies; it routes signals and data to the different computers on your network. If you have one computer, the router can act as a firewall or even as a network device leading to a print server (a gizmo that attaches to your router and allows you to print directly to a printer without having another computer on) or straight to a newfangled wireless printer.

✔ **Modem:** You need a modem for an Internet connection. You get one from your cable or phone company and plug it into an outlet with cable (just like your TV) or into a special phone jack if you have DSL. The modem connects to your router with an Ethernet cable.

 If you have broadband, you don't even need to have a main computer turned on to access the connection anywhere in the house. If you keep a printer turned on (and have a print server or a wireless printer), you can also connect that to your router and print from your laptop in another room — right through the network.

Using a Powerline Network

When I tell you how simple to install and inexpensive a powerline network is, you'll be shocked (no pun intended). It's a super alternative, as reliable as a wired connection, because it is — hard-wired! You can access your Internet connection from any power outlet in your home. Considering that I'm someone who likes to tinker with things, I was upset that setting it up was so easy!

All you need to have to share a high-speed Internet connection, files, and printers are

✔ **Electrical outlets:** I'll bet you have more than one in each room of your house.

✔ **An Ethernet connection on each computer:** These days all computers have one.

✔ **A wall-plugged Ethernet adapter for each computer:** The basis for the setup is a very small box, about the size of a pack of cigarettes that plugs into any two- or three-pronged electrical outlet. Take a look at one in Figure 47-1.

✔ **A router:** You only need this higher-end bit of gear if you intend to connect a high-speed Internet connection throughout your home or office (and isn't that really the point of all this?).

• **Figure 47-1:** Netgear's high-speed (85Mbps) wall-plugged Ethernet adapter.

Here are two especially nifty benefits of this little system:

✔ **It's inexpensive.** The requisite magic box costs for a powerline network can be as reasonable as $40. You need one for each computer.

✔ **You've already got the cabling.** The networking connection is made through your existing electrical wiring. It doesn't consume extra electricity.

If you have a high-speed Internet connection, no doubt you received a modem when you signed up. Since it's not sensible to connect the modem directly to your computer (a router does the work for you — as outlined in the accompanying Tip), you may already have a router.

 A *router* allows you to share a single Internet IP address among multiple computers. A router does exactly what its name implies; it routes signals and data to the different computers or devices on your network. If you have one computer, the router can act as a firewall, or even as a network device leading to a print sharer. But basically, to hook up more than one connection, you do need a router.

The integration works like this:

✔ The high-speed connection comes in through your DSL or cable line.

✔ The cable line plugs into your modem.

✔ An Ethernet cable goes from your modem into a router.

✔ One "out" Ethernet cable connection from the router goes to a local computer.

✔ Another "out" Ethernet cable goes to the power-line adapter.

✔ The powerline box is plugged into a convenient wall outlet.

Take a look at Figure 47-2 for a graphic display.

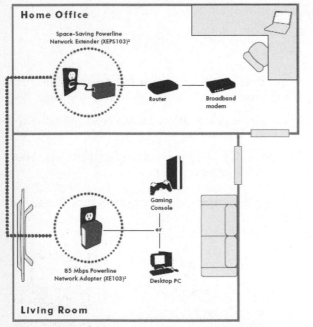

• **Figure 47-2: A typical basic setup for the powerline network.**

When you want to connect the computers in other rooms to the network, just plug in a magic box.

Going Wireless

Wireless networking — also known as Wi-Fi (or, to the more technically inclined, IEEE 802.11 networking) — is the hot technology for all kinds of networks. The abbreviation *Wi-Fi* is short for *Wireless Fidelity.* It's a very impressive system when

it works, with no cables or connectors to bog you down. And when it works well, it's flawless. You'll be so please to become non-tethered to cabling.

As a matter of fact, I was in New York recently, staying on the 16th floor of a hotel. I turned on my travel laptop to check e-mail and my laptop found signals for nine different wireless networks! I had to call the front desk to find out which one was the hotel connection. The whole world seems to be going wireless.

> Being a networked PowerSeller also means keeping an eye on network security — and going wireless means you're sending out a radio signal that other people can pick up. Some of those folks are way too interested in other people's business; they drive around with special equipment trying to pick up stray Wi-Fi signals to glean for information. It's called *wardriving* (I Googled it and got way over a million hits). In addition, the Wi-Fi hotspots you find out there in the world may not have any security encryption, and are free for all to use. What to do about possible snoopers? Well, for openers, see the "Encrypting Your Signal" section, later in this practice.

The types of wireless networks

If you've ever used a wireless telephone at home, you've used a technology similar to a wireless network. Most home wireless phones transmit to each other on the radio frequency band of 2.4 GHz, and they have the option to choose from several channels automatically to give you the best connection.

The two prevalent forms of wireless networks also work on the 2.4GHz band, and you generally will need to preset the channel when you set up the system. But there are three kinds:

✔ **802.11a:** This is a wireless format that works really well — pretty fast with good connectivity. It's used when you have to serve up a wireless connection to a large group of people, as in a convention center or dormitory. It delivers data at speeds as high as 54 Mbps (megabits per second). It also runs at the 5GHz band (hence its nickname *Wi-Fi5*), so it doesn't have any competition for bandwidth with wireless phones or microwave ovens. It's also very expensive.

✔ **802.11b:** My old laptop has a built-in 802.11b card, so I can connect to the ever-popular "hot spots" in Starbucks and airports. It's the most common wireless type, and it's used on the most platforms right now. The B version is slower than the A version, only capable of transferring data at 11 Mbps. It's a solid, low-cost solution when you have no more than 32 users per access point.

 The lower frequency of 2.4 GHz drains less power from laptops and other portable devices. So, if you're using a laptop, the battery will last longer. Also, 2.4GHz signals can travel farther — and pass through walls and floors more effectively — than 5GHz signals.

✔ **802.11g:** This is a widely used type of wireless connection, based on the 2.4GHz band. It speeds up data to a possible 54 Mbps, and it's backward-compatible so it works wherever the 802.11b service is available.

✔ **802.11n:** The latest fastest form of wireless, 802.11n is a dual-frequency connection that works through MIMO (multiple input/multiple output) technology. It travels farther than any of the other formats. (I'm using it at my home and it's amazing!) It can connect you to the Internet at speeds *averaging* 254 Mbps.

The wireless *n* speed can be a scorching 254 Mbps — but only if all your receiving equipment is fitted with 802.11n adapters. If you have different — that is, earlier — versions of wireless in your home system, you'll have to run at the slower (legacy) speed rate.

Setting up your wireless network

With a wireless network, you'll have to connect your computer (a laptop works best) to a wireless router (the gizmo that broadcasts your signal throughout your home or office) before you can perform some beginning setup tasks such as choosing your channel

and setting up your encryption code. (The wireless access point will come with instructions for your particular brand.)

After you complete the setup and turn on your wireless router, you will have a Wi-Fi hotspot in your home or office. Typically, your new hotspot will provide coverage for about 200 feet in all directions, although walls and floors definitely cut down on the range. Even so, you should get good coverage throughout a typical home. For a large home, you can buy wireless extenders to increase the range of your hotspot.

Simplified, this is how your network will be configured:

1. **Run a cable from your DSL line to your modem.**

2. **Connect an Ethernet cable from your modem to your router.**

3. **Connect the Ethernet cable to your Wireless Access Point.**

Take a look at the network diagram from Netgear in Figure 47-3.

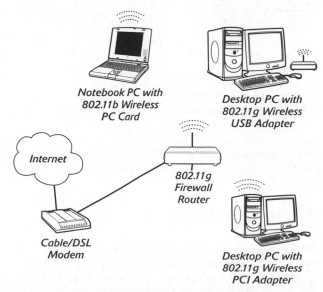

• **Figure 47-3:** A typical home wireless network.

Extending Your Wireless Connection

You can extend your network in one of two ways that you can extend your network. I've tried both and they seem to work really well. Here's the skinny . . .

Using a second router as a repeater

I was having major problems getting my wireless signal to the end of my house (a typical California ranch-style one-story with steel earthquake reinforcement). You can, depending on the brand of router, get one that can be configured as a repeater. I tried the Netgear wireless n WNR834b, and it sent an incredibly fast 802.11n signal to the farthest corners of my home (and even to my neighbors' homes). This technology shoots the fastest (as of now) signal as high as 278 Mbps.

Setup is easy; you put one router next to your DSL or cable modem, and put a second router somewhere in your home where your wireless signal begins to fall off. The second router picks up the signal from the first and sends its own signal to the rest of the house. Take a look at Figure 47-4 to see how it works.

Using a powerline wireless extender

An ingenious invention, a powerline extender uses your existing home electrical wiring to carry your network signals and your high-speed Internet connection. You access the network by connecting a powerline adapter to your router and then plugging it into an electrical outlet on the wall.

Hooking up a wireless powerline extender is so easy that it's a bit disappointing if you're braced for an engineering adventure — you'll wonder why it isn't more complicated. Most installations work immediately right out of the box. Hooking up the wireless/powerline network goes like this:

1. The high-speed connection comes in through your DSL or cable line.

2. Plug the cable line (or phone line for DSL) into your modem.

3. Connect one "in" Ethernet cable from your modem to a router.

4. Connect the "out" Ethernet cable to the wireless powerline extender.

5. Plug the wireless powerline extender into a convenient wall outlet.

6. Plug the wireless powerline receiver box into a convenient wall outlet, wherever you want to extend the signal.

That's it!

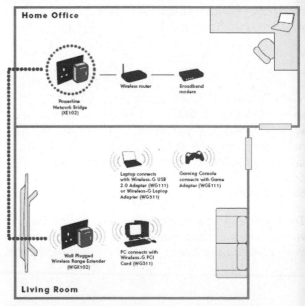

• **Figure 47-4:** Placing routers in your home wireless network.

Using a Hybrid Network

You may find that a wireless network may not work throughout your home. That's easy to fix. You can combine different networks and have (say) wireless connectivity in some rooms of your house or in your backyard, while keeping a wired network going inside the house.

At my house, I have a wireless *n* network. My router is a Netgear Rangemax Next and it plugs into my desktop computer with an Ethernet cable. The rest of the house is wireless, and I have no compatibility problems with any of the laptops. This way, no matter where I go, I can hook up with ease.

Encrypting Your Signal

It's not that I mind that my neighbors share my network, but if too many were to join, the speed would be massively reduced. There's also the not-to-be ignored issue that if you don't encrypt your signal, then anyone with a modicum of skill can pick up your wireless signal and learn all your passwords!

Wireless networks are protected by their own brand of security that encrypts your wireless transmissions and prevents others from getting into your network. Originally — and it's still available as a security option on wireless networks — people used WEP (Wireless Encryption Protocol) to secure their networks. Sadly, the security of this protocol didn't last long; these days even casual hackers and college kids can get into it. It's about as secure as Swiss cheese.

To solve the problem of confidentiality over the airwaves, a new system was invented, WPA or Wi-Fi Protected Access. That's what I use; it's the protocol that works best on all networks — even if you mix PCs and Macs on the same network.

When setting up your security settings on the router, you will have to come up with a Passphrase. It must be longer, more than your typical 6 to 8 character password. So come up with a good combination of letters and numbers (*not* your home street address) so it will be nearly impossible for a hacker to gain access to your transmissions. I use a PSK (pre-shared key) version that allows me to use one single passphrase for all my wireless secured devices. (Large networks use an authentication server, which distributes different keys to each user.) PSK also manages to mask the details of your network; it won't give out a bit of information about your network security.

To link your laptop or desktop to a wireless network with encryption, simply input your passphrase into your wireless setup and you should be good to go.

 I have a Nintendo Wii in my living room (for my home-business work breaks). It also picks up the wireless signal (with a WPA encryption) and allows me to access the internet from my television! For those of you who have Wiis and would like my Mii to join the Wii Parade, e-mail me at *mcollier@coolebaytools.com* with Wii Mii in your subject line and your Wii console code in the text. In return, I will send my Wii code to you and you can have my Mii running around your plaza. (For those who don't have a Wii, sorry about the interruption. Just remember: All work and no play makes Jack or Jill a dull PowerSeller.)

Glossary of eBay PowerSellers' Business Terms

AVS (Address Verification System): Used by PayPal and other credit card processors to see that the billing address given by the customer matches the credit card.

Above the fold: The part of the page or e-mail that is immediately visible without having to scroll. A preferred advertising spot, originally from newspapers.

About Me page: The free Web page given to every eBay user. It's an excellent promotional tool.

Accounts payable: Expenses that have been charged but not paid for.

Accounts receivable: The pending amount due from a sale to the seller. Merchandise has been sold, but money has not been collected.

Advance order: An order placed for merchandise to be delivered on a future date.

Advertising budget: The amount of money you set aside for advertising your items in any media (newspaper, radio, ad banner, and so on).

Affiliate Program: A promotional tool in which a particular Web site contracts with other Web sites to drive visitors to it. Those other sites earn paid commissions based on the traffic they bring in.

API: Application Program Interface. An application program that is created to interface with another computer (or another program).

Apparel/merchandise mart: A single building or complex filled with many wholesale sources where vendors lease space to provide buyers one-stop-shopping. Visiting one gives you the opportunity of checking out many wholesale sources in one area.

Archive: Moving an inactive file to another area for storage.

B2B: Business-to-business. Relationship in which a business targets other businesses rather than consumers; a business selling shipping supplies is usually B2B; a seller of recreational fishing supplies is usually B2C.

B2C: Business-to-consumer. Businesses that target the consumer market with their goods (versus the business market as in B2B).

Back order: (Something you don't want to hear if you're buying from a drop-shipper.) The merchandise you ordered is not available for delivery. Your vendor will usually supply you with a date if and when they'll be able to ship.

Barcode: A standardized set of lines and spaces of different widths that can be scanned (read) by a barcode reader to identify the product. It's accompanied by a Uniform Product Code (UPC).

Basic stock method: A method of stock planning in which you maintain a basic dollar amount of merchandise on hand. The amount remains constant from season to season.

Best Offer: A feature that allows a buyer to make an offer lower than the item's Buy It Now price. The seller can then decide whether to accept the offer or reject it.

Black Friday: The day after Thanksgiving when American retailers go from "in the red" to "in the black." Considered by many the heaviest brick-and-mortar shopping day of the year, but not on eBay.

BOM: Beginning-of-month stock or dollar-sales figure.

Bonding: A formal guarantee that a contract will be fulfilled. A surety bond can be issued by a third party (usually an insurance company) to guarantee a seller's performance within a transaction. (See Practice 46.)

Business formulas: Standard formulas that produce math calculations related to sales. Here are four standard examples:

- Specific amount = $\texttt{Total amount} \sqrt{} \texttt{percentage}$

- Percentage = $\texttt{Specific amount} \div \texttt{total amount}$

- Percent of increase (or decrease) = $\texttt{Difference between figures} \div \texttt{original amount}$

- Total Amount = $\texttt{Specific amount} \div \texttt{percentage}$

Buyer's premium: A percentage added to an auction's final bid that goes to the auctioneer. Used in brick-and-mortar and eBay Live auctions.

Buy It Now: An auction format on eBay that offers a buyout price that ends the listing.

Cannibalization: When you buy new products to resell that outdate your existing inventory.

COD (Collect On Delivery): When you ship an order to a buyer and they have to pay the shipping company upon receipt. Not recommended for eBay sellers.

COGS (Cost of Goods Sold): Costs directly related to the purchase or production of items you sell. Also a figure from the Profit and Loss statement for your business — it totals the full amount of all expenses involved in selling your items.

Chargeback: A credit-card transaction that is billed back to the merchant after the sale to cover disputed charges.

Consignment selling: Accepting merchandise to sell where the vendor is paid only when the merchandise sells. The seller takes a commission on the sale.

Co-op advertising: Allowances offered to sellers by some vendors and third-party sources — for example, by eBay to PowerSellers — toward advertising in print or other media. The third party shares the cost of preapproved advertising based on your dollar volume.

Cost of goods: A standard business-expense category that takes into account the actual cost of the merchandise plus shipping costs to get the item to you.

CPC (Cost Per Click): An online payment model where advertisers pay for each click-through made on their advertisements.

CPM (Cost Per Thousand): A price paid by an advertiser for a Web site displaying their banner a thousand times.

CTR (Click-Through Ratio): The number of times an online advertisement is clicked, divided by the times the ad is viewed or served to the page. This ratio helps you calculate whether your online ads are effective. The ratio of the number of times an ad is shown to the number of times it is clicked on. For example if the click-through ratio is 50:1, it means 1 in 50 people (that is, 2 percent) clicked the ad.

DSR (Detailed Seller Ratings): eBay Seller rating in a five-star system; buyers rate the seller for item as described, communication, shipping time, and shipping-and-handling charges.

Demographic data: Data that outlines the characteristics of your customers. It can include age, marital status, income, education, and other factors that influence buying.

Domain name: Your address on the Internet, as in www.coolebaytools.com.

Double Opt-In: The best way to ensure that your newsletter customers are "opt-in." When a customer requests to be on your e-mail list, you send a confirmation response asking the customer to verify their desire to receive your e-mails.

Drop-shipments: Items sold to you that are sent by a drop-shipping source directly to your customer. Technically, eBay's TOS state that you (the seller) must have control of any merchandise you sell on the site, making this an iffy situation.

Dumpster-diving: Acquiring the castoffs of others to resell on eBay. (Not necessarily accomplished by being lowered by the ankles headfirst into a garbage dumpster — but it *has* been done sometimes. Don't ask!)

Duty: A tax you may have to pay if you purchase merchandise from another country.

EAN: European Article Number. The international version of the Universal Product Code (UPC).

Early adopters: Consumers who seek out the newest trends in fashion or electronics in the earliest stages of the product cycle.

eBay Express: An eBay fixed-price marketplace.

Emotional buying motive: Trigger this motive in your description by plying the customers' emotions (that they "have to have" the product) versus selling with logic.

EOM: End-of-month stock or sales figure. The end of one month is the same figure as the *BOM* of the next month.

Escrow: A payment system to protect the buyer from fraudulent sales. The buyer's money is held by a third party until the buyer receives and approves of the item, and then the payment is released to the seller.

Even pricing: A merchandise-pricing strategy to create an upscale image for your item by pricing the item in full-dollar numbers — for example, $25.00 instead of $24.99.

Export: Goods shipped outside national borders to other countries (for example, from the U.S. to the U.K.).

Expos/trade shows: Shows generally held at large convention centers where manufacturers introduce their latest merchandise. These shows may offer general merchandise or only items from a particular category.

Fad: A short-lived fashion trend that comes and goes quickly.

Fashion followers: Those who look for apparel only after the trend has fully caught on and the general populace has accepted the style. Perfect eBay apparel customers!

Feedback: eBay's User-to-User rating system.

FIFO: First In First Out. An inventory control method, where merchandise that's first in is the first sold.

Fixed-price sale: Selling an item (or a number of items) on eBay at a set price with no option for auction.

FOB (Free On Board) shipping: When the seller has title to the goods until the merchandise reaches a certain point in the shipping process. From that point, the buyer takes title and is responsible for all further shipping charges. As in FOB Miami — the seller pays shipping to Miami, and the buyer pays all shipping charges from a Miami location.

FTC (Federal Trade Commission) Mail Order Rule: Also known as the "30-day" rule, this states that if you cannot ship a customer's order within the time you originally stated *or within 30 days,* you must obtain the customer's permission to delay the transaction. If you do not get permission, or you get no reply from the customer, you must refund all money paid to you for the unshipped merchandise.

FTP: File Transfer Protocol. The online communications protocol used to transfer files from one computer to another.

FVF (Final Value Fees): The commission paid by sellers to eBay based on a percentage of the final price achieved.

Global marketplace: An open online marketplace (such as eBay) where buyers can purchase from sources worldwide.

GMS: Gross Merchandise Sales. In dollars, your total merchandise sales figure.

Gross: A quantity of 12 dozen, or 144, of a single item. (Also: Finding a hair in your fried eggs.)

Growth stage: In the life cycle of a product, this is the stage at which the product or service is past the innovator's initial input and its sales grow through consumer acceptance.

Hammer fee: See *Buyer's premium.*

Hard goods: All merchandise other than apparel and accessories or home fashions. Hard goods would encompass furniture, appliances, high-tech goods, sporting goods, and so on.

Hot item: An item that's nearly impossible to keep in stock due to customer demand. This is the stuff you can generally sell for over *MSRP.*

Imports: Merchandise purchased from foreign countries and sources and brought into your home country (for example, from China to the United States) for resale.

Impression: One of a number of times an online ad is served to be viewed. One impression means there was one opportunity to see the ad.

Initial markup percentage: The percentage you're comfortable tacking onto an item to sell in a Buy-It-Now transaction.

Introduction stage: When merchandise is first introduced and has made it past the early adopters, but is new to the general merchandise scene.

Invoice: A bill that outlines the items in a specific transaction — including to whom the item is sold and all costs involved.

Irregulars: Merchandise that is not first quality and contains imperfections that may not be visible to the naked eye.

ISBN: International Standard Book Number. Like the UPC on a can of beans, the ISBN identifies the product (in this case, a book) by a universal number.

JPEG (or JPG): A file format used for storing graphic images, usually photographs.

Job lots: A varied assortment of merchandise that's left over at the end of a season. Usually sold to a buyer at a price discounted off the normal wholesale cost.

Just-in-time inventory: An inventory-management system set up to deliver all merchandise to the seller just as it's needed (or nearly so). Inventory is kept at minimal levels, freeing up cash by minimizing requisite storage space.

Keystone: Marking up your merchandise the amount that you paid for the item. Cost 50%, Markup 50% = 100% Keystone markup.

Layaway: Allowing someone to purchase an item and pay for it over time. You ship the item when the final payment is made.

LIFO: Last In First Out. An inventory-control method that assumes that merchandise that was received most recently (that is, last) should be first to sell.

List price: See *MSRP.*

Logo: A graphic symbol to identify a business. It may be an icon, or the business name in a distinctive type or graphic style.

Loss leader: Items you choose to sell at (or to start the bidding at) a price lower than the going rate. You may sell at a loss, but the goal is to sell other items from your eBay store to make up for the loss.

Mannequin: A representation of the human form made of wood, fiberglass, or plastic to model clothing for your eBay apparel sales.

Markdown: Reduction in selling price below your predetermined target price.

Markup based on cost: Pricing an item based on the price you paid for the items to be resold, rather than the "retail" price. The most common markup method used by eBay sellers.

Markup based on retail: Pricing your item to match full retail price.

Maturity stage: Toward the end of a product's life cycle, when prices and sales reach the maximum level. At this stage, the item is no longer hard to find.

Merchandise plan: Sales goals in dollar amounts, planned for a prescribed period of time.

Merchant account: A bank account that enables a business to accept credit cards for payment — in PayPal, a higher-level (lower-cost) account for larger sellers.

Middleman: The person between you and the manufacturer, if you're not buying direct.

MSRP: Manufacturer's Suggested Retail Price. The price (suggested by the manufacturer) that hardly anybody is willing to pay.

NARU: Not A Registered eBay User

Odd-cent pricing: Pricing your item with odd cents. A technique that creates the impression that the buyer will be getting a bargain. For example, Wal-Mart uses $.97 instead of $.98.

Off-price merchandise: Manufacturers' excess merchandise that's available to retailers at a considerable discount for resale.

Open to buy: In dollars, the amount left for acquiring merchandise within a specific season or time period.

Opt-in: When a customer requests to be put on a mailing list. (See *Double Opt-In.*)

Pay-per-click advertising: Ads placed on Google, Yahoo, or other search engines. The advertiser pays for the ad when the user clicks its advertisement and goes to its site.

Penetration pricing: Cutting your profits to generate more sales. A seller penetrates the market by gaining market share to overthrow the competition.

Physical inventory: The actual physical count of your merchandise versus what your bookkeeping or management program says you have.

Plagiarism: When another seller steals your description and/or images and uses those materials in their own sales. Report this eBay policy violation as *Image or description theft* in the Security Center.

Price skimming: Charging the highest price you can for merchandise, resulting in lower total transactions but a higher profit margin on the sales that are completed.

Price war: When two or more competitive sellers lower their product price to undercut the competition, thereby gaining market share.

Product life cycle: A chart depicting expected stages of low and high sales for a product during its time on the market.

Purchase order: A business form outlining the details of a merchandise purchase, usually from a retailer to a vendor.

Returns: Merchandise that has been sent back by the buyer and accepted by the seller after a retail transaction, normally resulting in a refund to the buyer. Often returns are resold to eBay sellers as part of liquidation-lot merchandise.

RSS (Really Simple Syndication): (The initials originally stood for Rich Site Summary.) A format for sharing content among different Web sites. Sites feed content to users who use an application called an RSS reader or aggregator to download feeds. RSS makes it possible for people to keep up with their favorite Web sites in an automated manner.

Seconds: Merchandise that clearly contains damage or imperfections. A step in quality below *irregulars*.

SEO (Search-Engine Optimization): The process of making your Web site attractive to search engines.

SKU (Stock-Keeping Unit): A number assigned to each piece of inventory for identification and/or tracking purposes. It may be your own number or it may relate to the item's UPC.

SSL (Secure Socket Layer): A set of standards used for encrypting data sent over the Internet, including e-commerce transactions and passwords.

STR (Sell-Through Rate): A percentage that represents the number of items sold compared to the number of items listed.

Sniping: The act *(or fine art)* of bidding at the very last possible second of an auction.

Spam: Unrequested and unwanted e-mail.

Staple merchandise: Items that people buy regardless of season, year in and year out.

Steamer: An electrical appliance used to remove wrinkles from fabric; essential equipment for PowerSellers of apparel.

Stock-to-sales ratio: A planning tool that shows the relationship between stock on hand and monthly sales. This shows the amount of inventory required to generate planned sales. Ideally it should be about 3:1, so you can have a three-month supply of inventory.

Street price: The typical price that merchandise can be purchased for at brick-and-mortar or online discounters.

Turnover: The number of times your average amount of stock sells during a given period — turning merchandise into cash.

UPC (Universal Product Code): The number that is part of the barcode that is used to identify almost any product. (You can also type a UPC into Google for identification.)

UVM (Universal Vendor Marking): The practice of premarking items so their origin may be identified. Many eBay sellers use a UV pen to mark their merchandise to prevent fraudulent returns. The marks of these pens can only be seen with a UV light.

Warranty: A written guarantee of the seller's or manufacturer's responsibility for ensuring the working order or usability of the product sold. It outlines the terms of return or repair.

Appendix B

Ten Other Places to Move Your Merchandise

As eBay moves more in the direction of fixed-price sales — even if your main business still thrives on the good old eBay auction — a familiar problem from the traditional retail world rears its head: excess inventory. (Don't feel bad about it; sooner or later, every business has some). Inevitably, *some* merchandise starts to look like it'll never scrape together a profit. If you're sick of looking at it but still have *some* cash tied up in it, you have to make storage room for this stuff immediately — or sell it fast. If a corner of your eBay merchandise area has turned into the Graveyard of Unsold Stuff (hey, it happens), you still have options.

You can't expect to bat a thousand every time you select a product to sell. The key is getting rid of the excess with minimum loss on your investment. None of your merchandise is trash (I hope); *someone* out there will want it and will pay *something* for it. If not, you can always donate it and take a tax write-off. In this chapter, I highlight the top ten ways to move that superfluous merchandise and still save your investment.

Donate to Charitable Organizations

Charitable donations are my favorite way of unloading unwanted items. Not only are you doing something good for someone else, but your donation may be a 100-percent business write-off. My community — yours too, no doubt — has many private schools, churches, and synagogues. What they have in common is that they put on fundraisers (auctions, raffles, tournaments, bingo) and they welcome donations. Consider giving the best of your unsold stuff to your schools or churches — especially if it will become some sort of prize. Some organizations make up gift baskets of varied items to put together a higher-value prize, or even take boxes of miscellaneous stuff (think Salvation Army and Goodwill).

Classy gifting

I like to put together gift baskets for charity auctions: I'll take a bunch of female-related, male-related, or kids' items, put them in a basket on a base of shredded Sunday comics, wrap the entire thing in clear cellophane, and top it off with a nice big bow. It's an appreciated donation (and wrapped up this way, it always gets a higher price at bazaars or silent auctions).

Online charities

`MissionFish.com` is the classic eBay example; with eBay, they organized eBay Giving Works (see Practice 16), helping nonprofit organizations support their missions by (in effect) "teaching them to fish." Select your charity from their approved list, and MissionFish does the rest. When an item sells, you (the donor) are responsible for shipping the item. You must use a shipping company that supplies a tracking number, which you submit to eBay Giving Works. (In addition to the item, the entire cost of shipping is tax deductible.) After the winner receives the item, all proceeds are sent from MissionFish to the designated nonprofit. You then receive a thank-you letter as proof of your gift for IRS tax purposes. Many sellers have found that contributing a portion of their sales to charity boosts their bids and final sale prices — while enhancing their image. Remember . . .

- Listings stand out with a Giving Works ribbon icon.

- Your chosen nonprofit's mission statement is on every listing that benefits them.

- Each donation is tax deductible (MissionFish provides the receipt for you).

- The eBay fee credit policy rewards your generosity.

Many other charities accept *gifts-in-kind,* items that are new or gently used that they resell to raise funds. I've brought excess eBay inventory to the American Cancer Society's Discovery Shop, and they've been very gracious about the donations. Now they also sell on eBay (aside from their many retail locations) under their own user ID.

Have a Garage Sale

Garage sales draw big crowds when promoted properly. An especially good time to have a garage sale is late fall or early winter — just in time for the holidays. (*Before* it freezes!) If you've been to a bunch of garage sales but haven't given one in a while, here's what works:

- **Plan the sale at least three weeks in advance:** Decide on the weekend of your sale well beforehand and be sure to set a specific opening time. If you welcome *early birds* (people who like to show up at 6:00 or 7:00 a.m.), be sure to put that in your ad and flyers.

- **Invite neighbors to participate:** The more the merrier! And the bigger the sale, the more customers you're likely to entice. Everyone can drum up at least a few items for a garage sale.

- **Gather and price items to go in the sale:** After you set a date, immediately start putting things aside and pricing them with sticky tags. That avoids a last-minute scramble.

- **Place a classified ad:** Call your local newspaper a week before the sale and ask the friendly classified department people when the best time is to run an ad. Take their advice — they know what they're talking about! Also consider placing the ad on their online site.

- **Make flyers to post around the neighborhood:** Fire up your computer and make a flyer; include your address, a map, the date, and the starting time. Be sure to mention special items that you've thrown into the sale to bring 'em in and mention also that many items are new. If two or three families are participating in the sale, mention that too. If you have small throwaway types of items, include the line "Prices start at 25 cents." Hang the flyers in conspicuous places around your neighborhood.

- **Post large signs on nearby corners:** The day before the sale, put up *large* posters (on brightly colored 22 × 28 poster board, lettered with thick black markers) to advertise it. Use few words; include only the basics — for example: "Garage Sale June 22–24, 8 a.m., Tons of Stuff, 1234 Extra Cash Blvd."

- **Clean up any dusty or dirty items:** If you want someone to buy an item for a good price, you have to make it look good.

- **Gather supplies:** Get lots of change; make sure you have plenty of tens, fives, a ton of singles, and several rolls of coins. Get a calculator for each person who'll be taking money. Designate a cash box. Collect shopping bags to offer those with multiple purchases.

- **Hang helium balloons to draw attention to your signs:** The day of the sale, go to the busiest corner near your sale and tie some helium balloons to your sign — that's sure to attract attention. Do the same thing at the corner near your sale and also at the curb of the sale.

- **Display everything in an orderly fashion:** Pull out your old card tables and arrange items so that people can easily see what's there; a literal pile of junk'll turn them off. Hang clothes on a temporary rack (or use a clothesline on the day of the sale).

- **Get ready to negotiate:** Talk to people when they approach, use your selling talents, and *make that sale!*

At the end of your sale, be sure to take down the signs you've plastered all over the neighborhood. It's the nice thing to do.

Rent a Table at the Local Flea Market

Local *swap meets* or *flea markets* (regularly scheduled — sometimes monthly — events where you can rent space for a token fee and sell your wares) can be a great place to meet other eBay sellers. But whatever you do, don't mention that you sell on eBay. If customers they're getting a bargain, so much the better. Offer great deals; give 'em a discount if they buy a *ton* of stuff. You can move lots of merchandise here. Don't forget to try selling your goods to other sellers; perhaps they can do with a little extra inventory. If you have a weekly Farmer's Market in your area, check it out. This might be a great place to buy a table for a few hours — especially if you're selling related items.

Consign Merchandise to the Local Antique Mall

An *antique mall* (a retail store that's often run by several people) may take your merchandise on consignment. Your items are sold in the store (which is good for you), and the store owners take a commission on each sale (which is good for them). They take your items, tag them with your identifying tag, and display them for sale. Antique malls usually see an enormous amount of foot traffic; this may be as close to brick-and-mortar retail as you'll ever get.

Take a Booth at a Community Event

Where I live, the local business community often holds special events such as street fairs, Fourth of July extravaganzas, and pumpkin festivals. You can buy a vendor's booth at such events to peddle your wares. For seasonal events, purchase a bunch of holiday-related items to make your table match the festivities. Your excess eBay inventory will just be part of the display — and a big part of your sales. You might even consider donating a percentage of your sales to a local nonprofit to help boost traffic.

 If the event is in the evening, purchase a few hundred glow-in-the-dark bracelets on eBay (you can often get one hundred for $20). The kids love them and will drag their parents to your booth. Be creative, support your community, have fun, and make some money!

Resell to Sellers on eBay

Sell your items to other eBay sellers. Just kidding (or *maybe not*). Maybe another seller (your competition) is selling the same items but is doing a better job with those items than you. If so, offer to sell your stock to that seller. It's a win-win situation. Perhaps some of the stuff you have may appeal to the locals in your community (some of whom probably sell on eBay). Package your items in related lots to appeal to sellers who are looking for merchandise online. One successful eBay seller often combines many lost packages into single lots to sell on eBay: the Post Office Mail Recovery Center. If you're overstocked with (say) stuffed animals, put together a lot of a dozen. If you don't have a dozen of any one item, make packages of related items that will appeal to a certain type of seller. And be sure to use the words *liquidation, wholesale,* or *resale* (or all three) in your title. A world of savvy sellers is out there looking for items to resell — maybe they can move yours at a later time or in a different venue.

Visit a Local Auctioneer

Yes, I mean a real *live* auctioneer, one who has pro credentials and holds live auctions at real auction houses that real people attend. Shopping at auctions can be addictive (duh), and live auctions attract an elite group of knowledgeable buyers. The basic idea is to bring your stuff to an auctioneer, who auctions off lots for you. Good auctioneers can get a crowd going, so the bidding is far more than an item was expected to sell for. Here are a few pointers to keep in mind when looking for an auctioneer:

✔ **Make sure that the auction house you choose is licensed to hold auctions in your state, insured, and bonded.** You don't want to leave your fine merchandise with someone who will pack up and disappear with your stuff before the auction.

✔ **Get the details before agreeing to the consignment.** Many auction houses give you at least 75 percent of the final hammer price. Before you consign your items, ask the auctioneer's representative about the details, such as these: When will the auction be held? How often are the auctions held? Have you sold items like this before? If so, how much have they sold for in the past? Will there be a printed catalog for the sale, and will my piece be shown in it?

 Get the terms and conditions in writing and have the rep walk you through every point so that you thoroughly understand each one.

✔ **Search the Internet.** Type *licensed auctions* and see what you come up with; it can't hurt.

✔ **Contact local auctioneers.** If your items are of good quality, a local auction house may be interested in taking them on consignment.

Find Specialty Auction Sites

If you have some specialized items that just don't sell very well on eBay, you might look for a different venue. You may have an item that only a specialist in the field can appreciate — one example: fine works of art. I searched Yahoo! for *art auctions.* Under the Web Results heading, I found more than six million Web sites that auction artwork. Refine your search with your telephone area code so you find auction locations in your immediate area. You may find an online auctioneer who specializes in the particular item you have for sale, something too esoteric for the eBay crowd that can sell well elsewhere.

Run a Classified Liquidation Ad

Sell your special items in the appropriate categories of the classifieds; sell the rest in bulk lots to other sellers. When you write the ad, make your lots sound fantastic. When a buyer calls, be excited about your merchandise. Be honest and say you're selling the stuff to raise cash.

Sell Everything on eBay for a $.99 Opening Bid . . .

. . . and take what you get.

Appendix C

About the CD

This appendix gives you the rundown on the contents of the CD that accompanies this book. Use this media as you would use the book — go directly to what interests you most and start there. Here's hoping you find the software, video training, and extra documents useful as you implement your PowerSeller practices. And, as always, have some fun!

System Requirements

Make sure that your computer meets the minimum system requirements shown in the following list. If your computer doesn't match up to most of these requirements, you may have problems using the software and files on the CD. For the latest and greatest information, please refer to the ReadMe file located at the root of the CD-ROM.

- ✔ A PC running Microsoft Windows XP or Windows Vista
- ✔ A Macintosh running Apple OS X or later
- ✔ A PC running a version of Linux with kernel 2.4 or greater
- ✔ An Internet connection
- ✔ A CD-ROM drive

If you need more information on the basics, check out these books published by Wiley Publishing, Inc.: *PCs For Dummies* by Dan Gookin; *Macs For Dummies* by Edward C. Baig; *iMacs For Dummies* by Mark L. Chambers; *Windows XP For Dummies* and *Windows Vista For Dummies*, both by Andy Rathbone.

Using the CD

To install the items from the CD to your hard drive, follow these steps:

1. **Insert the CD into your computer's CD-ROM drive.**

   The license agreement appears.

   Note to Windows users: The interface won't launch if you have autorun disabled. In that case, choose Start⇨Run. (For Windows Vista, choose Start⇨All Programs⇨Accessories⇨Run.) In the dialog box that appears, type **D:\Start.exe**. (Replace *D* with the proper letter if your CD drive uses a different letter. If you don't know the letter, see how your CD drive is listed under My Computer.) Click OK.

   Note for Mac Users: When the CD icon appears on your desktop, double-click the icon to open the CD and double-click the Start icon.

2. **Read through the license agreement and then click the Accept button if you want to use the CD.**

   The CD interface appears. The interface allows you to browse the contents and install the programs with just a click of a button (or two).

What You'll Find on the CD

The following sections are arranged by category and provide a summary of the software and other goodies you'll find on the CD. If you need help with installing the items provided on the CD, refer to the installation instructions in the preceding section.

For each program listed, I include the Web address where you can find more information and get upgrades or additional products. I also provide the program platform (Windows or Mac) plus the type of software. The programs you may find on the CD fall into one of the following categories:

- ✔ *Shareware programs* are fully functional, free, trial versions of copyrighted programs. If you like particular programs, register with their authors for a nominal fee and receive licenses, enhanced versions, and technical support.

- ✔ *Freeware programs* are free, copyrighted games, applications, and utilities. You can copy them to as many PCs as you like — for free — but they offer no technical support.

- ✔ *Trial, demo,* or *evaluation* versions of software are usually limited either by time or functionality (such as not letting you save a project after you create it).

DAZzle

For Windows and Mac, DAZzle is a 30-day free trial version of the software that offers small businesses mailing capabilities similar to those of large corporations. DAZzle uses a wizard interface that works with Microsoft Office 2000 and guides you through bulk mailing activities. You also get address verification and built-in mailpiece design. Visit www.endicia.com/store for more information or to purchase the full version.

Fast Photos

Fast Photos, from Pixby Software, promises to drastically cut the time you spend editing your auction photos. The software runs on Microsoft Windows Vista, XP, or 2000 operating systems, and is designed for convenient use by auction sellers to automate photo editing and resizing activities. Go to www.pixby.com for more information about the features of Fast Photos, as well as great user testimonials.

QuickBooks Simple Start Edition 2008

For Microsoft Windows XP or Vista operating systems, QuickBooks Simple Start is free, full-version financial accounting software especially for small businesses just starting out or having basic accounting needs. The program offers familiar forms to help with tracking sales and expenses. With these, business owners can stay in the know about how much money they are making. Also, QuickBooks Simple Start helps keep records organized for the inevitable tax time. Go to www.intuit.com for more information.

- ✔ **Recommended System Configuration:** At least 1.8 GHz Intel Pentium III (or equivalent) with 512 MB of RAM.

- ✔ **Minimum System Requirements:** 500 MHz Intel Pentium II (or equivalent) with 256 MB of RAM, Windows XP/Vista, 1 GB of disk space for QuickBooks Installation, at least 256 color SVGA video, optimized for 1024x768 with support for 800x600 with small fonts.

- ✔ **All online features/services** require Internet access with at least a 56 Kbps modem.

- ✔ **Upgrade information:** Simple Start 2008 is for first-time QuickBooks users or upgraders from prior versions of Simple Start. Simple Start cannot import data from prior versions of QuickBooks: Basic, Pro, or Premier Editions.

- ✔ **File Compatibility:** Data from Simple Start 2008 can be transferred to QuickBooks: Online Edition and can be viewed and edited in QuickBooks: Pro Edition and all Premier Editions 2008.

Training Videos

Training videos, used with permission of Santa Fe Productions, feature your author, Marsha Collier, in her role as e-commerce expert. To watch these training sessions, you need QuickTime media player. Included in these videos, you find training in the following areas:

- ✔ Image Editing

- ✔ Shipping: Carriers

- ✔ Packing Shipments

- ✔ Online Shopping Tips

- ✔ Taxes

Author-created material

In the Author directory on the CD, you find additional tools and documents provided by the author. These all work with computers running Microsoft Windows XP or Vista operating systems, and some documents may require other specific software, such as Adobe Acrobat for viewing PDF files, or Microsoft Word for doc files. Here's what you'll find in the Author directory:

- ✔ **Suggested Chart of Accounts:** A Word document that lists a set of account names and numbers developed for eBay sellers to use in an accounting program.

 Please remember to consult a tax professional prior to setting up any business.

- ✔ **Fee Calculator:** An Excel spreadsheet that allows you to plug in your starting values (for auctions) or selling price (for fixed price listings or store items) and figure your eBay fees. This fee calculator was created by Patti Louise Ruby, the book's technical editor and well-known eBay expert.

- ✔ **Listings That Sell:** An Adobe Acrobat PDF document that gives you illustrated tips on properly photographing your items and designing attractive listings.

- ✔ **Wholesale Merchandise Source Marts:** A Word document listing the name and Web address for wholesale merchandise sources marts around the U.S.

Troubleshooting

While I try to specify all system requirements and include files and programs that work on most computers (with the minimum system requirements), alas, your computer may differ, and some programs may not work properly for some reason.

The two likeliest problems are that you don't have enough memory (RAM) for the programs you want to use, or you have other programs running that are affecting installation or running of a program. If you get an error message such as Not enough memory or Setup cannot continue, try one or more of the following suggestions and then try using the software again:

- ✔ **Turn off any antivirus software running on your computer.** Installation programs sometimes mimic virus activity and may make your computer incorrectly believe that it's being infected by a virus.

- ✔ **Close all running programs.** The more programs you have running, the less memory is available to other programs. Installation programs typically update files and programs; so if you keep other programs running, installation may not work properly.

- ✔ **Have your local computer store add more RAM to your computer.** This is, admittedly, a drastic and somewhat expensive step. However, adding more memory can really help the speed of your computer and allow more programs to run at the same time.

Customer Care

If you have trouble with the CD-ROM, please call Wiley Product Technical Support at 800-762-2974. Outside the United States, call 317-572-3993. You can also contact Wiley Product Technical Support at www.wiley.com/techsupport. Wiley Publishing will provide technical support only for installation and other general quality control items. For technical support on the applications themselves, consult the program's vendor or author.

To place additional orders or to request information about other Wiley products, please call 877-762-2974.

Index

I

Wiley Publishing, Inc.
End-User License Agreement

READ THIS. You should carefully read these terms and conditions before opening the software packet(s) included with this book "Book". This is a license agreement "Agreement" between you and Wiley Publishing, Inc. "WPI". By opening the accompanying software packet(s), you acknowledge that you have read and accept the following terms and conditions. If you do not agree and do not want to be bound by such terms and conditions, promptly return the Book and the unopened software packet(s) to the place you obtained them for a full refund.

1. **License Grant.** WPI grants to you (either an individual or entity) a nonexclusive license to use one copy of the enclosed software program(s) (collectively, the "Software") solely for your own personal or business purposes on a single computer (whether a standard computer or a workstation component of a multi-user network). The Software is in use on a computer when it is loaded into temporary memory (RAM) or installed into permanent memory (hard disk, CD-ROM, or other storage device). WPI reserves all rights not expressly granted herein.

2. **Ownership.** WPI is the owner of all right, title, and interest, including copyright, in and to the compilation of the Software recorded on the DVD "Software Media". Copyright to the individual programs recorded on the Software Media is owned by the author or other authorized copyright owner of each program. Ownership of the Software and all proprietary rights relating thereto remain with WPI and its licensers.

3. **Restrictions on Use and Transfer.**

   (a) You may only (i) make one copy of the Software for backup or archival purposes, or (ii) transfer the Software to a single hard disk, provided that you keep the original for backup or archival purposes. You may not (i) rent or lease the Software, (ii) copy or reproduce the Software through a LAN or other network system or through any computer subscriber system or bulletin-board system, or (iii) modify, adapt, or create derivative works based on the Software.

   (b) You may not reverse engineer, decompile, or disassemble the Software. You may transfer the Software and user documentation on a permanent basis, provided that the transferee agrees to accept the terms and conditions of this Agreement and you retain no copies. If the Software is an update or has been updated, any transfer must include the most recent update and all prior versions.

4. **Restrictions on Use of Individual Programs.** You must follow the individual requirements and restrictions detailed for each individual program in the About the DVD appendix of this Book. These limitations are also contained in the individual license agreements recorded on the Software Media. These limitations may include a requirement that after using the program for a specified period of time, the user must pay a registration fee or discontinue use. By opening the Software packet(s), you will be agreeing to abide by the licenses and restrictions for these individual programs that are detailed in the About the DVD appendix and on the Software Media. None of the material on this Software Media or listed in this Book may ever be redistributed, in original or modified form, for commercial purposes.

SPORTS, FITNESS, PARENTING, RELIGION & SPIRITUALITY

0-471-76871-5

0-7645-7841-3

Also available:
- Catholicism For Dummies
  0-7645-5391-7
- Exercise Balls For Dummies
  0-7645-5623-1
- Fitness For Dummies
  0-7645-7851-0
- Football For Dummies
  0-7645-3936-1
- Judaism For Dummies
  0-7645-5299-6
- Potty Training For Dummies
  0-7645-5417-4
- Buddhism For Dummies
  0-7645-5359-3

- Pregnancy For Dummies
  0-7645-4483-7 †
- Ten Minute Tone-Ups For Dummies
  0-7645-7207-5
- NASCAR For Dummies
  0-7645-7681-X
- Religion For Dummies
  0-7645-5264-3
- Soccer For Dummies
  0-7645-5229-5
- Women in the Bible For Dummies
  0-7645-8475-8

TRAVEL

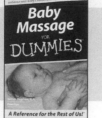

0-7645-7749-2

0-7645-6945-7

Also available:
- Alaska For Dummies
  0-7645-7746-8
- Cruise Vacations For Dummies
  0-7645-6941-4
- England For Dummies
  0-7645-4276-1
- Europe For Dummies
  0-7645-7529-5
- Germany For Dummies
  0-7645-7823-5
- Hawaii For Dummies
  0-7645-7402-7

- Italy For Dummies
  0-7645-7386-1
- Las Vegas For Dummies
  0-7645-7382-9
- London For Dummies
  0-7645-4277-X
- Paris For Dummies
  0-7645-7630-5
- RV Vacations For Dummies
  0-7645-4442-X
- Walt Disney World & Orlando
  For Dummies
  0-7645-9660-8

GRAPHICS, DESIGN & WEB DEVELOPMENT

0-7645-8815-X

0-7645-9571-7

Also available:
- 3D Game Animation For Dummies
  0-7645-8789-7
- AutoCAD 2006 For Dummies
  0-7645-8925-3
- Building a Web Site For Dummies
  0-7645-7144-3
- Creating Web Pages For Dummies
  0-470-08030-2
- Creating Web Pages All-in-One Desk
  Reference For Dummies
  0-7645-4345-8
- Dreamweaver 8 For Dummies
  0-7645-9649-7

- InDesign CS2 For Dummies
  0-7645-9572-5
- Macromedia Flash 8 For Dummies
  0-7645-9691-8
- Photoshop CS2 and Digital
  Photography For Dummies
  0-7645-9580-6
- Photoshop Elements 4 For Dummies
  0-471-77483-9
- Syndicating Web Sites with RSS Feeds
  For Dummies
  0-7645-8848-6
- Yahoo! SiteBuilder For Dummies
  0-7645-9800-7

NETWORKING, SECURITY, PROGRAMMING & DATABASES

0-7645-7728-X

0-471-74940-0

Also available:
- Access 2007 For Dummies
  0-470-04612-0
- ASP.NET 2 For Dummies
  0-7645-7907-X
- C# 2005 For Dummies
  0-7645-9704-3
- Hacking For Dummies
  0-470-05235-X
- Hacking Wireless Networks
  For Dummies
  0-7645-9730-2
- Java For Dummies
  0-470-08716-1

- Microsoft SQL Server 2005 For Dummies
  0-7645-7755-7
- Networking All-in-One Desk Reference
  For Dummies
  0-7645-9939-9
- Preventing Identity Theft For Dummies
  0-7645-7336-5
- Telecom For Dummies
  0-471-77085-X
- Visual Studio 2005 All-in-One Desk
  Reference For Dummies
  0-7645-9775-2
- XML For Dummies
  0-7645-8845-1

ALTH & SELF-HELP

0-7645-8450-2

0-7645-4149-8

Also available:

- Bipolar Disorder For Dummies
  0-7645-8451-0
- Chemotherapy and Radiation
  For Dummies
  0-7645-7832-4
- Controlling Cholesterol For Dummies
  0-7645-5440-9
- Diabetes For Dummies
  0-7645-6820-5* †
- Divorce For Dummies
  0-7645-8417-0 †

- Fibromyalgia For Dummies
  0-7645-5441-7
- Low-Calorie Dieting For Dummies
  0-7645-9905-4
- Meditation For Dummies
  0-471-77774-9
- Osteoporosis For Dummies
  0-7645-7621-6
- Overcoming Anxiety For Dummies
  0-7645-5447-6
- Reiki For Dummies
  0-7645-9907-0
- Stress Management For Dummies
  0-7645-5144-2

UCATION, HISTORY, REFERENCE & TEST PREPARATION

0-7645-8381-6

0-7645-9554-7

Also available:

- The ACT For Dummies
  0-7645-9652-7
- Algebra For Dummies
  0-7645-5325-9
- Algebra Workbook For Dummies
  0-7645-8467-7
- Astronomy For Dummies
  0-7645-8465-0
- Calculus For Dummies
  0-7645-2498-4
- Chemistry For Dummies
  0-7645-5430-1
- Forensics For Dummies
  0-7645-5580-4

- Freemasons For Dummies
  0-7645-9796-5
- French For Dummies
  0-7645-5193-0
- Geometry For Dummies
  0-7645-5324-0
- Organic Chemistry I For Dummies
  0-7645-6902-3
- The SAT I For Dummies
  0-7645-7193-1
- Spanish For Dummies
  0-7645-5194-9
- Statistics For Dummies
  0-7645-5423-9

Get smart @ dummies.com®

- **Find a full list of Dummies titles**
- **Look into loads of FREE on-site articles**
- **Sign up for FREE eTips e-mailed to you weekly**
- **See what other products carry the Dummies name**
- **Shop directly from the Dummies bookstore**
- **Enter to win new prizes every month!**